This book comprises papers examining recent developments in econometrics given at the Sixth World Congress of the Econometric Society in Barcelona in August 1990. It is the latest in a series of collections which cover the most active areas in econometrics over a five-year period. The individual papers are written by the world's leading specialists, and provide a unique survey of the most recent advances in the field.

Econometric Society Monographs No. 24

Advances in econometrics

Volume II

Advances in econometrics
Sixth World Congress

Volume II

Edited by

CHRISTOPHER A. SIMS

CAMBRIDGE UNIVERSITY PRESS
Cambridge, New York, Melbourne, Madrid, Cape Town, Singapore, São Paulo

Cambridge University Press
The Edinburgh Building, Cambridge CB2 2RU, UK

Published in the United States of America by Cambridge University Press, New York

www.cambridge.org
Information on this title: www.cambridge.org/0521444608

First published 1994

A catalogue record for this publication is available from the British Library

Library of Congress Cataloguing in Publication data
  'Sixth World Congress of the Econometric Society in
Barcelona'.
  1. Econometrics–Congresses.   I. Sims, Christopher A.
II. Econometric Society. World Congress (6th: Barcelona,
Spain)
HB139.A345   1993   330′.01′5195   92-42041

ISBN-10 0-521-44460-8 hardback

Transferred to digital printing 2005

Contents

Contributors

Richard Blundell
University College London

David Card
Princeton University

Albert Marcet
UNIVERSITAT Pompeu Febra, Barcelona

John Rust
The University of Wisconsin

Ariel Pakes
Yale University

Kenneth Judd
Hoover Institution, Stanford University

Kenneth Singleton
Graduate School of Business, Stanford University

Angelo Melino
University of Toronto

Sebastian Edwards
School of Management, University of California

Guido Tabellini
School of Management, University of California

Guillermo Calvo
International Monetary Fund, Washington

Carlos Végh
International Monetary Fund, Washington

I
Labour supply

CHAPTER 1

Evaluating structural microeconometric models of labour supply

Richard Blundell

1   SOME CHARACTERISTICS OF STRUCTURAL LABOUR SUPPLY MODELS

The choice between 'structural' models and data-descriptive, reduced-form representations of labour supply may appear straightforward. Structural models impose restrictions which may be invalid but, in exchange, provide economic interpretation. Where these structural restrictions are testable a standard approach to model selection is available. However, since labour supply is fundamentally dynamic, structural models usually require the separate specification and identification of expectation processes. Moreover, since many of the endogenous choice variables are censored or discrete, the ability to derive *explicit* reduced forms corresponding exactly to a given structural model is severely limited. In general, however, it would seem unwise to adopt some particular structural model without recourse to the usual battery of misspecification tests that reduced forms can provide; equally it would be sad not to recover structural parameters. The strategy developed in this chapter is to provide a sequential approach to estimation and testing, avoiding where possible unnecessarily strong structural assumptions. The theme is to assume only what is necessary to identify the structural parameters of interest, at the same time allowing the data the chance to reject the structural assumptions in question.

As economic models of labour supply have become increasingly sophisticated their econometric counterparts have become increasingly dependent on the imposition of structural theoretical restrictions in order to identify the parameters necessary to conduct policy and welfare analysis. This has been effectively illustrated by the results on econometric coherency and theory consistency in the analysis of taxation and labour supply. A well-defined econometric model of discrete or censored labour supply decisions requires a unique solution for labour supply for any wage/income combination. The restrictions this statistical condition places on the model parameters are equivalent to those of the Principal Assumption and Coherency Condition developed for more general models by Heckman (1978) and Gourieroux, Monfort and Laffont (1980) respectively. Tax and benefit systems typically introduce a non-linearity akin to censoring thereby ruling out an explicit 'reduced form' relationship between hours and the wage/income combination. However, a well-defined economic optimising model does, in general, guarantee uniqueness. Moreover, in the case of labour supply it is straightforward to show that the Slutsky negativity condition is sufficient for satisfaction of the uniqueness conditions noted above (see for example, MaCurdy, Green and Paarsch (1990) and Kooreman and Van Soest (1990)).

This observation raises two general issues. Firstly, to what extent is it possible to test structural assumptions, like the Slutsky condition? Secondly, if conditions like the Slutsky condition are to be assumed, what restrictions are implied for typically chosen (parametric) forms of labour supply? Both of these issues are critical for policy and welfare analysis. It is important to be able to assess the validity of the theoretical structure behind any chosen model for the data under analysis. Moreover, if theory consistency cannot easily be relaxed, it is important to assess the flexibility of the specific chosen parametric form *under* structural theoretical restrictions. In certain cases a non-parametric structure may be available. Structural models are often accused (in many cases quite rightly) of imposing untenable and unbelievable restrictions on behaviour. It is difficult to believe that this can be a generic property of structural models (although it may be generic to structural modellers!) and yet it is regularly used for rejection of the structural approach. This reaction seems to place unnecessary limitations on our ability to use empirical economic models for policy analysis.

The aim in this chapter is to bring together a selected sample of recent developments in the micro-econometrics of labour supply which relate to the estimation of structural parameters. The structural parameters of interest will be those that describe within-period allocations over consumption and labour supply as well as those that describe the intertemporal relationship between labour supply decisions and savings. It is hoped that by taking a simple illustration the arguments will be more transparent. The objective (not necessarily achieved!) will be to find empirical models that impose the least restrictions necessary to identify the structural parameters of interest. This then permits an assessment of the sensitivity of empirical results (and resulting policy prescriptions) to the imposition of more restrictive structural assumptions.

The empirical research reported here will refer, for the most part, to the analysis of the behaviour in and out of work and the hours of work for married women. It will turn out that the 'shape' of within-period labour supply behaviour can be assessed without the imposition of particularly strong assumptions on intertemporal behaviour. This is useful since for many policy problems the precise nature of within-period behaviour has become critical due to the non-linear nature of within-period budget constraints induced by taxation.[1] As noted above, with such budget constraints in place, the relationship between theory consistency and estimator consistency for the (full-information) maximum-likelihood approach is closely linked. However, this chapter suggests that this observation implies that rather more attention should be placed on misspecification tests and on finding estimators that, although less efficient, provide the ability to assess the empirical consistency of the theoretical model.

The parametric form for the theoretical model also becomes critical in the sense that economic theory usually allows a much wider class of parametric models than the single model chosen for analysis. Rejection of the 'theory' is often as suggestive of the use of more general theoretically consistent parametric (or even non-parametric) models as it is the rejection of the optimising theory itself. The linear labour supply model is a case in point. Theory consistency (together with linearity) essentially requires a positive sloping labour supply behaviour everywhere (see MaCurdy, Green and Paarsch (1990), for example). But theory allows more general shapes. We need to consider carefully the class of parametric models in the light of their behavioural properties under theory consistent restrictions given the range of variation in wage, income and hours under investigation.

The data used to illustrate these points in this chapter come from the repeated cross sections of the UK Family Expenditure Survey (FES) which provide a long time series of detailed information on wages, hours, consumption and household composition. The survey design is much like that of the US Consumers Expenditure Survey, although there is no panel element. Nevertheless, these data provide a consistent and accurate source of micro-level information over more than twenty years. They have also been the subject of considerable empirical application to date and have the distinct advantage of collecting accurate information on both hours worked *and* consumption expenditures across all household members.[2]

In summary the aim of this chapter is to provide a sequential framework for the estimation and identification of labour supply behaviour. Following this sequential approach, our attention naturally turns first to the analysis of within-period labour supply. This is then followed by a discussion of intertemporal allocations.

2   MODELLING WITHIN-PERIOD LABOUR SUPPLY DECISIONS

The objective of this section is to provide an analysis of within-period decisions over consumption and hours of work. A framework is developed that places the least restrictive structure on intertemporal optimising behaviour. The chosen structure will turn out to be fairly general, accounting for a number of the characteristics that are often considered to be important in modelling labour supply behaviour. We shall concentrate predominantly on female labour supply decisions and will condition on the earnings and labour market outcomes of other household members. There will be a number of separate features of the decision-making process which will have to be addressed. These include the role of children, the structure of the tax and benefit system, the importance of hours bunching and the endogeneity of gross wages and other household income.

Following from the contributions of Cogan (1981) and Mroz (1987) it is essential to acknowledge the importance of separating the participation and hours of work decisions. In particular, it is critical to place the participation decision in a setting that is sufficiently general to allow for the presence of fixed costs and also the significant number of women out of employment who record active search for work. Either of these two features is sufficient to rule out the Tobit corner solution model or standard reservation wage model of participation.[3] However, they do not in themselves rule out the standard analysis of within-period hours of work decisions provided the appropriate conditioning variables are chosen and an appropriate statistical selection model is adopted in estimation.

2.1   An intertemporal setting for within-period hours and consumption choices

We turn first to a dynamic extension of the standard labour supply model in which within-period hours of work are chosen in a labour market characterised by fixed costs and search costs. In any random sample of working-age individuals we may identify each with one of the following labour market states: (i) non-participation, (ii) active search and (iii) employment. Non-participants may receive job offers but usually at a rate less than that of searchers. Individuals who search incur time and money costs. Ignoring taxes, an individual who finds a job in period t has the option of employment in period $t + 1$ at the real hourly wage w_{t+1}. (Note that w_{t+1} is a random variable in period t.) Individuals in employment pay fixed time costs 'τ' and face a net layoff rate of δ. If they are employed in $t + 1$ they receive w_{t+1}.[4] In addition, individuals are allowed to borrow and save.[5] The overall model structure is the one analysed in Arellano and Meghir (1992) and Blundell, Ham and Meghir (1989). Here we shall just briefly sketch the main results.

Consider first the value function associated with employment in period t, V_t^e. An individual in employment achieves current-period utility level $U(T - h_t - \tau, C_t; z_t)$ where T is the maximum leisure time available, h_t is the hours of work, C_t is the level of real consumption and z_t a vector of taste shift characteristics and other conditioning variables. The total value V_t^e of employment in period t depends on expected future outcomes conditional on current employment. As a result it takes the following form

$$V_t^e = \max \{ U(T - h_t - \tau, C_t; z_t) + \phi E_t((1 - \delta) \max [V_{t+1}^0, V_{t+1}^s, V_{t+1}^e] \\ + \delta \max [V_{t+1}^0, V_{t+1}^s]), \tag{1.1}$$

where ϕ is a personal discount factor and V_{t+1}^0, and V_{t+1}^s are the value functions associated with non-participation and search in period $t+1$ respectively. Conditional expections $E_t(\cdot)$ refer to $E(\cdot | \Omega_t)$ where Ω_t is the individual's information set in period t. The asset accumulation constraint associated with (1.1) is given by

$$C_t = w_t h_t + (1 + r_t) A_{t-1} - A_t + y_t \tag{1.2}$$

where A_t is the level of end of period t assets, r_t is the real return on assets held at the end of period $t - 1$ and y_t is the level of other non-asset income in period t. The current value functions for search and non-participation can be similarly defined (see Blundell, Ham and Meghir (1989)).

The intertemporal model defined by (1.1)–(1.2) implies a very useful result for the empirical modelling of within-period behaviour: conditional on an individual being in employment, her marginal choice between hours h_t and consumption C_t can only affect the second term in (1.1) through A_t. As a result, her conditional hours of work can be modelled using a standard intertemporal two-stage budgeting approach. To see this, re-write (1.2) as

$$C_t = w_t h_t + \mu_t, \tag{1.3}$$

where $\mu_t = r_t A_{t-1} - \Delta A_t + y_t$ is a net dissaving measure. Then note that for an individual in employment, maximisation of (1.1) subject to (1.2) yields the marginal rate of substitution equation, $-U_h/U_c = w$. Combining this condition with the budget constraint (1.3) yields a standard Marshallian (or μ-conditional) *life-cycle consistent* labour supply model for hours of work (see MaCurdy (1983) and Blundell and Walker (1986)). For empirical purposes, we write this as

$$h_t^* = g(w_t, \mu_t; z_t, \theta) \tag{1.4}$$

where θ represents unknown preference parameters and may also reflect individual heterogeneity.[6]

The usefulness of (1.4), given our objective of sequential identification and estimation of the intertemporal model, is clear. Even in this fairly complex dynamic optimising framework, hours of work decisions for workers depend on the current wage and an appropriately defined other- (or virtual) income measure μ_t. The latter summarising all future expectations. Hence given w_t and μ_t (and demographic variables z_t), hours of work for those employed do not depend on the wage offer distribution, fixed costs, layoff and arrival rates or any other aspect of uncertainty. Moreover, the introduction of non-linear taxation on current earnings does nothing to upset this result. This simplicity disappears, however, when we consider optimal conditions across any of the discrete states. The conditions for two-stage budgeting *do not* prevail in general here since any pair-wise comparison of the second terms in each of the three state value functions indicates that labour market participation and search have an effect on the future that is above and beyond their effect through A_t.[7]

In analysing within-period hours and consumption choices the results above imply that *conditioning* on the employment state *and* μ_t is sufficient to capture *all* aspects of fixed costs and future expectations. Together they summarise all intertemporal considerations and allow identification of *all* within-period preference parameters. Since the selection mechanism into employment and the other-income variable μ_t are both likely to be endogenous we need to account for this in our estimated model. However, the analysis above can provide suitable overidentifying restrictions (simple exclusion restrictions) which allow the estimation of an employment selection probability and a reduced form equation for μ_t. It is important to note that breaking intertemporal separability either directly through habits in utility or indirectly through experience in the wage equation will invalidate the derivation of (1.4).[8]

2.2   Theory consistency and the issue of coherency in a model with taxation

There are many reasons why it may be desirable that an estimated model of the form in (1.4) describing desired hours of work should have properties that accord with choice theory. Apart from the difficulty of interpreting a model which is not theoretically consistent, welfare analysis is also pretty much ruled out. Nevertheless, constructing models that allow theoretical restrictions to be tested has been a major stimulation to the analysis of household behaviour. Rejection has often led both to the development of alternative (more flexible) theory consistent models as well as the introduction of new theories of individual decision making.

In discrete models or models with non-linear taxation, theoretical optimisation plays an important role in specifying a coherent statistical framework. Indeed, a strong argument behind the introduction of 'more appropriate' full-information maximum-likelihood methods for dealing with non-linear taxation in labour supply models was the belief that earlier instrumental variable estimation methods, by ignoring the important information in the individual's choice of position on the budget constraint, were partly responsible for the lack of theory consistency in much empirical work (see Pencavel (1986)). This previous work had been characterised by negatively sloped labour supply curves with small income effects. However, it has to be recognised that (full-information) maximum-likelihood methods, by utilising all information on the non-linearity induced by tax systems, impose strong restrictions for consistent estimation. These are the Coherency Condition referred to in the introduction. In the labour supply model with piece-wise linear taxation and in models of discrete choice these are satisfied when the parameters satisfy the integrability conditions.

The close relationship between the Coherency Condition and theory consistency has raised the question of whether theory restrictions are testable in such models. Indeed, why test theory? Having set the hours/consumption choice problem in a fairly unrestricted optimising environment we may hope for a closer relationship between data and theory. In particular, the model we have described is not static as was the case for many earlier labour supply models and it does not impose the simple reservation wage condition on employment. Nevertheless, there are many reasons why the model (or a particular parametric specification) may be invalid. In a two-good labour supply/consumption model the integrability conditions reduce to a simple non-negativity conditon on the compensated labour supply derivative (the Slutsky non-negativity condition). Typically in labour supply models the Slutsky condition is data dependent. If utility comparisons have to be made over a wide range of the budget constraint, as often occurs in kinked budget constraint models, concavity will be required over a large range of the data space. As a result it is clearly unattractive to consider a labour supply model whose properties are unreasonably restrictive under concavity. Estimated models are usually parametric and often linear. The linear labour supply model although popular would seem to be most unattractive since concavity essentially rules out backward-bending labour supply (assuming leisure is a normal good).

To illustrate this point let us consider the linear case which has been used extensively in tax reform analysis (see Hausman (1981) and Blomquist

(1983)). In the context of the model for hours of work (1.4) we may write this model as

$$h = a_0 + a_1 w + \beta_1 \mu \tag{1.5}$$

with the direct utility representation of preferences given by

$$U(h, c) = (\beta_1 h - a_1) \exp [\beta_1 (h - a_0 - \beta_1 c)/(a_1 - \beta_1 h)]. \tag{1.6}$$

For convenience we shall take a_0 to represent unobservable heterogeneity across individuals. The Slutsky condition reduces to $a_1 - \beta_1 h \geq 0$.

Imagine a single kink point in the budget constraint at h^t defined by a progressive tax structure and suppose that the budget constraint is convex and piece-wise linear. If we let w^t be the marginal wage above h^t and μ^t the corresponding virtual income, then (following Hausman (1985)) we may define the probability of being above h^t by

$$\Pr[h^t - a_0 - a_1 w^t - \beta_1 \mu^t > 0]. \tag{1.7a}$$

The probability of being below the tax kink is

$$\Pr[h^t - a_0 - a_1 w - \beta_1 \mu < 0], \tag{1.7b}$$

with the probability at the kink simply

$$\Pr[a_0 + a_1 w^t + \beta_1 \mu^t \leq h^t \leq a_0 + a_1 w + \beta_1 \mu]. \tag{1.7c}$$

For coherency we require that (1.7c) is non-negative and that the sum of probabilities is unity. Together these ensure $a_1 - \beta_1 h^t \geq 0$, precisely the Slutsky condition evaluated at h^t. Notice that if leisure is a normal good β_1 is negative and as a result a kink point (or corner solution) near zero hours ensures $a_1 > 0$, or forward-sloping labour supply behaviour everywhere.

Two conclusions can be drawn immediately from this analysis of coherency. Firstly, it may prove difficult to provide a formal test of theory consistency if a well-behaved likelihood depends on the imposition of a restriction close to concavity itself. Secondly, the properties of chosen (parametric) specifications should be evaluated under concavity. Concavity will require forward-sloping behaviour for labour supply at low hours but will not rule out backward-bending behaviour at higher hours. For example, figure 1.1 plots the non-parametric Kernel regression of hours of work on marginal wages for a sample of single mothers in the UK Family Expenditure Survey. The shift in the curves displays the usual income effect and the curvature suggests a declining wage response with hours.

To test choice theory, as defined in the chosen parametric utility-maximising model with piece-wise linear budget constraints, one clearly has to weaken the structure imposed by the full-information methods. This may take the form of approximating the budget constraint by a differenti-

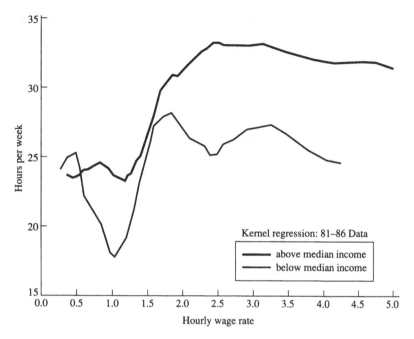

Figure 1.1 A picture of labour supply (single parents)
Source: Blundell, Duncan and Meghir (1992a)

able function. For example, where the tax constraint is heavily progressive with many small tax kinks, a smooth function will provide a good approximation and simple IV estimators are then consistent. MaCurdy *et al.* (1990) have used this approximation of the budget constraint to effectively analyse the labour supply responses of prime-aged males facing the 1975 US tax structure. Alternatively, if the budget constraint is made up of long linear segments, as is the case for the tax policy reforms of the 1980s, other robust estimators suggest themselves.

In the UK, and more recently in many other countries, the move to a relatively simple tax system at the outset of the 1980s suggests such an alternative scheme for robust estimation. The long linear segments that have resulted imply that for a large number of workers the marginal wage is constant for large variations in hours. Indeed, although many fewer than 50 per cent of married women in the UK work full time, around two-thirds face an effectively linear tax schedule. Selecting a sample of such working women provides us with a useful 'test bed' from which to evaluate the reliability of theoretical restrictions for alternative parametric models. By selecting 'deep' into the linear segments of the budget constraint Blundell,

Duncan and Meghir (1992) argue that optimisation error (and certain forms of measurement error) can also be allowed for by this procedure. Instruments for selection are given by the tax policy reforms themselves. Such an estimator goes hand in hand with the choice of suitably appropriate functional form for labour supply to which we turn first before we present some empirical results.

2.3   The shape of labour supply

Stern (1986) has provided a useful survey of popular functional forms for labour supply models and their properties. Attention below will be restricted to an assessment of model flexibility and the restrictions of theory consistency. Although the Slutsky condition places certain constraints on the 'shape' of labour supply behaviour, provided appropriate function forms are considered, we have noted above that these restrictions can be 'fairly' weak. A desirable property of labour supply functions, as is reflected in figure 1.1 above, is a positive wage effect at zero hours and the possibility of backward bending for higher hours. That is, provided the income effect is sufficiently negative, backward-bending supply curves can support Slutsky negativity.

In the linear model

$$h = a_0 + a_1 w + \beta_1 \mu \tag{1.8}$$

we have already seen that a non-negative Slutsky term guarantees $a_1 - \beta_1 h \geq 0$ which requires $a_1 \geq 0$ if h can be zero and is more likely to be satisfied the more negative is β_2.[9] The quadratic model

$$h = a_0 + a_1 w + a_2 w^2 + \beta_1 \mu \tag{1.9}$$

clearly relaxes this condition since a_2 can be negative. However, for very high μ, hours will tend to zero if β_1 is negative and as a result a negative $a_2 w^2$ term cannot be allowed to dominate for those close to non-participation. Since high μ and high w often occur together, the additivity between wage and μ terms in (1.9) appears undesirable.

We shall define models with a level of parameterisation as in (1.8) as *three parameter* models since they possess separate parameters for wage and income effects as well as a parameter a_0 that can be used to approximate individual (observed or unobserved) heterogeneity. Given the arguments raised against (1.8) and (1.9) we might look for three parameter representations that provide for a wider area for theory consistency. For example, consider

$$h = a_0 + a_1 \ln w + \beta_1 \frac{\mu}{w} \tag{1.10}$$

which can be shown to allow backward-bending behaviour provided a_1 is negative. Moreover, since β_1 is also negative, for large enough μ the β_1 term dominates the uncompensated wage derivative and as h tends to zero the labour supply curve becomes forward sloping as suggested by figure 1.1 above. Indeed, the Slutsky condition requires $a_1 - \beta_1(\mu/w) - \beta_1 h > 0$. The indirect utility associated with (1.10) is

$$V(w,\mu) = \frac{w^{1+\beta_1}}{1+\beta_1} \left\{ \frac{\mu}{w}(1+\beta_1)^2 + a_1 \ln w + a_0 - \frac{a_1}{(1+\beta_1)} \right\} \tag{1.11}$$

see Duncan (1990).[10] Both (1.10) and (1.11) can be extended to allow more flexibility if required by the data. In the empirical application we assess the importance of including $\ln w^2$ terms in (1.10). Such an extension would add a similar term to (1.11).

Although unobserved (as well as observed) heterogeneity is most conveniently entered through a_0, other parameters may be random and diagnostic tests against such misspecification are available and useful. Of course, the upper bound on hours provides some bound on the range of a_0 and if either a_1 or β_1 is assumed random, the Slutsky condition itself provides some bounds on the range of their distribution as in the Hausman illustration outlined above.

An attractive, yet underutilised, alternative procedure which yields flexible labour supply properties and convenient modelling of heterogeneity and kink points is the indirect labour supply function introduced by Heckman (1974c). It has been used in Blundell, Duncan and Meghir (1992a) to successfully model the labour supply of single mothers depicted in figure 1.1 above. Working from the marginal rate of substitution function Heckman introduced a three parameter model of the marginal rate of substitution of the form

$$\ln m = a_0 + a_1 h + \beta_1 \mu^* \tag{1.12}$$

with $\mu^* = wh + \mu - \frac{w}{a_1}(1 - e^{-a_1 h})$.

Since for positive hours the log of the marginal rate of substitution $\ln m$ is equated to the log real wage, the model is complete and relatively simple to estimate. Moreover, the indirect labour supply function (1.12) provides the *reservation* (real) wage directly and corner solutions can be dealt with simply. Indeed, the participation corner solution at $h = 0$ can be seen to occur if $\ln w \geq a_0 + \beta \mu$ since at $h = 0$ we have $\mu^* \cong \mu$. As a result, when h tends to zero the labour supply model reduces to a straightforward semi-log model in which concavity (and positive-sloping behaviour) is easily established. For h positive the Slutsky condition additionally requires $\beta_1 w(1 - e^{-a_1 h}) + a_1$ to be positive. This is precisely the condition required to derive a unique solution to h for any $\ln w$ (or a_0) and as a result it relates directly to the Coherency Condition described earlier. Note also that a_0 is in principle unbounded and therefore acts as a useful parameter to represent heterogeneity since no bounds on the distribution are required. Finally, since μ^* measures the indifference curve at zero hours it provides a welfare ranking equivalent to indirect utility.

2.4   Interpreting evidence on labour supply

In this section we provide estimates of within-period labour supply responses using data available in the UK FES over the 1980s and assess the properties of within-period behaviour. Attention is focussed first on the structure of the tax system and the distribution of hours of work for working women. This is then followed by an econometric analysis of within-period hours of work decisions.

2.4.1   The UK tax-benefit system and the distribution of working hours

The major tax policy reforms during the 1980s in the UK provide an ideal environment for measuring behavioural responses. They also possess many of the features of subsequent tax reforms in other western economies. Over the period of the 1980s under analysis, the UK tax and benefit system consisted of three main components: income tax, National Insurance Contributions (NICs hereafter) and the benefit system. Table 1.1 summarises some of the main policy experiments in the UK tax and benefit system over this period. It details the monotonic decline in basic and higher income tax rates. This is countered, to some degree, by the increase in the rate of NICs which is incident on all earnings above a lower earnings limit that is close to the basic personal allowance. Added to this is the rise in the VAT rate which displays the well-documented shift towards indirect taxation.

For many earners, reductions in the marginal rates were significant. At the bottom end, high rates of benefit withdrawal in excess of 100 per cent were largely removed although this often occurred at the cost of extending the range of earned income over which the lower withdrawal rates were effective.

It is also important to emphasise the wide distribution of weekly hours worked in our sample of married women. The frequency distribution of working hours for the sample of married women used in the estimation characterised by their position in the tax and benefit system is presented in figure 1.2. This appears to contrast strongly with the distribution of working hours in other European countries – see for example, the case for France in Bourguignon and Magnac (1990). Figure 1.2 also indicates the

Table 1.1. *UK tax and benefit changes, 1979–88*

	1979	1980	1981	1982	1983	1984	1985	1986	1987	1988
Basic rate tax	33–>30	30	30	30	30	30	30	29	27	25
Top rate	83–>60	60	60	60	60	60	60	60	60	40
Tax allowances	8% rise	—	−10%	—	8% rise	2 rise	2% rise	—	—	—
NIC	6.5	6.75	7.75	8.75	9	9	9	9	9	9
VAT (%)	9–>15	15	15	15	15	15	15	15	15	15

Notes:
Tax allowances denote real % changes. NIC is effective on all earned income
above a lower earnings limit (approx. the SA) and below an upper limit (approx.
the top of the basic rate tax band).
Source: Johnson and Stark (1989).

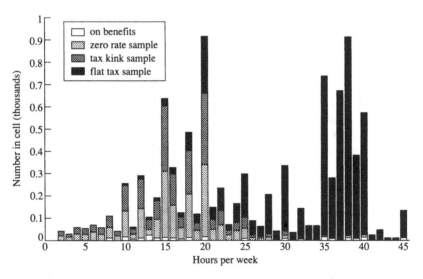

Figure 1.2 Hours distributions (married women)

large proportion of women who are either facing a zero marginal tax rate or
the basic tax rate. This despite the fact that figure 1.2 only places women on
such a linear segment if their hours of work are more than three hours from
an implied (tax) kink, thereby reducing the likelihood that any individual is
misplaced on a segment or is choosing labour supply with another marginal
tax rate in mind.

Table 1.2. *Hours of work for married women by occupation group, 1981–6*

Hours	Prof. (1)	Admin (2)	Teach. (3)	Clerical (4)	Shop wk (5)	Skilled (6)	Semi-s. (7)	Unskill. (8)
≤5	2.42	0.94	8.76	2.48	1.75	2.21	3.42	9.68
≤10	4.83	1.25	7.63	5.30	9.75	5.65	16.52	23.65
≤15	5.43	1.57	7.81	5.70	21.44	7.37	14.13	30.00
≤20	15.46	4.08	6.48	12.30	27.49	10.32	16.39	16.83
≤25	8.09	2.51	9.14	6.07	11.31	7.62	9.16	8.41
≤30	8.70	5.64	28.57	5.17	5.46	5.65	7.74	3.33
≤35	13.04	13.17	13.52	18.90	2.53	8.60	4.32	1.43
≤40	38.53	58.62	9.71	39.84	16.96	47.17	23.61	5.24
≤45	0.97	5.33	2.86	1.26	0.58	1.72	0.90	0.32
45<	0.72	3.76	3.24	0.29	0.19	0.25	0.77	0.00

Notes:
% figures. Armed forces were excluded throughout. Working women married to employed men.
Source: Own calculations.

For married women employees the wide spread of working hours is prevalent over most occupations and industries as is displayed in tables 1.2 and 1.3. However, the bunching in certain skilled and administrative occupations and manufacturing industries is suggestive of collective agreement on labour supply rather than pure individual choice. For this reason the first three occupations are excluded in the empirical analysis.

2.4.2   Estimation and testing

It is clear from the above discussion that for the large majority of working women employees the marginal tax rate associated with a small change in working hours is constant. As was shown in figure 1.2 most workers were either on the basic tax rate segment or the zero tax rate segment and, even though the position of the tax kink and the level of the basic tax rate has been subject to important changes over the period of our data, this feature has remained. Indeed, the independent movement of the tax system, which resulted from the many tax policy experiments during the 1980s, can be expected to help pin down the structural labour supply response coefficients.

In estimation, this structure of the tax system and hours of work can be exploited to provide a robust estimator of wage and income responses. This is the approach developed in Blundell, Duncan and Meghir (1992a,b). By

Table 1.3. *Hours of work for married women by industry, 1981–6*

Hours	Public serv. (1)	Prim. man. (2)	Heavy man. (3)	Light man. (4)	Print. (5)	Private serv. (6)	Transp. Comm. (7)	Financ. serv. (8)
≤5	2.06	1.64	2.14	2.65	4.32	3.28	0.72	4.50
≤10	5.18	1.64	4.28	5.04	4.94	11.72	4.35	9.24
≤15	11.55	8.20	3.83	5.80	7.41	18.60	6.88	8.53
≤20	10.57	5.74	8.11	11.22	8.02	18.88	10.14	11.49
≤25	14.99	4.10	5.63	8.32	6.17	9.07	5.43	4.38
≤30	8.59	0.00	3.15	6.81	4.32	6.43	2.90	2.96
≤35	10.55	9.84	8.78	11.85	17.28	6.20	10.14	36.37
≤40	8.12	68.85	58.45	40.73	40.12	19.43	48.19	19.08
≤45	26.04	0.00	0.56	1.26	0.62	1.50	7.25	0.47
45<	1.43	0.00	0.56	0.50	1.85	1.19	1.45	0.47
Total	3783	122	888	793	162	2193	276	844

Notes:
% figures. Armed forces were excluded throughout. Working women married to employed men.
Source: Own calculations.

selecting working women whose hours of work place them deep inside the linear segments, as in figure 1.2, we can remove the potential importance of optimisation error. The endogeneity in the marginal wage and virtual income generated by the non-linear tax system is allowed for by correcting for the selection of individuals on the linear segments. This can be achieved using the usual reduced form selectivity estimators in which the tax policy reforms themselves provide identifying instruments.

The selection process is modelled in two parts, reflecting the participation decision and the choice of linear segment respectively. Participation may reflect fixed costs and other constraints on entry and so this is modelled as a general binary choice model dependent on a large number of characteristics of the labour market and the individual. The estimates and their standard errors are presented in the first two columns of table A1 in appendix A. The choice of segment is modelled *conditional on participation*, using an ordered choice model whose estimated parameters and standard errors are presented in the second two columns of table A1. The explanatory factors are described in appendix A and in the notes to table A1. The diagnostic statistics based on the generalised residuals of Gourieroux *et al.* (1987) and presented at the foot of the table suggest that the normality assumptions utilised in these estimations are not seriously at odds with the data.

As argued above, by conditioning on the second of these two selection processes in the estimation of labour supply responses we are able to account for the possible endogeneity of marginal wages that occurs through the tax system. Conditioning on participation we are also able to adjust for the endogenous selection of individuals into the labour market. We must also allow for the possibility of endogeneity of the gross wage and other income. To construct this measure of other-income μ we use the consumption data available in the FES. Under normality of the reduced form disturbances for these variables we can control for endogeneity by adding the reduced form residuals (Smith and Blundell (1986)). The first two columns of table A2 in appendix A present the estimated reduced form log wage equation. The second two columns of table A2 present the reduced form other-income equation.[11]

Conditional on the inclusion of the other income and log wage residuals (ϵ_μ and ϵ_w) we can test for joint normality across the selection index probability distribution and the error term in the labour supply equation. To do this we may follow the general methodology of Lee (1984) but note that the nature of the selectivity models means that the testing procedure can be carried out sequentially and that the tests fit into the generalised residual score test (or Lagrange multiplier) procedures suggested by Chester and Irish (1987) and Gourieroux, Monfort, Renault and Trognon (1987). More specifically the normality of the marginal distribution of the selection probability index can be tested directly from the usual residual-based tests for skewness and kurtosis, see Bera, Jarque and Lee (1984) for example.

2.4.3   Evidence on the shape of labour supply

In estimating the labour supply model (1.10), all α and β parameters were allowed to vary with demographic characteristics and in table 1.4 some estimates (standard errors in parentheses) are presented for our selected sample of married women. Household composition is characterised by four zero-one child-age dummies (DK) which reflect the age of the youngest child. The AGE variable measures the age of the women. A brief data description is provided in appendix A, further details are to be found in Blundell, Duncan and Meghir (1992b).

The λ^p and λ^0 parameters reflect the correlation between the labour supply and the participation and tax segment selection processes respectively. The other-income residual coefficient is negative and significant, suggesting a significant negative bias in the β_1 parameters were we to exclude the residual term. The marginal significance of the wage residual suggests that most of the endogeneity of the marginal wage enters through

Table 1.4. *Labour supply estimates for married women*

α_0	28.156	(0.555)	β^1	-0.039	(0.003)
$\alpha_0(DK0–1)$	-3.242	(1.718)	$\beta^1(DK0–1)$	-0.048	(0.013)
$\alpha_0(DK2)$	-8.324	(1.615)	$\beta^1(DK2)$	-0.012	(0.013)
$\alpha_0(DK3–4)$	-10.633	(1.101)	$\beta^1(DK3–4)$	0.018	(0.006)
$\alpha_0(DK5–10)$	-10.205	(0.478)	$\beta^1(DK5–10)$	0.012	(0.002)
$\alpha_0(DK11+)$	-3.584	(0.544)	$\beta^1(DK11+)$	-0.016	(0.003)
$\alpha_0(AGE)$	-2.664	(0.127)			
$\alpha_0(AGE)^2$	-0.082	(0.100)			
α_1	1.657	(0.432)	ϵ_w	0.408	(0.368)
$\alpha_1(DK0–1)$	-7.372	(1.158)	ϵ_μ	-0.038	(0.002)
$\alpha_1(DK2)$	-4.926	(1.152)			
$\alpha_1(DK3–4)$	-4.479	(0.861)	λ^p	4.223	(0.840)
$\alpha_1(DK5–10)$	-2.291	(0.247)	λ^0	10.145	(0.154)
$\alpha_1(DK11+)$	-1.592	(0.317)	$\ln w^2$	$t=1.034$	

Notes:
Pooled FES regressions. Women married to employed men 1980–9.
Source: Blundell, Ham and Meghir (1992b).

non-linear taxation. It also turns out to be unnecessary to include terms in $(\ln w)^2$ as is indicated by the *t*-value provided in table 1.4.

Turning to the parameters themselves we see an overall significant and negative term on μ/w, indicating that leisure is indeed a normal good and that, for large enough values of μ, labour supply is forward sloping. The negative sign of the α_1 coefficient for women with children shows the possibility of backward-bending behaviour. Table 1.5 provides a detailed assessment of the corresponding estimated elasticities broken down by demographic subsamples. For each subsample the elasticities are evaluated at different quartile points from the distribution. Although small the uncompensated elasticities are largely positive and vary systematically with demographic type. The compensated elasticities show a close adherence with theory consistency across the sample. Blundell, Duncan and Meghir (1992b) also find that the elasticities rise with the exclusion of education from the reduced form equations of the Appendix. A grouping instrumental variable estimator based on tax year groups is shown to produce the largest elasticities and to be most robust.

The life-cycle consistent approach to modelling within-period labour supply decisions used in this section has proven to be a powerful tool in modelling hours of work. Together with a robust approach to dealing with piece-wise linear taxation, it has allowed the derivation of a data-coherent and largely theory-consistent model for within-period labour supply. It

Table 1.5. *Labour supply elasticities*

Youngest child	< 2	2	3–4	5–10	> 10	Childless
I. Uncompensated						
e(Q25)	− 0.008	0.014	0.010	− 0.052	− 0.040	0.008
e(Q50)	0.047	0.058	0.055	0.045	0.047	0.055
e(Q75)	0.099	0.103	0.100	0.079	0.079	0.093
e(mean)	0.103	0.074	0.050	0.023	0.024	0.052
II. Compensated						
e(Q25)	0.030	0.055	0.050	− 0.002	0.009	0.048
e(Q50)	0.088	0.099	0.095	0.086	0.087	0.096
e(Q75)	0.144	0.148	0.144	0.120	0.121	0.137
e(mean)	0.092	0.117	0.093	0.065	0.066	0.094
III. Income						
e(Q25)	− 0.101	− 0.084	− 0.087	− 0.121	− 0.116	− 0.088
e(Q50)	− 0.045	− 0.031	− 0.035	− 0.048	− 0.046	− 0.034
e(Q75)	− 0.010	− 0.009	− 0.009	− 0.016	− 0.016	− 0.011
e(mean)	− 0.095	− 0.079	− 0.091	− 0.119	− 0.139	− 0.089

also highlights the advantage of data sets, like the UK FES and the US CES, that collect information on both labour supply and consumption. As would be expected it turns out to be critical to allow for the endogeneity of the life-cycle consistent definition of other income as well as the selection on to each linear segment of the after-tax budget constraint.

3   A STRUCTURAL DYNAMIC MODEL WITH NON-PARTICIPATION

3.1   Preference restrictions and intertemporal models

Having considered a life-cycle consistent specification of within-period labour supply behaviour we return to the analysis of intertemporal allocations. Working within a time separable framework of the type described in section 2.1 allows relatively general interactions between labour supply and saving. The objective here is to briefly examine the type of structural restrictions typically imposed on empirical models of labour supply and saving, and to present a methodology for relaxing these as far as is possible within the time separable model. We then present some empirical results using the long time series of repeated cross sections available in the UK FES.

The stochastic life-cycle model of individual behaviour asserts that, in the face of new information about future wages, prices and other characteristics, individuals will alter their labour supply and consumption plans in a way that keeps the expected marginal value of wealth (appropriately discounted) constant across remaining periods. This does not necessarily imply that labour supply or consumption patterns themselves will be smooth since the marginal value of wealth may well not be proportional to labour supply or consumption across time; changes in the demographic structure of households, for example, may alter the marginal cost or marginal value of labour supply and consumption in any period and may lead to optimally lumpy life-cycle profiles.

In the time-separable intertemporal model, where life-cycle utility is additive across time, unobservable life-cycle variables capturing both past behaviour and forward-looking expectations can be summarised in the marginal utility of wealth 'λ'. Moreover, λ is dual to the other-income variable μ (as defined by (1.3) above) and there is a resulting equivalence between λ-conditional (Frisch) and μ-conditional (Marshallian) models. Following the theoretical discussion of section 2, separability over time implies that, conditional on μ or λ, only current-period variables enter the determination of current-period decisions. This is precisely the standard two-stage budgeting result and provides a useful way of choosing specifications that impose the fewest restrictions on preferences.

The attraction of thinking in terms of λ for intertemporal behaviour is that λ, after suitable discounting, is *constant* over the life cycle and can therefore be treated rather like an individual-specific fixed effect. This insight, attributable to MaCurdy (1981), implies that where panel data are available, *λ-constant* specifications of life-cycle utility-maximising behaviour can be estimated from the repeated observations on each individual. Actually, this analysis requires some care once we move from a world of perfect foresight, but even under uncertainty the λ-constant result remains correct under expectation. This is not altogether surprising since the separability assumption allows the application of the two-stage budgeting theory and ensures that life-cycle consistent current demands can be written in terms of a single sufficient statistic (λ or μ) capturing both past decisions and future anticipations.

More formally, defining q_s to be the leisure and consumption vector in period s and p_s as the corresponding price vector, lifetime utility in any period may be written as the expected discount sum of (concave twice differentiable) period-by-period utility (felicity) indices $U_s(q_s)$. Here p_s is defined to include the marginal wage rate. Life-cycle utility is then maximised subject to the combination of a within-period full income budget identity

$$p'_s q_s = m_s \qquad (1.13)$$

where m_s is full income in period s from the asset accumulation constraint

$$m_s = y_s + r_s A_{s-1} - \Delta A_s = \mu_s + \omega_s T_s \qquad (1.14)$$

where m_s is the sum of non-asset income y_s, interest income $r_s A_{s-1}$ and asset decumulation $-\Delta A_s$ as in equation (1.2) of section 2.

To complete this outline of the life-cycle framework it is useful to combine the two budget 'constraints' above to define the following lifetime wealth constraint

$$\sum_s p_s' q_s = (1 + r_t) A_{t-1} + \sum_s y_s = W_t \qquad (1.15)$$

where each $\sum_s$ refers to summation for $s = t, t + 1..$, and where for convenience we define all prices, wage rates and transfer incomes to be discounted back to period t.[12]

Turning to the first-order conditions for the intertemporal utility-maximising problem under perfect foresight (see Heckman and MaCurdy (1980)) we first write the usual within-period marginal conditions as

$$\partial U_t / \partial q_{it} = \lambda_t p_{it}, \text{ for each good } i. \qquad (1.16)$$

As described in section 2.1, in the labour supply/consumption model the parameters underlying within-period preferences may be estimated by eliminating λ as a function of μ and estimating the resulting μ-conditional labour supply models. The remaining parameters of U_t are identified from the following first-order condition, known as the Euler condition, that governs the evolution of marginal utility λ over time

$$\phi_{t+1} \lambda_{t+1} = \lambda_t \qquad (1.17)$$

where ϕ_{t+1} is the 'discount' factor $(1 + r_{t+1})$. In equation (1.17) the marginal utility of wealth in each period can be seen to provide the link between current and other-period decisions. Rearranging (1.16) to express within-period demands q_{it} in terms of p_t and λ_t generates the Frisch or λ-constant demand equations. In this formulation marginal utility λ_t acts as a summary of between-period allocations and therefore performs the same function as μ_t in the life-cycle consistent (Marshallian demand) analysis of section 2. Each Frisch or λ-constant demand may then be written

$$q_{it} = f_{it}(p_t, \lambda_t), \qquad (1.18)$$

which is homogeneous of degree zero in p_t and λ_t^{-1}.

The general properties of equations (1.18) are described in detail in Browning, Deaton and Irish (1985) and provide direct measures of the degree of intertemporal substitution. For example, the price and wage derivatives of (1.18) represent the effect of fully anticipated changes. An important advantage of using (1.18) directly is that the Euler equation

(1.17) can be usefully exploited to eliminate λ in empirical implementations on panel data.[13]

In most empirical representations of the life-cycle labour supply model the individual is allowed to be uncertain about future prices, wages and other relevant future events. Revisions to life-cycle wealth occur as new information or 'surprises' arise. In this case it is expected life-cycle utility that is maximised and the Euler equation (1.17) is replaced by

$$E_t(\phi_{t+1}\lambda_{t+1}) = \lambda_t. \tag{1.19}$$

where E_t represents expectations conditional on the information set available in period t as in (1.1). Hansen and Singleton (1982) use this moment condition directly to derive an optimal estimator for the intertemporal substitution parameters in the time separable model.

Removing the conditional expectation in (1.19) adds an innovation error or 'surprise' term to the model. This error is orthogonal to all past information according to (1.19) and, if there are no other stochastic unobservables, (1.19) defines an optimal set of instrumental variables. However, it should be noted that the empirical counterpart to this orthogonality condition refers to an averaging across *time* for a particular individual and not an averaging of (1.19) across individuals. For example, innovation errors may well be correlated across individuals according to their position in the other-income distribution and although past other incomes may be a perfectly valid instrumental variable over time for a particular individual, they may very likely be correlated with the distribution of current incomes across individuals. For this reason 'short' panels are to be avoided in the estimation of Euler equations.

Panel data applications to individual labour supply (and expenditure) decisions have generally required that the λ-constant demands take the form

$$g(q_{it}) = \gamma_i' f(p_t) + a_i \ln \lambda_t \tag{1.20}$$

where $g(.)$ refers to a log or linear transformation (see Heckman and MaCurdy (1980) and MaCurdy (1981), for example), γ_i is a vector of constant unknown parameters for the ith equation and $f(p_t)$ is a known of transformed prices p_t. Using (1.19) the model may then be written (assuming a constant discount factor) see (1.25) below as the following linear differenced specification

$$\Delta g(q_{it}) = \gamma_i' \Delta f_i(p_t) + a_i e_{t+1} \tag{1.21}$$

where e_{t+1} is an innovation error orthogonal to past information according to (1.19).

A number of recent papers (Blundell, Fry and Meghir (1990), Card

(1990) and Nickell (1986)) have noted the restrictions imposed both on life-cycle and within-period preferences from estimating structural models of the form (1.21). These restrictions are both strong and essentially unnecessary. The theoretical structure provides for much more general specifications. Using (1.20) Heckman and MaCurdy (1980) choose $g(.)$ to be log linear and $\gamma_i'f_i(p_i)$ to depend on p_{it} alone. This is equivalent to *explicit* additivity across time *and* goods, a situation sufficiently restrictive that all preference parameters relating to intertemporal substitution can be recovered from the μ-conditional models of section 2. Browning, Deaton and Irish (1985), on the other hand, assume g is linear and allow all prices to enter $g(.)$. However, this implies that within-period preferences are restricted to be Leontief and that the intertemporal substitution elasticity approaches zero as wealth increases. Both appear unreasonable prior assumptions.

It is useful to contrast these approaches with alternatives that relax the parametric structure and recover life-cycle consistent within-period preferences by substituting out the unobservable marginal utility of wealth across two or more contemporaneous decisions (see Altonji (1986)) or eliminate it using the within-period budget constraint (see MaCurdy (1983) or Blundell and Walker (1986)) as in our modelling of labour supply described in section 2. Where the monotonic transformation of within-period preferences is fixed and not estimated, as in Heckman and MaCurdy (1980) for example, the parameters estimated from such alternative representations are sufficient to identify all intertemporal substitution elasticities. However, given an estimated specification of within-period parameters, the remaining intertemporal parameters can be recovered from a single Euler condition without unduly restricting the parameterisation of interactions between savings and labour supply behaviour. We turn next to such a procedure.

3.2   A sequential approach to identification and estimation in intertemporal models

In the light of the above discussion, the aim in this section is to describe an alternative approach for the estimation of intertemporal preference parameters. We consider the implications of allowing individuals to go through periods out of the labour market. First, a specification for within-period preferences is chosen that is life-cycle consistent as described in section 2. Secondly, a Euler equation representing intertemporal allocations is chosen that encompasses this specification of within-period preferences. If we let $V(p_t, \mu_t; z_t)$ represent within-period preference estimated from the μ-conditional Marshallian life-cycle consistent models of section 2, the Euler condition can be thought of as identifying parameters of the monotonic transformation $F(V(p_t, \mu_t; z_t); z_t)$. It is worth emphasising at this point that the Euler condition on marginal utility (1.19) holds whether or not some elements of the q_t vector are at corner solutions or constrained in other ways (see Blundell, Meghir and Neves (1993)). At a constraint point λ must be evaluated at the corresponding reservation or support price (wage). As was shown in section 2, the Slutsky conditon on labour supply guarantees the existence of a unique support wage.

Setting up the intertemporal problem in this way will allow a number of problems to be addressed. In particular, corners in labour supply can be dealt with directly. We can study intertemporal substitution without imposing restrictions on within-period preferences (conditonal on intertemporal separability). We can also address the importance of separability of goods and leisure over time. Finally, we can study the effect of movements in and out of the labour market, and their importance as a mechanism of intertemporal adjustments, without assuming a priori the absence of constraints and frictions relating to such labour market transitions.

Turning to the estimation of the Euler equation (1.19) the methodology described in Blundell, Browning and Meghir (1989) can be used to identify intertemporal substitution elasticities. As an illustration take the following functional form for overall within-period utility

$$F(V_t; z_t) = \delta_t V_t^{\{1 + \rho_t\}} \equiv U_t \tag{1.22}$$

where the superscript in { } denotes the Box–Cox transform. As noted above all parameters in V_t are identified from the estimation of the μ-conditional labour supply equations described in section 2. The discount parameter δ_t and the parameter ρ_t may be allowed to vary across households and across time according to movements in demographic and other characteristics. Given this normalisation, the log of the discounted marginal utility of expenditure for any household in period t may be written as

$$\ln \lambda_t = \rho \ln V_t + \ln V_t' + \ln \delta_t \tag{1.23}$$

where V_t', is the μ_t derivative of V_t.

To estimate ρ_t and δ_t, the Euler equation (1.19) which governs the evolution of λ_t over time, may be exploited. To proceed, re-write (1.19) as

$$\phi_{t+1} \lambda_{t+1} = \lambda_t \epsilon_{t+1} \tag{1.24}$$

with $E_t \epsilon_{t+1} = 1$. For purposes of estimation we consider $\ln \epsilon_{t+1}$ which is distributed in such a way that

$$E_t(\ln \epsilon_{t+1}) = d_{t+1} + \ln(E_t(\epsilon_{t+1}))$$

where d_{t+1} is proportional to the conditional variance (or higher moments) of ϵ_{t+1}. In estimation, time effects will allow these conditional moments to vary systematically across time. Re-writing $\ln\epsilon_{t+1}$ as e_{t+1}, we have

$$\Delta\ln\lambda_{t+1} + \ln\phi_{t+1} + d_{t+1} = e_{t+1}, \qquad E_t(e_{t+1}) = 0 \qquad (1.25)$$

where Δ refers to the first difference operator. Since $\ln\lambda_t$ depends directly on ρ_t and δ_t through (1.23), equation (1.25) can be used to estimate these parameters noting that the orthogonality condition on e_{t+1} permits the use of lagged variables as identifying instrumental variables.

3.3   Some estimates using the repeated cross sections of the FES

In order to provide a sufficiently long period of time to estimate the Euler equation the period 1970 to 1986 is utilised. For the purposes of this empirical illustration, a simplified version of the labour supply model (1.10) was chosen of the form

$$h_{it} = a_0(z_{it}) + \beta_1(z_t)\frac{\mu_{it}}{w_{it}} + \epsilon_{it} \qquad (1.26)$$

where $a_0(z)$ and $\beta_1(z)$ reflect the dependence of these parameters on the child and age variables. Moreover, the complete sample of workers was used with a linearised budget constraint. However, both virtual income μ_{it} and marginal wage w_{it} were allowed to be endogenous following the discussion of the labour supply estimates in table 1.4 in section 2 above. Since, over such a long period, cohort and age effects will differ, a_0 was allowed to depend on cohort and age variables.[14]

Note again that the FES data rather than being a panel, following the same individuals across time, is a time series of repeated cross sections. As a result, to estimate our Euler equation (1.25) we follow Browning, Deaton and Irish (1985) and construct a pseudo panel using cohort averages.[15] Figures 1.3, 1.4 and 1.5 present the life-cycle pattern of real expenditure, female participation and the distribution of children in our cohort data base. Each line represents the path for a separate cohort.

To relate these cohort averages to the discussion in section 3.2 consider equation (1.25) which defines marginal utility 'λ' for each individual, and take population averages conditional on the person belonging to cohort c. With sufficiently large cohort groups these terms may be replaced by their corresponding sample averages. Taking cohort averages, (1.23) becomes

$$E_c\ln\lambda_t = E_c\,\rho(z_t)\ln V_t + E_c\ln(V'_t) \qquad (1.27)$$

where we have allowed the parameter ρ_t to depend on a vector of characteristics z_t. Providing entry into the cohort (through immigration)

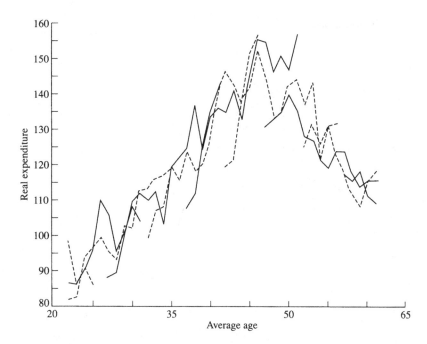

Figure 1.3 Real expenditure over the life cycle

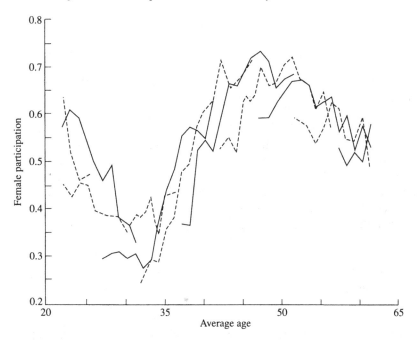

Figure 1.4 Female participation over the life cycle

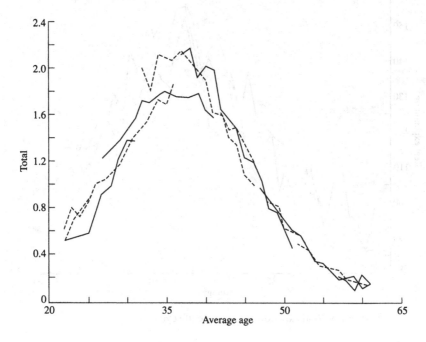

Figure 1.5 The life-cycle distribution of children

and exit (through death and emigration) are uncorrelated with the marginal utility of wealth, from (1.25) we obtain

$$\Delta E_c \ln\lambda_{t+1} + \ln\phi_{t+1} + d_{t+1} = E_c e_{t+1} \qquad (1.28)$$

where again Δ is the first-difference operator and $E_t E_t e_{t+1} = 0$.

Using (1.27) and (1.28) the counterpart to (1.24) can be constructed which is estimable on average cohort data provided the averages are constructed in a way that is consistent with (1.28) and provided all cohort members share the same information set. Using the cohort averages in this case maintains the orthogonality conditions (1.24) underlying the structural economic theory. For non-participants the indirect utility terms $\ln(V_t')$ and $\ln V_t$ can be constructed imputing the inverse labour supply equation at $h_t = 0$.

Specifying $\rho(z_t)$ to be

$$\rho(z_t) = \rho_0 + \Sigma_k \rho_t z_{tk} \qquad (1.29)$$

we see that (1.27) involves the cohort means of $\ln(V')_t$, of $\ln V_t$ and the cross moments of $\ln V_t$ with the characteristics z_t. We thus use the sample equivalents of these population moments. In other words the exact way in which the cohort averages in the pseudo panel are constructed are governed by the specification of the Euler condition and the estimated μ-conditional labour supply model.

Given this consistent aggregation procedure, the intertemporal parameters can be estimated using a Generalised Method of Moments estimator on

$$\Delta\ln(V'_t)_c + \rho^0\Delta\ln(V_t)_c + \sum_k\rho_k\Delta(z_{tk}\ln V_t)_c + \ln(1+r_t) + d_t + \Delta\ln\delta_t = (e_t)_c \tag{1.30}$$

where the subscript c on the differenced terms points to the fact that we are differencing cohort averages rather than individual's observations. The instruments used in the methods of moments estimator are lagged cohort averages and lagged differences in cohort averages. They do not involve any estimated parameters.

The stochastic process underlying the Euler condition does require careful attention in applications to micro-data as has been recognised by Chamberlain (1984) and Hayashi (1987). As we argued above large 'N' asymptotics may not be sufficient to guarantee the consistency of method of moments parameter estimates using lagged instruments in short panels. One solution to this potentially important problem is to exploit the comparatively long time series of cohort observations in the repeated cross-sections of the FES and to carefully assess the validity of chosen instrumental variables at each step of the estimation.

In the example here there are ten cohorts each covering a five-year band. This choice leads to cohorts with approximately 300–400 members each (per year). By removing any household whose head is sixty years of age or over we exclude the retired and can hope to minimise the effects of sample attrition due to death. After allowing for the different periods over which each cohort is observed and the loss of observations due to differencing and lagging the instrument set, the resulting data set comprised 100 observations. For the interest rate the simple after tax building society lending rate available at the end of period $t-1$ was used. Since most households hold such deposits this seemed an appropriate choice.

Column 1 of table 1.6 presents the estimated coefficients for the cohort model (1.30). The results of column 2 will be referred to below. The variables influencing ρ are fairly self-explanatory – HUNEMP refers to the husband out of work and WHC refers to whether the head of household is a white-collar worker. All interaction terms in (1.30) are treated as endogenous. A negative coefficient indicates a lower overall intertemporal elasticity.

All standard errors in table 1.6 are heteroscedasticity adjusted and the

Table 1.6. *The Euler equation estimates*

	Separable model	Non-separable model
HUEMP	−0.2308	−0.2215
	(0.1250)	(0.1280)
K2	−0.0542	−0.0608
	(0.0840)	(0.0860)
K3	0.0446	0.0422
	(0.0380)	(0.0390)
K4	0.0550	0.0522
	(0.0350)	(0.0340)
WHC	0.3447	0.3522
	(0.1120)	(0.1110)
Sargan (30)	46.053	45.451
r_1	1.2873	1.311
r_2	0.9776	0.976

Notes:
Generalised Methods of Moments used throughout. Standard errors in
parentheses. All instruments dated $t-2$.

Generalised Method of Moments estimator exploits this adjustment to
improve upon the efficiency of the simple IV estimator. All instruments
were dated $t-2$. This timing of instruments reflects the indication of first-
order autocorrelation in the errors. The r_1 diagnostic is a one degree of
freedom test of this hypothesis and is distributed asymptotically as $N(0,1)$
under the null. Such MA(1) errors may well be generated by time
aggregation but may also simply reflect the stochastic process underlying
$\Delta \ln \delta_t$ in (1.30).

Combining the Euler equation estimates of table 1.6 with the labour
supply model allows us to identify a set of elasticities relating to intertemporal behaviour. In particular we can construct the λ-constant labour
supply (h) and consumption (q) intertemporal substitution elasticities.
Browning (1987) provides an elegant description of the relationship
between these elasticities. These are presented for the non-separable model
in table 1.7 for particular demographic subsamples: e_{hw}^u refers to the wage
elasticity of hours of work holding utility u constant, the remainder follow
using the same notation.

The omission of the ln$w$ term in the labour supply model induces a
slightly larger μ constant (uncompensated) labour supply elasticity than

Table 1.7. *Some elasticities*

	DK3 = 1	DK4 = 1	K = 0
e^u_{hw}	0.185	0.213	0.164
e^{μ}_{hw}	0.127	0.142	0.085
e^{λ}_{hw}	0.199	0.234	0.181
e^u_{qp}	− 0.049	− 0.059	− 0.069
e^{λ}_{qp}	− 1.195	− 1.167	− 1.143

Note:
Elasticities using the non-separable model estimates evaluated at the mean for the sample of working women with children.

reported for the complete sample model in section 2. However, it is also interesting to note that for these samples β_1 is negative which guarantees the Slutsky condition and therefore a well-behaved indirect utility representation for V_t in (1.22) above. Moreover, the inverse labour supply equation is unique (Slutsky condition) and explicit, implying that the reservation wage for all individuals with $h = 0$ can be evaluated and included in V_t in the Euler equation (1.30) for individuals recording zero hours of work.

3.4   The importance of relative price changes and the separability of leisure from goods

There is no doubt that over the long time period considered in the empirical example of the previous subsection relative prices will have changed significantly. This only has serious implications for our model of intertemporal labour supply if the marginal rate of substitution between such goods is dependent on labour supply. That is, if labour supply and goods are non-separable. In this case the real wage deflator itself will depend on hours of work. There is a considerable body of empirical literature which suggests this is an important problem. Indeed a recent study by Browning and Meghir (1991) confirms the results of Blundell and Walker (1982) in rejecting separability using the Family Expenditure Survey. More important perhaps is the implication for intertemporal models that utilise labour supply and a single consumption item. All such models for the Michigan Panel Study of Income Dynamics are restricted to the use of food expenditures alone (see Altonji (1986) or MaCurdy (1983)).

To analyse the separability issue attention must be focussed on the determination of disaggregated expenditures. This can be carried out

Table 1.8. *The estimated conditional demand system*

(i) The γ_{ij}, α_{iF}, α_{iM}, β_i, β_{IF} and β_{im}, coefficient estimates

	Food	Alcl.	Fuel	Cloth	Trans.	Serv.	Other
PFOOD	-0.0314	0.0137	-0.0374	0.0091	-0.0068	0.0547	-0.0019
	(0.0153)	(0.0090)	(0.0073)	(0.0113)	(0.0162)	(0.0119)	(0.0114)
PALCL		-0.0428	0.0288	-0.0124	0.0479	0.0049	-0.0402
		(0.0104)	(0.0070)	(0.0079)	(0.0132)	(0.0096)	(0.0109)
PFUEL			0.0386	0.0034	-0.0593	0.0015	0.0244
			(0.0079)	(0.0062)	(0.0104)	(0.0079)	(0.0088)
PCLOTH				0.0073	0.0124	-0.0070	-0.0128
				(0.0127)	(0.0143)	(0.0101)	(0.0100)
PTRANS					0.0292	0.0268	0.0035
					(0.0323)	(0.0173)	(0.0185)
PSERV						0.0168	0.0056
						(0.0168)	(0.0217)
HM	0.0076	0.0056	0.0001	-0.0091	-0.0026	0.0057	-0.0073
	(0.0031)	(0.0022)	(0.0018)	(0.0032)	(0.0047)	(0.0031)	(0.0023)
HF	-0.0099	0.0009	-0.0036	0.0148	-0.0128	-0.0026	0.0132
	(0.0052)	(0.0037)	(0.0029)	(0.0054)	(0.0079)	(0.0054)	(0.0039)
LOGX	-0.0871	0.0362	0.0338	-0.0096	0.0036	0.0905	0.0001
	(0.0164)	(0.0115)	(0.0098)	(0.0182)	(0.0294)	(0.0176)	(0.0143)
HM*LOGX	-0.0009	-0.0006	-0.0002	0.0013	0.0003	-0.0009	0.0010
	(0.0004)	(0.0003)	(0.0003)	(0.0005)	(0.0007)	(0.0004)	(0.0003)
HF*LOGX	0.0013	-0.0001	0.0005	-0.0019	0.0018	0.0002	-0.0019
	(0.0007)	(0.0005)	(0.0004)	(0.0007)	(0.0011)	(0.0007)	(0.0005)

Note:
All HM, HF and LOGX terms are instrumented. Standard errors in parentheses.
Source: Neves (1991).

Table 1.9. *Statistical tests*

Homogeneity tests (*t*-ratios with 1 degree of freedom)						
Food	Alcl.	Fuel	Cloth	Trans.	Serv.	Other
0.83	-1.44	1.49	-1.67	0.00	0.77	0.59

Tests of weak separability	Degrees of freedom	Test statistic	*P*-value (%)
Female hours	12	43.04	2E-5
Male hours	12	284.39	9E-54

within a Marshallian life-cycle consistent demand framework using the repeated cross sections available in the FES. If expenditure decisions are not separable from labour supply, hours of work will enter the Marshallian demand system. Using an Almost Ideal (AI) demand system framework Browning and Meghir (1991) find this to be an important characteristic of demand equations. Drawing on their results, Neves (1991) has re-estimated the Almost Ideal demand system over the period used for the intertemporal model described in last subsection.[16]

The non-separability of labour supply decisions was introduced by extending the standard Almost Ideal indirect utility function to take the form

$$G(x,p;h) = \frac{\ln x - \ln a(p;h)}{b(p;h)} \tag{1.31}$$

where x is total expenditure (see Deaton and Muellbauer (1980)). In particular the price indices $a(p;h)$ and $b(p;h)$ were written:

$$\log a(p;h) = \sum_k (a_{k0} + a_{kF}.h_F + a_{kM}.h_M) \log p_k + \\ + 0.5 \sum_k \sum_j \gamma_{kj} \log p_k \log p_j \tag{1.32}$$

$$b(p,h) = \exp[\sum_k (\beta_k + \beta_{kF}.h_F + \beta_{kM}.h_M) \log p_k] \tag{1.33}$$

where h_F and h_M represent female and male hours of work, respectively.

The conditional expenditure of share equations implied by this parameterisation are given by

$$w_i = a(z) + a_{iF} \cdot h_F + a_{iM} \cdot h_M + \sum_j \gamma_{ij} \cdot \log p_j +$$

$$+ \beta(z) + \beta_{iF} \cdot h_F + \beta_{iM} \cdot h_M) \cdot \log(x/a(p, h; z)) \tag{1.34}$$

where the significance of the a_F, a_M, β_F, β_M, parameters reflect the importance of relaxing separability between goods and leisure. Summary parameter estimates are provided in table 1.8. Casual inspection of these results indicates the apparent strength of the separability restriction. This is confirmed in the tests performed in table 1.9.

Turning now to the labour supply estimates, to derive these labour supply estimates under non-separability we note that the AI model for preferences over goods implies a female labour supply equation of the form

$$h = \gamma_0 + \gamma_1 \frac{b(p; h)}{-\dfrac{w}{x} + a_F + \beta_F \ln(x/a(p; h))} \tag{1.35}$$

Under separability ($a_F = \beta_F = 0$ and $b(\ )$, $a(\ )$ independent of h) this reduces to

$$h = \gamma_0 - \gamma_1 b(p) \frac{x}{w}. \tag{1.36}$$

Noting that $x = \mu + wh$ and with $b(p) = 1$, we can re-write (1.36) as

$$h = \frac{\gamma_0}{1 + \gamma_1} - \frac{\gamma_1}{1 + \gamma_1} \frac{\mu}{w} \tag{1.37}$$

or

$$h = a_0 + \beta_1 \frac{\mu}{w} \tag{1.37'}$$

as in the labour supply model (1.26)

Although non-separability is an important issue for consumer behaviour over this period, its impact on the labour supply estimates (inclusive of time and cohort effects) appears negligible. Moreover, column (2) of table 1.6 provides the Euler equation estimates corresponding to this non-separable specification. These results confirm the robustness of the intertemporal results to the non-separability of goods and labour supply.

3.5   Intertemporal separability and endogenous experience

There are a number of serious and evident limitations to the intertemporal models that have been described thus far. Although these models are able to deal with non-participation and do not require the standard 'Tobit model' condition on non-participation, the time separability assumption is likely to be very restrictive, at least for certain types of individuals. It rules out endogenous on-the-job human capital formation and habit formation, for example.

Wage equations often include a measure of actual work experience for women (see Mroz (1987), for example). This typically differs significantly from potential experience (age minus age left school). As Mroz and others have pointed out, actual past work experience is likely to be endogenous. However, allowing for endogeneity in the wage equation is only half the problem. Experience reflects past labour supply choices and consequently breaks the time separability assumption.[17] When there is a significant payoff to experience an individual may decide to stay in employment despite a low current wage or a high current value of time because the cost of lost experience on future wages outweighs these current economic considerations. This is a very important point and invalidates even the hours/consumption trade-off model described in section 2. Indeed, in the structural labour supply model the current wage would require adjustment to account for the future payoff of current experience (see Altug and Miller (1990b) and Shaw (1989), for example). However, it should be pointed out that the Euler equation remains valid but now marginal utility λ_t depends directly on choice variables from outside the period.

As an illustration we can consider a simple extension of the wage equation to allow for the impact of past work experience. Suppose work experience for the past two years entered the wage equation. In the first-order conditions for optimal hours of work, conditional on μ, the current wage rate w would be replaced by terms in w_t, w_{t+1} and w_{t+3}. The effect of endogenous experience is to enter a 'smoothed' forward-looking wage into the labour supply decision. With uncertainty, conditional expectations need to be taken over all wage terms.

The distinct 'advantage' of breaking separability through endogenous experience is that a lot can be learned from examining the wage equation at the outset. To investigate the importance of endogenous experience for married women in the FES data source used in this study I considered the case of entering past experience in the wage equation. As these data are not a panel I divided women by education and demographic group and entered the participation proportion for women in the same cohort with similar education and demographic structure. Lagged cohort asset incomes and housing tenure variables were used to instrument these proportions. The results indicate that experience is most important for those with higher education.[18] Moreover, the experience effect is negligible after two years. As one might expect in most clerical, manual and shop assistant type occupations, the wage experience profile is relatively flat. This is not true for those with university entry level education where there was a significant 9 per cent return. These results are the major reason why professional and technical occupations were excluded from the sample used in the analyses of FES data in sections 2.4 and 3.3.

In general, it must be important to allow for the possibility of endogenous experience. This would seem most critical for the interaction of child timing and spacing decisions with labour market participation for women (see Eckstein and Wolpin (1989)), especially those having sufficient education to enter occupations with relatively steep experience/wage profiles. Naturally, educational choices may also be endogenous to this process but these usually enter in the time invariant initial condition in labour market studies.

4   CONCLUSIONS

Any attempt to provide a representative view of the rapidly expanding, yet historically large, field of structural micro-econometric models of labour supply would be fruitless. Instead this chapter has outlined a strategy for the sequential testing and estimation of a class of theoretically consistent labour supply models that portray the hours of work, and participation and intertemporal allocation decisions of married women. It has focussed on pointing out the unnecessarily severe preference restrictions in many empirical studies and on explaining the patterns of behaviour found in the UK, specifically that recorded in the repeated cross sections of the Family Expenditure Survey.

The approaches discussed, although not restricted to the FES data set, do exploit a number of features of this type of data source. Most notable is the long period over which the data set has been regularly and consistently recorded, together with the accurate measurement of consumption expenditures and earnings. The nature of the FES data source has also provided for some glaring omissions. In particular, the treatment of individual effects and measurement error has been necessarily limited. However, since the FES is a repeated random sample, individual effects do not induce autocorrelation over time as in the standard error-components panel data model. It is, nevertheless, important to include many individual conditioning variables. Since the models are non-linear, both through selectivity as well as preference flexibility, the ability to allow for correlated fixed effects is severely limited even if panel data were available (see Heckman (1981), Hsaio (1986) and Chamberlain (1984)). This is certainly the case for the models above which include weakly exogenous regressors. Finally, the presence of fixed effects in the life-cycle models of MaCurdy (1981) and Heckman and MaCurdy (1980) is circumvented to an extent by the ability to condition on observed consumption in our life-cycle consistent modelling framework.

In general, measuring consumption along with labour supply has been shown to carry some considerable advantages especially when labour supply is censored or discrete. Firstly, it allows the standard labour supply model describing the within-period trade-off between hours and consumption to be made consistent with a reasonably general intertemporal framework. Secondly, and perhaps more importantly, given the within-period preferences from the labour supply model, it allows the identification of the complete set of intertemporal substitution parameters through the Euler condition for consumption over time which was shown to retain its validity across discrete employment states. Since there is only one independent Euler condition in the time separable model, knowledge of within-period preferences together with the parameters of a single Euler condition are sufficient for full identification.

APPENDIX A   DATA DESCRIPTION AND BACKGROUND ESTIMATES

The data set used was drawn from the UK Family Expenditure Survey.

Sample selection criteria

(a)   Occupation: FES variable A210 with value 4, 5, 6, 7, 8. Clerical, shop assistant and manual workers only.

(b)   Age: Women with $16 < \text{age} < 60$, Men with $16 < \text{age} < 65$.

(c)   Two adult households living as a couple.

Sample statistics for the 1981 sample

Households with working women: 976.
Households with non-working women: 830.

	(i) Working women		(ii) Non-working women	
Variable	Mean	Standard deviation	Mean	Standard deviation
Female hours	25.451	11.591	—	—
Male hours	38.767	8.726	35.926	14.464
Children 0–2 (K1)	0.069	0.273	0.455	0.633
3–4 (K2)	0.054	0.231	0.260	0.478
5–10 (K3)	0.454	0.720	0.528	0.813
11+ (K4)	0.488	0.774	0.356	0.721

Sample statistics (*cont.*)

	(i) Working women		(ii) Non-working women	
Variable	Mean	Standard deviation	Mean	Standard deviation
Female wage	1.244	0.569	—	—
Male wage	2.022	0.747	2.135	1.017
Other income μ	39.246	34.721	66.183	38.676
Female age	36.930	10.645	35.539	11.124
Education (female)	15.431	1.210	15.671	1.696
Regional unempl.	13.495	3.129	13.822	3.092

Hours of work are normal weekly hours.
Wages are in £/hour. Other income is measured in £ per week. These units of measurement were used in estimation.
Education is the age at the end of full-time education.

Table A1. *Reduced-form selection equations*

	Participation model		Ordered probability model	
Variable	Coeff.	SE	Coeff.	SE
Constant	1.4563	0.7377	—	—
Ln (Personal allowance)	0.0945	0.1579	−0.8842	0.0241
Asset income	−0.0020	0.0001	−0.0003	0.0001
Basic tax rate	−2.3658	0.8091	−2.6772	0.9297
Age	−0.2993	0.0439	−0.2430	0.0500
Age^2	−0.1428	0.0208	0.0053	0.0230
Education	0.0628	0.0095	−0.0501	0.0099
(Age) × (Education)	−0.0026	0.0008	0.0012	0.0008
(Head ed.) × (Education)	−0.0034	0.0011	−0.0008	0.0011
1920s cohort	0.2552	0.1528	−0.0769	0.1793
1930s cohort	0.1484	0.1173	−0.0331	0.1387
1940s cohort	0.1139	0.0807	−0.1703	0.1003
1950s cohort	0.0925	0.0543	−0.2698	0.0710
Number of children	0.0914	0.0658	−0.2710	0.0893
(Number of children)^2	−0.0402	0.0143	0.0480	0.0202
DK0	−1.8168	0.1607	−0.2554	0.2690
DK1	−1.7736	0.1215	−0.3884	0.1737
DK2	−1.4949	0.1266	−0.3666	0.1869
DK3–4(NS)	−1.4817	0.1235	−0.4693	0.1761
DK3–4(S)	−1.2540	0.1214	−0.5019	0.1535

Table A1. (*cont.*)

Variable	Participation model		Ordered probability model	
	Coeff.	SE	Coeff.	SE
DK5–10	− 0.6736	0.0832	− 0.2863	0.1050
DK11 +	− 0.2381	0.0796	0.0576	0.0976
DK0 × (age)	0.2183	0.1124	0.3469	0.2017
DK1 × (age)	0.1745	0.0784	0.2544	0.1209
DK2 × (age)	0.1751	0.0898	0.3522	0.1410
DK3–4(NS) × (age)	− 0.0762	0.0983	0.2907	0.1506
DK3–4(S) × (age)	0.0357	0.1004	0.2352	0.1253
DK5–10 × (age)	0.0524	0.0495	0.1147	0.0570
DK11 + × (age)	− 0.0511	0.0608	− 0.0908	0.0636
Special school	− 0.1077	0.0916	− 0.0622	0.0869
North	0.1002	0.1959	0.1008	0.2245
Yorkshire	0.0642	0.1681	0.1473	0.1903
North-west	0.1700	0.1633	0.1371	0.1908
East Midlands	0.0470	0.1101	0.1081	0.1237
West Midlands	0.0092	0.1296	0.1067	0.1509
East Anglia	− 0.0916	0.0713	− 0.0316	0.0802
South-west	− 0.1756	0.1093	0.0287	0.1260
Wales	0.0558	0.1805	0.2200	0.2081
Scotland	0.0320	0.1175	0.2971	0.1313
Female unemp./age	− 0.2991	0.6062	0.7868	0.7053
Vacancies/region	0.0484	0.0275	− 0.0286	0.0299
Redundancies/region	0.0043	0.0092	− 0.0005	0.0098
Regional unemployment	− 2.2943	0.9603	2.3400	1.0544
Childcare density	0.2703	0.2291	0.4819	0.2341
Playgroup density	− 0.0580	0.0989	− 0.0822	0.1118
Skewness	2.093	—	2.098	
Kurtosis	1.788	—	3.989	

Notes:
DK0, DK2 etc. is a zero-one dummy indicating the age of the youngest child.
Childcare availability is measured by the number of full childcare places per
1,000 of the regional population (*source: Regional Trends* 1981–6). DK3–4(NS)
indicates the presence of the youngest child aged 3–4 not at school; DK3–4(S)
indicates the youngest child is aged 3–4 and attending school. Vacancies and
redundancies by region are taken from *Employment Gazette* 1981–6.
Participation dummy = 1 for individual working, 0 elsewhere.
Skewnes and Kurtosis are one degree of freedom chi-squared variate.

Table A2. *Reduced-form wage/other-income equations*

Variable	ln(wage)		Other income	
	Coeff.	SE	Coeff.	SE
Constant	5.3453	0.0727	76.2530	29.7041
Age	0.0580	0.0155	18.2868	2.3284
Age^2	−0.0210	0.0065	3.1493	1.0802
Education	0.1155	0.0060	4.4829	0.8909
Education^2	−0.0038	0.0007	−1.1057	0.1177
(Age) × (education)	0.0069	0.0022	0.1743	0.0438
(Head ed.) × (education)	0.0016	0.0003	0.5362	0.0605
1920s cohort	−0.0053	0.0534	−16.2199	8.1278
1930s cohort	−0.0512	0.0401	−5.7929	6.1099
1940s cohort	−0.0117	0.0281	−1.8660	4.1689
1950s cohort	0.0695	0.0181	−5.5760	2.7124
Number of children	—	—	27.9928	3.5123
(Number of children)^2	—	—	−3.3535	0.7587
DK0	—	—	45.7592	8.5423
DK1	—	—	31.2397	6.3947
DK2	—	—	48.9536	6.8828
DK3–4(NS)	—	—	34.4096	6.7804
DK3–4(S)	—	—	24.1376	6.7464
DK5–10	—	—	14.3133	4.4501
DK11+	—	—	11.4550	4.1620
DK0 × (age)	—	—	9.5136	5.8293
DK1 × (age)	—	—	−1.5628	4.0445
DK2 × (age)	—	—	13.0238	4.9147
DK3–4(NS) × (age)	—	—	6.0839	5.5418
DK3–4(S) × (age)	—	—	−7.2828	5.7484
DK5–10 × (age)	—	—	−9.1241	2.7149
DK11+ × (age)	—	—	−3.4837	3.1701
Special school	—	—	0.4359	4.6310
North	−0.2630	0.0484	−14.0954	12.2590
Yorkshire	−0.2089	0.0356	−17.3102	10.2225
North-west	−0.2282	0.0411	−8.1699	10.0714
East Midlands	−0.1543	0.0254	−16.7382	6.6182
West Midlands	−0.1972	0.0326	−8.7939	7.8805
East Anglia	−0.0845	0.0210	−12.9950	3.8609
South-west	−0.1407	0.0174	−9.8856	5.8545
Wales	−0.2324	0.0385	−15.5723	10.8543
Scotland	−0.2306	0.0376	−12.0668	7.9046
Female unemp./age	−0.2037	0.2354	12.4726	34.5730
Vacancies/region	0.0224	0.0130	−0.1717	2.0330
Redundancies/region	0.0236	0.0039	0.5320	0.5901

Table A2. (*cont.*)

Variable	ln(wage)		Other income	
	Coeff.	SE	Coeff.	SE
Regional unemployment	1.1653	0.6100	− 72.3842	92.5317
Childcare density	—	—	− 8.7152	13.1274
Playgroup density	—	—	1.5354	5.3438
Year = 1980	− 0.3522	0.0479	− 3.0150	8.7427
Year = 1981	− 0.3970	0.0484	− 0.6029	8.6989
Year = 1982	− 0.3827	0.0423	3.2509	7.8508
Year = 1983	− 0.3127	0.0392	9.9639	6.9792
Year = 1984	− 0.2664	0.0360	7.8645	6.2571
Year = 1985	− 0.2420	0.0371	9.5686	6.0319
Year = 1986	− 0.2016	0.0373	11.6562	5.8868
Year = 1987	− 0.1457	0.0303	6.1723	4.6994
Year = 1988	− 0.0182	0.0220	6.7778	3.4228
Selection correction	0.0283	0.0126		

Notes:
As for table A1.

Notes

Invited lecture at the Sixth World Congress of the Econometric Society, Barcelona, August 1990. I am grateful to a number of colleagues and co-authors for inspiration. In particular, I am indebted to Martin Browning, Richard Disney, Alan Duncan, John Ham, James Heckman, Francois Laisney, Costas Meghir, Robert Moffitt, Alice Nakamura, Pedro Neves, Richard Smith, Mark Stewart and Ian Walker. Financial support from the ESRC Centre for the Microeconomic Analysis of Fiscal Policy at IFS is gratefully acknowledged. Thanks are also due to the UK Department of Employment for providing the FES data used in this study. All errors are mine alone.

1 For example, Blomquist (1983), Bourguignon (1986), Burtless and Hausman (1978), Burtless and Moffitt (1985), Heckman (1974c), Moffitt (1986b) and Zabalza (1983).

2 Again the analogy with the Consumers Expenditure Survey for the US is striking.

3 Mroz (1987) has shown how critical the Tobit model assumption is in his study of married women in the USA. Blundell, Ham and Meghir (1987) reject it for the UK FES data. For the French data see Bourguignon and Magnac (1990). Of course, these models, still assume working individuals are not systematically off their labour supply curve. See Ham (1986b) for an excellent survey of evidence on this issue.

4 Individuals are assumed to be infinitely lived (see, e.g. Burdett and Mortensen (1978) for a discussion of this assumption) and maximise lifetime utility subject to an intertemporal budget constraint.

5 See Altonji (1986), Heckman (1974b) and Heckman and MaCurdy (1980). This is an important characteristic of female labour supply models.

6 Note that data on consumption expenditure, available in the FES, can be used to construct μ.

7 It should be noted, however, that the (intertemporal) Euler equation for consumption still holds across discrete labour market states, see Blundell, Meghir and Neves (1993). This will be exploited in section 3 of this chapter.

8 Clearly we are also ruling out the potentially important consideration of wage/ hours packages or hours dependent gross (hourly) wages, see Moffitt (1984) and Rosen (1976a). The importance of grouping hours is considered in the empirical application and intertemporal separability is discussed at the end of section 3.

9 If $a_1 w$ is replaced by $a_1 \ln w$ as in Mroz (1987) then the condition becomes $a_1/w - \beta_1 h \geq 0$.

10 Notice that random unobservable heterogeneity in a_0 simply leads to an additive random error on V. This provides a flexible specification which avoids the need for simulated moments (see Bloemen and Kapteyn (1990) for a useful discussion of the use of simulated moments in such labour supply models).

11 It should be noted that provided overlapping explanatory variables are available these reduced-form estimates need not come from the same sample. Indeed, Arellano and Meghir (1992) provide an ingenious example of the use of complementary data sets in just such a situation.

12 Under the two-stage budgeting allocation of full income over the life-cycle, m_t or μ_t is given by $\theta_t(p_t, p_{t+1}, \ldots, W_t)$ where θ_t is homogeneous of degree zero in discounted prices and wealth. If perfect foresight is relaxed to allow replanning all arguments of $\theta_t(.)$ are replaced by their conditional expectations given information in period t. It is clear from (1.15) that the $\theta_t(.)$ accounts for the influence of all future expectations concerning economic and demographic variables on current period as well as the influence of past decisions through A_{t-1} in W_t.

13 An equivalent derivation of the λ-constant model is given by Browning, Deaton and Irish (1985) using the individual's profit function defined by

$$\pi(p_t, 1/\lambda_t) = \max \{U_t/\lambda_t - C(p_t, U_t)\}$$

where $C(p_t, U_t)$ is the consumer's expenditure or cost function. The profit function $\pi(p_t, 1/\lambda)$ is linear homogeneous in p and $1/\lambda$, decreasing in p and increasing in $1/\lambda$. The λ-constant demands are derived from the negative price derivatives of π, i.e.

$$q_{it} = - \partial \pi(p_t, 1/\lambda_t)/\partial p_{it}$$

These are equivalent to demands derived from a rearrangement of (1.16).

14 This completes the set of possible 'time' effects since time dummies (trend) are perfectly co-linear with age and cohort dummies together.

15 Moffitt (1993) provides a useful overview of the use of repeated cross-sections. As will be noted below the orthogonality conditions in the Euler equation give extra power to the idea of taking cohort averages.
16 Blundell (1988) suggests the AI model provides a good statistical description of consumer behaviour recorded in the FES over this period.
17 Altug and Miller (1990b) provide the precise conditions under which there is no endogeneity of experience in current wage outcomes. These conditions are strong.
18 Joe Altonji has indicated to me that a similar ranking appears to be true for married women in the PSID.

References

Altonji, J.G. (1986), 'Intertemporal Substitution in Labour Supply: Evidence from Micro-Data', *Journal of Political Economy*, 94(3.2): S176–S215.

Altug, S. and Miller, R.A. (1990a), 'Household Choices in Equilibrium', *Econometrica*, 58: 543–70.

(1990b), 'Human Capital Accumulation, Aggregate Shocks and Panel Data Estimation', mimeo Carnegie-Mellon University.

Arellano, M. and Meghir, C. (1992), 'Female Labour Supply and On-the-Job Search: An Empirical Model Estimated using Complementary Data Sets', *Review of Economic Studies*, 59(3), No.200: 537–59.

Arrufat, J.L. and Zabalza, A. (1986), 'Female Labour Supply with Taxation, Random Preferences and Optimization Errors', *Econometrica*, 54: 47–63.

Atkinson, A.B., Micklewright, J. and Stern, N.H. (1982), 'A Comparison of the Family Expenditure Survey and the New Earnings Survey: Part II, Hours and Earnings', LSE Taxation and Incentives Discussion Paper 32.

Bera, A.K., Jarque, C.M. and Lee, L.F. (1984), 'Testing for the Normality Assumption in Limited Dependent Variable Models', *International Economic Review*, 25: 563–78.

Bloemen, H.G. and Kapteyn, A. (1990), 'The Joint Estimation of a Non-linear Labour Supply Function and a Wage Equation using Simulated Response Probabilities', mimeo, Center for Economic Research, Tilburg University, May.

Blomquist, N.S. (1983), 'The Effect of Income Taxation on the Labour Supply of Married Men in Sweden', *Journal of Public Economics*, 22: 169–97.

Blundell, R.W. (1987), 'Econometric Approaches to the Specification of Life-Cycle Labour Supply and Commodity Demand Behaviour', *Econometric Reviews*, 6(1): 147–51.

(1988), 'Consumer Behaviour: Theory and Empirical Evidence – A Survey', *Economic Journal*, 98: 16–65.

Blundell R.W., Browning, M. and Meghir, C. (1989), 'Consumer Demand and the Life-time Allocation of Household Expenditure', UCL Economics Discussion Paper 89–11, forthcoming *Review of Economic Studies*, January 1994.

Blundell, R.W., Duncan, A. and Meghir, C. (1992a), 'Taxation and Empirical Labour Supply Models: Lone Parents in the UK', *Economic Journal*, 102: 265–78.

(1992b) 'Robust Estimation of Labour Supply Responses in the Presence of Taxation', paper presented at the Fiscal Incentives and Labour Supply Conference, Institute for Fiscal Studies, June.

Blundell, R.W., Fry, V. and Meghir, C. (1990), 'Preference Restrictions in Micro-econometric Models of Life Cycle Behaviour under Uncertainty', in J.P. Florens, M. Ivaldi, J.J. Laffont and F. Laisney (eds.), *Microeconometrics: Surveys and Applications*, Oxford: Basil Blackwell, pp.41–54.

Blundell, R.W., Ham, J. and Meghir, C. (1987), 'Unemployment and Female Labour Supply', *Economic Journal*, 97: 44–64.

(1989), 'Unemployment, Discouraged Workers and Female Labour Supply', UCL Economics Discussion Paper No.90-02.

Blundell, R.W. and Laisney, F. (1988), 'A Labour Supply Model for Married Women in France: Taxation Hours Constraints and Job Seekers', *Annales d'Economie de Statistique*, 11: 41–71.

Blundell, R.W. and Meghir, C. (1986), 'Selection Criteria for a Microeconometric Model of Labour Supply', *Journal of Applied Econometrics*, 1: 55–81.

(1987), 'Bivariate Alternatives to the Tobit Model', *Journal of Econometrics*, 34: 179–200.

(1990), 'Panel Data and Life-Cycle Models', in J. Hartog, G. Ridder and J. Theeuwes (eds.), *Panel Data and Labour Market Studies*, Amsterdam: North Holland, pp.231–52.

Blundell, R.W. and Neves, P. (1992), 'Interpreting the Intertemporal Elasticities of Labour Supply', Discussion Paper, University College London.

Blundell, R.W., Meghir, C. and Neves, P. (1993), 'Labour Supply and Intertemporal Substitition', *Journal of Econometrics*, 59: 137–60.

Blundell R.W. and Walker, I. (1982), 'Modelling the Joint Determination of Household Labour Supplies and Commodity Demands', *Economic Journal*, 92: 351–64.

(1986), 'A Life Cycle Consistent Empirical Model of Labour Supply using Cross Section Data', *Review of Economic Studies*, 53: 539–58.

Bourguignon, F. (1986), 'Women's Participation and Taxation in France', in R.W. Blundell and I. Walker (eds.), *Unemployment, Search and Labour Supply*, Cambridge University Press.

Bourguignon, F. and Magnac, T. (1990), 'Labour Supply and Taxation in France', *Journal of Human Resources*, 25.

Bover, O. (1989), 'Estimating Intertemporal Labour Supply Elasticities using Structural Models', *Economic Journal*, 99: 1026–39.

Browning, M.J. (1987), 'Anticipated Changes and Household Behaviour: A Theoretical Framework', McMaster University Working Paper.

Browning, M.J., Deaton, A. and Irish, M. (1985), 'A Profitable Approach to Labour Supply and Commodity Demands over the Life-Cycle', *Econometrica*, 53.

Browning, M.J. and Meghir, C. (1991), 'Testing for Separability between Goods and Leisure Using Conditional Demand Systems', *Econometrica*, 59: 925–51.

Burdett, K. and Mortensen, D.T. (1978), 'Labour Supply under Uncertainty', in R.G. Ehrenberg (ed.), *Research in Labor Economics*, Vol. XII, Greenwich, Conn.: JAI Press, pp.109–158.

Burtless, G. and Hausman, J. (1978), 'The Effect of Taxes on Labour Supply', *Journal of Political Economy*, 86: 1103–30.

Burtless, G. and Moffitt, R. (1985), 'The Joint Choice of Retirement Age and Post-Retirement Hours of Work', *Journal of Labour Economics*, 3.

Card, D. (1990), 'Intertemporal Labour Supply: An Assessment', invited paper at the VIth World Congress of Econometric Society, Barcelona, August. Princeton University, Industrial Relations Section Working Paper No.249, see this volume.

Chamberlain, G. (1984), 'Panel Data', in Z. Griliches and M.D. Intriligator (eds.), *Handbook of Econometrics*, Vol. II, Amsterdam: North Holland, ch.22.

Chesher, A.D. (1984), 'Testing for Neglected Heterogeneity', *Econometrica*, 52: 865–72.

Chesher, A.D. and Irish, M. (1987), 'Residuals and Diagnostics for Probit, Tobit and Related Models', *Journal of Econometrics*, 34: 33–61.

Chesher, A.D. and Spady, R. (1988), 'Asymptotic Expansions of the Information Matrix Test Statistic', mimeo University of Bristol, March, forthcoming in *Econometrica*.

Cogan, J.F. (1981), 'Fixed Costs and Labor Supply', *Econometrica*, 49: 945–64.

Deaton, A.S. and Muellbauer, J. (1980), 'An Almost Ideal Demand System', *American Economic Review*, pp.312–26.

Dickens, W. and Lundberg, S. (1985), 'Hours Restrictions and Labour Supply', NBER Working Paper No.1638.

Duncan, A. (1990), 'Labour Supply Decisions and Non-Convex Budget Sets', IFS Working Paper 90/7.

Eckstein, Z. and Wolpin, K. (1989), 'Dynamic Labour Force Participation of Married Women and Endogenous Work Experience', *Review of Economic Studies*, 56: 375–90.

Flood, L. and MaCurdy, T. (1992), 'Work Disincentive Effects of Taxes: An Empirical Analysis of Swedish Men', paper presented at the Fiscal Incentives and Labour Supply Conference, Institute for Fiscal Studies, June.

Florens, J.P., Ivaldi, M., Laffont, J.J. and Laisney, F. (1990) (eds.), *Microeconometrics: Surveys and Applications*, Oxford: Basil Blackwell.

Fraker, T. and Moffitt, R. (1988), 'The Effect of Food Stamps on Labour Supply', *Journal of Public Economics*, 35: 25–56.

Gourieroux, C., Laffont, J. and Monfort A. (1980), 'Coherency Conditions in Simultaneous Linear Equation Models with Endogenous Switching Regimes', *Econometrica*, 3: 171–4.

Gourieroux, C., Monfort, A., Renault, E., and Trognon, A. (1987), 'Generalised Residuals', *Journal of Econometrics*, 34: 5–32.

Ham, J. (1982), 'Estimation of a Labor Supply Model with Censoring due to

Unemployment and Underemployment', *Review of Economic Studies*, 49: 335–54.

(1986a), 'Testing Whether Unemployment Represents Life-Cycle Labor Supply Behaviour', *Review of Economic Studies*, 54(4): 559–78.

(1986b), 'On the Interpretation of Unemployment in Empirical Labour Supply Analysis', in R.W. Blundell and I. Walker (eds.), *Unemployment, Search and Labour Supply*, Cambridge University Press, pp.121–42.

Hansen, L. (1982), 'Large Sample Properties of Methods of Moments Estimators', *Econometrica*, 50: 1029–54.

Hansen, L. and Singleton, K. (1982), 'Generalised Instrumental Variables Estimation of Nonlinear Rational Expectations Models', *Econometrica*, 50: 1269–86.

Hausman, J.A. (1979), 'The Econometrics of Labour Supply on Convex Budget Sets', *Economic Letters*, 3: 171–4.

(1980), 'The Effect of Wages, Taxes and Fixed Costs on Women's Labor Force Participation', *Journal of Public Economics*, 14: 161–94.

(1981), 'Labour Supply', in H.J. Aaron and J.A. Pechman (eds.), *How Taxes Affect Economic Behaviour*, Washington DC: Brookings Institution, pp.27–83.

(1985), 'The Econometrics of Nonlinear Budget Sets', *Econometrica*, 53: 1255–82.

Hayashi, F. (1982), 'Tests for Liquidity Constraints: A Critical Survey and some New Observations', in Bewley, T.F. (ed.), *Advances in Econometrics*, Fifth World Congress, Vol. II, pp.91–120.

Heckman, J.J. (1974a), 'Shadow Prices, Market Wages and Labor Supply', *Econometrica*, 42: 679–94.

(1974b), 'Life-cycle Consumption and Labour Supply: An Explanation of the Relationship between Income and Consumption over the Life-cycle', *American Economic Review*, 64: 188–94.

(1974c), 'Effects of Child-Care Programs on Women's Work Effort', *Journal of Political Economy*, 82(2): S136–S163.

(1976), 'A Life-Cycle Model of Earnings, Learning and Consumption', *Journal of Political Economy*, 84: S11–S44.

(1978), 'Dummy Endogenous Variables in a Simultaneous Equation System', *Econometrica*, 46: 931–59.

(1979), 'Sample Selection Bias as a Specification Error', *Econometrica*, 47: 153–61.

(1981), 'The Incidental Parameters Problem and the Problem of Initial Conditions in Estimating a Discrete Time – Discrete Path Stochastic Process', in Manski and McFadden (eds.), *Structural Analysis of Discrete Data with Econometric Applications*, Cambridge, Mass.: MIT Press.

Heckmann, J.J. and MaCurdy, T.E. (1980), 'A Life-Cycle Model of Female Labour Supply, *Review of Economic Studies*, 47: 47–74.

(1981), 'New Methods for Estimating Labour Supply Functions: A Survey', in Ehrenberg, R. (ed.), *Research in Labour Economics*, Vol. IV, Greenwich, Conn.: JAI Press.

(1986), 'Labour Econometrics', in Z. Griliches and M.D. Intriligator. (eds.), *Handbook of Econometrics*, Vol. III, Amsterdam: North Holland, ch.32.

Hotz, V.J., Kydland, F.E. and Sedlacek, G.L. (1988), 'Intertemporal Preferences and Labour Supply', *Econometrica*, 56: 335–60.

Hotz, V.J. and Miller, R. (1989), 'Conditional Choice Probabilities and the Estimation of Dynamic Discrete Choice Models', paper presented at ESEM 1989, Munich.

Hsaio, C. (1986), *Analysis of Panel Data*, Cambridge University Press.

Johnson, P. and Stark, G. (1989), 'Taxation and Social Security 1979–1989: The Impact on Household Incomes', IFS Commentary No. 12, London: Institute for Fiscal Studies.

Kapteyn, A., Kooreman, P. and Van Soest, A. (1990), 'Quantity Rationing and Concavity in a Flexible Household Labour Supply Model', *Review of Economics and Statistics*, 72: 55–62.

Kell, M. and Wright, J. (1989), 'Benefits and the Labour Supply of Women Married to Unemployed Men', *Economic Journal*, Conference Supplement, pp. 1195–265.

Killingsworth, M.R. (1983), *Labor Supply*, Cambridge University Press.

Kooreman, P. and Van Soest, A. (1990), 'Coherency of the Indirect Translog Demand System with Binding Nonnegativity Constraints', *Journal of Econometrics*, 44(3): 391–400.

Layard, R., Barton, M. and Zabalza, A. (1980), 'Married Women's Participation and Hours', *Economica*, 47: 51–72.

Lazear, E.P. (1983), 'A Competitive Theory of Monopoly Unionism', *American Economic Review*, 73: 631–43.

Lee, L.-F., (1984), 'Tests for the Bivariate Normal Distribution in Econometric Models with Selectivity', *Econometrica*, 52(4): 843–64.

MaCurdy, T.E. (1981), 'An Empirical Model of Labour Supply in a Life-Cycle Setting', *Journal of Political Economy*, 89: 1059–85.

(1983), 'A Simple Scheme for Estimating an Intertemporal Model of Labor Supply and Consumption in the Presence of Taxes and Uncertainty', *International Economic Review*, 24: 265–89.

(1985), 'Interpreting Empirical Models of Labour Supply in an Intertemporal Framework with Uncertainty', in J.J. Heckman and B. Singer (eds.), *Longitudinal Analysis of Labour Market Data*, Cambridge University Press, ch.3.

(1988), 'Problems with Testing the Intertemporal Substitution Hypothesis', in Florens *et al.* (1990).

MaCurdy, T., Green, D. and Paarsch, H. (1990), 'Assessing Empirical Approaches for Analysing Taxes and Labour Supply', *Journal of Human Resources*, 25: 415–90.

McFadden, D. (1989), 'A Method of Simulated Moments for Estimation of Discrete Response Models without Numerical Integration', *Econometrica*, 57: 995–1026.

Moffitt, R. (1984), 'Estimation of a Joint Wage-Hours Labour Supply Model', *Journal of Labour Economics*, 2: 550–6.

(1986a), 'Work Incentives in the AFDC System: An Analysis of the 1981 Reforms', *American Economic Review*, 76: 219–23.

(1986b), 'The Econometrics of Piecewise-Linear Budget Constraints: A Survey and Exposition of the Maximum Likelihood Method', *Journal of Business and Economic Statistics*, 4: 317–27.

(1990), 'The Econometrics of Kinked Budget Constraints', *Journal of Economic Perspectives*, 4(2): 119–39.

(1993), 'Identification and Estimation of Dynamic Models with a Time Series of Repeated Cross Sections', in *Journal of Econometrics*, 59: 99–124.

Mroz, T.A. (1987), 'The Sensitivity of an Empirical Model of Married Women's Hours of Work to Economic and Statistical Assumptions', *Econometrica*, 55: 765–800.

Neves, P. (1991), 'Commodity Demands and Labour Supply over the Life-Cycle', Ph.D. Thesis, UCL.

Newey, W.K., Powell, J.L. and Walker, J.R. (1990), 'Semiparametric Estimation of Selection Models: Some Empirical Results', *American Economic Review*, 80(2): 324–8.

Nickell, S. (1986), 'The Short-Run Behaviour of Labour Supply, in T.F. Bewley (ed.), *Advances in Econometrics*, Fifth World Congress, Vol. II, Cambridge University Press.

Pencavel, J. (1986), 'Labor Supply of Men: A Survey', in O. Ashenfelter and R. Layard (eds.), *Handbook of Labor Economics*, Amsterdam: North Holland.

Rosen H. (1976a), 'Taxes in a Labour Supply Model with Joint Wage-Hours Determination', *Econometrica*, 44: 485–507.

(1976b), 'Tax Illusion and the Labour Supply of Married Women', *Review of Economics and Statistics*, 58: 167–507.

Shaw, K. (1989), 'Life Cycle Labour Supply with Human Capital Accumulation', *International Economic Review*, 30(2): 431–57.

Smith, R.J. (1985), 'Some Tests for Misspecification in Bivariate Limited Dependent Variable Models', *Annales de l'INSEE*, 59/60.

Smith, R.J. and Blundell, R.W. (1986), 'An Exogeneity Test for the Simultaneous Equation Tobit Model', *Econometrica*, 54: 679–85.

Stern, N. (1986), 'On the Specification of Labour Supply Functions', in R.W. Blundell and I. Walker (eds.), *Unemployment, Search and Labour Supply*, Cambridge University Press.

Van Soest, A. (1989), 'Essays on Microeconometric Models of Consumer Demand and Labour Supply', Ph.D. Thesis, Tilburg University.

Van Soest, A., Kooreman, P. and Kapteyn, A. (1988), 'Coherent Specification of Demand Systems with Corner Solutions and Endogenous Regimes', Research Memorandum FEW 336, Department of Economics, Tilburg University.

(1990), 'Coherency and Regularity of Demand Systems with Equality and Inequality Constraints', Center Discussion Paper No.9001.

Wolpin, K. (1984), 'An Estimable Dynamic Stochastic Model of Fertility and Child Mortality', *Journal of Political Economy*, 92: 852–74.

Zabalza, A. (1983), 'The CES Utility Function, Nonlinear Budget Constraints and Labour Supply: Results on Female Participation and Hours', *Economic Journal*, 93: 312–30.

CHAPTER 2

Intertemporal labour supply: an assessment

David Card

The systematic study of intertemporal labour supply began only two decades ago.[1] In a remarkably short time the life-cycle model of individual hours choice has moved to the forefront of both micro- and macro-econometric research. This chapter begins with a look at the original questions that first led to the interest in the life-cycle approach. I then present a selective review of the evidence on various dimensions of intertemporal labour supply. I limit my discussion to micro-econometric studies of male labour supply, making no attempt at an exhaustive survey of even this branch of the literature.[2] Rather, my goal is to offer an assessment of the success and/or failure of the life-cycle model in providing a useful framework for understanding the main features of individual labour supply.

I conclude that the life-cycle labour supply literature sheds relatively little light on the questions that first generated interest in a life-cycle approach: What determines the shape of the life-cycle hours profile? How does labour supply respond to aggregate wage changes? What is the source of idiosyncratic changes in year-to-year labour supply? Part of the reason for this stems from a tendency in the literature to concentrate on one aspect of intertemporal hours variation – the response to wage growth along a known life-cycle trajectory – and to ignore another, namely, the response to unanticipated wage innovations. In addition, much of the literature has taken the position that average hourly earnings during the year are a 'sufficient statistic' for hours choices within the year. There is considerable evidence against this narrow reading of the life-cycle model.

1   THE QUESTIONS

A series of substantive questions first led to interest in life-cycle labour supply. Lucas and Rapping (1970), following a suggestion of Friedman

(1976, pp.206–7), posited a life-cycle framework as a way to reconcile an elastic short-run labour supply curve with an inelastic or even backward-bending long-run labour supply curve. Lucas and Rapping's idea was to model cyclical hours variation as a response to temporary wage changes. Subsequently, much debate in the macro-economics literature has focussed on the size of this intertemporal wage elasticity.

A second motivation arose from interest in human capital theory, and the recognition that the pattern of life-cycle hours is influenced by the pattern of life-cycle wages. This idea is clearly articulated by Heckman (1976, p.S12), who notes that a model with endogenous labour supply can potentially reconcile differences in the life-cycle profiles of earnings and hourly wage rates.[3]

A related question is whether wage growth over the life cycle can explain the parallel profiles of consumption and earnings. The simplest permanent income model (with fixed hours) predicts no systematic relation between earnings and consumption. The finding that individuals with steeper life-cycle profiles of earnings have steeper life-cycle profiles of consumption has therefore been used as evidence of credit constraints or other impediments to an optimal life-cycle consumption plan (Thurow (1969), Ghez (in Ghez and Becker, 1975), Carrol and Summers (1989)). As Heckman (1974) pointed out, however, a model with endogenous labour supply can explain the parallel age profiles of consumption and earnings if leisure and consumption are complements.[4]

Other questions have also emerged: What (if anything) can we conclude about the interpretation of measured unemployment (Ashenfelter and Ham (1979))? How does a life-cycle perspective affect the interpretation of the responses measured in the negative income tax experiments? How does an intergenerational transfer system (such as Social Security) affect the hours of young and old workers? Finally, and perhaps fundamentally, how can we explain the enormous year-to-year variation in individual-specific labour supply that appears in virtually every available panel data set?

The power of the life-cycle framework is illustrated by considering a decomposition of individual labour supply into aggregate time effects, systematic age effects, permanent person effects and person-and-year-specific effects. The life-cycle labour supply model has been proposed as an explanation for *all four* components! Lucas and Rapping (1970) proposed that a life-cycle model could explain aggregate year-to-year movements in labour supply (the time effects in a components-of-variance model). Heckman (1974, 1976), Ghez and Becker (1975), and others proposed that the life-cycle model could explain the systematic age effects in hours of work, and also differences across people in their amount of market work over the life cycle (i.e., the person-specific constants). Finally, models used by MaCurdy (1981), Altonji (1986), and others link person- and year-specific changes in hours to the corresponding changes in wages.

2   THE BASIC MODEL

A prototypical life-cycle labour supply model begins with a time-separable utility function defined over the consumption (c_{it}) and hours of work (h_{it}) of individual i in each of a sequence of periods $t = 0,1,2,\ldots$

$$\sum_t \beta^t U(c_{it}, h_{it}, a_{it}).\tag{2.1}$$

Here, $\beta = (1 + \rho)^{-1}$ measures subjective time discounting and a_{it} is a sequence of 'taste shifters' that capture heterogeneity across individuals and over time. In models with uncertainty, preferences are assumed to be additive over states and time (with the same $U(\ )$ function) so that the consumer's objective function is simply the expectation of (2.1) conditional on current information.

The second element of the model is the intertemporal budget constraint, which describes the change in the value assets (a_{it}) between periods

$$A_{it+1}/p_{t+1} = (1 + r_t)(A_t/p_t + w_{it}h_{it} - c_t).\tag{2.2}$$

Here, p_t is the price of consumption goods in t, r_t is the real interest rate between periods t and $t + 1$ (assumed to be known) and w_{it} is the real wage of individual i for hours worked in period t.

An interior solution for maximisation of the expectation of (2.1), subject to (2.2) and an appropriate terminal condition on assets, is characterised by first-order conditions for consumption and hours in period t, together with an intertemporal optimality condition for the marginal utility of wealth in period t (λ_{it}).[5]

$$U_c(c_{it}, h_{it}, a_{it}) - \lambda_{it} \qquad = 0 \tag{2.3a}$$

$$U_h(c_{it}, h_{it}, a_{it}) + w_{it}\lambda_{it} \qquad = 0 \tag{2.3b}$$

$$\lambda_{it} - \beta(1 + r_t)E_t[\lambda_{it+1}] \qquad = 0. \tag{2.3c}$$

Equations (2.3a) and (2.3b) can be solved for consumption and hours in terms of w_{it} and the current marginal utility of wealth. It is conventional to refer to the implied solution for hours as the 'intertemporal labour supply function'. With an appropriate transformation of the taste shift variable a_{it}, write the log-linear approximation[6] of this function as

$$\log h_{it} - a_{it} + \eta \log w_{it} + \delta \log \lambda_{it}.\tag{2.4}$$

The parameter η represents the elasticity of hours in period t with respect to wages in t, holding constant the marginal utility of wealth. Following the literature, I shall refer to η as the intertemporal substitution elasticity. This elasticity is necessarily positive, and is strictly greater than the (Hicksian) compensated labour supply elasticity associated with the same preferences if leisure is a normal good. The parameter δ represents the elasticity of hours with respect to the marginal utility of wealth, and also must be positive if leisure is a normal good. The two elasticities are related by the simple condition

$$\eta - \delta = \frac{c_{it}}{w_{it}h_{it}} \cdot \frac{\partial \log c_{it}}{\partial \log w_{it}}.$$

If consumption is independent of wages, holding constant the marginal utility of wealth (as is implicitly assumed in many versions of the permanent-income consumption model), then $\eta = \delta$.

Note the convenient form of the life-cycle labour supply function (2.4). As a consequence of the additive structure of preferences, the effects of asset income and future wages are completely summarised by the value of λ_{it}. With perfect foresight and constant real interest rates, (2.3a) implies that $\lambda_{it} = \partial_{i0}g^t$, where g is greater or less than unity depending on the gap between the real interest rate and the rate of time preference ρ. In this case, apart from taste changes and a geometric trend, the life-cycle profile of labour supply is completely determined by the profile of wages.

The implications of the life-cycle model under uncertainty are most easily seen by combining equation (2.3c) with equation (2.4) to describe the change in hours between periods $t-1$ and t

$$\Delta \log h_{it} = \Delta a_{it} + \eta \, \Delta \log w_{it} - \delta \cdot (r_{t-1} - \rho) + \delta \phi_{it} + \delta \xi_{it}, \qquad (2.5)$$

where $\phi_{it} \equiv \log \lambda_{it} - E_{t-1} \log \lambda_{it}$ is the one-period-ahead forecast error in the logarithm of the marginal utility of wealth, and $\xi_{it} \equiv -E_{t-1}[\exp(\phi_{it})]$.[7] The latter term is a constant if the distribution of ϕ_{it} is constant. In this case the change in labour supply consists of a component due to changes in tastes (Δa_{it}), a component due to variation in wages, a component due to the difference between the real interest rate and the rate of time preference and a component due to any updating in the logarithm of the marginal utility of income (ϕ_{it}).

The simple form of equation (2.5) has considerable appeal, and variants of it are used in many recent micro-econometric studies of labour supply. In a stochastic environment, however, it is important to keep in mind that the response of individual hours to an observed change in wages has two parts. The first of these is $\eta \, \Delta w_{it}$, as in the perfect foresight model. The second is the change in labour supply generated by the change in the marginal utility of wealth. The realisation of w_{it} provides new information that generates an update in the distribution of future wages and brings about a revision in the forecast of λ_{it}. Unfortunately, there are no closed-form expressions for λ_{it} in an uncertain environment.[8] Thus, the component of the change in labour supply attributable to wealth effects is usually treated as a 'nuisance', and is eliminated by an instrumental variables procedure. This is not to say that the wealth effects associated with observed wage changes are small. Indeed, my reading of the evidence suggests they are potentially significant. However, the difficulty of deriving a formal or even approximate expression for λ_{it} has led most researchers to concentrate on the intertemporal substitution effect.

3   EMPIRICAL IMPLICATIONS AND EVIDENCE

3.1   The life-cycle profile of hours

The first and most direct implication of the life-cycle model concerns the shape of the life-cycle hours profile. As noted earlier, with perfect foresight and constant real interest rates the model implies that the life-cycle profile of hours consists of a taste component, a trend and a component that is strictly proportional to wages. The presence of uncertainty adds other components with mean zero over a large sample of life cycles. To see this, re-write the life-cycle labour supply function as

$$
\begin{aligned}
\log h_{it} &= a_{it} + \eta \log w_{it} + \delta\{\log \lambda_{i0} + \sum_{j=0}^{t-1} (\rho - r_{t-j-1} + \phi_{it-j})\} \\
&= E_0 \log h_{it} + \eta(\log w_{it} - E_0 \log w_{it}) \\
&\quad - \delta\{\sum_{j=0}^{t-1} (r - r_{t-j-1} + \phi_{it-j})\},
\end{aligned}
\tag{2.4a}
$$

where E_0 denotes expectations at the beginning of the life-cycle and r is the expected real interest rate in period 0 (assumed to be constant). Hours at age t differ from hours planned at the beginning of the life cycle by a term representing the forecast error in wages, plus another representing the cumulative forecast errors in interest rates and the marginal utility of income. Over a large sample of life cycles (spanning different periods of calendar time), the average profile of observed life-cycle hours therefore converges to the mean of the planned profiles.[9]

The typical shapes of the life-cycle profiles of wages and hours for male workers are illustrated in figures 2.1 and 2.2. The underlying data for these figures are taken from the 1977–89 March Current Population Surveys (CPS), and pertain to annual hours and average hourly earnings (annual earnings divided by annual hours) for calendar years 1976–88.[10] Figure 2.1 shows annual averages of log wages for six single-year age cohorts. Each

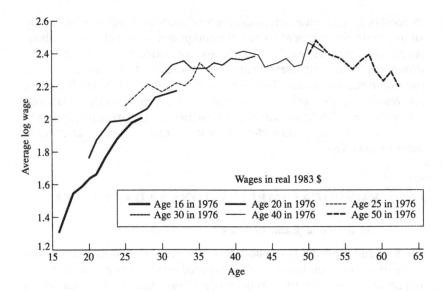

Figure 2.1 Life-cycle wage profiles for six cohorts

distinct line in the figure tracks the wage profile of a different cohort over the thirteen-year sample period. Figure 2.2 shows the corresponding profiles of average annual hours.

The data in figure 2.1 suggest that successive cohorts face similar expected wage profiles: real wages rise quickly between the ages of twenty and thirty, and then grow more slowly to a peak around age fifty. Nevertheless, there are common year effects in average hourly earnings,[11] and important cohort effects. During the 1980s, younger cohorts tended to earn lower real wage rates than older ones (at the same point in their life cycle). This negative wage growth provides an interesting opportunity to test Lewis' (1956) influential interpretation of the trend towards lower hours of work during the first half of the twentieth century. Lewis (1956, p.197) argued that the decline reflected an income effect, driven by higher average wages for successive cohorts of workers. If this interpretation is correct, one should detect an *increase* in hours for the most recent cohorts.

The life-cycle profiles of hours in figure 2.2 have a rather different shape than the profile of wages. Per-capita hours of work reach their peak in the early thirties, are roughly constant to age forty, fall slightly to age fifty, and then decline sharply. The pattern of hours among those who actually work is similar, reaching a peak of about 2,100 hours at age thirty, remaining stable to age fifty, falling to 1,900 hours at age sixty, and then declining sharply. The growth in per-capita hours at the beginning of the life cycle

Figure 2.2 Life-cycle hours profiles for six cohorts

coincides with a gradual withdrawal from school. Thirty per cent of all twenty-year-olds in the March CPS (1977–89) report their main activity in the previous week as 'in school'. This fraction falls to 11 per cent by age twenty-three and to 2 per cent by age thirty.[12] Much of the decline in per-capita hours at the other end of the life-cycle reflects withdrawal from the labour force. By age sixty-two, only 50 per cent of men are still working any hours. By age sixty-eight the fraction of workers has dropped to under 20 per cent.

The hours profiles in figure 2.2 suggest the presence of significant year effects, with all cohorts showing a downturn in hours in 1982. In contrast to the profiles of wages, however, the hours profiles of the younger cohorts are not systematically different from those of the older cohorts. Thus, there is no evidence of the intercohort income effects predicted by Lewis' explanation for the 1900–50 decline in per-capita hours.

How well does the life-cycle model explain the life-cycle profile of hours? Between the ages of twenty and thirty, wages grow by 40–45 per cent, per-capita annual hours grow by 55 per cent, the employment rate grows by 10 points, and hours conditional on working grow by 45 per cent. Between the ages of thirty and forty, wages rise another 10–15 per cent, conditional hours are constant, and the probability of working falls 5 points. Finally, between the ages of fifty and sixty, wages fall 5 per cent, conditional hours fall 5–10 per cent, and the employment rate falls by over 20 points. The life-

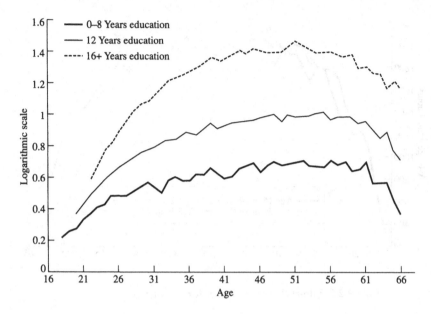

Figure 2.3 Life-cycle profiles of wages by education group (pooled
cohorts)

cycle profiles of wages and hours are far from parallel. Of course this does
not refute the life-cycle model, because tastes may vary systematically with
age and it is also possible that the intertemporal substitution elasticity
varies with the number of hours worked.[13]

A different test is provided by the data in figures 2.3 and 2.4, which
represent wage and conditional hours profiles for men in three education
classes: nought to eight years of schooling, exactly twelve years of schooling, and sixteen or more years of schooling.[14] Between the ages of thirty and
fifty the wage profiles of these three groups differ dramatically. Wages of
college graduates grow some 40 per cent, wages of highschool graduates
grow about 20 per cent, and wages of individuals with minimal schooling
grow only 10 per cent. However, for all three groups, hours (conditional on
working) are constant between ages thirty and fifty. In fact, the hours
profiles of the different education groups are very similar. To explain these
data with a simple life-cycle model requires a fairly elaborate set of taste
parameters.[15] A simpler interpretation is that the shape of the wage profile
bears no causal relation to the shape of the hours profile.

It is also interesting to compare the three education classes in terms of
their average lifetime hours and average lifetime wages. For simplicity,

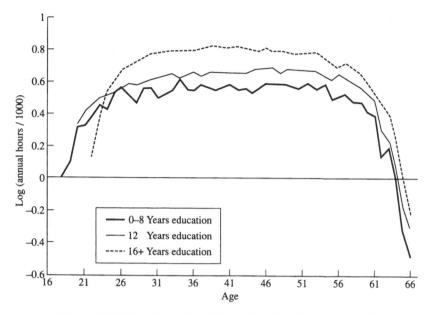

Figure 2.4 Life-cycle profiles of hours by education group (pooled cohorts)

assume that individuals with nought to eight years of schooling begin work at age sixteen, while highschool graduates begin work at eighteen and college graduates begin work at twenty-two.[16] Then average hours worked per year between the ages of sixteen and sixty-nine for the three education groups are as follows:

Years education	Hours/year	Hours/year when working
0–8	1,265	1,756
12	1,537	1,809
16+	1,638	1,833

Given the wage differentials between the three education groups, these data suggest that higher lifetime wages are associated with higher lifetime hours. This positive association calls into question the conventional view that long-run labour supply is negatively associated with wages.[17]

3.2 Economy-wide fluctuations

Much of the initial interest in life-cycle labour supply focussed on its potential role in explaining cyclical changes in employment and/or hours.

Since cyclical variation in real wages is modest, an equilibrium model with a stable aggregate labour supply function requires a relatively large elasticity of labour supply to generate large swings in employment or hours. In principle, a life-cycle framework can reconcile relatively elastic labour supply reponses over the business cycle with inelastic (or even negatively sloped) long-run labour supply.

To see the implications of the life-cycle model at the aggregate level, consider forming the average change in labour supply between periods $t-1$ and t for a sample of individuals. Equation (2.5) implies that

$$\Delta\log h_t = \Delta a_t + \eta\ \Delta\log w_t - \delta(r_{t-1} - \rho) + \delta\phi_t, \tag{2.5a}$$

where $\Delta\log h_t$ represents the average change in log hours in the sample, Δa_t represents the average change in the taste variable, $\Delta\log w_t$ represents the average change in log wages, and ϕ_t represents the mean of the forecast errors in λ_{it}. In principle it is possible to estimate (2.5a) on aggregate-level data. Something like this is actually carried out in Lucas and Rapping (1970), Altonji (1982) and Mankiw, Rotemberg and Summers (1985). Here I wish to discuss the implications of (2.5a) for the 'time effects' that emerge in micro-econometric studies of labour supply. This idea was suggested by Ashenfelter (1984) and is pursued by Angrist (1989, 1990).

Ashenfelter (1984) observed that aggregate changes in labour supply for a fixed cohort take a particularly simple form if (i) there are no aggregate components of taste variation, (ii) the real interest rate equals the rate of time preference and (iii) individuals have perfect foresight. In this case equation (2.5a) reduces to

$$\Delta\log h_t = \eta\ \Delta\log w_t.$$

Apart from sampling error, the mean change in hours is strictly proportional to the mean change in wages. This specification can be freed up by assuming that the taste components of individual labour supply follow a systematic life-cycle trend. For example, suppose that

$$a_{it} = a_i + b\ \mathrm{Age}_{it} + c/2\ \mathrm{Age}_{it}^2,$$

where a_i is a permanent person-specific component of tastes, Age_{it} denotes the age of individual i in period t, and b and c are common population parameters. Then equation (2.5a) implies

$$\Delta\log h_t = b - c/2 + c \cdot t + \eta\ \Delta\log w_t. \tag{2.6}$$

Since (by assumption) the only aggregate components of labour supply are taste and wage variation, equation (2.6) should fit the mean changes in hours and wages exactly, apart from sampling error in the estimated means.

Estimates of this equation are presented in Angrist (1991) using the

Table 2.1. *Estimated intertemporal substitution elasticities*

	Sample		
	PSID 1969–79	CPS 1963–74	CPS 1975–87
Preference trend:			
None	−0.13	−0.01	0.61
	(0.04)	(0.01)	(0.09)
Linear	0.56	0.25	0.58
	(0.12)	(0.08)	(0.09)
Quadratic	0.63	−0.04	0.94
	(0.21)	(0.10)	(0.14)

means of wages and hours for a panel of males in the Panel Study of Income Dynamics (PSID).[18] Similar estimates based on cohort-level data from consecutive CPS samples are presented in Angrist (1990). In analysing the CPS samples, Angrist (1990) divides the available data into two subsamples – 1963–73 and 1975–87 – and follows men aged twenty-three to fifty in 1964 in the first subsample, and men age twenty-five to fifty in 1976 in the second. Angrist's estimates of the intertemporal substition elasticity (with their estimated standard errors in parentheses) are as in table 2.1.

Angrist also reports a specification test based on the R^2 of the fitted models. The specifications that include either linear or quadratic taste components yield test statistics below conventional significance levels in the PSID sample. In the CPS sample, all of the test statistics are above conventional critical values, although it must be recognised that the sample sizes are large and the model is very parsimonious. Interestingly, none of the CPS results is substantively different when the analysis is repeated on samples of men with a fixed age distribution in each year.

Angrist's results suggest that there is a systematic positive relation between mean wages and mean hours, particularly in the post-1974 period. This relationship is illustrated in figure 2.5, which plots two measures of average annual labour supply for the cohort of men age twenty to fifty in 1976, along with a measure of their mean log wages. Both wages and hours for these men rose between 1976 and 1978, fell in the early 1980s, and then recovered. The timing of the post-1980 upturn differs slightly between wages (which grew between 1981 and 1982) and hours (which continued to fall until 1982). The covariation of wages and hours is also weak in the last four years of the data. Nevertheless, wage and hours changes from 1976 to 1988 are very highly correlated.

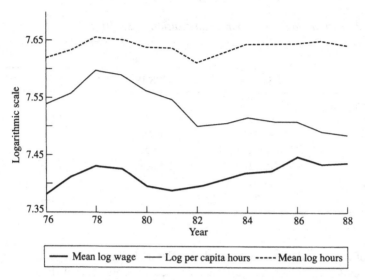

Figure 2.5 Aggregate wages and hours for men age 20–50 in 1976

Should we conclude that intertemporal labour supply does a good job of explaining the time effects that emerge in a micro-econometric model? My belief is that such a conclusion is premature. The reason is that the assumption of perfect foresight regarding the aggregate changes that occurred in the late 1970s and early 1980s is surely false. In the three decades before 1976, average real wages in the US economy grew fairly steadily at 2–3 per cent per year.[19] After 1975, real wage growth essentially stopped. This sharp downward adjustment in trend, coupled with the actual losses in real wages in the early 1980s, suggests that many individuals suffered unexpected reductions in their lifetime wealth. According to the life-cycle model, these changes should have affected hours decisions, and therefore should be modelled in the aggregate labour supply equation.

The difficulty is that very little is known about the evolution of the marginal utility of income or the size of the wealth elasticity δ. One approach is to write down an intuitively plausible or econometrically convenient model for λ_{it}. For example, Lucas and Rapping (1970) specified a labour supply function of the form

$$\log h_{it} = a_{it} + \eta(\log w_{it} - \log w_{it}^*) + \theta \log w_{it}^* \qquad (2.7)$$

where

$$\log w_{it}^* = \sum_{j=0}^{T-t} b_j E_t \log w_{t+j}, \; (\textstyle\sum b_j = 1)$$

This is equivalent to replacing $\delta \log \lambda_{it}$ with $-(\eta + \theta) \log w_{it}^*$ in the labour supply function (2.4).[20] As Altonji and Ashenfelter (1980) pointed out, the labour supply effects of aggregate wage changes in this model depend critically on the degree of persistence in innovations to the real wage. Empirically, it is difficult to reject the hypothesis that the aggregate real wage rate is a random walk with drift. If workers assume that the 'year effects' in individual wages have the same property, then the labour supply effect of a change in the aggregate component of wages depends only on the 'long-run' elasticity θ.[21] If this is negative (as Lewis (1956) and many subsequent authors have assumed) and if individuals expect aggregate-level changes in real wages to persist indefinitely (as is suggested by the random walk model) then the predicted correlation between the year effects in hours and wages from a panel of individual data is negative!

The only evidence in the micro-econometric literature pertaining to the sign of the 'long run' labour supply elasticity (i.e., the elasticity of hours with respect to a parallel shift in wage profiles) is from MaCurdy (1981, 1985). MaCurdy (1985) suggests a less restrictive specification for the marginal utility of income than Lucas–Rapping

$$\delta \log \lambda_{it} = \gamma_a A_{it} + \sum_{j=0}^{T-t} \gamma_j E_t \log w_{it+j}.$$

This specification implies that the elasticity of mean hours with respect to a permanent change in wages is $\eta + \kappa_{it}\bar{\gamma}$, where $\bar{\gamma}$ is the mean of the γ_j coefficients over the remaining life cycle and

$$\kappa_{it} = 1 - \frac{\gamma_a A_{it}}{\delta \log \lambda_{it}}$$

varies with the share of current assets in lifetime wealth. MaCurdy (1985) presents estimates for $\bar{\gamma}$ centring on -0.07 for individuals at the start of their life cycle. This is an upper bound on the absolute magnitude of the wealth effect of a permanent innovation in wages for older workers, since these individuals have a larger share of lifetime wealth in assets. MaCurdy's estimates, then, suggest that the wealth effect of a permanent change in wages is small, and that a permanent 10 per cent increase in wages is associated with a roughly 1 per cent increase in hours.[22]

In my opinion, more research is needed on the wealth effects of unexpected wage changes before we can conclude that the life-cycle model provides an adequate description of the year-to-year changes in average labour supply observed in a panel. One useful exercise that has not yet been carried out is to combine information on mean levels of consumption and hours for a panel such as the PSID. The assumption of perfect foresight implies that changes in mean consumption are described by an equation of the form

$$\Delta \log c_t = \Delta a_t^c + e \, \Delta \log w_t,$$

where a_t^c represents the mean across individuals of a taste shifter in consumption, and e (which is approximately equal to $\eta - \delta$) measures the degree of complementarity or substitutability between leisure and consumption, holding constant the marginal utility of wealth. At a minimum, the goodness-of-fit of this equation provides an indication of the magnitude of aggregate changes in the marginal utility of wealth.

3.3   Individual-specific components of wage and hours variation

In addition to its implications for the age and time effects in micro-econometric studies of labour supply, the life-cycle model offers a potential explanation for individual and period-specific hours variation. Specifically, suppose that individual wages are determined by an equation of the form

$$\log w_{it} = \omega_i + v_t + u_{it}, \tag{2.8}$$

where ω_i is a person-specific constant, v_t is an aggregate effect, and u_{it} is a person- and time-specific effect. Then equation (2.5) implies

$$\Delta \log h_{it} - \Delta \log h_t = (\Delta a_{it} - \Delta a_t) + \eta u_{it} + (\phi_{it} - \phi_t). \tag{2.9}$$

The person-specific component of hours variation in period t consists of person-specific taste variation, a person-specific intertemporal substitution effect ηu_{it}, and the difference between the person-specific forecast error in $\log \lambda_{it}$ and the average forecast error over the entire population.

The person-specific component of year-to-year changes in labour supply is large. For example, Altonji and Paxson (1986) estimate that the cross-sectional standard deviation of the change in log annual hours between consecutive years is 0.35 for men aged eighteen to sixty in the Panel Study of Income Dynamics (PSID). Using data constructed from survey information gathered every four months in the Survey of Income and Program Participation (SIPP), I estimate that the standard deviation of the change in log annual hours for men aged twenty-two to fifty-nine who worked in 1984 and 1985 is 0.54 (Card (1990)). Some of this variation is probably attributable to measurement error. Evidence reported by Duncan and Hill (1985) suggests that the signal-to-noise ratio in the measured change in log annual hours in the PSID is 1.22.[23] Applying this correction factor, the estimated standard deviation of true hours changes for continuously employed men in the PSID is 0.26, and somewhat larger for men in the SIPP panel.[24]

Nevertheless, virtually none of this variation is explained by the person-specific intertemporal substitution effect. Altonji (1986, tables 1 and 2) reports measures of R^2 for labour supply equations like (2.9) that instrument the individual-specific component of wage variation and treat the other two components (person-specific changes in taste and person-specific updating in the marginal utility of income) as residuals. The proportions of explained variance are essentially 0.

One reason for this low proportion of explained variance is the very small magnitude of the estimated intertemporal substitution elasticities that typically emerge from micro-econometric studies.[25] MaCurdy's (1981) estimates from the PSID range from 0.10 to 0.45. Altonji's (1986) estimates, also based on PSID data, range from 0 to 0.5, with the more precise estimates clustered near the bottom of this interval. A similar range of estimates emerges from other studies of the PSID, including Ham (1986), and from the detailed study of cohort-level data from the British Family Expenditure Survey by Browning, Deaton and Irish (1985). Taken together, the literature suggests that the elasticity of intertemporal substitution is surely no higher than 0.5, and probably no higher than 0.2. Given such small elasticities, the component of individual hours changes attributable to intertemporal substitution effects is tiny.

This leads to the question of whether there is *any* explanation for individual-specific hours variation. One source of systematic hours variation that is described by the labour supply model but ignored in most studies is idiosyncratic variation in the marginal utility of wealth. Some of this variation is potentially explainable by observed wage changes, particularly if person-specific wage innovations are highly persistent. To collect some evidence on the persistence of idiosyncratic wage shocks, I fit a very simple version of the components-of-variance model (2.8) to data on log wages for men in the PSID. Specifically, the model assumes that the measured log wage of individual i in period t is given by

$$\log w_{it} = \omega_i + v_t + u_{it} + \mu_{it}, \tag{2.10}$$

where

$$u_{it} = \alpha u_{it-1} + \zeta_{it},$$
$$\mathrm{var}(\zeta_{it}) = \sigma_t^2, \ \mathrm{cov}(\zeta_{is}, \zeta_{it}) = 0, \ t \neq s,$$
$$\mathrm{var}(\omega_i) = \sigma_\omega^2, \ \mathrm{var}(\mu_{it}) = \sigma_\mu^2,$$
$$\mathrm{cov}(\zeta_{it}, \omega_i) = \mathrm{cov}(\zeta_{it}, \mu_{it}) = \mathrm{cov}(\omega_i, \mu_{it}) = 0.$$

In this model the person- and period-specific wage shock consists of two components: a first-order serially correlated component with a time-varying variance (u_{it}), and a serially uncorrelated component (μ_{it}). One interpretation of the latter is a white-noise survey measurement error.

Table 2.2. *Auto-covariance structure of individual wages: continuously employed male household heads in PSID, 1971–8 (estimated standard errors in parentheses)*

	Auto-covariance of wage in							
	1971	1972	1973	1974	1975	1976	1977	1978
With wages in								
1971	0.243							
	(0.012)							
1972	0.196	0.252						
	(0.010)	(0.011)						
1973	0.185	0.199	0.251					
	(0.010)	(0.011)	(0.012)					
1974	0.180	0.188	0.194	0.240				
	(0.010)	(0.010)	(0.010)	(0.011)				
1975	0.173	0.187	0.187	0.193	0.253			
	(0.010)	(0.010)	(0.010)	(0.010)	(0.011)			
1976	0.168	0.178	0.180	0.188	0.206	0.271		
	(0.010)	(0.010)	(0.010)	(0.010)	(0.010)	(0.012)		
1977	0.163	0.177	0.180	0.183	0.185	0.205	0.254	
	(0.010)	(0.010)	(0.010)	(0.010)	(0.010)	(0.010)	(0.011)	
1978	0.151	0.166	0.164	0.170	0.180	0.196	0.205	0.293
	(0.010)	(0.010)	(0.010)	(0.010)	(0.010)	(0.011)	(0.011)	(0.016)
Average auto-covariance at lag								
	7	6	5	4	3	2	1	0
	0.151	0.165	0.169	0.175	0.182	0.188	0.200	0.257
	(0.010)	(0.009)	(0.009)	(0.009)	(0.009)	(0.009)	(0.009)	(0.009)

Note:
Sample consists of 1,374 male household heads from households with no change in head between 1969 and 1979, who earned positive labour earnings and worked positive hours in each year between 1969 and 1979, and whose hourly wage was between $0.75 and $100 (in constant 1967 dollars) in all years.

However, this is indistinguishable from a 'purely transitory' wage component. I have fitted this model (using minimum distance techniques) to the covariance matrix of individual wage data for 1,374 continuously employed male household heads in the PSID.[26]

The complete covariance matrix of 1971–8 wages for these men is presented in table 2.2, together with the estimated standard errors of the

Table 2.3. *Summary of estimated components-of-variance wage model (standard errors in parentheses)*

Parameter estimates	
1 Variance of permenant effect (σ_ω^2)	0.124
	(0.040)
2 Variance of white-noise component (σ_μ^2)	0.039
	(0.003)
4 Average variance of autoregression component (average of σ_t^2)	0.027
5 AR(1) coefficient (α)	0.886
	(0.077)
6 Goodness of fit (24 degree freedom)	35.314
Implied decomposition of the cross-sectional variance of wages	
7 Share attributable to permanent effect	0.50
8 Share attributable to white-noise component	0.16
9 Share attributable to autoregressive component	0.34

Note:
Model is fit by minimum distance to the 36 covariances displayed in table 2.2.

covariance elements and the average autocovariances at each lag. The autocorrelations of wages decline from 0.78 (at lag 1) to 0.59 (at lag 7). There is some evidence of non-stationarity in the data, with the variances and covariances rising in the last years of the panel.[27]

The simple model specified in equation (2.10) fits the covariance matrix of wages surprisingly well. The overall goodness-of-fit statistic is 35.51, which has a probability value of 8 per cent. The parameter estimates and their implications are summarised in table 2.3.[28] One half of the cross-sectional variance in wages is attributed to permanent person-effects. Another 15 per cent is attributable to the pure white-noise component. The remaining autoregressive component of variance is highly persistent: the estimated AR(1) coefficient α is 0.89.

To see the implications of this persistence, consider the effect of a unit innovation in the person-specific wage component on the discounted average of expected future wages

$$(1-\beta) \sum_{j=0}^{\infty} \beta^j E_t \log w_{it+j}.$$

Suppose that the white-noise component of variance (μ_{it}) is due to measurement error. Then a unit innovation in wages is purely an innovation in the first-order autoregressive component u_{it}. Assuming that

$\beta = 0.9$ (i.e., a real discount rate of 11.1 per cent), the effect of a unit innovation in current wages on the discounted average of expected future wages is $(1 - \beta)/(1 - a\beta) = 0.494$. When wages rise by 10 per cent in the current period, the discounted average of expected future wages rises by 5 per cent.

This calculation suggests that a typical person-specific wage innovation results in a significant revision to lifetime wealth. Accounting for these wealth effects could in principle increase the explanatory power of the life-cycle labour supply model rather substantially. Of course, it is possible that individuals have better information with which to forecast future wages than is available to an outside data analyst. In this case, wage innovations in the statistical model (2.10) do not necessarily represent new information. In my opinion, we need much more evidence on the predictability of individual wages before we can use the life-cycle model to describe the wealth effects of person-specific wage shocks.

One possible approach is to combine consumption and hours information to obtain direct estimates of λ_{it}, and then to consider projections of the forecast errors in log λ_{it} on wages and other information.[29] To see how this might work, write the log-linear version of the intertemporal consumption function implied by the first-order conditions (2.3a) and (2.3b) as

$$\log c_{it} = e \log w_{it} + f \log \lambda_{it}.$$

(For simplicity I will ignore any taste variation.) This consumption function can be combined with the labour supply function (2.4) to give

$$\log h_{it} = (\eta - \delta e/f) \log w_{it} + \delta/f \log c_{it}. \tag{2.11}$$

This equation is the within-period optimality condition implied by setting the marginal rate of substitution between goods and leisure equal to the wage.[30] An instrumental variables procedure can be applied to (2.11) to estimate the coefficients $(\eta - \delta e/f)$ and δ/f. Similarly, the intertemporal labour supply elasticity η can be estimated by conventional means, for example by applying instrumental variables to (2.8). Then, using the (approximate) restriction that $e = \eta - \delta$, it is possible to recover estimates of the coefficients e and f. (Alternatively, one can estimate the coefficient e in the intertemporal consumption function directly – see Altonji (1986) for example.) Finally, these can be used to form an estimate of log λ_{it} from the observed consumption and wage data for each person.

Given estimates of log λ_{it} it should be possible to estimate the relation between the marginal utility of income and observable information, such as current assets and current and lagged wages. One could then test a specific model for log λ_{it}, such as the one implied by the Lucas–Rapping labour supply function, or the one implied by perfect foresight. It would also be useful to estimate components-of-variance models for the change in the marginal utility of income. A recent paper by Altug and Miller (1990) shows that the assumption of complete contingent markets imposes a simple factor structure on λ_{it}: $\lambda_{it} = \lambda_i \cdot \lambda_t$. If this is correct, the idiosyncratic component of the estimated change in $\log \lambda_{it}$ is orthogonal to individual-specific information, controlling for a homogeneous time effect. Altug and Miller's results suggest that this restriction may be acceptable.

A major limitation to this entire line of research is the absence of panel data sets with information on consumption expenditures. The leading panel data source, the PSID, only contains information on food expenditures. Some progress may be possible using the cohort level data in the British Family Expenditure Survey, although the labour supply information contained in this survey is limited to weekly hours.

3.4   Other sources of variation in individual labour supply

Although careful modelling of wealth effects may go some way towards improving our understanding of the determinants of individual labour supply, I am not optimistic that a conventional life-cycle model can ever explain more than a tiny fraction of the year-to-year variation in the data.[31] One may be tempted to attribute the unexplained changes to tastes or measurement error. There is a growing body of evidence, however, which suggests that idiosyncratic changes in labour supply are systematically related to conditions on the demand side of the labour market. There are two complementary explanations for this link. On the one hand, individuals may be unable to sell all their offered labour supply. On the other, some form of fixed costs may enter into either the supply or demand sides of the labour market.

Ashenfelter and Ham (1979) and Ham (1986) present models of intertemporal labour supply which assume that reported unemployment contains information on hours constraints faced by workers. Specifically, these authors assume that desired hours of work are described by an equation such as (2.4). In the presence of labour market disequilibrium, actual hours sold may be lower. Following Ashenfelter (1978) suppose that a fraction θ of reported weeks of unemployment represent weeks in which an individual was unable to sell his or her labour. This leads to a specification of the life-cycle labour supply function that includes measured unemployment (or its first difference) on the right-hand side, with a coefficient of θ. Estimates of this coefficient reported in Ashenfelter and Ham (1979) and Ham (1986) are positive and significant. Furthermore, the inclusion of measured unemployment leads to a significant increase in the explanatory power of the labour supply equation.

The interpretation of such an augmented labour supply function is an issue of considerable dispute. Heckman and MaCurdy (1988), following Lucas and Rapping (1970), argue that measured unemployment is simply another component of leisure. Because total time is constrained, the sum of leisure and unemployment is *necessarily* negatively correlated with hours of work. According to Heckman and MaCurdy then, individuals with longer hours of unemployment are simply those who are consuming more leisure.

Evidence presented by Ham (1986) sheds some interesting light on the interpretation of reported unemployment, and also on the underlying question of what causes individual hours of work to vary from year to year. To understand the nature of this evidence, consider the following (simplified) intertemporal labour supply function

$$\Delta \log h_{it} = \eta \, \Delta \log w_{it} + l \, \Delta D_{it} + \delta \, \phi_{it} \tag{2.12}$$

where D_{it} is a vector of demand conditions in an individual's local labour market, industry and/or occupation. There is no mechanical connection between the measurement of h_{it} and the measurement of D_{it}. If the labour supply model is correctly specified, however, then $l=0$, since market-level information should be irrelevant to individual hours decisions, controlling for individual-specific wages. Although he does not report direct estimates of l in his 1986 paper, Ham's results using ΔD_{it} as instrumental variables for individual unemployment indicate that l is far different from zero. An earlier unpublished version of the paper (Ham (1984)) presents direct tests for the exclusion of industry, occupation and local unemployment rates from an individual labour supply equation. The test statistics are highly significant, indicating an explicit role for demand-side variables in the determination of individual labour supply. When Ham uses the demand-side variables to instrument reported unemployment in the labour supply equation, he continues to find evidence of a negative and significant effect of unemployment on hours of work. This is evidence against a strict labour supply model and in favour of a model in which reported unemployment conveys information about the demand conditions facing an individual worker.

One need not appeal to Keynesian-style labour market constraints to rationalise these findings. An alternative explanation is that labour supply decisions are made at a higher frequency time unit than the year (for example the week), and that there are significant fixed costs on either the worker's side or the employer's side of the labour market. A model along the latter lines is presented in Rosen (1985) and Card (1990).[32] In this model, effective labour input from a pool of N workers is $Ng(h)$, where g is an S-shaped function of hours worked per person. The optimal employment policy of a firm with this technology consists of a two-part rule: if product demand is sufficiently low, lay off a fraction of the labour force and employ the remainder at some minimum threshold level of hours. If product demand is sufficiently high, employ all available workers at hours above the threshold.

The implications of this firm-level behaviour for individual labour supply data are two-fold. Firstly, some component of annual hours variation will occur at a fixed hourly wage rate. In particular, individuals working at firms with relatively low product demand will vary their number of weeks worked, but in each week of employment they will supply the same number of hours, and (presumably) earn the same weekly wage. For these individuals, hours of work will vary directly with measures of the firm's product demand. Secondly, weekly hours will be observed to fluctuate above a (person-specific) minimum threshold. Evidence presented in Card (1990) indicates that the latter prediction is surprisingly close to the truth. In a sample of 2,800 men observed working for the same employer over a two-year period, reported hours per week in each of eight interviews were observed to fall below thirty-five hours per week in only 11 per cent of cases.[33]

A simple fixed-cost model of this kind suggests that employer demand conditions should affect weeks of employment per year. Predictions on the connection between employer demand and hours per week depend on the assumed form of employment contract. My paper (Card (1990)) presents a case in which, conditional on working, hours per week lie on a conventional supply schedule. In this case, controlling for the wage, employer demand should have no effect on hours per week. Some simple evidence on this prediction is presented in table 2.4, which shows the results of estimating the augmented labour supply function (2.12) on three measures of labour supply: hours per week, weeks per quarter and total quarterly hours.

The data summarised in table 2.4 pertain to men in the 1983 SIPP panel. The sample is restricted to individuals who are observed working for one employer over the nine quarters of the available sample period. Demand-side conditions are measured by the logarithm of employment in the individual's one-digit industry. Thus, ΔD_{it} refers to the percentage change in employment in an individual's industry in the most recent quarter. The equations are estimated by instrumental variables, using as an instrument for wages the changes in wages observed for the same person four quarters in the past or four quarters in the future. There is a small but highly significant seasonal correlation in individual wage changes that gives this instrumental variable its power.

The estimates suggest that measures of employment demand are significantly correlated with both hours per week and weeks per quarter. In comparison, the estimated intertemporal substitution elasticities are small

Table 2.4. *Estimated labour supply functions for quarterly hours outcomes: SIPP sample of men (standard errors in parentheses)*

	Log hours/wk	Log wks	Log total hrs	Log hours/wk	Log wks	Log total hrs
1 Log wage	0.10	0.05	0.16	0.10	0.05	0.14
	(0.14)	(0.13)	(0.22)	(0.14)	(0.13)	(0.22)
2 Industry	—	—	—	0.21	0.24	0.46
employment				(0.06)	(0.06)	(0.10)
3 *R*-squared	0.00	0.00	0.00	0.00	0.00	0.00

Note:
Sample consists of 19,566 observations on quarterly changes in labour supply of 4,814 men aged sixteen to sixty-four with same employer over nine quarters (1983-IV to 1985-I) in 1983 SIPP panel. All equations are estimated in first-difference form, and include nine unrestricted quarterly dummies as well as potential experience. Log wage is instrumented by the change in log wages of the same person four quarters in the past (or four quarters in the future, for observations from the first three quarters of the sample). The standard deviations of the dependent variables are: log hours per week – 0.142; log weeks per quarter – 0.147; log quarterly hours – 0.234.

and relatively imprecise.[34] One could easily conclude from this evidence that changes in labour supply are directly connected to employer demand conditions, and that wages play little or no role in the short-run labour–leisure decision.

The relatively weak connection between hours per week and wages illustrated in columns 1 and 4 of table 2.4 may seem puzzling, given that the Fair Labour Standards Act *mandates* overtime payments for individuals in many occupations who work over forty hours per week. Some additional evidence on the relation between weekly hours and wages is provided by data in the May 1985 CPS. This survey gathered information on usual hours per week, actual hours worked in the previous week, and whether or not the individual received any overtime payments. The responses suggest that there is substantial variation in actual weekly hours around 'usual' weekly hours: 13 per cent of men indicate that they worked less than their usual hours, while another 19 per cent indicate that they worked more.[35] Individuals in the latter group report ten extra hours per week on average, bringing their weekly total to fifty-one hours. However, only 47 per cent of these men report receiving any additional overtime compensation. For the majority, weekly hours are higher than usual but weekly earnings are fixed.[36]

Table 2.5. *Wages, hours, and overtime premiums for individuals working forty or more hours: May 1985 current population survey (standard errors in parentheses)*

	Paid overtime?	
	No	Yes
1 Number of individuals	1,651	2,416
2 Average hours last week	48.58	47.82
	(0.18)	(0.13)
3 Usual weekly hours	39.78	39.86
	(0.02)	(0.01)
4 Hours paid overtime	—	8.10
		(0.16)
5 Percentage paid time-and-a-half	—	92.34
6 Per cent female	41.67	32.37
7 Per cent paid by hour	38.10	85.67
8 Average hourly wage	10.65	8.97
	(0.27)	(0.16)

Note:
Sample consists of 4,067 individuals aged sixteen to sixty-four in May 1985 CPS who reported usual weekly hours between thirty-five and forty and who reported working forty-one or more hours in the survey week. Dual-job holders and self-employed workers are excluded. In the May 1985 CPS 62.4 per cent of all individuals report usual weekly hours between thirty-five and forty (62.3 per cent of men, 62.5 per cent of women). Of these, 13.5 per cent reported working forty-one or more hours last week.

Table 2.5 provides more detailed information on a very narrow subset of individuals – those who usually work thirty-five to forty hours per week and who report forty-one or more hours in the survey week.[37] Sixty-two per cent of all workers normally work thirty-five to forty hours per week. Of these, 13.5 per cent worked forty-one or more hours in the survey week, and are used in the table. The fraction receiving overtime compensation among this group is 59 per cent. Interestingly, however, extra hours worked are actually slightly higher for the group with no overtime pay.

These data suggest that even within the week, a simple labour supply model is inadequate for a large fraction of the population. Many individuals appear to be working extra hours for no extra pay. When this behaviour is added to the phenomenon of weekly layoffs, it becomes clear how a simple model of labour supply can fail to explain movements in annual hours.

Further work is obviously needed to isolate the systematic components of individual labour supply and to describe the links between employer demand and employee hours choices. While such work falls outside the narrow realm of a conventional life-cycle model, it seems to me that further understanding of individual hours outcomes will require a broader perspective than the standard model can provide. As it stands, the life-cycle model provides essentially no insight into the year-to-year variation in individual hours.

4   CONCLUSIONS

The life-cycle labour supply model offers an explanation for the four main components of individual hours choices: mean hours over the life-cycle, the age profile of hours, aggregate movements in hours, and individual-specific variation in hours around the life-cycle profile. All of these components are tied together by a combination of intertemporal substitution effects and wealth effects. In this chapter I have tried to gauge the success of the life-cycle model in explaining the various dimensions of male labour supply. My assessment is hardly positive: the only real success for the model has come as a description of aggregate patterns in wages and hours during the post 1970 period. Even here, my suspicion is that a careful consideration of wealth effects undermines the success of the model.

Much of the micro-econometric research over the past two decades has concentrated on the magnitude of the intertemporal substitution effect, and in particular on modelling the intertemporal substitution effect of individual-specific wage variation. As Pencavel noted in his 1986 survey, the available evidence suggests that this effect is of second-order importance. My view is that a similar conclusion holds with respect to the intertemporal substitution effect in the age profile of hours. With respect to the permanent component of hours, there is much ambiguity in the literature. A fairly widespread belief among labour economists is that a permanent increase in wages leads to a reduction in hours. Using modern panel data it is surprisingly hard to verify this hypothesis, and in fact the preponderance of the evidence suggests to me a positive association between long-run wages and average hours.

Two major avenues for further work are suggested. One involves a detailed effort to estimate the wealth effects in intertemporal labour supply. Existing methods can be used to estimate the marginal utility of wealth and test its properties. Progress in this direction will depend on the availability of data linking individual consumption and hours choices. A second involves a re-evaluation of the premise that average hourly earnings are a 'sufficient statistic' for current labour market opportunities. A variety of models suggest that individual hours are influenced directly by employer-specific demand conditions. Some limited empirical evidence confirms this suspicion. If true, our basic notions of labour supply, and in particular our notions about the degree of substitutability between current and future leisure, may be incomplete.

Notes

I am grateful to Dean Hyslop and John Penrod for outstanding research assistance, and to Robert Moffitt and my colleagues in the Industrial Relations Section for helpful comments and discussion.

1 Lucas and Rapping (1970) seem to be the first authors to use an explicit intertemporal model to describe short- and long-run labour supply phenomena, although Mincer (1962) distinguished between the effects of short-run unemployment and long-run wage increases in explaining the behaviour of female labour supply.

2 Excellent surveys are available in Killingsworth (1983) and Pencavel (1986).

3 Lucas and Rapping (1970, footnote 11) also noted in passing that their model had 'lifecycle as well as business-cycle implications'.

4 This same idea can potentially explain the 'excess' covariation of income and consumption growth in aggregate data.

5 See MaCurdy (1985) for example.

6 Of course one could start with a specification of U that *implies* the log-linear intertemporal labour supply function (2.4). Issues of functional form are discussed in Browning, Deaton and Irish (1985).

7 I have simplified (2.5) slightly using the approximation $\log(1 + \rho) = \rho$ and $\log(1 + r_t) = r_t$.

8 In fact, closed form expressions for λ_{it} under perfect foresight are not easily obtained. One case that can be solved uses an LES-form for the within-period utility function U. See Ashenfelter and Ham (1979).

9 Obviously, it may not be possible to recover an unbiased estimate of the planned life-cycle profile of hours from a sample of individuals in the same cohort, since these individuals share the same aggregate-level shocks in each year of their life.

10 The samples for each year consist of men aged sixteen to seventy, excluding those who are classified as self employed and those with allocated wage and salary earnings. Individuals who report positive wage and salary earnings, positive weeks of work, and positive usual hours per week for the previous year are counted as working. Individuals who were working and who report average hourly earnings less than $1.00 or greater than $75 (in 1983 dollars) are deleted from the sample. The sample sizes in each year range from 36,000 to 42,000.

11 Average real wage rates declined sharply between 1979 and 1981. For the youngest cohort in figure 2.1, this effect appears as a slowdown in the rate of growth of wages. For older cohorts, real wages actually declined.

12 The CPS does not ask 'weeks in school' during the previous year, or give any breakdown of hours per week into work and school time.

13 The wage profiles are also potentially biased estimates of the wage profiles for the whole population, since we only observe wages for workers. One way to evaluate the size of this bias is to assume that wages for those not working would be at some lower bound (say, the minimum wage) and then to recalculate the average wage. This procedure suggests that the bias in the wage profiles up to age fifty is trivial.

14 These profiles are estimated age coefficients from regressions of average log wages and average log hours on age effects, year effects, and a set of broad (ten-year interval) cohort effects.

15 One could also appeal to models with endogenous human capital accumulation. Evidence presented by Holt-Eakin, Newey and Rosen (1988), however, indicates that lagged hours have no influence on future wages. This seems to rule out simple capital accumulation models.

16 These assumptions clearly understate the total labour supply of the more-educated workers. First, many students work part time or part of the year. Second, actual time spent in school is arguably closer to work than leisure.

17 Finegan (1962) examined data on wages and weekly hours in different occupation and industry classes, and found a generally negative relation between them. On the other hand, Finegan's results indicate a positive association by level of education. However, he dismisses this evidence, asserting that wage differentials by education class include premia for training costs that should be netted out. I have attempted an analysis similar to Finegan's using data on 483 3-digit occupations for men in the March 1988 CPS. These data show a strong positive association between average hours and average wages in different occupations, even controlling for education and other demographic factors.

18 Actually, Angrist estimates the aggregated labour supply function in level form.

19 Between 1947 and 1976, for example, real average hourly earnings of non-supervisory workers rose at an average annual rate of 2.38 per cent.

20 One can derive an intertemporal labour supply function that is approximately equivalent to the Lucas–Rapping function (with $\theta = 0$) using the within-period preference function

$$U(c, h) = c - ah^{(1 + \eta)/\eta}.$$

However, this is only valid in the absence of uncertainty.

21 To see this, decompose $\log w_{it}$ into a permanent person effect, a year effect v_t, and a person and year specific effect, and suppose $E_t(v_{t+j}) = v_t$. Then (2.7) implies $\log h_t = a_i + \theta v_t$.

22 MaCurdy's estimates of the intertemporal substitution elasticity centre on 0.15 – see below.

23 This estimate is based on a sample of individuals working for a single employer over two years, and is surely an upper bound on the signal/noise ratio.

24 I suspect that a retrospective survey on annual hours in the previous year probably understates the true variation in average hours per week, since many individuals with substantial within-year variation in hours per week are likely to report a simple number like '40 hours per week'. This is especially problematic in the CPS survey, because interviewers are instructed to gather *modal* (rather than average) hours per week from such individuals. However, I have been unable to ascertain if the more frequent interview schedule in the SIPP accounts for the higher variation in annual hours changes.

25 One exception is MaCurdy's (1983) study using a sample of males in the control group of the Denver Income Maintenance Experiment. MaCurdy does not parameterise preferences in such a way as to imply a constant intertemporal substitution elasticity. However, his estimates imply that the intertemporal elasticity is high: in the neighbourhood of 2.0.

26 Specifically, I estimated the vector of parameters β by minimising $(m - f(\beta))' V^{-1}(m - f(\beta))$, where m is the vector of thirty-six second moments of the wage data, $f(\beta)$ is the vector of fitted moments, and V is the estimated variance matrix of the second moments.

27 The sample excludes 105 individuals who otherwise meet the data requirements but who are eliminated by virtue of reporting an hourly wage less than \$0.75 or greater than \$100 (in 1967\$) in one or more years. When these individuals are included, the variances and covariances are 25 per cent larger but the autocorrelations are very similar.

28 There are a total of twelve parameters in the model, including the eight period-specific variances σ_t^2 and the variance of the pre-sample shock u_{i0}.

29 This approach follows up on MaCurdy's (1983) method for estimating the parameters of the life-cycle model. MaCurdy's procedure is used by Blundell (1990).

30 Notice that if one maintains the assumption $e = 0$ (i.e., that wages have no effect on consumption, holding constant λ), then one can obtain estimates of the *intertemporal* substitution elasticity from cross-sectional data! This procedure is used by Altonji (1986), and seems to give estimates of η about the same size as those obtained by estimating (2.8).

31 For example, Altonji's (1986) use of observed food consumption as a control for the marginal utility of income results in only a small increase in the explanatory power of his fitted labour supply equations.

32 A class of models with similar properties is analysed in a macro context by Hansen (1985) and Rogerson (1988). In these papers, labour supply within the week is assumed to be either 0 or 1.

33 See Card (1990, table 3).

34 OLS estimates of the equation result in negative and significant wage coefficients, presumably as a consequence of measurement error in average hourly earnings. Further results are reported in Card (1990).

35 These statistics pertain to men aged sixteen to sixty-four who hold only one job and who are not self employed. Variation in weekly hours among the excluded group is even larger.
36 Unfortunately, the survey does not ask about reduced compensation for individuals who worked less than usual hours.
37 In an effort to obtain a reasonably large sample, this table includes both men and women.

References

Altonji, Joseph G. (1982), 'The Intertemporal Substitution Model of Labor Market Fluctuations: An Empirical Analysis', *Review of Economic Studies*, 49 (Supplement): 783–824.
    (1986), 'Intertemporal Substitution in Labor Supply: Evidence From Micro Data', *Journal of Political Economy*, 94 (Supplement, June): S176–S215.
Altonji, Joseph G. and Ashenfelter, Orley (1980), 'Wage Movements and the Labor Market Equilibrium Hypothesis', *Economica*, 47 (August): 217–45.
Altonji, Joseph G. and Paxson, Christina (1986), 'Job Characteristics and Hours of Work', in Ronald Ehrenberg (ed.), *Research in Labor Economics*, Vol. VIII (Part A), Greenwich, Conn.: JAI Press.
Altug, Sumru and Miller, Robert A. (1990), 'Household Choices in Equilibrium', *Econometrica*, 58 (May): 543–70.
Angrist, Joshua D. (1990), 'Does Labor Supply Explain Fluctuations in Average Hours Worked?', discussion paper 1476, Cambridge, Mass.: Department of Economics, Harvard University, March.
    (1991), 'Grouped Data Estimation and Testing in Simple Labor Supply Models', *Journal of Econometrics*, 47: 243–66.
Ashenfelter, Orley (1978), 'Unemployment as a Constraint on Labour Market Behavior', in M. Artis (ed.), *Proceedings of the 1977 Meeting of the Association of University Teachers of Economics*, Oxford: Basil Blackwell.
    (1984), 'Microeconomic Analyses and Macroeconomic Analyses of Labor Supply', in K. Brunner and A. Meltzer (eds.), *Carnegie-Rochester Conference Series on Public Policy*, Vol. XXI, Amsterdam: North Holland.
Ashenfelter, Orley and Ham, John (1979), 'Education, Unemployment and Earnings', *Journal of Political Economy*, 87 (Supplement, December): S99–S116.
Blundell, Richard (1990), 'Evaluating Structural Microeconometric Models of Labour Supply', unpublished manuscript, London: Department of Economics, University College, July.
Bound, John, Brown, Charles, Duncan, Greg J. and Rogers, Willard L. (1989), 'Measurement Error in Cross-Sectional and Longitudinal Labor Market Surveys: Results from Two Validation Studies', NBER Working Paper Number 2884, Cambridge, Mass.: National Bureau of Economic Research, March.

Browning, Martin, Deaton, Angus and Irish, Margaret (1985), 'A Profitable Approach to Labor Supply and Commodity Demands Over the Life-Cycle', *Econometrica*, 53 (May): 503–43.

Card, David (1990), 'Labor Supply with a Minimum Hours Threshold', Princeton University Industrial Relations Section Working Paper Number 262, Princeton, N. J., Industrial Relations Section, February, in A. Meltzer (ed.), *Carnegie Rochester Conference on Public Policy*, 33, Amsterdam: North Holland.

Carrol, Chris and Summers, Lawrence H. (1989), 'Consumption Growth Parallels Income Growth: Some New Evidence', unpublished Working Paper, Cambridge Mass.: Department of Economics, Harvard University.

Duncan, Greg J. and Hill, Dan H. (1985), 'An Investigation into the Extent and Consequences of Measurement Error in Labor-economic Survey Data', *Journal of Labor Economics*, 3: 508–32.

Finegan, T. Aldrich (1962), 'Hours of Work in the United States: A Cross-Sectional Analysis', *Journal of Political Economy* 70 (October): 452–70.

Friedman, Milton (1975), *Price Theory*, Chicago: Aldine Publishing.

Ghez, Gilbert and Becker, Gary S. (1975), *The Allocation of Time and Goods over the Lifecycle*. New York: Columbia University Press.

Ham, John (1984), 'Testing Whether Unemployment Represents Intertemporal Labor Supply Behavior', unpublished manuscript presented at University of Manchester, July.

(1986), 'Testing Whether Unemployment Represents Intertemporal Labor Supply Behavior', *Review of Economic Studies*, 53: 559–78.

Hansen, Gary (1985), 'Individual Labor and the Business Cycle', *Journal of Monetary Economics*, 16 (November): 309–27.

Heckman, James J. (1974), 'Life Cycle Consumption and Labor Supply: An Explanation of the Relationship Between Income and Consumption Over the Life Cycle', *American Economic Review*, 64 (March): 188–94.

(1976), 'A Life-Cycle Model of Earnings, Learning, and Consumption', *Journal of Political Economy*, 84 (Supplement, August): S11–S44.

Heckman, James J. and MaCurdy, Thomas E. (1988), 'Empirical Tests of Labor-Market Equilibrium: An Evaluation', in K. Brunner and A. Meltzer (eds.), *Carnegie-Rochester Conference Series on Public Policy*, Vol. XXVIII, Amsterdam: North Holland.

Holz-Eakin, Douglas, Newey, Whitney and Rosen, Harvey S. (1988), 'Estimating Vector Autoregressions with Panel Data', *Econometrica*, 56 (November): 1371–95.

Killingsworth, Mark R. (1983), *Labor Supply*, Cambridge University Press.

Lewis, H. Gregg (1956), 'Hours of Work and Hours of Leisure', in L. Reed Tripp (ed.), *Proceedings of the Ninth Annual Meeting of the Industrial Relations Research Association*, Madison Wis.: IRRA.

Lucas, Robert E. and Rapping, Leonard (1970), 'Real Wages, Employment and Inflation', in E.S. Phelps (ed.), *Microeconomic Foundations of Employment and Inflation Theory*, New York: Norton.

MaCurdy, Thomas E. (1981), 'An Empirical Model of Labor Supply in a Life-Cycle Setting', *Journal of Political Economy*, 89 (December): 1059–85.

(1983), 'A Simple Scheme for Estimating an Intertemporal Model of Labor Supply and Consumption in the Presence of Taxes and Uncertainty', *International Economic Review*, 24 (June): 265–89.

(1985), 'Interpreting Empirical Models of Labor Supply in an Intertemporal Framework with Uncertainty', in J.J. Heckman and B. Singer (eds.), *Longitudinal Analysis of Labor Market Data*, Cambridge University Press.

Mankiw, N. Gregory, Rotemberg, Julio J. and Summers, Lawrence H. (1985), 'Intertemporal Substitution in Macroeconomics', *Quarterly Journal of Economics*, 100 (February): 225–51.

Mincer, Jacob (1962), 'Labor Force Participation of Married Women: A Study of Labor Supply', in National Bureau of Economic Research, *Aspects of Labor Economics*, Princeton N. J.: Princeton University Press.

Pencavel, John (1986), 'Labor Supply of Men: A Survey', in O. Ashenfelter and R. Layard (eds.), *Handbook of Labor Economics*, Amsterdam: North Holland.

Rogerson, Richard (1988), 'Indivisible Labor, Lotteries, and Equilibrium', *Journal of Monetary Economics*, 21 (July): 3–16.

Rosen, Sherwin (1985), 'Implicit Contracts: A Survey', *Journal of Economic Literature*, 23: 1144–76.

Thurow, Lester C. (1969), 'The Optimum Lifetime Distribution of Consumption Expenditures', *American Economic Review*, 59 (June): 324–30.

II
Computation for stochastic equilibrium

CHAPTER 3

Simulation analysis of dynamic stochastic models: applications to theory and estimation

Albert Marcet

1 INTRODUCTION

The use of dynamic stochastic models in economics has grown very quickly during the last fifteen years. The importance of this type of models became evident in macro-economics after the paper of Lucas (1972); he argued that the basic relations that were taken as given in traditional macro-economic models (whether Keynesian or Monetarist), such as the money demand function, the consumption function, the investment function, were not invariant to the very type of policy intervention that those models were designed to analyse. Furthermore, these relations were often mutually inconsistent. The way around this problem was to study models where objects like preferences of consumers, production technology, information dissemination, etc. were fixed, and where a well-specified concept of equilibrium determined the outcome of the model. The research programme, then, was to analyse the equilibrium of the model under different environments (for example, under different policy rules) in order to study the effect of changes in the economic environment or policy interventions, taking consumption function, money demand, etc. as endogenous. Nowadays, dynamic stochastic models of equilibrium are being used in virtually all fields of economics.

One crucial element of how dynamic models behave is the assumption about how agents form their expectations. Nowadays, the standard assumption is that agents behave as if they had rational expectations. This avoids *ad hoc* assumptions about expectations that would not be likely to stay constant under policy changes if agents were rational. Furthermore, many recent papers argue that, in many models, the rational expectations equilibrium can be justified as the limit of a learning process.[1]

Economists have made a lot of progress on such basic issues as formulating equilibrium concepts for these models, finding conditions for existence and uniqueness of equilibria, determining the state variables, etc. But in order to *use* our models, that is, in order to characterise equilibria, evaluate different policy rules, learn about the importance of certain assumptions, and so on, it is necessary to obtain a solution for the law of motion of the equilibrium stochastic process. Unfortunately, progress in finding closed form solutions of dynamic stochastic models has been very slow; the only model that can be solved in any generality is the linear-quadratic model.[2] In non-linear models, very special assumptions have to be made in order to obtain analytic solutions; in effect, these assumptions limit the interest of the exercise.

Closed-form solutions are also needed in empirical applications, for example those using maximum-likelihood estimation. The GMM procedure of Hansen and Singleton (1982) can be used to estimate and test certain rational-expectations models from the Euler equations, even if a closed-form solution is not available, but this technique cannot be used if there are unobservables in the Euler equations. This is often the case in models with exogenous shocks to preferences, data aggregated over time or over agents, and models with inequality constraints

In the last five years, given the difficulties for finding closed-form solutions in models of interest, a growing number of researchers have turned to studying dynamic stochastic equilibrium models using computer simulations. With simulations, it is possible to implement empirical tests of the model and study the behaviour of the model under different environments. In this chapter we will discuss the usefulness of the simulation techniques, the progress that has been made in computer algorithms recently, and many applications of these techniques. Obviously, it is impossible to cite all the applications that have been done in economics, and we will discuss some applications to macro-economics and financial economics.

With the new algorithms, and refinements on the old ones, we are now able to simulate very complicated models on desktop computers. Besides increasing computational speed, the new algorithms have enlarged the class of models that can be approached by simulation; more precisely, it is no longer necessary to cast an equilibrium model into a planner's problem in order to solve it.

Studies of theoretical interest can be performed using computer simulations not only for illustrative purposes, as a complement to analytic results, but as the main tool for reaching conclusions of theoretical interest. We will argue that it is possible to do 'theory on the computer', much in the way that it is possible to do theory by proving theorems. In fact, this is probably the only way of making any progress in many models of interest, since analytic solutions are so difficult to obtain. Some issues that arise in doing theory on the computer are how to report results, how to choose the parameter values and issues about accuracy of the solution; we will discuss these below. On the issue of choosing parameter values, one alternative is to use those parameters that make the equilibrium of the model close to the observed series; in this respect, dynamic stochastic models are easy to handle, because they have very clear-cut implications for observed time series.

In section 2 we illustrate the difficulties for obtaining analytic closed-form solutions by studying a simple asset pricing model; we discuss the limitations of the model and some extensions that have been performed using simulation; we also review the literature on other topics where simulation studies have proved useful. Section 3 reviews some of the recent progress in solution algorithms and the usefulness of the new approaches. Section 4 discusses the use of simulations in theoretical exercises; we argue that this kind of exercise is as valid as analytic techniques and review some of the applications; we also discuss how to report the results, choose parameter values and issues about the accuracy of the solution. Section 5 discusses how to apply simulations in empirical studies; we discuss applications to maximum likelihood, the method of simulated moments and calibration. Section 6 is a response to Ken Judd's discussion of this chapter.

2   ANALYSING DYNAMIC ECONOMIES WITH SIMULATION: SOME APPLICATIONS

First of all, we want to illustrate the need for simulation in equilibrium dynamic stochastic models. To this end, we show the limitations of analytic solutions to a well-known asset pricing model and discuss how this and other models have been enriched by the use of simulations.

2.1   Analytic solution to Lucas' asset pricing model

Let us consider analytic solutions for asset prices in the model of Lucas (1978). Since this is a well-known model, the description will be brief.

There is an exogenous, stochastic stream of dividends $\{d_t\}$ that is produced exogenously by an infinitely lived productive unit. Agents have a right to this dividend if they hold shares of ownership of the productive unit for ever; shares can be bought and sold costlessly at any time period and all markets are perfectly competitive. There is only one type of agent, so it will simplify notation if we assume that there is only one representative agent who behaves competitively. Dividends are the only source of the only consumption good in this economy. At time t, the agent observes all current and past variables. The representative agent chooses streams of consumption and share holdings in order to solve[3]

$$\max E_0 \sum_{t=0}^{\infty} \delta^t u(c_t)$$

s.t. $c_t + p_t s_t = (p_t + d_t)s_{t-1}$ for $t = 0, 1, \ldots;$ $s_{-1} = 1$

taking the process for dividends and stock prices $\{d_t, p_t\}$ as given. Normalising the number of shares to one, the equilibrium conditions in this model are

$$s_t = 1 \text{ and } c_t = d_t.$$

The first-order conditions are

$$p_t u'(c_t) = \delta E_t[(p_{t+1} + d_{t+1})u'(c_{t+1})], \tag{3.1}$$

which, using recursive substitution and the equilibrium condition for the consumption good can be re-written as

$$p_t = E_t\left[\sum_{i=1}^{\infty} \delta^i d_{t+i} u'(d_{t+i})/u'(d_t)\right]. \tag{3.2}$$

To describe the behaviour of equilibrium asset prices in this economy we need to find a closed-form solution for the asset prices in terms of the dividend process. The above formulas are not closed-form solutions because they are written in terms of a conditional expectation that is difficult to solve unless special assumptions are introduced. So, we have to specialise this already very simple model in order to find a closed-form solution. Here are a few possibilities:[4]

Example 1
Assume that $\{d_t\}$ is identically independently distributed. Letting $C = E[d_t u'(d_t)]$, we obtain from (3.2)

$$p_t = C\delta/[u'(d_t)(1-\delta)]. \tag{3.3}$$

This is a closed-form solution up to the constant C, which could be found explicitly if more assumptions were placed on the functional form of $u(.)$ and on the distribution of d_t. Alternatively, this constant can be easily calculated by numerical integration.

Example 2
Assume that $u(c_t) = \log(c_t)$. Then $u'(d_t) = 1/d_t$ and (3.2) becomes

$$p_t = \delta d_t/(1-\delta). \tag{3.4}$$

This formula holds for any dividend process.

Example 3

Assume that $u(c_t) = (c_t)^{\gamma+1}/(\gamma+1)$ and that $d_t = d_{t-1}\epsilon_t$, where ϵ_t is i.i.d. Let $\mu = E(\epsilon_t^{\gamma+1})$; under the additional assumption that $\delta\mu < 1$ (which is guaranteed, for example, if $E(\epsilon_t) = 1$ and $\gamma < -1$), then the formula for asset prices is

$$p_t = \sum_{i=1}^{\infty} (\delta\mu)^i d_t^{\gamma+1}/d_t^{\gamma} = \delta\mu d_t/(1 - \delta\mu). \tag{3.5}$$

The point of having analytic examples in a paper that deals with simulation techniques is that, even in this simple model, very strong assumptions have to be made in order to find closed-form solutions. To the non-expert, the kind of exercise done in the above examples seems pure magic: we start with a complicated, hard to interpret formula like (3.2) and out come these neat, elegant formulas (3.3), (3.4) and (3.5). To the untrained eye, these formulas seemed to appear out of nowhere, but we all know that we put just the right cards in our sleeves (i.e., we made enough assumptions) to make the conditional expectation in (3.2) disappear.

Finding closed-form solutions after making these very extreme assumptions has certainly improved our knowledge about equilibrium asset pricing, but it turns out to be an exercise with limited possibilities. We would like to explore versions of that model where more general utility functions are used, perhaps allowing for shocks to preferences, non-time-separable utility functions, and for dividend processes that come closer to the dividend series observed in real data.

More importantly, there are many questions that cannot be addressed even in the most general version of Lucas' model. For example, the effects of liquidity constraints, market incompleteness, private information, heterogeneity of consumers, effects of transaction costs, limited enforcement of contracts are some of the features that play a potentially important role in securities markets, but they cannot be introduced in Lucas' model without major changes.

Also, one of the reasons that securities markets receive so much attention is probably that they may be the first markets to reflect news in the productive sector. But any relation between productivity and asset prices cannot be analysed in Lucas' model because production is exogenous. Brock (1982) provided a theoretical framework for formulating asset pricing models with endogenous production, but the properties of these models have not been explored until very recently.

Nevertheless, there is no general way of obtaining closed-form solutions in models with these type of generalisations and so the effect of market incompleteness, heterogeneity of agents, etc. has been largely unknown for a long time. Some exceptions are Scheinkman and Weiss (1986), Hansen (1987) and Hansen and Sargent (1990).

2.2   Beyond the representative agent asset pricing model

The main reason that so many important issues cannot even be addressed in asset pricing models with a representative agent is that there is *no* trading of securities in a representative agent model; for example, introducing or eliminating securities markets never has an effect on asset prices or on welfare; predictions about trading make no sense, etc.

Nevertheless, these are relevant problems in economics, nowadays. For example, there has been recently some political pressure to reduce the amount of securities trading in US stock exchanges by introducing a tax on securities trading, but in a representative agent model it is clear that this measure would not have any effect because there is no trading of assets to begin with. Another example: recently, options and futures markets started operating in some countries; presumably these markets are being established because somebody thinks they are useful, but the representative agent model would say that they serve no purpose and they will have no effect on the economy.

On the other hand, there are well-documented empirical failures of the representative agent model: from the popular equity premium puzzle of Mehra and Prescott (1985), to the excessive volatility of individual consumptions, to the excess volatility of asset prices of Grossman and Shiller (1981).

Starting in 1990 the study of equilibrium asset pricing models with heterogeneous agents, incomplete markets and liquidity constraints seems to have taken off. The papers by D. Lucas (1990), Marcet and Singleton (1990) and Ketterer and Marcet (1989) have two types of agents that can differ in their preferences or income processes. Only a few securities exist in this economy (stocks, bonds or call options); agents face liquidity constraints on the securities. Perfect competition and perfect information is assumed. The first two papers study empirical issues like volatility of individual consumption, how often the liquidity constraints are binding and the risk premium puzzle. The third paper discusses the effects of introducing derivative securities in a model with incomplete markets. Other papers by Hansen and Imrohoroglu (1992) and Diaz and Prescott (1990) study monetary models where money has value because of market incompleteness. Rios (1990) studies an overlapping generations model with uncertainty and a large number of generations alive at any point in time; he studies issues such as the life cycle, insurance among generations and the effects of market incompleteness. Finally, Brock and le Baron (1989) introduce liquidity constraints on the side of the firms.

Although it is impossible to summarise all the results from these papers in a short space we will remark on two features which they seem to have in common. The first feature is methodological: all of the above papers rely heavily on simulations for their results. The second point is a more substantive one: in most of these models market incompleteness on its own is not capable of generating results that are very different from the complete markets case. So, it turns out that there is barely any risk premium, individual consumptions are not very volatile, and the losses in utility from market incompleteness and liquidity constraints are not very large. It appears as if agents can do a great deal of consumption smoothing just by buying and selling stocks of their securities; in the terminology of Deaton (1991), assets act as a buffer stock that can be adjusted to cope with unforeseen shocks.

This is a nice example of how simulation can enhance our understanding of dynamic modelling. It seems as if these generalisations of Lucas' model do not automatically produce much better results than the representative agent, at least in the cases that have been explored up to now. This is striking because so many papers had suggested that incomplete markets would easily explain some empirical puzzles, for example Mehra and Prescott (1985), Hayashi (1987). We will discuss this further in section 4.1.

2.3   Recent applications of simulation techniques

Besides asset pricing with heterogeneous agents, there have been many other recent applications of simulation in economics. One example is asset prices and endogenous production, such as in the model of Brock (1982). In section 3 we will use this model as our main example for how different algorithms work. Some papers in this area are the following: Rowenhorst (1990) studies the effects of leverage on asset prices, the relationship between productivity and asset returns and studies some empirical implications; den Haan (1990b) studies the shape of the term structure of interest rates in an equilibrium monetary model with leisure; Marcet (1989) argues that a simple model with endogenous production can produce a complicated covariance structure for asset prices and can generate humped term structures of the interest rate.

Besides the more radical departures that we have discussed in the previous subsection, there have been many extensions of the representative agent asset pricing model where equilibria have been studied by simulations. Some of these applications are the following: Novales (1990) studies the effects of introducing habit persistence of consumption for the behaviour of interest rates; Ingram (1990a) studies a model with myopic agents in asset markets and Heaton (1990) studies the effects of habit persistence and time aggregation.

Other applications have been in monetary models with uncertainty.

Cooley and Hansen (1989) introduce monetary shocks in a real business cycle model; den Haan (1990a) studies the optimal monetary policy in a model where money reduces the shopping time; the Diaz and Prescott (1990) paper is also a paper on monetary theory. Coleman (1991) and Baxter (1990) study a cash-in-advance model, and Marshall (1988) studies the empirical implications for inflation of a representative agent where money is valued because of exogenously imposed transaction costs.

There have been also several applications to models with distortionary taxes. Braun (1989), Chang (1989) and McGratten (1989) study the business cycle properties of these models from an empirical point of view, Bizer and Judd (1989) discuss the optimality of a stochastic taxation scheme and Otker (1990) studies the welfare loss due to the presence of distortionary taxation. Jones, Manuelli and Rossi (1990) and Chari, Christiano and Kehoe (1990) study optimal distortionary taxes.

The formulation of models with incentive compatibility constraints and mechanism design has received great attention since the seventies. The implications of these models for empirical data and characterisation of equilibria in dynamic settings, however, have been difficult to study analytically. Using simulation, Phalen and Townsend (1991) characterise the sequentially optimal contracts in a non-growth economy with limited information and they document the welfare loss from private information; Phalen (1990) argues that the consumption choices of individual agents are better explained by incentive compatibility models; Marcet and Marimon (1992) study the effects of limited information and limited enforcement on the growth path of an economy.

We also find applications to game theoretical models. Rotemberg and Woodford (1992) argue that some features of the business cycle can be better explained with a model of monopolistic competition; Marimon, McGratten and Sargent (1990) show that in a monetary model with a multiplicity of Nash equilibria, if agents learn how to trade and how to maximise utility using rules that make them take more frequently those actions that provide higher rewards (more precisely, by using some genetic algorithms that have been used in biology to study the survival of species) then the economy would converge to the optimal Nash equilibrium. Judd (1989b) compares the equilibrium concepts of Bertrand and Cournot.

3   ALGORITHMS FOR SOLVING NON-LINEAR DYNAMIC STOCHASTIC MODELS

3.1   New developments in algorithms

Recently a large amount of research effort has been devoted to the development of new approaches to solving rational expectations equilibrium models. The fact that there exist several alternatives for finding numerical solutions may be confusing to the non-expert but it has several advantages. First of all, when several algorithms can be applied one can check the solutions that different algorithms provide and see if they are similar. Perhaps more importantly, different approaches work best in different models; for example, there is usually a trade-off between algorithms that can handle complicated models (with strong non-linearities) and algorithms that can solve larger models with higher speed.

When choosing an algorithm for application on a given model, one has to take into account several factors. Speed of computation is one of these factors, but not the only one.

Another important feature of a method is its flexibility. If the same method can be applied to many different and interesting models the researcher will be able to use his program and his expertise in other applications. For example, one algorithm might solve a model with one state variable very efficiently but, if this method relies on a discretisation of the state variables, the computation time will increase exponentially as the number of state variables increases.

In this section we will review some algorithms that have been used in a number of papers. The model we are going to use is Brock's model of asset pricing with endogenous production. There are two parts to solving this model: the first is to determine the consumption and investment allocations; this has to be done by solving the following growth model

$$\max E_0 \sum_{t=0}^{\infty} \delta^t u(c_t)$$

s.t.

$$c_t + k_t - (1-d)k_{t-1} = k_{t-1}^a \theta_t \tag{3.6}$$

$$\log(\theta_t) = \rho \log(\theta_{t-1}) + \epsilon_t,$$
$$\epsilon_t \sim N(O, \sigma^2), \text{ i.i.d.} \tag{3.7}$$

The first-order condition for this model is

$$c_t^\gamma = \delta E_t[c_{t+1}^\gamma[\theta_{t+1}k_t^{a-1}a + (1-d)]]. \tag{3.8}$$

With some side conditions that we are going to ignore in this chapter, a sufficient condition for an equilibrium consumption, investment and capital series is that the system (3.6)–(3.7)–(3.8) be satisfied. It is typical of equilibrium dynamic stochastic models to take the following general form

$$g(E_t[\phi(z_{t+1})], z_t, z_{t-1}, \epsilon_t) = 0, \tag{3.9}$$

of which the system (3.6)–(3.7)–(3.8) is a special case;[5] here z_t represents all the variables in the model, so that in the above simple growth model

$z_t = [k_t, c_t, \theta_t]$. A system like (3.9) is difficult to solve because it involves conditional expectations; we cannot solve for z_t until we know the conditional expectation, but we do not know this conditional expectation until we know the solution for z_t.

We will discuss briefly how to solve the simple growth model with five different methods. The first two methods are the linear-quadratic approximation and the value function iterations approach; these are fairly standard and they have been widely used in economics. The other three methods are much more recent: backsolving, iterations on Euler equations and parameterised expectations. Unfortunately, we will necessarily be unfair to each of these methods since they have been applied in much more sophisticated ways than the three line description we are forced to give in this chapter.

Linear-quadratic approximation

Substituting the technology restrictions in the objective function we obtain

$$\max E_0 \sum_{t=0}^{\infty} \delta^t u[k_{t-1}^a \theta_t - k_t + (1-d)k_{t-1}].$$ (3.10)

This objective function can be replaced by a linear-quadratic approximation to the term multiplying δ^t

$$\max E_0 \sum_{t=0}^{\infty} \delta^t [x_t A x_t' + x_t' B].$$ (3.11)

where $x_t = [k_t, k_{t-1}, \theta_t]$, and A, B are chosen so that the objective function in (3.11) is a good approximation of the objective function in (3.10).

As we said in the introduction, the linear-quadratic model is easy to solve (almost) analytically, so we can use these traditional techniques to solve the approximated problem (3.11).

Value function iterations

Using dynamic programming, the Bellman equation for the simple growth model is

$$V(k_{t-1}, \theta_t) = \max_{(c_t, k_t)} \{u(c_t) + \delta E_t V(k_t, \theta_{t+1})\}$$
$$\text{s.t. } c_t + k_t - (1-d)k_{t-1} = k_{t-1}^a \theta_t$$ (3.12)

If we replace V in the right-hand side of (3.12) by an arbitrary V^0, solve for the max at every possible point of the state variables (k_{t-1}, θ_t), find the implied V^1 and we iterate on the Bellman equation, this series of value functions will converge to the value function that solves the Bellman equation. To find the max, one usually imposes a grid of values on the space of (k_{t-1}, θ_t) and searches on this grid for a max. The expectation in the right-hand side of (3.12) is evaluated as an expectation on a random variable that can take only finitely many values, so it can be evaluated as a simple sum.

Backsolving

The idea here is to start by assuming a process for the endogenous variables. If this is done appropriately, then it may be quite easy to solve for all the variables in the system because we know the expectation in (3.8). For example, letting

$$\lambda_{t+1} = c_{t+1}^{\gamma}[\theta_{t+1}k_t^{a-1}a + (1-d)], \tag{3.13}$$

we assume a process for λ_t,

$$\lambda_t = \xi\lambda_{t-1} + \eta_t,$$

and then solve for consumption

$$c_t^{\gamma} = \delta\xi\lambda_t.$$

The solution for θ_t and k_t is found from the formula for λ_t and (3.6). The exogenous process that is finally backed out is the one that would be consistent with the assumption on λ_t.

Iterations on Euler equations

Several authors use methods with the following steps:

Impose a grid on (k_{t-1}, θ_t).

Start at a law of motion for k_t, say $f^0(k_{t-1}, \theta_t)$; this function is chosen from a family of functions that can approximate a continuous function and that depends on only finitely many parameters. Different types of polynomials, splines, linear interpolation or neural networks would qualify.

At each point in the grid evaluate the conditonal expectation in (3.8) by quadrature integration or other discrete expectations methods.

Iterate on the (finitely many) parameters of the law of motion until the left-hand side of the first-order condition (3.8) is as close as possible to the integral in the right-hand side.

The methods can vary widely in the way they perform the iterations, evaluate the integrals, approximating function chosen, etc.

Parameterised expectations

This method also works from the Euler equation. The idea is to parameterise the conditional expectations and then iterate until the series generated is such that the assumed conditional expectation is actually the best prediction of λ_t (where λ_t is given by (3.13)). The steps to follow are these:

> Substitute the conditional expectation on the right-hand side of the first-order condition (3.8) by a parameterised function $\psi(\beta; k_{t-1}, \theta_t)$, to obtain
>
> $$c_t^\gamma = \delta \psi(\beta; k_{t-1}, \theta_t). \tag{3.14}$$
>
> Create a long series of c_t and k_t with (3.14) and (3.6).
> Run a non-linear regression of
> λ_{t+1} on $\psi(\beta; k_{t-1}, \theta_t)$.

Iterate until β coincides with the result of non-linear regression.

This ends our discussion of the algorithms. For a more detailed description the reader is referred to the January 1990 issue of the *Journal of Business and Economic Statistics*, where different authors describe how to solve this simple growth model with alternative algorithms; comparisons are made by Taylor and Uhlig (1990), and some companion articles discuss how to solve it with different approaches in more detail. The methods discussed in that issue include different types of linear-quadratic approximations (by Christiano and McGratten), iterations on the Bellman equation (by Christiano), iterations on the Euler equation (Coleman and Baxter, Crucini and Rowenhorst), backwards solution (by Sims and Ingram), parameterised expectations approach (by den Haan and Marcet), the extended path algorithm (by Fair and Taylor), the Euler equation method of Labadie, and a quadrature method (by Tauchen).

Some of these methods do not have ways of obtaining arbitrary accuracy in their approximations. The linear-quadratic approximations, the extended path method and the backwards solution procedure are such methods. They have the disadvantage that they cannot be used to approximate the equilibrium arbitrarily well, and they may not produce solutions to models with complicated non-linearities like inequality constraints that are binding in some periods and non-binding in others. On the other hand, they tend to be much faster than the other methods discussed above; either they do not require any iterative procedure to find the equilibrium law of motion or the iterative procedure is very fast.

Many of the other iterative methods can obtain arbitrary accuracy to non-linear models by refining the approximations. For example, the value function iterations and the methods of Coleman, Bizer, Judd and Baxter provide arbitrarily good approximations by refining the grid on the state variables and on the stochastic shocks that these authors impose; the method of Marcet and Judd would obtain arbitrary accuracy by increasing the degree of the polynomials and calculating integrals with arbitrary accuracy.

3.2   Solutions without a planner's problem

There are many models in economics that yield suboptimal equilibria. This is usually the case, for example, in models with externalities, public goods, distortionary taxation, imperfect competition, monetary models, incomplete markets, etc. Until recently, a large amount of effort was devoted to finding some planner's problem whose solution would coincide with the equilibrium of the suboptimal model at hand. Jones and Manuelli (1989) show how to cast a large number of models in a planner's problem. Part of the reason for these efforts was that the most widely used techniques were the linear-quadratic approximation and the value function iterations, two techniques that had been constructed with the purpose of solving dynamic, stochastic maximisation problems, like the one involved in the planner's decision.

All the methods we have described above other than the linear-quadratic and value function iterations are designed to work independently of the specification of a planner's problem. These methods work directly from the Euler equations and the equilibrium conditions of the model, which are easy to find even if no equivalent planner's problem is at hand. Although casting suboptimal equilibria in some planner's problems is often useful, it is no longer a prerequisite for computing equilibria.

Actually, even LQ and VFI have been used in setups without a planner's problem. For example, Cooley and Hansen (1989) solve a cash-in-advance model, where one of the processes that is exogenous to the agent is the price level, but this process is in itself endogenous. Cooley and Hansen proceed by assuming a linear law of motion for the price level, and they iterate on this law of motion until it is consistent with the consumption allocations; in principle, the linearisation of the law of motion for prices introduces more inaccuracies in the solution, since they end up approximating not only the objective function of the agents but also the law of motion of the prices (which, in principle, is non-linear)[6] but it permits the use of linear-quadratic techniques which, as we said before, are very fast.

Also, Rios (1990) uses the linear-quadratic approach to solve an overlapping generations model. The equilibrium is again suboptimal, but it is still possible to apply the LQ approximation. In Rios' model agents live 150 periods (trying to mimick the number of trimesters of active life), so that the wealth of all agents are state variables of the model. With such a high dimensional model it is inconceivable to use most iterative methods, but linear-quadratic techniques make this model tractable.

Finally, Diaz and Prescott (1989) solve a suboptimal equilibrium using value function iterations. They assume a process for the price level and back out the level of government spending that is consistent with such a process. Once they have assumed a process for the price level they can do the value function iterations in the usual way. This idea of imposing a process for variables that are endogenous to the model has been used previously in the backwards solution procedure of Sims, Novales and Ingram; in order to solve the Euler equation instead of the value function.

3.3   Discretisation and the 'curse of dimensionality'

The 'curse of dimensionality' refers to the following problem: assume that we have a state variable that takes on continuous values; for example, in the simple growth model of section 3.1 the state variables, namely k_{t-1} and θ_t are both continuous. For a solution algorithm that must discretise the state variables or use a grid in the space where the state variables live, it is very expensive to find the solution as soon as more variables are added to the problem; for example, if we discretise the capital stock to take on 100 possible values, and if we add a second type of capital to the model,[7] the state vector now can take 10,000 possible values; in other words, the computational cost of the model increases, roughly, at the exponential rate of 100 with the number of (continuous) state variables.

Some of the methods we mentioned that suffer from this problem in different degrees are the following: value function iterations can only solve discrete problems, so they need very fine grids to get anywhere close to the true continuous solution; the method of Coleman, Bizer and Judd can produce continuous-valued series, but it uses a grid on the state variables where the Euler equation is evaluated; also, this method and that of Tauchen use quadrature integration, which means that a second grid has to be imposed on the space of stochastic shocks. This last group of methods does not need as fine a grid as the value function iteration approach, because by their own nature they produce continuous simulations so the computation time does not explode as quickly. For example, Judd uses twenty possible values of the capital stock. Nevertheless, the computation time still grows exponentially and a model with two or three continuous state variables would be very costly to solve.

The reader should now get an idea why this is called a 'curse'. Discretisation means that even models with only two continuous state variables are very costly to solve and means that we have to wait the time necessary for computer builders to increase computing power by 100 until we can add *one* more state variable.

There are, however, several methods that completely avoid discretisations and, therefore, they avoid the 'curse of dimensionality'. Obviously, models with more state variables are harder to solve with any method, but the key here is to use a procedure where the computational cost of the problem does not increase exponentially.

Clearly the 'fast' methods described before: linear-quadratic, backsolving and extended path, do not need any discretisation. It is possible to avoid the grids in evaluating integrals if quadrature is replaced by Monte Carlo integration,[8] in effect, the parameterised expectations approach of Marcet (1989) and the method of Smith (1989) substitute quadrature integration with Monte Carlo integration, since they evaluate expectations as time averages. It is true that as stochastic shocks are added to a model Monte Carlo integration is more costly, because more observations are needed in the averages that make up the calculation; but the number of observations increases at a speed much lower than exponential.[9]

3.4 Endogenous oversampling

One of the reasons for the 'curse of dimensionality' is that, when grids are imposed exogenously by the researcher, the algorithm explores all points in the grid, the space of state variables, giving equal importance to all possible points in this space, even though most of these points will rarely happen. This can be avoided with techniques that use endogenous oversampling, where the algorithm is designed in a way that only the relevant points of the state variables are explored by the algorithm.

Consider the simple growth model of section 3.1, assume that we are interested in finding the solution at the steady-state distribution. If we use a method that has to impose a grid on the state variables and in order for the productivity shock to have close to a continuous distribution we could impose a grid of, say, 100 points for the productivity shock and a grid of 100 points for the capital stock. Then, there are 10,000 possible values of the state variables (or pairs of θ_t and k_{t-1}) and we will spend equal computing time on all of them. In this case, all points are equally important for the algorithm, so that no oversampling is done. This is a waste of computing power, since many of these pairs happen very rarely; in fact, when the grid is imposed exogenously, many of these pairs will never happen. Let us see this problem in some more detail.

First of all, it is very hard to establish reasonable bounds for the endogenous state variables before knowing the solution. In the above

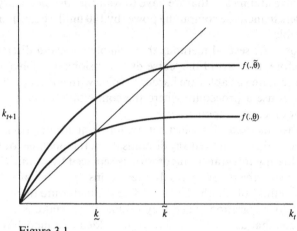

Figure 3.1

growth model one can easily place bounds on the productivity shock: we can limit θ_t to stay within, say, four standard deviations of the mean; we will denote these bounds by $\underset{\sim}{\theta}$ and $\tilde{\theta}$. But we know that the capital stock has to stay in the interval $(0, k')$, where k' is the maximum capital that is physically possible; this value depends on the depreciation rate 'd' and the maximum productivity shock. Nevertheless in the steady-state distribution and for most parameter values, the capital stock will never get anywhere close to these bounds.

To see this point, we can have a familiar picture with the optimal decision functions, represented by $f(., \theta)$ in figure 3.1. We know that the steady-state distribution will never leave the interval $[\underset{\sim}{k}, \tilde{k}]$. If the researcher *knew* the true law of motion, he could impose these bounds on the grid, but this law of motion *is* the solution we are seeking.

But even it we knew $\underset{\sim}{k}$ and $\tilde{k}$, we would still be wasting computer time by looking at all possible grid points within these bounds. The reason is that many combinations of the state variables never happen; for example, very high values of the shock θ_t never happen together with very low values of the capital stock, and vice-versa. Figure 3.2 describes this situation: out of all the possibilities in the set $[\underset{\sim}{k}, \tilde{k}] \times [\underset{\sim}{\theta}, \tilde{\theta}]$ only values in the parabola happen, but the discretisation methods will tend to spend as much time computing time in points near B that never happen, or in points near A that happen very frequently.

There has been a great deal of attention to this problem in other sciences. For example, the genetic algorithms used in biology and applied to economics by Marimon, McGratten and Sargent (1990) are designed to do

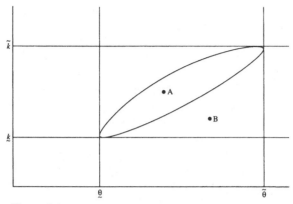

Figure 3.2

endogenous oversampling. The parameterised expectations approach described above is also designed to do endogenous oversampling. Integrals are
calculated by averaging out long-run simulations of the endogenous
variables; since in the long run the variables stabilise around the steady-
state distribution, the algorithm does not pay any attention to regions of the
state space that do not happen and the polynomial approximations are
good approximations precisely at values that happen often in the steady-
state distribution.

Obviously, when one is not interested in the steady-state distribution it is
not correct to oversample values that happen often in the steady-state
distribution. For example, in the simple growth model one may be
interested in calculating the growth path from a very low initial capital
stock towards the steady-state distribution. In this case, the initial capital
stock may be so low that it never happens in the steady-state distribution
and a good approximation around the steady state is not valid. It is clear
that some parts of the model behave very differently with low capital stocks;
for example, the marginal productivity of capital and the marginal utility of
consumption (which are the factors determining the investment decision)
are much higher than at any point in the steady-state distribution. In this
case we need to calculate the law of motion by oversampling at low capital
stocks. With the parameterised expectations approach, this can be easily
accomplished by using many independent draws of short simulations, each
simulation with enough periods for the capital stock to go from its low
initial level to the steady-state distribution; letting the number of draws go
to infinity one can obtain arbitrary accuracy in the integrals being evaluated. This scheme has been used in Marshall (1988) to deal with a non-
stationary growth rate of the money supply, and in Marcet and Marimon

(1992) to study a growth model where the capital grows from a very low initial capital stock to the steady-state value.

Techniques like value function iteration and the method of Coleman, Bizer and Judd do not use any kind of oversampling, so that their grids are bound to become unmanageable as soon as they solve problems with a high number of state variables. These techniques would improve in speed by introducing some scheme that eliminated the grid points that happen rarely, much in the way that genetic algorithms eliminate actions that give high payoffs with small probability.

On the other hand, these methods will perform better if a good approximation for any initial value of the state variables is needed. For example, in game theoretical models, if one looks for the *perfect* Nash equilibrium, then the equilibrium restrictions have to be satisfied at all nodes of the decision tree, even if they have zero probability in equilibrium; in this case endogenous oversampling would not look at equilibrium at those states.[10]

4   THEORETICAL RESEARCH BY SIMULATION

4.1   Economic theory on the computer

The use of computer simulations of structural models for empirical purposes, as will be discussed in section 5, is a common practice and its validity is generally accepted. More recent and perhaps more controversial is the use of simulations in theoretical work. There is a growing number of papers that study highly abstract models and reach conclusions about the behaviour of those models by studying computer simulations. These should be considered theoretical papers because they do not try to explain the real economy beyond, perhaps, some stylised facts.

For example, one result that seems to emerge from several papers we discussed in section 2.2, is that introducing market incompleteness by merely closing down some markets and introducing liquidity constraints does not produce many differences from the complete market or the representative agent case. This is a qualitative statement about how certain models behave, so it is a theoretical statement. It is also a statement that can be justified only because of the knowledge we have gained from computer simulations, and it stands in contrast with many negative theoretical results available in the literature about the behaviour of incomplete market models. These results claimed that these models would have very different equilibria from the complete market case, and that strong non-optimalities would be present with incomplete markets. Perhaps other departures from the complete market assumption, like private information, the possibility of default, introducing different types of heterogeneity, or having costly exchange of securities will yield more striking results.

Another use of simulation for theorists may be as a tool for acquiring intuition about results that can be proved analytically. Theorists have regulary used *ad hoc* models and graphical techniques for this purpose.

There are many other striking theoretical 'results' which we have learnt from simulation studies. For example, den Haan (1990a) argues that in a stochastic monetary model with a shopping time technology the k per cent rule is nearly optimal; this contradicts some statements in Hahn (1971) that, because in a stochastic model money serves as insurance, money could have a lower return in equilibrium and it may be optimal to run an inflation. Bizer and Judd (1989) argue that stochastic taxation can improve welfare over deterministic taxation when the tax is distorting. In the incentive compatibility literature, Marcet and Marimon (1992) argue that limited enforcement of contracts has a very significant effect in reducing growth, while limited information has very little effect. Phelan and Townsend (1991) argue that the optimal incentive compatible contract causes a very small utility loss.

It is necessary for economists to start considering theory on the computer as a necessary tool, due to the evolution of the models that we are working with. In fact, this has been a routine practice in the natural sciences like physics, biology, chemistry, etc. The discussion should not be about 'if', but about 'how' this type of exercise should be performed. In other words, we must think of the standards that theory on the computer should meet. Some of the questions that come up in this respect are: how to report results, how to choose parameter values and accuracy of the solution. We will discuss these points in the remainder of this section. The aim of the following discussion is not to close the debate on these matters, but of highlighting their importance.

4.2 Reporting simulation results

One of the reasons some people may be uncomfortable with theoretical results derived by simulation is that it seems easier to report results that are incorrect with a simulation than with a theorem. While with analytic methods it is possible to mention all the derivations in a paper, it is impossible to report all the calculations and all the programs used in simulation in a journal article, so, the issue of how to report simulation results is an important one; besides preventing careless work, adequate reporting should make the results more convincing to the reader.

Similar problems in reporting results are faced by the experimental sciences and, closer to our experience, by empirical work in economics.

Psychologists (and experimental economists) must detail carefully how their experiments have been conducted, how were the subjects of the experiment selected, what instructions were given to them, etc. Economists practising empirical work must report what data sources they are using, what observations they ignored, how the data were transformed. Similarly, economic simulators should give as much detail as possible about how the solution was actually implemented, what was the level of the approximation, what parameter values were used, some measure of computation time, etc.

Ideally, the actual law of motion should be reported in the paper; this would make it possible for some readers to easily write a computer program that calculates the simulations and study the simulation on their own, perform accuracy tests, and explore issues of the model that the authors may not have reported, without having to implement the whole iterative procedure that finds the corresponding fixed point.

4.3   Parameter selection

In order to obtain a simulation one must assume certain values for the parameters of the model. This is, perhaps, more of a problem in economics than in natural sciences, since we tend to have more uncertainty about the parameters of our models.

The usual practice is to use parameter values generating equilibria that closely reproduce some features of the data. Economists have accumulated by now considerable experience on this type of exercise. Part of the research agenda is to discover precisely what are interesting parameter values to use in a given model.

Some parameters are easy to choose because they have direct implications on the technology and they can be measured in a fairly direct way; for example, the depreciation rate 'd' in the simple growth model can be easily measured by the depreciation of aggregate capital observed on average in real data; measures of this depreciation rate in the United States put its value to about 10 per cent a year. Then we would have $d = 0.9$ in a yearly model, $d = 0.975$ in a quarterly model, and so on.

Other parameters for the simple growth model can be set using the equilibrium of the model. These are usually harder to choose, because the implications on this dimension are less clear. For example, in the representative agent asset pricing model the inverse of δ (the discount factor of the utility function) is close to the average gross return of a real riskless bond. In US data this return is around 1 per cent so that, if we used this asset to pin down the value of δ, we should choose $\delta = 0.99$ in a yearly model. But it turns out that in the simple growth model δ^{-1} is also close to the average return of a *risky stock* that pays the return on capital. In US data the average return of stocks is about 7 per cent, so by this measure δ should be set equal to 0.93. This is an example of how it may be hard to pin down some parameters due to the fact that our models do not replicate closely some aspects of the data. Most authors choose a compromise and they set δ somewhere in between these two values, but ideally one would want to explore different values of parameters like this that are not easily pinned down.

Assuming that the instantaneous utility function is defined as

$$u(c_t) = \frac{c_t^{-\gamma+1}}{-\gamma+1},$$

then γ is the coefficient of relative risk aversion. The implications of a parameter of this type are even harder to work out, so γ is even harder to choose convincingly. Mehra and Prescott (1985) report several micro-economic empirical estimations that set γ around one; to be safe, they explore all values of γ between 1 and 10.

If a researcher does not feel comfortable with choosing fixed values for the parameters,[11] then one should explore the parameter space in a systematic way. If this has to be done by imposing a grid on many parameters we will encounter similar problems as were discussed in section 3. More research on how to do this exploration would be useful.

4.4 Accuracy of simulations

So far there is no widely accepted measure of accuracy of numerical approximations. This may be an important issue since inaccurate solutions may distort considerably our conclusions.

First of all, a researcher has to be explicit about what is the approximation used: For example, in methods that use polynomial approximations some authors just state that a second- or third-degree polynomial was used, and the solution reported can be taken as the best approximation of second or third degree.

If one wants to claim that the solution is accurate, though, some testing of the solution needs to be done. Unfortunately, testing the accuracy for these solutions beyond any doubt is an impossible task. Finding the solution amounts to finding a non-linear function that can be changed in uncountably many directions, and it is impossible to check all of them. The best we can do is to challenge our solution with different tests of accuracy that experience indicates are good at selecting inaccurate solutions.

One such challenge is to compare solutions obtained with different methods that have been proved reliable in the past. The comparisons done by Taylor and Uhlig (1990) have proved useful in this respect. Much has been made about the differences in the solutions obtained with different methods in that *JBES* issue; rather than just observe that there are some differences it may be more instructive to try to explain where those differences arose. In particular, methods that simulated discrete series with relatively coarse grids tended to give different results; this is not surprising since the discreteness forces the solution for investment to be more variable.

Some methods have intrinsic ways of challenging the solution. For example, in the method of Coleman, Bizer and Judd one can change the grid points at which the Euler equation is evaluated and see if the solution changes considerably; the parameterised expectations approach can use different draws of stochastic shocks in order to find the non-linear regressions used in finding the law of motion in that method. These changes should not yield laws of motion that differ too much if the solution is accurate.

Another way of challenging a solution in order to test for accuracy is proposed in den Haan and Marcet (1994). They propose to test if the error in the Euler equation is orthogonal to functions of past variables; this amounts to testing the first-order conditions of a maximisation problem in certain directions. This test does not translate directly into bounds for the error in the simulated series, but in several examples it seems to select correctly the more accurate solution. Also, Taylor and Uhlig ran this test for the solutions of the different methods; they found that the methods that performed well in this test (namely, the solution of Coleman, backsolving, parameterised expectations and some of the linear-quadratic approximations) yielded similar solutions.

Finally, one can refine the approximation and check whether the solution changes considerably. For example, the value function iterations would use a finer grid, the methods of Coleman, Bizer and Judd and parameterised expectations would use a more refined approximation scheme in the class of functions used to approximate the solution (which can be either polynomials or splines). Christiano (1990b) has made comparisons between the linear-quadratic and the value-function iterations solution.

4.5   Multiplicity of equilibria and learning algorithms

It has been well documented in the literature of rational expectations that, in some models, there exists a multiplicity of equilibria. Often this multiplicity takes the form of a continuum of equilibria.

If we study a model with a multiplicity of equilibria by simulation, depending on the model and on the algorithm, two things may happen: the solution algorithm can have as a limit point any one of the multiple equilibria, or the algorithm can have only one equilibrium as a limit point. In the first case, there will be numerical problems because the algorithm may start drifting from one equilibrium to the other; in the second case, if the algorithm does converge to one equilibrium, we will never know if that equilibrium is more interesting than the others.

One way to approach this problem is to use algorithms that replicate learning schemes. There is now a large literature discussing how learning schemes can select one rational expectations equilibrium as a limit point in certain models with a multiplicity of equilibria; that is, only one rational equilibrium is stable under learning in these models. Learning schemes suggest computational algorithms that mimick the learning mechanism; these algorithms, then, will only converge to equilibria that are stable under learning. The remaining equilibria will go unnoticed but, if one believes that we should concentrate our study on solutions that are stable under learning, ignoring the other equilibria is the correct alternative. One such algorithm has been used by Marcet (1989) among many others, where the iterative scheme mimicks the evolution of least-squares learning about expectations, and, therefore, that algorithm only converges to solutions that are stable under learning.

5 EMPIRICAL RESEARCH BY SIMULATION

We will discuss two ways of estimating and testing dynamic models that are based on numerical simulations of structural models: maximum likelihood and the method of simulated moments.

5.1 Estimation: maximum likelihood and method of simulated moments

To see how maximum likelihood can be used and what its limitations are, let us consider, again, the simple growth model. Assume we have data on only the capital stock.[12] Given values for the parameter vector λ we have a law of motion of capital of the following form

$$k_t = h_\lambda(k_{t-1}, \theta_t). \tag{3.15}$$

Here $\lambda = [a, d, \rho, \sigma_\epsilon^2, \delta, \gamma]$, the fundamental parameters of the model. If we have a solution for the law of motion h_λ (which we have to find numerically), equation (3.15) allows us to back out θ_t from the observation on k_t and k_{t-1}; more explicitly, we can find the function f_λ that satisfies

$$\theta_{t-1} = f_\lambda(k_{t-1}, k_{t-2}); \tag{3.16}$$

that is consistent with (3.15). Then we can write down the likelihood of k_t

conditional on past observations (as is required in time series models). Applications of maximum likelihood estimation are surveyed in Rust (1988).

Unfortunately, in models with a larger number of unobservable than observable variables we cannot back out solutions for the unobserved shocks as in (3.16); in this case there is a manifold of unobservables that is consistent with the observations and a given parameter value, and putting probabilities on this type of manifolds is very cumbersome. There are many cases of interest where this problem arises: models with private information will typically have 'too many' shocks; applications with aggregation over agents have a similar problem, and the same happens with aggregation over time.

In the cases where maximum likelihood cannot be applied for the reasons just described, and if we are able to numerically solve our model, we can use the method of simulated moments. This procedure has been used in a time series framework by Ingram (1990a) to test an asset pricing model with myopic agents, Garcia-Mila (1987) in a model with both private and public capital, Heaton (1990) in an asset pricing model with habit persistence in the instantaneous utility function, Bossaerts and Hillion (1990) in an option pricing model with early exercise, Smith (1989) in a capital accumulation model. Applications to micro-economic problems are reviewed in Pakes and Rust (1991).

The idea in the simulated method of moments is very simple: the estimator is determined by finding the value of the parameters that make certain moments of the simulated series as close as possible to the analogous moments of the observed series. More formally, assume we have T observations on m time series denoted $\{z_t\}_{t=0}^{T}$, where each z_t is m dimensional; assume that we can generate simulations of the model to be estimated; let $\{\bar{z}_t(\lambda)\}_{t=0}^{s}$ be a simulation of length S of the model at a given parameter vector λ. Let $h: R^m \rightarrow R^q$ be a function such that $E(h(z_t))$ are moments we want to match; typically, $q > n$, where n is the number of parameters to be estimated. Finally, let H and $\bar{H}$ be the actual and simulated moments

$$H_T = (1/T) \sum_{t=0}^{T} h(z_t) \quad \text{and} \quad \bar{H}_S(\lambda) = (1/S) \sum_{t=0}^{S} h(\bar{z}_t(\lambda)).$$

Then, the method of moments estimator λ_T is defined as

$$\lambda_T = \underset{\lambda}{\text{argmin}} \ [H_T - \bar{H}_S(\lambda)]' W_{T,S} [H_T - \bar{H}_S(\lambda)], \tag{3.17}$$

where $W_{T,S}$ is a positive definite $q \times q$ matrix that defines the distance between the simulated moments $\bar{H}_S(\lambda)$ and the actual moments H_T.

This is a complete method for doing statistical inference: one can obtain consistency and asymptotic distribution results as T and S go to infinity. These results have been proved in the case of serially independent observations by Pakes and Pollard (1989) and, in a slightly different setup, by McFadden (1989); these authors allow non-differentiable simulations.[13]

The asymptotic results for the time series case has been analysed by Lee and Ingram (1991), and Duffie and Singleton (1990). The last paper allows for endogenous state variables; it handles the non-stationarity that arises in simulated series that start up at a fixed value for the state variable, and it provides conditions for checking ergodicity of the model. These authors have to assume that simulations are differentiable with respect to the parameter set λ; they need this assumption because they use the mean-value theorem in obtaining the asymptotic distribution for the estimator λ_T. Asymptotic results for time series assuming only continuity (but not differentiability) of the simulations have been partially analysed by Bossaerts (1989).

Under standard assumptions of stationarity, ergodicity, differentiability of the simulations and assuming that $\underset{T\to\infty}{\text{Lim}}\ T/S = \tau$, one can prove consistency and asymptotic normality of the method of simulated moments. Letting λ_0 be the true parameter value, and letting

$$S_w = \sum_{i=-\infty}^{\infty} E[[h(z_t) - Eh(z_t)] \circ [h(z_{t-i}) - Eh(z_{t-i})]'] \text{ and}$$

$$B = \frac{\partial}{\partial\lambda'} Eh(\bar{z}_t(\lambda_0)),$$

Assuming that $W_{T,S}$ converges in probability to a non-singular matrix W.

A necessary condition for identification is that B should have full column rank. This translates into the usual condition that the objective function in (3.17) has a unique local minimum at the true value of the parameters. With this condition it can be shown that the estimator is consistent and that $T^{1/2}$ $[\lambda_t - \lambda_0]$ asymptotically has a normal distribution with mean zero and variance-covariance matrix equal to

$$[B'WB]^{-1}B'\ WS_w\ W'\ B[B'WB]^{-1}(1+\tau). \tag{3.18}$$

The efficient matrix W in the sense of minimising this variance–covariance matrix is $W = S_w^{-1}$. To test the overidentifying restrictions of the model one can use the fact that under the null hypothesis that the model is correct and using the optimal weighting matrix $W = S_w^{-1}$, the test-statistic

$$T[H_T - \bar{H}_S(\lambda_T)]'S_w^{-1}[H_T - \bar{H}_S(\lambda_T)]$$

converges in distribution to χ^2_{q-n}. This is, then, a natural measure of goodness of fit. The interpretation is, as usual in these procedures, that we have n parameters so that we can fit q moments perfectly, but there are still $q - n$ dimensions that do not perfectly fit but, if the model is correct, they must be close to zero.

There are many aspects of this method that are yet to be explored. As we said, asymptotic results for the case of time series with discontinuous simulations have not yet been proved. Also, it is not known how to extend this procedure to non-stationary models that cannot be normalised in an obvious way. Another area for research is the robustness of this estimator: MSM is a parametric method in the sense that the results hinge on distributional assumptions about the underlying shocks. Finally, given that the numerical solutions are approximations and, therefore, they are not the correct solution, there is the issue of what effect these approximations have, if any, on the asymptotic results; as suggested by Pakes and Rust (1994), this problem can probably be handled by reinterpreting the parameter being estimated.

5.2   Calibration and the method of simulated moments

The paper by Kydland and Prescott (1982) was one of the earliest and most influential applications of simulation techniques to dynamic stochastic models. They applied the linear-quadratic approximation to a non-linear stochastic model; they simulated a capital accumulation model with a complicated delay structure for converting investment into capital, and durability of the utility from leisure. That paper also introduced the so-called 'calibration' approach for validating dynamic stochastic models; using this validation approach Kydland and Prescott argued that their aggregate real business cycle model came close to matching several moments of the data and a large literature has developed since over the issue of whether or not the business cycle can be explained by real models or whether some monetary aspects are essential to the business cycle. Calibration has been used recently in many papers, among many others, Hansen (1985), Rogerson (1988), Prescott (1986), and there has been debate about whether the calibration approach was called to replace traditional econometric procedures in testing dynamic models.

The principles of calibration can be summarised as follows: choose some moments of interest that the model at hand should explain, we will denote these as MTE (moments to be explained); choose the parameter values of the model from data or moments *different* from MTE; compare the MTE generated by the model at those parameters with the MTE from the real data. To decide if the simulated moments are close enough, Kydland and

Prescott obtain a large number of independent simulations and look at the dispersion of MTEs from these simulations; in this way they construct a confidence interval for each MTE. If the corresponding MTE from the real data falls within this interval, they declare this particular moment as being satisfactorily explained by the model.

This procedure can be interpreted as a simplified version of the method of simulated moments (MSM) and it may be instructive to look at it in this light. Using some of the moments for finding parameter estimates and the remaining moments for testing is equivalent to using a particular weighting matrix W in (3.18), putting n entries in the main diagonal equal to one and all other entries equal to zero. This matrix will pick out the n moments used for estimation and match them perfectly; then, in the part that tests the goodness of fit, one could derive a chi-square statistic analogous to (3.18) that, in effect, tests if the remaining $(q-n)$ moments are well explained by the simulated models.

Rather than testing all the overidentifying restrictions at once, calibration looks at each moment one by one. Also, instead of relying on asymptotic distribution as in the test statistic (3.18), it constructs short-sample confidence intervals by Monte Carlo integration, fixing the parameter values as if they were known with certainty.

From the point of view of statistical inference, this procedure ignores several important issues: by testing the moments one by one and ignoring uncertainty on the parameters the confidence intervals are incorrect; by using an arbitrary weighting matrix W the estimates contain a larger amount of sampling error than is necessary and by not reporting the uncertainty on the parameter estimates it is difficult to know how reliable the results are. Recently, Burnside, Eichenbaum and Rebelo (1990) have argued that by ignoring the uncertainty in the parameter estimates of the productivity shock of a business cycle model, some inadequacies of the real business cycle models are overlooked.

Nevertheless, calibration studies have helped to understand the working of dynamic models. The main advantage of calibration lies precisely in its simplicity. Estimating optimal weighting matrices, finding confidence intervals, reporting variance–covariance matrices, etc. is very cumbersome. Perhaps it is more instructive for economists to spend time thinking about economic modelling instead of dwelling on statistical issues!

Since we see econometricians too often forgetting about economic modelling, any voices that force econometricians to concentrate on the economics of their models are a welcome influence. But calibration contains too many arbitrary choices to be considered as the final word in testing a model.[14]

6   RESPONSE TO JUDD'S COMMENTS

What follows is a detailed analysis of the substance of Judd's discussion of this paper.

6.1   Monte Carlo integration

Judd seems to disagree with my claim that 'Monte Carlo integration is more efficient than quadrature in multi-dimensional integrals'; he writes that 'this claim is unsupported'. The reader will note, however, that his discussion argues that **quasi-Monte Carlo** techniques are superior to straight **Monte Carlo**. This is unrelated to my point, which was that 'Monte Carlo integration is more efficient than quadrature in multi-dimensional integrals', a well-known fact. Perhaps I should clarify that in most economic models of interest there are many random variables to integrate over: individual shocks, sectoral shocks etc., so multi-dimensional integration is often needed in economics. I saw no need to discuss quasi-Monte Carlo techniques due to the fact that they had not been applied in economics at the time of the Congress. In any event Ken Judd seems to further endorse Monte Carlo methods in the section on 'Theory by Computation'. This is a change from his original position expressed at the World Congress (among other places) where he argued that Monte Carlo was not a good procedure. In the last two years, a growing number of economists are switching to Monte Carlo-based simulation methods as they attack more complicated problems.

6.2   Endogenous oversampling

It is obviously true that endogenous oversampling will sometimes lead to bad approximations; this is also true of exogenous oversampling, and no oversampling at all. Endogenous oversampling reduces the amount of points in the state space that one looks at, and it permits solving models with a large number of continuous state variables, for the reasons explained in the main part of this chapter.

Judd disagrees with my comments in favour of endogenous oversampling; let us analyse his reasoning. First, he gives an example where, if there is a change in tax policy, then using the law of motion calculated before the change in policy would yield wrong results. This is just saying that one needs a different law of motion after a policy change; anybody who is acquainted with the Lucas' critique knows that, and nothing in my chapter suggests that we should ignore the Lucas critique.

In fact, parameterised expectations has been used successfully in Marcet and Marimon (1992) in a mechanism design problem and in Rojas (1992) in a differential game (of optimal taxation). Even for Nash perfect equilibria, the procedure can be modified in order to sample also regions that do not occur in equilibrium, so Judd's dismissal of techniques that use endogenous oversampling is unwarranted. It is not true that 'Marcet acknowledges, [that] any method which used endogenous oversampling ... is unsuitable to use in game-theoretic analysis'.

Judd claims that transitional paths to the steady state cannot be calculated with endogenous oversampling. I discuss in enough detail how to use independent realisations in PEA to calculate this transition in subsection 3.4, and I will not repeat my arguments. I have also made this argument in the original version of this chapter, in my presentation at the World Congress, and in many seminar presentations (the first one in January 1989 at Stanford University). Furthermore, now there are two published papers (Marshall (1988) and Marcet and Marimon (1992)) that use this scheme. So, my arguments seem to have been well received in the profession.

Judd claims that endogenous oversampling does not guarantee that the oversampled region will be approximated more accurately and he cites counterexamples where the outer regions should be sampled more frequently. This cannot be a generic case, since it is not hard to think of examples where oversampling the outer regions gives a bad approximation.

Judd cites an example that he does not work out, so it is very hard to respond precisely and I can only guess as to what is the reason for the bad approximations he has in mind. I suppose that those counterexamples are ones where the number of points in the fit is the same as the number of parameters in the polynomial. For example, if we fit five points on a function with a five degree polynomial, we may get the function fitting very poorly in some regions. But in algorithms that combine Monte Carlo simulation and endogenous oversampling (such as PEA, Smith's or Heaton's), we usually face a situation where the order of the polynomial that we fit is much smaller than the number of points where the fit is performed (typically the number of points is of several thousand, while the number of parameters is ten or twenty). In this case, when we oversample in region A we get more accuracy than in an undersampled region B. More precisely, and using Judd's example in the discussion, if we have two intervals of equal length A and B, and we sample at n equally spaced points, it is easy to show that for a given degree of the polynomial, if we choose the polynomial that minimises mean-square errors and we weight all points equally, as n goes to infinity, region A is better approximated than region B.

Also, our experience shows that this is the case. For example, in an earlier version of den Haan and Marcet (1994) we compare the true solution of a Brock and Mirman model with the approximated solution and the levels near the steady state are better approximated.

6.3   The curse of dimensionality

I do not see any justification to the claim that my discussion of the curse of dimensionality is at variance with conventional wisdom. If anything, Judd's discussion confirms that many methods suffer from this. I am sure that future adaptations of the current methods may partly solve the problem by performing some kind of endogenous oversampling.

6.4   Computational experience

One must discuss issues of speed of computation with great care.

First, the comparisons reported by Taylor and Uhlig (1990) were made within the NBER Rational Expectations Modelling Group. For example, the solution time that was reported by parameterised expectations was, in fact, solving ten different models, since it started with the solution for the capital growth model with 100 per cent depreciation and it gradually moved to the 90 per cent, 80 per cent until it got to the zero depreciation case. The reason for this was that den Haan and Marcet (1990) wanted to demonstrate how the homotopy approach could work in the simplest case; but the solution had to travel a long way, from the very low capital stock in the 100 per cent depreciation case to the very high capital stock of the no-depreciation case. By comparison, Judd performs the calculation by starting the law of motion at a constant level, equal to the deterministic steady state; if we use such excellent initial conditions, we cut the computation time to about one fifth.

Second, the Taylor and Uhlig comparisons were not meant as a race. Rather, the objective was to discern the applicability of the different methods to different models. Had we known we were in a race, we would have required much lower accuracy in the fixed point, we would have used better regression algorithms and much smaller number of observations. Also, we would have thought very hard about how to get good initial conditions and we would have probably asked the group to solve a model with more random variables and more state variables, where Monte Carlo integration and endogenous oversampling perform better. Finally, anybody in the mailing list could have sent solutions for the comparison before the comparisons were made.

The fact is that the algorithms based on Monte Carlo simulation and endogenous oversampling (the parameterised expectations approach among them) have produced many applications in a short period of time. Ultimately, the one and only test of an algorithm is if it produces interesting economic applications. There is no such a thing as a right or wrong algorithm; there are just algorithms that are more appropriate for certain models than others, and I tried to write the chapter in such a way as to help the reader distinguish the advantages.

6.5   Misinterpretation of sentences

Judd clearly misinterprets some of my words.

I never give the impression that 'numerical simulations of rational expectations models is a new technique'. I cite many early papers. The only thing that is new in economics is the use of simulation in theoretical papers.

Judd criticises my claim that a linear-quadratic approximation does not provide arbitrary accuracy in non-linear models. His reasoning is that linear quadratic is a special case of perturbation methods (although this is not the way in which it has been viewed in economics) and, therefore (?) my assertion is not correct. Perhaps, perturbation methods with higher-order terms provide arbitrary accuracy, but I never refer to these. One detail that is missing from Judd's discussion is that perturbation methods of order *higher* than one are considerably more complicated than the traditional linear-quadratic case; the reason is that in linear quadratic we can apply certainty equivalence, and the problem is nearly a deterministic one in terms of computational costs, while the same is not true with higher-order Taylor approximations.

In den Haan and Marcet (1990), we never 'have difficulty solving a six parameter case'. As we explain in that paper and in den Haan and Marcet (1994), the fact that multi-collinearity appears for higher-order terms just detects that some of these higher-order terms are irrelevant and the solution is equally accurate if these are not introduced.

About liquidity constraints, it is clear that I refer to asset pricing models and the effect of liquidity constraints on issues such as risk premium, risk sharing, etc.

6.6   Review of the literature

The references that Judd finds missing from the original version of my chapter are valuable, but they may give the impression that I was disrespectful of some authors. Any survey has to concentrate on part of the literature, and I say very clearly in the introduction to my paper and at the

World Congress presentation, that I review papers on simulation of dynamic, stochastic non-linear models, and I concentrate on applications in the last few years to macro-economics and financial economics.

The papers from agricultural economics are valuable references, but the fact is that it took a very long time for them to have an impact on the literature that I review. We have to thank Coleman, Baxter, Bizer and Judd for acquainting macro-economists with these methods. The study of why this happened may be an interesting subject for a historian of economic thought; I can only advance that, perhaps, one of the reasons is that these papers use very simplified models: linear production functions, constant prices, etc. This is true, at least, of the papers that I could access; Gustafson (1958) is a working paper from the Department of Agriculture that I could not obtain. It may not have been obvious to macro-economists in the 1980s interested in equilibrium models with non-linear utility and production functions how to apply the algorithms in those papers.

Judd points out that many numerical procedures were not discussed in my paper. For obvious reasons, I limited myself to numerical procedures that had been applied to economics. Writing down a large number of numerical techniques before actually checking if they are useful in economics is not an exercise that I ever wanted to perform. I have strong doubts about the usefulness of such an exercise, especially since numerical analysis textbooks are readily available.[15]

7   CONCLUSION

Simulation techniques are available to solve many stochastic dynamic models that cannot be handled with analytic methods. To the extent that these models can be used to ask interesting questions, and perhaps even to answer some of them, it seems necessary to use simulation techniques. Algorithms available for solving dynamic stochastic equilibrium models have progressd to a point that stumbling blocks of the past, like the 'curse of dimensionality' and the need for writing a planner's problem can be now sidestepped. Because of this we can now study very complicated models, with inequality constraints, suboptimal tax schemes, monetary models with uncertainty, discrete and continuous choices, incomplete markets, many types of agents, private information, limited enforcement of contracts, etc.

There are several techniques available for empirical work that have been used extensively. The use of simulations for theoretical purposes, however, is still uncommon and is now starting to be accepted in the economics profession; there should be active discussion on how these exercises should be done, in particular, on how to report the results, on how to justify the choice of parameter values and on what standards of accuracy are demanded.

Notes

Prepared for Invited Symposium, 6th World Congress of the Econometric Society, Barcelona, 1990. Comments from Wouter den Haan, David Marshall, Ramon Marimon and Tom Sargent are greatly appreciated. All errors are my own.

1 See, for example, Marcet and Sargent (1989a, 1989b) and references therein.

2 See Hansen and Sargent (1990) for a thorough review of applications of the linear-quadratic framework.

3 Strictly speaking, we have to add some constraints to the maximisation problem in order to avoid Ponzi schemes, where the agent sells arbitrarily large amounts of shares. Lucas introduces a constraint of the type $s_t \geq K$ for all t, where K is a sufficiently low number for this constraint never to be binding.

4 Some of these examples can be found, for example, in Sargent (1987).

5 Even models with inequality constraints take the form of (3.9), when the Kuhn and Tucker conditions are one of the equations in (3.9). See Marcet and Singleton (1990).

6 For example, their law of motion for prices does not hold exactly at the non-stochastic steady state, unlike in most LQ applications.

7 For example, by adding a second productive sector or by introducing public capital as in Garcia-Mila (1987).

8 Obviously, the Monte Carlo approach may give slightly different solutions for different draws of the random number generator. This is just a numerical error that has to be studied by the researcher in order to ensure that it is not marring the conclusions from his simulations. This is not more of a problem in Monte Carlo methods than it is in any numerical solution. For example, iterations on the Euler equations will depend on the grid imposed, and sensitivity to the choice of the grid should be explored.

9 See Geweke (1989) for some results on the increase of observations needed.

10 This point can be found in Judd (1989a).

11 In which case he should probably feel uncomfortable with analytic solutions like that of example 1, where the parameter $cov(d_t, d_{t-1})$ is arbitrarily set to zero.

12 Strictly speaking, the above growth model could not be estimated by maximum likelihood if we had data on consumption and investment because, having only one unobserved shock in the model, there exists a stochastic singularity.

13 Discontinuous simulations arise when the model contains some discrete decision: for example, in the case of Pakes (1986), firms have to decide whether or not to renew a patent. Then, by changing slightly the parameters λ it may happen that, in a given period, the firm changes its decision on whether to renew or not, causing a discrete jump in the simulated series.

14 Gregory and Smith (1991) have applied similar ideas to the ones presented here to evaluate the risk premium puzzle.

15 I did miss one application of perturbation methods. By the time of the World Congress, there was only one application, in the unpublished, and difficult to obtain, manuscript Judd (1985a).

References

Baxter, M. (1988), 'Approximation Suboptimal Dynamic Equilibrium: A Euler Equation Approach', Working Paper, University of Rochester.

Baxter, M., Crucini M., and Rowenhorst, K.G. (1990), 'Solving the Stochastic Growth Model by a Discrete-State-Space Euler Equation Approach', *Journal of Business and Economics Statistics*, 8 (January): 19–21.

Bizer, D. and Judd, K. (1989), 'Uncertainty and Taxation', Papers and proceedings of the *American Economic Review*, 79 (May): 331–6.

Bossaerts, P. (1989), 'The Asymptotic Normality of Method of Simulated Moments Estimators of Option Pricing Models', Working Paper, Carnegie Mellon University.

Bossaerts, P. and Hillion, P. (1990), 'Arbitrage Restrictions Across Financial Markets: Theory, Methodology and Tests', Working Paper, Carnegie Mellon University.

Braun, A. (1989), 'The Dynamic Interaction of Distortionary Taxes and Aggregate Variables in Postwar U.S. Data', Working Paper, University of Virginia.

Brock, W.A. (1982) 'Asset Prices in a Production Economy', in J.J McCall, (ed.), *The Economics of Information and Uncertainty*, Chicago: University of Chicago Press.

Brock, W.A. and le Baron, B. (1989), 'Liquidity Constraints in Production Based Asset Pricing Models', NBER Working Paper.

Brock, W.A., and Mirman L.J. (1972), 'Optimal Economic Growth and Uncertainty: the Discounted Case', *Journal of Economic Theory*, 4: 479–513.

Burnside, C., Eichenbaum, M. and Rebelo, S. (1990), 'Labor Hoarding and the Business Cycle', Working Paper, Northwestern University.

Chang, L.J. (1989), 'Distortionary Taxes, Monetary Policies and Business Cycles', Ph.D. Dissertation, Carnegie Mellon University.

Chari, V.V., Christiano, L. and Kehoe, P. (1990), 'Dynamic Ramsey Taxation in a Stochastic Growth Model', Working Paper, Federal Reserve Bank of Minneapolis.

Christiano, L.J. (1990a), 'Solving the Stochastic Growth Model by a Linear-Quadratic Approximation and Value-Function Iteration', *Journal of Business and Economics Statistics*, 8 (January): 23–6.

(1990b), 'Linear-Quadratic Approximation and Value-Function Iteration: A Comparison', *Journal of Business and Economics Statistics*, 8 (January).

Christiano, L.J. and Eichenbaum, M. (1990), 'Current Real Business Cycle Theories and Aggregate Labor Market Fluctuations', Working Paper, Federal Reserve Bank of Minneapolis.

Coleman, W.J. (1991), 'Equilibrium in a Production Economy with an Income Tax', *Econometrica*, 59: 1091–104.

(1990), 'Solving the Stochastic Growth Model by Policy Function Iteration', *Journal of Business and Economics Statistics*, 8 (January): 27–9.

Cooley, T. and Hansen, G. (1989), 'The Inflation Tax in a Real Business Cycle Model', *American Economic Review*, 79: 733–48.

Deaton, A. (1991), 'Saving and Liquidity Constraints', *Econometrica*, 59: 1227–98.

den Haan, W. (1990a), 'Optimal Inflation in a Sidrausky Model', *Journal of Monetary Economics*, 25: 389–409.

(1990b), 'The Term Structure of Interest Rates in Real and Monetary Production Economics', Working Paper, Carnegie Mellon University.

den Haan, W. and Marcet, A. (1990), 'Solving a Simple Growth Model by Parameterizing Expectations', *Journal of Business Economics and Statistics*, 8 (January): 31–4.

(1994), 'Accuracy in Simulations', *Review of Economic Studies* (forthcoming).

Diaz, J. and Prescott, E. (1990), 'Asset Returns in Computable General Equilibrium Heterogeneous Agent Models', Working Paper, Federal Reserve Bank of Minneapolis.

Duffie, D. and Singleton, K. (1990), 'Simulated Moments Estimation of Markov Models of Asset Prices', Working Paper, Stanford University.

Fair, R.C. and Taylor, J.B. (1983), 'Solution and Maximum Likelihood Estimation of Dynamic Nonlinear Rational Expectations Models', *Econometrica*, 51: 1169–85.

Gagnon, J. (1990), 'Solving the Stochastic Growth Model by Deterministic Extended Path', *Journal of Business and Economics Statistics*, 8 (January).

Garcia-Mila, T. (1987), 'Government Purchases and Real Output: an Empirical Analysis and Equilibrium Model with Public Capital', Working Paper, Universitat Autònoma de Barcelona. Published in Spanish in *Investigaciones Economicas*, 14: 369–89.

Geweke, J. (1989), 'Modeling with Normal Polynomial Expansions', in W.A. Barnett, J. Geweke and K. Shell (eds.), *Economic Complexity; Chaos, Sunspots, Bubbles and Nonlinearity*, International Symposia in Economic Theory and Econometrics, Cambridge University Press.

Gregory, A.W. and Smith, G.W. (1991), 'Calibration as Testing: Inference in Simulated Macroeconomic Models', *Journal of Business and Economic Statistics* (July).

Grossman, S. and Shiller, R. (1981), 'The Determinants of the Variability of Stock Market Prices', *American Economic Review*, 71: 222–7.

Hahn, F. (1971), 'Professor Friedman's Views on Money', *Economica*, pp.61–80.

Hansen, G. (1985), 'Indivisible Labor and the Business Cycle', *Journal of Monetary Economics*, 16: 309–28.

Hansen, G. and Imrohoroglu, A. (1992), 'The Role of Unemployment Insurance in an Economy with Liquidity Constraints and Moral Hazard', *Journal of Political Economy*, 100 (February): 118–42.

Hansen, L.P. (1987), 'Calculating Asset Prices in Three Example Economies', *Advances in Econometrics, Fifth World Congress*, Vol. I, Cambridge University Press, ch.6.

Hansen, L.P. and Sargent, T.J. (1990), 'Recursive Linear Models of Dynamic Economies', manuscript, Hoover Institution.

Hansen, L.P. and Singleton, K. (1982), 'Generalized Instrumental Variables Estimation of Non-linear Rational Expectations Models', *Econometrica*, 50: 1269–86.

Hayashi, F. (1987), 'Tests for Liquidity Constraints: a Critical Survey and Some

New Observations', *Advances in Econometrics, Fifth World Congress*, Vol. II, Cambridge University Press, ch.13.

Heaton, J. (1990), 'The Interaction between Time Non-separable Preferences and Time Aggregation', Working Paper, Massachussetts Institute of Technology.

Ingram, B. (1990a), 'Equilibrium Modelling of Asset Prices: Rationality Versus Rules of Thumb', *Journal of Business and Economic Statistics*, 8 (January).

(1990b), 'Solving the Stochastic Growth Model by Backsolving with an Expanded State Space', *Journal of Business and Economics Statistics*, 8 (January).

Jones, L.E. and Manuelli, R.E. (1989), 'Notes on a Model of Optimal Equilibrium Growth', Working Paper, Northwestern University.

Jones, L.E., Manuelli, R.E. and Rossi, P.E. (1990), 'Optimal Taxation in Convex Models of Equilibrium Growth', Working Paper, Northwestern University.

Judd, K. (1989a), 'Minimum Weighted Residual Methods in Dynamic Economic Models', Working Paper, Hoover Institution.

(1989b), 'Cournot versus Bertrand: a Dynamic Resolution', Working Paper, Hoover Institution.

Ketterer and Marcet (1989), 'Introducing Derivative Securities: A General Equilibrium Approach', Working Paper, Carnegie Mellon University.

Kydland, F.E. and Prescott, E.C. (1982), 'Time to Build and Aggregate Fluctuations', *Econometrica*, 50: 1345–70.

Labadie, P. (1990), 'Solving the Stochastic Growth Model by a Recursive Mapping Based on Least Squares Projection', *Journal of Business and Economics Statistics*, 8 (January).

Lee, B.S. and Ingram, B.F. (1991), 'Estimation by Simulation of Time Series Models', *Journal of Econometrics*, 47: 197–207.

Lucas, D. (1990), 'Asset Pricing with Undiversifiable Income Risk and Short Sales Constraints: Deepening the Equity Premium Puzzle', Working Paper, Northwestern University.

Lucas, R.E. (1972), 'Expectations and the Neutrality of Money', *Journal of Economic Theory*, 4: 103–24.

(1978), 'Asset Prices in an Exchange Economy', *Econometrica*, 46: 1426–46.

Marcet, A. (1989), 'Solving Non-Linear Dynamic Models by Parameterizing Expectations', Working Paper, Carnegie Mellon University.

Marcet. A. and Marimon, R. (1992), 'Communication, Commitment and Growth', *Journal of Economic Theory*, 58 (December): 219–49.

Marcet, A. and Sargent, T.J. (1989a), 'Convergence of Least Squares Learning Mechanisms in Self-Referential Linear Stochastic Models', *Journal of Economic Theory*, 48 (August): 337–68.

(1989b), 'Convergence of Least Squares Learning in Environments with Hidden State Variables and Private Information', *Journal of Political Economy*, 97 (December): 1306–22.

Marcet, A. and Singleton, K. (1990), 'Equilibrium Asset Prices and Savings of Heterogeneous Agents in the Presence of Portfolio Constraints', Working Paper , Carnegie Mellon University.

Marimon, R., McGratten, E. and Sargent, T.J. (1990), 'Money as a Medium of

Exchange in an Economy with Artificially Intelligent Agents', *Journal of Economic Dynamics and Control*, 14: 329–74.

Marshall, D. (1988), 'Inflation and Asset Returns in a Monetary Economy with Transaction Costs', Working Paper, Northwestern University. Forthcoming in the *Journal of Finance*.

McFadden, D. (1989), 'A Method of Simulated Moments for Estimation of Discrete Response Models without Numerical Integration', *Econometrica*, 57: 995–1026.

McGratten, E. (1989), 'The Macroeconomic Effects of Distortionary Taxation', *Journal of Monetary Economics* (forthcoming).

(1990), 'Solving the Stochastic Growth Model by Linear-Quadratic Approximation', *Journal of Business and Economics Statistics*, 8 (January): 41–3.

Mehra, R. and Prescott, E.C. (1985), 'The Equity Premium: A Puzzle', *Journal of Monetary Economics*, 15: 145–62.

Novales, A. (1990), 'A Stochastic Monetary Equilibrium Model of the Interest Rate', *Econometrica*, 58: 93–112.

Otker, I. (1990), 'The Welfare Implications of Fiscal Policy with Distortionary Taxation: A Numerical Analysis', Working Paper, Carnegie Mellon University.

Pakes, A. (1986), 'Patents as Options: Some Estimates of the Value of Holding European Patent Stocks', *Econometrica*, 54: 755–84.

Pakes, A. and Pollard, D. (1989), 'Simulation and the Asymptotics of Optimizations Estimators', *Econometrica*, 57(5): 1027–57.

Pakes, A. and Rust, J. (1994), 'Estimation of Dynamic Structural Models, Problems and Prospects', chs 4 and 5 this volume.

Phelan, C. (1990), 'Incentives, Insurance and the Variability of Consumption and Leisure', Working Paper, University of Wisconsin.

Phelan, C. and Townsend, R. (1991), 'Computing Multi-Period Information Constrained Optima', *Review of Economic Studies*, 58 (October): 853–82.

Prescott, E.C. (1986), 'Theory Ahead of Business Cycle Measurement', *Federal Reserve Bank of Minneapolis Quarterly Review*, 10: 9–22.

Rios, J.V. (1990), 'Life-Cycle Economies and Aggregate Fluctuations', Working Paper, Carnegie Mellon University.

Rogerson, R. (1988), 'Indivisible Labor, Lotteries and Equilibrium', *Journal of Monetary Economics*, 21: 3–17.

Rojas, G. (1992), 'Optimal Taxation in a Stochastic Growth Model with Public Capital', Working Paper, Universitat Pompou Fabra.

Rotemberg, J. and Woodford, M. (1992), 'Oligopolistic Pricing and the Effects of Military Purchases on Ecconomic Activity', *Journal of Political Economy*, 100 (December): 1153–207.

Rowenhorst, K.G. (1990), 'Asset Returns and Business Cycles: A General Equilibrium Approach', Working Paper, University of Rochester.

Rust, J. (1988), 'Maximum Likelihood Estimation of Discrete Control Processes', *SIAM Journal of Control and Optimization*, 26: 1006–23.

Sargent, T.J. (1987), *Dynamic Macroeconomic Theory*, Harvard University Press.

Scheinkman, J. and Weiss, L. (1986), 'Borrowing Constraints and Aggregate Economic Activity', *Econometrica*, 54: 23–45.

Sims, C.A. (1985), 'Solving Non-Linear Stochastic Equilibrium Models "Backwards"', manuscript, University of Minnesota.

   (1990), 'Solving the Stochastic Growth Model by Backsolving with a Particular Non-Linear Form for the Decision Rule', *Journal of Business and Economics Statistics* (January).

Smith, T. (1989), 'Solving Non-linear Rational Expectations Models: A New Approach', Working Paper, Queen's University.

Tauchen, G. (1990), 'Solving the Stochastic Growth Model by Using Quadrature Methods and Value-Function Iterations', *Journal of Business and Economics Statistics*, 8 (January): 49–51.

Taylor, J. and Uhlig, H. (1990), 'Solving Nonlinear Stochastic Growth Models: A Comparison of Alternative Solution Methods', *Journal of Business Economics and Statistics*, 8 (January): 1–18.

CHAPTER 4

Estimation of dynamic structural models, problems and prospects: discrete decision processes

John Rust

1   INTRODUCTION

This is the first in a two-part survey of recent developments in the rapidly growing literature on methods for solving and estimating dynamic structural models. Part I focusses on discrete decision processes (DDP), i.e., problems where the decision variable is restricted to a countable set. Most of this part deals with single-agent problems, though I do conclude by sketching a framework for inference of discrete dynamic games. Part II, by Ariel Pakes, considers extensions to mixed continuous discrete decision processes (MCDP), i.e., processes where some of the components of the decision variable can take on a continuum of values. Part II provides more extensive coverage of recent developments in estimation of dynamic multi-agent models. We have tried to make the parts relatively self contained, so that readers can feel free to skip to the sections that interest them. Both parts of the survey are restricted to problems formulated in discrete time, and, as a result, the words 'discrete' and 'continuous' will refer to the control rather than the time variable.[1]

I presume that readers are familiar with recent surveys of discrete decision processes by Eckstein and Wolpin (1989a) and Rust (1988a and 1994), and focus on issues that are not covered in these surveys. In keeping with the title, section 2 begins with some general comments on (my view of) the problems with the current literature on estimation of dynamic structural models. In section 3 I define the subclass of DDPs and in section 4 I discuss the identification problem. The identification problem can lead to potentially serious questions about the credibility of a structural approach to policy analysis. However, Rust (1992b) presents empirical examples that demonstrate that, despite the identification problem, one can formulate plausible, albeit abstract, structural models that yield far more accurate policy forecasts than reduced-form models. Section 5 reviews the main specifications for 'error terms' in DDP models. The predominant interpretation is that error terms represent unobserved state variables, i.e., state variables observed by the agent but not by the econometrician. Section 6 reviews the main results on maximum-likelihood estimation of DDPs with unobserved state variables that satisfy the conditional independence assumption. I note that development of tractable methods for handling serially correlated unobservables remains an unresolved problem. Section 7 surveys algorithms for solving and estimating DDP problems. The standard estimation/solution algorithm can be described as a 'nested numerical solution' consisting of an 'outer' hill-climbing algorithm that searches for a parameter θ that optimises the statistical objective function, and an 'inner' DP algorithm that computes the solution to the DDP model for each trial value of θ. Section 8 reviews several recent attempts to avoid the computational burden of the repeated nested numerical solution of the DDP model over the course of the estimation process. Several of these approaches involve innovative combinations of non-parametric and Monte Carlo simulation methods. Finally section 9 sketches a framework for estimation of discrete dynamic games. I show how one can avoid the computational burden of a full equilibrium solution by using non-parametric estimation methods to uncover opponents' reaction functions, allowing one to estimate a given player's preferences by treating his problem as a single-agent 'game against nature'.

2   DYNAMIC STRUCTURAL MODELS: PROBLEMS

One can characterise the class of 'dynamic structural models' by two key features: (1) time and uncertainty[2] are explicitly treated, and (2) agents are *rational*: they have well-defined objective functions and make their decisions sequentially based on their current information, their beliefs about nature, and their beliefs about the strategies of their opponents. The *primitives* of these models are agents' preferences and beliefs. Given specific functional forms for the primitives, it is often possible to solve the model to yield specific behavioural predictions. Structural models can usually be easily distinguished from 'reduced-form' approaches that do not attempt to derive behavioual predictions from an explicit solution to an underlying optimisation/equilibrium problem.

The concept of estimation is more difficult to define in a way that is uncontroversial. Currently there are a large number of competing methods for structural estimation, including 'calibration' approaches (Kydland and Prescott (1982), Hartley (1985)), 'classical' statistics approaches such as parametric maximum-likelihood estimation (Pakes (1986), Rust (1987), Wolpin (1984)), method of moments estimation (Hansen (1982), Hansen and Singleton (1982)), non-parametric and semi-parametric estimation methods (Hansen and Jagannathan (1991), Manski (1990)), as well as Bayesian approaches.[3] Some of the most bitter divisions in the profession stem from disagreements about the correct method of inference rather than arguments over substantive issues such as the interpretation of the data or the specification of the behavioural model. This problem is not unique to dynamic structural models, although the disagreements can be especially severe when pet theories are at stake. The divisions are unfortunate because, despite the differences in approach, the basic goal is the same: namely, to find specifications of preferences and beliefs that best fit the data according to some metric. It would be a shame to see disagreement over estimation methodology devolve to the level of the sterile debate in the statistics literature about whether Bayesian or classical methods are the 'right' way to do inference.[4] Of course having a multiplicity of estimation methods can make it hard to compare how well alternative models fit the data. It's not difficult to cite examples where a model appears to fit the data well according to one estimation method, but fits poorly when other methods are used.[5] At this point, there seems to be no easy resolution to the problem, other than to try to ensure that alternative models are sufficiently accessible to enable individual researchers to compare them using their own preferred notion of goodness of fit. Unfortunately the accessibility of different models is hindered by the fact that many models and solution procedures are closely linked to particular estimation methods.

We are starting to see similar conflicts arising out of the recent proliferation of solution methods for stochastic control problems. Ideally a good numerical method should be able to solve a given problem to an arbitrary degree of accuracy. However in practice, there is an obvious trade-off between the amount of computation required and the degree of approximation error. Unfortunately, it seems that it is just as difficult for the profession to agree on an appropriate metric for approximation error as it is to agree on an appropriate statistical metric for goodness of fit. While it seems desirable to have a wide menu of alternative solution methods, it is likely that in the near future a whole new set of controversies will emerge over which solution method is 'best'.

A positive approach is to compare alternative solution methods over a class of standard test problems as was done by the 'rational expectations modelling group' in the 1990 special issue of the *Journal of Business Economics and Statistics*. The group compared the performance of eight alternative solution methods for a simplified version of the Brock–Mirman stochastic growth problem. In their survey of the methods, Taylor and Uhlig (1990) may have foreshadowed the problems to come: 'The differences in the methods turned out to be quite substantial for certain aspects of the growth model. Therefore, researchers want to be careful not to rely blindly on the results of any chosen numerical method in applied work' (p.1). This raises the spectre of different researchers reaching very different conclusions about the ability of a given model to fit the data depending on which solution method they choose.

These problems have led some to question why one ought to go through the difficulty of estimating structural models in the first place. The two standard justifications for structural as opposed to reduced-form estimation are that the former leads to more direct tests of economic theory, and results in superior forecasts of the effects of policy changes. One can stereotype the structural approach to estimation and inference as a search for the 'true' specification. The typical approach is to estimate a parametric structural model by classical statistical procedures, performing hypothesis tests to see if the data reject the null hypothesis that the specification is correct. If the null is not rejected, then the estimated model is used to make various policy forecasts. Researchers frequently appeal to the arguments of Marschak (1953) or Lucas (1976) to justify why their structural forecasts are necessarily superior to forecasts from traditional reduced-form statistical models. Unfortunately the standard justification for doing structural estimation becomes significantly less potent if one admits that most structural models are typically crude approximations to reality. The fact that an estimated structural model 'passes' an hypothesis test often fails to convince many sceptics who believe that the only reason the model was not rejected is because the sample size was not large enough. However once we concede that the structural model is misspecified, then there is little reason to suppose that its forecasts are necessarily better than those from a reduced-form model.[6]

Of course we don't need to be backed into this corner if we are willing to take a more pragmatic view of structural estimation. The alternative view concedes that there is no such thing as a 'true specification', since even the most sophisticated structural models are still necessarily highly abstract representations of reality.[7] Under the alternative view, the process of specification and estimation of structural models is best understood from the standpoint of approximation theory: namely, as a more or less formal search over an expanding space of admissible specifications of preferences and beliefs in an attempt to find models that provide increasingly better approximations to real-world behaviour. This approach recognises that structural and reduced-form statistical models have different strengths and weaknesses, so we should select the approach that is appropriate for the problem at hand. Reduced-form models typically require fewer a priori restrictions, but are limited to summarising the historical distribution of observables. Structural models require stronger a priori restrictions, but have the potential to predict the impact of a wide class of policy interventions. These predictions are more credible in cases where the structural model provides a good approximation to what we observe, but this must be evaluated on a case-by-case basis. Although use of the 'Lucas critique' as a *carte blanche* justification for estimating structural models is an unfortunate hype, in a survey of the empirical literature (Rust (1992b)) I find a number of examples where economic theory has been successful in placing restrictions on a statistical model – albeit approximate and abstract – that appear to capture the essence of observed behaviour.

The problems that I have identified so far might be better thought of as disagreements (confusions?) that are potentially resolvable. There is a deeper set of problems concerning model complexity that may have no easy solution. While recent advances in computer hardware and solution software have enabled us to formulate and estimate a class of dynamic structural models that would have been unthinkable just ten years ago, nevertheless, the fact is that the class of estimable structural models is still quite limited. Even though computing power is increasing by at least an order of magnitude each decade, the 'curse of dimensionality' is sufficiently strong that estimation of even slightly more realistic models quickly becomes prohibitive. Indeed, the computational complexity of most dynamic structural models is exponential in any relevant measure of the size or realism of the model.[8]

In addition to computational complexity, there is a potentially more severe concomitant problem of 'estimation complexity'. The problem arises because beliefs and preferences are essentially very high-dimensional unknown parameters. Since economic theory often fails to deliver simple parsimonious parametric functional forms for these objects, many econometricians would be more comfortable if we could estimate them non-parametrically, perhaps using finite-cell approximations or series expansion techniques that expand the dimension of the parameterisation with the sample size. Unfortunately, the estimation complexity of preferences and beliefs is also exponential.[9] What I mean by this is that the number of observations needed to reliably estimate a finite-state approximation to a dynamic choice problem rises exponentially in any relevant measure of the size or realism of the choice problem.[10] This is especially true of the problem of estimating agents' 'beliefs', treated as conditional probability distributions over states of nature.

The final problem is 'data complexity' which is closely related, but distinct from, estimation complexity. The problem relates to the quality and level of detail of data needed to estimate a structural model, not just its sheer volume. In order to estimate more detailed and realistic structural models we will need much more detailed data sets that will allow us to obtain measurements of the required state and control variables. However the more detailed the data, the greater the opportunity for missing responses, response and coding errors, not to mention classification and programming errors on the part of econometricians using the data. In my experience, problems involved in solving and estimating more realistically specified dynamic choice models can be trivial in comparison to the problems involved in manipulating and comprehending the data, evaluating whether estimates of preferences and beliefs are sensible and determining whether the estimated model provides a good fit. The problem is that even though the underlying structural model may be conceptually simple and parsimoniously parameterised, its solution yields a very complicated multi-dimensional controlled stochastic process whose realisations can be difficult to concisely summarise and compare to observations, especially in cases where there are rare events. In my opinion, careful attention to the data is critical in order to dispel the growing view that structural estimation is merely a display of technique rather than a useful means of understanding the real world.

I will try to illustrate these problems more concretely in the following sections. I conclude this section by noting that while there are clearly exploitable trade-offs between computational, estimation and data complexity, in the end 'you can't fool mother nature'. What I mean by this is that it is unlikely that there is an undiscovered panacea that will somehow make arbitrarily complex structural models trivial to estimate.[11] Thus, methods like the non-parametric simulation methods outlined in section 8 that appear to significantly extend the class of estimable DP problems turn out to fall prey to serious problems of estimation complexity. Although it is unlikely that there is an magical fix (akin to solving the '$P = NP$ problem'), I think there still is considerable room for improvement in existing methods that will allow us to steadily expand the frontier of problems estimable by structural methods.

3   DYNAMIC STRUCTURAL MODELS: MDPs AND DDPs

Discrete decision processes (DDP) are a subclass of Markovian decision processes (MDP) for which the decision or control variable d is restricted to a countable set of alternatives.[12] Although the DP method can be used in some instances to solve problems with non-time separable preferences, the underlying theory and solution methods are much more developed in the time-separable case. However, by redefining the state variable, one can always re-write a non-stationary, time non-separable problem as a time-separable Markovian decision problem.[13] Perhaps a more significant restriction is the expected utility hypothesis, i.e., that preferences are state separable. The focus on expected utility appears to be due to the fact that theory and computational methods for solving non-expected utility models of dynamic choice are not yet well developed.[14] While it is unlikely that human decision makers are literally solving time-separable Markovian decision problems, it turns out that this class is sufficiently rich and flexible to enable one to construct detailed models of most types of behaviour. In section 4 I show that, if anything, this class is too rich; one can formulate MDP models that rationalise any observed behaviour.

Definition: A (discrete-time) *Markov decision process* consists of the following objects

A *time index* $t \in \{0,1,2,\ldots,T\}$, $T \le \infty$
A *state space* S
A *decision space* D
A family of *constraint sets* $\{D_t(s_t) \subseteq D\}$
A family of *transition probabilities* $\{p_{t+1}(\cdot | s_t, d_t)\}$
A discount factor $\beta \in (0,1)$ and a family of *single-period utility functions* $\{u_t(s_t, d_t)\}$ such that the utility functional $U(\mathbf{s}, \mathbf{d})$ over sequences $\mathbf{s} = (s_0, \ldots, s_T)$ and $\mathbf{d} = (d_0, \ldots, d_T)$ has the additively separable decomposition

$$U(\mathbf{s}, \mathbf{d}) = \sum_{t=0}^{T} \beta^t u_t(s_t, d_t). \tag{4.1}$$

The agent's optimisation problem can be stated formally as follows

$$\delta^* = \underset{\delta}{\operatorname{argmax}} \, E_\delta \{U(\tilde{\mathbf{s}}, \tilde{\mathbf{d}})\}. \tag{4.2}$$

This is equivalent to a static optimisation problem, except that rather than selecting a fixed sequence of *decisions* $\mathbf{d} = (d_1, \ldots, d_T)$, the agent can generally do better by selecting a sequence of *decision rules* $\delta^* = (\delta_1^*, \ldots, \delta_T^*)$, where each δ_t^* specifies the agent's best decision as a function of his information at time t: $d_t = \delta_t^*(H_{t-1}, s_t)$, where $H_{t-1} = \{s_0, \ldots, s_{t-1}, d_0, \ldots, d_{t-1}\}$ denotes the agent's history (information set) at time $t - 1$. The notation E_δ denotes the fact that the expectation in (4.2) is taken with respect to the controlled stochastic process $\{s_t, d_t\}$ induced by δ.[15] Although (4.2) is formally equivalent to a static optimisation problem, it involves searching over an infinite-dimensional space of alternative decision rules. A much more straightforward and computationally tractable solution procedure is *backward induction* using *value function* to serve the role of 'shadow prices' to decentralise a complicated multi-period decision problem into a sequence of simpler static problems. In the terminal period, T, V_T^* and δ_T^* are defined by

$$\delta_T^*(s_T) = \operatorname*{argmax}_{d_T \in D_T(s_T)} [u_T(s_T, d_T)], \tag{4.3}$$

$$V_T^*(s_T) = \max_{d_T \in D_T(s_T)} [u_T(s_T, d_T)]. \tag{4.4}$$

In periods $t = 0, \ldots, T-1$, V_t^* and δ_t^* are recursively defined by

$$\delta_t^*(s_t) = \operatorname*{argmax}_{d_t \in D_t(s_t)} [u_t(s_t, d_t) + \beta \int V_{t+1}^*(s_{t+1}, \delta_{t+1}^*(s_{t+1})) p_{t+1}(ds_{t+1}|s_t, d_t)], \tag{4.5}$$

$$V_t^*(s_t) = \operatorname*{argmax}_{d_t \in D_t(s_t)} [u_t(s_t, d_t) + \beta \int V_{t+1}^*(s_{t+1}, \delta_{t+1}^*(s_{t+1})) p_{t+1}(ds_{t+1}|s_t, d_t)], \tag{4.6}$$

It's straightforward to verify that at time $t = 0$ the value of function $V_0^*(s_0)$ represents the conditional expectation of utility over all future periods. Since dynamic programming has recursively generated the optimal decision rule $\delta^* = (\delta_0^*, \ldots, \delta_T^*)$, it follows that

$$V_0^*(s_0) = \max_{\delta} E_{\delta}\{U(\tilde{\mathbf{s}}, \tilde{\mathbf{d}})\}. \tag{4.7}$$

In infinite horizon MDPs there is no last period from which to begin backward induction, but in the special case of *stationary* MDPs (where $u_t = u$ and $p_t = p$ for all t) it is easy to see that the stationary Markovian structure of the problem implies that the future looks the same whether the agent is in state s_t at time t or in state s_{t+k} at time $t + k$ provided that $s_t = s_{t+k}$. In other words, the only variable which affects the agent's view about the future is the value of his current state s. This implies that the optimal decision rule and corresponding value function will be time invariant: i.e., for all $t \geq 0$ and all $s \in S, \delta_t^*(s) = \delta^*(s)$ and $V_t^*(s) = V^*(s)$. In analogy with equation (4.5), δ^* will satisfy

$$\delta^*(s) = \operatorname*{argmax}_{d \in D(s)} [u(s, d) + \beta \int V^*(s') p(ds'|s, d)], \tag{4.8}$$

where V^* is defined recursively by the solution to *Bellman's equation*

$$V^*(s) = \max_{d \in D(s)} [u(s, d) + \beta \int V^*(s') p(ds'|s, d)]. \tag{4.9}$$

It is not difficult to show that under certain regularity conditions (such as boundedness of u), Bellman's equation (4.9) is mathematically equivalent to a fixed point of a contraction mapping, which implies that it exists and is unique. The following theorem, known as *Blackwell's Theorem*, shows that the stationary decision rule δ^* computed from Bellman's equation in (4.8) is indeed an optimal decision rule to the original optimisation problem, i.e., it is a solution to (4.2). Subsequent work by Bhattacharya and Majumdar (1989) has substantially weakened the regularity conditions (such as boundedness of u) needed to establish Blackwell's Theorem.

Theorem 1 (Blackwell, Bhattacharya and Majumdar): Given an infinite-horizon, stationary MDP satisfying the regularity conditions in Bhattacharya and Majumdar (1989) we have

1   *A unique solution V^* to Bellman's equation (4.9) exists, and it coincides with the agent's expected disounted utility under an optimal policy.*

2   *An optimal decision rule δ^* exists and coincides with the stationary, non-randomised, Markovian optimal control δ^* given by the solution to (4.8).*

3   *δ^* can be approximated arbitrarily closely by the solution δ_N^* (computed by backward induction) to an N-period problem with utility function $U_N(\mathbf{s}, \mathbf{d}) = \sum_{t=0}^{N} \beta^t u(s_t, d_t)$ such that*

$$\lim_{N \to \infty} E_{\delta_N^*}\{U_N(\tilde{\mathbf{s}}, \tilde{\mathbf{d}})\} = \lim_{N \to \infty} \sup_\delta E_\delta\{U_N(\tilde{\mathbf{s}}, \tilde{\mathbf{d}})\} = \sup_\delta E_\delta\{U(\tilde{\mathbf{s}}, \tilde{\mathbf{d}})\}. \tag{4.10}$$

4   THE IDENTIFICATION PROBLEM

The goal of structural estimation is to uncover the primitives (u, p, β) of the DDP or MDP problem. The estimation problem can be posed as a dynamic form of 'revealed preference': given infinite observations $\{s_t, d_t\}$ on the states and decisions of an agent, under what conditions can we use this data to uniquely recover (u, p, β)? Unfortunately, without a strong a priori restrictions on (u, p, β), the answer to this question is 'none': the MDP model is non-parametrically unidentified in the sense that there is an equivalence class containing infinitely many distinct primitives (u, p, β) that are consistent with the observations $\{s_t, d_t\}$. Furthermore Blackwell's Theorem *per se* has no empirical content in the sense that we can always find primitives that rationalise any set of observations.

Note that these negative findings stand in contrast to the case of static choice models where we know that the hypothesis of optimisation *per se* does imply testable restrictions.[16] The absence of restrictions in the dynamic case may seem surprising given that the structure of the MDP problem already imposes a number of strong restrictions such as time-additive preferences, constant intertemporal discount factors, as well as the expected utility hypothesis itself. However many economists will probably not be surprised by this result since similar results have appeared in other areas such as the literature on choice under uncertainty, game theory and general equilibrium theory.[17]

To simplify notation, we establish these results in the context of stationary infinite-horizon MDPs, although the argument carries over almost without modification to the non-stationary, finite horizon case. In order to formulate the identification problem *à la* Cowles Commission, we need to translate the concepts of *reduced-form* and *structure* to the context of a non-linear MDP model.

Definition 1 The *reduced-form* of an MDP model is the agent's optimal decision rule, δ.

Definition 2 The *structure* of an MDP model is the mapping: $\Lambda(u, p, \beta) = \delta$ defined by

$$\delta(s) = \underset{d \in D(s)}{\operatorname{argmax}} [v(s, d)], \tag{4.11}$$

where v is the unique fixed point to

$$v(s, d) = u(s, d) + \beta \int \underset{d' \in D(s')}{\max} [v(s', d')] p(ds' | s, d). \tag{4.12}$$

The rationale for identifying δ as the reduced-form of the MDP is that it embodies all observable implications of the theory[18] and can be consistently estimated by non-parametric regression given sufficient number of observations $\{s_t, d_t\}$.[19] We can use the reduced-form δ to define an equivalence relation over the space of primitives.

Definition 3 Primitives (u, p, β) and $(\bar{u}, \bar{p}, \bar{\beta})$ are *observationally equivalent* if

$$\Lambda(u, p, \beta) = \Lambda(\bar{u}, \bar{p}, \bar{\beta}). \tag{4.13}$$

Thus $\Lambda^{-1}(\delta)$ is the equivalence class of primitives consistent with decision rule δ. Expected utility theory implies that $\Lambda(u, p, \beta) = \Lambda(au + b, p, \beta)$ for any constants a and b satisfying $a > 0$, so at best we will only be able to identify an agent's preferences u modulo cardinal equivalence, i.e., up to a positive linear transformation of u.

Definition 4 The stationary MDP problem (4.11) and (4.12) is *non-parametrically identified* if given any reduced-form δ in the range of Λ, and any primitives (u, p, β) and $(\bar{u}, \bar{p}, \bar{\beta})$ in $\Lambda^{-1}(\delta)$ we have

$$\begin{aligned} \beta &= \bar{\beta} \\ p &= \bar{p} \\ u &= a\bar{u} + b, \quad \textit{for some constants } a \textit{ and } b \textit{ satisfying } a > 0. \end{aligned} \tag{4.14}$$

Lemma 1 The MDP problem (4.11) and (4.12) is non-parametrically unidentified.

The proof of this result is quite simple. Given any δ in the range of Λ, let $(u, p, \beta) \in \Lambda^{-1}(\delta)$. Define a new set of primitives $(\bar{u}, \bar{p}, \bar{\beta})$ by

$$\bar{\beta} = \beta$$
$$\bar{p}(ds'|s, d) = p(ds'|s, d) \tag{4.15}$$
$$\bar{u}(s, d) = u(s, d) + f(s) - \beta \int f(s') p(ds'|s, d),$$

where f is an arbitrary integrable function of s. Then $\bar{u}$ is clearly not cardinally equivalent to u unless f is a constant. To see that both (u, p, β) and $(\bar{u}, \bar{p}, \bar{\beta})$ are observationally equivalent, note that if $v(s, d)$ is the value function corresponding to primitives (u, p, β) then $\bar{v}(s, d) = v(s, d) + f(s)$ is the value function corresponding to $(\bar{u}, \bar{p}, \bar{\beta})$

$$\bar{v}(s, d) = \bar{u}(s, d) + \beta \int \max_{d' \in D(s')} [\bar{v}(s', d')] p(ds'|s, d)$$
$$= u(s, d) + f(s) - \beta \int f(s') p(ds'|s, d) + \beta \int \max_{d' \in D(s')} [v(s', d') + f(s')] p(ds'|s, d)$$
$$= u(s, d) + f(s) + \beta \int \max_{d' \in D(s')} [v(s', d')] p(ds'|s, d)$$
$$= v(s, d) + f(s). \tag{4.16}$$

Since v is the unique fixed point to (4.12), it follows that $v + f$ is the unique fixed point to (4.16), so our conjecture $\bar{v} = v + f$ is indeed the unique fixed point to equation (4.12) with primitives $\{\bar{\beta}, \bar{u}, \bar{p}\}$. From (4.11) it is clear that $\{v(s, d), d \in D(s)\}$ and $\{v(s, d) + f(s), d \in D(s)\}$ yield the same decision rule δ. It follows that $(u + f - \beta Ef, p, \beta)$ is observationally equivalent to (u, p, β), but $u + f - \beta Ef$ is not cardinally equivalent to u.

We now ask whether Blackwell's Theorem places any restrictions on the decision rule δ. In the case of infinite-horizon MDPs, Blackwell's Theorem does provide two general restrictions: δ^* is Markovian and deterministic. In practice, it is extremely difficult to test these restrictions empirically. Presumably we could test the first restriction by seeing whether agents' decisions depend on lagged states s_{t-k} for $k = 1, 2, \ldots$. However, given that we have not placed any a priori bounds on the dimensionality of S, the well-known trick of 'expanding the state space' (Bertsekas (1987), chapter 4) can be used to transform an Nth order Markov process into a first-order Markov process. For example, by defining a new state x_t by $x_t = (H_{t-1}, s_t)$, we see that the general non-stationary, non-separable stochastic decision problem is actually a special case of an MDP where the objective is to maximise the utility of the terminal state and decision, $U(x_T, d_T) = U(H_{T-1}, s_T, d_T) = U(\mathbf{s}, \mathbf{d})$. The second restriction might be tested by looking for agents who make different choices in some state s in two different time periods: $\delta(s_t) \neq \delta(s_{t+k})$, for some state $s_t = s_{t+k} = s$. However this behaviour can be rationalised by a model where the agent is indifferent between several alternatives available in state s and simply chooses one at random.[20] The following lemma shows that there are no other restrictions beyond the two essentially untestable restrictions of Blackwell's Theorem.

Lemma 2 Given an arbitrary measurable mapping $\delta: S \to D$ *there exist primitives* (u, p, β) *such that* $\delta = \Lambda(u, p, \beta)$.
The proof of this result is straightforward. Given an arbitrary discount factor $\beta \in (0, 1)$ and transition probability p, define u by

$$u(s, d) = I\{d = \delta(s)\} - \beta. \tag{4.17}$$

Then it is easy to see that $v(s, d) = I\{d = \delta(s)\}$ is the unique solution to Bellman's equation (4.12), so that δ is the optimal decision rule implied by (u, p, β).

If we are unwilling to place any restrictions on (u, p, β), then lemma 1 shows that the resulting MDP model is non-parametrically unidentified and lemma 2 shows that it has no testable implications, in the sense that we can 'rig' an MDP model to 'rationalise' any decision rule δ. The identification problem was clearly foreseen by Sargent in his 1978 *JPE* article:

> The empirical results are moderately comforting to the view that the employment-real-wage observations lie along a demand schedule for employment. It is important to emphasize that this view has content (i.e. imposes overidentifying restrictions) because I have *a priori* imposed restrictions on the orders of the adjustment-cost processes and on the Markov processes governing disturbances. At a general level without such restrictions, it is doubtful whether the equilibrium view has content. (p. 1042)

Rather than end this survey right here, I suggest two ways around the problem. First, Bellman's principle does lead to empirically testable implications in the case of *laboratory experiments* where we have at least partial control over an agent's preferences or beliefs. A famous example of such an experiment is the *Allais paradox* which usually succeeds in rejecting the hypothesis that subjects are expected utility maximisers.[21] Second, it is clear that, from an economic standpoint, many of the utility functions $u + f - \beta Ef$ will be completely unreasonable, as is the utility function $u(s, d) = I\{d = \delta(s)\}$. By imposing additional *identifying restrictions* on (u, p, β) we can usually succeed in identifying a unique set of primitives that are consistent with the data and are plausible on a priori grounds. At the present time, almost all identifying restrictions are imposed by assuming that (u, p, β) belongs to a parametric family (i.e., u is quadratic, Cobb–Douglas, CES, etc.). The use of laboratory experiments as an additional source of identifying restrictions for structural models is still in its infancy.

Heckman (1994) has begun pioneering work on integration of experimental results and a priori identifying restrictions in structural estimation problems. However it seems unlikely that even extensive experimentation will be sufficient by itself to identify the structure of agents' decision-making processes.[22]

The point of this section is to show that there are strict limits on what we can learn from the data alone: the empirical content of any MDP theory is entirely a result of a priori identifying restrictions on (u, p, β). Although the results point out the futility of non-parametric estimation of (u, d, β), I definitely do not view them as suggesting that structural estimation and testing of parametric models is a futile exercise, and, given the huge and rapidly growing empirical literature on structural estimation, it is clear that most economists do not view it as a futile exercise either. The proofs of the lemmas do indicate that in order to obtain testable implications, we can get by with weaker identifying restrictions on p than on u and β. To see this, suppose we invoke the hypothesis of *rational expectations*: i.e., agents' subjective beliefs about the evolution of the state variables coincide with the objectively measurable population probability measure. This identifying restriction allows us to do structural estimation by semi-parametric methods: i.e., we can use non-parametric methods to consistently estimate $p(s_{t+1}|s_t, d_t)$ using observed realisations of the controlled process $\{s_t, d_t\}$, and parametric methods to estimate (u, β). However looking at proofs of lemmas 1 and 2 we can see that it's not possible to go non-parametric on (u, β) since the identification problem persists even if we assume that p is known a priori. Thus we must impose strong identifying restrictions on u and β: the usual way this is done is to assume that u and β are smooth functions of a vector of unknown parameters θ. As will be evident from section 6 this is sufficient to produce strong, empirically testable restrictions on the controlled process $\{s_t, d_t\}$.[23]

5   INCORPORATING 'ERROR TERMS' INTO DDP MODELS

Before we can start thinking about structural estimation, we need to give special consideration to the nature of error terms entering the DDP model. The need for some kind of error term is a consequence of Blackwell's Theorem, which shows that the optimal decision rule $d = \delta^*(s)$ is a deterministic function of the agent's state s. This implies that, if we were able to observe all components of s, then a correctly specified DDP model would be able to perfectly predict agents' behaviour. Since no theory is realistically capable of perfectly predicting the behaviour of human decision makers, there are basically four ways to reconcile discrepancies between the predictions of the DDP model and observed behaviour: (1) optimisation errors, (2) measurement errors, (3) approximation errors and (4) unobserved state variables.[24]

An optimisation error causes an agent who 'intends' to behave according to the optimal decision rule δ^* to take an actual decision d given by

$$d = \delta^*(s) + \eta, \tag{4.18}$$

where η is interpreted as an error that prevents the agent from correctly calculating or implementing the optimal action $\delta^*(s)$. This interpretation of discrepancies between d and $\delta^*(s)$ seems logically inconsistent: if the agent knew that there were random factors that lead to *ex post* discrepancies between intended and realised decisions, he would reoptimise taking these uncertainties into account. The resulting decision rule will generally be different from the optimal decision rule δ^* which assumes that intended and realised decisions coincide. On the other hand, if η is simply interpreted as reflecting irrational or non-maximising behaviour, it is not clear why this behaviour should take the peculiar form of random deviations from an optimal decision rule δ^*. Given these logical difficulties, I will ignore optimisation errors as a way of explaining discrepancies between d and $\delta^*(s)$.

Measurement errors, due to response or coding errors, must surely be acknowledged in most empirical studies. Measurement errors are usually much more likely to occur in continuous components of s than in the discrete values of d, although significant errors can occur in the latter as a result of classification error (e.g., defining workers as choosing to work full time versus part time based on noisy measurements of total hours of work). From an econometric standpoint measurement errors in s create more serious difficulties since δ^* is typically a non-linear function of s. Unfortunately, the problem of non-linear errors in variables has not yet been satisfactorily resolved in the econometrics literature. In certain cases (Wolpin (1987) and Christensen and Kiefer (1992)) one can account for measurement error in a statistically and computationally tractable manner, although at the present time this approach seems to be highly problem specific. See Rust (1993, 1994) for a more complete discussion and further examples.

Approximation errors amount to an up-front admission that any DDP model is inherently misspecified: by their very nature these models are simplified, abstract representations of human behaviour so we would never expect their predictions to be 100 per cent correct. Thus, we define an approximation error as the difference between the observed value of d and the model's prediction $\delta^*(s)$ with no auxiliary statistical assumptions about its distribution. Under this interpretation the econometric problem is to find a specification $\{\beta, u, p\}$ that minimises some metric of the approximation error such as mean-squared prediction error. While this approach seems quite natural, Rust (1994) shows that it leads to a 'degenerate' econometric model. The approximation error approach also suffers from ambiguity about the appropriate metric for determining whether a given model does or does not provide a good approximation to observed behaviour. As a result, the approximation error interpretation is typically associated with quasi-statistical 'calibration' approaches to estimating underlying structural parameters such as Kydland and Prescott (1982) and Hartley (1985).

The final approach, unobserved state variables, is the predominant interpretation of error terms in this literature is treated in detail in the next section.

6 STRUCTURAL ESTIMATION OF DDPs

Structural estimation of DDPs requires fundamentally different estimation methods from the Euler equation methods used to estimate continuous and mixed continuous discrete decision processes (CDPs and MCDPs, the topic of Pakes' chapter) since one cannot differentiate with respect to the control variable d to derive first-order necessary conditions characterising the optimal decision rule δ^*. Instead $\delta^*(s)$ is defined by a finite number of inequality conditions

$$d \in \delta^*(s) \Leftrightarrow \{\forall d' \in D(s) | u(s, d) + \beta \int V^*(s') p(ds' | s, d) \geq \\ u(s, d') + \beta \int V^*(s') p(ds' | s, d')\} \tag{4.19}$$

Econometric methods for DDPs borrow heavily from methods developed in the literature on estimation of static discrete-choice models.[25] The primary difference between estimation of static versus dynamic models of discrete choice is that agents' choices are governed by the relative magnitude of the value function V rather than the single-period utility function u.

To simplify the subsequent analysis, we assume that agents' choice sets are uniformly bounded: $|D(s)| \leq M < \infty$, for all $s \in S$.[26] We now review the theory of parametric estimation of DDPs, where the functional forms of the primitives $\{\beta, u, p\}$ are assumed to be specified up to an unknown vector $\theta \in R^N$. Under the maintained hypothesis that $\{s_t, d_t\}$ is a realisation of a controlled stochastic process, the econometric problem is to infer the unknown 'true' parameters θ^* of the primitives $\{\beta, u, p\}$ which generate it. The difficulty of estimating DDP models as opposed to static discrete-choice models is that, even if the functional form of the utility function u is specified a priori, the functional form of the value function V^* is generally unknown, although it can be computed for any value of θ. This suggests the possibility of using some sort of 'nested numerical solution of algorithm' that computes the estimate $\hat{\theta}$ and corresponding decision rule δ_t^* that best fits the data by repeatedly solving the dynamic programming problem for each trial value of the parameter vector θ.

Following the discussion of section 5, error terms entering the DDP model are interpreted as unobserved state variables. Without loss of generality, we can partition the state vector s into two components $s = (x, \epsilon)$ where x is a state variable observed by both the agent and econometrician and ϵ is observed only by the agent. The existence of unobserved state variables is quite plausible: it is unlikely that any survey could completely record all information that is relevant to the agent's decision-making process. It also provides a natural way to rationalise discrepancies between observed behaviour and the predictions of the DDP model: even though the optimal decision rule $d = \delta^*(x, \epsilon)$ is a deterministic function from the standpoint of the agent, it is random from the standpoint of the econometrician. If the specification of unobservables is sufficiently rich any observed (x, d) combination can be explained as the result of an optimal decision by an agent whose unobserved ϵ is a member of the set $\{\epsilon | d = \delta^*(x, \epsilon)\}$. Since ϵ enters the decision rule δ^* in a non-separable, non-additive fashion, it is infeasible to estimate θ by non-linear least squares. The method of choice for estimating θ is maximum likelihood using the *conditional choice probability*

$$P(d|x) = \int I\{d = \delta^*(x, \epsilon)\}q(d\epsilon|x), \qquad (4.20)$$

where $q(d\epsilon|x)$ is the conditional distribution of ϵ given x (to be defined). Even though δ^* is a step function, integration over ϵ in (4.20) leads to a conditional choice probability that is a smooth function of θ provided that the primitives $\{\beta, u, p\}$ are smooth functions of θ and the DDP problem satisfies certain general properties given in assumptions AS and CI below. These assumptions guarantee that the conditional choice probability has full support

$$d \in D(x) \Leftrightarrow P(d|x) > 0, \qquad (4.21)$$

which is equivalent to saying that the set $\{\epsilon | d = \delta^*(x, \epsilon)\}$ has positive probability under $q(d\epsilon|x)$. We say that a specification for unobservables is *saturated* if (4.21) holds for all possible values of θ. The problem with an unsaturated specification is the possibility that the DDP model will be contradicted in a sufficiently large data set: i.e., one may encounter observations (x_t^a, d_t^a) which cannot be rationalised by any value of ϵ or θ. This leads to practical difficulties in maximum-likelihood estimation, causing the log-likelihood function to blow-up when it encounters a zero probability observation. Although one might eliminate such observations

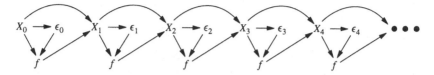

Figure 4.1 Pattern of dependence in a controlled Markov process

to achieve convergence, the impact on the asymptotic properties of the estimator is unclear. In addition, an unsaturated specification may yield a likelihood function whose support depends on θ or which may be a non-smooth function of θ. Little is known about the general asymptotic properties of these non-standard maximum-likelihood estimators.[27]

Borrowing from the literature on static discrete-choice models (McFadden (1981)) we introduce two assumptions which are sufficient to generate a saturated specification for unobservables in a DDP model:

> (AS): *The choice sets depend only on the observed state variable x:* $D(s) = D(x)$. *The unobserved state variable ϵ is a vector with at least as many components as the number of elements in $D(x)$.*[28] *The utility function has the additively separable decomposition*
>
> $$u(s,d) = u(x,d) + \epsilon(d), \qquad (4.22)$$
>
> *where $\epsilon(d)$ is the dth component of the vector ϵ.*
> (CI): *The transition density for the controlled Markov process $\{x_t, \epsilon_t\}$ factors as*
>
> $$p(dx_{t+1}, d\epsilon_{t+1} | x_t, \epsilon_t, d_t) = q(d\epsilon_{t+1} | x_{t+1}) \pi(dx_{t+1} | x_t, d_t), \quad (4.23)$$
>
> *where the marginal density of $q(d\epsilon | x)$ of the first $|D(x)|$ components of ϵ has support equal to $R^{|D(x)|}$ and finite first moments.*

CI is a conditional independence assumption which limits the pattern of dependence in the $\{x_t, \epsilon_t\}$ process in two ways. First, x_{t+1} is a sufficient statistic for ϵ_{t+1} implying that any serial dependence between ϵ_t and ϵ_{t+1} is transmitted entirely through the observed state x_{t+1}.[29] Second, the probability density for x_{t+1} depends only on x_t and not on ϵ_t. Intuitively, CI implies that the $\{\epsilon_t\}$ process is essentially a noise process superimposed on the main dynamics which are embodied by the transition probability $\pi(dx' | x, d)$ (see figure 4.1).

Under assumption AS and CI Bellman's equation has the following form

$$V(x, \epsilon) = \max_{d \in D(x)} [v(x, d) + \epsilon(d)], \qquad (4.24)$$

where

$$v(x, d) = u(x, d) + \beta \int V(y, \epsilon) q(d\epsilon | y) \pi(dy | x, d).   \tag{4.25}$$

Equation (4.24) is the key to subsequent results: it shows that the DDP problem has the same basic structure as a static discrete choice problem except that the value function v replaces the single-period utility function u as an argument of the conditional choice probability. In particular, AS-CI yields a saturated specification for unobservables: (4.24) implies that the set $\{\epsilon | d = \delta^*(x, \epsilon)\}$ is a non-empty intersection of half-spaces in $R^{|D(x)|}$, and since ϵ is continuously distributed with unbounded support, it follows that regardless of the values of $\{v(x, d)\}$ the choice probability $P(d|x)$ is positive for each $d \in D(x)$.

In order to formally define the class of DDPs, we need to embed the unobserved state variables ϵ (whose 'relevant' dimensions may vary with the number of elements in $D(x)$) in a common space E. Without loss of generality, we can identify each choice set $D(x)$ as a set of integers, $D(x) = \{1, \ldots, |D(x)|\}$, and let the decision space D be the set $D = \{1, \ldots, \sup_{x \in X} |D(x)|\}$. Then we define $E = R^{|D|}$, and whenever $|D(x)| < |D|$ the specification of $q(d\epsilon | x)$ for the remaining $|D| - |D(x)|$ 'irrelevant' components of ϵ is essentially arbitrary.

Definition 5 A Discrete Process *(DDP) is a Markov Decision Process satisfying the following restrictions:*

> The decision space $D = \{1, \ldots, \sup_{s \in S} |D(s)|\}$, where $\sup_{s \in S} |D(s)| < \infty$.
> The state space S is the product space $S = X \times E$, where X is a Borel subset of R^J and $E = R^{|D|}$.
> For each $s \in S$ and $x \in X$ we have $D(s) = D(x) \subset D$.
> The utility function $u(s, d)$ satisfies assumption AS.
> The transition probability $p(ds_{t+1} | s_t, d_t)$ satisfies assumption CI.
> The component $q(d\epsilon | x)$ of the transition probability $p(ds | s, d)$ is a non-zero density over $R^{|D|}$ with finite absolute first moments.

The conditional choice probability $P(d|x)$ is defined in terms of a function McFadden (1981) has called the *Social Surplus*

$$G(\{u(x, d), d \in D(x)\} | x) = \int_{R^{|D|}} \max_{d \in D(x)} [u(x, d) + E|d] q(d\epsilon | x).   \tag{4.26}$$

If we think of a population of consumers defined by ϵ, then $G(\{u(x, d), d \in D(x)\} | x)$ is simply the expected indirect utility of choosing alternatives

$d \in D(x)$. G has an important property that can be thought of as a discrete analogue of Roy's identity.

Theorem 1 If $q(d\epsilon|x)$ has finite first moments, then the Social Surplus (4.26) exists, and has the following properties:

1   *G is a convex function of $\{u(x,d), d \in D(x)\}$.*
2   *G satisfies the additivity property*

$$G(\{u(x,d)+a, d \in D(x)\}|x) = a + G(\{u(x,d), d \in D(x)\}|x).$$
(4.27)

3   *The partial derivative of G with respect to $u(x,d)$ equals the conditional choice probability*

$$\frac{\partial G(\{u(x,d), d \in D(x)\}|x)}{\partial u(x,d)} = P(d|x).$$
(4.28)

Looking at the definition of G in (4.26), it is evident that the proof of theorem 1 is simply an exercise in interchanging integration and differentiation: taking the partial derivative operator inside the integral sign we obtain[30]

$$\frac{\partial G(\{u(x,d), d \in D(x)\}|x)}{\partial u(x,d)} = \int \left\{ \frac{\partial[\max_{d \in D(y)}[u(x,d) + \epsilon(d)]]}{\partial u(x,d)} \right\} q(d\epsilon|x)$$

$$= \int I\{d = \underset{d' \in D(x)}{\operatorname{argmax}}[u(x,d') + \epsilon(d')]\} q(d\epsilon|x)$$

$$= P(d|x).$$
(4.29)

Note that the additivity property (4.27) implies that the conditional choice probabilities sum to 1, so $P(\cdot|x)$ is a well-defined probability distribution over $D(x)$.

The fact that the unobserved state variables ϵ have unbounded support implies that the objective function in the DDP problem is unbounded. Rust (1988b) provides extra assumptions to guarantee the existence of a solution, using the results of Bhattacharya and Majumdar (1989) to guarantee the existence and optimality of the decision rule implicitly defined by (4.24) and (4.25).

Theorem 2 If $\{s_t, d_t\}$ is a DDP satisfying AS and CI and the additional regularity conditions in Rust (1988b) then the optimal decision rule δ^* is given by

$$\delta^*(x, \epsilon) = \underset{d \in D(x)}{\operatorname{argmax}}[v(x,d) + \epsilon(d)],$$
(4.30)

where v is the unique fixed point to the contraction mapping $\Psi: B \to B$ defined by

$$\Psi(v)(x, d) = u(x, d) + \beta \int G(\{v(y, d'), d' \in D(y)\} | y) \pi(dy | x, d). \quad (4.31)$$

Theorem 3 If $\{s_t, d_t\}$ is a DDP satisfying AS and CI and the additional regularity conditions in Rust (1988b), then the controlled process $\{x_t, \epsilon_t\}$ is Markovian with transition probability

$$\Pr\{x_{t+1}, d_{t+1} | x_t, d_t\} = P(d_{t+1} | x_{t+1}) \pi(x_{t+1} | x_t, d_t), \quad (4.32)$$

where the conditional choice probability $P(d|x)$ is given by

$$P(d|x) = \frac{\partial G(\{v(x, d), d \in D(x)\} | x)}{\partial v(x, d)} \quad (4.33)$$

and G is the social surplus function defined in (4.26) and v is the unique fixed point to the contraction mapping Ψ defined in (4.31).

The proof of theorems 2 and 3 is straightforward: under assumption AS-CI the value function is the unique solution to Bellman's equation given in (4.24) and (4.25). Substituting the formula for V given in (4.24) into the formula for v given in (4.25) we obtain

$$v(x, d) = u(x, d) + \beta \iint \max_{d' \in D(y)} [v(y, d') + \epsilon(d')] q(d\epsilon | y) \pi(dy | x, d)$$
$$= u(x, d) + \beta \int G(\{v(y, d'), d' \in D(y)\} | y) \pi(dy | x, d). \quad (4.34)$$

The latter formula is the fixed point condition (4.31). It's a simple exercise to verify that Ψ is a contraction mapping, guaranteeing the existence and uniqueness of the function v. The fact that the controlled process $\{x_t, d_t\}$ is Markovian is a direct result of the CI assumption: the observed state x_{t+1} is a 'sufficient statistic' for the agent's choice d_{t+1}. Without the CI assumption lagged state and control variables would be useful for predicting the agent's choice at time $t+1$ and $\{x_t, d_t\}$ will no longer be Markovian. As we will see, this observation provides the basis for a specification test of CI.

For specific functional forms for q we obtain concrete formulas for the conditional choice probability $P(d|x)$, the Social Surplus function G, and the contraction mapping Ψ. For example if $q(\epsilon|x)$ is a multivariate extreme value distribution we have[31]

$$q(\epsilon|x) = \prod_{d \in D(x)} \exp\{-\epsilon(d) + \gamma\} \exp\{-\exp\{-\epsilon(d) + \gamma\}\}, \quad \gamma = 0.577 \quad (4.35)$$

then $P(d|x)$ is given by the well-known *multinomial logit* formula

$$P(d|x) = \frac{\exp\{v(x, d)\}}{\sum_{d' \in D(x)} \exp\{v(x, d')\}}, \quad (4.36)$$

where v is the fixed point to the contraction mapping Ψ

$$\Psi(v)(x,d) = u(x,d) + \beta \int \log[\sum_{d' \in D(y)} \exp\{v(y,d')\}] \pi(dy|x,d). \qquad (4.37)$$

The extreme-value specification is especially attractive for empirical applications since the closed-form expression for P and G avoid the need for multi-dimensional numerical integrations required for other distributions.[32] One of the characteristics of the extreme value specification is the property of *independence from irrelevant alternatives* (IIA). In static models where the utility function takes the form $u(x,d) = u(x(d))$, where $x(d)$ is interpreted as the attributes of alternative d, the IIA property can be stated as follows

$$\log\left\{\frac{P(d|x)}{P(1|x)}\right\} = u(x(d)) - u(x(1)), \qquad (4.38)$$

i.e., the odds of choosing alternative d over alternative 1 depend only on the attributes of those two alternatives. The IIA property has a number of undesirable implications such as the 'red bus/blue bus' problem denoted by Debreu (1960). Note, however, that in DDP models the IIA property no longer holds: the log-odds of choosing d over 1 equals the difference in the value functions $v(x,d) - v(x,1)$, but from the definition of $v(x,d)$ in (4.37) we see that it generally depends on the attributes of all of the other alternatives even when the single-period utility function $u(x,d)$ depends only on the attributes of the chosen alternative, say, $u(x(d))$. Thus, in dynamic models we benefit from the computational simplifications of the extreme value specification but avoid the IIA problem of static logit models.

The results in theorems 2 and 3 appear to apply only to infinite-horizon stationary DDP problems, but they actually include finite-horizon, non-stationary DDP problems as a special case. To see this, let the time index t be an additional component of x_t, and assume that the process enters an absorbing state with $u(x_t, t, d_t) = 0$ for $t > T$. Then theorems 2 and 3 continue to hold, with the exception that δ^*, P and v all depend on t. The value functions $v_t, t = 1, \ldots, T$ are given by the backward recursion formulas analogous to the finite-horizon MDP models described in section 3

$$v_T(x,d) = u_T(x,d)$$
$$v_t(x,d) = u_t(x,d) + \beta \int G(\{v_{t+1}(y,d'), d' \in D(y)\}|y) \pi(dy|x,d). \qquad (4.39)$$

Substituting these value functions into (4.33), we obtain choice probabilities P_t that depend on time. It is easy to see that the process $\{x_t, d_t\}$ is still Markovian, but the transition probability (4.32) is non-stationary.

Given panel data $\{x_t^a, d_t^a\}$ on observed states and decisions of a collection of individuals, $t = 1, \ldots, T_a$, $a = 1, \ldots, A$, the full information maximum-likelihood estimator $\hat{\theta}^f$ is defined by

$$\hat{\theta}^f = \underset{\theta \in R^N}{\text{argmax}}\ L^f(\{x_t^a, d_t^a\}, \theta) \equiv \prod_{a=1}^{A} \prod_{t=1}^{T_a} P(d_t^a | x_t^a, \theta) \pi(x_t^a | x_{t-1}^a, d_{t-1}^a, \theta).$$

$$(4.40)$$

Maximum-likelihood estimation is complicated by the fact that even in cases where the conditional choice probability has a closed-form solution in terms of the value functions v_θ (such as the extreme value case (4.35)), except in very rare cases these latter functions do not have a priori known functional form: they are only implicitly defined by the fixed-point condition (4.34). Theorems 2 and 3 suggest that a *nested fixed-point algorithm* can be used to estimate θ: an 'inner' contraction fixed-point algorithm computes v_θ for each trial value of θ, and an 'outer' hill-climbing algorithm searches for the value of θ that maximises L^f.

In practice, θ can be estimated by a simpler two-stage procedure which yields consistent, asymptotically normal but inefficient estimates of θ^*, and a three-stage procedure which is asymptotically equivalent to full-information maximum likelihood. These methods are based on factoring (4.40) into partial likelihoods and estimating parameters sequentially. Suppose we partition θ into two components (θ_1, θ_2), where θ_1 is a subvector of parameters that appear only in π and θ_2 is a subvector of parameters that appear only in $\{\beta, u, q\}$. In the first stage we estimate θ_1 using the partial-likelihood estimator $\hat{\theta}_1^p$

$$\hat{\theta}_1^p = \underset{\theta_1 \in R^{N_1}}{\text{argmax}}\ L_1^p(\{x_t^a, d_t^a\}, \theta_1) \equiv \prod_{a=1}^{A} \prod_{t=0}^{T_a} \pi(dx_t^a | x_{t-1}^a, d_{t-1}^a, \theta_1). \qquad (4.41)$$

Notice that maximisation of this likelihood does not require nested numerical solution of the DDP problem. In the second stage we estimate the remaining parameters θ_2 using the partial-likelihood estimator $\hat{\theta}_2^p$ defined by[33]

$$\hat{\theta}_2^p = \underset{\theta_2 \in R^{N_2}}{\text{argmax}}\ L_2^p(\{x_t^a, d_t^a\}, \hat{\theta}_1^p, \theta_2) \equiv \prod_{a=1}^{A} \prod_{t=0}^{T_a} P(d_t^a | x_t^a, \hat{\theta}_1^p, \theta_2). \qquad (4.42)$$

The second stage treats the consistent first stage estimates of $\pi\ (x_{t+1} | x_t, d_t, \hat{\theta}_1^p)$ as the 'truth', reducing the problem to estimating the remaining parameters θ_2 of $\{\beta, u, q\}$. It is well known that for any optimisation method the number of likelihood function evaluations needed to find a maximum increases rapidly (typically exponentially) with the number of parameters being estimated. Since the second stage estimation requires a nested fixed-point algorithm to solve the DDP problem at each likelihood function evaluation, any reduction in the number of parameters being estimated can lead to substantial computational savings. Note that due to the presence of estimation error in the first-stage estimate of $\hat{\theta}_1^p$, the covariance matrix formed by inverting the information matrix for the partial-likelihood function (4.42) will be inconsistent. Although there is a standard correction formula which yields a consistent estimate of the covariance matrix (Amemiya (1976), Rust (1994)), in practice it is just as simple to use the consistent estimates $\hat{\theta}^p = (\hat{\theta}_1^p, \hat{\theta}_2^p)$ from stages 1 and 2 as starting values for one or more 'Newton steps' on the full-likelihood function (4.40) yielding a three-stage maximum-likelihood estimator.

Establishing the asymptotic properties of the maximum-likelihood estimator requires one to verify that the likelihood function is a smooth function of the parameter vector θ. Assumptions (AS) and (CI) are sufficient to establish that the conditional choice probability is a smooth function of the value functions v_θ, so the problem reduces to establishing sufficient conditions under which v_θ is a smooth function of θ. This turns out to be a simple consequence of the Implicit Function Theorem, see Rust (1988b).

Note that the results in this section have relied heavily on the AS and CI assumptions. The main reason for imposition of these assumptions is to obtain a tractable econometric model: if the model has serially correlated unobservables ϵ, lagged values of these unobservables will necessarily enter as additional arguments (state variables) of the value function. Since ϵ is typically treated as a continuously distributed vector to obtain a non-degenerate econometric model, it is clear that the addition of serially correlated unobservables will significantly increase the computational burden of solving the DDP model. For example if the observed state variables can assume $|X|$ values and the choice variable can assume, say, four values, the total fixed-point problem has $4|X|$ dimensions under the CI assumption. With a four-dimensional serially correlated unobservable $\{\epsilon\}$ following a first-order Markov process, even a relatively coarse discretisation using ten cells for each component of ϵ magnifies the dimension of the problem to $10,000|X|$, which is generally infeasible using current technology.

The CI assumption is less problematic in models that are more comprehensive in their inclusion of observed state variables x, since the observables can be chosen to capture most of the serially correlated dynamics of the choice process, making it less implausible that the remaining unobserved state variables are conditionally independent. In any event, it is an easy matter to design a relatively powerful 'Holy Trinity' specification test of the CI assumption: simply add some function f of the previous period control variables $\{d_{t-1}, d_{t-2}, \ldots\}$ to the current-period value function: $v_\theta(x_t, d_t) + \alpha f(d_{t-1}, d_{t-2}, \ldots)$. Under the null hypothesis that CI is valid, the decision taken in period $t-1$ will have no effect on the decision made in period t once we condition on x_t since $\{v_\theta(x_t, d), d \in D(x_t)\}$ constitutes a set of 'sufficient statistics' for the agent's decision in period t. Thus, $a = 0$ under the null hypothesis that CI holds. However, under the alternative hypothesis that CI doesn't hold, ϵ_t and $\{\epsilon_{t-1}, \epsilon_{t-2}, \ldots\}$ will be correlated even conditional on x_t, so that $\{d_{t-1}, d_{t-2}, \ldots\}$ will generally be useful for predicting the agent's choice d_t. Thus, $a \neq 0$ under alternative hypothesis. The Wald, Likelihood Ratio or LM statistics can be used to test the hypothesis that $a = 0$. For example, the Wald statistic is simply $A\hat{a}^2/\hat{\sigma}^2(a)$, where $\hat{\sigma}^2(\hat{a})$ is the asymptotic variance of $\hat{a}$, and A denotes sample size (equal to the number of agents).

7   ESTIMATION/SOLUTION ALGORITHMS FOR DDP MODELS

This section provides a brief review of some of the methods and considerations involved in estimating DDP models. For a more comprehensive discussion of alternative solution and estimation methods, see Amman and Rust (1993).

To date most of the estimation methods for DDP models involve some form of nested numerical solution algorithm. These algorithms consist of an 'outer' non-linear optimisation algorithm that searches for the parameter value $\hat{\theta}$ that optimises the statistical objective function, and an 'inner' DP algorithm that solves the DDP model for each trial value of θ. An example is the 'nested fixed point' (NFXP) algorithm developed by Rust (1988b). In this case the outer algorithm maximises the likelihood function in θ and the inner algorithm computes the contraction fixed point. Most of the computational burden of such an algorithm is due to the need to repeatedly re-solve the DP problem for alternative values of θ. Thus, the feasibility of these algorithms depends critically on having a highly efficient inner algorithm to solve the DP problem. For practical purposes, the inner algorithm should be able to solve the DP problem in less than, say, one or two minutes of CPU time. The reason is that the likelihood for a DDP model is typically a highly non-linear function of θ. Depending on the dimensionality of θ, the outer optimisation algorithm can easily require several hundred function evaluations before converging on the estimate $\hat{\theta}$. If it takes much more than a minute to solve the DDP problem, the total time required to estimate a single specification becomes unacceptably long.

It is also important to use an efficient outer optimisation algorithm to find θ in the minimum number of function evaluations. Smoothness of the statistical objective function in θ is a key to successful estimation of DDP models since it permits use of more efficient gradient-based optimisation algorithms. Non-smooth objective functions associated 'frequency simulators' of the type proposed by McFadden (1989) and Pakes and Pollard

(1989) can be very difficult to optimise, requiring more robust but less efficient optimisation methods such as grid search, random search, or other derivative-free approaches such as the non-linear simplex algorithm of Nelder and Mead (1964). These methods can require an unacceptably large number of function evaluations to find the optimum, especially when the dimension of θ gets large. However, even when the objective function is smooth, many of the advantages of gradient optimisation algorithms are lost if it is difficult to compute the derivatives of the objective function with respect to θ. The usual approach of relying on numerical derivatives is extremely costly since evaluation of each partial derivative requires a separate function evaluation and hence an additional solution of the DP problem. The advantage of algorithms such as NFXP is that derivatives of the objective function are recovered as a by-product of the DP solution at small marginal cost.

Even if the objective function is smooth, it can be quite challenging to coax a gradient optimisation algorithm to convergence. A typical problem occurs when certain combinations of parameters are precisely identified and others are poorly identified, producing 'flats' or 'ridges' in the parameter space and consequent numerical problems in finding a search direction or choosing a step size. These problems can cause gradient optimisation procedures to wander or 'fall off the cliff', or break down entirely due to problems of numerical singularity or overflow. One way to avoid these problems is to use a two-stage optimisation procedure, starting with a robust but less efficient non-gradient method to get into a domain of attraction of a local optimum, and then switch over to a Newton-like gradient method to quickly converge to θ. An alternative approach is to adopt a homotopy path-following algorithm treating the discount factor β as the homotopy parameter. Let $\hat{\theta}(\beta)$ denote the optimised value of the other parameters conditional on a fixed value for β. The basic idea of the path following algorithm is to optimise a 'profile likelihood' in β starting with $\beta = 0$, increasing β in small steps towards $\beta = 1$. Since $\beta = 0$ corresponds to a static discrete-choice problem, there is no need to call the inner DP algorithm, and finding a local optimum is typically much easier (for example in the logit case (4.36), the likelihood function is globally concave at $\beta = 0$ when u is linear in parameters). Using $\hat{\theta}(0)$ as a starting point, one computes the parameter estimates corresponding to a new β slightly larger than zero. The smoothness of the objective function in β guarantees that by choosing β sufficiently small, $\hat{\theta}(0)$ will be in a domain of attraction of $\hat{\theta}(\beta)$. One can continue increasing β this way until an overall optimum $\hat{\theta}(\hat{\beta})$ is achieved. Garcia and Zangwill (1981) describe automatic procedures for choosing the increments in β to ensure that one follows a path to the solution.

The most important single part of the estimation algorithm is the subroutine that solves the DP problem. Porteus (1980), Puterman (1990) and Amman and Rust (1995) survey alternative solution methods for the 'inner' fixed point or DP problem. Most of these methods are based on discretisation of the state variables, solving the DP problem by backward induction (in the finite-horizon case) or using a variant of Howard's 'policy iteration' algorithm (in the infinite-horizon case). Both of these methods can also be used to solve DP problems with unobserved state variables. For DDP problems the backward induction procedure (also known as the method of *successive approximations*) has the general form

$$v_k = \Psi(v_{k-1}) = \Psi^k(v_0),$$ (4.43)

where Ψ is the operator defined in (4.31). Successive approximations for general operators Ψ can be accelerated using the McQueen–Porteus error bounds described in Bertsekas (1987) and Amman and Rust (1995). The policy iteration algorithm (also known as the *Newton–Kantorovich* method) has the general form

$$v_{k+1} = v_k - [I - \Psi'(v_k)]^{-1}(I - \Psi)(v_k),$$ (4.44)

where I denotes the identity operator on B and $\Psi'(v)$ denotes the Gateaux Derivative of Ψ evaluated at the point $v \in B$.[34] It is straightforward to show that $\Psi'(v)$ has the integral representation

$$\Psi'_\theta(v_\theta)(h)(x, d) = \beta \int \sum_{d' \in D(y)} h(y, d') P(d'|y, \theta) \pi(dy|x, d).$$ (4.45)

Using the analogy of a geometric series expansion, one can show that the linear operator $[I - \Psi'(v)]^{-1}$ exists, is continuous and has a convergent series expansion provided that $|\Psi'(v)| \in (0, 1)$.[35] It is easy to see than when Ψ is a contraction mapping, we have $|\Psi'(v)| \leq \beta$.[36] Thus, the iterations defined in (4.44) are always well-defined. Kantorovich's Theorem (Kantorovich and Aikilov (1982), p. 532) guarantees that given a starting point v_0 in a domain of attraction of the fixed point v^* of Ψ, the Newton–Kantorovich iterations will converge to v^* at a *quadratic rate*.

In order to implement these procedures on a computer, we need to discretise the state space into a finite number of cells, $|X|$. If we further assume there are a fixed number $|D|$ of feasible choices in all states, then the work or complexity of solving a finite-horizon DDP problem by backward induction is proportional to $(T-1)(|X||D|)^2$ since computation of each conditional expectation in (4.9) or (4.31) amounts to multiplying an $|X||D| \times |X||D|$ matrix by an $|X||D| \times 1$ vector. In the infinite-horizon case, the policy interation or Newton–Kantorovich algorithms (4.44 require solution of a system of linear equations of dimension $|X||D|$, which requires

$O((|X||D|)^3)$ algebraic operations. Since the policy iteration algorithm typically converges in a very small number of iterations (typically on the order of five to ten iterations), the overall complexity of solving an infinite-horizon DDP problem is of order $O((|X||D|)^3)$. Current supercomputers can perform up to a billion multiplications and additions per second, so it is now feasible to solve finite-horizon DP problems where $|X||D|$ is fairly large, on the order of 5,000 to 10,000. However even though computational complexity is at most a third-order polynomial in $|X||D|$, $|X|$ itself grows exponentially with the number of dimensions (or components) of the state variable. This is the 'curse of dimensionality' that Bellman (1957) referred to. Beyond use of pure brute force, there are a number of ways to reduce the computational burden of finite-horizon DP problems.

One strategy is to use massive parallel processing technology (such as the Connection Machine with over 30,000 individual processing elements) to solve the large linear systems involved in policy iteration algorithm. Pan and Rief (1985) have shown that with $O(N^\omega)$ processors (where ω is the exponent for the best method for fast matrix multiplication, currently around 2.5) one can solve systems on N linear equations in $O(\log\log(N))$ time.

Another strategy used by Wolpin (1989) is to formulate finite-horizon DDP problems with longer time intervals the further one is from the current period. This not only reduces the number of time periods T, but can also be accompanied with a coarsening of cell sizes used for future state variables. The idea is that since future utilities are discounted, only 'major' changes in future states are significant for current decisions so it is unnecessary to have a detailed model that accounts for 'small' fluctuations in distant future states. This strategy works well when all members of the survey are in a relatively homogeneous age group. An example is Wolpin's model of life-cycle search behaviour where interest focusses on tracking month by month transitions of young workers, even though workers' calculations formally extend to the end of their life span. It seems sensible in this case to structure a DDP model with monthly time periods at the beginning of the life span, gradually increasing to one- and five-year intervals in the middle and the end of the worker's life span. A related approach is to posit a parametric form for a 'terminal' value function, solving a more detailed DP problem up to the terminal period, and using the terminal value function to circumvent the solution for periods thereafter (see also the description of the Miller and Hotz 'conditional choice probability approach' in section 8 below).

Another strategy is to solve the DP problem via approximate solution methods. One such method, promoted by Judd (1992) is to approximate the value function by a polynomial function v_a of the state variables, and choose the coefficients a of this polynomial approximation to get as close as possible to a fixed point of the Ψ operator (4.31) by minimising the residual $v_a - \Psi(v_a)$ with respect to an appropriate norm. Pakes (1994) describes this approach in more detail in the next chapter and Pakes and McGuire (1992) provide a computational implementation in the context of solving for the equilibrium of a multi-firm model of entry, exit, and investment decisions. Keane and Wolpin (1992) describe a slightly different strategy for finite-horizon problems. They use Monte Carlo integration to compute the expectation with respect to ϵ in equation (4.34) at a subset of points x in the state space X. Then they use interpolation methods to compute estimates of $v(x', d)$ at other points x' not contained in this subset. Their results show that such approximate solution methods can yield highly accurate solutions while significantly reducing the amount of computation relative to a 'full solution' approach.

A final strategy is to exploit the recursive structure of many economic problems, which implies that the operator (transition probability matrix) $\Psi'(v)$ will have a particular *sparsity pattern* that permits very rapid recursive solutions of the linear systems involved in the policy/Newton–Kantorovich iterations. For example the bus replacement problem of Rust (1987) or the retirement problem of Rust (1992a) have banded and block-recursive structures, respectively, that can be exploited to greatly speed up the solution of the DP problem. I will briefly describe the approach taken by Rust (1992a) to solve finite and infinite-horizon models of retirement behaviour that are orders of magnitude larger than the largest problems solvable using 'dense' methods. Rust's work focussed on a problem of optimal retirement where Ψ' is a direct product of 'subtransition' matrices corresponding to the different state variables. In particular, Ψ' can be represented as a direct product of three matrices shown in figure 4.2: (1) a circulant matrix for age, a, (2) a banded matrix for wealth, w, and (3) a dense matrix for the remaining state and control variables, d. By varying the order in which the component matrices enter the direct product, we generate various sparsity patterns for the matrix $\Psi'(v)$. Figures 4.3, 4.4 and 4.5 depict the sparsity patterns for the orderings (d, w, a), (w, a, d) and (a, d, w), respectively. None of these patterns is particularly desirable, for they all lead to fairly irregular and dispersed memory reference patterns. Standard sparse matrix algorithms run into problems of 'fill-in' and 'bank-conflicts' that prevent supercomputers from running at maximum efficiency with continuously full vector pipelines.[37]

Figure 4.6 illustrates the 'optimal' sparsity pattern (a, w, d). This arrangement produces the maximum amount of local density in the storage pattern for the matrix elements. Observe that, under this ordering, solving for $[I - \Psi'(v)]^{-1}$ only requires LU factorisation of the lower (a, a) block followed by recursive back-substitution to compute the solution for the

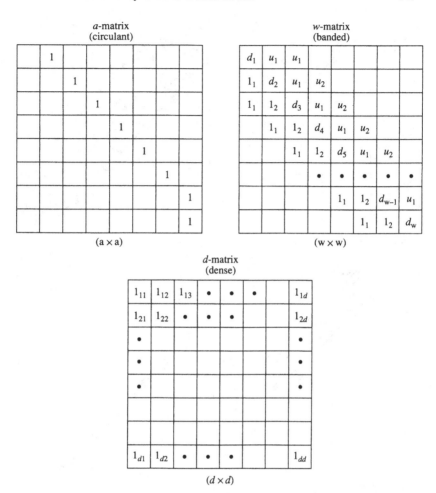

Figure 4.2 State transition matrices

other age groups $a - 1$ to 1. Since LU factorisation of an $N \times N$ matrix involves $O(N^3)$ operations, the time saved under the optimal ordering is proportional to a^3, which amounts to a speedup of 27,000 times when $a = 30$. Further speedups can be obtained by exploiting the block-banded structure of the non-zero blocks of $[I - \Psi'(v)]$. I designed a block elimination algorithm with LU factors the (a, a) block of $[I - \Psi'(v)]$ using a banded Crout decomposition, with elimination operations that are performed on the dense $d \times d$ blocks instead of individual matrix elements.[38] Thus, by using the optimal ordering of the state variables one can design a special

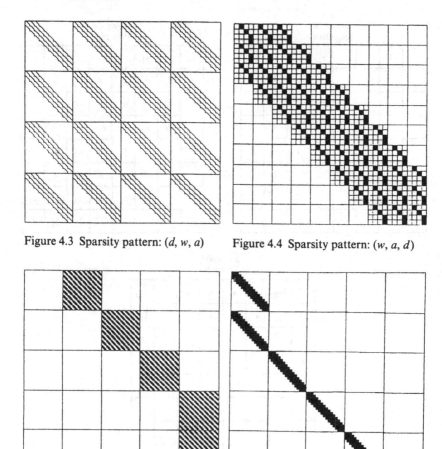

Figure 4.3 Sparsity pattern: (d, w, a) Figure 4.4 Sparsity pattern: (w, a, d)

Figure 4.5 Sparsity pattern: (a, d, w) Figure 4.6 Sparsity pattern: (a, w, d)

linear equation solver that fully exploits the sparsity structure of the $[I - \Psi'(v)]$ matrix without sacrificing the substantial speedups due to vector processing on supercomputers. The numerical results in table 4.1 show that this sort of strategy makes it feasible to solve very high-dimensional DP problems.

8   ALTERNATIVE ESTIMATION METHODS

This section presents alternative methods for estimating θ that completely avoid numerical solution of the DDP model. I review four different

Table 4.1. *Fixed-point computation times on the IBM PASC 3090.*

Item	Infinite horizon	Finite horizon
Age categories, a	30	25
Wealth income categories, w	100	100
Dense block size, d	18	108
Bandwidth $1 + u + 1$	10	100
Parameter dimension, $1 + \#\theta$	1	10
Fixed-point dimension $N = awd(1 + \#\theta)$	162,000	2,700,000
CPU time (seconds)*	84.3	36.5
Average rate (megaflops)**	54.3	56.9

approaches: Rust's (1988c) 'backward estimation' method, Manski's (1990) 'path utility' approach, Hotz and Miller's (1991) 'conditional choice probability' approach, and the 'simulated value function' estimation method proposed by Hotz, Miller, Sanders and Smith (1992). All of these methods incorporate unobserved state variables that satisfy the AS-CI assumption of section 6.

The idea behind the backward estimation method is that, under the conditional independence assumption, the choice probabilities of the DDP model have exactly the same form as static discrete-choice probabilities, except that the value function $v(x, d)$ replaces the single-period utility function $u(x, d)$. Recognising that we typically do not have very good prior knowledge of the appropriate functional forms for either v or u, the backward estimation method abandons the pretence of starting with an 'a priori' specification for u and instead conducts a specification search over the value functions v directly, using the estimated v functions to 'back out' estimates of the single-period utility functions u from the fixed-point condition (4.31):

$$\hat{u}(x, d) = \hat{v}(x, d) - \beta \int G(\{\hat{v}(x', d'), d' \in D(x')\} | x') \pi(dx' | x, d). \quad (4.46)$$

Notice that since the functional form of v is specified a priori, there is no need for repeated nested numerical solutions of the DP problem used in 'forward' estimation methods: standard estimation methods for static discrete-choice models can be used. The utility function can be recovered by a single evaluation of the mapping (4.46), and since this takes the form of an integral operator, one can achieve further computational simplifications by using Monte Carlo integration methods instead of direct numerical integration. Using the simulation estimators of McFadden (1989) and Pakes and Pollard (1989), we can also estimate v for more general distributions for unobservables q than the i.i.d. extreme value specification (4.35). In an empirical application comparing the backward and forward approaches using the bus replacement model Rust (1988c) shows that both methods generate basically similar estimates of u and v, and that variations in the estimates are not due so much to use of forward or backward methods *per se*, as they are to variations in the specifications of u and v.

Manski's (1993) 'path utility' approach encompasses a more general class of problems than the stationary time separable MDPs outlined in section 3. The path utility approach differs from the nested solution approach by using observations on the future states and decisions of other agents ('future paths') to estimate $v(s,d)$ rather than calculating it directly. Thus, if we have sufficient data on the future paths $\{s_t^a, d_t^a\}$ for a 'reference group' of agents, then we can form a semi-parametric estimate of $\hat{v}_\theta(s,d)$ by simply evaluating the summation

$$\hat{v}_\theta(s,d) = \frac{1}{A} \sum_{a=1}^{A} \sum_{t=1}^{T_a} \beta^t u_\theta(s_t^a, d_t^a), \tag{4.47}$$

where $s_1^a = s, d_1^a = d, a = 1, \ldots, A$. Formula (4.47) yields a consistent estimate of an agent's value function provided the following conditions hold: (1) the number of periods T_a over which agents in the reference group are observed must be as long as the decision-making horizon,[39] (2) agents are homogeneous: i.e., the reference group has the same primitives $\{u, p, \beta\}$ as the agent in question. However if agents have identical primitives, and the econometrician is assumed to observe the entire state vector s_t, we run into the logical difficulty discussed in section 5: Blackwell's Theorem implies that agents will be behaving according to the deterministic optimal decision rule $d = \delta^*(s)$ which implies that we will never observe any of the agents choosing a non-optimal action, $d' \neq \delta^*(s)$. Thus, unless the model contains unobserved state variables, it will be impossible to estimate $v_\theta(s,d)$ for all $d \in D(s)$, which is needed to calculate the decision rule δ_θ^* and the conditional choice probabilities $P_\theta(d|x)$ for any of the estimation methods presented so far. However, if we acknowledge the existence of unobserved state variables, then it is not clear how to calculate an estimate of the value function in (4.47). To get around the problem Manski assumes that unobserved state variables enter the utility function, but only in the period t in which the agent is observed, not at subsequent times $t+j, j > 0$. Manski assumes that the unobservables entering at the date of observation satisfy the AS-CI assumptions of section 6, so that by integrating the time t optimal decision rule with respect to a distribution $q(\epsilon|x)$ he obtains a conditional choice probability of the form (4.36) and a partial likelihood function similar to (4.42), allowing θ to be estimated by maximum likelihood. The advantage of the path utility approach is that it avoids nested numerical solution of v_θ: instead the simpler semi-parametric estimate $\hat{v}_\theta$ in (4.47) is re-evaluated for each trial value of θ. Since the estimated value function enters the choice probability non-linearly, we have a problem akin to non-linear errors in variables due to the estimation error in $\hat{v}_\theta(x, d)$. However Ahn and Manski (1993) show that, if the observed state variable x is discrete, then the errors in variables problem has no asymptotic consequences and $\sqrt{A}(\hat{\theta} - \theta)$ is consistent and asymtotically normally distributed.[40]

The 'conditional choice probability' approach of Hotz and Miller (1993) is similar to the backward estimation method in that it circumvents numerical solution of the fixed-point problem by estimating the value function v directly. However Hotz and Miller's method only requires parametric specification of v for a single alternative, say, $v_\theta(x, 1)$, instead of for all alternatives $d \in D(x)$. In some problems $v_\theta(x, 1)$ can be specified as the value corresponding to a 'terminating decision' that takes the DDP process into an absorbing state. An example is a woman's sterilisation decision in Hotz and Miller's fertility application, or a firm's exit decision in the Ericson–Pakes (1989) model of firm dynamics. Given $v_\theta(x, 1)$, the functional forms of the remaining value functions $v(x, d)$ are uncovered non-parametrically by inverting the mapping (4.33) from value functions into choice probabilities. The inverse mapping reduces to a simple log-odds transformation when $\{\epsilon_t\}$ has an i.i.d extreme value distribution, see (4.36). In this case the fixed-point condition (4.37) can be re-written as

$$
\begin{aligned}
\hat{v}_\theta(x, d) = &u_\theta(x, d) + \beta \int \log \left[\sum_{d' \in D(x')} \exp\{v_\theta(x', d') - v_\theta(x', 1)\} \right] \pi(dx'|x, d) \\
&+ \beta \int v_\theta(x', 1) \pi(dx'|x, d) \\
= &u_\theta(x, d) + \beta \int \log \left[\sum_{d' \in D(x')} \hat{P}(d'|x')/\hat{P}(1|x') \right] \pi(dx'|x, d) \\
&+ \beta \int v_\theta(x', 1) \pi(dx'|x, d).
\end{aligned}
\tag{4.48}
$$

The odds ratio $\hat{P}(d'|x')/\hat{P}(1|x')$ can be estimated by non-parametric regression, allowing one to avoid solving the contraction fixed-point problem to compute $\hat{v}_\theta(x, d)$. Once we have $\hat{v}_\theta$ we can estimate θ using the partial likelihood estimator (4.42) or by the generalised method of moments:

$$
\hat{\theta} = \operatorname{argmin} H_A(\theta)' W_A H_A(\theta),
$$

$$
H_A(q) = \sum_{a=1}^{A} \sum_{t=1}^{T_a} \sum_{d \in D(x_t^a)} [I\{d = d_t^a\} - P_\theta(d|x_t^a)] Z_t^a.
\tag{4.49}
$$

Note that in (4.49) P_θ is not the non-parametric estimate but rather the parametric logit conditional choice probability (4.36) evaluated using $\hat{v}_\theta$ from (4.48). The instrument vector Z_t^a used in (4.49) has K elements, where K exceeds the dimension of θ. Estimation requires repeated recalculation of

$\hat{v}_\theta$ in (4.48) each time θ is updated, but this typically involves much less work than computing the contraction fixed point. Similar to Manski's path utility estimator, non-parametric estimation of $P(d|x)$ introduces a problem of non-linear errors in variables due to estimation error in $\hat{v}_\theta$. However Hotz and Miller show that provided the estimation error in the log-odds ratio disappears quickly enough, the method of moments estimator is consistent and asymptotically normal.[41]

The final estimation method, introduced by Hotz, Miller, Sanders and Smith (1993), combines Monte Carlo simulation and non-parametric estimation to avoid the need for a prior parametric specification of $v_\theta(x, 1)$ required by the Hotz–Miller conditional choice probability approach. I present a modified version of their estimator, which I refer to as the simulated value estimator (SV), consisting of five steps. For simplicity I assume that the observed state variable x has finite support and that there are no unknown parameters in the transition probability π, and that q is an i.i.d. extreme value distribution.

Step 1 Invert non-parametric estimates of $P(d|x)$ to compute a consistent estimate of the normalised value function $\Delta v(x, d) = v(x, d) - v(x, 1)$

$$\Delta\hat{v}(x, d) = \log\left\{\frac{\hat{P}(d|x)}{\hat{P}(1|x)}\right\}. \tag{4.50}$$

Step 2 Use the consistent estimate of $\Delta\hat{v}$ to uncover a consistent estimate of the decision rule δ^*

$$\hat{\delta}(x, \epsilon) = \underset{d \in D(x)}{\text{argmax}}[\Delta\hat{v}(x, d) + \epsilon(d)]. \tag{4.51}$$

Step 3 Using $\hat{\delta}, q$ and π simulate realisations of the controlled stochastic process $\{x_t, \epsilon_t\}$. Given an initial condition (x_0, d_0), this consists of the following steps:

(a)   given (x_{t-1}, d_{t-1}) draw x_t from the transition probability $\pi(x_t|x_{t-1}, d_{t-1})$,
(b)   given x_t draw ϵ_t from the density $q(\epsilon_t|x_t)$,
(c)   given (x_t, ϵ_t) compute $d_t = \hat{\delta}(x_t, \epsilon_t)$,
(d)   if $t > S(A)$, stop, otherwise set $t = t + 1$ and return to step (a).[42]

Repeat step 3 using each of the sample points (x_t^a, d_t^a), $a = 1, \ldots, A, t = 1, \ldots, T_a$ as initial conditions.

Step 4 Using the simulations $\{\tilde{x}_t, \tilde{d}_t\}$ from step 3, compute the *simulated value function* $\tilde{v}_\theta(x_0, d_0)$

$$\tilde{v}_\theta(x_0, d_0) = \sum_{t=0}^{S(A)} \beta^t [u_\theta(\tilde{x}_t, \hat{\delta}(\tilde{x}_t, \tilde{\epsilon}_t)) + \tilde{\epsilon}_t(\hat{\delta}(\tilde{x}_t, \tilde{\epsilon}_t))], \tag{4.52}$$

where (x_0, d_0) is the initial condition from step 3. Repeat step 4 using each of the sample points (x_t^a, d_t^a) as initial conditions.

Step 5 Using the normalised simulated value functions $\Delta\tilde{v}_\theta(x_t^a, d_t^a)$ and corresponding non-parametric estimates $\Delta\hat{v}(x_t^a, d_t^a)$ as 'data', compute the parameter estimate θ as the solution to

$$\hat{\theta}_A = \text{argmin } H_A(\theta)' W_A H_A(\theta)$$

$$H_A(q) = \frac{1}{A} \sum_{a=1}^{A} \sum_{t=1}^{T_a} [\Delta\hat{v}(x_t^a, d_t^a) - \Delta\tilde{v}_\theta(x_t^a, d_t^a)] Z_t^a, \tag{4.53}$$

where W_A is a $K \times K$ positive definitive weighting matrix, where K is the dimension of the instrument vector, Z_t^a. The SV estimator has several attractive features: (1) it avoids the need for repeated calculation of the fixed point (4.37), (2) the simulation error in $\Delta\tilde{v}_\theta(x_t^a, d_t^a)$ averages out over sample observations, so that one can estimate the underlying parameters using as few as one simulated path of $\{\tilde{x}_t, \tilde{\epsilon}_t\}$ per (x_t^a, d_t^a) observation, (3) since each term $\Delta\tilde{v}_\theta(x, d)$ is a smooth function of θ, the objective function (4.53) is a smooth function of θ allowing use of gradient optimisation algorithms to estimate $\hat{\theta}_A$. Note that the simulation in step 2 needs to be done only once at the start of the estimation, so the main computational burden is the repeated evaluation of (4.52) each time θ is updated. Hotz *et al.* proved that their version of the SV estimator is consistent and asymptotically normally distributed, and present Monte Carlo evidence that suggests that their estimator compares favourably to full-information maximum-likelihood when the optimal weighting matrix W_A is used.

Overall, the methods outlined in this section represent some clever alternatives to 'nested numerical solution' methods described in section 7. However as I mentioned in section 2, they are not a panacea: the methods attempt to reduce computational complexity at the expense of increased estimation complexity. Thus, these methods are likely to work well only when we have sufficient data to obtain good estimates of the value function. The empirical application in the Hotz and Miller paper is a case in point. They attempt to estimate a fertility model with 2^{20} possible birth sequences, thirty-one age cohorts, fifteen wife education classifications, fifteen husband education classifications, and 1,500 values for the Lagrange multipliers for the wife's labour supply choice (estimated separately as fixed effects). The implied conditional choice probabilities have approximately 10^{13} cells, which Hotz and Miller 'non-parametrically estimate' using a data set with 9,000 observations (which is large relative to most economic data sets).

In cases where there is a paucity of data relative to the dimensionality of the problem being estimated, it's unclear whether empirical results that rely on non-parametric estimation methods aren't simply artifacts of the particular method used (kernel, nearest neighbour, series estimators, regressograms, etc.) and the associated somewhat arbitrary choices of various smoothing parameters, kernel functions, window widths, etc. Indeed, the Monte Carlo results in Hotz *et al.* show that even in a relatively small-scale problem (the bus-replacement problem of Rust (1987) where the state variable, bus mileage, is discretised into ninety possible values) the regressogram estimator of P (i.e., estimating the choice probabilities based on sample frequencies in each mileage cell) can lead to significant biases resulting from 'zero cell probabilities, empty cells, or, more generally, poorly estimated replacement probabilities [choice probabilities] that can bias the estimates of the log-odds ratios in finite samples. Thus it appears that poorly estimated [choice probabilities] – as opposed to poorly simulated valuation functions – are accounting for much of the downward bias in the [parameter] estimates when simple cell frequencies are used to estimate the [choice] probabilities' (p.20). Although they found that in certain cases the biases could be reduced by using a kernel estimator of the choice probabilities (with sufficiently high bandwidth), when there are few observations per cell the simulation estimator based on the kernel estimates of the choice probabilities were 'biased downward to an even greater extent than those using sample frequencies' (p.22), leading them to conclude that 'the potential for the greatest bias in the parameter estimates arises from using poorly estimated conditional choice probabilities ... Bias resulting from the simulation of the conditional valuation function appears to be much less important' (p.23).

Of course direct solution methods are also subject to criticisms about the arbitrariness of the choice of functional forms for the primitive objects. However it seems probable that economists have more prior information guiding their choice of a utility function or discount factor than their choice of a kernel function or bandwidth parameter. Despite these problems, I think that these methods offer promising alternatives when used judiciously. The results of Ahn and Manski (1993), Hotz, Miller, Sanders and Smith (1993), McFadden (1989) and Pakes and Pollard (1989) offer the hope that we can get good estimates of the parameters of interest (θ) even though various 'nuisance parameters' (the value function v and conditional choice probability P) are estimated/simulated with considerable noise.

9   STRUCTURAL ESTIMATION OF DISCRETE DYNAMIC GAMES

I conclude this survey by sketching a framework for formulating and estimating a class of discrete dynamic multi-player games. I argue that repeated direct computation of the equilibria in a nested numerical solution estimation algorithm appears to be currently infeasible for all but the simplest games. However, by substituting non-parametric estimates of opponents' reaction functions into a given player's optimisation problem, one can reduce the equilibrium problem to a simpler 'game against nature' which is computationally feasible to estimate using any of the estimation methods described in the previous sections.

I start with simplest case, a static N-player game. Player i has N possible actions, and receives utility $u_i(x, d_i, d_{-i})$ when the other $N-1$ players take actions $d_{-i} = (d_1, \ldots, d_{i-1}, d_{i+1}, \ldots, d_N)$. The vector x represents characteristics of the players, the environment, etc. Note that the actual game may not be static: this could be a normal form representation of a dynamic game in extensive form. However, except for the simplest games it is generally difficult to translate from the extensive to the normal form, which is why I treat this as a static game and model dynamics explicitly below.

I incorporate unobservables into the game in a special way, by assuming that the variables that are unobserved by the econometrician are also unobserved by the other players in the game. Let the unobservables be represented by a vector $\epsilon = (\epsilon_1, \ldots, \epsilon_N)$ where $\epsilon_i(d)$ is the unobserved component of utility that player i receives from taking action d_i. Notice that this part of the utility only depends on player i's action d_i and not on the actions d_{-i} of player i's opponents. While player i knows the vector ϵ, neither the econometrician nor any of the other players know it. I assume, however, that it is common knowledge among the players (and econometrician) that ϵ is a random variable from a density function $q(\epsilon|x)$ (although the econometrician may not know the true parameter θ^*) that satisfies the AS-CI assumptions of section 6. In addition, I assume that conditional on x, ϵ_i and ϵ_j are independently distributed for any two players $i \neq j$. The decision rule for player i is given by

$$\delta_i(x, \epsilon) = \operatorname*{argmax}_{d \in D_i} \sum_{d_{-i}} u(x, d, d_{-i}) P(d_{-i}|x) + \epsilon_i(d). \tag{4.54}$$

The CI assumption implies that the joint probability $P(d_{-i}|x)$ entering (4.53) is given by

$$P(d_{-i}|x) = \prod_{k \neq i} P_k(d_k|x), \tag{4.55}$$

where the conditional choice probability $P_i(d_i|x)$ for player i is defined by

$$P_i(d_i|x) = \int_{\epsilon_i} I\{d_i = \delta_i(x, \epsilon_i)\} q_i(d\epsilon_i|x). \tag{4.56}$$

Note that (4.54) and (4.55) implicitly define player i's choice probability as a function of his opponent's choice probabilities:

$$P_i(x) \equiv \{P_i(d|x)|d \in D_i\} = \Gamma_i(P_1(x), \ldots, P_N(x)|x). \tag{4.57}$$

Stacking equation (4.57) over players $i = 1, \ldots, N$ we obtain a system of equations defining a Bayesian Nash equilibrium of the incomplete information game

$$\mathbf{P}(x) = [P_1(x), \dots, P_N(x)]' = \Gamma(\mathbf{P}(x)). \tag{4.58}$$

Fixing x, equation (4.58) defines agents' choice probabilities as a fixed point of a mapping $\Gamma : S \rightarrow S$, where $S = S_1 \times \dots \times S_N$, and S_i is the simplex of dimension $|D_i| - 1$. This fixed point must be solved separately for each x to obtain the conditional choice probability function $\mathbf{P}(x)$.[43] The convexity of the social surplus function implies that Γ is a differentiable function of $\mathbf{P}(x)$, so that Newton's method can be used to compute a solution. Inference proceeds by parameterising agents' utility functions as $u_\theta(x) = \{u_1(d_1, d_{-1}, x, \theta), \dots, u_N(d_N, d_{-N}, x, \theta)\}$, yielding corresponding parametric choice probabilities $\mathbf{P}_\theta(x)$ implicitly defined by the fixed-point condition (4.58). Given observations on a cross-section of T identical, independent N-player games the likelihood function is given by

$$L(\theta) = \prod_{t=1}^{T} \mathbf{P}_\theta(\mathbf{d}_t | x_t). \tag{4.59}$$

where $\mathbf{d}_t = (d_{1t}, \dots, d_{Nt})$ is the vector of actions taken by the N players in game t. Computation of the maximum-likelihood estimate of θ requires a nested fixed-point algorithm: for each trial value of θ, the fixed point (4.58) must be calculated in order to evaluate the likelihood function (4.59). Given the differentiability of the best-response probability function defined in (4.58) the Implicit Function Theorem guarantees that $P_\theta(x)$ and $L(\theta)$ are differentiable functions of θ. For relatively small problems, this sort of nested fixed-point algorithm is computationally feasible.

However an alternative method is to use non-parametric estimation of players' response probabilities (4.58) to avoid the need to repeatedly recompute the Nash equilibrium at each trial value of θ. Observe that if we have sufficient data to compute a non-parametric estimate $\hat{P}(d_{-i} | x)$ for all d_{-i} and x, then we can plug this estimate into agent i's decision problem (4.54) to yield a static single-agent discrete-choice problem. The parameter vector θ can be estimated by standard methods using the quasi-likelihood function (4.59) where the non-parametric estimates $\hat{P}(d|x)$ have been substituted for the parametric values $P_\theta(d|x)$ that would otherwise be repeatedly calculated in the nested fixed-point algorithm. Building on Ahn and Manski (1993) it seems possible that one could prove that the resulting quasi-maximum-likelihood estimator θ is consistent and asymptotically normal.

I will now briefly illustrate how this framework extends naturally to finite and infinite-horizon N-player Markov games. In a Markov game player i has a discount factor β_i and utility function $u_i(d_{it}, d_{-it}, x_t) = u(\mathbf{d}_t, x_t)$ where x_t

is the state of the game at time t, and $\mathbf{d}_t$ is the vector of actions taken by the players at time t. To avoid technical issues of existence of equilibrium discussed in Dutta and Sundaram (1993), I assume x_t can assume only a finite number of possible values. The state vector evolves according to a controlled Markov process with transition probability $p(x_{t+1}|x_t, \mathbf{d}_t)$ which depends on the joint action $\mathbf{d}_t$ taken by the players at time t. I assume that at each time t, player i's action depends on a vector of private state variables ϵ_{it} known only by player i. In each period t, I assume that the econometrician and other players believe that ϵ_{it} is a draw from a density $q_i(\epsilon_{it}|x_t)$. These distributions are common knowledge among the players, and for each time t and state x_t it is also common knowledge that ϵ_{it} is independent of ϵ_{jt} for $i \neq j$.

In the finite horizon case, one solves the game by backward induction from the terminal period, T. In the last period we have a simple one-shot game that was analysed above. Equilibrium choice probabilities in period T, $\mathbf{P}_T(x)$, are therefore defined by the fixed-point condition in equation (4.58). In periods $t = 1, \ldots, T-1$ the players choose their actions with knowledge of equilibria that will be played from periods $t+1$ onwards.[44] Player i's decision rule is given by

$$\delta_{it}(x_t, \epsilon_{it}) = \operatorname*{argmax}_{d \in D_{it}} E_{-i}\{u_i|d, d_{-i}x_t\} + \beta_i E_{-i} E_y\{v_{it+1}(y)|x_t, d\} + \epsilon_{it}(d), \tag{4.60}$$

where the value function $v_{it}(x_t)$ is defined recursively by

$$v_{it}(x_t) = G_i(\{E_{-i}\{u_i|d, x_t\} + \beta_i E_{-i} E_y\{v_{it+1}(y)|x_t, d\}|d \in D_{it}\}|x_t), \tag{4.61}$$

where G_i is player i's social surplus function (defined in (4.26)) and the conditional expectation operator E_y is defined by

$$E_y\{f(y)|x, \mathbf{d}\} = \int_y f(y)p(dy|x, \mathbf{d}), \tag{4.62}$$

and the expectation operator E_{-i} is defined by

$$E_{-i}\{f(x, d_i, d_{-i})|d, x\} = \sum_{d_{-i}} f(x, d_i, d_{-i})P(d_{-i}|x). \tag{4.63}$$

It is straightforward to show that for each x the individual choice probabilities $P(d|x)$ entering (4.63) are solutions to the fixed-point condition (4.58). It follows that the solution of a Markov-perfect equilibrium of a T-period finite-horizon game involves T solutions of the fixed-point condition (4.58) (each of which must in turn be solved for all possible values x) combined with N dynamic programming recursions for players $i = 1, \ldots, N$ for periods 1 to T. The solution provides a T-fold vector of conditional choice probabilities, $\mathbf{P}(x) = \{\mathbf{P}_1(x_1), \ldots, \mathbf{P}_T(x_T)\}$ which can be used to form the likelihood function for the data in an obvious way (see

(4.42) and (4.59)). If there are sufficient data to compute non-parametric estimates of the choice probabilities of player i's opponents, then one can substitute these into the DP recursion calculations eliminating the need to repeatedly recalculate the T fixed-point problems each time the trial value of θ is updated.

Finally, consider the infinite-horizon case. The relevant notion of equilibrium is a stationary, Markov-perfect equilibrium. The decision rule for player i will be given by

$$\delta_i(x_t, \epsilon_{it}) = \operatorname*{argmax}_{d \in D_i} E_{-i}\{u_i|d, x_t\} + \beta_i E_{-i} E_y\{v_i(y)|x_t, d\} + \epsilon_{it}(d), \quad (4.64)$$

where the value function $v_i(x)$ is the unique solution to

$$v_i(x) = G_i(\{E_{-i}\{u_i|d, x\} + \beta_i E_{-i} E_y\{v_i(y)|x, d\}|d \in D_i\}|x). \quad (4.65)$$

Solving the game amounts to solving a coupled fixed-point problem. To see this, stack the individual player Bellman fixed-point problems in (4.65) as $\mathbf{v} \equiv \{v_1, \ldots, v_N\}$ noting their implicit dependence on conditional choice probability vector $\mathbf{P}$ in (4.63)

$$\mathbf{v} = \Psi(\mathbf{v}, \mathbf{P}). \quad (4.66)$$

The conditional choice probabilities are given by the partial derivatives of the social surplus function, which I re-write in general notation to emphasise its dependence on the value functions

$$\mathbf{P} = \Gamma(\mathbf{P}, \mathbf{v}). \quad (4.67)$$

A stationary Markov-perfect equilibrium is any solution to the coupled fixed-point problem (4.66), (4.67). It is straightforward to prove that there exist $(\mathbf{v}, \mathbf{P})$ that solve (4.66) and (4.67) simultaneously, thereby guaranteeing the existence of a stationary Markov-perfect equilibrium.[45] Owing to the convexity of the social surplus functions G_i, $(\mathbf{v}, \mathbf{P})$ could be simultaneously computed using the Newton–Kantorovich algorithm. This appears to be computationally tractable only in the simplest of problems. However once again we can avoid the equilibrium calculation if we have sufficient data to get good estimates of the choice probabilities. Substituting these estimates into (4.65), we see that the problem then reduces to computing N separate contraction fixed points. For moderate N, decomposing a single multi-agent game into separate 'games against nature' for purposes of estimation appears to be feasible using any of the methods outlined in this survey.

Notes

Acknowledgements: This paper was originally written jointly with Ariel Pakes in 1990, but due to the large volume of material we decided to split the survey into two separate pieces. This first section was subsequently revised several times, the last revision occuring in July, 1992 while I was a fellow at the Hoover Institution. In addition to extensive and insightful comments from my co-author Ariel Pakes, I am grateful to John Dagsvik, Mita Das, Joseph Hotz, Charles Manski, James Walker and Ken Wolpin for additional comments which led to significant improvements of the final version of this paper. Parts of the my research described in this paper benefited from financial support from the National Science Foundation, the National Institute on Aging, a grant from the IBM Corporation's Research Support Program, and release time at the Institute for Empirical Macroeconomics at the Federal Reserve Bank of Minneapolis.

1 This is justified by the fact that a continuous-time Markov decision process can be arbitrarily closely approximated by a discrete-time Markov decision process (van Dijk (1984)). In fact one of the most powerful and general numerical methods for solving continuous-time stochastic control problems involves simply solving an approximate version of the problem in discrete time (Kushner (1990)). Of course this is not to ignore problems of 'time aggregation' and 'aliasing' that arise when the discrete-time approximation is too coarse. For discussions of these problems in related contexts see Hansen and Sargent (1983), the thesis of Marcet (1986), and Hansen and Scheinkman (1992).

2 Other authors, such as Dagsvik (1983), have developed continuous-time theories of discrete dynamic choice under perfect foresight. In this framework there is no uncertainty from the standpoint of the agent, although there is uncertainty from the standpoint of the econometrician who does not fully observe all relevant characteristics of the agent. One can view Dagsvik's model as a limiting case of a DDP model where agent-specific uncertainty and the decision time interval go to zero. See also the recent paper by Resnick and Roy (1992) who develope a parallel perfect-foresight model for continuous choices in continuous time.

3 There has been negligible use of Bayesian methods for structural estimation due to the high cost of evaluating the likelihood. While computational advances such as Geweke (1989) offer hope for Bayesian inference in relatively complex reduced-form models, it still appears infeasible for all but the simplest types of structural models.

4 See Rust (1988d) for one approach towards reconciling the Bayesian and classical viewpoints.

5 An example is Kydland and Prescott's (1982) model of real business cycles. Using a calibration approach, they claimed that 'the fit of the model is very good, particularly in light of the model's simplicity' (p.1363). In subsequent work Kydland and Prescott (1989) claimed that the productivity shocks in their model account for '70% of U.S. postwar cyclical fluctuations'. Altüg (1989) used the method of maximum likelihood to estimate the unknown parameters of

an extension of the Kydland–Prescott model and concluded that 'an aggregative model in which persistent technology shocks are the only driving force cannot rationalize the joint behavior of per capita hours with the remaining series' (p.912). More recently Eichenbaum (1991), having estimated versions of the model by the method of moments, questioned the degree of confidence in Kyland and Prescott's claims: 'What the data are telling us is that, while productivity shocks play some role in generating the business cycle, there is simply an enormous amount of uncertainty about just what percent of aggregate fluctuations they actually do account for' (p.1). For further examples see Rust (1992b).

6 This is especially true when one estimates reduced-form models using flexible or non-parametric estimation methods that don't require the host of rigid main-tained assumptions that are typically imposed in structural models. See also Rust (1993) for a discussion of some of the logical problems involved with the standard 'comparative static' approach to policy evaluation in dynamic models.

7 Acknowledgement of the possibility of misspecification does not force us to abandon classical statistical procedures and concepts such as consistency, or hypothesis testing. Hypothesis test statistics can be re-interpreted as providing a measure of the goodness of fit of the parametric model. Consistency can be re-interpreted as convergence to a parameter which minimises the asymptotic statistical distance between the parametric model and the data generating process. See, for example, White (1982) who shows that standard results on the consistency and asymptotic normality of maximum likelihood hold despite misspecification, and that maximising the likelihood is asymptotically equivalent to minimising the 'Kullback-Liebler' distance between the parametric model and the true distribution function generating the data.

8 Infinite-horizon DP problems can be solved by a variety of algorithms such as policy iteration (discussed in section 7) whose space and time complexity increases as a third degree polynomial in N, the number of distinct action/state pairs in the DP model. However Bellman's curse of dimensionality implies that N itself increases exponentially as a function of any sensible measure of the 'size' or 'realism' of the model.

9 In models with continuous state or control variables, complexity also increases exponentially in any relevant measure of the grid size governing the distance of a discrete-state approximation to its continuous-state limit.

10 This is subject to the constraint, of course, that the number of discrete cells or parameters in the finite approximation increases with the complexity of the underlying dynamic choice problem so that the approximation error (however measured) tends to zero.

11 Unless, of course, you believe there is a solution to the '$P = NP$' problem (Garey and Johnson (1979)) that once discovered, will allow us to solve all NP-complete problems, including DP problems, in polynomial time.

12 The state variable x may be modelled as discrete or continuous. Most of the comments in this section also apply to the mixed discrete/continuous case (MCDP) where some components of the decision variable can assume a continuum of values.

13 For an example of how this is done, see section 4.

14 A promising beginning along these lines is the recent work by Epstein and Zin (1989) who extend the work of Kreps and Porteus (1978) to develop an infinite-horizon non-expected utility theory of dynamic choice under uncertainty. For a class of CES aggregator functions, they show that the implied intertemporal utility function has a recursive structure that enables them to derive analogues of the Bellman and Euler equations. They have used this framework to derive implications for asset pricing, applying standard econometric techniques to empirically test their results.

15 The expectation in (4.2) is taken with respect to the initial information set $H_{-1} = \phi$.

16 These restrictions include the symmetry and negative-semi-definiteness of the Slutsky matrix (Hurwicz and Uzawa (1971)), the generalised axiom of revealed preference (Varian (1987)), and, in the case of discrete choice, restrictions on conditional choice probability (Block-Marshak (1960) and McFadden and Richter (1970)).

17 For example it is well known that in 'subjective expected utility' models with state dependent preferences, one cannot separately identify the agent's subjective beliefs p from preferences u (see Kreps (1988), proposition 7.4 or Myerson (1991), theorem 1.2). In game-theoretic models Ledyard (1986) has shown that any undominated strategy profile can be rationalised as a Bayesian Nash equilibrium outcome of a game of incomplete information given enough freedom in selecting agents' beliefs (priors) and utility functions. Mantel (1974) and Sonnenschein (1973) and others have shown that at an aggregate level, static demand theory implies no testable restriction beyond Walras' Law. Finally, even in the simplest context of deterministic optimal growth model with a single capital stock k_t, Boldrin and Montrucchio (1986) showed that any continuous law of motion $k_{t+1} = f(k_t)$ is optimal for some specification of preferences and technology provided the discount factor β is not too close to 1.

18 We use δ^* as the reduced-form rather than the transition probability $\Pr\{s_{t+1}, d_{t+1} | s_t, d_t\} = I\{d_{t+1} = \delta^*(s_{t+1})\} p(s_{t+1} | s_t, d_t)$ since if p represents the agent's subjective beliefs, there is no objective way to estimate it except through its observable implications via δ^*. However if we assume that agents have 'rational expectations' then p can be estimated non-parametrically (Basawa and Prakasa Rao (1980)) and all remaining observable implications of the theory are determined by δ^*.

19 Since the econometrician observes all components of (s, d) the non-parametric regression used to estimate δ^* is degenerate in the sense that the model $d = \delta^*(s)$ has an 'error term' that is identically 0. Nevertheless, a variety of non-parametric regression methods will be able to consistently estimate δ^* under very general regularity conditions. See, for example, Häerdle (1990). For further discussion, see section 5.

20 In addition, if the data do not record all relevant components of s, the agent's actions may appear to be stochastic from the standpoint of the econometrician even though it is deterministic from the standpoint of the agent. I treat this case in detail in section 5.

21 See Machina (1987) for a survey of other examples of laboratory experiments of choice under uncertainty. Machina (1982) identifies the *independence axiom* as a potential source of many of the rejections.

22 Experiments have been predominantly used as a means of rejecting candidate models, rather than identifying their primitives. A classic example is the study by LaLonde (1986) and LaLonde and Maynard (1987) who found that forecasts of earnings differentials due to job training programmes produced by 'selection regression' models were substantially different from the results of randomised experiments. However in my opinion they go too far in interpreting their findings as 'further evidence that the current skepticism surrounding the results of nonexperimental evaluations is justified'. Heckman (1994) has shown that experimental methods have many limitations that structural forecasting methods avoid, so that our best hopes for policy evaluation is via an integration of the methods rather than a rejection of structural forecasts. Note that in experienced hands (Heckman, Hotz and Dabos (1987)), the forecasts of the structural selectivity model are found to be much closer to the experimental findings.

23 Identification of β is particularly problematic and in many cases its value is specified a priori. For example in life-cycle models it is very difficult to discriminate between a model with a high β without bequests from a model with a low β that allows for bequests: both models imply a slow rate of asset decumulation that we observe in the data. If we assume a particular parametric functional form for the bequest function B we may be able to identify β 'by virtue of functional form', but the estimates are likely to be very sensitive to the specification of B.

24 Another method, *unobserved heterogeneity*, can be regarded as a special case of unobserved state variables in which certain components of the state vector vary over individuals but not over time.

25 See McFadden (1981) and (1984) for surveys of estimation methods and functional forms for econometric models of discrete choice.

26 The notion $|D(s)|$ denotes the number of elements in the set $D(s)$. In cases where the state space S is also a finite set, the class of DDPs is identical to the class of finite MDPs described in section 3.

27 Results are available for certain special cases, such as Christensen and Kiefer's (1991) analysis of the job search model. If wages are measured without error, this model generates the restriction that any accepted wage offer must be greater than the reservation wage (which is an implicit function of θ). This implies that the support of the likelihood function depends on θ, resulting in a non-normal limiting distribution with certain parameters converging faster than the $\sqrt{N}$ rate that is typical of standard maximum-likelihood estimators.

28 For technical reasons ϵ may have a number of superfluous components so that we may formally embed the ϵ state vectors in a common state space E. For details, see definition 5.

29 If $q(d\epsilon|x)$ is independent of x then $\{\epsilon_t\}$ is an i.i.d. process which is independent of $\{x_t\}$.

30 The interchange is justified by the Lebesgue dominated convergence theorem, since the derivative of $\max_{d \in D(x)}[u(x, d) + \epsilon(d)]$ with respect to $u(x, d)$ is bounded (it equals either 0 or 1) for almost all ϵ.

31 The constant γ in (4.35) is *Euler's constant*, which shifts the extreme value distribution so it has unconditional mean zero.

32 Closed-form solutions for the conditional choice probability are available for the larger family of multivariate extreme value distributions (McFadden, (1981), Resnick and Roy (1989)). This family is characterised by the property that it is *max-stable*, i.e., it is closed under the operation of maximisation. Dagsvik (1991b) showed that this class is dense in the space of all distributions for ϵ in the sense that the conditional choice probabilities for an arbitrary density q can be approximated arbitrarily closely by the choice probability for some multivariate extreme value distribution.

33 Using arguments similar to Cox (1975) one can show that under standard regularity conditions, the partial-likelihood estimators will be consistent and asymptotically normally distributed.

34 The Gateaux derivative is defined by $\Psi'(v_0(v)) = \lim_{t\to 0}[\Psi(v_0 + tv) - \Psi(v_0)]/t$. For each $v_0 \in B$ we require that $\Psi'(v_0) \in L(B, B)$, the space of all continuous linear operators from B into itself. If the above limit is uniform for all v such that $|v| = 1$, $\Psi'(v_0)$ is known as the *Fréchet derivative* (evaluated at the point v_0).

35 This is *Banach's Theorem*, Kantorovich and Aiklov (1982), p.154.

36 The norm $|A|$ of a linear operator $A \in L(B, B)$ is defined by $|A| = \sup\{|A(v)| : |v| = 1\}$.

37 Indeed, Duff (1984) reports that even after extensive modification and optimisation of standard sparse linear equation solvers, the resulting code typically runs only at scalar speeds. In Duff's work on the Cray-1, the sparse matrix code ran at twelve megaflops which is significantly lower than the Cray-1's peak rate of 160 megaflops on the dense linear algebra problems.

38 One can show that $[I - \Psi'(v)]$ has sufficient diagonal dominance that the block elimination algorithm is numerically stable even though pivot operations only occur within the elementary $d \times d$ diagonal blocks as they are inverted as part of the block elimination process. A simple check of numerical accuracy is to compute a fixed point with u identically equal to 1. It is easy to show that v must then be identically equal to $1/(1 - \beta)$, so the numerical results can be checked against the exact solution. Running the algorithm in sixty-four bit double precision on very large problems with β as large as 0.9999999, I found that the computed solution agreed with the exact solution to ten significant digits.

39 In infinite horizon problems, we should have both $A \to \infty$ and $T_a \to \infty$ for $a = 1, \ldots, A$.

40 If x contains continuous variables, Ahn and Manski show that their asymptotic results continue to hold provided that the sample average estimator (4.47) is replaced by a kernel-type estimator for which $\hat{v}_\theta(x, d)$ converges to $v_\theta(x, d)$ uniformly in (x, d, θ) at a sufficiently rapid rate. Note that there is a price to be paid in terms of efficiency, since the asymptotic covariance matrix of the path utility estimator will be larger than the asymptotic covariance matrix when v_θ is computed exactly.

41 This will always be the case when x_t assumes only a finite number of values. In cases where x_t contains continuous components, one must verify that the non-parametric estimator of $P(d|x)$ converges uniformly at a sufficiently rapid rate, similar to the results of Ahn and Manski (1993).

42 Here $S(A)$ denotes any stopping rule (possibly stochastic) with the property that with probability $1, S(A) \to \infty$ as $A \to \infty$.

43 Given the regularity conditions assumed for the distribution of ϵ, Brouwer's fixed-point theorem guarantees the existence of at least one fixed point to (4.58).

44 In the case where there are multiple solutions to (4.58), there is common knowledge of which particular solution will obtain in each state x and each time t.

45 To see this, note that Ψ is a system of contraction mappings, so that given any choice probability $\mathbf{P}$, there is a unique solution $\mathbf{v}(\mathbf{P})$ which depends continuously on $\mathbf{P}$. Substituting this implicit function into (4.67) and appealing to Brouwer's fixed-point theorem guarantees the existence of a stationary Markov equilibrium.

References

Aedo, M. (1990), 'The Schooling Decision: A Dynamic Model', Ph.D. dissertation, University of Minnesota.

Ahn, H. and Manski, C. (1993), 'Distribution Theory for the Analysis of Binary Choice Under Uncertainty with Nonparametric Estimation of Expectations', *Journal of Econometrics*, 56: 291–32.

Altûg, S. (1989), 'Time-to-Build and Aggregate Fluctuations: Some New Evidence', *International Economic Review*, 30(4): 889–920.

Amemiya, T. (1976), 'On A Two-Step Estimation of a Multivariate Logit Model', *Journal of Econometrics*, 8: 13–21.

Amman, H. and Rust, J. (1995), 'Numerical Dynamic Programming', in H. Amman, D. Kendrick and J. Rust (eds.), *Handbook of Computational Economics*, Vol. 1, Amsterdam: North Holland.

Basawa, I.V. and Prakasa Rao, B.L.S. (1980), *Statistical Inference for Stochastic Processes*, New York: Academic Press.

Bellman, R. (1957) *Dynamic Programming*, Princeton, N. J.: Princeton University Press.

Bellman, R. and Hartley, M. (1985), 'The Tree Crop Problem', manuscript, Development Research Department, The World Bank.

Berkovec, J. and Stern, S. (1991), 'Job Exit Behavior of Older Men', *Econometrica*, 59(1): 189–210.

Bertsekas, D. (1987), *Dynamic Programming Deterministic and Stochastic Models*, New York: Prentice Hall.

Bhattacharya, R.N. and Majumdar, M. (1989), 'Controlled Semi-Markov Models – The Discounted Case', *Journal of Statistic Planning and Inference*, 21: 365–81.

Blackwell, D. (1962), 'Discrete Dynamic Programming', *Annals of Mathematical Statistics*, 33: 719–26.

(1965), 'Discounted Dynamic Programming', *Annals of Mathematical Statistics*, 36: 226–35.

(1967), 'Positive Dynamic Programming', *Proceedings of the 5th Berkeley Sym-*

posium on Mathematical Statistics and Probability, 1: 415–18.

Block, H. and Marschak, J. (1960), 'Random Orderings and Stochastic Theories of Response', in I. Olkin (ed.), *Contributions to Probability and Statistics*, Stanford: Stanford University Press.

Boldrin, M. and Montrucchio, L. (1986), 'On the Indeterminacy of Capital Accumulation Paths', *Journal of Economic Theory*, 40(1): 26–39.

Brock, W.A. and Mirman, L.J. (1972), 'Optimal Economic Growth Under Uncertainty: The Discounted Case', *Journal of Economic Theory*, 4: 479–513.

Christensen, B. (1990), 'Estimation of Dynamic Programming Models with Applications to Intertemporal Equilibrium Asset Pricing Models', manuscript, New York University.

Christensen, B.J. and Kiefer, N.M. (1991), 'The Exact Likelihood Function for an Empirical Job Search Model', *Econometric Theory*, 7: 464–86.

(1992), 'Estimation and Inference in an Optimal Stopping Model', manuscript, Cornell University.

Cox, D.R. (1975), 'Partial Likelihood', *Biometrika*, 62(2): 269–76.

Cox, D.R. and Hinkley, D.V. (1974), *Theoretical Statistics*, London: Chapman and Hall.

Dagsvik, J. (1983), 'Discrete Dynamic Choice: An Extension of the the Choice Models of Luce and Thurstone', *Journal of Mathematical Psychology*, 27: 1–43.

(1991a), 'Discrete and Continuous Choice, Max-Stable Processes and Independence from Irrelevant Alternatives', manuscript, Central Bureau of Statistics, Oslo.

(1991b), 'A Note on the Theoretical Content of the GEV Model for Discrete Choice', manuscript, Central Bureau of Statistics, Oslo.

Das, M. (1992), 'A Micro Econometrica Model of Capital Utilization and Retirement: The Case of the Cement Industry', *Review of Economic Studies*, 59(2): 277–98.

Daula, T. and Moffitt, R. (1991), 'Estimating a Dynamic Programming Model of Army Reenlistment Behavior', in C. Gilgo, D. Horn and D.A. Smith (eds.), *Military Compensation and Personnel Retention: Models and Evidence*, US Army Research Institute for Behavioral and Social Sciences.

Debreu, G. (1960), 'Review of R.D. Luce *Individual Choice Behavior*', *American Economic Review*, 50: 186–8.

(1974), 'Excess Demand Functions', *Journal of Mathematical Economics*, 1: 15–23.

Dongarra, J.J. and Hewitt, T. (1986), 'Implementing Dense Linear Algebra Algorithms Using Multitasking on the Cray X-MP-4', *SIAM Journal on Scientific and Statistical Computing*, 7(1): 347–50.

Duff, I. (1984), 'The Solution of Sparse Linear Equations in the Cray 1', in J.S. Kowalik (ed.), *High Speed Computation*, NATO ASI Services, F7, 293–309.

Duff, I.S. and Reid, J.K. (1982), 'Experience of sparse matrix codes on the CRAY-1', *Computational Physics Communications*, 26: 293–302.

Dutta, P. and Sundaram, R. (1993), 'The Non-Existence of Perfect Equilibrium in Infinite Dynamic Games', manuscript, Department of Economics, University of Wisconsin.

Eckstein, Z. and Wolpin, K. (1989), 'The Specification and Estimation of Dynamic Stochastic Discrete Choice Models', *Journal of Human Resources*, 24(4): 562–98.

(1989a), 'Dynamic Labour Force Participation of Married Women and Endogenous Work Experience', *Review of Economic Studies*, 56: 375–90.

(1989b), 'Interpreting Duration of Job-Search and Wage Dispersion Using Estimable Matching-Bargaining Models', manuscript, University of Minnesota.

(1990), 'Estimating a Market Equilibrium Search Model from Panel Data on Individuals', *Econometrica*, 58(4): 783–808.

(1992) 'Duration to First Job and the Return to Schooling: Estimates from a Search-Matching Model', manuscript, University of Minnesota.

Eichenbaum, M. (1991), 'Real Business-Cycle Theory: Wisdom or Whimsy?', *Journal of Economic Dynamics and Control*, 15: 607–26.

Epstein, L.G. and Zin, S.E. (1989), 'Substitution, Risk Aversion, and the Temporal Behavior of Consumption and Asset Returns: A Theoretical Framework', *Econometrica*, 57(4): 937–70.

Ericson, R. and Pakes, A. (1989), 'Observable Implications of Firm Dynamics', manuscript, Yale University.

Fafchamps, M. (1991), 'Sequential Labor Decisions Under Uncertainty: An Estimable Household Model of West-African Farmers', manuscript, Stanford University.

Garcia, C.B. and Zangwill, W.I. (1981), *Pathways to Solutions, Fixed Points and Equilibria* Prentice Hall Series on Computational Mathematics, Englewood Cliffs, N. J.

Garey, M.R. and Johnson, D.S. (1979), *Computers and Intractibility: A Guide to the Theory of NP-Completeness*, New York: W.H. Freeman and Company.

Geweke, J. (1989), 'Bayesian Inference in Econometric Models Using Monte Carlo Integration', *Econometrica*, 57(6): 1317–40.

(1990), 'Efficient Simulation from the Multivariate Normal Distribution Subject to Linear Inequality Constraints and the Evaluation of Constraint Probabilities', manuscript, University of Minnesota.

Gotz, G.A. and McCall, J.J. (1980), 'Estimation in Sequential Decisionmaking Models: A Methodological Note', *Economics Letters*, 6: 131–6.

(1984), 'A Dynamic Retention Model for Air Force Officers', Report R-3028-AF, the RAND Corporation, Santa Monica, Calif.

Häerdle, W. (1990), *Applied Nonparametric Regression*, Econometric Society Monographs, Cambridge University Press.

Hansen, L.P. (1982), 'Large Sample Properties of Method of Moments Estimators', *Econometrica*, 50: 1029–54.

Hansen, L.P. and Jagannathan, R. (1991), 'Implications of Security Market Data for Models of Dynamic Economies', *Journal of Political Economy*, 99: 225–62.

Hansen, L. and Sargent, T. (1983), 'The Dimensionality of the Aliasing Problem in Models with Rational Spectral Densities', *Econometrica*, 51(2): 377–88.

Hansen, L.P. and Scheinkman, J.A. (1992), 'Back to the Future: Generating Moment Implications for Continuous Time Markov Processes' manuscript, University of Chicago.

Hansen, L.P. and Singleton, K. (1982), 'Generalized Instrumental Variables Estimation of Nonlinear Rational Expectations Models', *Econometrica*, 50: 1269–81.

Hartley, M. (1985), 'Neoclassical Econometrics: Non-negativity Constraints', manuscript, Development Research Department, The World Bank.

Heckman, J.J. (1994), 'Randomization and Social Policy Evaluation', in C. Sims and J. Laffont, *Advances in Econometrics: Proceedings of the 1990 Meetings of the Econometric Society*.

Heckman, J.J., Hotz, V.J. and Dabos, M. (1987), 'Do We Need Experimental Data to Evaluate the Impact of Manpower Training on Earnings?', *Evaluation Review*, 11(4): 395–427.

Hotz, V.J. and Miller, R.A. (1993), 'Conditional Choice Probabilities and the Estimation of Dynamic Programming Models', *Review of Economic Studies*, 60: 497–529.

Hotz, V.J., Miller, R.A., Sanders, S. and Smith, J. (1993), 'A Simulation Estimator for Dynamic Models of Discrete Choice', *Review of Economic Studies* (forthcoming).

Hurwicz, L. and Uzawa, H. (1971), 'On the Integrability of Demand Functions', in J. Chipman *et al.* (eds.), *Preferences, Utility, and Demand*, New York: Harcourt Brace Jovanovich.

Judd, K. (1992), *Numerical Methods in Economics*, Hoover Institution.

Kantorovich, L.V. and Akilov, G.P. (1982), *Functional Analysis*, Oxford: Pergamon Press.

Keane, M. and Wolpin, K.I. (1992), 'The Solution and Estimation of Discrete Choice Dynamic Programming Models by Simulation: Monte Carlo Evidence', manuscript, University of Minnesota.

Kennet, M. (1993), 'Did Deregulation Affect Aircraft Maintenance? An Emprical Policy Analysis', *Rand Journal*, 24(4): 542–58.

(1994), 'A Structural Model of Aircraft Engine Maintenance', *Journal of Applied Econometrics* (forthcoming).

Koopmans, T.C. (ed.) (1950), *Statistical Inference in Dynamic Economic Models* Cowles Commission Monograph 10, New York: John Wiley.

Kreps, D.M. (1988), *Notes on the Theory of Choice*, Underground Classics in Economics, Boulder: Westview Press.

Kreps, D. and Porteus, E. (1978), 'Temporal Resolution of Uncertainty and Dynamic Choice Theory', *Econometrica*, 46: 185–200.

Kushner, H.J. (1990), 'Numerical Methods for Stochastic Control Problems in Continuous Time', *SIAM Journal on Control and Optimization*, 28(5): 999–1048.

Kydland, F. and Prescott, E.C. (1982), 'Time to Build and Aggregate Fluctuations', *Econometrica*, 50: 1345–70.

(1989), 'Hours and Employment Variation in Business Cycle Theory', Discussion Paper 17, Institute for Empirical Macroeconomics, Federal Reserve Bank of Minneapolis.

LaLonde, R. (1986), 'Evaluating the Econometric Evaluations of Training Programs with Experimental Data', *American Economic Review*, 76: 604–20.

LaLonde, R. and Maynard, R. (1987), 'How Precise are the Evaluations of

Employment and Training Programs: Evidence from a Field Experiment', *Evaluation Review*, 11: 428–51.

Ledyard, J. (1986), 'On the Scope of the Hypothesis of Bayesian Equilibrium', *Journal of Economic Theory*, 39(1): 59–82.

Lucas, R.E. Jr. (1976), 'Econometric Policy Evaluation: A Critique', in K. Brunner and A.K Meltzer (eds.), *The Phillips Curve and Labour Markets*, Carnegie-Rochester Conference on Public Policy, Amsterdam: North Holland.

Lumsdaine, R., Stock, J. and Wise, D. (1990), 'Three Models of Retirement: Computational Complexity vs. Predictive Validity', NBER Working Paper 3558.

Machina, M.J. (1982), 'Expected Utility without the Independence Axiom', *Econometrica*, 50(2): 277–324.

(1987), 'Choice Under Uncertainty: Problems Solved and Unsolved', *Journal of Economic Perspectives*, 1(1): 121–54.

Manski, C.F. (1993), 'Dynamic Choice in Social Settings', *Journal of Econometrics*, 58: 121–36.

Mantel, R. (1974), 'On the Characterization of Excess Demand', *Journal of Economic Theory*, 7: 348–53.

Marcet, A. (1994), 'Simulation Analysis of Stochastic Dynamic Models: Applications to Theory and Estimation', in C. Sims and J. Laffont, *Advances in Econometrics: Proceedings of the 1990 Meetings of the Econometric Society*.

Marschak, T. (1953), 'Economic Measurements for Policy and Prediction', in W.C. Hood and T.C. Koopmans (eds.), *Studies in Econometric Method*, New York: John Wiley.

McFadden, D. (1973), 'Conditional Logit Analysis of Qualitative Choice Behavior', in P. Zarembka (ed.), *Frontiers in Econometrics*, New York: Academic Press.

(1981), 'Econometric Models of Probabilistic Choice', in C.F. Manski and D. McFadden (eds.) *Structural Analysis of Discrete Data with Econometric Applications*, Cambridge, Mass.: MIT Press.

(1984), 'Econometric Analysis of Qualitative Response Models', in Z. Griliches and M.D. Intriligator (eds.), *Handbook of Econometrics*, 2: 1395–457.

(1989), 'A Method of Simulated Moments for Estimation of Discrete Response Models without Numerical Integration', *Econometrics*, 57(5): 995–1026.

McFadden, D. and Richter, M. (1970), 'Revealed Stochastic Preference', manuscript, University of Minnesota.

Miller, R. (1984), 'Job Matching and Occupational Choice', *Journal of Political Economy*, 92(6): 1086–120.

Montgomery, M. (1990), 'A Dynamic Model of Contraceptive Choice', manuscript, State University of New York.

(1991a), 'Migration and Job Search in Malaysia: Estimates from Dynamic Models', manuscripts, SUNY-Stony Brook.

(1991b), 'The Transmission of Human Capital in the Marriage Market: The Case of Singapore', manuscript, SUNY-Stony Brook.

Myerson, R. (1991), *Game Theory Analysis of Conflict*, Cambridge, Mass.: Harvard University Press.

Nelder, J.A. and Mead, R. (1964), 'A Simplex Method for Function Minimization', *Computer Journal*, 7: 308–13.

Pakes, A. (1986), 'Patents as Options: Some Estimates of the Value of Holding European Patent Stocks', *Econometrica*, 54: 755–85.

(1994), 'Estimation of Dynamic Structural Models: Problems and Prospects Part II: Mixed Continuous-Discrete Controls and Market Interactions', in C. Sims and J. Laffont, *Advances in Econometrics: Proceedings of the 1990 Meetings of the Econometric Society*.

Pakes, A. and McGuire, P. (1993), 'Computing Markov Perfect Nash Equilibria: Numerical Implications of a Dynamic Differentiated Product Model', *Rand Journal of Economics* (forthcoming).

Pakes, A. and Pollard, D. (1989), 'Simulation and the Asymptotics of Optimization Estimators', *Econometrica*, 57(5): 1027–57.

Pan, V. and Reif, J. (1985), 'Efficient Parallel Solution of Linear Systems', *ACM Transactions on Computing*, 143–52.

Phelan, C. and Rust, J. (1991), 'U.S. Social Security Policy: A Dynamic Analysis of Incentives and Self-Selection', manuscript, University of Wisconsin.

Porteus, E.L. (1980), 'Overview of Iterative Methods for Discounted Finite Markov and Semi-Markov Decision Chains', in R. Hartley *et al.* (eds.), *Recent Developments in Markov Decision Processes*, New York: Academic Press.

Puterman, M.L. (1990), 'Markov Decision Processes', in D.P. Heyman and M.J. Sobel (eds.), *Handbook of Operations Research and Management Science*, Vol. II, Amsterdam: North Holland, pp.331–434.

Resnick, S. and Roy R. (1989), 'Random USC Functions, Max-Stable Processes and Continuous Choice', manuscript, Cornell University.

(1992), 'Super-Extremal Processes, Max-Stability and Dynamic Continuous Choice', manuscript, Cornell University.

Rozenzweig, M. and Wolpin, K. (1989), 'Credit Market Constraints, Consumption Smoothing and the Accumulation of Durable Production Assets in Low Income Countries: Investments in Bullocks in India', manuscript, University of Minnesota.

Rust, J. (1987), 'Optimal Replacement of GMC Bus Engines: An Empirical Model of Harold Zurcher', *Econometrica*, 55(5): 999–1033.

(1988a), 'Statistical Models of Discrete Choice Processes', *Transportation Research B*, 22B–2: 125–58.

(1988b), 'Maximimum Likelihood Estimation of Discrete Control Processes', *SIAM Journal on Control and Optimization*, 26(5): 1006–23.

(1988c), 'A Backward Solution Algorithm for Structural Estimation of Discrete Control Processes', manuscript, University of Wisconsin.

(1988d), 'The Subjective Perspective of a "Spiritual Bayesian"', *Journal of Economic Perspectives*, 2(1): 145–51.

(1992a), 'A Dynamic Programming Model of Retirement Behavior', in K.R. Billingsley, H.U. Brown III and E. Derohanes (eds.), *Computer Assisted Modelling on the IBM 3090: The IBM Contest Prize Papers*, Vol. II, Place: Baldwin Press, pp.885–912.

(1992b), 'Do People Behave According to Bellman's Principal of Optimality?',

Hoover Institution Working Paper, E-92-10.

(1993), 'Stochastic Decision Process: Theory, Computation and Estimation', manuscript, University of Wisconsin.

(1994), 'Structural Estimation of Markov Decision Processes', forthcoming in R. Engle and D. McFadden (eds.), *Handbook of Econometrics*, Volume IV, Amsterdam: North Holland.

Sargent, T.J. (1978), 'Estimation of Dynamic Labor Demand Schedules Under Rational Expectations', *Journal of Political Economy*, 86(6): 1009–44.

(1981), 'Interpreting Economic Time Series', *Journal of Political Economy*, 89(2): 213–48.

Sonnenschein, H. (1973), 'Do Walras Law and Continuity Characterize the Class of Community Excess Demand Functions?', *Journal of Economic Theory*, 6: 345–54.

Stock, J.H. and Wise, D.A. (1990), 'Pensions, The Option Value of Work, and Retirement', *Econometrica*, 58(5):1151–80.

Sturm, Roland (1990), 'A Structural Economic Model of Operating Cycle Management in European Nuclear Power Plants', manuscript, RAND Corporation.

Taylor, J.B. and Uhlig, H. (1990), 'Solving Nonlinear Stochastic Growth Models: A Comparison of Alternative Solution Methods', *Journal of Business and Economic Statistics*, 8(1): 1–17.

van den Berg, G. (1990), 'Structural Dynamic Analysis of Individual Labour Market Behavior', Ph.D. dissertation, Tilburg University.

van Der Klaauw, Wilbert (1990), 'Female Labor Supply and Marital Status Decisions: A Life-Cycle Model', manuscript, New York University.

van Dijk, N.M. (1984), *Controlled Markov Processes: Time Discretization*, CWI Tract 11, Center for Mathematics and Computer Science, Amsterdam.

Varian, H. (1982), 'The Nonparametric Approach to Demand Analysis', *Econometrica*, 50: 954–74.

White, H. (1982), 'Maximum Likelihood Estimation of Misspecified Models', *Econometrica*, 50: 1–26.

Wolpin, K. (1984), 'An Estimable Dynamic Stochastic Model of Fertility and Child Mortality', *Journal of Political Economy*, 92(5): 852–74.

(1987), 'Estimating a Structural Search Model: The Transition from Schooling to Work', *Econometrica*, 55: 801–18.

(1989), 'The Determinants of Black-White Differences in Early Employment Careers: Search, Layoffs, Quits, and Endogenous Wage Growth', *Journal of Political Economy*, 100(3): 535.

CHAPTER 5

Dynamic structural models, problems and prospects: mixed continuous discrete controls and market interactions

Ariel Pakes[1]

1   INTRODUCTION

This chapter reviews dynamic structural econometric models with both continuous and discrete controls, and those with market interactions. Its goal is to highlight techniques which enable researchers to obtain estimates of the parameters of models with these characteristics, and then use the estimates in subsequent descriptive and policy analysis. In an attempt to increase the accessibility of structural modelling, emphasis has been laid on estimation techniques which, though consistent with the underlying structural model, are computationally simple. The extent to which this is possible depends on the characteristics of the applied problem of interest, so the chapter ends up covering more than one topic. To help the reader who has more focussed interests, we now provide an outline of what can be found in the various subsections of the chapter.

Section 2 introduces the examples used to illustrate the points made in the chapter. We begin with single-agent problems involving continuous, as well as discrete, controls, and later place the agent explicitly into a market setting. The availability of continuous controls raises the possibility of using stochastic Euler equations to estimate some of the parameters of the model, and section 3 begins the substantive discussion of the chapter by considering this possibility.

We first show that the fact that there are discrete, as well as continuous, controls does not destroy our ability to generate stochastic Euler equations off of perturbations to the continuous controls, and that, provided the data are handled with care, these equations can be used to generate computationally simple estimators of the form developed by Hansen and Singleton (1982). Next we show that modified Euler equations can also be developed to analyse situations in which there are boundaries on the choice of the continuous control that are binding with positive probability (3.1; we consider both the case of boundaries whose values evolve endogenously, and the case of exogenously set boundaries), and to analyse certain special cases of models with unobserved state variables (3.2). Finally we consider conditions for the use of Euler equations when the impact of the controls on future values of the state variables are stochastic (section 3.3), and when the realisations of the state variables determining behaviour are not necessarily conditionally independent across agents (conditional on past history; section 3.4).

For long enough panels probably the most troubling aspect of the assumptions needed to generate desirable estimators out of Euler equations is the fact that Euler equation techniques can only accommodate very limited forms of serial correlation, or dependence, in unobserved state variables. Moreover, the problem of obtaining consistent estimators of the parameters of models with serially correlated unobserved state variables persists when we consider estimators based on the complete solution to the control problem, and not limit ourselves to the restrictions embodied in Euler equations. As a result we devote section 4 to the problem of incorporating serially correlated unobserved state variables into the structural models we estimate.

That section begins by noting that the problem of serially correlated unobserved state variables can be reduced to an 'initial conditions' problem almost identical to the problem discussed in Heckman's (1981) analysis of estimation in discrete-state, discrete-time, stochastic processes. Section 4.1 provides some comments on the applicability of the results from previous analysis of the initial conditions problems to estimating structural economic models with serially correlated unobserved state variables.

Section 4.2 provides an alternative method for dealing with serially correlated unobserved state variables that arises naturally in certain economic models with continuous (as well as discrete) controls, and provides proofs of its validity for the two examples used extensively in this chapter. Where applicable, the alternative can often be combined with semi-parametric estimation techniques to enable one to derive computationally simple estimators for problems that are inherently very complex (such as those that allow for market interactions). We illustrate with an empirical example taken from Olley and Pakes (1992). It derives estimates of a Cobb–Douglas production function in the presence of a serially correlated unobserved productivity shock which generates both a simultaneity and a selection problem (the first because of the endogeneity of input choices, and the second because of the fact that firms which draw better productivity sequences are more likely to survive).

Section 5 of the chapter begins by making the agent's payoff in a given period depend on the state variables of other agents in that period, thereby formally incorporating market ineractions into the problem. Once we do this we are faced with the issue of specifying the nature of the equilibria established among the various (potential and actual) actors. We limit ourselves to a discussion of the estimation and computational issues that arise in models with Markov Perfect Nash equilibria (see Maskin and Tirole (1987, 1988a, 1988b)).

Our attitude towards the empirical analysis of dynamic models with market interactions is to separate the problem of estimation from the problem of computing the equilibrium implications of the parameters estimated. The estimation problem is broken into smaller parts, each of which is both consistent with the overall dynamic equilibrium framework, and provides an estimator (with desirable properties) for a subvector of the model's parameters. We assume estimation will have to proceed in this fashion because, for most problems of current interest, neither our computational resources, nor our data, are rich enough to allow us to estimate all the model's parameters in a single unified iterative estimation algorithm. This procedure also turns out to be helpful in providing a framework which enables us to separate out and empirically analyse single primitives from richer, and hopefully more realistic, economic environments.

Once we have estimated the primitives of the problem, we will want to compute and analyse the distribution of equilibrium, or market, responses to policy and environmental changes. Section 5.1 turns to this computational problem. It begins with an algorithm for computing Markov Perfect Nash equilibria. We use this algorithm to compute a differentiated products version of the Ericson–Pakes model of industry dynamics (Ericson and Pakes (1992)) and then use the output of this computation to illustrate the many aspects of reality that can be captured by the current generation of structural models.

The example also has the useful property that the Markov process which defines its equilibrium lives on a finite set of points. So we can calculate the value functions and policies it generates to any desired degree of precision and then compare the true values to the values obtained from alternative approximation methods. We show that for exact calculations the number of grid points that need to be evaluated at every iteration of the recursive fixed-point calculation grows polynomially in the (least upper bound to the) number of agents (ever) active in the market. The time per grid point evaluation grows as a polynomial of lower order. So we turn to an examination of the possibility of using polynomial expansions to approximate the value function at each iteration of the computational algorithm; an idea which, in somewhat different form, has been used extensively in a variety of recent research (see Judd (1990) the chapter by Marcet in this volume, and the literature cited in those articles).

The major analytic result in this section shows that provided the value function of a given agent is symmetric (more precisely exchangeable) in the state vectors of its competitors, the number of polynomial coefficients one needs to determine for a given order of approximation is independent of the number of agents active in the market. This implies that the number of grid points which we need to use at each iteration of the fixed-point calculation will also become independent of the number of agents active in the market – a result which may enable us to devise relatively straightforward algorithms for computing equilibria for large markets. The computational part of the chapter concludes by fitting the actual value functions for our example to the exchangeable basis of polynomials, and then examining the quality of the fit from the polynomial approximation.

There is also a short concluding section to the chapter. It provides a more personal view on the use of structural economic modelling, and its role in helping to interpret data.

Notation, and the role and choice of examples

The following notation will be augmented at various points in the chapter.

> s is the state variable, assumed to be an element of some metric space S. In this chapter $s = (y, \hat{s})$, where y is understood to be the vector of state variables whose values are agent specific, and $\hat{s}$ consists of the y vectors of all other agents operating in the market.
>
> $C_s = Y_s \times \Gamma_s$: where $Y(\cdot)$ specifies a finite (but strictly positive) number of feasible alternatives for the discrete control (χ) and $\Gamma(\cdot)$ specifies a compact valued continuous correspondence which provides the feasible values for the continuous control (x).
>
> $d = (\chi, x)$: where d is the decision vector, χ is the discrete control, and x is the continuous control.
>
> In all our examples the one period return function will be written as $\pi(s, d) - c(s, d)$, where $\pi(\cdot)$ is the single-period 'profit' function and $c(\cdot)$ provides the cost of the chosen policy (note also that the feasible levels of d depend on s although Γ_s).

There are, of course, many possible state variables whose values do not differ across agents (examples include prices, technology and regulatory rules). It will be understood here (for notational convenience) that these individual invariant variables are also included in y. Under standard regularity conditions the agent's policy solves the Bellman equation

$$V(s) = \sup_{\{d \in C_s\}} \{\pi(s, d) - c(s, d) + \beta \int V(s') P(ds' | s, d)\}, \qquad (5.1)$$

with $V(s)$ given by the unique solution to the implied contraction mapping. We let $\{d_s, s \in S\}$ be the associated stationary optimal policy.[2]

At this level of generality the notation hides distinctions which become important in both choosing specifications which are appropriate for different applied problems, and for determining the availability and properties of alternative estimators. Rather than cataloguing special cases in an abstract way, we carry particular examples along in the various subsections of the chapter. The examples have been chosen for their ability to allow us to illustrate the issues we thought were important in as simple a setting as possible. Using examples in this way has the additional advantage that it allows us to comment on some of the more detailed specification issues that arise in choosing appropriate assumptions for certain classes of applied problems.

The first example we deal with is a production–investment model, similar to those which have been used extensively in both the macro (see Stokey, Lucas and Prescott (1989)) and in the industrial organisation (see Tirole (1989)) literatures. Section 2, which allows for both continuous and discrete controls but not market interactions, considers a monopolist who accumulates physical capital according to a deterministic law of motion but faces a stochastic environment. The monopolist makes two decisions in each period; whether or not to exit and, if not, how much to invest in capital accumulation. The second example is also a production investment model; but this time one that allows for stochastic accumulation. This model is also somewhat more detailed, and we use it more intensively in the later sections of the chapter where we revoke the monopoly assumption and consider estimation and computation in models that allow for market interactions.

2   AN INTRODUCTORY EXAMPLE

We begin with what is probably the simplest model with both continuous and discrete controls that one would attempt to take to panel data. It has one continuous control (investment), a choice between two discrete alternatives (remaining active or exiting), an exogenous state variable which evolves stochastically, and no market interactions. For simplicity we will take the exogenous stochastic state variable to be unobserved, but in general it could be a vector process with an unobserved component. The unobservable is needed to rationalise the heterogeneity in both the outcome paths and the investment choices observed in the data. Also, in a more general framework we would want to allow for separate disturbances affecting the value of all but one of the discrete alternatives (this to rationalise the discrete choices in the data). Provided the discrete state-specific disturbances are included in an additive fashion and are serially independent, as in the discussion of the chapter by Rust (1991), they have no substantive effects on the points to be made using this simple example, and therefore, have been omitted from the discussion.[3]

In terms of our previous notation, we make the following assumption.

Assumption 1

$$y = (k, \omega) \in K \times \Omega \subset \mathcal{R}_+^2,$$

where it is understood that we only observe y for firms that are active at the beginning of the period $(\chi = 1)$, while if $d = (\chi_t, x_t) = (1, x)$

$$k_{t+1} = k_t(1 - \delta) + x,$$

with probability one, and the distribution of ω_{t+1} conditional on y_t is determined by the family of distributions

$$\mathcal{P}_\omega = \{P(\cdot|\omega), \omega \in \Omega\},$$

which are assumed to have densities w.r.t some domination measure, to be stochastically increasing in ω, and to possess the property that if $h(\cdot)$ is continuous and bounded then

$$\int h(\omega')(d\omega'|\omega)$$

is a continuous function of ω.

We also assume that $\pi(y; \theta)$ is bounded, increasing in both its arguments, differentiable (with bounded derivative) and concave in k, and has $\lim_{k \to 0}$ $\partial\pi(\cdot)/\partial k = \infty$ while $\lim_{k \to \infty} \partial\pi(\cdot)/\partial k = 0$, for each $\omega \in \Omega$; that $c(x, s; \theta) = c(x; \theta)$ which is increasing, differentiable (with bounded derivative), and convex in x (for every k); and that both $\partial c(\ )/\partial x$, and $\partial\pi(\ )/\partial k$, are differentiable in θ (a.s.).

The assumption that the cost of adjustment depends only on the amount of investment (and not on the capital in place) is made solely for expositional convenience. Remark 1 following theorem 1 generalises the results in this section to the case where the cost of adjustment depends also on k.

There are, however, at least two aspects of these assumptions that are more problematic. First (assumption 1) assumes that the accumulation relationship between the continuous control and the state variable is deterministic. Though this has become a traditional assumption in the literature on the accumulation of physical capital, it is a special case of a more general model in which the impact of investment is stochastic. One might argue the relevance of the special deterministic case for investment in physical capital, but it seems much less appropriate for the accumulation of the 'intangible' capital stocks that emanate from a firm's investment in research and exploration, or in advertising and goodwill. Here the randomness in the outcome from the investment activities often seem both to have strikingly large variances, and to underlie many of the 'simultaneity' and 'selection' issues that generated the interest in structural modelling of the phenomena of interest in the first place.[4] Similar distinctions occur among the different types of stocks accumulated by households (compare, for example, investments in health to investments in consumer durables).

There are several differences between models with deterministic and stochastic accumulation which are important for the discussion which follows. First, when a state variable evolves deterministically knowledge of past investments implies knowledge of the current stock (at least up to an initial condition and the parameters describing the decay process). So deterministically controlled state variables are generally assumed to be observed by the econometrician. In contrast, unless there is a separate reading on the outcome of (in contrast to the input into) the investment process, a stock that accumulates stochastically will be unobserved, and will therefore generate a serially correlated unobserved state variable (of course, there may well be serially correlated unobserved state variables in models with deterministic accumulation also; section 4 discusses estimation in the presence of serially correlated unobserved state variables). Also, though one can derive 'Euler equations' for some models with stochastic accumulation, both their form, and the assumptions needed to justify them, differ from those needed for models with deterministic accumulation (see section 3.3). On the plus side, models which allow for stochastic accumulation, but presume smoothness in the relationship between the continuous choice and the transition probabilities, generate first-order conditions with relative ease. This, in turn, both enables more detailed analytic treatment of optimal policies, and simplifies computational issues (section 5). Our second example is a model with stochastic accumulation, and it will be used to illustrate these points.

The assumption of a convex and differentiable cost of investment function can also be problematic. Non-convexities can often be handled by adding additional dimensions to the set of discrete alternatives (see Das (1992)). In models of capital accumulation one often worries about the differentiability of $c(x)$ at the point $x = 0$, as this is the point at which small movements carry with them the difference between selling, and purchasing and installing, units of the stock. A count of the number of observations at which x is exactly zero in the data ought to provide some indication of whether this is likely to be an important problem in any given application (and it often is).

With assumption 1 the Bellman equation for our problem (equation (5.1)) reduces to

$$V(\omega,k)=\max\{\Phi,\sup_{[x\in\Gamma(\omega,k)]}[\pi(\omega,k)-c(x) \\ +\beta\int V[\omega',k(1-\delta)+x]P(d\omega'|\omega)]\}, \tag{5.1'}$$

where Φ is the return of closing down the firm (the return to $\chi=0$) and transferring its salvageable assets to another activity[5] and, here and below, it is understood that all functions are indexed by θ_0.

We pause here to fill in two details. First, to complete the specification of the model we need to specify $\Gamma(y)$, the choice set for x. This is a primitive of the problem and we will want to consider different assumptions on it and investigate their implications below. For starters assume there are no restrictions on $\Gamma(y)$, or that $\Gamma(y)=\mathcal{R}$. Now note that boundedness of $\pi(\cdot)$ together with the fact that $\beta<1$ implies boundedness of the expected discounted value of any feasible programme, and, therefore, that there exists a (finite) $\bar{x}$ such that $\sup_y x(y)<\bar{x}$. Similarly the fact that $\lim_{k\to 0}\partial\pi(\ )/\partial k=\infty$, implies that it will never be optimal for an active firm to drive its capital stock to zero, so for all k $\inf_\omega x(\omega,k)>-k$. So ω l.o.q we take, $\Gamma(y)=[-k,\bar{x}]$, and note that

$$x(\omega,k)\in\overset{0}{\Gamma}(y), \tag{5.2a}$$

for every $(\omega,k)\in K\times\Omega$ (here $\overset{0}{\Gamma}(y)$ is notation for the interior of the set $\Gamma(\cdot)$). That is, investment will never be at a 'corner' of its choice set (we come back to the problems generated by corners below).

Second, note that policies for this problem are couples, (χ,x), where $\chi:K\times\Omega\to[0,1]$, provides the exit decision, and $x:K\times\Omega\to\mathcal{R}$ determines investment. Given assumptions it is straightforward to show that $V(\cdot)$ is non-decreasing in both its arguments, and that, as a consequence, there is a function $\underline{\omega}(\cdot)$, which is decreasing in k, such that $V(\omega,k)\le\Phi$ if and only if $\omega\le\underline{\omega}(k)$. So the exit policy is a stopping rule, $\underline{\omega}(\cdot):K\to\Omega$, with the property that

$$\chi_{t+1}=0 \text{ iff } \omega\le\underline{\omega}(k), \quad k\in K. \tag{5.2b}$$

3   EULER EQUATIONS FROM MIXED CONTINUOUS–DISCRETE-CHOICE MODELS

Having added a continuous alternative to the discrete-choice problem, it is natural to begin with the question of whether we can go back to the computationally simple estimation techniques based on stochastic Euler equations to estimate at least some of the parameters of this mixed continuous–discrete-choice model. To this end we compare the discounted cash flow earned from the optimal policy to that from the starred alternatives to that policy given by

$$\chi^*(y_{t+\tau}) = \chi(y_{t+\tau}), \text{ for all } \tau,$$

$$x^*(y_t, \epsilon) = x(y_t) - \epsilon, \quad x^*(y_{t+1}, \epsilon) = x(y_{t+1}) + (1 - \delta)\epsilon,$$

$$x^*(y_{t+\tau+1}, \epsilon) = x(y_{t+\tau+1}), \text{ for } \tau \geq 1, \tag{5.3}$$

and alternative values of ϵ.

An important property of the alternative programmes (5.3) is that they all hold the discrete choice the same as the discrete choice would have been in the optimal programme (no matter what the realised state of the world), and they only perturb the continuous control in periods t and $t + 1$. Also all programmes are constructed so that $y_{t+\tau}^* = y_{t+\tau}$ for all $\tau \geq 2$ with probability one. Thus the difference between the cash flows generated by the ϵ-alternative and the optimal policy is only a function of the costs of adjustment and profits in periods t and $t + 1$. Now note that boundedness of the return function and the fact that $\beta < 1$ ensure that this difference in cash flows is well defined, while the feasibility of the ϵ-alternative programme for sufficiently small $|\epsilon|$ (see (5.2a)) together with the optimality of the original programme, insure that this difference must be non-positive in a neighbourhood of $\epsilon = 0$. Thus, provided this difference is differentiable, its derivative must be 0 at $\theta = \theta_0$. Differentiability follows from the assumptions that $c(\ )$ and $\pi(\ )$ have bounded derivatives, the fact that $\chi(\ )$ is differentiable almost everywhere (see 5.2b), and the Lebesgue Dominated Convergence Theorem. Taking that derivative, and evaluating it at $\epsilon = 0$, we get the Euler equation in lemma 1.

Lemma 1
A necessary condition for a policy couple $\{\chi(y), x(y)\}$ to be optimal is that

$$-\partial c(x)/\partial x + \beta \int \chi[\omega', k(1 - \delta) + x]\{\partial \pi[\omega', k(1 - \delta) + x]/\partial k$$
$$+ (1 - \delta)\partial c[x(\omega', k(1 - \delta) + x)]/\partial x\}P(d\omega'|\omega) = 0,$$

at $\theta = \theta_0$.

Lemma 1 makes it clear that the presence of discrete, as well as continuous, controls does not destroy our ability to generate stochastic Euler equations. We simply substitute the observed value of the discrete control into the return functions and then proceed in precisely the same way we did in the continuous problem. The Euler equation formed in this way can then be used as a basis for forming moment conditions which can be fed into a method of moments estimation algorithm of the form developed by Hansen and Singleton ((1982); for further notes on the estimation algorithm see the discussion at the end of section 3). Note, however, that if we were to use an equation such as lemma 1 as a basis for estimation we would have to select the observations used to form the sample moments on variables which are *measurable at date t*. If an agent satisfies the selection criteria in year t and transfers discrete states in year $t+1$, the agent must be kept in sample for the purpose of the period t Euler equation, even if the relevant date $t+1$ variables are not 'reported'. In our example then, when a firm actually does exit in period $t+1$, we use the period t observation by substituting the actual x_t in for the first term for that observation in lemma 1, and setting the second term *equal to zero*, as would be the case if $\chi_{t+1} = 0$.

There are, of course, several problems that actually can destroy our ability to use stochastic Euler equations, at least those as simple as the one in lemma 1, as a basis for estimating parameters of dynamic models from panel data, but they have little to do with the addition of discrete alternatives to the choice set. We now move on to a brief review of some of them. Section 3.1 considers the possibility of binding constraints on the choice set, section 3.2 considers unobserved state variables, 3.3 considers stochastic (in contrast to deterministic) accumulation, and 3.4 considers cases in which the realisations of the state variables are not conditionally independent across agents in the panel. Since the extent to which any of these problems are likely to be important will vary with the characteristics of the economic model and of the data one is analysing, we have tried to ensure that each subsection is self-contained.[6]

3.1   Binding constraints on the choice set

We begin with the possibility that the optimal choice is not in the interior of the feasible set, i.e., of constraints in the correspondence defining the feasible choices for the continuous control that are binding for a set of values for the state variables that have positive probability. In this case condition (5.2a) is not always satisfied and, as a result, it is not always possible to construct the alternative programme in (5.3) for all $|\epsilon|$ less than some positive κ.

There are at least two types of characterisations of the economic environment that have led to binding boundaries in empirical work. In the first the location of the relevant boundary is both known to the econometrician and independent of the actions of the agent. This would have occurred in our example if we had not assumed a market for used capital goods, since this would change the choice set for x from $[-k, \bar{x}]$ to $[0, \bar{x}]$ and we could not rule out the possibility that the optimal investment choice is 0 for a set of

$y = (k, \omega)$ values with positive probability. A similar problem occurs when one of the primitive functions is non-differentiable at zero (or at any other prespecified point), and the modification of the Euler equation in lemma 1 developed below will cover this case also. Both these cases generate zero investment with positive probability, and when $x = 0$ the x choice need not satisfy a first-order condition (like the Euler equation) with equality.

In the second type of problem with binding boundaries the location of the boundary is endogenous, being determined, in part, by the actions of the agent in previous periods. This latter case has been studied extensively in both the consumption and the investment literatures under the heading of liquidity and/or financial constraints (see Hubbard and Kashyap (1989), Gilchrist (1989) and Himmelburg (1990), and the literature cited there for the investment problem, and Hayashi (1987), Runkle (1983), Zeldes (1989) and the literature cited in these articles for the consumption problem).[7] This problem would have occurred in our example were we to have introduced another state variable for the firm, its financial assets in period t, or $A(t)$, and assumed that the firm cannot borrow more than $A(t)$. This would restrict the choice set for x to equal $[-k, A]$, and we could not ensure that $x < A$ for all possible y.

We begin with binding boundaries of the first kind using our example with the additional restriction that $\Gamma(y) = [0, \bar{x}]$. Note first that the conditions we required for the proof of lemma 1 can now be violated in one of two different ways. First it is possible that $x(y_t) = 0$. Second, even if $x(y_t) > 0$, it is possible that there is a set of y_{t+1} that has positive probability conditional on y_t, for which $x(y_{t+1}) = 0$. In either one of these cases the alternative programme in (5.3) will not be feasible for all values of $|\epsilon| \leq \kappa$ (and some $\kappa > 0$), and, as a result, the logical basis for constructing the Euler equation in lemma 1 breaks down. Note, however, that provided $x(y)$ is observable the first requirement, i.e., that $x(y_t) > 0$, does not, in itself, destroy our ability to obtain parameter estimates from a Euler equation for a selected sample. That is, since, x is measurable at date t, we can select only those observations with $x(y_t) > 0$. Consider the sample analogue to the restriction in lemma 1 for this subsample, and base estimation on the fact that the expected value of the Euler equation for the subsample will equal zero at the true θ_0. So provided x is observable, the difficulty in deriving Euler equations that rely on compensating perturbations in *adjacent* periods (like those in (5.3) above) when there is a possibility of binding corners, is that we do not directly observe $x(y_{t+1})$ for all values of y_{t+1} that have positive probability conditional on period t information.

One way around this problem is to relax the requirement that we base our Euler equations on perturbations in adjacent periods.[8] As we now show, this will allow us to push the compensating ϵ-perturbation forward to some (random) future period in which the agent is not at a corner, thereby making it feasible for all values of $|\epsilon| \leq \kappa$ with probability one. With this in mind define

$$\tau^* = \min_{\tau \geq 1}\{\chi(y_{t+\tau}) = 0 \text{ or } x(y_{t+\tau}) \geq \kappa\}. \tag{5.4a}$$

τ^* is a positive, integer-valued, random variable determined either by the first time the agent's programme calls for positive investment, or by the period in which the agent exits, whichever comes first (formally if $F_{t+i} = \sigma$ $(y_t, \ldots, y_{t+i})$, the σ-algebra generated by $(y_t, \ldots, y_{t+i})$, then τ^* is a stopping time with respect to the sequence $\{F_{t+i}\}$). Now select out a subsample with $x(y_t) \geq \kappa$, and for that subsample consider the alternative programmes

$$\chi^*(y_{t+\tau}, \epsilon) = \chi(y_{t+\tau}), \text{ for all } \tau \text{ and } \epsilon,$$

and

$$x^*(y_{t+\tau}, \epsilon) = \begin{cases} x(y_{t+\tau}) - \epsilon, & \text{for } \tau = 0, \\ x(y_{t+\tau}), & \text{for } \tau < \tau^*, \\ x(y_{t+\tau^*}) + (1-\delta)^{\tau^*-1}\epsilon, & \text{for } \tau = \tau^*, \\ x(y_{t+\tau}), & \text{for } \tau > \tau^*. \end{cases} \tag{5.4b}$$

For fixed τ^* the ϵ-alternative policy in (5.4b) is feasible for all $|\epsilon| < \kappa$. Moreover any such policy generates the same values for the state variables in all $\tau > \tau^*$ as does the optimal policy (with probability one). Conditional on a value for τ^* then, the difference between the expected discounted values of net cash flows generated by the optimal and these ϵ-alternative policies just depends on cash flows between times t and $t+\tau^*$. τ^* is a random variable, but one whose realisation is *independent* of ϵ.

Now construct the difference in discounted net cash flows between the optimal and the ϵ-alternative policies given in (5.4b), and note that an argument analogous to that proceeding lemma 1 leads to the conclusion in lemma 2.

Lemma 2
When investment is restricted to be non-negative, but the rest of the assumptions underlying lemma 1 remain intact, then a necessary condition for a policy couple $\{\chi(y), x(y)\}$ to be optimal is that

$$-\partial c(x_t)/\partial x + E_{(t)}\{\textstyle\sum_{\tau=1}^{\tau^*-1} \beta^\tau[\partial\pi(\omega_{t+\tau}, k_{t+\tau})/\partial k](1-\delta)^{\tau-1}$$
$$+ \beta^{\tau^*}\chi_{t+\tau^*}\{[\partial\pi(\omega_{t+\tau^*}, k_{t+\tau^*})/\partial k](1-\delta)^{\tau^*-1} + \beta[\partial c(x_{t+\tau^*})/\partial x](1-\delta)^{\tau^*}\} = 0,$$

where $E_{(t)}f(\ )$ provides the expectation of $f(\ )$ conditional on F_t, and τ^* is defined as in (5.4a).

Provided that τ^* is observable (in our example this requires observations on both investment and on whether or not the firm liquidated in a given year), and that τ^* is always less than $T - t$, where T is the final year of the panel, lemma 2 can be used to generate Euler-equation-based estimators in the same way lemma 1 does. Note, however, that the requirement that $\tau^* \leq T - t$ is a probability one requirement. If we simply select out those observations for which it ends up being true, we will be selecting the sample on the basis of behaviour determined by information not available at date t, and any selection procedure based on such information will generate an inconsistency in the estimation procedure. The importance of this censoring problem is likely to vary from sample to sample, but one ought to be able to get an indication of just how important it is in any given sample by examining the empirical distribution of the realisations of τ^*, and by adjusting the estimation algorithm accordingly (that is using only those years for which there is a sufficiently long subsequent period observed in the panel).

As an empirical example of the magnitude of the issues raised by the existence of discrete controls and of binding corners, we consider Olley's (1991) study of the telecommunications equipment industry (most of SIC 3661, and part of SIC 3663). The study constructs a thirteen-year panel of enterprise level data (the basic data sources are the various censuses and surveys of manufacturing as combined in the LRD, see McGuckin and Pascoe (1988) for details on the LRD). The telecommunications equipment industry is an industry with large plants, but one which went through a major restructuring during the period covered by the data (this was caused by both a gradual deregulation process, and by technological change). Of the 376 plants that are in the data at some time during the sample period, ninety-nine, or approximately 25 per cent, had shut down by the end of the sample. So liquidation does occur quite frequently and should be accounted for in the analysis. Of the 2,569 plant/year observations available (this includes the observations on plants which liquidated in the following year) 168, or about 6.5 per cent, report exactly zero investment. Thus there is some evidence of there being a 'boundary' at zero. These 168 zero observations, however, include only sixteen sequences with two consecutive years of zero investment, and there is not one sequence with three consecutive zero investment years. Thus it seems that for this data set Euler equation techniques would be appropriate provided we used data on all plant-year observations at t (including those who liquidate in $t + 1$) for all $t \leq T - 2$, or possibly, $t \leq T - 3$.

We now move on to consider boundaries whose values are determined, at least in part, by the actions of the agent in previous periods. There are really two differences from the last case. The first is due to the fact that once we have partial control over the value of the boundary in the coming period we can often, though not always, ensure that we will be away from that boundary with probability one by appropriate choice of control, and this simplifies the estimation problem considerably. The second difference is that models which have endogenous boundaries generally involve an extra (often quite difficult) set of measurement problems that arise from the need for a measure of that boundary. We come back to this measurement problem below.

We should note at the outset that not all models with endogenous boundaries will be able to generate Euler equations from simple compensating variations in adjacent periods. There is, therefore, room for developing necessary and sufficient conditions for Euler equations when boundaries are endogenous. Here we suffice with the simpler task of illustrating the logic of the argument that allows one to use Euler equations when they are available. To do so in as simple a fashion as possible we have to modify our example to allow for consumption, as well as production (this because the simple model with an added finance constraint does not admit Euler equations based on compensating perturbations in adjacent periods.)[9] Now the agent is allocating consumption and investment expenditures to maximise the expected discounted value of a time-separable utility function. The boundary condition is obtained by constraining the agent to satisfy the 'credit constraint' that the sum of investment and consumption expenditures cannot exceed the value of the agent's financial assets. These are denoted by $A(t)$, so that if the two continuous controls (investment and consumption) are given by $x_{1,t}$ and $x_{2,t}$, the credit constraint is written as

$$A_t \geq x_{1,t} + x_{2,t}. \tag{5.5a}$$

$A(t)$ (which is the boundary of the correspondence determining the feasible choices for the continuous control) evolves according to

$$A_{t+1} = \frac{A_t(1+r) + \pi(\omega_t, k_t) - x_{1,t} - x_{2,t}, \text{ if } \chi_t = 1,}{A_t(1+r) + (\chi_{t-1} - \chi_t)\Phi - x_{2,t}, \quad \text{ if } \chi_t = 0,} \tag{5.5b}$$

where for simplicity we have assumed a deterministic rate of return on financial assets (r). Note that the effect of a change in the discrete state here is to change the nature of the accumulation relationship.[10] If the agent shuts down the firm, he or she obtains a one-period payoff of Φ, and then must live off asset income. We shall assume that the primitives of this model have been chosen so that the optimal programme is kept away from any lower bound on the x-choices.

With these assumptions consider the following family of alternative policies. Leave the discrete shutdown decision the same as in the optimal programme in every period, and the continuous controls unchanged for all periods after $t+1$, but change the continuous controls in periods t and $t+1$ to

$$x_{1,t} = x^*_{1,t} - \epsilon_1, \text{ and } x^*_{2,t} - \epsilon_2 \qquad (5.6)$$

$$x_{1,t+1} = x^*_{1,t+1}(y_{t+1}) + (1-\delta)\epsilon_1, \text{ and } x_{2,t+1} = x^*_{2,t+1}(y_{t+1}) + g(y_{t+1}, \underline{\epsilon}),$$

where

$$g(y_{t+1}, \underline{\epsilon}) = \Delta\pi[y_{t+1}, \epsilon_1] - (1+r)\epsilon_2 - (r+\delta)\epsilon_1,$$

and $\Delta\pi[\cdot]$ is the difference in profits resulting from the difference in period $t+1$ capital stocks induced by ϵ_1, and $\underline{\epsilon} = (\epsilon_1, \epsilon_2)$. Without going into details we simply note that it is easy to show both that the alternative programme in (5.6) has been constructed so that it will be feasible with probability one for all sufficiently small $|\epsilon_1| + |\epsilon_2|$ provided *only* that the credit constraint is not binding in period t, and that the alternative and optimal programmes generate the same value for the state variables after period $t+2$ (with probability one).

Given these facts, a simple extension to the logic of lemma 1 for the subsample which is not at the boundary in the current period leads us to two Euler equations. These are obtained from the derivatives of the function defining the difference between the expected discounted value of utility from the alternative and from the optimal programme with respect to ϵ_1 and ϵ_2 (evaluated at $\underline{\epsilon} = 0$). The first Euler equation is familiar from the finance literature (see Lucas (1978)). It states that the expected discounted value of the marginal-utility weighted returns from the two forms of savings (investing in physical and in financial capital) must be equated at the margin. The second Euler equation is familiar from the literature on the life-cycle hypothesis (see Hall (1979)). It states that, if consumption expenditures are interior, the marginal utility of consumption should be a martingale (with respect to $\{F_t\}$).

The fact that this latter Euler equation is not destroyed by credit constraints, provided only that the credit constraint is not binding in the initial period, was exploited to do estimation and testing of a stochastic consumption model with credit constraints by Zeldes (1989) (see also the literature he cites; similar reasoning has been used to derive and analyse Euler equations for the investment decisions of firms in situations in which firms face credit constraints, see Gilchrist (1989), Himmelburg (1990) and Hubbard and Kashyap (1989)). Our discussion only generalises to the extent that it allows for discrete controls (a fact which might allow one to integrate the closely related phenomena of shutdown and/or bankruptcy into the analysis).

In terms of our notation, those articles assume that all expenditures and assets are perfectly observed, and then proceed as follows. Calculate the right-hand side of (5.5a). If it is greater than $A(t)$ for a given agent, that agent could not have faced a binding finance constraint in the given period. Now separate the sample and use only the unconstrained agents in the estimation algorithm. Again, provided the selection is on variables which are measurable at date t, the selected sample should abide by the constraints generated from the Euler equation at θ_0. Moreover a comparison of diagnostic tests done on the selected and the unselected parts of the sample can be illuminating (see Zeldes (1989)).

Note that these procedures for generating Euler equations, when there are boundaries which evolve endogenously, assume that we can select out a subsample that we *know* is not at a boundary in the current period. Empirically the question of whether this is possible depends on our ability to measure the variables determining the boundary condition. The reason to bring out measurement problems here, after ignoring them for the most part of this subsection, is that the variables determining the boundary conditions for the applications which have used these techniques to date are among the poorest measured of economic variables. For example, to determine whether the agent is at a boundary in the credit constraint example we need information on both *total* expenditures and *total* assets, two variables which are notoriously hard to measure. Most of the micro-empirical literature to date has treated this measurement problem in an informal manner, using more or less stringent selection criteria, and focussing on the parameter estimates obtained from the more stringent criteria. Little has been done on more formal treatments of this problem (though a preliminary discussion of it is contained in Hajivassiliou and Ioannides (1990)).

Once we allow for the case in which we do not know with certainty whether a given observation was at a boundary, the conditional expectation of the Euler equation is no longer necessarily zero at θ_0. Instead it becomes a sum of its expectation conditonal on the constraint not being binding (which equals zero at θ_0) times the probability of the constraint not being binding, plus the expectation of the Euler equation conditional on the constraint being binding, times the probability of this latter event. A question that then arises is whether we can use the structure implied by the measurement problem, together with the constraints implied by the model at θ_0, to restrict the moments obtained from this 'generalised' Euler equation at $\theta = \theta_0$ in a way that allows us to narrow the admissible range for (and, if possible, estimate) that parameter. We do know that at θ_0 the expectation of the Euler equation conditional on being at the boundary must be non-negative everywhere (this follows from the fact that a negative perturbation to the current choice is always feasible), and we will often be able to show that both it, and the probability of being at a corner, is non-increasing in the observed asset measure (as a case in point, in the credit constraint example the expectation of the Euler equation becomes the 'Lagrange multiplier' for the credit constraint). This gives us another set of constraints to use in obtaining information on θ. Just how far theory, together with some combination of parametric and non-parametric estimation procedures, can get us in this context, is an open question, but one that might well be worth pursuing, at least for problems to be analysed on large data sets see Matzkin (1992) for both an analysis of how qualitative characteristics derived from theory can be used to empirically analyse some static choice problems, and for a discussion of related computational issues).

There are, of course, more complicated constraints on the choices of continuous controls possible than those considered here. Our examples, however, do serve to illustrate the following points. First, if we have the ability to observe whether an agent is currently at a boundary of the feasible correspondence, the difficulty in establishing the conditions needed to generate stochastic Euler equations is in constructing a perturbation to the optimal policy which will be feasible in the following periods *with probability one* for all ϵ in an open neighbourhood of zero. When the boundary is endogenous, this problem can often be circumvented by appropriate choice of controls in the alternative programmes (this presumes sufficient markets to trade over time or between continuous controls). However in the case of endogenous boundaries measurement problems often make it difficult to determine whether an agent is at a boundary in the current period, and little work has been done to date on incorporating measurement error into the analysis. When the boundaries are set exogenously, modified Euler equation techniques can still be constructed, but we will generally require data that allows us to follow each agent over more than two periods of time to implement them (though the data itself ought to be able to tell us approximately how many consecutive periods are required). Finally, note that the presence (or absence) of discrete controls has little to do with our ability to generate Euler equations from perturbations to the continuous control (no matter whether there is the possibility of binding boundaries).

3.2   Unobserved state variables

To date our ability to estimate the parameters of structural models with unobserved state variables, whether using Euler-equations-based estimators, or some other form of estimation technique, is severely limited. As a result we will pay special attention to it in this review. Section 4 discusses the problems associated with integrating serially correlated unobserved state variables in estimation algorithms based on actually solving for the value function at different values of the parameter vector. This subsection explores the extent to which unobserved state variables can be incorporated into Euler-equation-based estimation algorithms.

We begin by setting out the problem generated by unobserved state variables, and then move on to discuss two special cases for which we can circumvent that problem. These cases are neither nested to, nor more general than, either the conditional independence assumption discussed extensively in Rust (1991), or the assumptions we develop in section 4 for estimation in the presence of serially correlated unobserved state variables. More generally, the assumptions that are relevant for the problem at hand determine our ability to derive consistent estimators from alternative estimation techniques, and no single technique nests the others.

Our ability to obtain Euler-equation-based estimators when there are unobserved state variables depends on particular functional-form assumptions. In order to be clear about precisely what assumptions are needed, we will have to move out of the confines of our example, and into a more general setting. Letting the state vector for a given individual be, $y(z, v)$, with z observed, and v not observed, and recalling that $d(\cdot)$ is the vector of decision, or control, variables we write the Euler equation as

$$E_{(t)}h[d(z_{t+1}, v_{t+1}), z_{t+1}, v_{t+1}, d(z_t, v_t), z_t, v_t; \theta_0] = 0, \qquad (5.7)$$

where the expectation is conditional on all information available to the agent in period $t(F_t)$. The estimation problem is that, since we do not observe v, we cannot calculate the sample analogues to the moment conditions that can be generated from (5.7).

The first special case we consider mixes a partial conditional independence assumption with an exclusion restriction. Formally what we require is that we can partition the vector of unobservables, v, into two components, v_1 and v_2, and then write the function $h(\cdot)$ in (5.7) as

$$h[d(z_{t+1}, v_{2,t+1}), z_{t+1}, v_{1,t+1}, d(z_t, v_{2,t}), z_t, v_{1,t}; \theta_0], \qquad (5.8a)$$

with v_1 and v_2 subvectors of v, and

$$P(dv_1', dv_2', dz' | v_1, v_2, z) = P(dv_1' | z') P(dv_2', dz' | v_2, z), \qquad (5.8b)$$

with $P(dv_1' | z')$ a known family of distributions.

Equation (5.8a) assumes that one of the components of the partitioned vector of state variables (i.e., v_2) only impacts on the value of the Euler equation through its effects on the controls (i.e., through $d_t(\cdot)$), while the other (v_1) can have an independent effect on the Euler equation but does not affect the control at all. Equation (5.8b) states that v_1, the unobserved component which has an independent effect on the value of the Euler equation, must be from a known family of conditionally independent distributions. However the conditional distribution of v_2, the unobserved component that only affects the Euler equation through its impacts on the control, need be neither known, nor restricted (v_2 can, for example, be freely serially correlated).

To illustrate the content of the restrictions in (5.8) we go back to our example (assumption 1 and lemma 1), and augment it with unobserved state variables. Assume then that there is both an unobserved component in the ω process determining productivity (our v_1), and randomness in the process determining the liquidation value of the firm (this value was previously the constant Φ). Call the unobserved component of the liquidation value v_2, and assume v_1 and v_2 obey (5.8b). That is v_1 is generated by a known family of conditionally independent distributions, but v_2 may be freely serially correlated. z_t in this example contains the capital stock and any observed components of the ω process (for simplicity we ignore these in what follows).

There are two controls in this problem; the investment (x), and the shutdown (χ), decisions. For (5.8a) to be satisfied neither can depend on v_1. If v_1 is conditionally independent, investment cannot depend on it (investment only depends on the conditional distribution of future v_1 values and that distribution is independent of v_1. $\chi(\cdot)$ will not depend on v_1 provided either that the exit decision must be made before the realisation of v_1, or that the exiting firm exits at the end of the period and obtains the profits from that period. Of the assumptions needed for (5.8a), then, the one that seems to be more problematic for our example is that the unobserved component of the productivity process is conditionally independent. Whether it is a reasonable assumption for the problem at hand depends on the nature of the factors which cause shifts in productivity in the industry being studied, and on the variables measured in the data being used.

The Euler equation for this example (the extension to lemma 1) is

$$-\partial c(x)/\partial x + \beta \int_{v_2'} \int_{v_1'} \chi[v_2', k(1-\delta)+x]\{\partial \pi[v_1', k(1-\delta)+x]/\delta x$$
$$+(1-\delta)\partial c[x(v_2', k(1-\delta)+x)]/\partial x\}P(dv_1'|k(1-\delta)+x)P(dv_2'|k, v_2) = 0,$$

at $\theta = \theta_0$. This is a special case of (5.8a) (one in which the initial value of v_1 does not affect the Euler equation). We now note how combining this equation with a simulation technique (McFadden (1989), and Pakes and Pollard (1989)) allows us to obtain consistent estimates of θ_0 (as will become clear, numerical integration would do equally well). Draw v_1^* from $P[dv_1|k(1-\delta)+x]$, then construct

$$-\partial c(x_t)/\partial x + \beta \chi_{t+1}[\partial \pi(k_{t+1}, v_1^*)/\partial k + (1-\delta)\partial c(x_{t+1})/\partial x],$$

and form the product of this function with alternative functions of observables known at data t. Now note that, since the expectation of the product function is zero at $\theta = \theta_0$, sample moments obtained in this fashion can be used as a basis for a GMM estimation algorithm à la Hansen and Singleton (1982) (for more detail see the discussion at the end of section 3). Note, however, that since (5.8a) was not an assumption directly on the primitives of the model, we needed to verify it for our example before we could proceed with this estimation technique (there are alternative sets of assumptions on primitives that would lead one to (5.8a), and it was not clear that a listing of them would be any more useful than just stating (5.8a) directly).

The more general case is only slightly more complicated. Note that (5.7) and (5.8) imply that

$$E_{(t)} \int h(d_{t+1}, z_{t+1}, v', d_t, z_t, v_{1,t}) P(dv'|z_{t+1}) = 0$$

for almost every (d_t, v_t, z_t). Consequently the integral of this expression with respect to $P(dv_{1,t}|z_t)$ must equal zero. Let $g(\cdot)$ be any square integrable function of (d_t, z_t). Then, from Fubini's Theorem

$$E_{(t)}\{[\int\int h(d_{t+1}, z_{t+1}, v'', d_t, z_t, v')g(d_t, z_t)P(dv''|z_{t+1})P(dv'|z_t)]|z_t, d_t\} = 0.$$

Now simply substitute the observed values of the vector $(d_{t+1}, z_{t+1}, d_t, z_t)$ into $h(\ )$, and simulate both v' and v'', for each individual. The sample average of these equations should converge to zero at $\theta = \theta_0$, and therefore can also be used as a basis for a method of moments estimation algorithm.

There is at least one more special case in which unobserved state variables do not hamper our ability to obtain consistent parameter estimates from Euler equations. This case also partitions the unobserved state vector into two components. The first only affects the Euler equation through its effect on the control (v_2), while the second (v_1) can also have a direct effect on the Euler equation. However the logarithm of the Euler equation must be additively separable into a function of v_1 and a function which is independent of v_1, and v_1 must be constant over time. More formally the requirements of this special case are that

$$v_{1,t+1} = v_{1,t} = v_1, \tag{5.9a}$$

and

$$h(\ ) = h_1(v_1; \theta_0)h_2(d_{t+1}, z_{t+1}, d_t, z_t; \theta_0), \tag{5.9b}$$

with $h_1(v_1; \theta_0) \neq 0$ (a.s.). Equation (5.9a) assumes that the value of v_1 is constant over (at least one) two-period interval; an assumption which has been used extensively in panel data estimation problems (see Mundlak (1963) for an early discussion of its relevance, and the more recent discussion in Chamberlain (1982), and the literature cited therein). Equation (5.9b) is a strong assumption on the form of the Euler equation. It has been used in investigations of Euler equations for optimal intertemporal consumption choices; in these cases differences in instantaneous utility functions across agents that appear multiplicatively in the marginal utility of consumption will, when combined with (5.9a), generate Euler equations of the form in (5.9b) (Zeldes (1989) uses one variant of this assumption).

Given (5.12) estimation and testing is straightforward. Together (5.7) and (5.9) ensure that the expectation of $h_2(\ )$ conditional on all observed variables must be zero. Since $h_2(\ )$ does not contain any unobservables, we can simply treat it as the Euler equation (ignoring ν_1) and base estimation on the restrictions implied by the fact that its conditional expectation is zero at θ_0.

We do not want to conclude this subsection with the wrong impression. *All* of the assumptions used to date to account for unobservables in structural estimation problems are quite restrictive. At this point all we can say is that (more or less simple) estimation algorithms have been developed under alternative sets of assumptions, and one or more of them may be appropriate to the problem at hand. The alternatives do have the saving grace that they usually generate overidentifying restrictions which can be used to formulate test statistics. The tests, however, are usually omnibus tests that do not distinguish very well between alternative possible sources of error, and the models we are dealing with are quite complicated. Good model selection criteria are likely to be more dependent on a detailed knowledge of the problem one is dealing with, and of the data that are available. The researcher will simply have to be familar enough with his or her problem to have reasonably strong priors about what the major unobservable sources of differences in behaviour across agents are, on how they relate to the alternative estimation procedures available, and, if there is a worry left over, on which diagnostic tests are likely to pick up problems in the more questionable assumptions.

3.3 Stochastic accumulation

We now sketch the basics of a model that allows for stochastic accumulation – a model that we will elaborate on when we introduce market interactions later in the chapter.[11] Our purpose in this subsection is simply to illustrate the logic that allows one to generate Euler equations from models with stochastic accumulation when it is possible to do so. The deeper question of the conditions that allow one to generate Euler equations in models with stochastic accumulation is left for future research.

For simplicity assume that there is only one state variable, ω, or the efficiency of the firm, and that profits are increasing in it. The firm invests in research and exploration to improve its efficiency in future years but the outcomes of the research process are uncertain. That is the distribution of ω_{t+1} conditional on information at time t depends upon ω_t and x_t, so that $\{\omega_t\}$ is a controlled Markov process. Its primitives are given by the family of conditional distributions

$$\mathscr{P} = \{P(\cdot|x, \omega), (x, \omega) \in \mathscr{R}_+ \times \Omega \subset \mathscr{R}^2\}.$$

The family $\mathscr{P}$ is assumed to be stochastically increasing in x for each value of ω (increases in investment lead to better, in the stochastic dominance sense, distributions for future efficiency), stochastically increasing in ω for each given x (conditional on x the higher the current ω the better the distribution of tomorrow's ω), and continuous in the sense that when integrated against a continuous bounded function of ω', it produces a continuous bounded function of both x and ω.

The rest of the structure of this example is taken from the model with deterministic accumulation. In each period an active firm makes two decisions. One discrete decision (whether to remain active or to liquidate and receive the sell-off value of Φ), and, if the discrete decision is positive ($\chi = 1$), one continuous decision (the quantity to invest in research or x). The Bellman equation which defines the value function for this problem is then

$$V(\omega) = \max\{\Phi, \sup_{x \in \mathscr{R}_+}[\pi(\omega) - c(x) + \beta \int V(\omega')P(d\omega'|\omega, x)]\}. \quad (5.10)$$

Let $\{\chi(\omega), x(\omega)\}$ be the optimal policy. Then substituting that in (5.10) and re-writing in terms of the expected value of profits in the following period and the value of continuing thereafter we have

$$V(\omega) = \max\{\Phi, \pi(\omega) - c[x(\omega)] + \beta \int \{\chi(\omega')[\pi(\omega') \\ - c(x(\omega'))]\}P[d\omega'|\omega, x(\omega)] + \beta\Phi \int [1 - \chi(\omega')]P[d\omega'|\omega, x(\omega)] \\ + \beta^2 \int \chi(\omega')V(\omega'')P[d\omega''|\omega', x(\omega')]P[d\omega'|\omega, x(\omega)]\}.$$

We want to find a set of alternative programmes that leave the last term in this expression unchanged (then the difference between the value of the alternative and optimal programmes just depends on actions and outcomes in periods t and $t+1$). The continuity properties of the family $\mathscr{P}$ ensure that the following set of policies would suffice (were they feasible). Leave the shutdown policy the same as the optimal shutdown policy, and the investment policy the same as the optimal investment policy for all $t + \tau$ with $\tau \geq 2$. However substract ϵ from $x(\omega_t)$ and add $\Delta(\epsilon, \omega_{t+1})$ to $x(\omega_{t+1})$, where ϵ and $\Delta(\cdot)$ are chosen such that $\Delta(\epsilon, \cdot) = 0$ at $\epsilon = 0$, and the *distribution* of ω_{t+2} conditional on ω_t and each alternative policy, is the same as the distribution of ω_{t+2} conditional on ω_t and the optimal policy. More formally choose ϵ and $\Delta(\cdot)$ such that for every $\tilde{\omega} \in \Omega$

$$\int_{\omega'} P[\omega'' > \tilde{\omega} | \omega', x(\omega')] P[d\omega' | \omega, x(\omega)]$$
$$= \int_{\omega'} P[\omega'' > \tilde{\omega} | \omega', x(\omega') + \Delta(\epsilon, \omega')] P[d\omega' | \omega, x(\omega) - \epsilon]. \tag{5.11}$$

The optimal policy produces a distribution of ω_{t+2} conditional on ω_t, as a convolution of $P[\cdot | \omega_t, x(\omega_t)]$ and $P[\cdot | \omega_{t+1}, x(\omega_{t+1})]$. Equation (5.11) states that we can obtain the same convoluted distribution by perturbing x_t by $-\epsilon$ and x_{t+1} by $\Delta(\epsilon, \omega_{t+1})$. When this is so the difference in the expected discounted value of cash flows generated by the alternative and optimal programmes just depends on the cash flows in periods t and $t+1$.

More formally, if the alternative (5.11) is feasible and we let $V(\epsilon, \omega)$ be the value generated by the alternative programme, then

$$V(\omega) - V(\epsilon, \omega) = - c[x(\omega)] + \beta \int \{\pi(\omega') - c[x(\omega')]\} \chi(\omega') P[d\omega' | \omega, x(\omega)]$$
$$+ c[x(\omega) - \epsilon] - \beta \int \{\pi(\omega') - c[x(\omega') + \Delta(\epsilon, \omega')]\} \chi(\omega') P[d\omega' | \omega, x(\omega) - \epsilon]. \tag{5.12}$$

By optimality (5.12) is non-negative for every feasible value of ϵ and equals zero at $\epsilon = 0$. Thus provided we can show that there is a feasible ϵ-alternative policy that abides by (5.11) for all $|\epsilon| \leq \kappa$ (for some $\kappa > 0$), and that (5.12) is differentiable in ϵ in the appropriate region, that derivative must be zero at $\epsilon = 0$ – giving us a 'Euler equation' for the problem with stochastic accumulation.

Whether or not these conditions are satisfied, and the form of the derivative if they are, depend on the properties of the family $\mathscr{P}$ (as well as on the differentiability of $c(\cdot)$ and the continuity of $\pi(\cdot)$). Though it is beyond the scope of this chapter to do a detailed investigation of the appropriate necessary and sufficient conditions, a simple example where the required conditions are satisfied will help illustrate how to proceed.

Let the family $\mathscr{P}$ have densities (with respect to some dominating measure) and assume those densities can be written as

$$p(\omega_{t+1} | \omega_t, x_t; \theta) = p_\xi[\omega_{t+1} - \mu(\omega_t, x_t; \theta)], \tag{5.13}$$

for every $(\omega_{t+1}, \omega_t, x_t) \in \Omega^2 \times \mathscr{R}_+$, as would be the case if differences in ω and in x only caused a change in the mean of the distribution of future efficiencies (condition (5.13) is also satisfied in the computed version of the Ericson–Pakes model we discuss below; though for different reasons). Assume also that $p_\xi(\cdot)$ is differentiable in its argument for every possible value of ξ, that $\mu(\cdot)$ is everywhere differentiable in both its arguments, and that $\partial \mu(\cdot)/\partial x$ is both positive everywhere and goes to ∞ as x approaches zero (for all ω). This last condition ensures that x is kept away from its lower bound of zero. The others ensure (via the implicit function theorem) that there exists a differentiable function $\Delta(\epsilon, \omega')$ that satisfied (5.11).

Now $\omega_{t+1} = \xi_{t+1} + \mu(\omega_t, x_t)$, so for the family of alternative programmes to satisfy (5.11) we need

$$\mu[\xi_{t+1} + \mu(\omega_t, x_t), x_{t+1}] = \mu[\xi_{t+1} + \mu(\omega_t, x_t - \epsilon), x_{t+1} + \Delta(\epsilon, \xi_{t+1})].$$

This, in turn implies that

$$\partial\Delta(\epsilon = 0, \omega_{t+1})/\partial\epsilon = \{[\partial\mu(\omega_{t+1}, x_{t+1})/\partial\omega][\partial\mu(\omega_t, x_t)/\partial x]\}/\{\partial\mu(\omega_{t+1}, x_{t+1})/\partial x\},$$

Now go back to (5.12), substitute in (5.13), and note that our assumptions together with the Lebesgue Dominated Convergence Theorem imply that the result is a differentiable function ϵ. Taking that derivative and setting it equal to zero we obtain

$$- \partial c[x_t]/\partial x + \beta[\partial\mu(\omega_t, x_t)/\partial x]E_{(t)}\chi_{t+1}\{[\partial\pi(\omega_{t+1})/\partial\omega] - [\partial c(x_{t+1})/\partial x]$$
$$[\partial\mu(\omega_{t+1}, x_{t+1})/\partial\omega]/[\partial\mu(\omega_{t+1}, x_{t+1})/\partial x]\} = 0.$$

This is not much more complicated than the Euler equation in lemma 1 (the equation for the model with deterministic accumulation). However, we should emphasise that the procedure outlined here did rely heavily on the index restriction in (5.13).

3.4   Conditional distributions which are not independent across agents

Thus far we have assumed that the conditional distribution of the vector of the period $t + 1$ state variables of the different agents (conditional on information known at date t) factors into the product of the distributions that those agents actually use in forming their own expectation. In addition to rational expectations, this requires independence of the conditional distributions of $\{y_{t+1,i}\}_{i=1}^N$. It is this independence which ensures that the average of the Euler equation disturbances, averaged over the individuals in the sample, converges to zero at the true θ_0, a property which lies at the heart of the proof of the convergence, as N grows large, of the Euler-equation-based estimator to the true θ_0.

Recall that y_{t+1} must include all variables which have either an independent effect on the value of the Euler equation, or are determinants of the value of control variables which, in turn, are arguments in the Euler equation. Frequently this leaves a lot of room for state variables whose realisations will either be common, or highly correlated, across agents (typical examples include prices, levels of technology and governmental policy variables). At this point we should note that the fact that there is dependence in the conditional distribution of the $y_{t+1,i}$ across i does not necessarily rule out our consistency condition. That is, the same random variable may affect different agents in different ways, so that the dependence it induces in the realisation of the Euler equation errors may not be strong enough to invalidate the convergence of the sample average of the true Euler equation disturbances to zero. On the other hand, when there are state variables that have important impacts on behaviour that are likely to induce dependence across agents, then the arguments we have been implicitly relying on for the consistency of the Euler-equation-based estimators are at best incomplete (and may be seriously misleading).

There are at least two ways to investigate the possibility that dependence in the realisations of the state variables generates significant biases in Euler-equation-based estimators. The first is empirical, using a combination of formal tests and less formal descriptive statistics to analyse the possible impact of dependence for the problem at hand. There are several computationally straightforward ways of proceeding here, and we come back to a more detailed discussion of them below. The second possibility is to provide *theoretical* conditions under which any dependence would impact on the Euler equation in a particular (and analysable) way, and then check for, and possibly estimate, subject to them.

The latter possibility has recently been used in the literature on consumption choices, where the theory of complete markets has been used to structure the relationship between the increment in the marginal utility of consumption across households (see Altug and Miller (1990) and Altonji, Hayashi and Kotlikoff (1992)). To date the empirical specifications used in this literature have focussed on the opposite extreme to the one that is implicitly employed in the estimation procedures that do not allow for dependence – with complete markets the only source of uncertainty is one whose realisations are common to all agents. The truth, no doubt, lies somewhere in the middle (and much more difficult) case with only partial markets for future income streams. Note, however, that if any such markets exist they will, in and of themselves, induce conditional dependence in the realisations of the state variables of agents operating in the same submarket (for some eye-opening empirical evidence on such dependence, see Townsend (forthcoming)). In applications involving choices by firms, the implications of the dependence induced by the aggregate factors we often worry about (demand, factor price, technological and policy changes) will depend on the nature of the dynamic equilibria established among the various actors (see section 4.3).

We now move on to consider what can be done to salvage Euler-equation-based estimation techniques that have desirable limit properties in dimension N when there is dependence across agents. Unfortunately, there has been little progress here. Empirical papers often attempt to account for the problem of dependence by adding time-specific dummy variables, say a_t, to the Euler equation, assuming that $E_{(t)}[h(\cdot;\theta) - a_t] = 0$, and then minimising (by choice of both the vectors α and θ) a quadratic form in the sample analogues of the population restrictions implied by this equation. One way to see the implications of this procedure is to partition the vector of state variables, y_t, into a subvector whose conditional distribution is independent across agents, say z_t, and one that is not, say l_t, and then consider conditions which would imply the consistency (as N grows large) of the estimator of θ we obtain when we use the time-specific dummy variables. Using the more general notation introduced in section 3.2 where $h(\cdot)$ is the Euler equation and $d(\cdot)$ is the vector of controls, one set of such conditions is

$$h(d_{t+1}, y_{t+1}, d_t, y_t) = h_1(d_{t+1}, z_{t+1}, d_t, y_t) + h_2(l_{t+1}) \tag{5.14a}$$

$$d(y_{t+1}) = d(z_{t+1}), \tag{5.14b}$$

and

$$P(dz_{t+1}, dl_{t+1}|z_t, l_t) = P(dz_{t+1}|z_t)P(dl_{t+1}|l_t), \tag{5.14c}$$

Equation (5.14a) states that the impact of l on the Euler equation is additively separable, while (5.14b) requires that l not effect the control at all. There are few, if any, empirical examples where the additive separability in (5.14a) arises naturally from the underlying primitives of the model, and, as we can now show, it can be relaxed at the cost of a small change in the specification of the estimating equation. Replace assumption (5.14a) with

$$\begin{aligned} h(d_{t+1}, y_{t+1}, d_t, y_t) &= h_1(d_{t+1}, z_{t+1}, d_t, z_t)h_2(l_{t+1}) \\ &\quad + h_3(d_{t+1}, z_{t+1}, d_t, y_t) + h_4(l_{t+1}). \end{aligned} \tag{5.14a$'$}$$

Equation (5.14a$'$), by itself, is a condition which, though clearly restrictive, arises quite frequently in applied work. It would, for example, apply to our leading investment example (assumption 1) if we were worried about a common price (or demand) uncertainty, and those prices (or demand factors) had a multiplicatively separable effect on the current profit function (it also arises in the consumption example discussed by Hall (1979) once one allows for interest rate uncertainty). Now note that (5.14a$'$), (5.14b), (5.14c) and (5.7) imply that

$$h_{2,t+1}E_{(t)}h_1[d(z'), z', d, l, z] + E_{(t)}h_3[d(z'), z', d, z, l] + h_{4,t+1} = 0, \tag{5.15}$$

where $h_{2,t+1} = \int h_2(l_{t+1})P(dl_{t+1}|l_t)$, and $h_{4,t+1}$ is defined accordingly. It follows that the sequence of couples $\{[h_{2,t+1}, h_{4,t+1})]\}_{t=1}^T$ can be treated as parameters to be estimated along with θ, in a Euler-equation-based estimation procedure that will, given our assumptions and some standard regularity conditions, yield a consistent and asymptotically normal estimator as N, the number of agents, grows large (with T held fixed).

Note, however, that these results rely not only on (5.14a'), but also on (5.14b). The latter assumption requires that the controls in $t+1$ not be a function of the factor which induces the dependence in the state variable across agents (l_{t+1}). For most problems of interest, including our investment problem with common price uncertainty, this would be unlikely unless the common price process were serially independent (in which case its current realisations would not impact on the perceived distribution of its future values, and therefore would not impact on investment and exit decisions). Serial independence of the process leading to the dependence in the realisations of the state variables of the various agents is often an unattractive assumption. On the other hand, the assumptions underlying estimators based on equations such as (5.15) are testable, just as those based on an assumption of a lack of conditional dependence in the process generating the state variables are, and (5.15) is clearly less restrictive. Before moving away from the discussion of providing Euler-equation-based estimators with desirable asymptotic properties as N grows large holding T fixed when there is conditional dependence, it should be noted that neither we, nor other published work we are aware of, have attempted a very detailed investigation of the possibilities here, so that this is an area in which further research may well be warranted.[12]

We now move to a brief comparison of Euler-equation-based estimators that rely on limits in dimension T, holding N fixed, to those that rely on limits in dimension N, holding T fixed. We do this even though the vast majority of panel data problems have N much larger than T, for two reasons.[13] First, a comparison of limits will lead to simple sets of tests for conditional dependence in the state variable. Second, whether or not T is large for a given application is not only a function of the length of the panel, but also of the variance that the common factor induces in the sample average of the true Euler equation disturbances in the different years of the panel. If the average (over time) of these cross-sectional average disturbances has a 'small enough' variance, then the asymptotic approximations that rely on T growing large will be accurate (and recall that if the theory is correct the average cross-sectional Euler equation disturbances in the different years of the panel should be mutually uncorrelated so its variance should go down at rate T^{-1}). Moreover, if the approximations that rely on T growing large are accurate, *and* we choose an *appropriate* Euler-equation-based estimator (see below), we can often obtain estimators with desirable properties even in the presence of dependence.[14]

Once we allow for the possibility of conditionally dependent state variables, we have to be more careful about distinguishing differences in the properties of Euler-equation based estimators obtained from different restrictions. To this end we introduce some additional notation. Let, $h[d(y_{i,t+1}), y_{i,t+1}, d(y_{i,t}), y_{i,t}; \theta] = h_{i,t}(\theta), x_{i,t} \in F_t$, and define

$$N^{-1}\sum_{(i)} h_{i,t}(\theta) x_{i,t} = g^x_{*,t}(\theta), \tag{5.16a}$$

$$T^{-1}\sum_{(t)} h_{i,t}(\theta) x_{i,t} = g^x_{i,*}(\theta), \tag{5.16b}$$

and

$$T^{-1}N^{-1}\sum_{(t)}\sum_{(i)} h_{i,t}(\theta) x_{i,t} = g^x_{*,*}(\theta). \tag{5.16c}$$

We consider estimators of θ obtained from minimising a quadratic form in restrictions formed by: (i) averaging over i for fixed t (as in (5.16a)), (ii) by averaging over t for fixed i (as in (5.16b)) and (iii) by averaging over i and t (as in (5.16c)).

Given appropriate regularity conditions, the first will yield consistent and asymptotically normal estimators as N grows large regardless of T provided that the evolution of the state variables are conditionally independent across agents. Note, however, that the first-order conditions which define the estimator of θ in this case have terms which converge to the expectation of

$$g^x_{*,t}(\theta) \, \partial g^x_{*,t}(\theta)/\partial \theta,$$

and, if there is dependence in the conditional distributions of the state variables of the various agents, then the covariance between the cross-sectional average of the Euler equation disturbance, and its derivative with respect to θ, will not generally be zero at the true θ_0. As a result, if there is dependence in the realisations of the state variables across agents, the estimator based on minimising a quadratic form in restrictions of the form in (5.16a) will *not only* be inconsistent when N grows large holding T fixed, but will *also be inconsistent as T grows large*.[15]

On the other hand, given appropriate regularity conditions, estimators based on minimising a quadratic form in the time-averaged Euler equation restrictions of the different individuals (as in (5.16b)) will result in consistent and asymptotically normal estimators of θ as T grows large, for fixed N, even if the conditional distributions of the state variables of the various agents are dependent.[16] However, an analogous argument to the one used to show that conditional dependence destroys the consistency of Euler-equation-based estimators obtained from averaging over i for fixed t, shows that if T is not large enough the estimator obtained from restrictions such as those in (5.16b) will be *inconsistent regardless* of whether the observations are conditionally independent.

Finally the estimators obtained from averaging the restrictions over both i and t are consistent and asymptotically normal if *either* N is sufficiently large and the state variables are conditional independent, *or* if there is conditional dependence but T is large enough.

One way of deciding between the various possibilities is to obtain estimators from restrictions that are averaged over both i and t (as in (5.16c), and then use a combination of formal testing and descriptive statistics to decide on whether any of the more restrictive alternatives seem relevant. An intuitive starting point would be to do a decomposition of the variance in the value of either the Euler equation or the restrictions (evaluated at the estimator obtained by averaging over both i and t) between time, individual and idiosyncratic components. In building formal test statistics for various hypotheses (e.g., the time effects are zero) care has to be taken to account for the fact that we are using an estimate of θ_0 rather than its true value.

That concludes our discussion of the use of Euler equations in structural estimation. It is incomplete in several ways. In addition to leaving several questions open on the topics we did discuss, we left several important topics totally untouched. Perhaps foremost among the latter is the issue of the choice of estimator given only the restrictions that are embodied in the Euler equations (and, perhaps, some regularity conditions).

There is a large related econometric literature on the efficiency of estimators based on moment conditions that can guide us here. In their initial article Hansen and Singleton (1982) use the Euler equations to generate a finite number of moment restrictions, and then consider estimators based on minimising a quadratic form in those restrictions. A result in Hansen (1982) shows that, given appropriate regularity conditions, the optimal weighting matrix is the inverse of the variance covariance matrix of the moment restrictions themselves (evaluated at the true value of the parameter vector). Chamberlain (1987) shows that, again subject to regularity conditions, the same result applies if we do not limit ourselves to estimators based on quadratic forms in the (finite number of) moment restrictions. Chamberlain then goes on to provide an efficiency bound (for regular estimators) when the restrictions we have to work with are specified directly as conditional moment restrictions (this generates an infinite number of moment restrictions, one for each possible value of the conditioning set; see also Hansen (1985) and Hansen, Heaton and Ogaki (1988) for related work in the time series literature). Recall that the Euler equation restrictions are in fact conditional moment restrictions (conditional on the σ-algebra generated by variables known in period t); so, provided we are only using the Euler equations, we would ultimately like to obtain estimators which achieve the efficiency bound from the conditional moment restrictions they generate.[17]

If there are K parameters to be estimated, there will (again subject to regularity conditions) to be a set of K 'instruments' (measurable functions of the conditioning set) which generate moments (orthogonality conditions) whose sum of squares will be minimised at a value of the parameter vector whose limit distribution will achieve the efficiency bound. However, these 'efficient' instruments involve the derivative of the conditional moments with respect to the parameter vector (they equal the derivative of the vector of conditional moments times the inverse of the conditional variance of those moment conditions; all evaluated at the true value of the parameter vector). In the Euler equation (and most other non-linear) examples, computation of the derivative of the conditional moments requires knowledge of the conditional distribution of the endogenous variables (conditional on the state variables of the model), and then use of either numerical integration or simulation to calculate the appropriate integral.

Use of an instrument which requires a complete solution for all the endogenous variables destroys the *raison d'être* for using Euler-equation-based estimation techniques in the first place. Chamberlain (1987) touches on the possibility of obtaining an estimator which achieves the efficiency bound by adding instruments sequentially from a sequence of functions which, in the limit, form a basis for a function space which is rich enough to include the efficient instruments. Newey (1990) considers the special case of homoskedastic conditional moments, and then provides conditions for achieving the efficiency bound using non-parametric (series and nearest neighbour) estimators of the efficient instruments (see also the related work on feasible GLS for heteroskedasticity by Carroll (1982) and Robinson (1987)). Newey (1990) also provides a Monte Carlo example whose results show that use of the series estimator for the optimal instruments does amazingly well (though the nearest neighbour estimator did not). The interested reader should consult the rapidly developing related literature on semi-parametric efficiency bounds (see Chamberlain (1992) Newey (1990b) and the literature cited in those articles).

One final point. It is often worthwhile to examine the form of the 'efficient' instruments even if one is unlikely (for whatever reason) to attempt to generate an estimator that attains the efficiency bound that results from them. This is because an examination of the form of the efficient instruments frequently suggests sets of instruments which, though not strictly speaking efficient, should get one close to the efficiency bound, and be fairly easy to construct.

4   ALTERNATIVE ESTIMATION STRATEGIES, SERIALLY CORRELATED UNOBSERVABLES AND INVERTIBILITY CONDITIONS

It is natural to next ask what can be done in cases where Euler-equation-based estimation techniques cannot provide estimators with desirable properties for at least some of the parameters of interest. Generally, the alternative estimation strategies that are available depend on the model and data being investigated, but, at least in the context of models as simple as those used in our examples, it is probably most natural to look next at the possibility of specifying all the primitives of the model up to a vector of parameters, solving for the optimal choices implied by the different possible values for this vector, and then using either a maximum likelihood, or a minimum distance, estimator to fit the model to data.

Though estimation techniques which require computation of the value function are generally more computationally burdensome then Euler-equation-based techniques, their computational burden in models with a mixture of discrete and continuous choices is comparable to their burden in discrete-choice models, and this is discussed extensively in the chapter by Rust (1991). Indeed, the computational issues only become significantly more difficult when we introduce interactions among agents, and are, therefore, required to solve for market equilibria. As a result we postpone further discussion of computation until we bring the market back in. For now we simply assume that we can compute the value function and the optimal policy, and look to see if this enables us to estimate the parameters of the model in situations where, because of the reasons noted above, Euler-equation-based estimation techniques are likely to fail.

To compute the value function we will generally also be required to make more detailed assumptions on the exogenous 'forcing' processes than the assumptions we required for the Euler-equation-based estimators discussed in the last section. What we gain for these assumptions, and for the additional computational burden, is a set of predictions for the controls conditional on any given value of the parameter vector, all state variables and the correspondence defining the feasible choices. Note that our ability to obtain these controls is independent of whether or not they are continuous or discrete (or, if continuous, are at a boundary of the choice set), of the form of the accumulation relationship (stochastic or deterministic), or of whether the distributions of the state variables are conditionally independent across agents.

However, the model's predictions for the controls are calculated as a function of *all* the state variables and the parameters of the problem. To match these predictions to data we need to express them in terms of only the *observed* state variables and these parameters. This requires an assumption on the distribution of the unobserved state variables. Consider first the case where these are serially independent so that their distribution at time t does not depend on their realisations at time $t-1$. Then, given any value for the parameter vector, we can integrate out over the current values of the unobservables that the model indicates would generate the observed controls, obtain the likelihood as a function of only *observable* magnitudes, and compute maximum-likelihood estimators in the usual way (alternatively, we could compute, or simulate, the expected value of the controls for different values of the parameter vector, and obtain a method of moments estimator for θ). Though this may be a computationally difficult estimation procedure, it is always available, and requires no additional assumptions.[18]

On the other hand, when there are serially correlated unobservables the likelihood we calculate for the controls conditional on alternative values for θ is a function of the period $t-1$ value of the unobserved state variable. Thus, direct application of maximum likelihood is not possible. We could, of course, iterate backward, using the distribution of the period $t-1$ value of the unobserved state variable conditional on its value in period $t-2$ to form the distribution of the control in period t conditional on information in period $t-2$, and so on (see below), but we will still be left with the problem of an unknown value for the unobserved state variable in the initial period of the data. Alternatively, we could attempt to obtain the joint distribution of the values of the unobserved and observed state variables in some (preferably the initial) period, and use this to integrate out over the unobservable in forming the likelihood (again see below). However, given serial correlation in the unobservable and even partial control of any of the observable state variables, the model itself will predict particular forms of dependence in the joint distribution of the observed and unobserved state variables. Thus before we can integrate out over the unobserved component we need to solve explicitly for the form of the *conditional* distribution of the unobserved state variable (conditional, that is, on the observed state variables), and this will require both additional assumptions, and an additional level of computational complexity. Analogous problems occur in developing method of moments estimators when there are serially correlated unobserved state variables.

As noted earlier the same issue arises in all stochastic dynamic programming models (discrete, continuous or mixed). Indeed, the problem has a longer history than this; it has an almost identical structure to the problem labelled the 'initial conditions' problem in Jim Heckman's discussion of discrete-time, discrete-data, stochastic processes (see Heckman (1981)). Several solutions have been suggested in the literature. We begin by providing a brief review of some of them, focussing on their applicability to estimating structural models. Then we suggest an alternative which arises naturally for certain theoretical models with continuous (as well as discrete) controls, and provide proofs of its validity for the two leading examples used in this chapter. Where applicable, the alternative is easy to adapt to the more complicated settings in which we allow for market interactions. We illustrate this below by looking at the problem of estimating the parameters of a Cobb–Douglas production function in the presence of a simultaneity (endogenous investment and labour choices) and a selection (attrition due to exit behaviour) problem induced by a (serially correlated) unobserved productivity variable.

4.1 The problem

We illustrate with the simple example introduced above; that of a firm choosing investment and exit strategies to maximise the expected discounted value of future net cash flow. Recall that $x(\cdot)$ provided the investment, and $\chi(\cdot)$ the exit, policies, of the firm. We shall assume here that k (capital) and ω (the state of productivity or demand) are, respectively, an observed and an unobserved state variable. Then

$$m_t = (k_t, x_t, \chi_t) \in M \subset \mathcal{R}^2 \times [0,1], \qquad (5.17a)$$

is the vector of observables for each firm in each period while

$$A(m_t; \theta) = \{\omega : x(\omega, k_t; \theta) = x_t \text{ and } \chi(\omega, k_t; \theta) = \chi_t\} \subset \Omega, \qquad (5.17b)$$

is the set of possible values for the unobservble, ω, that are consistent with the observable m_t vector, for different values of θ.

Capital accumulates deterministically, so conditional on $y_{t-1} = (\omega_{t-1}, k_{t-1})$, the only source of randomness in $A(m_t; \theta)$ is the alternative possible realisations of ω_t. $\{\omega_t\}$ is a Markov process with transition probabilities given by the family $\mathcal{P}_\omega$ in (2). Assuming (for simplicity) that these have densities with respect to Lebesgue measure (these densities will be denoted by $p(\cdot|\omega, \theta), \omega \in \Omega, \theta \in \otimes$), the likelihood for the sequence of observables for a given firm *conditional* on the *initial* value of its *unobserved* state variable, is given by

$$\Pr(m_T, \ldots, m_1 | \omega_1, \theta) = \prod_{t=1,\ldots,T} \Pr[m_t | m_{t-1}, \ldots, m_1, \omega_1, \theta], \qquad (5.18)$$

where

$$\Pr[m_t | m_{t-1}, \ldots, m_1, \omega_1, \theta] = \int_{\omega_{t-1}} \Pr[A(m_t; \theta) | \omega_{t-1}, \theta]$$
$$p(\omega_{t-1} | m_{t-1}, \ldots, m_1, \omega_1, \theta) d\omega_{t-1} = \int_{\omega_{t-1}} \ldots \int_{\omega_2} \Pr[A(m_t; \theta) | \omega_{t-1}, \theta]$$
$$p(\omega_{t-1} | m_{t-1}, \omega_{t-2}, \theta) \ldots p(\omega_2 | m_2, \omega_1, \theta) d\omega_{t-1} \ldots d\omega_2$$

and

$$p(\omega_j|m_j, \omega_{j-1}, \theta) = \begin{cases} p(\omega_j|\omega_{j-1}, \theta)/\Pr[A(m_j; \theta)|\omega_{j-1}, \theta)], \\ \text{for } \omega_j \in A(m_j; \theta), 0, \end{cases}$$

elsewhere, while

$$\Pr[A(m_j; \theta)|\omega_{j-1}, \theta] = \int_{\omega_j \in A(m_j; \theta)} p(\omega_j|\omega_{j-1}, \theta)d\omega_j.$$

The conditional likelihood for the sample, conditional on the initial values of all state variables, is formed as the product (across agents) of the likelihoods in (5.18). If either the initial value of the ωs of the different agents are known, or if there was no dependence in the process generating the $\{\omega_t\}$ so that $\Pr[A(m_t; \theta)|\omega_{t-1}, \theta] = \Pr[A(m_t; \theta)|\theta]$, we could maximise the likelihood obtained in this fashion with respect to θ, and obtain a consistent and asymptotically normal estimator of that parameter (this presumes standard regularity conditions).

When there is a serially correlated unobservable, several possibilities present themselves. The simplest is the conditional maximum-likelihood estimator that treats the ω_1 of each individual in the sample as a parameter to be estimated (i.e., we maximise the likelihood in (5.18) with respect to both θ and the vector of ω_1 values). As is well known, if limits of this estimator are taken as N grows large holding T fixed the estimator can, in general, be shown to be inconsistent (the number of parameters being estimated grows with the size of the sample and this generates a classic incidental parameter problem; see Neyman and Scott (1948)). On the other hand, if limits are taken in dimension T, and the family $\mathcal{P}_\omega$ is sufficiently regular, then consistency and asymptotic normality are assured.

Panels are getting longer and it is reasonable to ask just how long they need to be before the conditional maximum-likelihood estimator is reasonably well behaved. Surprisingly little research has been done on this point. Heckman (1981) reports simulation results for a problem with a single discrete alternative (no continuous control) and a disturbance process which is the sum of a (normally distributed) permanent effect and an i.i.d. (again normal) deviate, on an eight-year-old panel. He concludes that when there are only exogenous determinants of the discrete choice, the conditional maximum-likelihood estimator does well enough. However, when lagged values of the discrete choice also determine the current choice, the performance of the conditional maximum-likelihood estimator is markedly worse. One's guess is that structural models that treat unobserved initial conditions as parameters to be estimated will perform more like the simulated models that allow for lagged endogenous variables (the current choices in the structural models build up the values of the state variables that determine the choices in future periods). On the other hand, there is enough of a difference between the models whose bias has been evaluated to date, and the current generation of structural models, that further Monte Carlo analysis seems to be warranted.

We next consider a class of solutions to the problem of serially correlated unobserved state variables that dates back, in a slightly different form, at least to the work of Kiefer and Wolfowitz (1956). In terms of the models considered here the Kiefer–Wolfowitz suggestion is to formulate the likelihood conditional on the initial value of the unobserved state (as in (5.18)), obtain information on the joint distribution of the observed and unobserved initial values of the state variable, and then use the conditional distribution of the initial value of the unobserved state variable, say $p^*(\omega_1|k_1,\theta_2)$, to integrate ω_1 out of (5.18), forming, thereby, a marginal likelihood (note that $p^*(\cdot|\cdot,\theta_2)$ will, in general, depend on a different set of parameters than those involved in the original choice problem). The Kiefer–Wolfowitz suggestion is to maximise this marginal likelihood with respect to the vector (θ,θ_2).

To do so we need the conditional density of the unobserved initial state, $p^*(\cdot|\cdot,\theta_2)$; a density which is typically unknown. There are at least two possible ways of proceeding. One is to look for a non-parametric estimator of $p^*(\cdot|\cdot,\theta_2)$ that allows us to find a semi-parametric estimator for θ. Note that this requires a non-parametric estimator for a family of distributions for the unobserved initial state, one for each possible initial value of the observed state vector. We know of no research which has systematically explored this non-parametric alternative, so at this stage we simply relegate it to a topic for future research.

The second possibility is to use economic theory to derive the $p^*(\cdot)$ associated with the alternative possible values of θ. The way of proceeding here depends on the relevant model. We consider first models in which the joint distribution of the state variables of the agents active in a given market converges to some unique invariant measure (invariant to both the passage of time and to initial conditions). Models of markets with many agents, and exogenous forcing processes which are both independent across agents and ergodic, often have this characteristic (see Jovanovic and MacDonald (forthcoming) and Hoppenhayn and Rogerson (1990) for examples). Assuming that the data are a random sample from this invariant measure, what we will need is the form of this invariant measure over (couples of) state variables. This generally requires knowledge of the parameters defining all the primitives of the model, and, in addition, an ability to compute the invariant measure associated with them. Since some of the parameters defining these primitives are the parameters we are trying to estimate, we would have to nest the problem of estimating the distribution of the initial conditions inside the estimation algorithm. That is, an evaluation of the marginal likelihood for a given value of the parameter vector would begin by calculating the invariant distribution associated with that value, and then use it as the $p^*(\cdot)$ needed to form the marginal likelihood.

Though in principle feasible, this is a very computationally intensive procedure. Moreover, in models with finite numbers of agents, and/or forcing processes which are not independent across them, both the analytic and computational problems get even more difficult. In these models the limiting characteristics of the market are often an ergodic distribution over the distribution of state vectors of the agents (as in the Ericson–Pakes model described below), and in order to integrate the unobservable initial condition out of the likelihood we would have to integrate also over the ergodic distribution of the distribution of state vectors. Though, as we show below, it might not be as difficult as once thought to calculate this ergodic distribution for one particular value of the parameter vector, calculating it repetitively for each different function evaluation required to find the maximum-likelihood estimator is probably beyond our current computational capabilities.

Though in any given period there is an *endogenous* joint distribution of the observable and unobservable state variables, there may well be an initiation date for the process for each agent at which the required distribution of state variables is either a primitive to be estimated (at least up to a parameter vector) or easy to derive in terms of such primitives. Typical examples are models of firm behaviour in which there is an entry date, or models of labour market behaviour in which there is a date of first entry into the labour force. Given an initiation date for the process, a complete model will generate a joint distribution for the observed and unobserved state variables in the first period of the data conditional on the 'age' of the agent at that time, any other presample information available, and the vector of parameters defining all the primitives of the model. This distribution is the $p^*(\ )$ needed to obtain the marginal likelihood.

Note that the vector of parameters which define this marginal likelihood now contains also the parameters describing the entry process, and, perhaps, parameters describing changes in the environment that have occurred between the initiation of the process for the agent and the start of the panel. Thus this 'solution' to the problem of serially correlated unobserved state variables does add an additional layer of computational complexity to the problem (deriving the conditional distribution of the unobserved state variables at the initiation date of the sample as a function of the parameters determining the distribution of the state variables at the initiation date of the process). However, it is an additional layer which has proven not to be too difficult in some applications, and, as a result, it is the only coherent treatment of the problem of serially correlated unobserved state variables that has been used in the estimation of structural discrete dynamic programming problems to date (see, e.g., Miller (1984) and Pakes (1986)).

The procedures discussed in the previous paragraphs are closely related. They both derive a form for the need $p^*(\cdot)$ distribution from economic theory. Indeed they only differ in that the latter makes use of presample information, and assumes that any relevant market outcomes that occur between the initiation date of the process and the beginning of the sample can be captured by a simple exogenous process. It will, therefore, be both easier to implement, and more realistic in its assumptions, when there is an exogenous 'entry' date for the process we are trying to model which is close to the first sample year for each observation, and when the important sources of randomness are well described by a simple Markov process.[19]

4.2   Invertibility conditions

Once we have a fully specified choice model, and the possibility of continuous controls, an additional procedure for dealing with the problem of serially correlated unobserved state variables presents itself. Where feasible, this solution is no more computationally burdensome than the inconsistent (in dimension N) conditional maximum-likelihood estimator which treats the initial values of the unobserved state variables as parameters to be estimated. Additionally, it can often be combined with semi-parametric estimation procedures to produce computationally simple estimators for models in which the value functions themselves are too difficult to compute (such as in models which allow for interactions among agents).

The technique does, however, require an invertibility condition. This condition states that there is a set of values for the observable vector each of which could only have been generated by a single value of ω – though the associated ω value can depend on θ. Below we formalise this condition and show that it is satisfied for the two leading examples used in this chapter; the deterministic accumulation investment example used in this section, and the stochastic accumulation example used in the next. The proofs are, however, particular to these two classes of models. So both the feasibility of using the invertibility condition, and the form of the invertibility condition where feasible, must be investigated separately for each problem. This is the additional burden of the procedure we suggest. It is not computational, but it does require a detailed knowledge of the model one is using and the data at hand (and, as will become clear, whether or not one can obtain an invertibility condition depends on the observables available). On the other hand, provided the intuition underlying the invertibility condition is clear, one can sometimes circumvent the need for a formal proof of the condition by building a check for it into the estimation algorithm.

We first provide a formal statement of the invertibility condition (condition 1), and then show how it can be used to circumvent the initial condition problem generated by serially correlated unobservables. Recall that $m \in M$ is the vector of observables (controls *and* state variables), and $A(m; \theta)$ provides the set of ω values that could generate m given θ.

Condition 1 (the invertibility condition)
There is a subset of M, say M^*, such that

$$\#A(m; \theta) = 1, \text{ for all } \theta \in \otimes \text{ and } m \in M^*,$$

In condition 1, $\#$ provides the cadinality of a set, so the condition is that $A(m; \theta)$ is a singleton for m in M^*. Also, it is important to note that we do not require the condition to hold for all $m \in M$, but rather just for m in the subset M^*, as M^* will tend to be a proper subset of M in problems with discreteness in the choice set or the possibility of binding boundaries (see below).

Now assume condition 1. Then if m_τ is in M^* we know the value of ω_τ for any value of θ; i.e., $\omega_\tau = \omega^*(m_\tau; \theta)$ for $m_\tau \in M^*$. So substitute $\omega^*(m_\tau; \theta)$ for the unobserved ω_τ in (5.18), and use this as the initial condition needed to compute a maximum-likelihood (or a method of moments) estimator from the predictions of the model for periods $\tau + 1$ to T. The product of this likelihood across agents will depend only on the period τ vector of *observables* for each agent, and the finite dimensional parameter vector to be estimated.

More formally, define the stopping time

$$\tau = \begin{cases} T \text{ if } \cup_t m_t \cap M^* = \emptyset \\ \min\{t : m_t \in M^*\} \end{cases} \tag{5.19a}$$

otherwise.

And form the truncated conditional likelihood

$$\prod_{t=\tau+1,\ldots,T} \Pr[m_t | m_{t-1}, \ldots, m_\tau, \omega^*(m_\tau; \theta)], \tag{5.19b}$$

where

$$\Pr[m_t | m_{t-1}, \ldots, m_\tau, \omega^*(m_\tau; \theta)] = \int_{\omega_{t-1}} \cdots \int_{\omega_{\tau+1}} \Pr[A(m_t; \theta) | \omega_{t-1}, \theta]$$
$$p(\omega_{t-1} | m_{t-1}, \omega_{t-2}, \theta) \ldots p(\omega_{\tau+1} | m_{\tau+1}, \omega^*(m_\tau; \theta)) d\omega_{t-1} \ldots d\omega_{\tau+1},$$

and the terms in the integral are defined as in (5.18).

Assume the set M^* has positive probability. Then maximisation of the product (across agents) of the truncated conditional likelihood in (5.19b), with respect to θ, will, subject to 'standard' regularity conditions (see Andersen (1973), section 2.8, or Huber (1967)) produce consistent and asympotically normal estimators of that parameter.

We now go back to our example of a firm making investment and exit decisions to maximise the expected discounted value of future net cash flow. To prove that it satisfies the invertibility condition, at least for the subset of M for which $x > 0$, we will have to restrict its primitives somewhat. The additional restriction that has empirical bite is that the derivative of the profit function with respect to capital must be increasing in the unobserved state variable, ω (more generally, $\pi(\omega, k)$ must be supermodular in the sense of Topkis (1978), see also Milgrom and Roberts (1990)). Though this condition is satisfied for most specifications used in empirical work (where ω generally represents either Hicks' neutral efficiency differences in production, or quality differences among a group of differentiated products firms; see the examples below), it is easy to generate counter examples where it is not. In addition we will (partly to keep matters simple) impose additional regularity conditions on the family of probability distributions, $\mathscr{P}_\omega$. We begin with a lemma which ensures that under our conditions the investment policy is non-decreasing in ω.

Lemma 3 (monotonicity of the investment policy in the investment example)
Assume 1, that $\partial \pi(\omega, k)/\partial k$ is increasing in ω (everywhere), and that if $h(\cdot)$ is continuous (everywhere) and uniformly integrable with respect to a subset of $\mathscr{P}_\omega$, say $\mathscr{P}^*$, then provided $P(\cdot|\omega_1)$ and $P(\cdot|\omega_2)$ are contained in $\mathscr{P}^*$, $|\int h(\omega')[P(d\omega'|\omega_1) - P(d\omega'|\omega_2)]| \leq \psi(h, \mathscr{P}^*)|\omega_1 - \omega_2|$. Then

$$x(\omega, k) \text{ is non-decreasing in } \omega \text{ for each } k.$$

Proof See appendix 1.

Theorem 1 provides the invertibility condition for the investment example.

Theorem 1
Conditional on the assumptions underlying lemma 3, condition 1 is satisfied for the subset of M on which $x > 0$.

Proof
From lemma 1 the investment choice must satisfy the Euler equation.

$$F(x, k, \omega) \equiv -\partial c(x)/\partial x + \beta \int \chi[\omega', k(1 - \delta) + x]\{\partial \pi[\omega', k(1 - \delta) + x]/\partial k + (1 - \delta)\partial c[x(\omega', k(1 - \delta) + x)]/\partial x\}P(d\omega'|\omega) = 0.$$

Assumption 1, together with the form of the optimal policy (see (5.2)) ensures that $F(\cdot)$ is a continuous function of ω for every (x,k). So it will suffice to show that for each (x,k), $F(\cdot)$ is strictly increasing in ω. Equation (5.2) ensures that $\chi(\cdot)$ is non-decreasing in ω', and the convexity of the adjustment cost function together with lemma 3 ensure that $\partial c(\cdot)/\partial x$ is also, while $\partial \pi(\cdot)/\partial k$ is strictly increasing in ω' by assumption. Thus the integral is non-decreasing in ω' everywhere and strictly increasing for all ω' in the region where $\chi = 1$. To complete the proof, then, one need only note that if $x > 0$, $\chi[\omega', k(1-\delta)+x]$ must be 1 on a set of ω' with positive $P(\cdot|\omega)$ probability (else $x = 0$ would generate a more profitable programme).

Remark 1
The statement of lemma 3 given in the appendix allows the cost of adjustment function to depend also on k. The condition on $c(x,k)$ that suffices for the lemma in this more general case is that it be non-increasing in k for each fixed x. When the adjustment cost function depends on k the Euler equation for the investment choice becomes,

$$
\begin{aligned}
F(x,k,\omega) = &- \partial c(x,k)/\partial x \\
&+ \beta \int \chi[\omega', k(1-\delta)+x]\{\partial \pi[\omega', k(1-\delta)+x]/\partial k \\
&+ (1-\delta)\partial c[x(\omega', k(1-\delta)+x), k(1-\delta)+x]/\partial x \\
&- \partial c[x(\omega', k(1-\delta)+x), k(1-\delta)+x]/\partial k\} P(d\omega'|\omega) = 0.
\end{aligned}
$$

Now to obtain the strong monotonicity result in (1) we need also that $-\partial c(\cdot)/\partial k$ is non-decreasing in x. If $c(\cdot)$ is appropriately differentiable, then what we require is that $\partial^2 c(x,k)/\partial x \partial k < 0$, a condition which is satisfied for most investment functions used in empirical work.

Remark 2
Theorem 1 does not depend on the feasibility of negative investment. That is, if we constrained investment to be non-negative we could use the modified Euler equation in lemma 2 to prove the same condition (the proof would only be true for the subset of M for which the modified Euler equation is indeed satisfied, but that would include all observed vectors for which $x > 0$).

Theorem 1 implies the existence of a function $\omega^*(x,k;\theta)$ with the property that if $m \in M^*$, then $\omega = \omega^*(x,k;\theta)$. Following the discussion above, a truncated conditional maximum-likelihood estimator for this problem can then be constructed by defining the $\tau(i)$ in (5.19a) to be the first observation on firm i for which we observe positive investment, substituting $\omega^*(x_{\tau(i)}, k_{\tau(i)}; \theta)$ for the needed initial condition into (5.19b), and then maximising the sum (over firms) of the resulting log likelihoods with respect to θ.

Once we know the inverse function exists, alternative estimation strategies present themselves. Of particular interest are estimation techniques that use a non-parametric estimator of the inverse function, thereby circumventing the need to compute that function for different possible values of the parameter vector. Non-parametric alternatives are often feasible in situations where we want to control for ω in order to attenuate biases resulting from the presence of this serially correlated unobserved state variable.

Olley and Pakes (1992) study of productivity in the telecommunications equipment industry provides one example of the use of such a semiparametric estimation procedure. To construct their measure of productivity they required estimates of the industry's production function. This is specified in Cobb–Douglas form as

$$q_{i,t} = a_0 + a_a a_{i,t} + a_1 l_{i,t} + a_k k_{i,t} + \omega_{i,t} + \eta_{i,t}, \qquad (5.20)$$

where q, k, and l are the logarithms of output (value added), capital (constructed from a geometric decay assumption and data on the book value of the plant in the initial year the plant enters any of the census' files), and labour (man hours), while 'a' is the plant's age (this allows for vintage effects, or for an initial sunk factor of production whose impacts decay from birth). The data are taken from the Longitudinal Research Data File at the US Bureau of the Census (see McGuckin and Pascoe (1988)). This is a thirteen-year (1973–86) panel which follows information at the enterprise (plant) level of aggregation.

The model has two disturbances affecting observed productivity, ω and η. The distinction between them is that the firm is allowed to adjust its decisions to realisations of ω, but not to those of η (so that η is either measurement error, or a serially uncorrelated productivity shock that is realised after input decisions are made). Since ω affects the firm's decisions, it is the source of concern about the consistency of the OLS estimates of the parameters in (5.21). There are two reasons for these concerns. The first, which dates back to Marschak and Andrews' (1944) classic article, is that if ω is serially correlated, and input decisions are at least partially subject to control, then inputs in place will be correlated with current ω, and this will generate a simultaneous equation bias in the OLS coefficients. The second, which though discussed in the empirical literature for some time (see, e.g., Wedervang, 1965) had not been previously incorporated into the econometric analysis of production functions, is that we only observe firms that do not close down and, if more productive firms tend to be more profitable and survive longer, the selection on survival is, in part, a selection on ω, producing a selectivity bias in the OLS coefficients (for a review of the literature on selectivity biases in the labour of econometrics literature, see Heckman and Robb (1985) and the literature cited therein).

To devise an estimation procedure which takes account of the simultaneity and selectivity biases we need a model for input and exit decisions. For this Olley and Pakes (1992) use the model in our example, augmented to allow for a labour choice and for an additional state variable (age). Labour is assumed to be variable so that it is contracted for at the beginning of the period and can be adjusted, perhaps at increasing cost, to realisations from the conditional distribution of ω_t. As in the model outlined above exit occurs whenever $\omega_t \leq \underline{\omega}_t(k_t, a_t)$, with $\underline{\omega}_t(\cdot)$ decreasing in k, while $x_t = x_t(\omega_t, k_t, a_t)$ with $x_t(\cdot)$ strictly increasing in ω for each (k, a) whenever $x > 0$. The investment and exit function are indexed by t to allow for changes in market conditions over the period covered by the data (see Olley and Pakes (1992)).[20]

Since we are only interested in the use of the invertibility condition, we only reproduce the initial stage of their estimation algorithm, the stage that obtains the labour coefficient, a_1. The simultaneity problem here is a result of the correlation of l and k (through the past choices) with ω, while the selection problem is a result of the fact that the survival process truncates the distribution of the ω observed in the data (and the truncation point is a function of the right-hand side variables in the equation we want to estimate). We could account for both of these problems if we could condition also on ω. The invertibility condition tells us that for those observations with $x > 0$ we can do just that by substituting $\omega_t^*(\cdot)$ for ω_t in (5.20) producing the equation

$$q_{i,t} = a_0 + a_1 l_{i,t} + \phi_t(x_{i,t}, k_{i,t}, a_{i,t}) + \eta_{i,t} \qquad (5.21)$$

where,

$$\phi_t(x_{i,t}, k_{i,t}, a_{i,t}) = \omega_t^*(x_{i,t}, k_{i,t}, a_{i,t}) + a_a a_{i,t} + a_k k_{i,t}.$$

The first stage of the estimation algorithm uses a polynomial approximation to the $\phi_t(\cdot)$ function to obtain a semi-parametric estimator of $a_1(\cdot)$. Since $\omega_t^*(\cdot)$ is a function of all the state variables of the problem (all the determinants of the investment choice), the semi-parametric procedure does not allow us to separate out the effects of k and a on investment, from their direct effects on output. Olley and Pakes (1992) proceed to show how, by considering also the restrictions from the expectation of $y_t - b_1 l_t$ conditional on k_t, a_t and ω_{t-1}, one can also obtain consistent estimates of a_k and a_a (here b_1 is the first stage root n consistent estimate of a_l).

Alternative estimates of a_1 and a_k (standard errors in parenthesis) and the relevant sample sizes, are presented in table 5.1. The estimates in the first two columns are computed from a 'balanced panel'. The balanced panel is obtained by using only the information on the plants that were active for the entire thirteen-year period. Balanced panels are the traditional way of

Table 5.1. *Alternative estimates of Cobb–Douglas production function parameters*

Sample	Balanced panel		Unbalanced or full panel	
Estimation technique	OLS	Within	OLS	Olley/Pakes
Coefficient of	(1)	(2)	(3)	(4)
Labour	0.87	0.77	0.70	0.62
	(0.04)	(0.05)	(0.02)	(0.02)
Capital	0.16	0.05	0.31	
	(0.03)	(0.05)	(0.02)	
Number of observations	886	886	2,397	2,397

Source: Olley and Pakes (1991), table 6. Estimated standard errors are in parenthesis. Other variables in all equations are plant age and a time trend. The balanced panel uses only the data on plants which were active in every year of the thirteen years of the panel. The unbalanced panel uses data on all plants that were ever active in every year they were active.

drawing samples for use in production analysis. Columns (3) and (4) use the 'full' sample; this contains information on all plants ever active in all years that they are active (except those plant year observations that have zero investment, as these observations do not satisfy the invertibility condition).

The first point to note is that by using the balanced panel we discard about two-thirds of the observations, so the potential for selection problems is large. Column 1 provides the OLS, while column 2 provides the within estimator from the balanced panel (the within estimator uses deviations from firm-specific means for all variables; see Chamberlain (1982) for a detailed discussion). The within estimator would be appropriate if the effects of selection and simultaneity differed by firm but were constant for a given firm over time (note how much at odds this is with the model; according to the model the firms who exited were firms who changed their perceptions of their future profitability over the period, and one would expect perceptions to be correlated with realisations).

The total and within coefficient estimators from the balanced panels are not unusual for production function estimates from balanced panels. The labour coefficient is higher than what seems plausible for the elasticity of output with respect to labour, and the capital coefficient is noticeably lower than what we think plausible for the capital elasticity. Theory suggests at least two explanations. First labour, being easier to adjust, is more highly correlated with the current value of ω (simultaneity). Second, the exit rule is decreasing in k, so low capital firms who survive need to be firms who drew exceptionally good productivity sequences, while firms with more capital will survive on much poorer productivity draws. This induces a negative correlation between capital and productivity among survivors. Note also that since labour and capital are positively correlated, positive biases in one coefficient will tend to be associated with negative biases in the other.

Column 3 provides the OLS estimates on the full sample. We expect moving to the full sample to alleviate much of the selection problem, though not necessarily the simultaneity problem. The results are quite striking. The capital coefficient more than doubles, and the labour coefficient moves down by over 20 per cent. There should still be a bias in these coefficients that can be eliminated by substituting the polynomial approximation to the $\omega^*(\cdot)$ function for the unobserved value of ω_t. Just as theory says it should, use of the polynomial approximation to the inverse function forces the labour coefficient down still further, by another 10 per cent, so that the final estimate of the labour coefficient was close to labour's share in value added (the final estimate of the capital coefficient, which is not reported in the table, was 0.345 with a standard error of 0.05).

Where applicable, this combination of the use of theory (to prove the existence of an inverse function), and of semi-parametric estimation techniques (that allow us to use that inverse function without ever computing its form), should be quite useful, as it ought to allow us to account for the problems induced by serially correlated unobservables with estimation algorithms which are computationally quite simple. There may, of course, be many cases in which difficulties arise in checking for the regularity conditions which ensure the consistency and asymptotic normality of the semi-parametric estimator, or in computing its variance–covariance matrix and ensuring there is a consistent estimator of it, or, perhaps, in finding an efficient semi-parametric estimator for the structure at hand. However, the econometric literature on semi-parametric estimation has been advancing at an extremely rapid rate (see Ahn and Powell (1993), Andrews (1991, 1993) Chamberlain (1992), Newey (1993a and 1990b), Powell, Stock and Stocker (1989), Robinson (1988), Sherman (1991) and the literature cited in those articles); and it may not be too long until many of the relevant issues are clarified. Then the major problem facing the applied researcher will be to formulate the invertibility condition for the problem at hand and to show how it can be used to identify the finite dimensional parameter vector of interest – a task that generally requires a deep understanding of both the appropriate model and of the data at hand.

Having provided detail on one example where the invertibility condition takes on a relatively simple form, it is worth re-emphasising that the results

on that form are model specific. Indeed, our ability to use investment
(conditional on capital) as a proxy for the unobserved state variable in this
model depends crucially on the fact that, in models with deterministic
accumulation that satisfy the assumptions in lemma 3, the expected
increment to the value of the firm arising from a given increment in *capital* is
increasing in the unobserved state variable. In models in which there is
stochastic accumulation (such as the one outlined in section 3.3) this
monotonicity condition, and hence the associated invertibility condition, is
unlikely to be satisfied.

In these models the role of investment is to improve the distribution of
ω_{t+1} conditional on ω_t, and the increment to the value of the firm generated
by given increments in ω are not characteristically monotonic in ω. In
particular, boundedness of the value function implies that the increment in
value per increment in ω must eventually be concave in ω, and there is often
reason to expect the value function to be convex in ω at lower levels of
development (see, for example, Ericson and Pakes (1989), part I). As a
result we have to look for alternative ways of controlling for efficiency
differences in situations in which the stochastic accumulation model seems
appropriate.

The version of the stochastic accumulation model presented in the next
section is one in which firms are differentiated by the quality of the product
they produce. Consumers have a distribution of tastes over the alternative
products, and an increase in the quality of any one product (in its
unobserved ω) will increase demand for that product conditional on any
vector of prices and any vector of the ωs of a firm's competitors. Firms are
price-setters, and the equilibrium in the spot market for current output is
Nash in prices conditional on the ωs of all active firms. The ωs of the firms
evolve over time according to the stochastic outcomes of the firms'
investment decisions (and investment, entry and exit decisions are made to
maximise the expected discounted value of future net cash flows).

Berry (forthcoming, appendix 1) shows that under these conditions, and
some mild restrictions on the distribution of preferences over consumers,
there is a one to one map between the vector of market shares of the various
competitors and the vector of unobserved efficiency differences. This map
can therefore be inverted to obtain the unobserved efficiency differences as a
function of the observed market shares and the parameters of the model. So
there is an inverse function for this model, but it has a different form, and
requires different data, then the inverse function for the model with
deterministic accumulation.

The point to emphasise here is that the existence of the invertibility
condition, and its form where available, depends on the details of the model
that is appropriate for the problem one wants to analyse, and the data

available. There is simply no substitute for a deeper understanding of the major sources of unobserved variation in the data, and on how these unobservables are likely to interact with the observed deviates.

Given the possible complexity of the invertibility condition, there may be cases where the intuition underlying it is clear enough, though the formal justification for its use is difficult to obtain. Our suggestion here is to begin by simply computing the value function (or the equilibrium condition) underlying the invertibility condition for different values of the parameter vector, and then inspecting the solution for the required properties. If one finds that the condition is satisfied, but the proof is still not available, one may be able to extend this numerical procedure one step further, and actually programme a check of the invertibility condition into the computations at each iterative stage of the estimation algorithm.

This suggestion presumes that the estimation algorithm requires computation of the necessary relationships. As shown above, for more complicated models where computation of the needed functions can be very difficult, it is often easy to simplify the computational burden of the estimation procedure by combining an invertibility condition with a semi-parametric estimator for the inverse function. When formal proofs of the invertibility condition for these more complicated cases are not available, but the intuition underlying it is still strong, the suggestion is to use it, together with the semi-parametric estimator for the inverse function, to provide a simple 'diagnostic' test for the presence of a serially correlated unobservable, and some indication of just how much of an effect it may have on the parameter estimates.

The idea behind using an invertibility condition is essentially the same as the idea of using a 'proxy' to substitute for an unobserved variable; albeit a proxy whose values typically depend on the parameters being estimated as well as a vector of observables, and a proxy which can typically only be justified for a subset of the possible realisations of the vector of observables. The connection to the use of proxy variables makes it clear that there is a long history of related research on accounting for unobservables in econometric models; most recently in a non-linear form in the semi-parametric selection models (see Ahn and Powell (1993), Choi (1990), Newey (1988), and the literature cited in these articles).

Much of the prior literature on 'proxy' variables focussed on linear models. Latent variable models (see the review by Aigner, Hsiao, Kapetyn and Wansbeek (1984)) and dynamic factor analysis models (see Geweke (1977) and Sargent and Sims (1977)) are two of the more successful examples. Also related is the analysis of the initial condition problem for dynamic linear models on panel data (see Andersen and Hsiao (1982) Pakes and Griliches (1984) and the literature cited in those articles). For the most part neither of these literatures worried about deriving the linear system analysed from the primitives of a behavioural model, so the issue of the relationship of the inverse function to those primitives did not arise (for notable exceptions in the context of dynamic representative agent models, see Hansen and Sargent (1990), in static equilibrium contexts with hetero-geneity, see Heckman and Scheinkman (1987)). Also, once one incorporates either discreteness in the choice set, or interactions among agents, non-linearities typically appear in the relationship between the observable vector and the unobserved deviates we want to control for.

On the other hand, most of the linear models did allow for disturbances in all the relationships of interest. In contrast our discussion has assumed that the non-linear relationship between the observables and the unobserved state variable holds exactly. Perhaps, then, a logical next step for our analysis would be to allow for measurement error in the observables used as proxies (in our example, in investment). The truncated conditional likelihoods, or the truncated conditional moment restrictions, would then be in terms of the 'true' unobserved variables, and, since we would only observe the error-prone deviates, estimation would require a solution to a non-linear errors-in-variables problem. Research on non-linear errors-in-variables models (see Fuller (1987), chapter 3; Hausman, Ichimura, Newey and Powell (forthcoming), Newey and Powell (1992) and Newey (1990)) has been proceeding rather rapidly, so it may well be possible to incorporate errors of measurement into the analysis of invertibility conditions.

It is appropriate to conclude this section on a more general point. What is clear is that once we allow for serially correlated unobserved state variables, the properties of our estimators are going to have to depend on a set of very detailed assumptions on the way those variables affect the primitives of the model. A successful researcher, then, is likely to have to develop a fairly detailed understanding of what are the major sources of unobserved variation that affect behaviour, and of how they interact with the other primitives of the problem. The alternative is to assume that all unobserved deviates are serially uncorrelated. This is, of course, even more of a restriction than those needed for the models that allow for serially correlated state variables. Moreover, at least for many problems of current interest, it is an additional restriction which is simply untenable.

5   MARKET INTERACTIONS AND THE COMPUTATION OF EQUILIBRIUM RESPONSES

We now consider one way of incorporating market interactions into our examples, make some brief comments on related estimation problems, and then focus on computing equilibrium responses assuming that the parameters defining the primitives of the equilibrium problem have already been estimated.

To incorporate market interactions we allow the returns an agent earns in a given period to depend not only on the value of the agent's own state vector (y), but also on the vector of state variables of the other agents active in the market ($\hat{s}$). Recall that $s = (\hat{s}, y)$, is the list of state variables of all active agents. It will be assumed that there is a finite upper bound to the number of agents active in a given period (a condition which should, in general, be shown to be a consequence of the primitives of the model). So a particular value of s is a finite list of the state vectors of the firms currently active in the industry, and will be called an industry structure. In the deterministic accumulation example, then, the state vector for a given firm is a couple (ω, k), so s is a finite counting measure on $\Omega \times K$. Note also that the vectors (s, y), and $(\hat{s}, y)$, carry precisely the same information so, for notational convenience, we will use (s, y) where possible.

The assumption that the current returns the agent earns depends on s, as well as the agent's y, implies that the likely profitability of a firm's investments depend on the investments of its (potential and actual) competitors. As before we shall assume that all decisions are made to maximise the expected discounted value of the future net cash flow conditional on the current information set. That information set includes a distribution for the counting measure of possible industry structures in future years conditional on the current structure. The equilibrium notion we use to close the model insists that this distribution is in fact consistent with optimal behaviour by all incumbents and potential entrants.

It is important to note that though we do allow the firm's profits to depend on the state variables of competing firms, we will, throughout, restrict those state variables to the set of variables which determine either current production costs or current demand conditions (to use the terminology of Tirole, 1989, to 'payoff relevant' state variables). Strategies, in turn, will be restricted to depend only on the vector (s, y) (in particular they cannot depend on previous actions). Our assumptions, then, require the equilibrium to be Markov Perfect Nash in investment strategies (in the sense of Maskin and Tirole (1987, 1988a and 1988b)).

The extent to which the focus on the Markov Perfect Nash assumption limits the nature of the equilibria we study depends on the dimensionality of y. Since the burden of the computational algorithm also goes up (and quite rapidly) in the dimensionality of y (see below), there will often be a trade-off between the richness of the equilibria that the applied researcher allows for and the computational burden of the subsequent analysis (and, as in other trade-offs discussed above, our feeling is that it should be decided on a case by case basis according to the characteristics of the applied problem one wants to analyse). Note also that our discussion does not allow for non-pecuniary spillovers among firms (à la Romer (1986)) or for asymmetric information (for recent empirical work on structural models with asymmetric information in static contexts see Hendricks, Porter and Wilson (1993) and Wolak (1990)). These are reasonably glaring omissions which impose serious limits on the applicability of the results developed here. On the other hand, one has to start somewhere, and it is not analytically difficult to bring more detail into the current structure provided the basic behavioural assumptions used here are appropriate.

Our attitude towards structural estimation in applied problems where the interactions among heterogeneous agents are important, is that the stategy of estimating the model's parameters by solving for the complete set of dynamic equilibrium responses for different candidate values of the parameter vector, and then fitting these into an iterative maximum-likelihood (or minimum-distance) search procedure, has both computational and data requirements that are unlikely to be satisfied in the near future (at least for many problems of current interest). It therefore becomes essential to develop techniques that allow one to break the estimation problem down into smaller parts. Each part should allow the researcher to obtain an estimator for a subvector of the total vector of the model's parameters. This estimator should be obtainable without having to solve for the complete set of equilibrium responses, but should be consistent and asymptotically normal under the *complete* set of equilibrium assumptions. A typical breakdown will involve splitting off the static return function from the complete dynamic system and obtaining consistent estimates of its parameters in one part of the estimation algorithm, and then splitting off the problem of estimating the parameters defining the impact of investments on subsequent values of the state variables into another estimation subroutine. Part of the reason for our focus on Markov Perfect Nash equilibria is that they make it relatively easy to separate out the estimation of the parameters defining the one-period return function from those defining the dynamic impacts of decisions.

On the other hand, once we have our estimated parameters, we will still want to use them to compute the equilibrium they imply, and then investigate how that equilibrium varies with policy and environmental changes. Thus we are still in need of an algorithm capable of computing equilibrium responses, but not one that needs to be fast enough to enable us to nest it into an iterative estimation algorithm. Section 5.2 provides an algorithm for computing the equilibrium implications for the class of Markov Perfect Nash equilibria we focus on.

When we modify the deterministic accumulation example (assumption 1) to allow profits to depend also on the list of state variables of competing firms and then close it with an entry process, the example becomes a version of the Hoppenhayn–Rogerson (1990) model of industry dynamics (a model which is, pehaps, the most straightforward heterogeneous agent extension of the traditional production–investment model). This is the equilibrium model that underlies estimation of the Cobb–Douglas production function in the example in section 4.2. When we modify the stochastic accumulation example (section 3.3) for the same factors, the example becomes a version of the Ericson–Pakes (1992) model of industry dynamics. This will be the example used to illustrate the computational algorithm introduced below.

The last section mentioned estimation algorithms for subvectors of both these model's parameter vectors that do not require iterative computation of equilibrium responses. We emphasised there that the availability and form of these estimation techniques depended on detailed characteristics of the model relevant for the data at hand. Though there are interesting and important general estimation issues here, we have chosen not to discuss them in this chapter. Instead we focus on the problems involved in computing equilibrium responses conditional on having an estimate of the value of the model's parameter vector in hand. It would be inappropriate, however, to proceed directly to the computational issues without at least noting some of the problems that arise in generalising the estimation techniques discussed in the last sections to models where there are market interactions.

Since much of our discussion of invertibility conditions already incorporated market interactions, we do not have much to add to our discussion of the use of invertibility conditions. So we go directly to the potential for integrating market interactions into Euler-equation-based estimation techniques. Here the prognosis is not as bright . At least in 'small' markets, that is markets in which marginal changes in one firm's state variables in the current period generate non-trivial reactions by the firm's competitors in the following period, Euler-equation-based estimators will not generally be feasible. That this is so despite the fact that in some of these cases one can in fact use perturbations to the continuous control to derive Euler equations (e.g., the alternating move games discussed in Maskin and Tirole; see in particular their 1987 article) is a result of the fact that the restrictions that result from these Euler equations will involve a term giving the reactions of the firm's competitors to the perturbation in the given firm's control. The needed 'reaction function' is not a primitive of the model, but rather an endogenous construct, and to determine its form we generally have to know the form of the solution for the equilibrium responses. Without either more work, or more assumptions, then, we will be unable to use the restrictions embodied in the Euler equations to derive estimators for the model's parameters without solving first for the equilibrium responses generated by the different trial values of the parameter vector – a strategy which, as noted earlier, we want to avoid.

In some cases, of course, there will be ways around this problem. For example, in special cases where we can show that the reaction functions must have a simple form (e.g. linear, as in the linear quadratic game literature; see, for example, Kydland (1975)), we should be able to estimate the parameters of the reaction function along with the other parameters in the Euler equation from the restrictions that the Euler equation generates. A second possibility is to obtain a non-parametric estimate of the reaction function, substitute it into the Euler equation, and then derive a semi-parametric estimator for the rest of the parameters that determine the restrictions emanating from the Euler equation (see the literature on semi-parametric estimation referred to in the last section). Finally, we should note that even in cases where 'dynamic first-order' conditions cannot be used as a basis for estimation, one still may be able to use them to derive analytic characteristics of the optimal policy that ensure that other forms of estimators are feasible. Of particular importance here is the use of first-order conditions to show that invertibility conditions are indeed satisfied for some subset of the possible set of values of the observable vector.

We now leave the topic of estimation to consider computation of equilibrium responses.

5.1 Equilibrium responses

An underlying purpose of structural modelling is to obtain a deeper understanding of the responses to policy and environmental changes. This will require, in addition to estimates of the appropriate parameters, an ability to compute the equilibrium implications of those estimates. This sub-section assumes that we have estimated the model's parameters, and focusses on the problem of computing their implications.[21]

Once our models acknowledge the fact that agents do differ, and grant that their actions may impact on one another, then the computation of the responses we are typically after can become quite demanding. That this is so even if we are only after the aggregate impact of a given change, is a result of the simple fact that agents responses in realistic models are typically *different non-linear* functions of the changing variable (the non-linearity becomes most obvious once one allows for discréte alternatives) and the aggregate response we are after is usually a weighted average of the individual responses. Note that an analysis of aggregate impacts in such a world requires not only the distribution of responses of the agents currently active in the given market, but also, if agents can enter or exit that market, the equilibrium response of that distribution to the policy or environmental change.

Moreover, we are often specifically interested in the relationship of policy, or environmental, variables to the more detailed structure of the distribution of agents' characteristics, and in how the equilibrium distribution of those characteristics is likely to react to the policy or environmental change. Obvious examples where more detailed knowledge of the determinants of the equilibrium distribution is of overriding importance are easy to come by in almost all aspects of economics. The analysis of the link between default probabilities and the market for finance capital, and of the effects of the various deregulatory changes on market structure, are examples that occur repeatedly in the finance and industrial organisation literatures. More recently, the finding that almost all of the variance in gross job creation and gross job destruction is within-time-period, within-industry, variance (see Davis and Haltwinger (1990)) makes any analysis of the causes or the effects of job turnover in labour markets highly dependent on the detailed characteristics of the equilibrium from dynamic heterogeneous agent models (see Hoppenhayn and Rogerson (1990) for a start at such an analysis).[22] This section focusses on problems involved in computing the equilibria from dynamic stochastic heterogeneous agent models (assuming that all the parameters defining the primitives of that model are known).

As noted earlier we focus on Markov Perfect Nash equilibria, and again we find it convenient to illustrate our points with a particular example. The theoretical structure of the example is taken from Ericson and Pakes (1992), and it generalises the single-agent stochastic accumulation example used in section 3.3 to allow for market interactions. The differentiated product special case for the spot market for current output used in the computations is adapted from Berry (forthcoming), and the structure of the computational algorithm is taken from Pakes and McGuire (forthcoming).

The example provides us with a special case to use to test the computational algorithm. It has the additional, and at least for testing purposes desirable, characteristic that the Markov Process which defines the equilibrium in this example lives on a finite collection of points. We can, therefore, calculate the value functions and policies the equilibrium generates exactly (or at least to any desired degree of precision) and then compare the exact results to results based on various approximations.

We begin by calculating the exact solution. Then we illustrate the richness of the solutions one gets from structural heterogeneous agent models by simulating the ergodic distribution of market structures, and characterising firm behaviour, for a particular numerical example.

We also show, however, that the number of points at which we have to evaluate the value function to obtain the exact solution goes up as a polynomial in the number of agents ever active in the market. The number of computations per point evaluated also grows as a polynomial in this number. Exact calculation will, therefore, become computationally impossible for a market with a large enough number of agents. For our example we cannot really go beyond a seven agent equilibrium on our SPARC 1.

We therefore move on to show how one can use procedures based on polynomial approximations (and/or interpolation) to cut down the number of points at which we must calculate the value function in the computational algorithm. Our major result in this context is analytic. We prove that provided the value function of a given agent is symmetric (more precisely exchangeable) in the state vectors of its competitors, the number of polynomial coefficients one needs for a given order of polynomial approximation is *independent* of the number of agents active in the market.

To get some idea of how good the polynomial approximations could be, we fit polynomials directly to the exactly calculated value functions for our example. It is reasonably clear that the fit of a polynomial with a given number of coefficients does not depend on the number of agents active in the market (at least when we measure fits by a simple R^2 criteria). Two other points come out of these exercises. First, one can often do a lot better than using simple polynomial expansions, particularly if one knows something about the problem being analysed. Second, and most encouraging, it seems that one can fit the polynomials, or the other approximating functions, to a small but reasonably diffuse subset of the total number of points, use the approximating functions obtained in this fashion to fit all the points, and do just about as well as one would have done by fitting the whole set of points directly.

5.2   The example

Recall that in the model with stochastic accumulation firms invest to explore, and if warranted, develop, profit opportunities (improved goods or techniques of production). The outcomes of the investment process are uncertain. Positive outcomes lead the firm to states where the good or service can be marketed more profitably. If the outcomes generate lesser increments than those of its competitors (both inside and outside the industry) the firm's profits deteriorate, and may lead to a situation in which it is optimal to abandon the whole undertaking (thus generating exit). A firm's supply to the spot market for current output, and its current profits, depend on its own level of development, a counting measure which provides the levels of development of its competitors in the industry, and on the level of development of an alternative outside of the industry. The level of development of the outside alternative evolves exogenously. Entry and investment decisions (which determine the levels of development of the actors in the industry) are made to maximise the expected discounted value of future net cash flow conditional on the current information set. The equilibrium notion is Markov Perfect Nash in investment strategies.

We begin by providing a brief description of each of the primitives of the model, starting with the profit function, then turning to the other primitives determining incumbent behaviour, and finally to those determining the behaviour of entrants. We then give a verbal characterisation of the aspects of the model's equilibrium that we want to investigate (for more detail, see Ericson and Pakes (1992)).

The state variables determining the firm's perception of its opportunities are

$$(\omega, s) \in \Omega XS \subseteq \mathscr{X}_+^{\mathscr{X}},$$

where ω is an index of its own efficiency, s is a counting measure providing the number of firms at each possible efficiency, and $\mathscr{X}$ is notation for the integers. 's_t' defines the structure of the industry at each t.

Thus

$$\pi(\cdot, \cdot) : \Omega XS \to \mathscr{R},$$

provides the 'reduced' form of the current profit function. In the general case we need only that

(i) $\pi(\omega, s)$ is increasing in ω for all s,
(ii)   that there exists a complete preorder on S, say $\geq$, s.t. if $s_1 \geq s_2$, then $\pi[\omega, s_1] \geq \pi[\omega, s_2]$ for all ω, and that
(iii) $\sup \pi[\omega, s] \leq \pi^*$ and for each ω, $\pi[\omega, s] \leq (1 - \beta)\Phi$ for sufficiently large s.

In (iii) β is the discount rate, and Φ is the scrap or exit value (the value of the firm and its entrepreneur in its best alternative use) so $(1 - \beta)\Phi$ is the per-period return on the firm's transferable assets.

The special case we actually compute is a differentiated product model. Good '0' is the outside good, and goods $1, \ldots, N$ are the goods produced by the firms competing in the industry. Each consumer purchases at most one good from the industry. The utility consumer 'i' derives from purchasing and consuming good 'j' is given by

$$U(i,j) = v_j - p_j^* + \epsilon(i,j),$$

where v_j is the quality or efficiency index, and p_j^* is the price, of the good, and $i = 1, \ldots, M$. Consumer 'i' chooses good 'j' if and only if it is preferred over all the alternatives, that is if for $q = 0, 1, \ldots, N$

$$\epsilon(i,j) - \epsilon(i,q) \geq [v_q - v_j] + [p_j^* - p_q^*]$$
$$= [v_q - v_0] - [v_j - v_0] + [p_j^* - p_0^*] - [p_q^* - p_0^*]$$
$$= g[\omega_q] - g[\omega_0] + p_j - p_q,$$

where $g(\cdot)$ is increasing, $\omega_q = g^{-1}[v_q - v_0]$, and $p_q = p_q^* - p_0^*$. Let the set $c[\omega_j; p, s]$, where s is the counting measure providing the number of firms at each ω, be the set of ϵs that satisfy the above set of inequalities, and hence induce the choice of good j.

Note that choices are determined entirely by the firm's efficiency relative to the efficiency of the outside good. So an increase in the firm's efficiency means that its efficiency has gone up relative to the outside alternative, and its efficiency will decrease only if the improvements to the firm's own product are not as great as the improvements in the outside alternative. Also, movements in v_0 will cause synchronised movements in the relative efficiencies, in the ωs, of all firms in the industry, which in turn will generate a *positive* correlation in their profits (of course movements in the v_j will generate a negative correlation in the profits of firm 'j' and its competitors). Finally, it is the 'real' price of the good that matters.

Let $G(\cdot)$ provide the distribution of ϵ. Then the probability that a random consumer will choose good 'j' is

$$\sigma[\omega_j; p, s] = \int_{\epsilon \subseteq c[\omega_j; p, s]} dG(\epsilon) = \exp[g(\omega_j) - p_j]/\{1 + \sum \exp[g(\omega_q) - p_q]\},$$

where the last equality assumes that $G(\cdot)$ is multivariate extreme value. If there are N firms in the market, no fixed costs of production and constant marginal costs equal to mc, then it can be shown that if firms choose prices to maximise profits a unique Nash equilibrium exists (Caplin and Nalebuff (1991)) and satisfies the vector of first-order conditions

$$-[p_j - mc]\sigma_j[1 - \sigma_j] + \sigma_j = 0$$

for $j = 1, \ldots, N$. Profits are given by

$$\pi[\omega_j, s] = \{p[\omega_j, s] - mc\}M\sigma[\omega_j - s],$$

where it is understood that the price and share vectors are calculated from the spot-market equilibrium conditions.

The distribution of ω_{t+1} conditional on ω_t depends on the amount the firm is willing to invest in developing its product. We let the family of distributions for the increment in ω, i.e., for $\omega_{t+1} - \omega_t = \tau_t$, conditional on different values of x_t, be

$$\mathscr{P} = \{P(\cdot | x), x \in \mathscr{R}_+\},$$

which we assume to have finite support. This family is built as a convolution of two random variables. The first, say v_1 is the increment in efficiency the firm gets from its own research process, and is stochastically increasing in x.

The second, say v, is an exogenous random variable which represents the force of the competition from outside of the industry (the efficiency of the outside alternative in the example above). Note that the possibility of advances by outside competitors implies both that; $P(\cdot)$ puts positive probability on negative values of τ, and that the realisations of τ are not independent across the firms that are active in a given period.

The example used in the computations puts $\tau = v_1 - v$, where

$$v_1 = \begin{cases} 1 \text{ with probability } ax/(1+ax) \\ 0 \text{ otherwise,} \end{cases}$$

and

$$v = \begin{cases} 1 \text{ with probability } \delta \\ 0 \text{ otherwise.} \end{cases}$$

By making the time period per decision small relative to the time period in the data, we generate distributions of increments that make large changes in τ possible.

To choose optimal investment and exit policies, incumbents need also a perceived distribution for

$$\hat{s}_{t+1} = s_{t+1} - e[\omega_{t+1}],$$

where $e[\omega_{t+1}]$ is a vector which puts one in the ω_{t+1} spot and zero elsewhere, conditional on s_t and ω. This will be denoted by

$$q_\omega\{\hat{s}_{t+1}|s_t\} = \sum q_\omega\{\hat{s}_{t+1}|s_t, v_{t+1}\}p\{v_{t+1}\}.$$

Note that this distribution embodies the incumbent's beliefs about entry and exit.

We assume that the functions $q_\omega[\hat{s}|s]$ can be derived as the transition probability for $s_{t+1} - e[\omega_{t+1}]$ from some regular Markov transition kernel, say $Q[\cdot|\cdot]: S \times S \to [0,1]$ and that S is compact. Ericson and Pakes show that the Markov Perfect Nash equilibrium will generate transition kernels with these properties (i.e., that these conditions are indeed satisfied in equilibrium).

Given that $q_\omega(\cdot|s)$ provides the incumbent's perceived distribution of future market structures, the Bellman equation for the firm's maximisation problem is

$$V(\omega, s) = \max \{\Phi, \sup_{(x \geq 0)}[\pi(\omega, s) - cx \\ + \beta \sum V(\omega + \tau, \hat{s} + e[\omega + \tau])q_\omega[\hat{s}|s, v]p(\tau|x, v)p(v)]\}.$$

Ericson and Pakes (1992) provide a reasonably detailed exposition of the nature of optimal policies in this framework. What we require here is the fact that boundedness of the value function implies that if ω is high enough, the value of additional increments in ω can be made as small as we like. Since the return to investment in this model is determined by the increment in the value function generated by higher values of ω, the boundedness assumption ensures that investment will be zero for all ω greater than some $\hat{\omega}$. Since firms cannot improve their quality index without some investment, states above $\hat{\omega}$ are 'coasting states' from which the firm's ω can only deteriorate (and will stochastically). So there is an upper bound to the achievable ω states. Similarly, the possibility of exit generates a lower bound for the observed ω states. So we can, without loss of generality, take the set $\Omega = \{1, \ldots, K\}$.

To complete the description of the model we need also to specify the primitives which determine entry behaviour. We have chosen a very simple model of entry where:

(i)   entry is sequential from an unlimited pool;
(ii)   entrants pay a (sunk) setup fee of $x_e(m)$, which is non-decreasing in the number of entrants (m), then obtain a draw from a distribution $P[\omega_0]$, and begin operation in the next period at the ω-location generated by the draw;
(iii) each potential entrant enters if the EDV of net cash flow from entry exceeds $x_e(m)$.

Formally, if

$$V^e[s, m] = \beta \sum V[\omega_0, \hat{s} + e_{\omega_0}] q_{m-1}[\hat{s}|s, v] p[\omega_0|v] p(v)$$

then

$$m_s = \begin{cases} 0 \text{ if } V^e[s,1] < x_1^e, \text{ else} \\ \min \{m \in I_+ : x_m^e \leq V_{s,m}^e, V_{s,m+1}^e < x_{m+1}^e\}, \end{cases}$$

with $\{q_{m-1}[\hat{s}|s, v]\}$ consistent with some Markov transition kernel on a compact set.

Note that the distribution of entering ωs is fixed over time. Thus the 'ability' of entrants progresses at the same pace as the 'ability' of the outside world (in terms of our example it advances with the ability of the outside alternative). If this were not the case entry would eventually go to zero and stay there. Also in the computational example we set $x_1^e = x^e$, and $x_2^e = \infty$, so the maximum number of entrants in any given period is one (the maximum number of entrants in any time interval depends on the number of decision-making periods in that time interval), and

$$p[\omega_0|v] = \begin{cases} 1 \text{ for } \omega_0 = \omega^*, & \text{if } v = 0 \\ 1 \text{ for } \omega_0 = \omega^* - 1 & \text{if } v = 1. \end{cases}$$

Ericson and Pakes show that under these conditions

(i) $\forall s, m_s \leq m^*$.

(ii) $\exists N^*$ s.t $\sum s_j \geq N^* \Rightarrow m_s = 0$.

Hence $\#S \leq K^{N^* + m^*}$, i.e., there is only a finite number of industry structures possible. They also provide a formal proof of the existence of a rational expectations, Markov Perfect Nash equilibrium under these assumptions.

The industry structures generated by this equilibrium will all be counting measures on Ω with a finite number of firms, i.e.

$$S = \{s = [s_1, \ldots, s_K]: \sum s_j \leq N^* + m^*\}.$$

So the heart of the equilibrium is a stochastic process for $\{s_t\}$, defined on $(S^\infty, \underline{S}, \underline{P})$. This process is a stationary Markov process, i.e., if $s^t = (s_1, \ldots, s_t)$, then

$$\Pr\{s_{t+1} = s' | s^t\} = \Pr[s' | s_t] = Q[s' | s],$$

with transition kernel $Q[\cdot|\cdot]$, and initial condition s_0 (assumed in S).

The Ericson–Pakes paper also proves that the Markov kernel, $Q[\cdot|\cdot]$, implied by the model's assumptions generates an ergodic distribution of industry structures. In particular it is shown that

(i)   the state space, S, contains a unique, positive recurrent communicating class, say $R \subseteq S$;

(ii) $\exists$ a unique probability measure, say μ^*, whose support is R, and which satisfies, $\mu^* Q = \mu^*$.

(iii)   if $\mu_T[s_0, s]$, gives the fraction of time periods for which $s_t = s$, then $\mu_T[s_0, s] \to \mu_s^*$ a.s. uniformly over $s \in S$.

Note that though $(1/T)\sum s_t \to \mu^*$, s_t itself never settles down. Rather the structure of the industry is in perpetual flux. Depending on the nature of μ^* we can expect the industry to go through periods when output is concentrated in the hands of a small number of large firms, and then, perhaps as a reaction to a sequence of new inventions, to fracture into an industry composed of a large number of approximately equally sized firms. Of course even over periods when the industry structure remains relatively stable there will be heterogeneity in the outcomes of the active firms, with rank reversals, and simultaneous entry and exit as the normal course of affairs.

It is worth emphasising, however, that the actual nature of the limit distribution, i.e., of μ^* (whether in fact it does include both relatively fractured and relatively concentrated structures), and the nature of the pattern of likely transitions between elements in that limit distribution (do we cycle over the divergent types of structures, or are there Poisson type events that take us more directly from one type of structure to another?)

depends on the precise values of the parameters that determine the primitives of our model. What the ergodic theorem tells us is that, if we are willing to suffice with limit properties, we can analyse them, and see how they react to different values of the parameter vector, without specifying initial conditions.

5.3 Computation of equilibria

We now come back to the task of tracing out the characteristics of $Q[\cdot|\cdot]$ implied by different values of the parameters defining the primitives of the model, and of describing how sample paths are likely to change in response to policy and environmental changes. This brings us back to the need for a computational algorithm that allows us to solve for (or simulate) the stochastic process generating $\{s_t\}$ for different values of the parameters of the model.

$Q[\cdot|\cdot]$ is calculated from the optimal policy and the primitives, as together these generate the transition probabilities for all incumbents and potential entrants from any initial state. Though the actual computation may well be complicated (see Ericson and Pakes (1992)), given the optimal policies, i.e., $\{\chi(\omega,s), x(\omega,s), V^e(s,m)\}$, and an initial s, it is easy to simulate different sample paths and then derive an empirical distribution which will converge (uniformly) to the true $Q[\cdot|\cdot]$. So the whole computational problem is in finding the optimal policies. We turn now to a description of a computational algorithm (taken from Pakes and McGuire (forthcoming)), designed to find these policies, and a discussion of its properties. The algorithm, together with the functional forms given in the example provided above, is then used to generate and characterise the evolution of that industry.

A computational algorithm
We work off value functions for problems with a limited number of active firms, and then push that limit up. Start with the value function for one active firm. This is a straightforward contraction which sets the support of (the upper and lower limits for) ω, i.e., it sets Ω.

For $N=2$ we need to calculate $V[\omega_1, \omega_2]$ for $\{\omega_1, \omega_2\} \in \Omega^2$. Start with $V_0[,] = \pi[\omega_1, \omega_2]$. Then get $V^n[\omega_1, \omega_2]$ as the solution to

$$V^n[\omega_1, \omega_2] = \pi[\omega_1, \omega_2] - cx$$
$$+ \beta \sum_{\tau_1, \tau_2, v} V^{n-1}[\omega_1 + \tau_1 + v, \omega_2 + \tau_2 + v] p[\tau_1|x_1, v] p[\tau_2|x_2, v] p(v),$$
(5.22a)

where the couple $[x_1 x_2]$ satisfy the Kuhn–Tucker conditions

$$x_i \{ -c + \beta \sum_{\tau_i, \tau_j, v} V^{n-1}[\cdot, \cdot] p_j (\partial p_i / \partial x_i) p(v) \} = 0, \qquad x_i \geq 0, \qquad (5.22b)$$

for $i \neq j, i, j = 1, 2, \ldots, p_i = p[\tau_i | x_i, v]$, and so on. One procedure for calculating the fixed point defining the equilibrium would be to repeat this step iteratively until $\|V^n - V^{n-1}\|$ was below an acceptable tolerance for an appropriate norm $\|\cdot\|$.

Note that this procedure differs from a straightforward 'doubly nested' fixed-point calculation. The latter would begin with a candidate function for the process generating the competitors' states (for $p(\tau_2 | s, v)$ in our two firm example), use it to solve the implied contraction for $V[\cdot | p(\tau_2 | \cdot)]$ and the associated investment policy, then use that investment policy to update the process generating the competitors' states (to update $p(\tau_2 | s, v)$), and then iterate on this double nest until convergence. By solving for all the xs simultaneously at each iteration we have done away with one of the 'nests' in this fixed-point algorithm. However, the procedure in (5.22) requires the solution to an implicit non-linear system of equations at each iteration of the fixed point, and the fact that the system of equations does not have an explicit solution increases computational time dramatically.

An alternative is to use x_j^{n-1} in the Kuhn–Tucker condition that solves for x_i (for $j \neq i$). If we ignore the constraint that $x \geq 0$, this gives an explicit solution for each x_i. If $x_i \leq 0$, set it equal to zero. This does away with the requirement of a non-linear search at each iteration, and decreases computational time accordingly. Of course we could iterate on this 'policy step' until convergence and (provided convergence is achieved) obtain an exact solution without ever having to simultaneously solve the non-linear system. Though it did not prove helpful to iterate on this step in the examples presented here, it is more likely to prove helpful once we substitute polynomial approximations into the computational algorithm (see below).

For expositional simplicity we ignored entry in the discussion above. To account for entry, consider states where $V[\omega_2, \omega_1] = \Phi$. In such cases we use $\pi[\omega_1]$ instead of $\pi[\omega_1, \omega_2]$, and calculate $V^e[\omega_1]$. If this term is greater than x^e, we calculate $V[\omega_1, \omega_0]$ for $V[\omega_1, \omega_2]$, where the transition probabilities for ω_0 are given by $P[\omega_0]$.

We still continue iterating until $\|V^n - V^{n-1}\|$ is within a given tolerance, but now we also check $\|x^n - x^{n-1}\|$. A fixed point to this problem can be shown to satisfy all the requirements for our equilibrium if the maximum number of firms, set either endogenously by the model's parameters, or by an artificial barrier to entry, call it N, is 2. Now push N up to 3 and do the fixed-point calculation again starting at

$$V^{n=0,3}[\omega_1, \omega_2, \omega_3] = V^{n=\infty,2} \{\omega_1, \max[\omega_2, \omega_3]\}.$$

This procedure should be repeated until we reach an n where, for all industry structures at which $\sum s(i) = n$, $V^e(s, 1) < x^e$. The n which satisfies this condition is an upper bound to the number of firms ever in the industry (i.e., it is N; of course this is only true if the initial s has no more than N firms).

Some caveats are in order before proceeding. We have not proved a contraction property for our algorithm, so we have no way of ensuring that it converges. On the other hand, it has converged for every set of parameter vectors we have tried. We have not proven uniqueness either. We did calculate all results we describe here thrice, starting each at different initial conditions (once at $A(\cdot)$, once at zero, and once at $V(\cdot)$ from the smaller N, see above). In each case we got to precisely same answer.

Computational burden
Roughly, the computational burden of this algorithm is the product of: (1) time per grid point evaluation, (2) number of grid points evaluated at each iteration, (3) number of iterations until convergence.

An explicit calculation can be provided for the number of grid points. First note that one does not have to evaluate all of them since symmetry implies that $V[\omega,1,k]=V[\omega,k,1]$, for all $\omega,k,1$. Indeed the number of points one needs to evaluate are the number of distinct N-element vectors with $\omega_1 \geq \omega_2,\ldots, \geq \omega_N$, (and, $1 \leq \omega_i \leq K$, for $i=1,\ldots,N$). Lemma 4 provides an exact calculation for the number of distinct N-element vectors that satisfy this condition. Note that it can be re-written as a (K^{th}-order) polynomial in N.

Lemma 4
The number of distinct sequences $[\omega_1,\ldots,\omega_n]$ with $\omega_i \geq \omega_{i-1}$ and $\omega_i \in [1,\ldots,K]$ $(i=1,\ldots,N)$, say $E[K,N]$, is given by

$$E[K,N]=\binom{K+N-1}{N}=\frac{(K+N-1)!}{(K-1)!N!}$$

Proof
First note that for $N \geq 2$

$$E[K,N]=\sum_{j=1}^{K} E[j,N-1]$$

since when we put the number 'j' in the Nth slot we have $E[j,N-1]$ sequences of $[\omega_1,\ldots,\omega_{N-1}]$ with $\omega_i \geq \omega_{i-1}$ for $i=1,\ldots,N-1$ and $\omega_i \in [1,\ldots,K]$. Given this fact we can proceed with an inductive proof for the theorem (in N). The initial condition of the inductive argument $[N=2]$ is true by enumeration, so what we need to show is that if $E[K,N]$ satisfies the equation in the statement of the lemma so does $E[K,N+1]$. From above

$$E[K,N+1]=\sum_{j=1}^{K} E[j,N]=\sum_{j=1}^{K}\binom{j+N-1}{N}=\binom{K+N}{N+1}$$

as required, where the last equality can be shown by induction on K.

The approximation methods we discuss below are designed to overcome the problem that the number of grid points evaluated grows as a polynomial in the least upper bound to the number of active firms. There will still be the issue, however, that the time per grid point evaluation grows as a similar (though not quite so large) polynomial in N (it would be exactly the same if all industry structures were connected in the sense that it was possible to pass from any one to any other in a single period; though this is definitely not the case in our example). That is at each grid point we do evaluate, we need to evaluate the value function at every achievable industry structure in the following period.

On the other hand, we expect the number of iterations needed for convergence to go down as N goes up. As we increase N, the effect of an additional active firm on the value of being at a particular point ought to diminish, so the final iteration for the value function calculated at the $N-1$ firm equilibrium should be closer to the N-firm value function we are looking for. However, we have no formula for the rate at which this will occur.

We calculated 2 to 6 firm equilibria (i.e., $N^* = 2, \ldots, 6$) for different values of the parameter vector for our example, and found that the computational time for the 6 firm equilibria was about 5.5 hours on our SPARC station. The no-entry barrier equilibria value of N^* for most of these runs was six firms. However, the time required to calculate the equilibria went up by a factor of about 5 every time we went from an N to an $N+1$ firm equilibria. This in spite of the fact that the number of iterations required before our convergence criteria was met typically got multiplied by fractions between 0.5 and 0.7 when we moved up N in units of one (though this varied between runs).

Thus, though the computational techniques presented here may suffice for computing equilibria for markets with a small number of agents, we will need to improve on them in order to analyse many of the markets of interest. We come back to this point below. First we glance at some of the summary statistics from one run of our example.

Descriptive output from one set of computations
To illustrate the type of dynamic stochastic equilibrium that results from this class of dynamic heterogeneous agent models, we briefly go over some summary statistics from one set of parameter values. Those values are: δ (the probability that the outside alternative moves up) $= 0.7$; $\beta = 0.925$, x^e (sunk entry cost) $= 0.2$, Φ (scrap value) $= 0.1$ m (size of market) $= 5$, spread $= 3$ and $a = 3$ (parameters determining the efficacy of own investment in increasing the probability of quality improvements), mc (marginal cost) $= 5$.

Table 5.2. *Characteristics of ergodic distribution*

$\delta = 0.7$ $a = 3$ $\beta = 0.925$ $x^e = 0.2$ phi $= 0.1$ spread $= 3$ $m = 5$ $c = 5$

	Number of periods	10,000
Panel A	% with 6 firms active	0.3
	% with 5 firms active	1.9
	% with 4 firms active	27.9
	% with 3 firms active	69.9
	% with 2 firms active	0.0
Panel B	% with entry and exit	10.10
	% with entry only	4.44
	% with exit only	2.18
	% with entry or exit	16.75

Table 5.2 provides some statistics which help describe the ergodic distribution for this industry. Part A of the table indicates that the erdogic process characteristically has either three or four firms active in a given period. There is, however, lots of entry and exit, so the firms active in equilibrium are not always the same three or four firms. Note also that entry and exit are positively correlated; in most years when there is entry there is also exit (part B of the table: this is in stark contrast to models of industry dynamics that do not allow for idiosyncratic sources of change).

During the 10,000 periods simulated 1,451 firms participated in the industry; however, most were active only a short period of time (table 5.3, part A). Almost half of them dropped out after their first year of operation. Both mortality and hazard rates decline markedly over the first seven or eight years, giving the indication that this initial period looks very much like a 'learning' period. About 11 per cent of new entrants survive eight years, and after that the hazard has no particular shape (one should be aware that these are estimated mortality rates; their standard errors are on the order of 0.005).

Part B of table 5.3 provides characteristics of the realised values of the firms which participated. The first point to note is that over 90 per cent of the firms which participated in this industry had a net loss from their endeavour (generated negative realised values). Most lose about 0.1 (the difference between the entry and exit fees), but there are those who invest for awhile, never move up the 'quality ladder', and eventually drop out, losing also their investments in the interim. Among the 10 per cent whose realised values were positive, the mean realised value was very high (9.3, giving a benefit/cost ratio of 46.5), and the distribution was very skewed.

Table 5.3A. *Lifetime distribution*

(Based on 1,451 'lives' in 10,000 time periods)

$\delta = 0.7$ $a = 3$ $\beta = 0.925$ $x^e = 0.2$ phi $= 0.1$ spread $= 3$ $m = 5$ $c = 5$

Mean $= 22.7$, Median $= 2$, Standard deviation $= 101.8$

Lifetime	Frequency	Per cent	Implied hazard	Cumulative per cent
1	617	42.5	42.5	44.5
2	401	27.6	48	70.2
3	126	8.7	29.2	78.8
4	55	3.8	17.9	82.6
5	36	2.5	14.3	85.1
6	20	1.4	9.4	86.5
7	16	1.1	8.2	87.6
8	14	1.0		88.6
9	7	0.5		89.0
10	5	0.3		89.4
≥ 10	146	10.06		
≥ 50	96	6.6		
≥ 100	77	5.32		

The industry is most often reasonably fractured (the one-firm concentration ratio averaged 0.37 in an industry in which there are almost always either three or four active firms), but periodically a firm will surge ahead of its competitors and stay there for reasonable lengths of time (the standard deviation of the one-firm concentration ratio was 0.11).

These parameter values generate an industry in which it is relatively cheap to start up and explore some new idea. Most startups are not successful. The few that are grow to become major actors in the industry, and earn phenomenal rates of profit. Of course, eventually, even the most profitable firms are passed over by the developments of their competitors and find it optimal to exit.

At this point it would be useful to perturb the model in ways that correspond to possible policy or environmental changes, do additional computations, and compare the results. One of the great advantages of structural modelling is that it generates an ability to do such comparisons, and Pakes and McGuire (forthcoming) illustrate this by considering the effects of alternative possible regulatory changes on market structure and welfare (see also Judd's (1990) numerical analysis of alternative duopolies). However, these comparisons are topics for wholly different papers, so we now return to computational issues.

Table 5.3B. *Realised value distribution*

$\delta = 0.7$ $\alpha = 3$ $\beta = 0.925$ $x^e = 0.2$ phi $= 0.1$ spread $= 3$ $m = 5$ $c = 5$

Mean $= 0.58$, Median $= -0.1$, Standard deviation $= 3.60$

128 positive entries, mean is 9.3

1,223 negative entries, mean is -0.28

Obs/num	RV	Lifetime	Sum/rv
1	72.8	79	72.8
2	24.0	70	96.9
3	22.2	182	119.1
4	21.9	501	141.0
5	20.2	530	161.2
10	17.8	54	253.4
50	10.44	78	779.4
100	4.39	334	1,135.9
128	0.21	9	1,192.2
129	-0.06	4	1,191.9
1,000	-0.1		
1,451	-4.03		846.7

5.4 Computational approximation

We now consider computational techniques that attempt to reduce the computational burden of obtaining the equilibrium by fitting the value function at only a small fraction of the points in S, and then using the information obtained from those values to predict the value function at other points as needed. More generally, all we require is an approximation to a function which determines policies at any point in S, and there are many different ways of doing this. The symposium in the *JBES* (1990) reviews and compares several different approximating techniques in the context of computing equilibria for a *representative agent* stochastic growth model. Judd (1990) sketches a general framework and computes equilibria from models with two agents (no entry or exit), and the article by Marcet (1994) in this volume reviews progress in this field to date.

Many of these techniques fit polynomials in a set of functions that span, or form a basis for, a 'rich enough' collection of approximating functions (the Chebyshev or Legendre polynomials for example) to a small set of points, and then use the fitted polynomial to predict the other points as needed. An alternative is to fit the function directly at a small number of points, and then interpolate, either linearly, or using a spline, to other points. We begin by showing how to embed such approximations into the computational algorithm described above. Note that the heterogeneous agent problems we are interested in are by nature multi-dimensional, the dimensionality of the state vector for any given agent going up with the number of other agents active in the market.[23]

Recall that a function $f: \Omega^N \to \mathscr{R}$ is a polynomial of order λ if for all $\omega \in \Omega^N$

$$f(\omega_1, \ldots, \omega_N) = \sum_{p=0}^{\lambda} \sum_{h_N=0}^{p-\sum h_i} \cdots \sum_{h_1=0}^{p} a(h_1, \ldots, h_N) \omega_1^{h_1} \cdots \omega_N^{h_N}$$

$$\equiv \sum_{h \in H^N} a(h)\omega(h)$$

with $a(h) \in \mathscr{R}$ for all $h = \{h_1, \ldots, h_N\} \in H^N$, where $H^N = \{h \in \mathscr{Z}_+^N : \sum h_i \le \lambda\}$. The collection of all such polynomials (obtained by varying a), together with the usual operations of addition and scalar multiplication, is a vector space (over the real numbers), say $\mathscr{V}_\lambda$. A basis for this vector space is the set of tensor products of the $\omega_i^{h(i)}$ with h varied over H^N (see Hoffman and Kunze (1972), section 5.6), truncated to keep the sum of the coefficients less than or equal to λ (this produces the 'complete' polynomial basis). These are just the functions implicit in the $\omega(h)$ in the equation above. Though we do not pursue it here, the following discussion could be generalised by looking for an approximation in a vector space spanned by the tensor products of $g(\omega_i)$ for suitably chosen $g(\cdot)$.

The iterative procedure used to calculate the fixed point defining the value function for our problem can be modified to find an approximating polynomial, a $\hat{V} \in \mathscr{V}_\lambda$ as follows. Define a set of basis points, say $\omega(j) \in \Omega^N$, for $j = 1, 2, \ldots$ If there are J basis functions, the basis points must generate at least J linearly independent values for those functions. Starting at some initial guess for the vector a, let the estimate of the coefficients at the $n-1$th-iteration of the recursive calculation be a^{n-1}. Now calculate the value function at the basis points by substituting

$$\hat{V}^{n-1}[\omega(j)] = \omega(j)'a^{n-1},$$

into the nth iteration of the recursive calculation in (5.22). Equation (5.22b) then produces an x^n, which when substituted back into the (5.22a) that used $\hat{V}^{n-1}$ produces a new value function, say $V^{*n}(\ )$, at each of the basis points. We choose a^n to minimise the Euclidean distance between $\omega' a^n$ and $V^{*n}(\ )$ at the basis points. That is, if W is the matrix formed from the rows $\omega(j)$

$$a^n = [W'W]^{-1}W'V^{*n}.$$

This procedure can be generalised slightly by approximating a monotone function of $V(\cdot)$ by a polynomial in the basis functions, instead of approximating $V(\cdot)$ itself.

Without further restrictions the number of functions needed to form a basis for $\mathscr{V}_\lambda$, and hence the minimum number of points at which we need to fit the value function for this approximation, still grows as a polynomial in N. However, we have not yet used the fact that the value function is symmetric, more precisely exchangeable, in the vector $(\omega_2, \ldots, \omega_N)$. If we restrict our search to the subspace of $\mathscr{V}_\lambda$ that satisfies the restriction that, for all $\omega^N \in \Omega^N$

$$\hat{V}(\omega_1, \ldots, \omega_N) \equiv \hat{V}(\omega_1, \pi_2, \ldots, \pi_N), \tag{5.23}$$

for any $N-1$ dimensional vector $\pi = (\pi_2, \ldots, \pi_N)$ which is a permutation of $(\omega_2, \ldots, \omega_N)$, we reduce the number of required basis functions dramatically. Indeed, provided $N \geq \lambda$, the number of required basis functions becomes *independent of N*. That is the content of the following theorem.

Theorem 2
The space of polynomials of order λ satisfying equation (5.23), together with the usual operations of addition and scalar multiplication, is a vector space, say $\mathscr{V}_\lambda^{\mathscr{E}} \subseteq \mathscr{V}_\lambda$, with dimension

$$\dim \mathscr{V}_\lambda^{\mathscr{E}} \leq \sum_{p=0}^{\lambda} \sum_{i=0}^{p} \Delta(i) = \varphi(\lambda), \tag{5.24}$$

where $\Delta(i)$ is the number of partitions of the number i (see below). Further, 5.24 holds with equality if $N \geq \lambda$. Note that $\varphi(\lambda)$ is independent of N.

Proof
The fact that addition and scalar multiplication preserves partial exchangeability proves that the subspace of functions satisfying (5.23) is a vector space. The proof of 5.24 is a result of the following lemma.

Lemma 5 (proved in appendix 2)
An $f \in \mathscr{V}_\lambda$ is also a member of $\mathscr{V}_\lambda^{\mathscr{E}}$ if and only if for all $h \in H^N$

$$a_f(h_1, h_2, \ldots, h_N) = a_f(h_1, \pi_2, \ldots, \pi_N),$$

for any $(\pi_2, \ldots, \pi_N)$.

Define $m_j(h)$ to be the jth largest element in the vector $(h_2, \ldots, h_N)$ for $j = 1, \ldots, N-1$ (using any tiebreaking rule that preserves the natural order of pairs that are ordered). Then lemma 5 implies that we can form a basis for $\mathscr{V}_\lambda^{\mathscr{E}}$ by simply adding together the basis functions from $\mathscr{V}_\lambda$ that have

$$a_f(h_1, \ldots, h_N) = a_f(h_1, m_2, \ldots, m_N),$$

for each distinct value of the vector $(h_1, m_2, \ldots, m_N)$. What remains is to determine the number of distinct a coefficients this generates. Let $p(h)$ be the order of the basis function corresponding to $a(h)$, that is $p(h) = \sum h(i)$. Then the number of distinct a coefficients generated by h vectors with $p(h) = p$, and a particular value of h_1, is the number of ways the number $p - h_1$ can be allocated among $N - 1$ locations (without regard to order). If $N \geq \lambda \geq p - h$, this is simply the number of partitions of $p - h_1$, or $\Delta(p - h_1)$ (see below). Consequently, the number of distinct a coefficients required to generate all distinct coefficients of the pth order basis functions is $\Psi(p)$, where

$$\Psi(p) = \sum_{i=0}^{p} \Delta(i)$$

$\varphi(\lambda)$ is derived by summing this equation over $p = 0, 1, \ldots, \lambda$.

The theorem implies that there are only two distinct first-order coefficients

$$a(1, 0, \ldots, 0), \text{ and } a(0, 1, \ldots, 0)$$

with associated basis functions

$$\omega_1, \text{ and } \sum_{i=2} \omega_i.$$

Similarly, there are four distinct second-order coefficients

$$a(2, 0, \ldots), a(1, 1, 0, \ldots), a(0, 1, 1, \ldots), \text{ and } a(0, 2, 0, \ldots)$$

with basis functions

$$\omega_1^2, \omega_1 \sum_{i=2} \omega_i, \sum_{i_1=2} \sum_{i_2=2} \omega_{i_1} \omega_{i_2}, \text{ and } \sum_{i=2} \omega_i^2.$$

More generally, there are $\Delta(p-j)$ p^{th} order coefficients with $h_1 = j$

$$a(j, p-j, 0, \ldots), \quad a(j, p-j-1, 1, 0, \ldots), \quad a(j, p-j-2, 2, 0, 0, \ldots),$$
$$a(j, p-j-2, 1, 1, 0, \ldots), \ldots, a(j, 1, 1, \ldots, 1, 0, \ldots),$$

with associated basis functions

$$\omega_1^j \sum_{i=2}^{N} \omega_i^{h-j}, \ \omega_1^j \sum_{i_1=2}^{N} \sum_{i_2=2}^{N} \omega_{i_1}^{h-j-1} \omega_{i_2}, \ \omega_1^j \sum_{i_1=2}^{N} \sum_{i_2=2}^{N} \omega_{i_1}^{h-j-2} \omega_{i_2}^2,$$

$$\omega_1^j \sum_{i_1=2} \sum_{i_2=2} \sum_{i_3=2} \omega_{i_1}^{p-j-2} \omega_{i_2} \omega_{i_3}, \ldots, \omega_1^j \sum_{i_1} \cdots \sum_{i_{p-j}} \omega_{i_1}, \ldots, \omega_{i_{p-j}}.$$

For convenience, we provide a listing of $\Delta(q)$ (taken from Abramowitz and Stegun (1972)), and $\varphi(q)$ for $q = 1, \ldots, 12$, in table 5.4.

Recall that if a λ-order polynomial is a good approximation to the value function, then we need only calculate the value function at $\varphi(\lambda)$ points. For comparison, the point-wise technique used to calculate the results reported earlier required calculating the value function at 639,000 points; and this for a vector of parameters that generated an ergodic distribution of

Table 5.4. *Dimension of partially exchangeable basis*

q	0	1	2	3	4	5	6	7	8	9	10	11	12
$\Delta(q)$	1	2	3	4	5	7	11	15	21	30	41	55	75
$\varphi(q)$	1	3	7	14	26	45	75	120	186	276	407	593	854

industry structures with an upper bound of six active firms. Thus, at least for industries with a moderate number of firms, polynomial approximations restricted to the subspace of exchangeable polynomials should allow us to cut the number of points at which we evaluate the value function by several orders of magnitude.

The other point to remember is that the CPU time required to compute the value function is a product of the number of points evaluated at each iteration, the time per point evaluated and the number of iterations required before convergence. Though the number of points evaluated will fall dramatically as a result of imposing the restriction that $\hat{V} \in \mathcal{V}_\lambda^\delta$, the complexity of the calculations at each point evaluated will increase. The reason is that at each point we require the integral of the value function over the states achievable from that point in the next period, and the values of the value function required for the integrand in this computation must now be computed as a product of basis functions and polynomial coefficients (instead of just calling them up from memory, which is what is done when we calculate the value function point-wise). On this count alone, then, we would not expect substitution of the approximation technique to cut computational time by the same factor as it cuts the number of points at which we need to evaluate the value function. In addition, substitution of the approximating technique is likely to change the number of iterations needed before convergence is achieved (though it is not clear in which direction this change will go). Thus, the crucial question of just how much of a saving in CPU time we will generate by approximating the value function by a $\hat{V} \in \mathcal{V}_\lambda^\delta$ is still unresolved, and all we can say at this stage is that this form of approximation *may* enable us to calculate the equilibria in problems for which the number of active agents is quite large.

To begin our examination of the use of a $\hat{V} \in \mathcal{V}_\lambda^\delta$ to approximate the value function, we fit the approximating basis to the *actual* value function for our example (recall that we obtained the value function from an 'exact' point-wise calculation). We started here for two related reasons. First, we thought that if the polynomial coefficients obtained by fitting the approximating basis to the true numbers did not provide an adequate approximation to the value function, then we could not expect the polynomial coefficients obtained by fitting the approximating technique into our computational algorithm to provide an adequate approximation. Second, there are several ways of modifying the procedure used to obtain the polynomial approximation to the value function, and one simple way of comparing the alternatives is to compare how well they do in approximating the true numbers.

In this latter context we mention four points. First, since the sum of (partially) exchangeable functions is an exchangeable function, one can add any exchangeable function to an exchangeable basis and still maintain the exchangeability of the approximating function. This is one way of embodying exogenous information into the approximation algorithm, and we illustrate below by adding the profit function to the basis used for approximating the value function with quite dramatic results. Second, we have proceeded throughout as though the basis were being fit directly to the value function. Instead, we could fit the basis to any monotone transformation of the value function, and modify the computational algorithm accordingly. The Ericson–Pakes (1992) paper proves that for some simple cases of their model the value function is 'S-shaped' in the firm's own ω, and it is presumed that this general shape characteristic persists for a larger class of primitives, including the primitives used in our calculations. So we present results from fitting the logit transform of the value function, as well as the value function *per se*. Third, it is possible to use different degrees of polynomial approximation for the ω_1 dimension, then for the $(\omega_2, \ldots, \omega_N)$ dimension, and, finally, we need not restrict ourselves to fitting $\varphi(\lambda)$ points (any number greater than $\varphi(\lambda)$ will do).

Table 5.5 present some results from the fitting exercise. The entries in the table are the R^2s obtained from OLS fits of the value function to alternative approximations. For most of the approximations we present the fits from the value function when the number of active firms is restricted to be no more than 4, and 5 as well as for the unrestricted case (where the least upper bound on the number of active firms in the ergodic distribution is 6). We also present most results as the order of the polynomial being used in the basis functions varies from 2 to 6 (this gives us the alternative rows of the table).

The columns labelled V provide the R^2s from fitting the value function to the partially exchangeable basis of polynomials. The columns labelled LOV fit the logit transform of the value function, but then transform back to the actual numbers to calculate the fit. The columns labelled A fit the actual value functions, but add the profit function to the set of basis functions. The columns labelled A2 add both the profit function and an interaction of the profit function with the first-order polynomials to the basis functions. The numbers above all these columns refer to the number of points at which we

Table 5.5. *R^2s for alternative approximations**

Firms	4						5				
# of points	25270			mod3 = 588			138958			mod3 = 1470	
Order	V	LOV	A	A2	mod3	mod3a	V	A	A2	mod3	mod3a
2	0.804	0.905	0.977	0.986	0.802	0.976	0.807	0.971	0.982	0.804	0.970
3	0.877	0.911	0.987	0.992	0.873	0.985	0.880	0.985	0.991	0.877	0.982
4	0.927	0.947	0.993	0.995	0.919	0.992	0.928	0.991	0.994	0.922	0.990
5	0.951	0.974	0.995	0.996	0.939	0.994	0.953	0.994	0.996	0.941	0.993
6	0.968	0.977	0.996	0.997	0.942	0.995	0.968	0.996	0.997	0.943	0.994

Firms	6							Interpolation-6 firms		
# of points	639331			mod3 = 3235			ergodic = 2485	3234	8778	1064
Order	V	erg	ergA	ergA2	erg-mod3	erg-mod3A	erg-mod3A2	mod3	mod3 (2–6)	mod6 (2–6)
2	0.815	0.834	0.971	0.988	—	—	—	0.989	0.993	0.902
3	0.887	0.908	0.986	0.994	—	—	—			
4	0.932	0.957	0.993	0.996	0.865	0.979	0.990			
5	0.954	0.978	0.996	0.998	0.917	0.987	0.993			
6	0.969	0.988	0.998	0.999	0.942	0.993	0.993			

Note:

* For the approximating technique relevant for the alternative columns, see the explanation in the text.

obtain values for the value function, or the cardinality of S (this is the number of observations for the OLS regressions).

The entries for the columns labelled mod3 and mod3A are found in a slightly different way. Here we took only the value function at those ω points that were mod3 in the vector sense (i.e., each element of the ω vector was divisible by 3) and projected these on to the basis functions to obtain the polynomial coefficients. We then use the polynomial coefficients obtained in this way, to predict the value function at all points, and calculate the R^2 obtained from fitting the true values to these predicted values. The 'number of points' headings above these columns refer to the number of points used in the first stage of this procedure (the number of mod3 points). The column labelled mod3A adds the profit function to the basis used in the first stage. Finally, in subpanel 6 we also present results from fitting only the 2,485 points in the ergodic distribution of industry structures.

Several points stand out from the table. First, as expected, the same order of polynomials (and hence approximately the same number of basis functions) produce about the same fit regardless of N, or the number of firms ever active in equilibrium (at least if fit is measured by R^2). Second, in comparing the alternative ways of approximating the value function, it seems that using the logit transform only improves the fit marginally (at least when the fit is already quite good), but adding the profit function to the set of basis functions improves the fit rather dramatically. When one has exogenous information on either the form of the value function, or on an alternative function which is expected to 'mimic' the properties of the value function, one should probably use it directly.

Third, and probably most importantly, when we fit the exchangeable basis to a small number of (reasonably diffuse) points (the mod3 points), and then use the coefficients obtained from that fit to predict the value function at all possible points, we seem to do just about as well as we do when we fit the basis to the entire set of points directly – at least if the polynomial basis is rich enough to give a good direct fit.

We now move on to examine how well we fit the 2,485 points in the ergodic distribution. Since they are less than 1 per cent of the total points being fit in the six-firm equilibria, we were worried that the fit of the points in the ergodic distribution (weighted by their probabililty in the invariant measure) might not be similar to the overall fit of the points in the six-firm equilibria (and it is the ergodic points that we want accurate estimates of for most subsequent analysis). The columns labelled erg, ergA, and ergA2, fit the ergodic points directly. The columns labelled ergmod3, ergmod3A, and ergmod3A2, take the polynomial coefficients obtained from fitting the set of mod3 points from the entire six-firm equilibria, and use those to predict the points in the ergodic distribution. If anything we seem to fit the points with positive probability in the ergodic distribution better than we fit the entire space of points (even in cases where we use the coefficients predicted from the entire set of points). This gives some reason to believe that the points at which our approximation is not fitting well are points which would not be used intensively in policy and descriptive simulations.

The last subpanel of the table presents some results from fitting interpolated values of the value function. The points from which we interpolate are, respectively in the three columns: all mod3 points, mod1 for the ω of the firm in question and mod3 for the other firms' ωs, and mod1 for the ω of the firm in question and mod6 for the other firms' ωs. It seems that in order to obtain the same fit as obtained from the polynomial approximations, the interpolation procedure requires a larger number of interpolation points than either the number of basis functions required to achieve this fit in the polynomial approximations, or the number of points we used to obtain the polynomial coefficients.

Since the value function *per se* is not what we are interested in, we also did some limited experiments on whether the investment strategies implied by these approximations were sufficiently close to the investment strategies calculated from the point-wise solution. To do this we simply substituted the approximations into (5.22b) and calculated the implied investment strategies. We used three measures of fit. The first was the R^2 obtained from comparing the two investment strategies. The second separately substituted the alternative investment strategies into the simulation programme used to compute ω_{t+1} and then computed the R^2 from comparing the two ω_{t+1} series, and the third did the same but computed the R^2 from the two series for $\omega_{t+1} - \omega_t$. The three R^2s were, respectively, 0.98, 0.99 and 0.91. These were obtained using polynomial approximations made directly to the ergodic points, and if we use instead the polynomial coefficients obtained by fitting polynomials to the mod3 points from the entire six-firm equilibrium, and then fit to the ergodic distribution, the results are somewhat worse: 0.91, 0.98 and 0.78, respectively. Still, an R^2 of 0.8 for first differences, and of 0.98 for levels seems reasonable, and we could do better by increasing the order of the polynomial we fit.

For a 'first cut' we view these results as encouraging. Still they do leave two unanswered questions. First, will we get as good an approximation if we obtain the approximating functions directly from the recursive algorithm described above? Second, are fits as good as those shown in the table 'good enough' either for estimation, or for descriptive and policy simulations. At this stage all we can say is that there is work in progress which should help to clarify these points, at least for models similar to those discussed in this chapter.

6   CONCLUSION

This chapter has attempted to clarify some of the modelling, econometric and computational issues that arise in bringing dynamic structural models into empirical use. The discussion focussed on selected technical issues that have been of concern in applied work; the uses and limitations of Euler equations, incorporating serially correlated unobservables into our models, and computing equilibrium responses to dynamic heterogeneous agent models. Throughout we used examples to illustrate the main points. The exposition of the examples also carried with it an implicit view of structural modelling – so much so that it did not seem necessary to add a section with a more general discussion of when, why and how one might engage in it.

It might, however, be useful to conclude with some practical points that often get lost in the more abstract debates on the methods and merits of structural modelling. Our discussion of these points will be premised on the following 'fact'. We, as applied researchers, attach a 'structural' interpretation to the numbers we eke out of our data every time we use those numbers to analyse the interactions between economic agents, or between an agent and his or her environment. This is just as true when the numbers we use in the analysis are simple 'reduced form' correlations, as it is when the numbers used in the analysis are parameter estimates from a complex structural model. So there is really no room for debate on the issue of whether structural models are 'useful'. The debate must, therefore, be about whether the cost of formalising the structural models being implicitly used in the analysis, and then possibly parameterising them with the data, is worth the benefits from this (sometimes quite costly and time-consuming) endeavour.

The answer to this question is undoubtedly that sometimes it is worthwhile, and sometimes it is not; and when it is, it is to varying degrees. The cost–benefit calculation depends on a myriad of factors including: the complexity of the problem being analysed and the possibilities for drawing misleading conclusions from simpler forms of analysis, the quality of the data, computational difficulties, prior knowledge on the likely appropriateness of the assumptions that need to be fed into the structural model, and the comparative advantages of the researcher. General rules are hard to come by when so many of the important dimensions of the decision are problem specific. There are, however, a few considerations that one might keep in mind in formulating one's own strategy.

First, it is often useful to begin an empirical project with a reasonably detailed 'reduced-form' analysis of the data. This for several reasons. First it is likely to suggest just why a more detailed structural model might be useful. Second, the reduced-form analysis should indicate the aspects of reality that will need to be built into a structural model for that model to be able to account for that data, and, finally, thoughtful reduced-form analysis often allows one to get some feel for the likely benefits from a structural modelling effort.[24]

Second, given a set of reduced-form results, it is often helpful to write down a simple structural model that captures the essence of what one thinks might lie behind them regardless of whether one intends to take that model to data (note that by this we mean writing down a model all of whose assumptions, including the assumptions on its disturbances, are formulated entirely in terms of the primitives affecting economic behaviour). The understanding that comes from this modelling exercise is typically useful in several ways. First, it clarifies the problems associated with placing any given interpretation on the reduced-form estimates. Second, it crystallises the trade-off between assumptions, computational problems, and data requirements that will be faced in attempting to build a structural estimation algorithm. Finally the modelling exercise will frequently lead to simple diagnostic tests and/or correction procedures for problems that seem likely to be important in interpreting a particular relationship; corrections that might not require either all the assumptions, or the computational burden, that would be needed in order to estimate a complete structural model. The developments in semi-parametric estimation (see the references in the text) are particularly exciting in this context. Semi-parametric techniques often allow one to circumvent many of the computational issues and some of the more detailed assumptions that would need to be addressed had we to solve the complete model for alternative possible values of its parameter vector before we engage in any estimation.

Third, given the complexity of the issues we typically want to analyse, and the limited data and computational resources available, any successful effort at structural modelling is going to have to abstract from certain aspects of reality. The choices of what to abstract from, and the issue of how that abstraction impacts on what we can learn from our estimates, are both legitimate topics for discussion. In engaging in such discussion, however, a few general points should be kept in mind.

First, given the limitations of our data sets and computational procedures, it seems reasonably clear that one should lean heavily on any prior knowledge available about the applied problem at hand (and there is frequently quite a bit of it available). This, in turn, is going to make the modelling problem more complex; there will be no single framework that is likely to abstract from just the 'right' features of reality for a multitude of problems, so that modelling flexibility is going to be required.

Second, even given diligent prior work we are unlikely to come down to exactly the 'right' model. The reason we engage in structural modelling in spite of this fact is the belief that there is continuity in the map between the assumptions and the implications of interest, so that the more we know about our problem and the better we are able to incorporate that knowledge into our model, the closer our model will be to mimicking reality.

The fact that structural models cannot be rich enough to encompass all aspects of reality does, however, make it easy to pick them apart. All of the assumptions used are laid out in front of the reader, so it is easy to find transgressions from reality, and these transgressions are frequently large enough to be picked up in formal test statistics. Again, what has to be kept in mind when evaluating a structural modelling exercise is that some model is going to be implicitly used in the subsequent descriptive and policy analysis whether we like it or not. As a result the relevant question is often not whether the model is exactly correct, or whether it satisfies some formal statistical test. Rather it is whether we believe the implications of the internally consistent structural model whose parameters have been obtained from the data more than we believe the implications of the alternative lines of reasoning available (there is also the possibility of mixing the results of the structural model with other forms of analysis). Of course we also have to be careful not to fall into the habit of accepting the implications of the structural estimates as gospel (forgetting that corners had to be cut to obtain them). There is always room (indeed a need) for doubt (especially if it is constructive), and it will always be possible to make further improvements (though sometimes it might not be worthwhile).

It is easy to close this chapter on an optimistic note. The one fact that seems clear from the developments over the last decade of modelling is that advances in theory, computation, statistical methods, and data sources have generated dramatic increases in our ability to take economic models to data and come back with useful interpretations of reality. Moreover, if anything, the rate of increase in our abilities to engage in such endeavours has been accelerating, making it an exciting time to be engaged in empirical research.

APPENDIX I: PROOF OF LEMMA 3

(Monotonicity of the investment policy with deterministic accumulation)

Lemma 3
Assume 2, that $\partial\pi(\omega, k)/\partial k$ is increasing in ω, that $\partial c(x, k_1)/\partial x \leq \partial c(x, k_2)/\partial x$ whenever $k_1 \geq k_2$, and that if $h(\cdot)$ is continuous (a.e.) and integrable with respect to a subset of $\mathscr{P}_\omega$, say $\mathscr{P}^*$, then provided $P(\cdot|\omega_1)$, and $P(\cdot|\omega_2) \in \mathscr{P}^*$, $|\int h(\omega')[P(d\omega'|\omega_1) - P(d\omega'|\omega_2)]| \leq \psi(h, \mathscr{P}^*)|\omega_1 - \omega_2|$.

Proof

The proof assumes that the optimal policy is unique. Given this we show that the solution to the finite horizon problem, say $x^T(\omega,k)$, is, for all T, weakly increasing in ω for each k. It is straightforward to show that this implies that the limit function, $x(\omega,k)$ must also be weakly increasing.

For every T define

$$V^T(\omega,x,k) = -c(x,k) + \pi(\omega,k) + \beta \int V^{T-1}[\omega',k(1+\delta)+x]P(d\omega'|\omega)$$

where $V^{T-1}(\omega,k)$ provides the value of a $T-1$ horizon problem. Two properties of this function will be used below. First we use the fact that maximisation implies that $V^T(\omega,x,k) \leq V^T(\omega,k)$ for all $x \in \Gamma(k)$, and all $(\omega,k) \in \Omega \times K$. Second we need the fact that if $V^T(\omega,x,k)$ has isotone differences in (ω,x), i.e., if

$$[V^T(\omega_1,x_1,k) - V^T(\omega_1,x_2,k)] - [V^T(\omega_2,x_1,k) - V^T(\omega_2,x_2,k)] \geq 0$$

whenever $\omega_1 \geq \omega_2$ and $x_1 \geq x_2$, then $x^T(\omega,k)$ is non-decreasing in ω (briefly, since both Ω and K are totally ordered, the fact that $V^T(\cdot)$ has isotone differences implies that it is supermodular; see Topkis (1978), theorem 3.2). This, together with the fact that $\Gamma(\cdot)$ is independent of ω, implies the result; see theorem 6.1 of Topkis (1987).

This latter result implies that to prove the theorem we need only show that for any T, $V^T(\cdot)$, has isotone differences. We now use induction to prove this fact. For the initial condition of the inductive argument we need only note that

$$[V^1(\omega_1,x_1,k) - V^1(\omega_1,x_2,k)] - [V^1(\omega_2,x_1,k) - V^1(\omega_2,x_2,k)]$$
$$= \beta \int \{\pi[\omega',k(1-\delta)+x_1] - \pi[\omega',k(1-\delta)+x_2]\}[P(d\omega'|\omega_1) - P(d\omega'|\omega_2)] \geq 0,$$

where the inequality follows from the supermodularity of $\pi(\ )$ and the fact that the family $\mathcal{P}_\omega$ is stochastically increasing in ω (see assumption 2).

For the inductive step assume that $\{V^t(\omega,x,k)\}_{t=1}^{T-1}$ is supermodular in (ω,x) for each k. Lemma * below shows that this implies that $V^{T-1}(\omega,k)$ is supermodular in (ω,k). Consequently

$$[V^T(\omega_1,x_1,k) - V^T(\omega_1,x_2,k)] - [V^T(\omega_2,x_1,k) - V^T(\omega_2,x_2,k)]$$
$$= \beta \int \{V^{T-1}[\omega',k(1-\delta)+x_1] - V^{T-1}[\omega',k(1-\delta)+x_2]\}$$
$$[P(d\omega'|\omega_1) - P(d\omega'|\omega_2)] \geq 0,$$

where the inequality follows from lemma *, and the fact that $\mathcal{P}_\omega$ is stochastically increasing in ω.

Lemma *

$V^T(\omega,k)$ is supermodular in (ω,k) on $\Omega \times K$, if $\{V^t(\omega,x,k)\}_{t=1}^T$ are supermodular in (ω,x) on $\Omega \times \Gamma(k)$, for each $k \in K$.

Proof

Again by induction on T. The initial condition of the inductive argument is analogous to the initial condition of the inductive argument in lemma 3 and need not be repeated. For the inductive step assume that $\{V^t(\omega,k)\}_{t=1}^{T-1}$ are supermodular on $\Omega \times K$. Then, using the shorthand that for any $f: \Omega \times K \to \mathcal{R}, f(i,j) = f(\omega_i, k_j)$

$$
\begin{aligned}
[V(1,1) - V(1,2)] - &[V(2,1) - V(2,2)] \geq \{V^T[\omega_1, x(\omega_2, k_1), k_1] \\
&- V^T(\omega_1, k_2)\} - \{V^T(\omega_2, k_1) - V^T[\omega_2, x(\omega_1, k_2), k_2]\} \\
&\equiv \Delta + \beta \int \{V^{T-1}[\omega', k_1(1-\delta) + x(\omega_2, k_1)] - V^{T-1}[\omega', k_2(1-\delta) \\
&+ x(\omega_1, k_2)]\} [P(d\omega'|\omega_1) - P(d\omega'|\omega_2)],
\end{aligned} \tag{5.1A}
$$

where

$$
\Delta \equiv [\pi(1,1) - \pi(1,2)] - [\pi(2,1) - \pi(2,2)] > 0.
$$

Consequently if

$$
k_1(1-\delta) + x(\omega_2, k_1) \geq k_2(1-\delta) + x(\omega_1, k_2)
$$

the proof is complete. So assume to the contrary that

$$
x(1,2) - x(2,1) - (k_1 - k_2)(1-\delta) \equiv \kappa > 0.
$$

The assumption that $\partial c(x,k)/\partial x$ is non-increasing in k, together with the Euler equation in lemma 1, and the convexity of the investment cost function implies that $x(1,1) + k_1(1-\delta) > x(1,2) + k_2(1-\delta)$ whenever $k_1 > k_2$. Hence by continuity of the optimal policy, and the hypothesis of the inductive argument (which ensures that $x^T(\omega,k)$ is weakly increasing in ω) there exists an $\omega^* \in [\omega_1, \omega_2]$ such that

$$
k_1(1-\delta) + x(\omega^*, k_1) = k_2(1-\delta) + x(\omega_1, k_2) \equiv \bar{k}.
$$

Substituting ω^* for ω_1 in (5.1A) we have

$$
\begin{aligned}
[V^T(\omega^*, k_1) - V^T(\omega^*, k_2)] &- [V^T(\omega_2, k_1) - V^T(\omega_2, k_2)] \\
&\geq [\pi(\omega^*, k_1) - \pi(\omega^*, k_2)] - [\pi(\omega_2, k_1) - \pi(\omega_2, k_2)] \geq 0,
\end{aligned}
$$

where the last inequality follows from the supermodularity of $\pi(\ )$.

Next we show that $\omega_1 - \omega^* \geq J(k_1, k_2)$. That will complete the proof because it will imply that we can break the move from ω_1 to ω_2 into a finite number of steps (each of which preserves isotone differences). To this end note that lemma 1 implies that

$$
\begin{aligned}
\partial c[x(\omega_1, k_2), k_2]/\partial x &- \partial c[x(\omega^*, k_1), k_1]/\partial x \\
&= \beta \int \chi(\omega', \bar{k}) \{\partial \pi(\omega', \bar{k})/\partial k + \partial c[x(\omega', \bar{k}), \bar{k}]/\partial x\} [P(d\omega'|\omega_1) - P(d\omega'|\omega^*)] \\
&\equiv \int h(\omega') [P(d\omega'|\omega_1) - P(d\omega'|\omega^*)].
\end{aligned}
$$

The convexity of $c(\cdot)$ and the assumptions on $\mathcal{P}_\omega$ then imply that

$$\beta^{-1}[\partial c(x=0,k_1)/\partial x][k_1-k_2](1-\delta)\leq\psi(h,\mathscr{P}^*)(\omega_1-\omega^*),$$

or

$$\omega_1-\omega^*\geq\beta^{-1}[\partial c(x=0,k_1)/\partial x][k_1-k_2](1-\delta)/\psi(h,\mathscr{P}^*)\equiv J(k_1,k_2),$$

where $\mathscr{P}^*$ includes the interval $[\omega_1,\omega_2]$, as required.

APPENDIX 2: PROOF OF LEMMA 5

Lemma 5
An $f\in V_\lambda$ is also a member of V_λ^δ if and only if for all $h\in H^N$

$$a_f(h_1,h_2,\ldots h_N)=a_f(h_1,h_{\pi(2)},\ldots h_{\pi(N)}),$$

for any $(\pi_2,\ldots,\pi_N)$ which is a permutation of $(2,\ldots,N)$.

Proof
We need only prove that partial exchangeability of the value functions implies partial exchangeability of the coefficients (the other direction of causation is immediate).

Consider any $V\subset V_\lambda$. Then there is a sequence $\{a_j\}_{j=1}^J$ such that

$$V=\sum_{j=1}^J a_j b_j(\omega_1,\omega_2,\ldots,\omega_n) \tag{5.2A}$$

where the sequence $\{b_j(\omega_1,\omega_2,\ldots,\omega_n)\}_{j=1}^J$ forms a basis for V_λ.

For any $f:\Omega^n\to\mathscr{R}$ define the linear operator $*$ as

$$*f(\omega_1,\omega_2,\ldots,\omega_n)=1/(n-1)!\sum_{\pi\in\Pi}f(\omega_1,\omega_{\pi(2)},\ldots,\omega_{\pi(n)}),$$

where Π is the set of permutations of the sequence $\{2,3,\ldots,n\}$.

If $V\in V_\lambda^\delta\subset V_\lambda$, then

$$V(\omega_1,\omega_2,\ldots,\omega_n)=*V(\omega_1,\omega_2,\ldots,\omega_n)=\sum_{j=1}^J a_j *b_j(\omega_1,\omega_2,\ldots,\omega_n), \tag{5.3A}$$

where the last equality follows from (5.2A).

Now define the equivalence relationship

$$iRj<=>*b_i=*b_j,$$

and use it to define the equivalence classes,

$$\{1,\ldots,J\}/R=S=\{S_1,\ldots,S_m\}, \text{ for } m\leq J.$$

Note that two functions are in the same equivalence class if and only if one can be obtained by permuting the last $(n-1)$ arguments of the other. By the axiom of choice there exists $\{s_1,\ldots,s_m\}$ such that $s_i\in S_i$ and $1\leq s_i\leq N$, for $i=1,\ldots,m$. Therefore using (5.3A)

$$V(\omega_1, \omega_2, \ldots, \omega_n) = \sum_{j=1}^{J} a_j {}^*b_j(\omega_1, \omega_2, \ldots, \omega_n)$$
$$= \sum_{i=1}^{m} \sum_{j \in S_i} a_j {}^*b_j(\omega_1, \omega_2, \ldots, \omega_n)$$
$$= \sum_{i=1}^{m} {}^*b_i(\omega_1, \omega_2, \ldots, \omega_n)[\sum_{j \in S_i} a_j] = \sum_{i=1}^{m} \underline{a}_i {}^*b_i(\omega_1, \omega_2, \ldots, \omega_n)$$
$$= \sum_{i=1}^{m} [\underline{a}_i/(n-1)!] \sum_{\pi \in \Pi} b_i(\omega_1, \omega_{\pi(2)}, \ldots, \omega_{\pi(n)}),$$

where $\underline{a}_i = \sum_{j \in S_i} a_j$, as required.

Notes

1 This is one part of a two part tour of dynamic structural modelling prepared for the Sixth World Congress of the Econometric Society, Barcelona, 1990. The second part, by John Rust, comprises chapter 4 of this volume. Both parts are self contained. I have benefited from discussions with many individuals in the course of writing this chapter, among them: Don Andrews, Steve Berry, Gary Chamberlain, Sam Kortum, Jim Heckman, Ken Judd, Werner Ploberger, John Rust, Chris Sims and Stephen Zeldes. Special thanks go to John Rust who read over several previous drafts and made very helpful comments. The chapter also borrows liberally from my previous work with Rick Ericson, and with Steve Olley, and therefore, also owes them a special debt. All errors, of course, remain my own responsibility. The research reported here was funded, in part, by the National Science Foundation, through grant number SES-882172.

2 Uniqueness of the policy function for the continuous control is often more difficult to obtain; see Benveniste and Scheinkman (1979), Blume, Easely and O'Hare (1982), the discussion in Stocky, Lucas and Prescott (1989), and for the case where the impact of the continuous control on the family of measures $\{P(\cdot|\cdot, x)\}$ is sufficiently smooth in x, Ericson and Pakes (1992). At the very least non-uniqueness generates non-uniqueness in behavioural responses to policy and/or environmental changes, and this becomes a problem for policy analysis. It may also generate an additional set of estimation problems (see Jovanovic (1989) for a discussion of the related problem of estimation in models with multiple equilibria). Note, however, that once the value function in (5.1) is computed for a given set of primitives one can simply inspect the solution for uniqueness of the policy.

3 To add them back in simply assume that ϕ, the exit value in the discussion that follows, is random. Provided the distribution of the discrete state specific disturbance is sufficiently rich, the saturation condition discussed in Rust (1991) will amount to the condition that the observed combinations of the continuous control and observable component of the state vector can be generated by the primitives of the model and the alternative possible values of the unobservable state. A partial discussion of this issue can be found in the related literature on continuous choice using extremal processes; see Cosslett (1988), Dagsvick (1988), Resnick and Roy (1989).

4 For an early model with stochastic accumulation see Roberts and Weitman (1981). Tirole (1989), chapter 10 and Ericson and Pakes (1992) discuss some of the more recent contributions to the literature.

5 One could make this return depend on y, but then, to preserve the form of the optimal stopping policy below, we would need to ensure that $\Phi(y)$ does not increase at as rapid a rate in y as the return from staying in operation does.

6 Throughout we derive our Euler equations by constructing a set of alternative feasible policies and checking for differentiability of the implied perturbations to the value function. This makes the problems that arise in constructing Euler equations in applications with a single continuous control transparent. An alternative would be to nest a system of random Lagrange multipliers into the control problem, and derive the Euler equations from their properties; see Kushner (1965a) and (1965b). This latter technique is more detailed notationally, but would have advantages in applications with a system of continuous controls in which case we might want to use the relationships between the various constraint sets to help structure estimation.

7 This heading does not adequately describe the richness of the issues at hand. These are not so much a result of any notion of the illiquidity of assets, as they are a result of the incompleteness of markets for future income streams. Moreover, different formulations for market opportunities lead to different budget constraints, and the precise formulation of the budget constraint will generally affect the properties of alternative estimators; see, for example, the discussion in section 5 of Hayashi (1987) and the literature referred to below.

8 Another possibility is to impose restrictions which make it possible to develop a semi-parametric estimator which uses the information in the data to select out a subsample for which both $x(y_t) > 0$ and $x(y_{t+1}) > 0$ with probability one, and then generate a Euler equation from this subsample that allows one to obtain consistent parameter estimates.

9 If we did not allow for consumption expenditures we would have two state variables, A_t and k_t whose laws of motions are different linear functions of the same, single, control, x_t. Thus, it would in general be impossible to construct compensating perturbations for the control that would return *both* state variables to what their values would have been in the optimal programme after two periods.

10 This is analogous to the situation that would arise if we were to apply the Euler equation methodology to analysing retirement decisions, or to choices among entering various welfare programmes, see the references in Rust (1991).

11 This model is taken from Ericson and Pakes (1992), Part I.

12 We have not attempted, for example, to use any additional restrictions that might result from the sampling process, for example, the possible exchangeability of the vector of observations on different individuals; for a review of the implications of exchangeability see Aldous (1983). Similarly we have not attempted to make use of the fact that the factors generating the dependence across observations are often observed, which would allow us to compare different years with similar realisations in that factor.

13 The exceptions here are usually data sets that follow industries or countries over time.

14 To illustrate I asked Stephen Zeldes to supply the values (and standard errors) of the coefficients of the time dummy variables he estimated in his analysis of the consumption Euler equation ((1989), see the discussion in 3.2). The estimates of

the time dummies for the nine-year panel on his preferred equation ranged from -0.05 (0.12) to $+0.03$ (0.06). It is reasonably clear from his estimates that one could accept the null that they are all zero, but this seems to be as much a function of the fact that the averages are estimated imprecisely as of any inherent smallness in the point estimates. On the other hand, the grand average of the Euler equation errors in Zeldes' study was -0.01 with a standard error which was also 0.01, and these are numbers that one might be willing to accept as close enough to zero with high enough probability.

15 There are, of course, special cases for which the required covariance is zero. This occurs when the derivative of $g(\cdot)$ with respect to θ depends only on variables that are measurable F_t. A case in point is the literature which tests for the rationality of price forecasts, see Keane and Runkle (1990) and the literature cited there. The linear framework typically used in this literature generates estimators which are unbiased regardless of the presence of dependence in the process generating the forecast error. As stressed by Keane and Runkle, however, the standard errors of the coefficients obtained from the OLS regression still need to be adjusted for the presence of dependence, and this adjustment can have very large impacts on the relevant test statistics.

16 The required regularity conditions here are generally both more delicate, and harder to verify. We need the dependence in the $y_{i,t+1}$ to induce a dependence in the $h_{i,t+1}()$ that is weak enough to justify the use of a uniform law of large numbers in the consistency proof, and a stochastic equicontinuity condition in the proof of asymptotic normality. 'Strong mixing' conditions will often suffice (see Billingsley (1964)), but these are not always satisfied for the problems of interest. For recent contributions to the literature on conditions that generate uniform laws of large numbers, and central limit theorems, in the presence of dependence, see Andrews (1991) and the literature cited there.

17 There remains the question of whether the conditional expectation of the Euler equation depends on the entire past history of all variables in the data set, or on just a subset of them. If one were willing to specify the entire structure of the underlying control problem, then the model itself would answer this question. Alternatively, one could try to determine the relevance of different variables empirically by using an initial consistent estimate of the parameter vector to construct estimates of the realised value of the Euler equation for the alternative sample points, and then examining its conditional expectation.

18 Apart, perhaps, for those required to verify the regularity conditions needed to ensure consistency and asymptotic normality of the maximum-likelihood estimator. We should note that all we actually need for this procedure is the somewhat weaker assumption of conditional serial independence described in Rust (1987).

19 The Markov assumption is not innocuous, especially when we are trying to model a group of agents active in the same market. For example, though it may be reasonable to assume that agents take prices parametrically, it is much less reasonable to assume that agents think the distribution of price tomorrow just depends on today's price (and no other characteristic of today's market) especially since current price is not a sufficient statistic for future price in most dynamic models; see the more detailed discussion in the next section.

20 The framework used in Olley–Pakes allows for interactions among agents. They assume that the profits a firm earns in a given period depend not only on its own state variables, but also on the list of state variables of competing firms, and that the data are generated by a Markov Perfect Nash equilibrium in investment, exit and entry strategies (see the next section). The model then becomes a modified version of the Hoppenhayn–Rogerson (1990) model of industry dynamics, and the firm's decisions depend on both the firm's own state variables, and the measure providing the list of state variables of the competing firms.

21 This section draws heavily on Pakes and McGuire (forthcoming).

22 The Hoppenhayn and Rogerson (1990) paper is also one of the few that worries about computation in heterogeneous agent models. They assume that all agents are zero measure and all sources of uncertainty are idiosyncratic, show that under their conditions the industry structure converges to a fixed s^* (and stays there) and then provide a simple way of computing s^*. Judd (1990) has computed Markov Perfect Nash equilibria for two-agent models with no entry and exit, and Hansen and Sargent (1990) provide a computational algorithm for a class of heterogeneous agent models that allow for linear decision rules and equilibria (they assume quadratic preferences, linear technologies and information sets, no discrete choices, and that continuous choices are always interior).

23 Throughout we will consider the case where N, the least upper bound to the number of agents ever active in a given period, is less than or equal to $K = \#\Omega$. In this case the dimensionality of the state vector is smaller when we calculate value functions as a function of the vector of ω values of all active agents. When $N > K$, use of a counting measure on Ω as the state vector minimises the dimensionality of the state space.

24 Unless one has large amounts of data and is extremely careful about how it is used, the preliminary reduced-form analysis will often also call into question the interpretation of subsequent standard errors and test statistics. However, without a more detailed theory of learning that allows for the mix of inductive and deductive reasoning actually used in empirical work, this seems like a cost we will just have to bear.

References

Abramowitz, M. and Stegun, I. (1972), *Handbook of Mathematical Functions*, New York: Dover Publications.

Ahn, H. and Powell, J.L. (1993), 'Semiparametric Estimation of Censored Selection Models with a Nonparametric Selection Mechanism', *Journal of Econometrics*, pp.3–29.

Aigner, D., Hsiao, C. Kapetyn, A. and Wansbeek, T. (1984), 'Latent Variable Models in Econometrics', in Z. Griliches and M. Intrilligator (eds.), *The Handbook of Econometrics*, Amsterdam: North Holland.

Aldous, D.J. (1983), 'Exchangeability and Related Topics', *Springer Lecture Notes in Mathematics*, No. 117, Ecole D'ete de Probabilities de Saint-Flour XIII, pp.2–199.

Altonji, J., Hayashi, F. and Kotlikoff, L. (1992), 'Is the Extended Family Altruistically Linked: Direct Tests Using Micro Data', *American Economic Review*, 82(5): 1177–98.

Altug, S. and Miller, R. (1990), 'Household Choices in Equilibrium', *Econometrica*, 58: 543–70.

Andersen, E.B. (1973), *Conditional Inference and Models for Measuring*, Kopeernhavn: Mentalhygiehnisk Forlag.

Andersen, T. and Hsiao, C. (1982), 'Formulation and Estimation of Dynamic Models Using Panel Data', *Journal of Econometrics*, 18: 47–82.

Andrews, D.W.K. (1988), 'Laws of Large Numbers For Dependent Non-Identically Distributed Random Variables', *Econometric Theory*, 4: 458–67.

(1991), 'Asymptotic Normality of Series Estimators for Various Nonparametric and Semiparametric Models', *Econometrica*, 59: 307–45.

(1991), 'An Empirical Process Central Limit Theorem For Dependent Non-Identically Distributed Random Variables', *Journal of Multivariate Analysis*, 38: 187–203.

(1993), 'Nonparametric Kernel Estimation for Semiparametric Models', Revision of Cowles Foundation Discussion Paper No. 909, Yale University.

Benveniste, Lawrence M. and Scheinkman, Jose A. (1979), 'On the Differentiability of the Value Function in Dynamic Models of Economics', *Econometrica*, 47: 727–32.

Berry, S. (forthcoming), 'Discrete Choice Models of Oligopoly Product Differentiation', *Rand Journal of Economics*.

Billingsley, P. (1968), *Convergence of Probability Measures*, Wiley Series in Probability and Statistics, New York: John Wiley.

Blume, L., Easley, D. and O'Hara, M. (1982), 'Characterization of Optimal Stochastic Dynamic Programs', *Journal of Economic Theory*, 28: 221–34.

Caplin, A. and Nalebuff, B. (1991), 'Aggregation and Imperfect Competition: the Existence of Equilibrium', *Econometrica*, 59: 25–59.

Carroll, R. (1982), 'Adapting for Heteroskedasticity in Linear Models', *Annals of Statistics*, 10: 1224–33.

Chamberlain, G. (1982), 'Multivariate Regression Models For Panel Data', *Journal of Econometrics*, 18: 5–46.

(1986), 'Panel Data', in Z. Griliches and M. Intrilligator (eds.) *Handbook of Econometrics*, Amsterdam: North Holland, pp.1247–318.

(1987), 'Asymptotic Efficiency in Estimation with Conditional Moment Restrictions', *Journal of Econometrics*, 34: 305–34.

(1992), 'Efficiency Bounds for Semiparametric Regression', *Econometrica*, 60(3): 569–96.

Choi, K. (1990), 'The Semiparametric Estimation of the Sample Selection Model Using Series Expansion and The Propensity Score', mimeo, Department of Economics, University of Chicago.

Christiansen, Bent (1990), 'Dynamic Programming, Maximum Likelihood, Stock Price Volitability and the ICAPM', mimeo, NYU, Business School.

Cosslett, S. (1988), 'Probabilistic Choice Over a Continuous Range: An Econometric Model Based on Extreme Value Stochastic Processes', mimeo, Department of Economics, Ohio State University.

Dagsvick, J.K. (1988), 'The Generalized Extreme Value Utility Model for Continuous Choice', mimeo, Central Bureau of Statistics, Oslo.

Das, S. (1992), 'A Micro-Econometric Model of Capital Utilization and Retirement: The Case of the U.S. Cement Industry', *Review of Economic Studies*, 59: 277–97.

Davis, S. and Haltwinger, J. (1989), 'Gross Job Creation, Gross Job Destruction: Microeconomic Evidence and Microeconomic Implications', *NBER Macroeconomics Annual*, 5: 123–68.

Ericson, R. and Pakes, A. (1992), 'An Alternative Theory of Firm and Industry Dynamics', Cowles Foundation Discussion Paper No. 1041.

Fuller, W. (1987), *Measurement Error Models*, Wiley Series in Probability and Mathematical Statistics, New York: John Wiley.

Geweke, J. (1977), 'The Dynamic Factor Analysis of Economic Time-Series Model', in D.J. Aigner and A.S. Goldberger, *Latent Variables in Socio-Economic Models*, Amsterdam: North Holland.

Gilchrist, S. (1989), 'An Empirical Analysis of Corporate Investment and Financing Hierarchies Using Firm Level Panel Data', unpublished Ph.D. dissertation, University of Wisconsin.

Hajivassiliou, V. and Ioannides, Y., (1990), 'Dynamic Switching Regression Models of the Euler Equation: Consumption and Liquidity Constraints', mimeo, Department of Economics, Yale University.

Hall, R. (1979), 'Stochastic Implications of the Life-Cycle Permanent Income Hypothesis: Theory and Evidence', *Journal of Political Economy*, 86: 971–87.

Hansen, L. (1982), 'Large Sample Properties of Generalized Method of Moments Estimators', *Econometrica*, 50: 1029–54.

(1985), 'A Method for Calculating Bounds on the Asymptotic Covariance of Generalized Method of Moments Estimators', *Journal of Econometrics*, 30: 205–38.

Hansen, L., Heaton, J. and Ogaki, M. 'Efficiency Bounds Implied by Multiperiod Conditional Moment Restrictions', *Journal of the American Statistical Association*, 863–71.

Hansen, L. and Sargent T. (1982), 'Two Difficulties in Interpreting Vector Autoregressions', in L. Hansen and T. Sargent (eds.) *Rational Expectations Econometrics*, Westview Press, forthcoming.

(1990), 'Recursive Linear Models of Dynamic Economies', mimeo, Hoover Institution.

Hansen, L. and Singleton, K. (1982), 'Generalized Instrumental Variable Estimation of Nonlinear Rational Expectations Models', *Econometrica*, 50: pp.1269–86.

Hausman, J., Ichimura, H. Newey, W. and Powell, J. (forthcoming), 'Semiparametric Identification and Estimation of Polynomial Errors-in-Variables Models', *Journal of Econometrics*.

Hayashi, F. (1987), 'Tests for Liquidity Constraints: A Critical Survey and Some New Observations', in T. Bewley (ed.), *Advances in Econometrics* (Econometric Society 5th World Congress), Cambridge University Press, pp.91–120.

Heckman, J. (1981), 'The Incidental Parameter Problem and the Problem of Initial Conditions in Estimating a Discrete Time-Discrete Data Stochastic Process', in C. Manski and D. McFadden (eds.), *Structural Analysis of Discrete Data with Econometric Applications*, Cambridge, Mass: MIT Press, pp.179–97.

Heckman, J. and Robb, R. (1985), 'Alternative Methods for Evaluating the Impact of Interventions', in J. Heckman and B. Singer (eds.), *Longitudinal Analysis of Labor Market Data*, Cambridge University Press.

Heckman, J. and Scheinkman J. (1987), 'The Importance of Bundling in a Gorman-Lancaster Model of Earnings', *Review of Economic Studies*, 54: 243–55.

Hendricks, K., Porter, R.H. and Wilson, C.A. (1993), 'Auctions for Oil and Gas Leases with an Informed Bidder and a Random Reservation Price', mimeo Northwestern University.

Himmelburg, C. (1990), 'Essays in the Relationship Between Investment and Internal Finance', unpublished Ph.D. dissertation, Northwestern University.

Hoffman, K. and Kunze, R. (1972), *Linear Algebra*, Second edn, Englewood Cliffs, N. J.: Prentice Hall.

Hoppenhayn, H. and Rogerson R. (1990), 'Labor Turnover and Policy Evaluation In A Model Of Industry Equilibrium', mimeo, Graduate School of Business Stanford University.

Hubbard G. and Kashyap, A. (1989), 'Internal Net Worth in the Investment Process: An Application to U.S. Agriculture', *Journal of Political Economy*, 100(5): 501–34.

Huber, P.J. (1967), 'The Behaviour of Maximum Likelihood Estimates Under Nonstandard Conditions', *Proceedings of the Fifth Berkeley Symposium*, 1: 221–33.

Journal of Business and Economic Statistics (1990), 'Solving Nonlinear Stochastic Growth Models: A Comparison of Alternative Solution Methods', symposium edited by J. Taylor and H. Uhlig, in the *Journal of Business and Economic Statistics*, 8(1): 1–55.

Jovanovic, B. (1989), 'Observable Implications of Models with Multiple Equilibria', *Econometrica*, 57: 1431–9.

Jovanovic, B. and MacDonald G. (forthcoming), 'Competitive diffusion', *Journal of Political Economy*, 102(1) (February 1994).

Judd, K. (1989), 'Minimum Weighted Residual Methods in Dynamic Economic Models', mimeo, Hoover Institution.

(1990), 'Cournot Versus Bertrand: A Dynamic Resolution', mimeo, Hoover Institution.

Keane, M. and Runkle, D. (1990), 'Testing the Rationality of Price Forecasts: New Evidence From Panel Data', *American Economic Review*, 80: 714–35.

Kiefer, J. and Wolfowitz, J. (1956), 'Consistency of the Maximum Likelihood Estimator in the presence of Infinitely Many Incidental Parameters', *Annals of Mathematical Statistics*, 27: 887–906.

Kushner, H. (1965a), 'On the Stochastic Maximum Principle: Fixed Time of Control', *Journal of Mathematical Analysis of Application*, 11: 78–92.

(1965b), 'On Stochastic Extremum Problems: Calculus', *Journal of Mathematical Analysis and Applications*, 10: 354–67.

Kydland, F. (1975), 'Noncooperative and Dominant Player Solutions In Discrete Dynamic Games', *International Economic Review*, 16: 321–35.

Lucas, R. (1978), 'Asset Prices In An Exchange Economy', *Econometrica*, 46: 1429–45.

Marcet, Albert (1994), 'Simulation Analysis of Dynamic Stochastic Models: Applications to Theory and Estimation', in this volume.

Marschak, J. and Andrews, W.H. (1944), 'Random Simultaneous Equations and the Theory of Production', *Econometrica*, 12: 143–205.

Maskin, E. and Tirole, J. (1987), 'A Theory of Dynamic Oligopoly, III: Cournot Competition', *European Economic Review*, 31: 947–68.

(1988a), 'A Theory of Dynamic Oligopoly, I: Overview and Quantity Competition with Large Fixed Costs', *Econometrica*, 56: 549–69.

(1988b), 'A Theory of Dynamic Oligopoly, II: Price Competition, Kinked Demand Curves, and Edgeworth Cycles', *Econometrica*, 56: 571–99.

Matzkin, R. (1992), 'Nonparametric and Distribution-Free Estimation of the Binary Threshhold Crossing and the Binary Choice Models', *Econometrica*, 60: 239–70.

McFadden, D. (1989), 'A Method of Simulated Moments for Estimation of Discrete Response Models Without Numerical Intergration', *Econometrica*, 57: 995–1026.

McGuckin, R. and Pascoe, G. (1988), 'The Longitudinal Research Data Base (LRD): Status and Research Possibilities', *Survey of Current Business*, 68 (11): 30–36.

Milgrom, P. and Roberts, J. (1990), 'Rationalizability, Learning and Equilibrium in Games with Strategic Complementarities', *Econommetrica*, 58 (6): 1255–78.

Miller, R. (1984), 'Job Matching and Occupational Choice', *Journal of Political Economy*, 92: 390–409.

Mundlak, Y. (1963), 'Estimation of Production and Behavioral Functions From A Combination of Time Series and Cross Section Data', in C. Christ (ed.), *Measurement in Economics; Essays in Honor of Yehuda Grunfeld*, Stanford Calif.: Stanford University Press.

Newey, W. (1990a), 'Efficient Instrumental Variables Estimation of Nonlinear Models', *Econometrica*, 58: 809–39.

(1990b), 'Semiparametric Efficiency Bounds', *Journal of Applied Econometrics*, 5: 99–135.

(1991), 'Two-step Series Estimation of Sample Selection Models', mimeo, Department of Economics, MIT.

(1993), 'Distribution Free Simulated Moments Estimation of Nonlinear Errors-in-Variables Models', mimeo, MIT.

(1993), 'The Asymptotic Variance of Semiparametric Estimators', mimeo, Department of Economics, MIT.

(forthcoming), 'Series Estimation of Regression Functionals', *Econometric Theory*.

Newey, W.K. and Powell, J.L. (1992), 'Nonparametric Instrumental Variables Estimation', manuscript, Department of Economics, Princeton University.

Neyman, J. and Scott, E. (1948), 'Consistent Estimates Based on Partially Consistent Observations', *Econometrica*, 16(1): 1–32.

Olley, S. (1991), 'An Econometric Study of the Telecommunications Equipment Industry', unpublished Ph.D. Dissertation, University of Wisconsin.

Olley, S. and Pakes, A. (1992), 'The Dynamics of Productivity in the Telecommunications Equipment Industry', NBER, Working Paper, January.

Pakes, A. (1986), 'Patents as Options: Some Estimates of the Value of Holding European Patent Stocks', *Econometrica*, 54: 755–84.

Pakes, A. and Griliches, Z. (1984), 'Estimating Distributed Lags in Short Panels with an Application to the Specification of Depreciation Patterns and Capital Stock Constructs', *Review of Economic Studies*, 51(2): 243–62.

Pakes, A. and McGuire P. (forthcoming), 'Computation of Markov Perfect Equilibria: Numerical Implications of a Dynamic Differentiated Product Model', the *Rand Journal of Economics*.

Pakes, A. and Pollard, D. (1989), 'Simulation and the Asymptotics of Optimization Estimators', *Econometrica*, 57: 995–1026.

Resnick, S. and Roy, R. (1989), 'Random USC Functions, Max-Stable Processes, and Continuous Choice', mimeo, Cornell University.

Roberts, K. and Weitzman, M. (1981), 'Funding Criteria for Research, Development, and Exploration Processes', *Econometrica*, 49: 1261–88.

Robinson, P. (1987), 'Asymptotically Efficient Estimation in the Presence of Heteroskedasticity of Unknown Form', *Econometrica*, 55: 875–91.

(1988), 'Root-N-Consistent Semiparametric Regression', *Econometrica*, 56: 931–54.

Romer, P. (1986), 'Increasing Returns and Long-Run Growth', *Journal of Political Economy*, 94: 1002–37.

Runkle, D. (1983), 'Essay in Empirical Macroeconomics', Unpublished Ph.D. Dissertation, MIT.

Rust, J. (1987), 'Optimal Replacement of GMC Bus Engines: An Empirical Model of Harold Zurcher', *Econometrica*, 55: 999–1034.

(1994), 'Dynamic Structural Models; Problems and Prospects: Discrete Decision Processes', ch.4 in this volume.

Sargent, T.J. and Sims, C.A. (1977), 'Business Cycle Modeling without Pretending to Have Too Much A Priori Economic Theory', in C.A. Sims (ed.), *New Methods in Business Cycle Research: Proceedings from a Conference*, Federal Reserve Bank Minneapolis, Minneapolis.

Sherman, R. (1991), 'U-Processes and Semi-Parametric Estimation', Unpublished Ph.D. Dissertation, Department of Statistics, Yale University.

Stokey, N., Lucas, R.E. and Prescott, E.C. (1989), *Recursive Methods in Economic Dynamics*, Cambridge, Mass.: Harvard University Press.

Tirole, J. (1989), *The Theory of Industrial Organization*, Cambridge, Mass.: MIT Press.

Topkis, D.M. (1978), 'Minimizing a Submodular Function on a Lattice', *Operations Research*, 26: 305–20.

Townsend, R. (forthcoming), 'Risk and Insurance in Village India', *Econometrica*.

Wedervang, F. (1965), *Development of A Population of Industrial Firms*, Oslo: Scandinavian University Books.

Wolak, F. (1990), 'Estimating Regulated Firm Production Functions with Private

Information: An Application to California Water Utilities', mimeo, Stanford University.

Zeldes, S. (1989), 'Consumption and Liquidity Constraints: An Empirical Investigation', *Journal of Political Economy*, 97: 305–46.

Comments on Marcet, Rust and Pakes

Kenneth L. Judd

While these chapters are concerned with both econometric and computational issues, I will follow the principle of comparative advantage and confine my comments to issues related to the numerical solution of dynamic economic models. This is an area which has received increasing attention lately and these chapters report progress in both the micro-economic and macro-economic literature. While these literatures have different objectives and methods, they have much in common when it comes to computational techniques.

I shall first discuss aspects of numerical dynamic programming related to all three chapters. I shall now focus on Marcet's paper and related literature in detail since it focusses on computation; however, the methodological comments are just as applicable to micro-economic problems discussed in Pakes' and Rust's chapters. In my comments, I will aim to, first, put Marcet's chapter and the literature he reviews in a more complete historical perspective, and, second, point out the many ways in which Marcet's conjectures and recommendations differ from standard numerical practice. While Marcet has done a nice job in describing some of the numerical work going on today, he has prematurely dismissed some methods as being impractical for future work. I think that it is premature to focus on the few methods Marcet endorses since we have so little experience with the problems which arise in economics.

DYNAMIC PROGRAMMING SOLUTIONS AND ESTIMATION

Since the Pakes and Rust chapters focus largely on econometric issues, I have little to say about them except for one point. On the computational side, both chapters represent a careful, almost timid, approach to numerical solutions. In the micro-econometric literature, authors generally formulate dynamic problems so that there are only a finite number of states. Such finite-state models are comfortable since dynamic programming problems with a finite-state space and Markov transition rules are easy to solve with high accuracy. However, substantial approximation error results when one replaces a continuous economic problem with a finite-state problem. The only way to reduce this error is to make more refined discretisations. Such discretisation procedures have rapidly increasing costs of increasing accuracy since the number of states grows rapidly as one increases the accuracy target, and the time used to solve the dynamic programming problem generally grows superlinearly in the number of states.

Approximating continuous-state problems with finite-state Markov chains limits the range of problems which can be analysed. Fortunately, state-space discretisation is unnecessary. For the past thirty years, the standard procedure in operations research literature (see Bellman *et al.* (1963), Dantzig *et al.* (1974) and Daniel (1976) has been to approximate value functions and policy rules over continuous state spaces with orthogonal polynomials, splines or other suitable families of functions. This results in far faster algorithms and avoids the errors associated with making the problem unrealistically 'lumpy'. These methods clearly would have substantial value in computing pareto-optima and recursive equilibrium in general. In fact, Kotlikoff, Shoven and Spivak (1986) used these procedures in their study of intergenerational wealth transmission.

I strongly suspect that the empirical techniques which Pakes and Rust discuss in their chapters can be applied to models where more sophisticated numerical approaches are used to solve the dynamic economic models. In fact, the dynamic game example at the end of Pakes' chapter strongly supports this conjecture. The use of more modern approaches to the solution of continuous-state dynamic programming problems will substantially increase the usefulness of the empirical techniques discussed in the Pakes and Rust chapters.

EARLY NUMERICAL SOLUTIONS OF RATIONAL EXPECTATIONS MODELS

Marcet's review of the literature on numerical solution methods gives the reader the impression that numerical simulations of rational expectations models is a new technique, asserting that 'In the last five years . . . a growing number of researchers have turned to studying dynamic stochastic equilibrium models using computer simulations'. A closer examination of the economics literature reveals that this trend has been present for much longer.

In fact, such methods have been extensively used in the agricultural economics literature for over thirty years. Since those of us working on computational methods can learn, and have learned, much about computing numerical solutions and their usefulness from that earlier literature, I shall briefly discuss this literature and other important original work. The first numerical solution of a non-linear stochastic rational expectations model I am aware of was Gustafson's (1958) analysis of grain stockpiling policies. Gustafson considered the following problem. Each year a random output of grain is realised, the resulting output is added to the existing stockpile, and the total amount allocated between current consumption and saving in the stockpile. There is one important constraint: that negative stockpiles are not feasible. Gustafson developed a method to compute the function expressing consumption decisions and/or equilibrium prices as functions of the total amount of grain currently available. His method (similar to that later used in Bizer and Judd, Coleman, and Baxter, *et al.*) computes a piece-wise linear function which approximately solves a Euler equation, and finds it through 'time iteration', that is, given tomorrow's equilibrium rule, find today's equilibrium, which in turn determines yesterday's equilibrium rule, etc. However, Gustafson's problem is more difficult than a stochastic growth problem since he had to handle the non-negativity constraint on stocks.

Following Gustafson (1958), the agricultural economics literature grew substantially in sophistication, including several papers published in standard economics journals, such as papers by Williams and Wright (1982a,b) and Miranda and Helmburger (1988). These papers have addressed several important extensions of Gustafson's model and serve as very good examples of how to take a numerical approach to important economic questions. Those of us who have been aware of this literature have also found it valuable. The recent book by Williams and Wright (1991) is a comprehensive survey of this literature.

I must also disagree with Marcet's claim that 'the new algorithms have enlarged the class of models that can be approached by simulation; more precisely, it is no longer necessary to cast an equilibrium model into a planner's problem in order to solve it'. The old algorithms were solving distorted stochastic rational equilibrium problems for thirty years, as the many applications in the agricultural economics show. In general, there is much that current researchers can learn by reading the substantial body of innovative work in the agricultural economics literature.

THE CHANGING STATUS OF NUMERICAL METHODS

I agree with Marcet that something has changed and that is why we have an invited chapter on this topic. What is new is a greater recognition of the potential these methods offer for economic analysis and an increased willingness to think of these methods as alternatives to and complements of theorem proving. These realisations have led economists to think systematically about solution methods and evaluate alternative methods. Outside of the work associated with computational general equilibrium (see the survey by Shoven and Whalley (1984)) and applications in public finance, numerical methods did not have as wide an acceptance as today and there was less focus on the methods. That situation is improving, as the papers cited in Marcet make clear.

There are problems associated with publishing work taking a numerical approach. These problems were stumbling blocks to those who have used numerical approaches in the past. Authors of the earlier papers have told me that they often wanted to highlight the methodological innovations of their work but were blocked by journal editors who wanted only a summary of the economic implications. That policy was not consistent with other aspects of typical editorial policy. For example, when it comes to theory or econometrics, journals generally demand that authors provide proofs of theorems. Often the value of a theoretical analysis lies in the innovations in the proofs more than in the economic content of a particular application. Similarly, the value of many of the papers cited above and in Marcet's chapter lies as much in their techniques as in their applications. It is unclear why journals did not demand as much of authors using numerical methods, and why they blocked the diffusion of methodological innovations. Fortunately, current practice has improved somewhat.

None of this is to deny that documenting a numerically intensive study is difficult and presents unique challenges to the author and journal. Space constraints and the lack of a universal programming language argues against the publication of code. An exhaustive listing of all the results is similarly impractical. However, these problems can be handled in much the same way we handle similar problems in reporting empirical work. For example, in recognition of the importance of diffusing this material as well as holding authors accountable, the NSF now encourages grantees to file documented programmes in a public database just as it requires the filing of data and empirical procedures. Hopefully, this together with an increased willingness on the part of journals to publish some of the details of the numerical procedures will increase the rate at which sophisticated numerical techniques are diffused among economists.

LIQUIDITY CONSTRAINTS

One particular substantive area discussed by Marcet was liquidity constraints. Because of their recent vintage and unpublished status as of this writing I am not well acquainted with the papers he discusses, but I was struck by his description of what we have learned from them. He argues that there is a general conclusion that 'market incompleteness on its own is not capable of generating results that are very different from the complete contingent markets case'. This conclusion differs sharply from several other papers on liquidity constraints which have been published in the past five years. Kotlikoff, Shoven and Spivak (1986) found that liquidity constraints had enormous impact on the distribution of income over time. Auerbach (1986) documents the importance of carry-forward and carry-back provisions in the tax code. Hubbard and Judd (1987) found that the inclusion of liquidity constraints altered the desirability of a social security programme designed to compensate for a missing annuity market. Hubbard and Judd (1986) showed that the relative ranking of income and wage taxation was changed when one included liquidity constraints in the analysis. These papers have used a variety of numerical procedures since closed-form solutions are generally unavailable. In general, public finance economists consider liquidity constraints to be of some importance, and have shown that they can generate results substantially different from the complete markets model.

PERTURBATION METHODS AND LINEAR-QUADRATIC APPROXIMATION

Marcet's opinion about perturbation methods differs a great deal from the literature. He asserts that 'some of these methods ... do not have ways of obtaining arbitrary accuracy in their approximations ... Linear-quadratic approximations [is one] such method', but that 'the method of Marcet (1989) ... would obtain arbitrary accuracy by increasing the degree of the polynomials ...'. I was confused by this assertion since there are so many similarities between Marcet's method and the methodology behind linear-quadratic approximations. To see this we must recall what linear-quadratic approximations really are.

What Marcet calls a 'linear-quadratic' approximation is just the result of a standard first-order perturbation method around the deterministic steady state. This is the approach taken by Fleming (1971), Magill (1977), Kydlund and Prescott (1982), Judd (1985a, b), Laitner (1987, 1989, 1990), Christiano (1990) and McGrattan (1990). The method is essentially one of writing down a functional equation which defines equilibrium, finding a case where the solution can be determined analytically, taking a Taylor approximation of the defining functional equation around that point, and computing a Taylor expansion of the solution by matching coefficients of like powers.

While these papers only discussed linear approximations, this is not a limitation of the method since Taylor's theorem, extended to Banach spaces, can be used to attain higher-order approximations. This, in fact, occurs frequently in applications of perturbation theory in the physical sciences, particulary general relativity theory. It is obvious from the treatment in Judd (1985a) that this can be done in deterministic growth models. Higher-order approximations have been used in analysing dynamic games in Judd (1985b) and Budd, Harris and Vickers (1990). If the function being approximated is analytic over some interval, then one can gain an arbitrary order of approximation for that function over that interval. In any case, one expects that one can do much better than linear-quadratic approximations by going to higher-order asymptotic expansions. This is demonstrated in Judd (1990).

There is substantial literature which tells us that these formal power series are asymptotically valid in these dynamic equilibrium real business cycle models (see Bensoussan (1988)). The linear-quadratic and higher-order approximations are very fast to compute relative to any alternative. The same techniques could be used to approximate moments of the resulting time series. Furthermore, the related methods of Adomian (1986) can also be used to obtain good higher-order approximations to non-linear problems.

The comparison Marcet makes in his comparison of linear-quadratic methods and his method is not appropriate. A fair exercise is to compare the linear-quadratic approximation to the method of Marcet similarly restricted to a linear solution. If Marcet restricts the policy function to be linear, then his method is not capable of obtaining arbitrary accuracy. In order to improve accuracy, he must allow higher-order terms. But one could also compute a Taylor series expansion which allows higher-degree terms. Marcet's claim that his method has some advantage over asymptotic methods is particularly confusing in light of the fact that parameterised expectations endeavours to get a good approximation only where the solution visits frequently, which, in many models, is also close to the point around which asymptotic expansions are centred and have high accuracy. Furthermore, den Haan and Marcet attempt to compute a higher-order approximation but give up because of multi-collinearity problems with their method. Such multi-collinearity problems do not arise in computing higher-order perturbation solutions. In summary, Marcet's description of perturbation methods is inconsistent with the economic and mathematical literature, and his dismissal of them as a useful higher-order approximation method appears unwarranted.

CONVERGENCE

This discussion of arbitrary accuracy brings us to the very important issue of just how well can numerical methods solve the problem. One way to address this is to prove convergence of the solution in some norm as the flexibility of the method, such as the degree of the approximating polynomial or the number of nodes used, increases. Convergence theorems attempt to show that, as the degrees of freedom increase to infinity, a method will converge in some appropriate norm to the true solution.

Marcet claims that arbitrary accuracy can be obtained for parameterised expectations. Unfortunately, he gives no documentation of this. There is some work on the problem but so far it has not produced a useful limit theorem. For Galerkin methods applied to non-linear functional equations, there are some theorems which give sufficient conditions for convergence (see Zeidler (1989) and Krasnosel'skii and Zabreiko (1984)). Unfortunately, checking the sufficient conditions is non-trivial work since they often involve degree theory in Banach spaces. I am not aware of any work showing that they apply to any of these economic problems. One paper which has made some progress in this dimension for the finite element approach is Miranda (1987). While I share Marcet's optimistic conjecture about the convergence of these methods, it must be made clear that the issue is far from settled but will hopefully attract serious attention in the near future.

THE 'CURSE OF DIMENSIONALITY'

The other area in which Marcet's comments are at variance with conventional wisdom in the numerical analysis literature is his discussion of what will happen as we take these methods to higher dimensions. In moving to higher dimensions, problems do arise since the number of unknowns does increase. If one discretises the state space then the costs rise exponentially since n points in each of d dimensions results in a lattice of n^d points. However, there are many alternative procedures.

In all of the problems discussed in Marcet, the basic problem is one of determining the values of a finite set of unknowns. The critical index of the size of the problem is the number of unknown parameters in some parametric representation of the solution. As the dimensionality of a problem grows, the minimally adequate number of parameters will also grow. The tensor product approach taken in Bizer and Judd, and Coleman, would have a 'curse of dimensionality' as Marcet claims. However, no one would take such an approach to high-dimensional problems. One standard way to avoid this is to use complete families of polynomials, as discussed in Davis and Rabinowitz (1984), which grow polynomially in the dimension. Furthermore, if Marcet is to avoid the curse of dimensionality he must also avoid the tensor product approach to approximation. Also, perturbation methods will naturally avoid the curse of dimensionality since they automatically use complete polynomials. Hence, there is little difference here among the algorithms in the problems they face as dimensionality increases.

MONTE CARLO INTEGRATION

As dimensionality increases, computing integrals representing conditional expectations will become more difficult; this is a problem faced by all the methods except perturbation methods. He claims that 'several methods . . . avoid the curse of dimensionality', and appears to claim that this will happen 'if quadrature is replaced by Monte Carlo integration'. That claim is unsupported by, and appears to contradict, the current state of knowledge in numerical analysis. The main use of Monte Carlo methods in these algorithms is to compute a conditional expectation, an integral. Davis and Rabinowitz (1984), show that Monte Carlo methods are just one of several ways to handle multi-dimensional integration. They also argue that for well-behaved domains of integration of moderate dimension, and moderately well-behaved integrands (conditions which are satisfied by the economic applications discussed by Marcet), quasi-Monte Carlo methods are superior to Monte Carlo procedures, some achieving order N^{-1} or greater convergence, where N is the number of sampled points. Neiderreiter (1978) is a good survey of these superior techniques.

Marcet refers to the work of Geweke (1989) on applying acceleration schemes to Monte Carlo integration. This does not really address the issues for two reasons. First, Monte Carlo acceleration schemes do not increase the rate of convergence to the true answer as we increase the number of draws since that is $N^{-\frac{1}{2}}$ by the logic of the central limit theorem. Second, as Davis and Rabinowitz point out, these acceleration schemes are subject to dimensional effects and that, outside of special cases, none of them appears to be of any value for large dimension problems.

Monte Carlo schemes may have some tractability advantages. The theory of equidistributional sequences and discrepancy measures and related acceleration methods based on Fourier expansions of integrands clearly shows that integration formulas which carefully choose which points to evaluate dominate randomly (or pseudo-randomly) chosen nodes. The problem is in developing tractable methods for determining good nodes. If that problem is computationally difficult then Monte Carlo methods may dominate. However, Marcet gives us no reason to think that the integrals we are likely to encounter in economic problems are necessarily of a difficult variety, just that they will have high dimension. While research in multi-dimensional quadrature is ongoing[1] and perhaps future developments will favour Monte Carlo methods, Marcet provides no foundation for his endorsement of Monte Carlo integration methods over the numerous alternatives offered by the mathematical literature.

ENDOGENOUS OVERSAMPLING

Another aspect of Marcet's presentation which differs from standard numerical practice is his discussion of the endogenous oversampling inherent in his parameterised expectations method. He asserts that it is an advantage of his method. This discussion came as a surprise to me since it differs so much from standard numerical results in approximation theory. The flavour of Marcet's argument is that if one cares more about accuracy in region A than in region B than one should sample more points in region A. An implication of this rule is that if one cared equally than one should sample equally. Suppose that I were trying to approximate a function on $[-1, 1]$ with a polynomial. This argument would seem to argue for sampling at $x = k/n - 1, k = 0, 1, 2, \ldots, 2n$. This approach, however, is well known to be inefficient, and sometimes leads to great errors even when one is approximating continuous functions (see Atkinson (1989)). In contrast, Chebyshev approximation theory says that the set of nodes which generally gives the best uniform approximation oversamples the outer regions of $[-1, 1]$, and undersamples the middle region. In general, approximation theory does not say that sampling should occur in proportion to the desired accuracy in a region, and deviates substantially from that rule. Marcet gives the reader no idea of why he disagrees with standard approximation theory, or how his stated objective is related to his sampling scheme.

As Marcet acknowledges, any method which uses endogenous oversampling, such as parameterised expectations, is unsuitable to use in game-theoretic analyses. It must also be noted that it is unsuitable to use in evaluation of policy changes. One use of these models, as in Bizer and Judd, is to examine the economy under various government policies and to map the economy's response to a change in those policies. Suppose that the current tax policy causes the economy to have an average capital stock of 10 with a standard deviation of 0.2, but that a new policy will cause the capital stock to have a mean level of 12 with a standard deviation of 0.2. Suppose that the current level of capital under the current policy is at its mean, 10. Such a level occurs infrequently under the new policy and hence is likely to be poorly approximated in the solution of the new policy. This poor approximation will mean that the transition path caused by the change will be poorly modelled, implying a poor approximation to the welfare impact of the policy change. The key point is that in computing the welfare impact of a policy change, we do not care only about accuracy in the ultimate ergodic distribution, but also on the transition. Hence, in order to model non-marginal policy changes, one cannot use any method which relies on endogenous oversampling. Since endogenous oversampling is inappropriate in so many contexts, methods which use them are of limited value.

COMPUTATIONAL EXPERIENCE

Above I have highlighted how Marcet's suggestions differed from conventional wisdom in numerical analysis. Of course, numerical analysis is as much art as science, and the conventional wisdom could be wrong. Perhaps Marcet's suggestions are helpful when applied to economic problems. One way to test this is to compare performance of the various algorithms.

The stochastic growth model is the only problem where all these methods have been applied. When we compare the times in den Haan and Marcet for Marcet's method with the times for conventional numerical procedures described in Judd (1990) we find that, holding fixed the number of unknown parameters, conventional numerical techniques ran hundreds of times faster than Marcet's method using Monte Carlo integration and endogenous oversampling. This is despite the fact, criticised by Marcet, that the conventional techniques attempt to approximate the equilibrium over a larger region. Furthermore, in the time that Marcet's method took to compute a three-parameter approximation, the standard procedures computed a sixty-parameter approximation. In contrast, den Haan and Marcet reported difficulty solving the six-parameter case.

Marcet argues against such time comparisons. While relative performance across different problems may vary significantly, having some solid information about performance is valuable since ultimately the only important attribute of a numerical procedure is how much time it takes to achieve an answer with the desired accuracy. Of course, there are two kinds of time costs which are important – researcher time and machine time. A procedure which can solve a problem in a second but takes a year to programme is not attractive. I have ignored human time in my comparison. To the extent that human time is the critical limit, it may be appropriate to use procedures which economise on human time at the expense of machine time.

However, for most problems I can imagine, the machine time will be the limiting factor. The critical fact is that researcher time for programming is a fixed cost, but machine time is a marginal cost, that is, a fixed amount of time per case examined. If one is doing a broad search through parameter space to establish a proposition or compute a maximum-likelihood estimate, it is important to reduce the marginal cost of a computation.

THEORY BY COMPUTATION

One way in which computation can be useful is to provide evidence for a theoretical proposition which is as yet unproven. As Marcet discusses, if the proposition depends on a finite number of parameters, one can either choose a parameter which best describes the world, or explore the parameter space to determine the proposition's validity. There are two procedures which could be used here.

Suppose that empirical analysis gives us a posterior belief about the true parameters. One could then sample from the posterior distribution to compute the expected truth of the question. This procedure is far better than just evaluating the issue at the point estimate whenever there are non-linearities. This was done by Harrison (1986) in his study of a trade liberalisation proposal.

In some situations we don't have any belief about the appropriate parameters except for some crude bounds. In that case, I suggest that one take a statistical approach to determine the truth of a proposition. Suppose that we confine the parameters to a bounded set P. If we make many independent and random draws (using, say, the uniform distribution) of parameters from P and find that the proposition is true at each of those parameter choices, we can make a statistical statement. If 1 per cent of P actually invalidated the proposition, the probability of making 300 draws without finding one of them is 4.9 per cent. Therefore, speaking in a classical statistical fashion, if our hypothesis is 'the proposition is true at 99 per cent of the points in P', then we can accept it at a 95 per cent confidence level. Such Monte Carlo exercises and statistical statements can compactly express the results of a computational approach to a theoretical question.[2]

CONCLUSION

Let me conclude by saying that I am fully sympathetic to expanded use of computation in economics in both theoretical and empirical work. By bringing to bear the full range of techniques available in the numerical analysis literature, we will be able to attack many important and complex problems. However, before doing this economists need to acquaint themselves with the basics of numerical analysis. Just as basic probability theory and statistics are necessary for doing econometrics, basic numerical analysis is crucial to developing accurate, efficient and useful numerical solution procedures for economic problems.

Notes

1 In fact, Wozniakowski (1991) computes an upper bound on the average performance of deterministic quadrature rules. Such a bound applies to Monte Carlo integration procedures which use pseudorandom number generators. He showed that a quasi-Monte Carlo scheme achieves that upper bound. There is no evidence that any Monte Carlo procedure based on a pseudorandom number generator is capable of achieving that bound.

2 Dan McFadden has also made this suggestion.

References

Adomian, George (1986), *Nonlinear Stochastic Operator Equations*, Orlando: Academic Press.

Atkinson, Kendall (1989), *An Introduction to Numerical Analysis*, New York: John Wiley.

Auerbach, Alan (1986), 'The Dynamic Effects of Tax Law Asymmetries', *Review of Economic Studies*, 53(2): 205–26.

Baxter, Marianne, Crucini, Mario J. and Rouwenhorst, Geert K. (1990), 'Solving The Stochastic Growth Models by a Discrete-State-Space, Euler-Equation Approach', *Journal of Business and Economic Statistics*, 8(1) (January): 19–21.

Bellman, Richard, Kalaba, Robert and Kotkin, Bella (1963), 'Polynomial Approximation – A New Computational Technique in Dynamic Programming: Allocation Processes,' *Mathematics of Computation* 17: 155–61.

Bensoussan, Alain (1988), *Perturbation Methods in Optimal Control*, New York: John Wiley.

Bizer, David and Judd Kenneth L. (1988), 'Capital Accumulation, Uncertainty, and Taxation', mimeo.

(1989), 'Taxation and Uncertainty', *American Economic Review*, 78 (May): 331–6.

Budd, Christopher, Harris Christopher and Vickers John (1990), 'A Model of the Evolution of Duopoly: Does the Asymmetry Between Firms Tend to Increase or Decrease?', Nuffield College, mimeo, February.

Christiano, Lawrence J. (1990), 'Solving The Stochastic Growth Model by Linear-Quadratic Approximation and by Value-Function Iteration', *Journal of Business and Economic Statistics*, 8(1) (January): 23–6.

Coleman, Wilbur John, II (1990), 'Solving The Stochastic Growth Model by Policy

Function Iteration', *Journal of Business and Economic Statistics*, 8(1) (January): 27–9.

Daniel, J.W. (1976), 'Splines and Efficiency in Dynamic Programming', *Journal of Mathematical Analysis and Applications*, 54: 402–7.

Dantzig, G.B., Harvey, R.P., Lansdowne, Z.F. and McKnight, R.D. (1974), 'DYGAM – A Computer System for the Solutions of Dynamic Programs', Control Analysis Corporation, Palo Alto, Calif., August, 1974.

Davis, Philip, and Rabinowitz, P. (1984), *Methods of Numerical Integration*, 2nd edition, New York: Academic Press.

Fleming, W.H. (1971), 'Stochastic Control for Small Noise Intensities', *SIAM Journal of Control*, 9: 473–517.

Fletcher, C.A. (1984), *Computational Galerkin Methods*, New York: Springer.

Gustafson, Robert L. (1958), 'Carryover Levels for Grains: A Method for Determining Amounts that are Optimal under Specified Conditions', USDA Technical Bulletin 1178.

den Haan, Wouter J. and Marcet, Albert (1990), 'Solving The Stochastic Growth Model by Parameterizing Expectations', *Journal of Business and Economic Statistics*, 8(1) (January): 31–4.

Harrison, G.W. (1986), 'A General Equilibrium Model of Tariff Reductions', in *General Equilibrium Trade Policy Modelling*, edited by T.N. Srinivasan and John Whalley, MIT Press.

Hubbard, R. Glenn and Judd, Kenneth L. (1986), 'Liquidity Constraints, Fiscal Policy, and Consumption', *Brookings Papers on Economic Activity*, 1–50.

(1987), 'Social Security and Individual Welfare: Precautionary Saving, Liquidity Constraints and the Payroll Tax', *American Economic Review*, 77 (September): 630–46.

Judd, Kenneth L. (1985a), 'Short-run Analysis of Fiscal Policy in a Simple Perfect Foresight Model', *Journal of Political Economy*, 93 (April): 298–319.

(1985b), 'Closed-Loop Equilibrium in a Multistage Innovation Race', mimeo.

(1989), 'Minimum Weighted Residual Methods for Solving Dynamic Economic Models', Hoover Institution mimeo.

(1990), 'Asymptotic Methods in Dynamic Economic Models', mimeo (October).

Kotlikoff, Laurence, Shoven John and Spivak, Avia (1986), 'The Effect of Annuity Insurance on Savings and Inequality', *Journal of Labor Economics*, 4: S183–S207.

Krasnosel'skii, Mark A. and Zabreiko, Petrovic (1984), *Geometrical Methods of Nonlinear Analysis*, New York: Springer-Verlag.

Kydland, F.E. and Prescott, E.C. (1982), 'Time to Build and Aggregate Fluctuations', *Econometrica*, 50: 1345–70.

Laitner, John. (1987), 'The Dynamic Analysis of Continuous-Time Life Cycle Saving Growth Models', *Journal of Economic Dynamics and Control*, 11: 331–57.

(1989), 'Transition Time Paths for Overlapping-Generations Models', *Journal of Economic Dynamics and Control*, 7: 111–29.

(1990), 'Tax Changes and Phase Diagrams for an Overlapping-Generations Model', *Journal of Political Economy*, 98(1): 193–220.

Magill, Michael J.P. (1977), 'A Local Analysis of N-Sector Capital Accumulation under Uncertainty', *Journal of Economic Theory*, 15 (June): 211–19.

Marcet, Albert (1989), 'Solving Non-Linear Stochastic Models by Parameterizing Expectations', CMU mimeo.

McGrattan, Ellen R. (1990), 'Solving The Stochastic Growth Model by Linear-Quadratic Approximation', *Journal of Business and Economic Statistics*, 8(1) (January): 41–3.

Miranda, Mario J. (1987), 'A Computational Rational Expectations Model for Agricultural Price Stabilization Programs', University of Connecticut, mimeo.

Miranda, Mario J. and Helmburger, Peter G. (1988), 'The Effects of Commodity Price Stabilization Programs', *American Economic Review*, 78 (March): 46–58.

Niederreiter, Harold (1978), 'Quasi-Monte Carlo Methods and Pseudo-Random Numbers', *Bulletin of the American Mathematical Society*, 84(6) (November): 957–1041.

Shoven, John and Whalley, John (1984), 'Applied General Equilibrium Models of Taxation and International Trade: An Introduction and Survey', *Journal of Economic Literature*, 22: 1007–51.

Tauchen, George (1990), 'Solving The Stochastic Growth Model by Using Quadrature Methods and Value-Function Iterations', *Journal of Business and Economic Statistics*, 8(1) (January): 49–51.

Taylor, John B. and Uhlig, Harald (1990), 'Solving Nonlinear Stochastic Growth Models: A Comparison of Alternative Solution Methods', *Journal of Business and Economic Statistics*, 8(1) (January): 1–18.

Williams, Jeffrey, and Wright, Brian (1982a), 'The Economic Role of Commodity Storage', *Economic Journal* 92 (September 1982): 596–614.

(1982b), 'The Roles of Public and Private Storage in Managing Oil Import Disruptions', *Bell Journal of Economics*, 13 (Autumn): 341–53.

(1991), *Storage and Commodity Markets*, Cambridge University Press.

Wozniakowski, H. (1991), 'Average Case Complexity of Multivariate Integration', *Bulletin of the American Mathematical Society*, 24: 185–94.

Zeidler, Eberhard (1989), *Nonlinear Functional Analysis: Volume II*, New York: Springer-Verlag.

III
Econometrics of finance

CHAPTER 6

Econometric analysis of representative agent intertemporal asset pricing models

Kenneth J. Singleton

1   INTRODUCTION

This chapter attempts to augment and critique recent econometric work on the relations between aggregate consumptions and equilibrium asset prices. The increased interest in the econometric implications of intertemporal asset pricing relations during the past decade can be traced to several important developments in economic theory and econometric method. In the latter half of the 1970s, Rubinstein (1974, 1976), Cox, Ingersoll and Ross (1985), Lucas (1978) and Breeden (1979) deduced general equilibrium relations between consumption decisions and asset prices under the assumptions that agents had common information sets, access to a complete set of contingent claims markets, identical preferences and equal access to all production technologies. These models served to significantly expand our understanding of the characteristics of asset prices and the nature of hedging demands in dynamic, stochastic models.

However, the implied asset pricing relations were typically highly non-linear and not easily analysed with existing econometric techniques. Not surprisingly, then, early empirical studies explored the properties of several very special cases of these models. Hall (1978), Sargent (1978) and Flavin (1981), as well as many others subsequently, investigated versions of the permanent income-life-cycle model of consumption. Preferences were assumed to be quadratic and constraints were assumed to be linear. These assumptions imply that interest rates on discount bonds are constants and that consumption follows a random walk. Empirical studies of the permanent income model have typically not supported the random walk implication, and the implication of constant real interest rates is also counterfactual.

Grossman and Shiller (1981) were the first to study the relation between consumption and asset returns implied by the representative agent models of Rubinstein (1976), Lucas (1978) and Breeden (1979). They studied the co-movements of consumption and returns in the context of a model in which consumers were risk averse and had perfect foresight about the future. Subsequently, Hansen and Singleton (1982, 1983) developed methods for estimating the parameters of asset pricing relations implied by stochastic dynamic models that incorporate fairly general specifications of concave preference functions. These methods have been applied to study asset pricing relations implied by a wide variety of specifications of preferences, including the HARA class and certain CES-type functions.

The theoretical underpinnings of all of these econometric studies are essentially those of the pioneering studies by Rubinstein (1976) and Lucas (1978). Though extended versions of these models have incorporated non-time-separable utility and multiple goods, the complete market structure and homogeneity conditions have been maintained. By proceeding in this manner, the probability models estimated have retained easily interpretable links to the formal theory. Consequently, recent econometric studies have provided useful feedback on the strengths and weaknesses of these theories for explaining intertemporal consumption and investment decisions.

A primary objective of this chapter is to summarise the large body of empirical evidence on the goodness-of-fit of intertemporal consumption-based asset pricing models. In section 2 I briefly describe the representation of asset prices implied by a representative agent economy in which preferences are a member of the family of S-branch utility functions. Most of the recent empirical studies of dynamic asset pricing models have examined special cases of this model. Several non-linear asset pricing models in which agents have time-separable preferences defined over a single consumption good ('non-durable goods') are discussed in section 3. The limitations of these models in representing the historical co-movements of consumption and real returns on stocks and bonds are explored in depth. Among the issues addressed are the autocorrelation properties of the variables, the sensitivity of the results to the length of the holding period of the investments, and the relation between the average growth in consumption, the average real returns and the estimated parameters for the post-war period. The findings from this analysis suggest that the single-good, representative agent model with time-separable preferences is incapable of explaining several important features of the data.

Three possible explanations for these findings are explored in sections 4 and 5. First, in section 4, the role of non-time separability of preferences is investigated. Specifically, the possibilities that the single consumption good is durable in character or the agents exhibit habit formation in consumption decisions are explored empirically. A single-good model in which goods are durable and provide services over time was explored by Dunn and Singleton (1986). More recently, Ferson and Constantinides (1991) and Heaton (1991) examined the empirical fit of models accommodating both durability of goods and habit formation.

Models in which utility is not separable across non-durable goods and durable goods or leisure are explored in section 5. Most of this discussion focusses on the properties of models in which utility is defined over the service flows from goods that are durable in character, though models incorporating leisure are also discussed briefly. The implications of these models for the relative volatility of assets returns and the decision variables of agents, as well as the behaviour of the implied risk premia are reviewed. In addition, the extent to which these models overcome some of the empirical failings of the single-good models is assessed.

All of the models examined in section 3 through 5 assume agents have von Neumann–Morgenstern expected utility functions. Epstein and Zin (1989, 1990) and Weil (1989), among others, have investigated models in which agents have non-expected utility functions of the type introduced by Kreps and Porteus (1978). The empirical properties of these models are discussed in section 6.

Overall, the results presented in sections 3 through 6 suggest that a very large class of representative agent models is not supported by the historical asset return–consumption relations. Several possible explanations for the empirical limitations of representative agent models and suggestions for future research are presented in section 7.

2   THE ECONOMIC ENVIRONMENT

Suppose that there is a complete set of markets for contingent claims to future quantities of a finite number of goods in the economy; and there are no taxes, short-sale restrictions or transactions costs. Also, suppose agents have a common information set I_t at date t and that utility is concave. Let q_{t+1} denote the payoff on a traded asset denominated in the numeraire good. Then the price at date t of this asset, denoted by $\pi_t(q_{t+1})$, can be expressed as a conditional inner product of q_{t+1} with the marginal rate of substitution of the numeraire good at date t for the numeraire good at date $t+1$ $(m_{t+1}^1)^1$

$$\pi_t(q_{t+1}) = E[m_{t+1}^1 q_{t+1} | I_t]. \tag{6.1}$$

In principle, (6.1) holds for each individual consumer. For the purpose of empirical work with time series data, however, it is often convenient to work with aggregate data on consumption and leisure decisions. Hence, one must either ignore distributional effects or impose sufficient structure to permit aggregation up to a representative 'stand-in' consumer.

Under the assumptions of complete markets and additively separable, concave, state independent utility for individual agents, there exists a utility function in the same class defined over aggregate consumption at prices q_{t+1} (Constantinides (1982)). That is, if m_{t+1}^1 in (6.1) is set equal to the marginal rate of substitution associated with this utility function of aggregate consumption, then (6.1) yields the same prices as those obtained with the individual agents' m_{t+1}^1. In general, the functional form of the utility function defined over aggregate consumption will not be the same as any of the individual agents' utility functions. Also, the demands of the stand-in consumer must agree with the aggregate demands only at the equilibrium price. Thus, many interesting economic issues, including the consequences of many interventions by policy authorities, cannot be addressed using this framework.

Most of the utility functions that have been studied empirically admit a stronger, exact form of demand aggregation. Rubinstein (1974) proved that there is exact demand aggregation for single-good models in which agents' preferences reside in the HARA class and markets are complete. Subsequently, Eichenbaum, Hansen and Richard (1985) showed that aggregation extends to certain multi-good models in which goods are durable in character and the service flows from goods are produced according to linear technologies. Consistent with most of the recent literature, economic environments that imply exact demand aggregation will be explored in this chapter.

To be concrete, consider the following version of the S-branch utility function discussed by Eichenbaum, Hansen and Richard (1985). Let s_{jt} denote an m-dimensional vector of services from consumption goods for consumer j at date t, and suppose the jth consumer ranks alternative streams of consumption services using the utility function

$$[1/(\delta\sigma)]E\left[\sum_{t=1}^{\infty}\beta^t\{U(s_{jt})^\sigma - 1\}|I_0\right], \tag{6.2}$$

where $\delta = (1 - \sigma)$ and U is given by

$$U(s_{jt}) = \left\{\sum_{i=1}^{m}\theta_i\{\delta[s_{jt}^i]\}^\alpha\right\}^{1/\alpha}. \tag{6.3}$$

The parameter β is a subjective discount factor between zero and one and the θ_i satisfy $0 < \theta_i < 1$ and $\sum\theta_i = 1$. There are two branches to this utility function corresponding to whether α is less than or greater than one. Special cases of (6.2) and (6.3) include period utility functions that have the Cobb–Douglas form ($\sigma < 1, \alpha = 0$), and quadratic utility ($\sigma = 2, \alpha = 1$). These cases are discussed in more detail in sections 3 through 5.

I shall assume that the dimension (m) of the vector of service flows s_{jt} is the same as the number of consumption goods in the economy.[2] Additionally, the service flows are assumed to be generated by the linear technology

$$s_{jt} = A(L)e_{jt}, \tag{6.4}$$

where e_{jt} is the m-dimensional vector of endowments of the m goods for consumer j at date t and $A(L)$ is a polynomial in the lag operator given by

$$A(L) = \sum_{\tau=0}^{\infty} a_{\tau} L^{\tau}. \tag{6.5}$$

A positive value of the il^{th} entry of $a_{\tau}, \tau > 0$, implies that acquisition of the lth good in period $t - \tau$ contributes to the production of services from the ith good in period t, while a negative entry implies that the lth good contributes disservices to the service flow from good i. Examples of both positive and negative a_{τ} are discussed subsequently. Eichenbaum, Hansen and Richard (1985) show that if there is a complete set of contingent claims to services from goods, and agents have identical utility functions given by (6.2)–(6.5), then equilibrium prices for securities in a representative consumer economy are identical to those of the underlying multi-consumer economy. Thus, for the purposes of empirical work, one can proceed with the use of aggregate per-capita data even though consumers are heterogeneous with regard to their endowments (e.g., 'rich' and 'poor').

Even with the flexibility and generality of (6.2)–(6.5), the models to be examined in subsequent sections remain very restrictive in several potentially important respects. First, strong homogeneity assumptions are imposed – agents have common utility functions and a common information set. Second, unobserved (by the econometrician) taste shocks are excluded. The economic environment is also one where all agents are interior with regard to their consumption and labour supply decisions, so the 'frictions' that would preclude such equilibria are assumed to be absent.

In particular, exchange via fiat money is a key feature of economic activity in modern industrial economies, and most securities have payoffs denominated in terms of domestic currencies. There is no role for fiat money in the economic environment set forth above. Strictly speaking then there are no securities with nominal payoffs in terms of money; all payoffs are in terms of a numeraire good. Exact counterparts to the latter securities are not traded in the US. Therefore, it has become common practice to substitute real returns on claims to the dividend streams of common stocks or real holding period returns on government and corporate bonds for the purposes of econometric analyses of relation (6.1). In principle, this substitution may not be innocuous, since the pricing relations implied by models which formally incorporate the frictions underlying the desire for monetary exchange may lead to quite different pricing relations. Examples of these differences are presented in the studies of monetary models with cash-in-advance constraints by Lucas (1984) and Townsend (1984).

Another consequence of the homogeneity and complete markets assumptions typically made in deducing (6.1) is that the determination of quantities demanded and supplied in asset markets is simplified. The representative agent prices assets correctly and holds all of the fixed outstanding supply of capital assets. When agents receive different endowments, they will in general actively trade claims to future dividends and borrow and lend among themselves in these environments. However, it might be argued that these models exclude many additional and potentially important motives for trade in security markets. This possibility is discussed further in the concluding section of this chapter.

3   TIME-SEPARABLE PREFERENCES FOR A SINGLE CONSUMPTION GOOD

Much of the recent econometric analysis of representative agent models has examined the restrictions implied by the stochastic Euler equation (6.2). An attractive feature of this approach is that it permits substantial flexibility in specifying preferences. Nevertheless, it is instructive at the outset to examine in depth the simple case of a single-good economy in which the consumption good is non-durable. This environment is sufficiently rich to gain substantial insight into the degree to which representative agent models of intertemporal consumption and investment decisions are consistent with the historical time paths of aggregate consumption and real returns.

Hansen and Singleton (1982), Dunn and Singleton (1983) and Brown and Gibbons (1985) investigated single-good economies in which agents have constant relative risk-averse preferences. Therefore, for illustrative purposes, much of my discussion will also focus on this model. This utility function is obtained as a special case of the S-branch utility function as follows. Let $m = 1$ (single good) and suppose that the consumption good is non-durable so that acquisitions at date t are consumed at date t $[A(L) = 1]$. Also, suppose that $\alpha = 0$ and $\sigma < 1$. Then the period utility function simplifies to

$$U(c_t) = (1/\sigma)(c_t)^\sigma, \tag{6.6}$$

where c_t is the level of consumption of the non-durable good. The marginal rate of substitution for the jth agent, m_{jt+n}^n, is $\beta^n(c_{jt+n}/c_{jt})^{\sigma-1}$. Thus, the stochastic Euler equation underlying these studies is

$$E[\beta^n(c_{t+n}/c_t)^{\sigma-1} r_{t+n} | I_t] = 1, \tag{6.7}$$

where $r_{t+n} = (q_{t+n}/\pi_t(q_{t+n}))$. Interpreting the variable

$$u_{t+n} = \beta^n (c_{t+n}/c_t)^{\sigma-1} r_{t+n} - 1 \tag{6.8}$$

as the disturbance for an econometric analysis, Hansen and Singleton (1982) show how to use the fact that $E[u_{t+n}|I_t] = 0$ to construct instrumental variables estimators of the unknown parameters (β, σ) and to test overidentifying restrictions implied by (6.7).

Briefly, the conditional mean restriction (6.7) implies that $E[u_{t+n}z_t] = 0$, for all $z_t \in I_t$, and therefore elements of agents' information set at date t can be used as instrumental variables for the disturbance u_{t+n}. After selecting s instruments to be used in estimating q parameters $(s \geq q)$, the parameter estimates are chosen by minimising a quadratic form in the sample means of $u_{t+n}z_{jt}, j = 1, \ldots, s$. In this manner, these sample means are made close to their population value of zero under the null hypothesis according to the distance measure defined by the quadratic form. This approach amounts to setting q linear combinations of the s sample orthogonality conditions to zero. If $s > q$, then there are $s - q$ independent linear combinations of the s orthogonality conditions that are not set to zero in estimation, but that should be close to zero if the model is true. Chi square goodness-of-fit tests of these overidentifying restrictions are described in Hansen (1982) and Hansen and Singleton (1982).

These tests of (6.7) accomodate heterogeneity across consumers, in the sense that agents may have different endowment processes (see section 2), as well as certain econometric difficulties. In particular, the model accommodates geometric growth in real per-capita consumption over time, since only the ratio (c_{t+n}/c_t) appears in (6.7). Also, the disturbance u_{t+n} may be conditionally heteroskedastic; that is, $\text{Var}[u_{t+n}|I_t]$ may be an essentially arbitrary function of the elements of agents' information set I_t. Thus the model allows for the possibility that the volatility of stock and bond returns varies across different stages of the business cycle. More generally, this model does not assume that the returns or consumption be drawn from any particular family of distributions in contrast, for example, to log-linear expectations models of asset prices.

In spite of the significant weakening of the assumptions underlying the linear expectations models embodied in (6.7), Hansen and Singleton (1982, 1984) found that relation (6.7) is generally not supported using monthly data on aggregate stock and Treasury bill returns for the period January 1959 through December 1978. When consumption was measured as National Income and Product Accounts (NIPA) 'non-durables plus services' and the monthly return $(n = 1)$ was the value-weighted return on the NYSE, the probability values of the test statistics ranged from 0.57 to 0.30. However, for one choice of instruments the estimate of the parameter

σ was outside the concave region of the parameter space (i.e., $\hat{\sigma} > 1$). Replacing the value-weighted with the equally weighted aggregate stock return resulted in probability values ranging between 0.24 and 0.02. Moreover, three of the four sets of instruments considered lead to estimates of σ exceeding unity. When combinations of returns were examined (several stock returns or stock and bill returns), $\hat{\sigma}$ was again greater than unity *and* the probability values of the test statistics were typically less than 0.01. Similar findings are reported in Dunn and Singleton (1986) for real returns on several investment strategies using Treasury bills. The principal difference is that they also find substantial evidence against the model for individual returns on bills, as well as combinations of returns. Finally, using a different approach, Mehra and Prescott (1985) calculate the equity premiums implied by their equilibrium model for a range of plausible values for the risk-free rate and with the second moments of consumption fixed at the values of the sample second moments for the period 1889–1978. They conclude that their model is not consistent with the average excess return of a security that pays off the aggregate endowment stream over the risk-free return.

There are, of course, many possible explanations of these findings including the misspecification of the agents' objective function and constraint set, mismeasurement of consumption, misspecification of the decision interval and associated problems with temporal aggregation, and the omission of taxes. Some insight into the plausibility of these explanations can be gained from further exploration of the empirical evidence. Consider first the problem of mismeasurement of aggregation consumption. Although much of the variation in aggregate consumption of non-durable goods is due to changes in retail sales, which is collected monthly, various interpolations and extrapolations are used to construct the monthly and quarterly data. These approximations may distort both the autocorrelation function of non-durable goods and the correlations between consumptions and returns. This in turn may explain why sample versions of the orthogonality conditions $E[u_{t+n}z_t] = 0, z_t \in I_t$, cannot be made close to zero for values of (β, σ) in the admissible region of the parameter space.

If the mismeasurement of consumption distorts the lower-order autocorrelations more than higher-order autocorrelations, then this problem may be alleviated somewhat by working with monthly data point-sampled at long intervals. That is, instead of using monthly returns one would use longer-term securities so that $m_{t+n}^n = \beta^n (c_{t+n}/c_t)^{\sigma-1}$ involves monthly consumptions sampled at widely separated points in time. Table 6.1 displays the results from estimating the parameters of the model studied by Hansen and Singleton (1982, 1984) using monthly data on real returns with one, six

Table 6.1. *Parameter estimates and test statistics for single-good models and individual returns for various maturities, August 1963–December 1978[a]*

Return	$\hat{\beta}$	$\hat{\sigma}$	χ^2	DF
TBILL1	1.0003	0.7254	19.54	3
	(0.0003)	(0.0867)	(0.0002)	
TBILL6	1.0002	0.7816	16.27	3
	(0.0006)	(0.2467)	(0.0010)	
TBILL12	1.0007	0.3931	6.603	3
	(0.0007)	(0.2922)	(0.0857)	
VWR1	0.9963	1.646[b]	1.010	3
	(0.0056)	(2.091)	(0.7990)	
VWR6	0.9926	3.955[b]	0.2086	3
	(0.0103)	(4.261)	(0.9762)	
VWR12	1.0003	−0.3143	6.027	3
	(0.0047)	(1.972)	(0.1103)	
TBILL12 &	1.0019	0.0036	1.451	4
VWR12	(0.0010)	(0.4814)	(0.8350)	
TBILL12 &	0.998	1.3666[b]	50.718	5
VWR12		(0.043)	(0.0000)	

Notes:

[a] Standard errors of the parameter estimates and probability values of the test statistics are indicated in parentheses.

[b] The estimated value of σ is outside the concave region of the parameter space.

and twelve month maturities. In the case of stocks, the investment strategy involves rolling over the value-weighted portfolio of stocks on the NYSE for the stated number of months (i.e., VWRn is the n-month rollover strategy); similary, TBILLn denotes the return on an n-month Treasury bill. The time period of analysis is August 1963 through December 1978. Earlier months were omitted, because trading of twelve-month Treasury bills was initiated in 1963.[3] For the Treasury bill returns, there is a tendency for the fit of the model to improve as the maturity is lengthened. Not only do the test statistics decline, but the coefficient of relative risk aversion increases to a value closer to logarithmic utility ($\sigma = 0$). Though, in spite of this improvement in fit, the test statistic remains quite large for TBILL12.

The pattern of results for the stock returns is altogether different. For the one and six-month returns, $\hat{\sigma}$ is well outside the concave region of the parameter space. Correspondingly, the chi square statistics are very small relative to their degrees of freedom. In contrast, for VWR12, $\hat{\sigma}$ is within the concave region of the parameter space. Also, the test statistic is substantially larger, although there is not strong evidence against the model. Overall, there is no systematic improvement in fit as n increases across stock and bill returns, which suggests that mismeasurement that distorts primarily the low-order autocorrelations of consumption growth is not the explanation for previous findings.

Nevertheless, for a given type of security the length of the holding period does affect the results. Also, there are systematic differences in the fit of the model across securities. Further insight into these results is obtained by examining the autocorrelation properties of the variables comprising this single-good model. An immediate implication of (6.7) is that the disturbance (6.8) follows a moving average process of order $(n-1)$ (see Hansen and Singleton 1982). This is an implication of the fact that u_{t+n} is in agents' information set at date $t + n$ and $E[u_{t+n}|I_t] = 0$. It follows that, if the model is correct, then the autocorrelation properties of $\beta^n(c_{t+n}/c_t)^{\sigma-1}$ and $r_{t,n}$ must interact in a manner that leads to an $MA(n-1)$ representation for their product.

The moving average representations of (c_{t+6}/c_t), TBILL6, VWR6, and the corresponding versions of the disturbance (6.8) (u_{t+6}^{T6} and u_{t+6}^{V6} for TBILL6 and VWR6, respectively) are displayed in table 6.2. The coefficients in the MA representation for u_{t+6}^{T6} are significantly different from zero at the 2 per cent level out to lag seven.[4] Thus, the implication of the theory that this disturbance follows an $MA(5)$ process is not satisfied. Moreover, disturbance u_{t+6}^{T6} seems to be inheriting the autocorrelation properties of TBILL6; compare the coefficients in the third and fourth columns of table 6.7 to each other and to those for the consumption ratio in the second column. Next, consider the results for VWR6. Again, u_{t+6}^{V6} seems to be inheriting the autocorrelation properties of the return (in this case VWR6) and not that of the consumption ratio. Though, in contrast to the results for TBILL6, the return VWR6 and u_{t+6}^{V6} exhibit only low-order serial correlation, much less correlation than is implied by an $MA(5)$ process.

The findings that the disturbances are inheriting the autocorrelation properties of the returns may well explain why the probability value of the test statistics for TBILL6 is much larger than the test statistic for VWR6 – the disturbance u_{t+6}^{T6} exhibits too much autocorrelation, while the disturbance u_{t+6}^{V6} exhibits less autocorrelation than might be expected from the theory. Additional evidence consistent with this interpretation is displayed in the last column of table 6.2. The MA representation for the disturbance u_{t+12}^{T12} associated with TBILL12 indicates that there is not significant autocorrelation beyond lag eight, whereas the theory accommodates correlation out to lag eleven. At the same time, the probability value of the chi square statistic for TBILL12 is relatively small. In sum, it is the autocorrelation properties of the returns that largely explain the differences

Table 6.2. *Moving average representations of variables in the single-good models and individual returns for various maturities, August 1963– December 1978[a] (Dependent variable)*

Lag	(c_{t+6}/c_t)	TBILL6	u_{t+6}^{T6}	VWR6	u_{t+6}^{V6}	u_{t+12}^{T12}
1	0.7883*	1.023*	1.005*	1.020*	1.086*	1.015*
	(0.085)	(0.081)	(0.079)	(0.079)	(0.080)	(0.083)
2	0.7823*	1.015*	0.966*	0.911*	1.124*	0.948*
	(0.101)	(0.114)	(0.111)	(0.115)	(0.119)	(0.118)
3	1.118*	1.114*	1.062*	0.209	0.430*	1.052*
	(0.129)	(0.137)	(0.131)	(0.137)	(0.150)	(0.141)
4	1.030*	0.974*	0.944*	0.160	0.279	0.952*
	(0.127)	(0.146)	(0.140)	(0.136)	(0.153)	(0.164)
5	0.072*	0.932*	0.891*	0.265	0.319	0.919*
	(0.131)	(0.146)	(0.140)	(0.138)	(0.153)	(0.179)
6	0.143	0.451*	0.458*	0.149	0.129	0.734*
	(0.122)	(0.137)	(0.132)	(0.137)	(0.151)	(0.180)
7	0.336*	0.284**	0.279**	−0.284	0.131	0.534*
	(0.130)	(0.115)	(0.111)	(0.115)	(0.120)	(0.190)
8	0.252*	0.067	0.087	−0.199**	−0.167	0.446**
	(0.085)	(0.081)	(0.079)	(0.080)	(0.082)	(0.179)
9						0.277
						(0.164)
10						0.244
						(0.141)
11						0.187
						(0.117)
12						0.013
						(0.082)
Constant	1.021	1.003	0.0015	1.003	0.0009	−0.0013
	(0.0017)	(0.0018)	(0.0016)	(0.012)	(0.016)	(0.0042)
R^2	0.724	0.847	0.851	0.678	0.732	0.877

Notes:
[a] Standard errors are displayed in parentheses. A *(**) denotes a coefficient that is significantly different from zero at time 1%(2%) level based on a two-sided test and the standard normal distribution.
[b] The variables u_{t+6}^{T6}, u_{t+6}^{V6}, and u_{t+12}^{T12} are the versions of the disturbance (6.8) for the returns TBILL6, VWR6, and TBILL12, respectively.

in test statistics both across maturity, holding fixed the type of security, and across types of securities.

There are also striking differences in the point estimates of (β, σ) across Treasury bills and common stocks. Notice that, whenever $\hat{\beta}$ exceeds unity, $\hat{\sigma}$ is less than unity and vice versa. The results in the previous studies of this model display a similar pattern. This finding can be interpreted both in terms of the means and covariances of consumption growth and returns. To interpret the pattern in terms of mean growth rates, consider the unconditional expectation of (6.7)

$$E[\beta^n(c_{t+n}/c_t)^{\sigma-1}r_{t+n}] = 1. \tag{6.9}$$

The estimation algorithm selects estimates of β and σ so as to make sample versions of the moment conditions, including (6.9), as close to zero as possible. Now the results in table 6.2 suggest that, for the sample period August 1963 through December 1978, the variation in $\beta^6(c_{t+6}/c_t)^{\sigma-1}r_{t+6}$ is due primarily to variation in r_{t+6}. Thus, letting μ_{c6} denote the mean of (c_{t+6}/c_t), in order to satisfy (6.9), β and σ should be chosen such that $\delta_6 = \beta^6(\mu_{c6})^{\sigma-1}E[r_{t+6}] \approx 1$. For this sample period, $\mu_{c6} = 1.0133$. The mean of TBILL6 is 1.0035 and the estimated value of β^6 from table 6.1 is 1.0012. Thus, a value of σ less than unity is required to make δ_6 close to unity. Similarly, the mean of VWR6 is 1.0047 and the estimated value of β^6 is 0.9564, which is consistent with a value of $\hat{\sigma}$ that is much larger than unity. In other words, the growth rate of consumption during the sample period was on average too large relative to real returns on both stocks and Treasury bills for this model to yield plausible parameter estimates. Consumption growth was positive a large majority of the months while there were long periods during which the real rates of return on stocks were negative.

Why is $\hat{\beta} < 1$ and $\hat{\sigma} > 1$ for the value-weighted return on the NYSE? An explanation of this pattern comes from examining the covariance properties of the returns and consumption growth. Campbell and Shiller (1988) found that a high dividend–price ratio at the beginning of a year forecasts low consumption growth over the year. Hence, low consumption growth tends to be associated with a high one-period discount rate on common stock, which requires that σ exceed unity in (6.7).

An obvious question at this juncture is whether the omission of taxes from these studies might explain the findings. This omission works in favour of, not against, the model. If r_{t+n} is replaced by an after-tax real return, then the average value of this return will be lower on average than the unadjusted return. This in turn means that, for a given mean μ_{c6}, β will have to exceed unity by an even wider margin for the condition (6.9) to be satisfied in the sample. In the context of a model with leisure (see section

Table 6.3. *Parameter Estimates and test statistics for single-good models and stock returns for various maturities, January 1959–December 1985[a]*

Returns	$\hat{\beta}$	$\hat{\sigma}$	χ^2	DF
VWR1	0.9945	1.730[b]	2.077	3
	(0.0040)	(1.980)	(0.5565)	
VWR6	0.9995	0.3769	2.414	3
	(0.0070)	(3.532)	(0.4910)	
VWR12	0.9840	6.006[b]	4.610	3
	(0.0047)	(2.336)	(0.2027)	

Notes:

[a] Standard errors of the parameter estimates and probability values of the test statistics are indicated in parentheses.

[b] The estimated value of σ is outside the concave region of the parameter space.

5.2), Eichenbaum, Hansen and Singleton (1988) estimated the parameters of the corresponding Euler questions using before and after tax real returns on Treasury bills. Consistent with this discussion, they found that in both cases $\hat{\beta}$ exceeded unity and $\hat{\beta}$ was much larger when after tax real returns were used.

It can also be shown that there are not two (approximately equal) local minima to the criterion functions used in estimation, one with $(\beta < 1, \sigma > 1)$ and one with $(\beta < 1, \sigma > 1)$. For example, the results from estimating the one-good model for TBILL12 and VWR12 simultaneously are displayed in the seventh row of table 6.1.[5] Interestingly, for this run $\hat{\sigma}$ is well inside the concave region of the parameter space, although $\hat{\beta}$ is slightly larger than unity. Furthermore, the chi square statistic is small relative to the degrees of freedom. Nevertheless, the apparent good fit of this model is deceiving. When β is restricted to be 0.998, corresponding to an annualised real rate of interest of approximately 2.5 per cent, $\hat{\sigma}$ is greater than unity and the probability value of the chi square statistic is essentially zero (row 8, table 6.1). This sensitivity of the results to the choice of β highlights the important influence of the average values of the returns and the consumption growth rate on the values of the parameter estimates.

For comparability with earlier studies, the statistics displayed in tables 6.1 and 6.2 were calculated for a sample period ending in December 1978. The corresponding estimates for the value-weighted return over the sample period January 1959 through December 1985 are displayed in table 6.3. While the test statistics do not provide much evidence against the model, estimates of σ are again outside the concave region of the parameter space in

two out of three cases. Evidently, the qualitative nature of the results is not
sensitive to extending the sample period through 1985.

From the results in tables 6.1–6.3, it seems that mismeasurement alone is
not sufficient to explain such a poor fit of the single-good model. Another
explanation is that problems of temporal aggregation, perhaps combined
with mismeasurement, underlie the results. Christiano (1984) has shown in
the context of a log-linear model that aggregation over time may distort
both the parameter estimates and the magnitudes of the test statistics. One
approach to circumventing these difficulties is suggested by the analysis in
Rubinstein (1976). If agents have logarithmic utility, then for certain
production and exchange economies the intertemporal marginal rate of
substitution of consumption is proportional to the inverse of the total
return on the aggregate wealth portfolio. It follows that

$$E[r_{t+n}/r_{t+n}^{\omega}|I_t] = k_n,\qquad(6.10)$$

where r_{t+n}^{ω} is the n-period return on the wealth portfolio and k_n is a constant
that depends on n. The assumption of logarithmic utility can be replaced by
the more general assumption of constant relative risk-averse utility, but at
the expense of assuming independently and indentically distributed growth
rates in consumption over time.

Hansen, Richard and Singleton (1981) and Brown and Gibbons (1985)
have studied relation (6.10) empirically using the value-weighted return on
the NYSE (VWRn) as a measure of r_{t+n}^{ω}. Brown and Gibbons did not test
overidentifying restrictions implied by (6.10). The implication of (6.10) that
the ratios of returns r_{t+n}/r_{t+n}^{ω} are serially uncorrelated was tested using
returns on individual stocks by Hansen, Richard and Singleton, however.
For an economy in which there is a single non-durable good and VWRn is
an accurate measure of the return r_{t+n}^{ω}, this test avoids the problems of
temporal aggregation and measurement of consumption or the deflator
($(r_{t+n}/r_{t+n}^{\omega})$ can be formed as the ratio of two nominal returns). The findings
suggest that the model underlying (6.10) is not consistent with the data.

In sum, and without denying that some mismeasurement is surely
present, I believe that the more important factors underlying previous
findings are likely to be misspecification of preferences or violation of the
conditions for aggregation across consumers. For instance, non-time
separability of preferences may be an important factor in explaining asset
return–consumption relations. This possibility is explored in the next
section of this paper.

4   SINGLE-GOOD MODELS WITH NON-TIME
SEPARABLE PREFERENCES

There are several dimensions along which the structure of preferences in the
single-good models examined in section 3 may be misspecified. First, the

functional form for utility may have been misspecified, though the variety of functional forms studied (e.g., quadratic, power and exponential) suggests that this is not the primary explanation for the poor fit. Second, the assumption that utility is separable across the decision variables of agents may be incorrect. For instance, utility may be a non-separable function of consumption of non-durable goods and consumption of leisure. Third, preferences may be non-separable across time even if they are separable across goods at each point in time. This section explores the latter explanation and examines the properties of single-good models of asset prices with non-time separable preferences. The properties of models with non-separable utility across decision variables and time are explored in section 5.

Two sources of non-time separability of preferences have been investigated in the literature: durability of goods and habit formation. If goods are durable in character, then acquisitions of goods will not coincide with the consumption of these goods. The misclassification of goods in the National Income and Product Accounts (NIPA) as being non-durable on a monthly basis is a potentially important source of misspecification, because it may distort both the autocorrelation properties of consumption growth, as well as the mean and variance of consumption. In the NIPA, goods are classified as non-durable if they have a typical lifetime of less than three years. Clearly, it will be the case that many of the goods called non-durable should be considered durable for the purpose of analyses of models with monthly or quarterly decision intervals. This possibility was pursued empirically in a single-good model by Dunn and Singleton (1983, 1986).

Alternatively, agents may exhibit habit formation. That is, an increase in consumption at date t increases the marginal utility of consumption at adjacent dates relative to the marginal utility of consumption at distant dates. Consumptions at adjacent dates are complementary. The implications of habit formation for asset pricing has recently been explored by Sundaresen (1989), Constantinides (1990), Ferson and Constantinides (1991) and Heaton (1991).

A convenient parameterisation preference that accomodates the possibility of durability or habit formation is the special case of (6.3) with $m = 1, \sigma < 1$ and $\alpha = 0$,

$$U(s_{jt}) = (s_{jt})^\sigma / \sigma \qquad (6.11)$$

and the service technology given by

$$s_{jt} = A(L)e_{jt}, \qquad (6.12)$$

where $A(L)$ is a scalar lag polynominal with $A(0) = 1$, and, in equilibrium, c_{jt} equals the jth agent's endowment of the good, e_{jt}. Positive values of the coefficients of $A(L), a_r$, imply that acquisitions of goods in the past continue to provide services in the current period; i.e., the good is durable. On the other hand, negative values of a_τ, for $\tau \geq 1$, can be interpreted as the weights on past consumptions that enter the agent's 'subsistence' level of consumption services. The presence of this subsistence level induces habit persistence; as c_t approaches $\sum_{\tau=1}^{\infty} a_\tau c_{jt-\tau}$, the marginal utility of s_{jt} becomes infinite if $\sigma < 0$.

Tests of the overidentifying restrictions implied by models with durability and/or habit formation have been based on the Euler equation

$$E_t \left[\sum_{\tau=0}^{\infty} a_\tau \beta^\tau (c_{t+\tau})^{\sigma-1} \right] = E_t \left[\left(\sum_{\tau=0}^{\infty} a_\tau \beta^{\tau+1} (c_{t+\tau+1})^{\sigma-1} \right) r_{t+1} \right]. \qquad (6.13)$$

The expectation appears on the LHS of (6.13), because acquisitions of goods at date t affect utility in future periods. Dunn and Singleton (1986) estimated the model (6.11)–(6.12) with $A(L) = 1 + a_1 L$. For this specification, a_1 captures the combined effects of durability and habit persistence, with the sign of a_1 being positive if durability is the dominant reason for non-separability and negative if habit persistence dominates. A higher-order polynomial is required to identify the separate effects of durability and habit persistence. Consumption was measured as monthly NIPA non-durables plus services over the period 1959:1–1985:12. Exponential growth was accommodated in this economy by scaling both sides of (6.13) by $c_t^{\sigma-1}$, which led to the econometric disturbance.

$$u_{t+2} = \sum_{\tau=0}^{1} a_\tau \beta^\tau (c_{t+\tau}/c_t)^{\sigma-1} - \left[\sum_{\tau=0}^{1} a_\tau \beta^{\tau+1} (c_{t+\tau+1}/c_t)^{\sigma-1} \right] r_{t+1}. \qquad (6.14)$$

Since, by (6.13), u_{t+2} can be interpreted as a two-period ahead expectational error, $\{u_{t+2}\}$ follows an MA(1) process. The estimated value of a_1 was positive, consistent with the presumption that 'non-durables plus services' provide consumption services over time. However, the probability value of the chi square statistic for this model was 0.001 indicating that the introduction of non-time separability did not markedly improve the fit.

In contrast, Ferson and Constantinides (1991) estimated a version of (6.11)–(6.12) with $A(L) = 1 + a_1 L$ using post-war quarterly data and annual data for the period 1929–86. To accommodate real growth they scaled (6.13) by $(c_t + a_1 c_{t-1})^{\sigma-1}$, which gives the econometric model

$$u_{t+2} = \sum_{\tau=0}^{1} a_\tau \beta^\tau \left(\frac{c_{t+\tau} + a_1 c_{t+\tau-1}}{c_t + a_1 c_{t-1}} \right)^{\sigma-1} - \left[\sum_{\tau=0}^{1} a_\tau \beta^{\tau+1} \left(\frac{c_{t+\tau+1} + a_1 c_{t+\tau}}{c_t + a_1 c_{t-1}} \right)^{\sigma-1} \right] r_{t+1}. \qquad (6.15)$$

As instruments, they used dividend yields, nominal Treasury bill returns, industrial production, and measures of nominal term and default premiums. The best fit of the model for real returns on Treasury bonds and

Table 6.4. *Analysis of single-good models with habit formation using quarterly data from 1959:1 to 1986:4*

Returns	$\hat{\beta}$	$\hat{\sigma}$	$\hat{a}^1$	χ^2	DF
VWR3 & TBILL3	1.004	−0.2980	0	28.95	12
	(0.0021)	(0.4024)		(0.004)	
VWR3 & TBILL3	0.9906	0.4492	−0.5	10.66	12
	(0.0019)	(0.1426)		(0.559)	
VWR3 & TBILL3	0.9947	0.0274	−0.9	7.835	12
	(0.0025)	(0.0161)		(0.798)	

Autocorrelations of $\{u_{t+2}\}$ in equation (6.15) with $\beta = 0.99$ and $\sigma = 0$

$a_1 = -0.9$	u^{VWR}	−0.5864	−0.0477	0.1622	0.1296	−0.3312	0.1737
	u^{TB3}	−0.5836	−0.0565	0.1684	0.1254	−0.3447	0.2002
$a_1 = -0.5$	u^{VWR}	0.0896	−0.1420	−0.0683	−0.0062	−0.0307	−0.1445
	u^{TB3}	−0.4312	−0.0094	0.2082	−0.1286	−0.2539	0.2172
$a_1 = 0$	u^{VWR}	0.1323	−0.1677	−0.0612	−0.0250	−0.0451	−0.1056
	u^{TB3}	0.6512	0.5764	0.5577	0.4460	0.4104	0.4263
$a_1 = 0.5$	u^{VWR}	0.1316	−0.1696	−0.0588	−0.0261	−0.0493	−0.0990
	u^{TB3}	0.7824	0.6799	0.6098	0.5207	0.5194	0.4610
$a_1 = 0.9$	u^{VWR}	0.1315	−0.1698	−0.0585	−0.0262	−0.0499	−0.0983
	u^{TB3}	0.7819	0.6845	0.6109	0.5256	0.5137	0.4621

NYSE decile portfolios was obtained with $a_1 < 0$. In other words, preferences exhibit habit formation. Furthermore, they did not reject the implied overidentifying restrictions at conventional significance levels. With quarterly data and c_1 measured as non-durable consumption expenditures, the estimate of a_1 obtained by Ferson and Constantinides was −0.95, suggesting a very high level of habit formation. Moreover, when durable goods expenditures were substituted for non-durable expenditures, the estimates continued to suggest habit formation; $\hat{a}_1 = -0.65$.

The pronounced degree of habit formation obtained by Ferson and Constantinides with quarterly data seems surprising since many 'non-durable goods' provide services for up to three years and, of course, durable goods provide services for much longer periods. Some insight into whether values of a_1 close to −1 are symptomatic of model misspecification or mismeasurement is obtained by examining the properties of the disturbances in a model with habit formation for various values of a_1. The top part of table 6.4 displays the estimates of the model (6.15) using quarterly data over the sample period 1959:1 through 1986:4. Estimates were obtained for the real return on three-month Treasury bills and the real three-month holding period return on the value-weighted NYSE portfolio, using the constant unity and two lagged values of consumption growth and the real returns as instruments. In the latter respect, I followed previous studies rather than Ferson and Constantinides in choosing instruments.[6] Also, estimates were obtained for three different fixed values of a_1 in order to evaluate the effects on the other preference parameters and test statistics of changes in a_1. When $a_1 = 0$, there is substantial evidence against the model, which is consistent with the results in Hansen and Singleton (1982) for the analogous monthly model. Consistent with the results in Ferson and Constantinides, the test statistic declines markedly as a_1 decreases to -0.9.

The second part of table 6.4 displays the first six autocorrelations of $\{u_t^{VWR}\}$ and $\{u_t^{TB3}\}$ given by (6.15) with VWR3 and TBILL3 as returns, respectively, for various values of a_1. The disturbances were all computed with $\beta = 0.99$ and $\sigma = 0$. (log utility). Consider first the correlations for $a_1 = 0$. In this case, the disturbances are serially uncorrelated under the null hypothesis. In fact, the autocorrelations of $\{u_t^{TB3}\}$ are substantially larger than zero and decay relatively slowly. This is a manifestation of the positive persistence in TBILL3. Positive values of a_1 increase the autocorrelation of $[(1 + a_1\beta L)(c_{t+1}^*/c_t^*)^{\sigma-1}]$, where $c_t^* \equiv c_t + a_1 c_{t-1}$, but have relatively little affect on the volatility of the disturbances or their correlation.

When $a_1 \neq 0$, the disturbances follow MA(1) processes under the null hypothesis. The computed autocorrelations of both $\{u_t^{VWR}\}$ and $\{u_t^{TB3}\}$ are much closer to an MA(1) autocorrelation structure for $a_1 = -0.5$ and -0.9. In particular, the second and third autocorrelations, which are aligned in time with the instruments, are quite small. On the other hand, positive values of a_1 tend to increase the autocorrelations of the disturbances and thereby lead to larger departures from the null of zero autocorrelations. The reason for this pattern can be seen immediately from the following version of (6.15)

$$u_{t+2} = \left[\beta\left(\frac{c_{t+1}^*}{c_t^*}\right)^{\sigma-1} + a_1\beta^2\left(\frac{c_{t+2}^*}{c_t^*}\right)^{\sigma-1}\right]r_{t+1} - a_1\beta\left(\frac{c_{t+1}^*}{c_t^*}\right)^{\sigma-1} - 1. \qquad (6.16)$$

When $a_1 < 0, (c_{t+1}^*/c_t^*)$ is more volatile than (c_{t+1}/c_t) and increasingly dominates the volatility of $\{u_t\}$. At the same time, the autocorrelation of $\{c_{t+1}^*/c_t^*\}$ declines as a_1 approaches -1. Thus, for a_1 near $-1, \{u_t\}$ is approximately a quasi-difference of a nearly serially uncorrelated process. In other words, the time-series properties of $\{u_t\}$ are determined almost entirely by the terms involving $\left(\frac{c_{t+1}^*}{c_t^*}\right)$ and not r_{t+1} as a_1 approaches -1. As $\{u_t\}$ becomes increasingly dominated by the consumption term the test statistics decline. This pattern is what would be expected from the discussion of tables 6.1 and 6.2.

Further confirmation of this interpretation is provided by the correlation matrix of (u_t^{VWR}, u_t^{TB3}): when $a_1 = -0.9$, the correlation between u_t^{VWR} and u_t^{TB3} is 0.994 and the corresponding standard deviations and autocorrelations of these shocks are essentially equal. In contrast, when $a_1 = 0$, corr $(u_t^{VWR}, u_t^{TB3}) = 0.04$, the standard deviation of u_t^{VWR} is more than ten times larger than the standard deviation of u_t^{TB3}, and as in table 6.2, the properties of these disturbances are determined largely by the returns.

In sum, the near perfect correlation between u_t^{VWR} and u_t^{TB3} may be, as the theory presumes, a manifestation of a very high degree of habit persistence over quarterly decision intervals for consumption of services from durable and non-durable goods. Alternatively, the preceding observations suggest that it may also be a consequence of misspecification of the model or mismeasurement of consumption. Computation of the asset prices and MRSs implied by values of a_1 as small as -0.9 may be informative about the economic plausibility of prices with this high degree of habit persistence.

Additional evidence on the goodness-of-fit of single-good models with non-time separable preferences is presented in Gallant and Tauchen (1989). They assumed that the first-order conditions of an agent's intertemporal optimum problem could be expressed in terms of a general, scaled period utility function of the form

$$U(c_t/c_{t-1}, c_{t-1}/c_{t-2}, \ldots, c_{t-l}/c_{t-l-1}). \tag{6.17}$$

This utility function was then approximated by a flexible functional form. Furthermore, the joint conditional density of asset returns and consumption growth was approximated by a flexible parameterisation that accomodated various departures from normality. Then the parameters of the model were estimated by maximum likelihood subject to the conditional moment constraints implied by their counterparts to (6.16). Their point estimates of the utility function were consistent with a positive value of a_1 (durability of goods). Moreover, when stock and bond returns were studied simultaneously, they found that the overidentifying restrictions implied by the Euler equations were not supported by the data. Though they allowed for more general specifications of preferences and quite flexible distribution functions, their results were very similar to those from previous studies assuming CRRA preferences and using limited information estimation procedures.

There is, of course, the mixed case in which goods are durable in character and agents' preferences exhibit habit persistence. This case has been investigated in depth by Heaton (1991). His findings with monthly data suggest that goods are locally durable, but that over long horizons there is evidence of significant habit formation. These conclusions were reached from fitting bivariate time series models of consumption of non-durable goods and dividends, while accomodating time aggregation in the measurement of consumption. Furthermore, allowing for both local dura-bility and habit persistence over longer horizons substantially improves the fit of the model compared to the simple time-additive model. Nevertheless, the overidentifying restrictions were rejected at conventional significance levels.

5   MULTI-GOOD MODELS OF ASSET PRICES

The time series properties of intertemporal marginal rates of substitution are also affected by the composition of the goods (services) entering the period utility function. Two notable omissions from the set of decision variables in sections 3 and 4 are leisure and services from durable goods. The properties of asset pricing relations based on preferences which are non-separable across non-durable consumption expenditures and either durable expenditures or leisure are explored in this section.

5.1   Models with durable goods

There are notable co-movements in durable goods purchases and the levels of interest rates. Accordingly, by introducing the services from durable goods into the model explicitly, and assuming that utility from the services of NIPA non-durable and durable goods are not separable, the model may better represent the 'consumption risk' inherent in asset returns.

This possibility was pursued empirically by Dunn and Singleton (1986) and Eichenbaum and Hansen (1989), who considered the following exten-sions of the model in Hansen and Singleton (1982). The function $U(s_{jt})$ was chosen to be the special case of (6.3) with $\sigma < 1, a = 0$, and $m = 2$

$$U(s_{jt}) = (s_{jt}^1)^\delta (s_{jt}^2)^{(1-\delta)}. \tag{6.18}$$

Additionally, the service technologies were given by

$$\begin{vmatrix} s_{jt}^1 \\ s_{jt}^2 \end{vmatrix} = \begin{vmatrix} 1+aL & 0 \\ 0 & \theta(1-\theta L)^{-1} \end{vmatrix} \begin{vmatrix} e_{jt}^1 \\ e_{jt}^2 \end{vmatrix}, \tag{6.19}$$

here e_{jt}^1 and e_{jt}^2 are the endowments of NIPA 'nondurable goods plus services' and 'durable goods', respectively. In this model, NIPA non-durable goods provide services for two periods (months), while durable goods provide a perpetual flow of services that decline geometrically in magnitude over time.

Substituting (6.18) into (6.19) gives an indirect period utility function defined over acquisitions of goods. Let MU_{1t} and MU_{2t} denote the partial derivatives of $\sum_{t=0}^{\infty}\beta^t U(s_{jt})$ with respect to e_{jt}^1 and e_{jt}^2 respectively; and P_t denote the relative price of durables in terms of non-durables. The Euler equations that have typically been studied for this model are

$$E_t MU_{1t} - E_t[MU_{1,t+1}r_{t+1}] = 0, \tag{6.20}$$

$$P_t E_t MU_{1t} - E_t MU_{2t} = 0. \tag{6.21}$$

Upon estimating the model for the period January 1959 through December 1978, Dunn and Singleton (1986) and Eichenbaum and Hansen (1989) found that overidentifying restrictions were typically not rejected at conventional significance levels for individual returns. The returns considered were the three-month real holding period returns on US Treasury bills for buy-and-hold and rollover investment strategies (Dunn and Singleton) and one-month holding period returns on one-month bills and an aggregate stock portfolio (Eichenbaum and Hansen). The lack of evidence against this model, especially using Treasury bill returns, stands in sharp contrast to the results for the single-good model with preferences given by (6.6). On the other hand, when the Euler equations for two different returns were examined simultaneously, there was substantial evidence against the overidentifying restrictions. In this respect, the results are similar to the earlier findings for the model (6.7).

Eichenbaum and Hansen (1989) also investigated a quadratic version of the S-branch utility function with the linear technology (6.19). Specifically, the function $U(s_{jt})$ was chosen to be the special case of (6.3) with $\sigma = 2$ and $\alpha = 2$:

$$U(s_{jt}) = -\{[s_{jt}^1 - \frac{\alpha_1}{2}(s_{jt}^1)^2] + [\alpha_2 s_{jt}^2 - \frac{\alpha_3}{2}(s_{jt}^2)^2] + \alpha_4 s_{jt}^1 s_{jt}^2\}, \tag{6.22}$$

$\alpha_1, \alpha_2, \alpha_3 > 0$. Preferences are non-separable across goods when $\alpha_4 \neq 0$, which is consistent with their results. A potentially important difference between the specifications (6.18) and (6.22) is that the quadratic model does not restrict the substitution elasticity between the service flows from 'non-durable' and 'durable' goods to unity. However, in spite of its more flexible substitution possibilities, chi square statistics with probability values of 0.004 and 0.006 are obtained using TBILL1 (Eichenbaum and Hansen (1989) and VWR1 (Singleton (1985)).

Three patterns of results emerge from these empirical studies of asset pricing models with multiple goods. First, for power utility, the introduction of durable goods seems to improve the fit of the models when individual returns are examined, perhaps with the exception of the one-month Treasury bill. For quadratic utility, the p-values remain small for

Table 6.5. *Parameter estimates for one- and two-good models of treasury bill returns[a], January 1959–December 1978*

Returns	$\hat{\beta}$	$\hat{\sigma}$	$\hat{\delta}$	$(1-\hat{\theta})$	$\hat{a}$	χ^2	DF
Unrestricted one-good model – Dunn and Singleton							
TBILL1	0.7843	*	*	*		18.37	3
	(0.0796)					(0.001)	
TBILL3	1.0095	*	*	*		11.113	3
	(0.1029)					(0.011)	
TB6H3	0.8260	*	*	*		9.97	3
	(0.0953)					(0.019)	
Unrestricted two-good model – Dunn and Singleton							
TBILL1	1.0025	−0.2194	0.8963	0.9908	0.2669	13.83	5
	(0.0013)	(0.5557)	(0.0415)	(0.0094)	(0.0465)	(0.017)	
TBILL3	1.0036	−0.9139	0.9228	0.9961	0.5460	6.38	5
	(0.0030)	(1.212)	(0.1552)	(0.0188)	(0.2241)	(0.301)	
TB6H3	1.0028	−0.6124	0.9322	0.9975	0.5577	76.38	5
	(0.0023)	(0.9110)	(0.1133)	(0.0116)	(0.2131)	(0.271)	
Restricted two-good models: $\sigma = 0$							
TBILL3	1.0016	0	0.8981	0.9933	0.6494	16.65	6
	(0.0003)		(0.0688)	(0.0121)	(0.3732)	(0.011)	
TB6H3	1.0140	0	0.8863	0.9914	0.5420	12.06	6
	(0.0003)		(0.0340)	(0.0081)	(0.2649)	(0.061)	
Restricted two-good model: $\beta = 0.996$							
TBILL3	0.996	0.9999	0.8860	0.9988	−0.7387	248.9	6
			(0.1175)	(0.0153)	(0.1183)	(0.000)	
TB6H3	0.996	0.9999	0.8294	1.0057	−0.8413	714.31	6
			(0.0602)	(0.0073)	(0.0129)	(0.000)	

Note:
[a] Standard errors of the coefficients and probability values of the test statistics are indicated in parentheses.

both TBILL1 and VWR1. Second, the fit of the consumption-based models is typically better for aggregate stock indexes and long-term bonds than for real Treasury bill returns. Third, there is substantial evidence against the overidentifying restrictions in models with durable goods, and for power and quadratic utility, when two or more returns are studied simultaneouly.

The improvement in fit from introducing durable goods into the single-good model (6.7) is documented in table 6.5. The first six rows are taken from tables 1 and 2 in Dunn and Singleton (1986). The probability values of the test statistics in rows 4 through 6 are substantially larger than the corresponding values in rows 1 through 3. There are two differences between the models with preferences given by (6.6) and (6.18)–(6.19) that might explain these results: services from NIPA durable goods enter (6.18) in a non-separable way and NIPA non-durable goods provide services for two periods according to the technology (6.19). The results reported in section 4 suggest that the introduction of durable goods is the source of the improvement in fit.

More direct evidence on this question is displayed in the seventh and eighth rows of table 6.5. The two-good model (6.18)–(6.19) was re-estimated with power utility and σ constrained to equal 0. With $\sigma = 0$, preferences are of the logarithmic form

$$U(s_{jt}) = \xi \log s_{jt}^1 + (1 - \xi) \log s_{jt}^2, 0 < \xi < 1, \tag{6.23}$$

which is separable across the decision variables s_{jt}^1 and s_{jt}^2. Although $\sigma = 0$ is well within a one standard deviation confidence interval for the runs with TBILL3 and TB6H3 (rows 5 and 6), restricting σ to equal zero leads to a substantial increase in the chi square statistic for the models (rows 7 and 8).[7] These results corroborate those of Eichenbaum and Hansen for quadratic utility and TBILL1, which also support non-separable specifications of preferences.

Comparable results for VWR1 are presented in table 6.6. Unlike the findings for Treasury bills, there is little evidence against either the one- or two-good models for the instruments chosen. Moreover, restricting σ to equal zero (logarithmic utility) in the two-good model leads to a comparable test statistic and more plausible point estimates of the share parameter δ and the decay parameter θ. It turns out that the hypothesis $\alpha_4 = 0$ cannot be rejected at conventional significance levels for the quadratic specification (6.22) (Singleton (1985)). Thus, there is not much evidence against the separable specification of utility (across service flows) when returns on common stocks are studied.

A plausible explanation for the results in tables 6.5 and 6.6 lies in the differences in the properties of the second moments of returns on stocks and Treasury bills. The aggregate stock return is much more volatile than Treasury bill returns. Also, bill returns exhibit large and significant autocorrelations at much longer lags than the aggregate stock return (table 6.2). Accordingly, the introduction of the smooth series 'services from durable goods', which is highly autocorrelated and correlated with bill rates, may well improve the fit of the model. On the other hand, because of their high volatility and low autocorrelation, stock returns continue to dominate the behaviour of the disturbance from the Euler equation (6.20),

Table 6.6. *Parameter estimates for one- and two-good models of the value-weighted return on the NYSE (VWR1)ª, January 1959–December 1978*

$\hat{\beta}$	$\hat{\sigma}$	$\hat{\delta}$	$(1-\hat{\theta})$	$\hat{a}$	χ^2	DF
One-good model – Hansen and Singleton						
0.9982	−2.035	*	*	*	1.07	1
(0.0045)	(1.876)				(0.301)	
Unrestricted two-good model						
1.0083	−4.181	0.9734	1.0029	0.3735	5.68	5
(0.0257)	(4.8345)	(0.5583)	(0.0319)	(0.0747)	(0.338)	
Restricted two-good model: $\sigma=0$						
0.9985	0	0.8452	0.9752	0.6279	5.96	6
(0.0024)		(0.0104)	(0.0092)	(0.4889)	(0.427)	
Restricted two-good model: $\beta=0.996$						
0.996	0.9999	0.9936	1.0053	−0.7651	5.56	6
	(0.2337)	(0.0116)	(0.4200)	(0.474)		

Note:
ª Standard errors of the coefficients and probability values of the test statistics are indicated in parentheses.

so the introduction of 'services from durable goods' does not affect the fit of the model.

In section 3 it was shown that the autocorrelation of the disturbance was not the only factor in the poor fit of the model. There was the additional consideration of the average values of the growth rate of consumption and the asset returns. The last two rows of table 6.5 display the results from estimating the two-good model with β restricted to equal 0.996 and σ restricted to be less than unity (utility to be concave).[8] The deterioration in the fit of the model with the imposition of these restrictions is even more striking when durable goods are included in the analysis. The chi square statistic is now enormous. Also, the estimated value of σ is essentially on the boundary of the parameter space, which is why a standard error is not reported for $\hat{\sigma}$. Finally, the estimated value of a indicates that past acquisitions of NIPA non-durable goods provide *disservices* in the current periods as in the presence of habit formation.

For comparison, the restricted two-good model was re-estimated using VWR1 as the return and the results are displayed in the last row of table 6.6. Once again σ is on the boundary of the parameter space and a is negative. However, in contrast to the results for Treasury bills, the chi square statistic has changed little from the value for the unrestricted model. This seems to be yet another piece of evidence supporting the view that, with the high variability and low autocorrelation of VWR1, little information can be extracted about the structure of preferences of agents from aggregate stock return and consumption data alone over the holding periods considered here.

Would a smaller value of σ improve the fit of the model? Certainly more risk aversion will induce more volatility in the intertemporal marginal rate of substitution of consumption. Nevertheless, it turns out that decreasing σ leads to a *deterioration* in the fit of the model. This deterioration can be documented in three complementary ways. First, for the single-good utility function (6.6) with $\sigma < 0$, a smaller value of σ increases $|\sigma - 1|$ and, hence, $\mu_{cn}^{\sigma-1}$ falls, where $\mu_{cn} (>1)$ is the average value of (c_{t+n}/c_t). Consequently, for the orthogonality condition (6.9) to be satisfied using Treasury bill returns, $\hat{\beta}$ would have to exceed unity by more than it does in table 6.1. In particular, the data do not support a smaller value of σ and a value of β less than unity.

Second, Dunn and Singleton (1986) investigated the implications of changing σ for the 'unconditional' risk premiums implied by the utility functions (6.18)–(6.19). An implication of the Euler equation (6.20) for any two n-period returns is that

$$E[r_{t+n}^1] - E[r_{t+n}^2] = - \text{Cov}[r_{t+n}^1 - r_{t+n}^2, MU_c^*(t+n)]/E[MU_c^*(t+n)], \tag{6.24}$$

where $MU_c^*(t)$ is the marginal utility with respect to c_t scaled by $[(s_t^1)^{\delta\sigma-1}(s_t^2)^{(1-\sigma)\sigma}]$ (in order to allow for real growth in acquisitions of goods). Letting $n = 3$ and choosing r_{t+3}^1 and r_{t+3}^2 to be the returns TBILL3 and the three-month real return on a six-month bill (TB6H3), Dunn and Singleton found that the sample estimate of $(E[r_{t+3}^1] - E[r_{t+3}^2])$ was -0.0012, while the estimate of the right-hand side of (6.24) (calculated at the point estimate $\hat{\sigma} = -1.66$) was 1.37×10^{-7}. The estimated risk premium is much too small and has the wrong sign. Moreover, decreasing $\hat{\sigma}$, holding all of the other parameters fixed at their estimated values, leads to a larger positive value of the sample unconditional premiums. Thus, as risk aversion is increased the difference between the sample excess return and the premium (which according to the theory should be equal to the excess return) increases.

Third, Hansen and Jagannathan (1989) recently derived admissible regions for the means and standard deviations of the MRSs implied by the ICAPM. These regions are non-parametric in that they can be computed using return data alone, are preference free and, therefore, can be used to assess the goodness-of-fit of a wide class of preference specifications. This is accomplished by computing the mean and standard deviation of the MRS for a candidate parametric model and then checking whether this pair lies in the admissible region implied by the time series properties of the returns being investigated. A special case of the Hansen–Jagannathan bound was computed by Dunn and Singleton (1986) for their preferences defined over non-durable and durable goods. They found that a value of σ less than -200 was required for the sample variance of the marginal utility to exceed its sample lower bound computed for short-term bill returns. The admissible mean-standard deviation region for the MRS was not explored.

Hansen and Jagannathan (1989) and Heaton (1991) have computed mean-standard deviation frontiers for single-good, non-time separable models. For values of a near zero and values of σ near zero, the implied mean-standard deviation pair for the MRS lies well outside the admissible region. Decreasing σ (increasing relative risk aversion) increases the standard deviation of the MRS. However, it also leads to a substantial decline in the mean of the MRS and, hence, an increase in the implied real interest rate. This unfavourable trade-off is amplified by positive values of a (durability), consistent with the findings in Dunn and Singleton.

Introducing habit formation through negative values of a does lead to fitted mean-standard deviation pairs for the MRS that are close to the admissible region. For instance, Heaton (1991) finds that with $a = -0.8$ and σ near -30, the computed moments for the MRS are close to satisfying the Hansen–Jagannathan bounds. The high degrees of habit persistence and relative risk aversion used in these computations are notable and indicative of the difficulty of fitting the first and second moments of returns using aggregate consumption data. In the estimation of Euler equations using instrumental variables procedures, the point estimate σ is often much smaller in absolute value and a has often been estimated to be positive. This conflict between the mean-standard deviation frontier calculations and IV estimates of Euler equations is explained by the use of different sets of moment conditions in the two estimation procedures. As implemented by Dunn and Singleton (1986) and Ferson and Constantinides (1991), the moment restrictions used in estimation and testing of the Euler equations were more comprehensive than those used to compute standard deviation bounds on the MRS.

5.2   Introducing leisure into asset pricing models

The intertemporal asset pricing models discussed up to this point have all assumed implicitly or explicitly that preferences are separable across consumption and leisure choices. Two recent studies have replaced this assumption with the assumption that utility can be represented as a non-separable function of non-durable goods and leisure plus a separable function of the services from durable goods.[9]

Mankiw, Rotemberg and Summers (1985) examined models in which the period utility function was given by

$$U(c_t, l_t) = \frac{1}{1-\gamma} \left[\frac{c_t^{1-\alpha} - 1}{1-\alpha} + d\frac{l_t^{1-\xi}}{1-\xi} \right]^{1-\gamma}, \tag{6.25}$$

where c_t and l_t denote consumptions of non-durable goods and leisure at date t, respectively. When $\alpha = \xi$, (6.25) becomes the CES form of the utility function. This particular utility function is not a special case of the S-branch function introduced in section 2. Thus, empirical studies using this function should be interpreted as studies of a 'representative stand-in consumer', and not of a representative agent obtained from exact demand aggregation across a large number of individual consumers with possibly different endowments. In addition, the model implies the following deterministic relation between consumption, leisure and the real wage rate

$$\frac{w_t \partial U/\partial c_t}{\partial U/\partial l_t} - 1 = 0. \tag{6.26}$$

Relation (6.26) is not satisfied by the data and, therefore, if (6.26) is required to hold then the model is trivially inconsistent with the data. To circumvent this difficulty, Mankiw, Rotemberg and Summers assume that, because of measurement problems or the presence of contracts, (6.26) holds only up to an additive error term.

Upon estimating the model using the three-month Treasury bill as the asset in their version of (6.1), the authors found substantial evidence against the model. In several cases, the concavity parameter $\hat{\sigma}$ was outside the concave region of the parameter space. Also, the chi square goodness-of-fit statistics were often in the 1 per cent critical region.[10] However, the utility specification (6.25), when combined with the econometric procedures used by Mankiw, Rotemberg and Summers, does not accommodate growth in per-capita consumption or the real wage. Also, implicit in (6.25) is the assumption that leisure provides services only in the current period. Thus, (6.25) does not permit the rich intertemporal substitution possibilities for leisure that Kydland and Prescott (1982) have shown to emerge from allowing leisure to provide services over time.[11]

An alternative model of consumption and leisure choice that avoided these limitations of the utility function (6.25) was studied by Eichenbaum, Hansen and Singleton (1988). They considered a version of the utility function (6.18)–(6.19) with s_t^1 denoting services from NIPA 'non-durables plus services' and s_t^2 denoting leisure services (durable goods were excluded from the analysis). The technology linking the service flow s_t^1 to acquisitions of 'non-durable' goods was given by the first row of (6.19). Two versions of the technology for producing leisure services were examined: the first was given by $[1 + bL/(1 - \eta L)]l_t$; and the second was given by $(l_t + bl_{t-1})$. The first specification is identical to the leisure service specification proposed by Kydland and Prescott (1982).

Eichenbaum, Hansen and Singleton estimated this model using TBILL1 as the return and several measures of hours worked for the period 1959 through 1978. Interestingly, the estimates of the parameter b in the leisure service technologies were always less than zero when the counterpart to the intertemporal relation (6.26) was included in the econometric analysis. In other words, the findings are consistent with current leisure providing *disservices* in future periods, which is not consistent with intertemporal substitution of leisure.[12]

Another interesting feature of their results is that $\hat{\sigma}$ was always less than unity (concave utility) and $\hat{\beta}$ always exceeded unity. Furthermore, for most of the specifications considered, $(\hat{\beta} - 1)$ was more than five standard deviations from zero. The probability value of the chi square goodness-of-fit statistics ranged between 0.0001 and 0.02, so even with β unconstrained there was evidence against the model. It seems likely that restricting β to be less than unity would lead to a further deterioration in the fit of the model.

These observations suggest that many of the limitations of models with single or multiple consumption goods carry over to models that incorporate leisure in a non-separable way. This is perhaps not surprising in light of the fact that per-capita hours of leisure time have not grown substantially over this period and the variation in l_t is small relative to asset returns. Consequently, the estimate of β is still largely determined by the relative values of the growth rate of consumption and the average real interest rate. Introducing leisure does not help in explaining the co-movements of aggregate consumption and interest rates observed historically.

6   NON-STATE SEPARABLE PREFERENCES

The preferences examined in sections 3 through 5 are in the class of von Neuman–Morgenstern preferences. Recently, Epstein and Zin (1990), Giovannini and Jorian (1989) and Hansen and Singleton (1990) among others investigated the empirical properties of a particular class of non-state separable preferences for which agents are not indifferent to the timing of the temporal resolution of uncertainty. The Euler equations implied by their models may be fundamentally different from those, for example, implied by the HARA class in that the representative agent's marginal rate of substitution is a function of the return on the aggregate wealth portfolio. In this section we briefly describe the models in these papers and then assess the extent to which they fit the consumption and return data better than the corresponding state separable models.

Agents are assumed to maximise the following recursive utility function

$$U_t = [c_t^{\gamma-1} + \beta(E_t U_{t+1}^a)^{(1+\gamma)/a}]^{1/(1+\gamma)}, \qquad a \neq 0, \tag{6.27}$$

$$U_t = [c_t^{\gamma-1} + \beta\exp\{(\gamma+1)E_t(\log U_{t+1}|I_t)\}]^{1/(1+\gamma)}, \qquad a = 0. \tag{6.28}$$

The parameter a may be interpreted as the relative risk-aversion parameter and $-1/\gamma$ is the intertemporal elasticity of substitution of consumption. Thus, (6.28) is the case of logarithmic risk aversion.

The first-order conditions for this model are

$$\beta^{a/(\gamma+1)}E_t\{[c_{t+1}/c_t]^{a\gamma/(\gamma+1)}\mathcal{M}_{t+1}^{a/(\gamma+1)}\} = 1, \tag{6.29}$$

$$\beta^{a/(\gamma+1)}E_t\{[c_{t+1}/c_t]^{a\gamma/(\gamma+1)}\mathcal{M}_{t+1}^{a/(\gamma+1)-1}R_{t+1}\} = 1, \tag{6.30}$$

where $\mathcal{M}_{t+1}$ and R_{t+1} are the one-period holding period returns on the wealth portfolio and any security in the agent's choice set, respectively. Notice that the return on the wealth portfolio appears in (6.30). In light of the significant correlation between the returns on common stocks and typical measures of the return $\mathcal{M}$, the marginal rate of substitution in (6.30) may have very different properties from those which are functions of consumption variables alone.

The empirical results in Epstein and Zin were mixed, however. The expected utility hypothesis was strongly rejected. At the same time, the overidentifying restrictions implied by their non-expected utility model were rejected for most instrument sets when returns on a common stock and a US Treasury bond were studied simultaneously. There was less evidence against the model when common stock returns were studied individually. Recall that the test statistics exhibited a similar pattern for the state separable, CRRA models.

The point estimate of a indicated that risk preferences were close to logarithmic. With logarithmic risk preferences, the asset return equations (6.30) reduce to those tested by Hansen, Richard and Singleton (1981) and Brown and Gibbons (1985). The test results reported in the former paper were generally not supportive of the model. Futhermore, equation (6.29) simplifies to a log-linear version of the Euler equation for the return on the wealth portfolio

$$E[\gamma\log(c_{t+1}/c_t) + \log\mathcal{M}_{t+1} + \log\beta|I_t] = 0. \tag{6.31}$$

This equation is nearly identical to the log-linear relation studied by Hansen and Singleton (1983), but here it is obtained without assuming log-normality of returns or consumption growth. The difference is in the constant term; in the expected utility models under log-normality, a constant conditional variance term also appears in the intercept. Also, (6.31) holds only for the return on the wealth portfolio, so these two models are not observationally equivalent for all returns.

Up to this point we have assumed that the decision interval of the agents coincides with the sampling interval of the data (typically monthly or quarterly). Christiano (1984), Grossman, Melino and Shiller (1987) and Hall (1988), among others, have emphasised that aggregation over time may lead to inconsistent estimates of the parameters of (6.31). They derived the following temporally aggregated version of (6.31)

$$E[\gamma(c^a_{t+1} - c^a_t) + r^a_{t+1} + k|I_{t-1}] = 0, \tag{6.32}$$

where c^a_t is the logarithm of the geometric average of instantaneous consumption flows over the sampling interval of the data and r^a_{t+1} is the logarithm of the geometric average return on an asset between dates $t+1$ and t. Also, the information set is lagged one period relative to the dating in (6.31), because temporal aggregation induced a moving-average error of order one. Hall estimated γ in (6.32) using monthly data on consumption and Treasury bill and aggregate stock returns, and with the coefficient on $(c^a_{t+1} - c^a_t)$ normalised to unity and the coefficient on r^a_{t+1} set to $(1/\gamma)$.[13] His estimate of $(1/\gamma)$ was near zero, which led him to conclude that agents have very small intertemporal elasticities of substitution.

However, this conclusion is not robust to the normalisation used in estimating γ. Campbell and Mankiw (1989) compared the results from estimating (6.32) with Treasury bills to those obtained from Hall's normalisation. If $(1/\gamma)$ is small, then γ should be estimated to be large. In fact, the estimates of γ were closer to unity. Similarly, Hansen and Singleton (1990) re-examined Hall's findings using estimation procedures that are invariant to renormalisation of (6.32). Their estimates of γ, obtained using the time-averaged value weighted return on the NYSE as M, were typically outside the concave region of the parameter space and imprecisely estimated. In addition, when r^a_{t+1} was taken to be the Treasury bill rate, the chi square goodness-of-fit statistics were large relative to their degrees of freedom. Thus, there was no evidence that accommodating temporal aggregation in this manner does not improve substantially the fit of the model or lead to more economically reasonable point estimates compared to previous studies of log-linear models.

7   CONCLUDING REMARKS

The research summarised in this chapter is best viewed as an early step towards providing a better understanding of the relations between movements in consumpion, production and asset prices. The results indicate that co-movements in consumption and various asset returns are not well described by a wide variety of representative agent models of asset price determination. There are several dimensions along which the models fit poorly. First, the average consumption growth rates were too large relative to average real asset returns during the post-war period in the USA to be consistent with these theories. In addition, the serial correlations of the disturbances do not match those implied by the models. Because of the relatively small volatility of aggregate consumption, the disturbances inherit the autocorrelation properties of the returns in the econometric equations. Finally, precise statements about the values of the parameters characterising preferences and the covariances of stock returns and consumption are not possible. The fit of the models with stock returns did improve some when the holding period was extended to one year, however, and the results on the autocorrelations of stock returns and industrial production over longer holding periods suggest that further analyses of these links over long holding periods is warranted.

There are several directions in which this research is currently proceeding. The paper by Scheinkman and Weiss (1986) illustrated the potential importance of incomplete insurance for consumption behaviour. Townsend (1986) has explored the properties of consumption and savings in dynamic models in which incomplete insurance arises endogenously due to private information. This work is at an early state and has not yet addressed return–consumption linkages. Similarly, Rogerson (1986) has explored some implications of fixed costs and the associated non-convexities for optimal labour supply decisions by households. All of these studies provide models which may imply substantial differences between the time series properties of aggregate and individual household consumption, leisure and savings.

At the individual security market level, work is also proceeding on the incorporation of heterogeneous beliefs into models of asset price determination. Hellwig (1980), Diamond and Verrechia (1981), Kyle (1984) and Altug (1986) among others, have deduced the properties of asset prices in a one-period model in which traders are heterogeneously informed and learn about the information of other traders from the equilibrium price. In Singleton (1987), a repeated version of these models is solved in order to study the autocorrelation properties of asset prices in a multi-period model. It is clear from these studies that noise introduced at the individual market level (see also Black (1986)) can lead to substantial volatility of prices on a week-to-week basis that obscures the influence of underlying fundamentals on asset prices. The empirical results presented in section 3 suggest that there are systematic links between stock returns and aggregate output over long holding periods. An interesting area for future research is the integration of these considerations into a model with multi-period consumption and leisure choices.

Third, and related to the first issue, progress is being made on modelling explicitly the motives for transacting in fiat money and the pricing of assets in monetary economies. Lucas (1984) and Townsend (1984) deduced asset pricing formulas in cash-in-advance economies and contrasted these relations to the counterparts in non-monetary economies. These and related models offer economic environments in which the negative correlation between stock returns and inflation can be explored.

Notes

Prepared for the *World Congress of the Econometric Society*, August 1990, in Barcelona, Spain. Comments were provided by Ken West. This research was supported by the National Science Foundation.

1 See, for example, Lucas (1978) and Hansen and Richard (1987). Hansen and Richard (1987) explore the inner product representation of asset pricing functions in much more general setups than the one considered here.

2 Eichenbaum, Hansen and Richard (1985) also discuss the case where the dimension of the endowment vector does not equal the dimension of s_{jt}.

3 The instruments were the constant unity, $(c_t/c_{t-1}), (c_{t-1}/c_{t-2}), r_{t-n}$ and r_{t-n-1}, where $n = 1, 6,$ or 12. Thus, five orthogonality conditions were used to estimate two parameters, leaving three overidentifying restrictions that are tested.

4 The moving-average representations were estimated using the non-linear least-squares algorithm in RATS. The standard errors displayed in table 6.2 should be interpreted with caution for at least two reasons. First, the disturbances u_{t+6}^{T6} and u_{t+6}^{V6} involve estimated parameters and the standard errors have not been adjusted for the randomness in the first-stage estimates. Second, the shocks underlying the MA representation may be conditionally heteroskedastic.

5 The instruments were unity, (c_t/c_{t-1}), and r_{t-12}^j for the jth disturbance, $j = 1,2$. This gives six othogonality conditions for use in estimating two parameters.

6 This model and instrument set corresponds most closely to the model underlying the second part of table 4, panel 3 in Ferson and Constantinides (1991). They used the return on the largest decile portfolio instead of VWR3 and the three-month return from rolling over the one-month Treasury bill instead of TBILL3.

7 The discrepancy between the test of $\sigma = 0$ using the large sample t ratio and the difference between the minimised objective functions as test statistics suggests that the large-sample distribution is not an accurate approximation to the small-sample distribution of one or both of these statistics.

8 Comparable results were obtained with $\beta = 0.998$.

9 There is an enormous literature on the linkages between consumption and leisure choices, but most of this literature does not consider explicitly the linkages between these choices and asset price behaviour.

10 Complementary evidence against similar models of consumption and leisure choice is presented in Clark and Summers (1982).

11 Mankiw, Rotemberg and Summers (1985) also did not allow 'non-durable' consumption goods to provide services over time, which is another potentially important source of misspecification.

12 Deaton (1985) provides complementary evidence against the representative agent model of consumption and leisure choice by comparing the co-movements of consumption and hours worked over the post-war period.

13 Grossman, Melino and Shiller (1987) and Hall (1988) also assumed that the first-order autocorrelation of the MA(1) expectational error associated with (6.32) was 0.25. It turns out that this is not an implication of their model when r^a_{t+1} is a short-term bond return; see Hansen and Singleton (1990) for a further discussion of this issue.

References

Altug, S. (1986), 'The Effect of Insider Trading by a Dominant Trader in a Simple Securities Model', manuscript, University of Minnesota.

Black, F. (1986), 'Noise', *Journal of Finance*, 41: 529–43.

Breeden, D. (1979), 'An Intertemporal Asset Pricing Model with Stochastic Consumption and Investment Opportunities', *Journal of Financial Economics*, 7: 265–6.

Brown, D.P. and Gibbons M.R. (1985), 'A Simple Econometric Approach for Utility-Based Asset Pricing Models', *Journal of Finance*, 40: 359–81.

Campbell, J. and Shiller, R. (1988), 'The Demand–Price Ratio and Expectations of Future Demands and Discount Factors', *Review of Financial Studies*, 1: 195–228.

Christiano, L. (1984), 'The Effects of Temporal Aggregation over Time on Tests of the Representative Agent Model of Consumption', manuscript, Carnegie-Mellon University.

Clark, K.B. and Summers L.H. (1982), 'Labor Force Participation: Timing and Persistence', *Review of Economic Studies*, 49: 825–94.

Constantinides, G. (1982), 'Intertemporal Asset Pricing with Heterogenous Consumers and Without Demand Aggregation', *Journal of Business*, 55: 253–67.

(1990), 'Habit Formation: A Resolution of the Equity Premium Puzzle', *Journal of Political Economy*, 98: 519–43.

Cox, J., Ingersoll, J. and Ross, S. (1985), 'A Theory of the Term Structure of Interest Rates', *Econometrica*, 53: 385–408.

Deaton, A. (1985), 'Life-cycle Models of Consumption: Is the Evidence Consistent with the Theory?', manuscript, Princeton University.

Diamond, D.W. and Verrecchia, R.E. (1981), 'Information Aggregation in a Noisy Rational Expectation Economy', *Journal of Financial Economics*, 9: 221–35.

Dunn, K.D. and Singleton K.J. (1983), 'An Empirical Analysis of the Pricing of Mortgage Backed Securities', *Journal of Finance*, 36: 769–99.

(1986), 'Modeling the Term Structure of Interest Rates Under Nonseparable Utility and Durability of Goods', *Journal of Financial Economics*, 17: 27–55.

Eichenbaum, M. and Hansen, L.P. (1989), 'Estimating Models with Intertemporal Substitution Using Aggregate Time Series Data', manuscript, University of Chicago.

Eichenbaum, M., Hansen, L.P. and Richard, S.F. (1985), 'The Dynamic Equilibrium Pricing of Durable Consumption Goods', manuscript, Carnegie-Mellon University.

Eichenbaum, M., Hansen, L.P. and Singleton, K.J. (1988), 'A Time Series Analysis of a Representative Agent Model of Consumption and Leisure Choice Under Uncertainty', *Quarterly Journal of Economics* (February): 51–78.

Epstein, L. and Zin S. (1989), 'Substitution, Risk Aversion, and the Temporal Behavior of Consumption and Asset Returns: A Theoretical Framework', *Econometrica*, 57: 927–69.

(1990), 'Substitution, Risk Aversion, and the Temporal Behavior of Consumption and Asset Returns II: An Empirical Analysis', manuscript, University of Toronto.

Ferson, W. and Constantinides, G. (1991), 'Habit Persistence and Durability in Aggregate Consumption: Empirical Tests', manuscript, University of Chicago.

Flavin, M.A. (1981), 'The Adjustment of Consumption to Changing Expectations about Future Income', *Journal of Political Economy*, 89: 974–1009.

Gallant, R. and Tauchen G. (1989), 'Seminonparametric Estimation of Conditionally Constrained Heterogeneous Processes: Asset Pricing Applications', *Econometrica*, 57: 1091–120.

Giovannini, A. and Jorian, P. (1989), 'Time-series Tests of a Non-expected Utility Model of Asset Pricing', NBER Working Paper No. 3195.

Grossman, S., Melino, A. and Shiller, R. (1987), 'Estimating the Continuing Time Consumption-Based Asset Pricing Model', *Journal of Business and Economic Statistics*, 5: 315–27.

Grossman, S.J. and Shiller, R.J. (1981), 'The Determinants of the Variability of Stock Market Prices', *American Economic Review*, 71: 222–7.

Hall, R.E. (1978), 'Stochastic Implications of the Life-Cycle-Permanent Income Hypothesis: Theory and Evidence', *Journal of Political Economy*, 86: 971–87.

(1988), 'Intertemporal Substitution and Consumption', *Journal of Political Economy*, 96: 339–57.

Hansen, L.P. (1982), 'Large Sample Properties of Generalized Method of Moment Estimators', *Econometrica*, 50: 1029–54.

Hansen, L.P. and Jagannathan, R. (1989), 'Implications of Security Market Data for Models of Dynamic Economies', NBER Technical Working Paper No.89.

Hansen, L.P. and Richard, S.F. (1987), 'The Role of Conditioning Information in Deducing Testable Restrictions Implied by Dynamic Asset Pricing Models', *Econometrica*, 55: 587–614.

Hansen, L.P., Richard, S. and Singleton, K.J. (1981), 'Econometric Implications of the Intertemporal Asset Pricing Model', manuscript, Carnegie-Mellon University.

Hansen, L.P. and Singleton, K.J. (1982), 'Generalized Instrumental Variables Esimation of Nonlinear Rational Expectations Models', *Econometrica*, 50: 1269–8.

(1983), 'Stochastic Consumption, Risk Aversion, and the Temporal Behavior of Asset Returns', *Journal of Political Economy*, 91: 249–65.

(1984), 'Addendum', *Econometrica*, 52: 267–8.

(1990), 'Efficient Estimation of Linear Asset Pricing Models with Moving-Average Errors', manuscript, Stanford University.

Heaton, J. (1991), 'An Empirical Examination of Asset Pricing with Temporally Dependent Preference Specifications', manuscript, MIT.

Hellwig, M.F. (1980), 'On the Aggregation of Information in Competitive Stock Markets', *Journal of Economic Theory*, 22: 477–98.

Kreps, D. and Porteus, E. (1978), 'Temporal Resolution of Uncertainty and Dynamic Choice Theory', *Econometrica*, 46: 185–200.

Kydland, F. and Prescott, E. (1982), 'Time to Build and Aggregate Fluctuations', *Econometrica*, 50: 1345–70.

Kyle, P. (1984), 'Equilibrium in a Speculator Market with Strategically Informed Trading', manuscript, Princeton University.

Lucas, R.E., Jr. (1978), 'Asset Prices in an Exchange Economy', *Econometrica*, 46: 1429–46.

(1984), 'Money in a Theory of Finance', in K. Brunner and A. Meltzer (eds.), *Carnegie-Rochester Conference on Public Policy Vol.21*, Amsterdam: North Holland.

Mankiw, G., Rotemberg, J. and Summers, L. (1985), 'Intertemporal Substitution in Macroeconomics', *Quarterly Journal of Economics*, 100: 225–52.

Mehra, R. and Prescott, E. (1985), 'The Equity Puzzle', *Journal of Monetary Economics*, 15: 145–61.

Rogerson, R. (1986), 'Nonconvexities and the Aggregate Labor Market', manuscript, University of Rochester.

Rubinstein, M. (1974), 'An Aggregation Theorem for Security Markets', *Journal of Financial Economics*, 1: 225–34.

(1976), 'The Valuation of Uncertain Income Streams and the Pricing of Options', *Bell Journal of Economics and Management Science*, 7: 407–25.

Sargent, T.J. (1978), 'Rational Expectations, Econometric Exogeneity, and Consumption', *Journal of Political Economy*, 86: 673–700.

Scheinkman, J. and Weiss, L. (1986), 'Borrowing Constraints and Aggregate Economic Activity', *Econometrica*, 54: 23–46.

Singleton, K.J. (1985), 'Testing Specifications of Economic Agents' Intertemporal Optimum Problems Against Non-Nested Alternatives', *Journal of Econometrics*, 30: 391–414.

(1987), 'Asset Prices in a Time Series Model with Disparately Informed, Competitive Traders', in W. Barnett and K. Singleton (eds.), *Austin Symposium in Econometrics*, Cambridge University Press.

Sundaresen, S.M. (1989), 'Intertemporally Dependent Preferences and the Volatility of Consumption and Wealth', *Review of Financial Studies*, 2: 73–89.

Townsend, R.M. (1984), 'Asset Prices in a Monetary Economy', manuscript, Carnegie-Mellon University.

(1986), 'Private Information and Limited Insurance: Explaining Consumption Anomalies', manuscript, University of Chicago.

Weil, P. (1989), 'The Equity Premium Puzzle and the Risk-free Rate Puzzle', *Journal of Monetary Economics*, 24: 401–21.

CHAPTER 7

Estimation of continuous-time models in finance

Angelo Melino

1   INTRODUCTION

Continuous-time stochastic processes arise in many applications in economics, but perhaps nowhere do they play as large a role as in finance. Following the pathbreaking work of Merton (1969, 1973) and Black and Scholes (1973), the use of continuous-time stochastic processes has become a common feature of many applications, especially asset pricing models. Even a casual comparison of the textbooks of the seventies (e.g., Fama and Miller (1972), Fama (1976)) with the current crop (e.g., Ingersoll (1987), Duffie (1988)) serves to demonstrate the remarkable speed with which the tools of stochastic process theory have been assimilated into mainstream finance. This survey will look at the specification and estimation of continuous-time stochastic processes. Although much of the discussion is relevant for other applications, I have chosen to write it from the perspective of someone interested in evaluating the empirical content of current continuous-time asset pricing models and in contributing to their future development.

It is interesting to speculate on the reasons for the widespread adoption of continuous-time models in asset pricing. Although many come to mind, I would argue that they have been widely adopted not because of their empirical properties but in spite of them.[1] The explosion and sophistication of theoretical research simply has not been matched by empirical work. Continuous-time asset pricing models typically involve restrictions linking the parameters of the price process to those of some underlying 'forcing' variables. In general equilibrium models, the forcing variables may be taste and technology. In option pricing models, they may be the term structure and/or the price of the underlying security. Tests of these models are invariably joint tests of 'nuisance' assumptions, including the specification of the forcing variable process. Although theoretical work allows for quite general specifications, most empirical work has used implausibly restrictive specifications.

One reason for the relative backwardness of empirical research in this area is that, except for a small number of specifications, estimation of continuous-time stochastic processes can be a daunting challenge. In large part, the difficulties stem from 'measurement' problems. Economic data do not come in the form of a continuous-time record. Available data are a sequence of observations. The data are often irregularly or randomly spaced. Moreover, the observations on the continuous-time process can take on a variety of forms. They may be measurements on the level of a process ('stocks'), such as an asset price, or on the integral of a process between two points in time ('flows'), such as consumption, or a mixture of both types.

The mapping that relates observed data to the parameters of the underlying process is generally very messy. The specifications for which this mapping is fairly tractable have therefore received most of the attention of empirical researchers. But this inordinate attention to 'tractable' functional forms has been costly. Although these popular functional forms may make estimation easier, they are often inappropriate for providing useful answers to substantive questions. For example, the popular geometric Brownian motion specification does a notoriously poor job of mimicking high frequency asset price data. As a result, practical men simply ignore empirical tests of asset pricing models that take seriously this specification. The absence of estimation strategies for more 'realistic' stochastic specifications has led to a variety of *ad hoc* empirical strategies that are less than satisfactory.

Recent developments promise to finally break the reliance on a few special functional forms and provide a strategy for estimating a variety of interesting processes. Although much remains to be done, with these conceptual and computational advances in estimation, perhaps soon empirical work can focus on the more interesting and challenging questions of model specification and testing.

This chapter has several goals. I hope it will serve as a useful guide to those seeking an introduction to the literature on estimation of continuous-time processes that arise as solutions to stochastic differential equations. I will focus principally on the details of estimation, with very little discussion of other issues such as identification or the sampling properties of the resulting estimators. There is a close link between model specification and estimation. I hope to provide a useful summary of the deficiencies and advantages of currently common specifications and estimation strategies, as well as some directions for future research.

The chapter is organised as follows. Section 2 provides a brief introduction to continuous-time stochastic processes. Notation and terminology is introduced and some common specifications are described. For the benefit of those unfamiliar with process theory, I have included an appendix that contains a summary of the relevant definitions and results. Section 3 provides a brief bibliometric evaluation of the importance of continuous-time stochastic processes in the major finance journals over the last two decades. I document current tendencies in specification and estimation strategies, and provide some critical discussion of these choices. I argue that there is a need to develop continuous-time specifications to empirical work which are multivariate and display conditional heteroskedasticity. The remainder of the chapter focusses on models with one or both of these properties. A fairly mature treatment of linear models is now available, and these models are examined in section 4, along with extensions that are 'essentially' linear. For a small but growing number of non-linear specifications it is possible either to characterise explicitly the likelihood or (generalised) moments of observed data in terms of the parameters of the underlying process. Section 5 looks at 'exact' methods for non-linear models of the Itô-Skorokhod variety. Given the difficulty in linking the observed data to the parameters of the underlying process, it is not surprising that approximations have a long history in literature on estimation of continuous-time models, and some of these strategies are reviewed in section 6. These strategies by their very nature have tended to be model specific. Section 6 concludes with an introduction to simulation estimators for continuous-time models. Although a variety of outstanding issues remain to be solved, simulation estimators are an exciting recent development with potentially very general applicability.

2   CONTINUOUS-TIME PROCESSES

2.1   General discussion and statement of the estimation problem

The following model arises often in finance. We are given a filtered probability space $(\Omega, \mathscr{F}, \mathbf{F}, P)$. On this space is defined an adapted process X, taking values in $\mathscr{R}^G$, of the form

$$X_t(\omega) = X_0(\omega) + \int_0^t \sigma(\tau, \omega) dS_\tau(\omega) \tag{7.1}$$

where X_0 is an $\mathscr{F}_0$ measurable random vector, S denotes an L-vector of semi-martingales, and σ is a $G \times L$ matrix of coefficients. The dimensions of

X and S are finite but otherwise unrestricted (i.e., we can have $G < L$, $G = L$, or $G > L$). It is sometimes convenient to write (7.1) in differential form, i.e., as

$$dX_t = \sigma(t)dS_t \qquad (7.2)$$

where the dependence on ω is suppressed (here and below) for convenience. The differential form is simply a shorthand notation. Although it serves to provide a heuristic representation of the process X, it has no meaning beyond (7.1). A more recent and compact notation for (7.1) is $X = X_0 + \sigma \cdot S$.

Developments in the theory of the stochastic integral over the last thirty years have been fairly rapid and are ongoing.[2] Historically, the stochastic integral was first proposed for Brownian motion, then for square-integrable martingales, and finally for processes which can be written as the sum of a locally square-integrable local martingale and an adapted RCLL process with paths of finite variation on bounded intervals. In Doléans-Dade and Meyer (1970), the (what is already referred to as 'classical') definition of a semi-martingale was first introduced. Alongside the advances in the class of integrators considered has been an evolution in the class of integrands, particularly in terms of informational requirements. Itô's original work considered Brownian motion and Lebesgue integrators and coefficients that were allowed to depend only upon time and the level of the process X_t. This theory was intimately linked to the study of Markov processes. Subsequent work breaks this link by considering coefficients which are adapted to the filtration $\mathbf{F}$. Since the natural filtration is contained in $\mathbf{F}$, in particular this allows the coefficients to depend upon the history of X in a very general way.

A wide variety of processes can be written in the form of (7.1) or (7.2). The class of semi-martingales includes as special cases: (i) adapted RCLL processes that have bounded variation a.s. P (e.g., $S_t(\omega) \equiv t$), (ii) point processes, (iii) processes with independent increments (including all Lévy processes), (iv) square integrable martingales, (v) martingales, and (vi) sub- and supermartingales. Since the class of semi-martingales is a vector space and is closed under localisation, it also includes linear combinations of the localised class of (i)–(vi). It is of some interest to note that both a variety of discrete-time processes and stopping times (i.e. durations) can also be treated under the rubric of (7.1). In particular, the process given by (7.1) can be a mix of what economists have traditionally considered to be discrete- and continuous-time processes.

Having noted that (7.1) allows for a good deal of generality, it must also be admitted that in some respects it may be too general. It may be difficult to identify the separate contributions of the coefficients and the semi-martingale integrators to the process X. These identification problems are exacerbated by the measurement problems that typically arise with economic data. Also, available estimation strategies that have been proposed for models of the form (7.1) have considered only a fairly narrow set of particular special cases.

For our purposes, the integral equation (7.1) is defined component-wise,[3] and for it to make sense certain restrictions must be imposed on the component functions σ_{ij}. The specific details of these restrictions is an area of ongoing research (see Jacod and Shiryaev (1987) or Protter (1990) for a discussion of the trade-offs). The restrictions generally take two forms: (a) measurability conditions on σ_{ij} (essentially, that it is predictable), and (b) restrictions on the range or rate of growth of σ_{ij}. The integral is always well-defined if the component functions of σ belong to the class of locally bounded predictable processes – indeed the class of semi-martingales is the largest class of processes with respect to which one can 'reasonably' integrate such integrands. On the other hand, for many of the special cases of semi-martingales listed above, more general integrands can be considered.

The estimation challenge posed by (7.1) is as follows. In applications, the coefficients σ and/or the probability law of the semi-martingales are assumed to depend upon a finite vector of parameters. The data available for analysis are produced by a measurement scheme that may itself depend upon parameters and yields a finite set of observations $Y = \{y_i; i = t_1, \ldots t_n\}$, where $y_i = g_i(X)$, for some functional g_i. Analysis of the measurement scheme, g_i for $i = 1, \ldots n$, alongside (7.1) is an integral part of the econometric problem. Although in some physical applications the data come in a complete-record analog form, the measurement scheme in economic applications can be very complicated. It may involve sampling some (or all) of the components of X at discrete points in time ('flows'), or as integrals over an interval of time ('stocks'). The observed data may be and/or include the range of the process ('high' and 'low') over an interval, or some other statistic calculated from the sample path. Components may be sampled at different, possibly irregular frequencies. The time between observations may be random. In finance, the measurement scheme may also include data on the prices of derivative assets which are deterministically linked to X by theory. Finally, the observed data may be corrupted by measurement error. Given the data Y, the task is to estimate the unknown parameters of (7.1) and the measurement scheme.

2.2 Examples

Some examples will help to clarify notation. For a leading example, set $G = 1$, $L = 2$, with the semi-martingale components t and W_t, where W_t

denotes a standard Brownian motion (or Wiener process). In differential form

$$dX_t = a(t, \omega)dt + b(t, \omega)dW_t \qquad (7.3)$$

where $a(t)$ is called the drift coefficient and $b(t)$ is called the dispersion coefficient. These coefficients are assumed to satisfy some conditions of the sort described above. The process X given by (7.3) will have, among other properties, continuous sample paths. If the coefficients are 'Markov', i.e., $a(t)$ and $b(t) \in \sigma(X_t)$ then X will be a Markov process, and in fact a diffusion process with diffusion coefficient $b^2(t, X_t)$. Three special cases which appear prominently in the empirical finance literature are the so-called Ornstein–Uhlenbeck (or arithmetic Brownian motion) process

$$dX_t = (a + AX)dt + bdW_t, \qquad (7.4)$$

the geometric Brownian motion process

$$dX_t = AXdt + BXdW_t, \qquad (7.5)$$

and the square-root process

$$dX_t = (a + AX)dt + c\sqrt{X}dW_t, \qquad (7.6)$$

where a, b, c, A, and B denote constants. All three of these processes are usefully viewed as special cases of the constant elasticity of variance (CEV) family. For our purposes, the CEV family will be defined by

$$dX_t = a(t, X_t)dt + cX^\gamma dW_t \qquad (7.7)$$

where the coefficient a is locally bounded and γ is a non-negative parameter.[4]

Conceptually, it is rather straightforward to replace the Brownian motion in (7.3)–(7.6) with any continuous local martingale (see Karatzas and Shreve (1988)), but this possibility has not been much pursued in empirical work. One reason might be due to the result that any continuous martingale can be represented in terms of a Brownian motion 'up to a random time change'. This topic is pursued in section 4.

In many physical applications, X_t might represent the position of a particle, so path properties such as continuity are compelling. In finance, this is seldom the case. Many assets (e.g., equities) are traded on regulated exchanges which have explicitly stated discrete increments (e.g., $\pm 1/8$) that price changes must take. Aside from these 'micro' discontinuities, rapid changes in asset prices (e.g., October 1987 crash) may also be usefully viewed as arising from a discontinuity. Assuming that X is RCLL, then any discontinuities are of the form $\Delta X_t > 0$, where $\Delta X_t \equiv X_t - X_{t-}$. Modelling jumps requires a joint distribution for the number of jumps in a given interval along with the size of jumps when they occur. The canonical example assumes that the number of jumps in a given interval of time is Poisson. One often sees in financial models the specification

$$dX_t = a(t, X_{t-})dt + b(t, X_{t-})dW_t + c(t, X_{t-})dN_t \qquad (7.8)$$

where N_t denotes the Poisson process with intensity $\lambda = E(N_1)$. Heuristically, the interpretation of (7.8) is that X_t looks like a solution of (7.3) until a jump $\Delta X_t > 0$ occurs. At the time of the jump, the process is increased by $c(t, X_{t-})$. Beginning from this new value, the process once again looks like a solution of (7.3) until the next jump occurs. Merton (1971) suggested using $c(t, X_t) = -X_t$, along with geometric Brownian motion coefficients for a and b, as a way of modelling bankruptcy. Related specifications for modelling jumps include the serially correlated Poisson process (Oldfield *et al.* (1977)), and a Bernoulli process (Ball and Torous (1983)). Shimko (1989) suggests an interesting specification where the intensity of the Poisson process is random and assumed to be a diffusion.

A more general treatment would replace the Poisson contribution in (7.8) by an integer-valued random measure. Both the distribution of the times between jumps and conditional distribution for the size of the jumps could then be allowed to depend on all the available information (such as the history of the process), essentially subject only to the requirement of predictability (see Jacod and Shiryaev (1987), chapter 2).

2.3   On the continuity of paths and time

Within the class of processes given by (7.1), jump processes are conceptually simpler but asset pricing models for diffusion processes are more developed. One might well ask what (if anything) is lost in restricting attention exclusively to either continuous-path or jump processes.

Although path continuity is compelling in many physical applications, it is hard to make the same argument in finance. Recent work dealing with the micro-structure of markets often examines data on a transaction by transaction basis. Data at this frequency are becoming increasingly available and force the researcher to take seriously the path properties of asset prices. For example, on organised exchanges, asset prices are discrete and there are often institutional regularities that govern the set of possible transitions. In fact, since the bid–ask spread is large relative to the changes in observed transactions prices, one must recognise when working at such high frequencies that there are really two prices – one if you are buying and another if you are selling. It may even be necessary to think of these prices as points on schedules with values depending upon the size and timing of the order flow (e.g., Kyle (1985)). It is unsettling that diffusion models of asset prices should look so inappropriate for describing extremely high frequency data, since this is exactly the setting where they should be most relevant. Diffusion models can describe these data, but only if they are combined with some fairly complicated measurement scheme (e.g., recorded trades only occur in some subset of those times where the 'true' price crosses either the bid or the ask).

In many cases, the data are available at some fixed frequency such as daily, weekly, monthly, etc. Ironically, as we go to these lower frequencies, the 'micro' details about path properties seem much less important, and a diffusion model for asset prices (with point sampling) appears less questionable. Indeed, given even daily data one might well ask how can continuity (much less non-differentiability) of sample paths have any empirical content?

Path continuity by itself is not restrictive if we simply wish to describe the distribution of an asset's price measured at some fixed frequency, such as daily. It may be convenient and fruitful to model an asset price as a semi-martingale driven by Brownian motion and Poisson processes (e.g., Jorion (1988)), but the identification of the jump contribution in such a specification is due to the restriction that the continuous component be a Brownian motion. However, path continuity does seem to matter if we impose restrictions suggested by economic theory on the joint distribution of asset prices and other variables. Economic theory gives empirical content to sample path properties, because the links across asset prices and other variables are sometimes sensitive to path properties. Consider, for example, the case of an option written on an asset. If the asset's price follows a diffusion process, then the options payoff can be replicated by a dynamically weighted portfolio of the asset and 'cash'. This is the insight behind the Black–Scholes formula linking the price of the asset to options written on it. If the asset's price follows a diffusion process with jumps, then this replication is no longer possible. The price of the option relative to the underlying asset will be sensitive to the decomposition of the asset's price into its continuous and jump components.

Just as theorists have revealed a preference for continuous-time continuous-path models of asset prices, empirical researchers have tended to prefer to work with discrete-time models (which can be viewed as a particularly simple kind of jump process). From a statistical perspective, data measured at some fixed frequency, such as daily or weekly, is simply a stochastic sequence. There exist a rich variety of modelling strategies to capture the 'structure' in these data. For example, ARMA models can be used to summarise the linear structure in the conditional mean, and ARCH models provide a convenient summary of the conditional second moment. These two approaches can be combined and the conditioning set can be expanded easily. With enough data, non-parametric approaches can be used to approximate quite general distributions. Any underlying continuous-time model that is introduced as a data-generating process for the stochastic sequence must be viewed as a latent variable. Why bother with it at all?

The most common assumption in empirical work is that economic agents make and act upon decisions at the same frequency as the available data. For example, given quarterly observations, the applied researcher often begins with a model where the economic agent has preferences defined over quarterly integrals of the consumption flow. The association of the timing of decisions to the frequency of observations is convenient for empirical work but leads to its own difficulties. The predictions of economic models are not invariant to the length of the decision interval. Changes in the frequency at which decisions are made and acted upon constitute a real change in the economic environment and can have important implications for model predictions. For example, an investor choosing to allocate his wealth between common stocks and Treasury bills and who is allowed to rebalance his portfolio once a year faces a very different risk/return trade-off than the investor who is allowed to rebalance much more frequently.

In the best of all worlds, economic theory would endogenise the frequency of decisions and actions by agents. Such a model would probably not involve a fixed frequency at all, and would introduce some fascinating heterogeneity as individuals and institutions would undoubtedly choose to work at different frequencies, given their specific circumstances and abilities.

An often useful and powerful alternative to the assumption that agents make decisions at the same frequency as the available data is to assume that decisions are made in continuous time. From a purely statistical point of view, introducing the latent continuous-time process can be a convenient way of handling some measurement difficulties, such as time-averaging or irregular spacing of observations.[5] In addition, the latent process may have parameters that are invariant to some class of interventions (such as varying the observation frequency). However, the main justification for introducing an imperfectly observed continuous-time process must be that the restrictions imposed by theory are most conveniently imposed on the parameters of the latent process.[6] If these restrictions impose some over-identifying structure on the class of distributions for the stochastic sequence, then parsimony and estimation efficiency provide a justification for introducing the latent process. It is true that applied researchers can appeal to either discrete- or continuous-time asset pricing theories as a source of restrictions. At nearby frequencies, such as daily versus continuous, the distinctions are probably not very large. However, the continuous-time theories seem to produce sharper predictions. Merton (1975), and more recently in his preface to Merton (1990), provides some nice discussion of the relative merits of discrete versus continuous-time theorising.

3   A LOOK AT CURRENT PRACTICE

What sort of stochastic processes appear in the finance literature and how are they currently estimated? This section presents the results of a simple bibliometric exercise that provides a partial response to this question.[7] The data are culled from four prominent finance journals: *Journal of Finance*, *Journal of Financial Economics*, *Journal of Financial and Quantitative Analysis* and *Review of Financial Studies*. All papers and shorter notes, beginning with the first issue available in 1970 or thereafter, are included in the analysis.

Table 7.1 documents the rapid and remarkable growth of continuous-time stochastic models in finance. Virtually non-existent in the early seventies, continuous-time models have grown steadily in importance, and in the late eighties they appeared in about 15 per cent of the papers published in these journals. A disproportionate number of these papers are concerned with asset pricing and, in particular, option pricing.

In order to obtain information on the relative importance of various specifications and how they are used, I divided all the papers concerned with continuous-time stochastic models into the exclusive categories of 'Empirical' or 'Other'. I define 'Empirical' broadly to consist of papers that report estimation or simulation results, or are concerned with algorithms to improve the speed and/or accuracy with which these results are computed. Papers not falling into this category (such as this survey!) are classified as 'Other'. This dichotomy serves to highlight the differences in specification tendencies between papers where the specifications are actually used to compute something observable, and those that don't. For each paper, the specification of the continuous-time processes was recorded and some summary statistics calculated. Many papers considered a variety of specifications. For any papers labelled 'Empirical', I followed the convention of recording those specifications that were actually used in the estimation or simulation results. For the papers labelled 'Other', I made some judgement as to the paper's value added in deciding which specification(s) to highlight. Since the results reflect a good deal of subjective judgement, the usual caveats apply. Nonetheless, I think the exercise is informative.

Table 7.2 summarises the main findings. Using my generous definition, just over 60 per cent of the papers concerned with continuous-time processes are classified as 'Empirical'. Within this group, the great majority

Table 7.1. *Continuous-time stochastic models in finance journals 1970–89*

Year	No. of continuous-time articles	Total no. of articles	% of articles dealing with continuous-time
1970	1	125	0.8
1971	0	143	0.0
1972	1	173	0.6
1973	1	176	0.6
1974	1	214	0.5
1975	2	186	1.1
1976	13	187	7.0
1977	17	253	6.7
1978	17	203	8.4
1979	14	186	7.5
1980	20	174	11.5
1981	14	159	8.8
1982	20	155	12.9
1983	15	203	7.4
1984	24	172	14.0
1985	21	164	12.8
1986	27	166	16.3
1987	19	160	11.9
1988	23	186	12.4
1989	31	181	17.1

Sources: Based on articles and shorter notes appearing in *Journal of Finance, Journal of Financial Economics, Journal of Financial and Quantitative Analysis,* and *Review of Financial Studies.*

of applications (85.6 per cent) deal with univariate specifications. Many papers in this category look at more than one univariate specification, but geometric Brownian motion stands out prominently as the most common specification. Jumps and/or jump-diffusions appear in just over 13 per cent of the papers. There has been a growing trend towards bivariate specifications in the 'Empirical' literature, and they constitute 11.5 per cent of the papers over the entire sample. In this sample, multivariate specifications appear rarely in 'Empirical' papers. The distribution of specifications in the 'Other' category shows some interesting contrasts. In a nutshell, about 20 per cent fewer of these papers look at geometric Brownian motion, but posit a multivariate specification instead.

The bottom half of table 7.2 provides some summary statistics on the sort

Table 7.2. *Part A: Specifications used in continuous-time models*

Type of process appearing	Empirical		Other	
	No. of papers	% of all empirical	No. of papers	% of all other
Univariate	149	85.6	69	63.9
Constant elasticity of variance	134	77.0	49	45.4
Geometric Brownian motion	106	60.9	41	40.0
Square-root process	9	5.2	2	1.9
Ornstein–Uhlenbeck	3	1.7	4	3.7
Jump or jump-diffusion	23	13.2	11	10.2
Bivariate	20	11.5	9	8.3
Multivariate	5	2.9	31	27.8
Totals (% of total)	174	(61.7)	108	(38.3)

Part B: Type of empirical work presented

	No. of papers	% of empirical papers
Estimation	76	44.8
Implicit estimation	38	21.8
Maximum likelihood	24	13.8
Method of moments	6	3.4
Approximation strategy	20	11.5
Simulation	87	50.0
Algorithm	17	9.8

Sources: Data are based on the same sample period and journals as in table 7.1.

of empirical work presented. Simulations are the most popular kind of empirical work in this sample. Exactly half of the papers used simulations to convey a sense of the empirical consequences of their model. About 10 per cent of the papers were concerned with algorithms, principally for pricing options. A little less than half of the 'Empirical' papers actually presented estimation results. A few papers (most of which looked at jump processes) used method of moments. Any papers estimating a geometric Brownian motion that reported the historical standard deviation were classified as using maximum likelihood. Even so, less than one quarter of the papers reporting estimation results used this estimation strategy. About as common as maximum likelihood is some sort of approximation strategy. Typically, this involves taking a discrete-time approximation to the continuous-time process and then estimating the parameters of the discrete-time approximation. Approximation strategies are the modal choice for bivariate and multivariate specifications. Implicit estimation was used by almost one-half of the papers reporting estimation results, with the fraction over the second half of the sample being even larger.

The patterns reported in table 7.2 prompt a number of observations. In particular, the popularity of the geometric Brownian motion specification merits some scrutiny. This specification appears prominently in over half of all the papers in the sample dealing with continuous-time stochastic processes. Geometric Brownian motion enjoys the benefits of tractability and historical precedent. What makes its popularity puzzling, however, is that it is well known that it does a remarkably poor job of mimicking the stochastic properties of asset price data. Returns on a wide variety of assets measured at high frequencies, such as daily or weekly, display a number of regularities. In particular, it is well documented that their frequency distribution has fat tails (Fama (1965) is a classic reference), and displays predictable conditional heteroskedasticity (see Bollerslev *et al.* (1990)). The geometric Brownian motion specification is also inconsistent with a number of regularities in first and second moments linked to calendar time, such as day-of-the-week effects, day-of-the-month effects, and seasonal patterns. Estimates of the variance of returns vary widely across sample periods and give little support to the hypothesis of homoskedasticy (Schwert (1989)). Discrete-time specifications which reflect these regularities are fairly well developed and are an area of ongoing research. Yet, with a few exceptions, these regularities are ignored in empirical work that uses continuous-time specifications. I'm at a loss to understand why. Shouldn't we impose the same standard of conformity with the data on continuous-time specifications?

Bob Solow once declared, 'There are no interesting bivariate relationships in economics.'[8] Anyone glancing at table 7.2 can take some comfort that the great majority of continuous-time work, especially in empirical applications, considers only univariate specifications. Nonetheless, there is clearly a need to develop multivariate specifications that are tractable but capture the salient features of financial data. The contrast in table 7.2 is clear – multivariate specifications abound in finance, but (in general) applied researchers simply don't have available to them the tools required to estimate and test these specifications.[9]

The last set of comments that I would like to make on tendencies and trends in the specification of continuous-time processes is motivated by the popularity of 'implicit estimation' in finance applications. To take a leading example, consider the problem of pricing a European option (call or put) on a stock. The justly famous Black–Scholes formula is derived under a number of assumptions, such as the underlying stock price follows a geometric Brownian motion. It expresses the price of the option as a deterministic function of a number of variables, including the diffusion coefficient or volatility (but not the drift) of the stock price process. A so-called 'historical' estimate of volatility is defined by estimating the parameters of the Brownian motion from stock price data. An 'implicit' estimate of volatility is obtained by inverting the Black–Scholes formula to solve for that unknown value of volatility for which the formula gives the 'best' fit to observed option prices. Implicit estimates of the stock volatility ignore the data on stock prices, except to the extent that the current price is required as an input into the Black–Scholes formula (of course, it can be estimated implicitly as well). Implicit estimators have the non-trivial advantage of being robust to misspecification of the drift. However, the deterministic link between inputs and the predicted option price, which accounts for much of the theory's appeal, is also the source of considerable embarrassment. In theory, one only needs the price of one option on any given day to estimate exactly the value of the stock's volatility. In practice, implicit estimates of the volatility vary both with the characteristics of the option (maturity, call or put, in-or out-of-the-money, etc.) and with time. Current practice is to select some loss function for the various prediction errors on, say, any given day and then to choose the implicit estimate of volatility by minimising the loss function. Taken literally, the implicit estimation strategy is fraught with internal inconsistencies. There should be considerable unease about a procedure that uses the assumption that volatility is constant to produce estimates of volatility that often change significantly from day to day![10] A more generous interpretation is that volatility is not assumed to be constant and that implicit estimators are actually estimating some sort of 'average' volatility expected to obtain over the life of the option. This turns out to be a rather loose statement that is hard to make precise. It holds literally (in the sense that there is a known model that generates this prediction) only if the path of volatility over the life of the option is deterministic, or at least measurable with respect to current information. Otherwise, both lack of indifference to volatility risk and Jensen's inequality introduce an error. In any case, because the option's predicted price is linked deterministically to inputs, this line of reasoning still has the strong and empirically doomed prediction that once the researcher has appropriately controlled for maturity, implied estimates of volatility will not vary across option characteristics at any point in time.[11]

Clearly, information about the stochastic properties of an asset's price is contained both in the history of the asset's price and the price of any options written on it.[12] Current strategies for combining these two sources of information, including implicit estimation, are uncomfortably *ad hoc*. Statistically speaking, we need to model the source of prediction errors in option pricing and to relate the distribution of these errors to the stock price process. Absent this, we have a variety of 'approximate' predictions with absolutely no sense of how big or regular 'approximate' errors should be.

4   LINEAR MODELS

Stochastic integrals with linear (in X) coefficients have been extensively studied. For such processes, explicit solutions of X in terms of its initial value and the driving semi-martingales are available. These solutions are interesting in their own right and often can be used to suggest an estimation strategy. In many examples, an explicit solution makes it straightforward either to characterise the conditional moments of X_t (given X_0), or even to write down the conditional likelihood of X_t.

Before considering extensions, it is useful to begin with a relatively simple case. Consider the process $X = (X_t \in \mathscr{R}^G; t \in \mathscr{R}_+)$ which satisfies the stochastic differential equation

$$dX_t = (a(t, \theta) + A(t, \theta)X_{t-})dt + \sum_1^L b_i(t, \theta)dM_t^i \qquad (7.9)$$

where $\theta \in \mathscr{R}^K$ is a vector of parameters, $M \equiv (M^1, \ldots, M^L)'$ is an L-tuple of orthogonal locally square-integrable martingales, and the coefficients $a(t, \theta), b_i(t, \theta) \in \mathscr{R}^G$ and $A(t, \theta) \in \mathscr{R}^{G \times G}$ are non-stochastic, measurable and locally bounded (but need not be continuous). Equation (7.9) generalises in an obvious way the univariate Ornstein–Uhlenbeck process and plays a large role in empirical applications. Solutions to (7.9) closely mimic the development in the deterministic case. To simplify notation, suppress the dependence on θ and let $b(s)$ denote the matrix whose columns are $b_i(s)$.

Let $\Phi(t)$ denote the solution to the matrix differential equation

$$d\Phi(t) = A(t)\Phi(t)dt \qquad \Phi(0) = 1. \qquad (7.10)$$

It can be shown, for each θ, that Φ is unique and non-singular. Using Itô's formula (put $Y = (t, X)$ and $f(Y) = \Phi^{-1}X$) for semi-martingales, we see that X has the representation

$$X_t = \Phi(t)[X_0 + \int_0^t \Phi^{-1}(s)a(s)ds + \int_0^t \Phi^{-1}(s)b(s)dM_s]. \qquad (7.11)$$

Note that the second integral in (7.11) is an L^2-martingale on $[0, t]$. It follows immediately that the conditional mean of X_t (given X_0) is

$$E(X_t|X_0) = \Phi(t)[X_0 + \int_0^t \Phi^{-1}(s)a(s)ds]. \qquad (7.12)$$

The calculation of the conditional variance is a little bit more involved. For simplicity assume the local martingales have deterministic quadratic variation (i.e., they are Levy processes) and normalise $<M^i, M^i>_t = t$. The conditional variance (assuming that X_0 and M are independent) is given by

$$V(X_t | X_0) = \int_0^t \Phi^{-1}(s) b(s) b'(s) \Phi^{-1\prime}(s) ds. \tag{7.13}$$

In the important special case where M is a vector of standard Brownian motions, then the conditional distribution is multivariate normal.

Most econometric analysis of models such as (7.9) has proceeded in a slightly different framework.[13] Bergstrom (1983, 1984) considers a class of stochastic integrals that are closely related. Let ξ denote a vector of random measures on $\mathcal{R}^G$, i.e., each component of ξ is a family $(\xi^i(\omega; dt); \omega \in \Omega)$ of signed measures (for our purposes) defined on $(\mathcal{R}_+, B(\mathcal{R}_+))$ satisfying $\xi_i(\omega; \{0\}) = 0$ identically. Random measures arise in a variety of contexts (see Jacod and Shiryaev (1987), chapter 2). Many semi-martingales naturally induce a random measure. For example if $A(t, \omega)$ is a finite variation process, we can set $\xi^i([0, t]) = A(t, \omega) - A(0, \omega)$. The Wiener measure satisfies $P(\xi^i([0, t]) \le c) = P(W(t, \omega) - W(0, \omega) \le c)$, where c is any constant and W is a standard Brownian motion. The Poisson measure is given by $\xi^i([0, t]) = N(t, \omega) - N(0, \omega)$, where N_t is a Poisson process with intensity $\lambda = E(N_1)$. Note that we could also use a standardised (compensated) Poisson process to induce the random measure, namely $(N_t - \lambda t)/(\lambda t)^{1/2}$.

Let A and B denote two sets in $B(\mathcal{R}_+)$, and let $\lambda_{A \cap B}$ denote the Lebesgue measure of the set $A \cap B$. Bergstrom restricts attention to random measures that satisfy $E(\xi(A)) = 0$ and $E(\xi(A)\xi(B)') = \lambda_{A \cap B} \Sigma$, where Σ is a symmetric, positive-definite matrix.[14] Bergstrom uses random measures to develop a theory for linear stochastic differential equations of the form

$$dX_t = (a(t, \theta) + A(t, \theta) X_t) dt + b(t, \theta) \xi(dt). \tag{7.14}$$

The solution can be expressed as

$$X_t = \Phi(t)[X_0 + \int_0^t \Phi^{-1}(s) a(s) ds + \int_0^t \Phi^{-1}(s) b(s) \xi(ds)]. \tag{7.15}$$

Notationally and conceptually, (7.11) and (7.15) are very similar. Bergstrom's approach interprets the integral in (7.15) as an L^2-limit of a sequence of approximating sums, and leads to a second-order theory. The distinction between (7.11) and (7.15) seems unimportant in practice. Both approaches lead to the same characterisation of the first two (conditional) moments and allow for an asymptotic sampling theory that does not rely on Gaussianity of the process X_t. Much has been made of the fact that the random measure solution (7.15), by allowing discontinuities, does not restrict the conditional distribution of X_t given X_0 to be Gaussian. The same can be said about (7.12) if we allow discontinuities in the sample paths of M.[15]

A large and important part of the continuous-time econometric literature has dealt with the problem of estimation of higher-order continuous-time AR models. Following Bergstrom (1983), such processes can be represented by

$$D^{p-1}X_t = D^{p-1}X_0 + \int_0^t (a + A_1 X_s + \ldots + A_{k-1}D^{p-1}X_s)ds + \xi([0, t])$$

(7.16)

where the vector a and the matrices A_i are non-stochastic and constant. If the vector a depends upon time (either explicitly or through exogenous variables), the model is referred to as 'open'. Using the method of expansion of states, (7.16) can be put in the first-order form (7.14). Bergstrom (1983) shows that if X_t is point-sampled at regular intervals, then it will follow an ARMA$(p, p-1)$ process. By contrast, if X_t is measured as a stock, it will have an ARMA(p, p) representation. Bergstrom (1983) shows how to use these representations to construct Gaussian quasi-likelihoods for X_t. Initially, his strategy was restricted to the stable case (which rules out processes displaying unit roots or cointegration), but this limitation has since been relaxed (Bergstrom (1985)). Although the representations are of direct interest, computational strategies that attempt to exploit Bergstrom's discrete-time representations for X_t are algebraically and computationally tedious beyond $p = 2$.

Harvey and Stock (1985) represents a computational watershed. They showed how to use a continuous-time Kalman filter to construct the quasi-likelihood. The Kalman filter approach embeds a treatment of measurement problems which is extremely powerful and well suited to continuous-time applications. Harvey and Stock (1985) show how to handle mixed observations on flows and stocks, irregular spacing, classical measurement error and partial observability. Open systems are treated transparently. The initialisation of the filter also provides a good deal of flexibility in specifying initial information $\mathcal{F}_0$. Zadrozny (1988), building on these results, provides a variety of useful improvements. He shows that the mixed case can be handled with a smaller state vector than originally proposed. Zadrozny generalises (7.16) to a class of continuous-time ARMA processes. The Kalman filter is well suited to dealing with the case where the components of X_t are measured at different frequencies, and Zadrozny fills in the details for this application. He also incorporates the results of Van Loan (1978) to provide compact expressions for the various matrix exponentials and integrals of matrix exponentials that appear in the calculation of the quasi-likelihood.

In summary, estimation of processes that satisfy (7.16) is very well developed for a rich variety of measurement schemes. To date, however, applications in finance have tended to ignore these tools. A justification for this neglect is not hard to find. Unfortunately, these models are ill-suited for many applications in finance. The emphasis in (7.16) is in capturing the linear structure in the conditional first moment. The conditional second moment is posited to be constant. For high frequency financial data, specifications with the opposite features are needed. High frequency asset returns display very little linear structure in the mean. However, the symptoms of autoregressive conditional heteroskedasticity are not hard to find. Moreover, in many financial applications (such as option pricing) all the interest is in capturing the second-moment structure. Specifications of processes with constant second moments may be ubiquitous in finance, but it is generally conceded that empirical tests which take this feature seriously should be ignored.

4.1   General linear stochastic difference equations

One way to specify a more interesting second-moment structure is to allow the coefficients on the martingale integrators in (7.9) to depend upon the process X. If we make this dependence linear, we are led to the specification

$$dX_t = (a(t, \theta) + A(t, \theta)X_{t-})dt + \sum_1^L (b^i(t, \theta) + B^i(t, \theta)X_{t-})dM_t^i \quad (7.17)$$

where the non-stochastic coefficients $A(t, \theta)$, $B^i(t, \theta)$ are in $\mathcal{R}^{G \times G}$ and a, b^i are in $\mathcal{R}^G$. Wu (1985) examines in detail the case where the martingales in (7.17) are assumed to be independent Brownian motions, and also treats the case of continuous semi-martingales. Specification (7.17) generalises in a natural way both the univariate Ornstein–Uhlenbeck and geometric Brownian motion processes. The special case $b^i = 0$ appears prominently in many term structure applications (Brennan and Schwartz (1979, 1980, 1982), Courtadon (1982) and Ogden (1987)).

In order to solve (7.17), it is useful to embed it in a more general problem. Notice that we can express (7.17) in the form

$$X_t = H_t + \sum_0^L \int_0^t B^i(s)X_{s-}dS_s \quad (7.18)$$

where H_t is a vector of semi-martingales given by

$$H_t = X_0 + \int_0^t a(s)ds + \sum_1^L \int_0^t b^i(s)dM_s^i \quad (7.19)$$

and the coefficients B^i, and the semi-martingales S^i have the obvious definitions. Define $V = \sum_{0 \le i \le L} \int B^i(s)dS^i$. Note that V is a $G \times G$ matrix of semi-martingales. Let U denote the right stochastic exponential of V (see Protter (1990), chapter 5), i.e., the (unique) matrix valued solution to

$$U_t = I + \int_0^t dV_s U_{s-}. \tag{7.20}$$

U_t is invertible if V is continuous, or if the jumps of V satisfy some regularity conditions (Protter (1990), theorem 5.63). In the case where all the components of V are continuous, the solution of (7.18) can be written as

$$X_t = U_t[X_0 + \int_0^t U_s^{-1}(dH_s - \sum_{i=0}^L B^i(s)d[H, S^i]_s)]. \tag{7.21}$$

It is immediate to verify that (7.11) emerges as a special case if $B^1 = \ldots = B^L = 0$. Using the representation (4.13), one can compute the conditional first and second moments of the point-sampled X_t given X_0, and build a second-order theory similar to that available for (7.11). It is fairly straightforward to show that the conditional first moment for this process is also given by (7.12); in fact this is true even if the martingales are possibly discontinuous and correlated. However, expressions for the conditional second moments are messy. Courtadon (1982) provides conditional moments for the univariate case, assuming $b = 0$ and the martingale is a Brownian motion (see also Karatzas and Shreve (1988), section 5.6). The general linear specification (7.17) aptly demonstrates one of the important difficulties in estimating continuous-time processes. Aside from the prominent special cases of arithmetic and geometric Brownian motions, the conditional distribution of X_t given X_0 is not known.

4.2 Time deformation

A relatively simple strategy for introducing conditional heteroskedasticity into models such as (7.11) is to distinguish between calendar and operational time, as described in Stock (1987, 1988). In his time deformation model, the process X operates in 'operational' time τ. Operational time is linked to calendar time by a transformation $\tau = g(t)$, so the observed data vector (assuming point sampling) is $Y_t = X(g(t))$. A simple example of the separation of operational and calendar time is the common asssumption in empirical finance that a process evolves in 'market time'. This assumption is used to justify the practice of treating data sampled only on days when organised markets are open as equally spaced observations on the latent process X. Clark (1973) proposed that the transformation $g(t)$ be treated as random (see also the discussion by Mandelbrot (1973)). In particular, he argued that trading volume was a good proxy for 'operational time'. By allowing the increments of the time-scale deformation g to be random or depend upon 'forcing variables' it is possible to induce interesting non-linearities that can be interpreted as conditional heteroskedasticity.

General specifications for 'operational time' lead to models that are difficult to estimate. Stock's approach essentially maintains the linear structure of (7.11). Let z_{t-1} denote an m-vector of forcing variables that are measurable with respect to the information available to the econometrician at time $t-1$. Stock suggests choosing a time-scale transformation by setting $g(0)=0$ and specifying piece-wise the time derivative $\dot{g}(\tau; z_{t-1})$ for $\tau \in (t-1, t]$. Although $\dot{g}(\tau; z_{t-1})$ can be very general, he suggests the parametric representation[16] $\dot{g}(\tau; z_{t-1}) = \exp(c'z_{t-1})$. This specification ensures that operational time cannot 'reverse' itself. It also implies that between observations the process runs at a constant speed, so that the increment to operational time between observations satisfies $g(t) - g(t-1) = \exp(c'z_{t-1})$. If $c=0$, then operational and calendar time coincide. Variations in $g(t) - g(t-1)$ affect both the conditional mean and the conditional second moment. A large change $g(t) - g(t-1)$ means that these conditional moments will tend to resemble their unconditional counterparts. In many applications in finance, the effect on the first moment won't be noticeable (since there is very little first-moment predictability). Serial correlation in z, however, can induce serial correlation in second moments which will resemble ARCH. Stock (1988) considers the class of models given by (7.16) for the latent X process. He estimates a variety of models, including a bivariate relationship involving GNP and interest rates. His time deformation variables (z) include lagged values of X and a business cycle indicator. A major advantage of the time-deformation model as implemented by Stock is that it ties in very easily to the continuous-time Kalman filter. The specification reduces to a linear model with uneven but measurable spacing. This permits the important flexibility in dealing with measurement problems and computational advantages described above.

4.3   Linear model with continuous martingale integrators

The derivation of the conditional second-moment matrix (7.13) required the assumption that the predictable quadratic co-variations satisfied $< M^i, M^j >_t = \delta_{ij} t$. Relaxing this assumption is a natural way of introducing conditional heteroskedasticity that also provides an interesting perspective on the time-deformation model. For simplicity, consider the first-order univariate case with $a=0$, $b=1$, and A constant. The solution (7.11) can then be written as

$$X_t = e^{AT} X_0 + \int_0^t e^{A(t-s)} dM_s \qquad (7.22)$$

where M is assumed to be a continuous local martingale. Define the stopping time $T(s) = \inf\{t \geq 0; <M,M>_t > s\}$. Under mild regularity conditions (Karatzas and Shreve (1988), section 3.4), the process $W_s = M_{T(s)}$ is a standard one-dimensional Brownian motion and $M_t = W<M,M>_t$. Moreover, we have the following equality

$$\int_0^t e^{A(t-s)}dM_s = \int_0^{<M,M>_t} e^{A(<M,M>_t - T(s))}dW_s. \tag{7.23}$$

To develop further the analogy with the time-deformation model, let $g(t) = <M,M>_t$ and follow Stock's suggested procedure for specifying $g(t)$ described above. Because of the piece-wise linearity of $g(t)$, we obtain that the conditional distribution of X_t given X_{t-1} is Gaussian with mean $e^A X_{t-1}$ and variance

$$V(X_t|X_{t-1}) = \exp(c'z_{t-1}) \int_{t-1}^t e^{2A(t-s)}ds. \tag{7.24}$$

The expression in (7.24) makes it clear that variations in z can generate conditional heteroskedasticity. In the multivariate case, each martingale can be given it's own 'clock' to capture multivariate ARCH effects. With Stock's specification for $g(t)$, the continuous-time Kalman filter can be employed to estimate the process. Other specifications for the predictable quadratic variation are available, but unfortunately lead us out of the class of linear models. For example, if we assume that the predictable quadratic variation is absolutely continuous with respect to Lebesgue measure, i.e., $d<M,M>_t = \sigma(\omega,t)dt$, then we are led to a random volatility model (e.g., Melino and Turnbull (1990)). The relative simplicity of Stock's specification is obtained by combining a linear continuous-time model for the process X with a discrete-time specification for the 'conditional variance' or 'clock speed'.

5   NON-LINEAR MODELS

Outside the class of linear (or essentially linear) models described above, most estimation strategies used by applied researchers are 'approximate' in the sense that they involve approximations either to the likelihood or the moments of the point-sampled continuous-time process. However, an 'exact' theory is available for some special cases where the coefficients and driving semi-martingales are suitably restricted. Consider once again the class of processes satisfying

$$dX_t = a(t, X_t)dt + b(t, X_t)dW_t + c(t, X_{t-})dN_t \tag{7.25}$$

where W_t is a standard Brownian motion, and N_t is an independent Poisson process with intensity λ. Processes satisfying (7.26) go by a variety of names including Itô–Skorokhod, generalised Itô, and jump diffusion. Whatever the name, there is an extensive literature.

Itô–Skorokhod processes are a subclass of the family of continuous-time (strong) Markov processes. Results from that literature can be used to derive sufficient conditions for the existence and uniqueness (in terms of probability of law) of the Markov process given by (7.25). The transition probability function for X is characterised by certain analytic properties. In some happy cases, this characterisation can be used to solve explicitly for the transition probability function. It is then a short step to solve for the likelihood function of the sample, assuming the data are point-sampled (at possibly irregular intervals) and free of the various measurement difficulties described in section 2.1.

Before considering the general equation (7.25), it is useful to specialise to the pure diffusion case ($c = 0$),

$$dX_t = a(t, X_t)dt + b(t, X_t)dW_t. \tag{7.26}$$

For clarity, sometimes the solution to (7.26) initialised at $X_s = x$ will be denoted $X_t^{(s,x)}$. Feller suggested studying the distribution of the process X through the transforms

$$u(s, t, x) = T_{s,t}f = Ef(X_t^{(s,x)}) \tag{7.27}$$

for functions $f \in L \subset BC(\mathscr{R}^G)$, the space of bounded continuous functions. If the space of functions L is 'big enough' (such as any superset of $C_0^\infty(\mathscr{R}^G)$, the space of infinitely differentiable functions having compact support), then the transforms uniquely determine the transition probability function $P(s, x, t, \Gamma) \equiv P\{X_t \in \Gamma | X_s = x\}$, and hence, since X is Markov, the distribution P^x of X.

Suppose there exists a solution to (7.26) that is unique in probability. The set of functions u that satisfy (7.27) have a number of special properties, that are most easily expressed as properties of the associated operator $T_{s,t}$. For example, it is immediately apparent that $T_{s,t}$ is a linear operator that maps bounded functions into bounded functions. Among other properties, the two-parameter family of operators $\{T_{s,t}\}$ is a semi-group (because X is Markov) with generator A_s given by

$$A_s = \frac{1}{2}\sum_{i,j}^{G} a^{i,j}(s, x)\frac{\partial^2}{\partial x_i \partial x_j} + \sum_i^{G} a^i(s, x)\frac{\partial}{\partial x_i} \tag{7.28}$$

where $a \equiv bb^T$. One approach to studying the distribution of the process X is to turn these properties around: Given the generator A_s, does it uniquely determine a two-parameter family of operators with the requisite properties? Posing this question for arbitrary generators provides a vehicle for studying general Markov processes (including diffusions).[17] Our interest is in processes with generators that are second-order differential operators of the form (7.28).

Stroock and Varadhan (1979) show that if the coefficients α and a are sufficiently regular (i.e., bounded or satisfy a Lipschitz condition) then u in (7.27) satisfies the following partial differential equation

$$\frac{\partial u}{\partial s} + A_s u = 0 \qquad (7.29)$$

with

$$\lim_{s \uparrow t} u(s, t, x) = f(x). \qquad (7.30)$$

(7.29)–(7.30) is known as the Cauchy problem. Existence and uniqueness of a solution to the Cauchy problem for all $0 \le s < t < \infty$ and $f \in L$ is therefore linked to existence and uniqueness of a probability measure for the process X that solves (7.26). A fundamental solution of the Cauchy problem is a non-negative function $p(s, x, t, y)$ defined for $0 \le s < t < T$ with the property that for every $f \in C_0(\mathscr{R}^G)$ the function

$$v(t, x) = \int_{\mathscr{R}^G} p(s, x, t, y) f(y) dy \qquad (7.31)$$

is bounded, of class $C^{1,2}$, and satisfies (7.29) and (7.30). If the coefficients are suitably regular (see Karatzas and Shreve (1988) section 5.7 for sufficient conditions and references) a fundamental solution exists and is unique. Comparing (7.31) to (7.27), we see that the fundamental solution is the transition probability density for the process $X^{(s,x)}$.

The connection with the Cauchy problem suggests a strategy for computing the transition probability density. For fixed (t, y), the fundamental solution $p(\cdot, \cdot, t, y)$ satisfies (7.29), also called the backward Kolmogorov equation. With additional regularity conditions on the coefficients, and for fixed (s, x), $\phi = p(s, x, \cdot, \cdot)$ will also satisfy the forward Kolmogorov equation

$$\frac{\partial}{\partial t} \phi(t, y) = \frac{1}{2} \sum_{i,j}^{G} \frac{\partial^2}{\partial y_i \partial y_j} [a^{i,j}(t, y)\phi(t, y)] - \sum_{i}^{G} \frac{\partial}{\partial y_i} [a_i(t, y)\phi(t, y)]. \qquad (7.32)$$

If we can solve (7.29) and (7.30), or (7.32) along with the boundary condition that $P(t, x, t, \Gamma)$ is the indicator function, we have the conditional likelihood of X_t given X_s.

The pure jump case ($a = b = 0$) is relatively straightforward. Given $X_s = x$, the waiting time to the next jump is exponentially distributed with expectation $1/\lambda$, where λ is the intensity of the Poisson process. The magnitude of a jump that occurs at time t is given by $c(t, X_{t-})$.[18]

Lo (1988) discusses the general stochastic differential equation (7.25). He shows, under suitable regularity conditions of the coefficients, that the transition probability density for X (if it exists) must solve a partial differential equation that is closely related to the forward Kolmogorov equation. Unfortunately, he does not provide existence or uniqueness results. However, he suggests that this partial differential equation can be used to verify any conjectured solution, and provides an example to illustrate his point.

The link between the probability law for Itô–Skorokhod processes and problems involving the solution of partial differential equations is useful in establishing existence and uniqueness results. More to the point, for some specifications (e.g., Feller (1951), Lo (1988)) it has led to explicit solutions for the transition probability laws in cases where more direct probabilistic reasoning fails. This is particularly true for problems displaying special boundary behaviour, such as absorbing barriers (but see Ikeda and Watanabe (1989), section 4.7). Nonetheless the limitations of this 'exact' approach are numerous. Even if the coefficients satisfy the requisite regularity conditions, solving a second-order partial differential equation such as (7.32) in a 'closed form' so that the likelihood can be computed is akin to a measure zero event. In my opinion, this has led to an inappropriate emphasis on those specifications whose coefficients lead to a partial differential equation (such as those of classical physics) that has been extensively studied.[19] This class of specifications is much too narrow, and does not lead to models which adequately mimic asset price data. As a final comment, it is not obvious how to go beyond the likelihood for the point-sampled data and deal with the various measurement issues described in section 2.1.

6   APPROXIMATION STRATEGIES

Given the difficulty in deriving and/or computing the exact likelihood or moments of the sample of observations $\{Y_1, \ldots, Y_n\}$ on the continuous-time process X, it is not surprising that applied researchers have often turned to some sort of approximation. Approximation strategies often exploit special features of the model at hand, so it is difficult to provide a general framework that encompasses the wide variety of strategies that have been pursued.

A fairly common approach is to approximate the continuous-time model of interest by a more tractable model, usually a discrete-time specification. The researcher proceeds as if the data were generated by the discrete-time model and estimates the parameters of the approximating model by maximum likelihood or (generalised) method of moments. In some applications, the objective function associated with these estimators of the approximating model is itself approximated in order to simplify further.

To fix ideas, consider a leading special case. Suppose X is a univariate Itô process and the observed data are obtained by point-sampling X at regular intervals, denoted h. We have

$$X_t - X_{t-h} = \int_{t-h}^{t} a(s, X_s; \theta_0)ds + \int_{t-h}^{t} b(s, X_s; \theta_0)dW_s \qquad t = 0, h, \ldots, nh \tag{7.33}$$

and the measurement scheme $Y_i = X_{ih}$. An approximating discrete-time model for (7.33) is obtained by approximating the two integrals that appear. One suggestion is

$$X_t - X_{t-h} \approx a(t-h, X_{t-h}; \theta_0)h + b(t-h, X_{t-h}; \theta_0)[W_t - W_{t-h}]. \tag{7.34}$$

By analogy to the deterministic case, (7.34) is called the stochastic Euler approximation. The approximate model for the observed data is then

$$Y_i = Y_{i-1} + a(ih-h, Y_{i-1}; \theta_0)h + b(ih-h, Y_{i-1}; \theta_0)h \cdot u_i \tag{7.35}$$

where $u_i \sim \text{NID}(0,1)$. Using the approximation (7.35), one can construct the quasi-loglikelihood

$$QL(Y; \theta) = -\frac{n}{2}\ln(2\pi) - \sum_{i=1}^{n} \ln(b(ih-h, Y_{i-1}; \theta)h)$$

$$\frac{1}{2}\sum_{i=1}^{n}\left[\frac{Y_i - Y_{i-1} - a(ih-h, Y_{i-1}, \theta)h}{b(ih-h, Y_{i-1}, \theta)h}\right]^2. \tag{7.36}$$

Maximising the quasi-loglikelihood (7.36) provides an estimator $\hat{\theta}$.

Even this very simple example leads to several variations. Dietrich–Campbell and Schwartz (1986) recommend transforming X (and therefore the measurement equation), if possible, to set $b(\cdot, \cdot)$ equal to a constant function, so that only the first integral in (7.33) needs to be approximated. The simple Euler approximation used to obtain (7.34) can be replaced by alternative schemes. For example, the first integral in (7.33) can be approximated by

$$\int_{t-h}^{t} a(s, X_s; \theta_0) \approx \frac{a(t, X_t; \theta_0) + a(t-h, X_{t-h}; \theta_0)}{2}. \tag{7.37}$$

Similarly, there are several suggestions for improving the approximation to the stochastic integral in (7.35).[20] The important question is how well the estimators induced by these various approximations behave in practice. Unfortunately, there are few available results.

There is a relatively large literature on the ability of continuous-time models to approximate discrete-time models and vice versa, e.g., Jacod and Shiryaev (1987), Nelson (1990a, 1990b), and He (1989). Nonetheless, papers that investigate the properties of an estimator based on the approximating model are much rarer, and (ironically) most of these deal with situations where exact methods are also available.

Sargan (1976) considers the linear stochastic differential equation (7.14), with constant coefficients. He assumes the data are point sampled at equally spaced intervals of length h. Sargan studies the properties of various estimators (2SLS, 3SLS and ML) of the drift coefficients based on the approximation (7.35), but with the drift term replaced by (7.37). He shows that the biases tend to be $O(h^2)$, and that the differences between the plims of the 3SLS and ML estimators is $O(h^5)$. Bergstrom (1984) shows that using the approximation for the drift term in (7.35) produces biases that are $O(h)$.

Results about the quality of the approximation (7.35) for non-linear specifications is sketchy. Melino and Turnbull (1991) provide some specific evidence for various members of the CEV family. Using daily data on six exchange rates, they computed both the exact ML estimator and the quasi-ML estimator based on (7.36). They report that the point estimates of the drift parameters were sensitive to the use of an exact or approximate method. However, the drift parameters tended to be inaccurately ·estimated, and the differences in the point estimates were never large compared to the standard errors obtained from either the exact or approximate likelihood. Both exact and quasi-likelihood estimates of the volatility parameter had small standard errors and were found to be virtually identical. Melino and Turnbull (1991) also report that the maximised values of the exact and approximate log-likelihood were virtually identical. In a more systematic comparison, Tse (1990) uses Monte Carlo methods to compare the properties of the exact and approximate ML estimators for the arithmetic and geometric Brownian motion models. His design is meant to mimic the behaviour of a stock price process sampled at one-, four-, and thirteen-week intervals. Tse's conclusions are similar to those of Melino and Turnbull (1991), although he finds more noticeable differences, for his longest sampling interval.

In summary, available results about the quality of simple approximations such as (7.35) for high frequency, point-sampled financial data are encouraging. However, economists have had very limited computational experience with continuous-time models and must be cautious about extrapolating these results. This is particularly true for measurement schemes aside from the point-sampled case. The applied researcher needs to know for a specific model and data set at hand if the biases and/or losses of efficiency induced by approximations are large relative to either sampling error or some substantive economic yardstick. With minor exceptions, available results do not provide a simple way to obtain such a quantitative estimate. Results such as those of Sargan (1976) and Bergstrom (1984) are sometimes useful in ranking approximations or estimators, but only computational experience can provide the judgement required to decide when an $O(h^2)$ error is large! Ultimately, to be able to judge the quality of computationally attractive approximations such as (7.35), we will have to develop more powerful estimation strategies that are computationally feasible and allow us to *control* arbitrarily well for the effects of approximation.

6.1 Simulation models

Many latent variable models have the property that it is difficult to compute the likelihood or (generalised) moments of the observed data. Nonetheless, for a particular candidate parameter vector, it is often fairly straightforward to simulate the latent process and compute statistics, such as averages or event frequencies, that can be compared in a natural way to statistics based on the observed data. By comparing observed statistics to analogous simulated statistics, it is possible to form a heuristic judgement about the plausibility that a given data set was generated from the model under consideration. Repeating the exercise with different choices of the parameter vector to see which provides the closest fit between observed and simulated statistics amounts to an *ad hoc* estimation procedure. As the bottom half of table 7.2 documents, using simulation as a heuristic procedure for estimation and specification testing of continuous-time models has been very popular in the finance literature. In an exciting new development, formal estimators that build on the simple intuition of this heuristic procedure have been introduced. Originally proposed for cross-section applications (such as limited dependent variable models) by Pakes and Pollard (1989) and McFadden (1989), simulation estimators have been adapted to continuous-time problems by Duffie and Singleton (1988), and Bossaerts and Hillion (1990).

Before considering extensions, it is useful to begin with a fairly simple example that illustrates the basic approach and results. Consider a process X that satisfies the stochastic differential equation

$$dX_t = a(t, X_t; \theta_0) + b(t, X_t; \theta_0)dW_t \tag{7.38}$$

with X_0 fixed, and where $\theta_0 \in \Theta$ denotes the true parameter vector. Assume the observed data are point sampled, so we have a sample $Y = \{y_1, \ldots, y_N\}$, where $y_i = X_{t_i}$ for time $t_i \in T = \{t_1, \ldots, t_N\}$. Suppose further that the coefficients are sufficiently regular for strong uniqueness. We can think of (7.38) as a mapping from the particular Brownian motion W into the process X. If we randomly draw another Brownian motion $\hat{W}$, then we can construct the process $\hat{X}(\theta)$ that solves (for fixed $\theta \in \Theta$)

$$d\hat{X}_t(\theta) = a(t, \hat{X}_t(\theta); \theta)dt + b(t, \hat{X}_t(\theta); \theta)d\hat{W}_t \qquad (7.39)$$

with $\hat{X}_0(\theta) \equiv X_0$. Put $\hat{y}_i = \hat{X}_{t_i}(\theta)$ and denote the simulated sample by $\hat{Y}(\theta) = \{\hat{y}_1(\theta), \ldots, \hat{y}_N(\theta)\}$. It is easy to see that Y and $\hat{Y}(\theta_0)$ have the same multivariate distribution. In particular, for any integrable p-valued function f, we have

$$E[f(y_i, \ldots, y_{i-J}) - f(\hat{y}_i(\theta_0), \ldots, \hat{y}_{i-J}(\theta_0))] \equiv E[f_i(Y) - f_i(\hat{Y}(\theta_0))] = 0. \qquad (7.40)$$

The component functions of f may include first and uncentred second moments, auto-covariances, etc. Subject to identification and other regularity conditions, (7.40) suggests a moment-type estimator, namely

$$\hat{\theta}_a = \underset{\theta \in \Theta}{\mathrm{argmin}} \left\| \frac{1}{N} \sum_i [f_i(Y) - f_i(\hat{Y}(\theta))] \right\| \qquad (7.41)$$

for some suitably chosen norm $\|\cdot\|$.

We can think of $f_i(\hat{Y}(\theta_0))$ as providing an unbiased estimator of the expected value of $f_i(Y)$. This leads to a useful interpretation which links $\hat{\theta}_a$ to the more familiar GMM estimator. To simplify notation, I will suppress dependence on θ.

Manipulating the argument in (7.41) leads to

$$\frac{1}{N}\sum_i [f_i(Y) - f_i(\hat{Y})] = \frac{1}{N}\sum_i [(f_i(Y) - Ef_i(Y)) + (Ef_i(Y) - f_i(\hat{Y}))]$$

$$\equiv \frac{1}{N}\sum_i [(f_i(Y) - Ef_i(Y)) + (Ef_i(Y) - \hat{E}_a f_i(Y))]$$

$$\equiv \frac{1}{N}\sum_i [(f_i(Y) - Ef_i(Y)) + u_a(i)]. \qquad (7.42)$$

By construction, the two terms in (7.42) are independent and $Eu_a = 0$. If u_a were exactly zero, then $\hat{\theta}_a$ would reduce to the GMM estimator. As a point of reference, it is helpful to imagine a case where the GMM estimator is consistent and asymptotically normal, and ask how these properties are affected by the introduction of the simulation error u_a.[21] Loosely speaking, there are two important changes. The simulation error u_a can induce additional dependence among the summands in (7.43). This temporal dependence can interfere with the application of laws of large numbers and/or central limit theorems. Assuming the temporal dependence of the simulation error does not interfere with establishing the asymptotic normality of $\hat{\theta}_a$, the major difference between it and the GMM estimator is asymptotic efficiency: Duffie and Singleton (1988) show that the asymptotic covariance matrix of $\hat{\theta}_a$ is twice that of the GMM estimator.

Relatively simple changes in the way the simulations are performed can produce estimators with significantly better sampling properties. Intuitively, simulation strategies that produce a more precise estimator of $Ef_i(Y)$ will lead to more efficient estimators of θ. In particular, there is no point in simulating a moment if closed-form expressions are readily available.

One strategy that is generally applicable in simulation contexts is to average independent estimates of $Ef_i(Y)$. Suppose that we draw M independent Brownian motions $(\hat{W}^1, \ldots, \hat{W}^M)$, and for each Brownian motion construct the process, call it $\hat{X}^m$, that solves (7.35). Proceeding as before, we can compute M simulated samples $(\hat{Y}^1, \ldots, \hat{Y}^M)$. By averaging the estimates $f_i(\hat{Y}^m)$, we can construct a new estimator of $Ef_i(Y)$, namely

$$\hat{E}_a^{(M)} f_i(Y) \equiv \frac{1}{M} \sum_{i=1}^{M} f_i(\hat{Y}^m).$$

Replacing $f_i(\hat{Y})$ by $\hat{E}_a^{(M)} f_i(Y)$ in (7.41) leads to a new estimator, $\hat{\theta}_a^{(M)}$. Since averaging provides a more precise estimator of $Ef_i(Y)$, we would expect the precision of $\hat{\theta}_a^{(M)}$ to increase with M. In their application, Duffie and Singleton show that the asymptotic covariance matrix of $\hat{\theta}_a^{(M)}$ is $(1 + M^{-1})$ times that of the GMM estimator, a ratio that also arises in other simulation contexts.

Averaging independent estimates provides a useful way of improving the efficiency of simulation estimators. However, the computational burden imposed by choosing M large can be quite onerous so there is ample incentive to exploit special features of the problem at hand. There has been very little computational experience with using simulation to estimate the parameters of a continuous-time process, but it seems possible to improve on the Duffie and Singleton (1988) scheme, described above.

Suppose $G = 1$ and the first component function of f is the identity mapping: $f^1(y_i) = y_i$. For fixed θ, the Duffie and Singleton simulation scheme leads to an estimator for Ey_i of the form

$$\hat{E}_a y_i = \hat{X}_0 + \int_0^{t_i} a(s, \hat{X}_s) ds + \int_0^{t_i} b(s, \hat{X}_s) d\hat{W}_s. \tag{7.43}$$

But the second integral in (7.43) is a martingale and has expectation zero, so a more precise estimator for Ey_i is given by

$$\hat{E}_b y_i = \hat{X}_0 + \int_0^{t_i} a(s, \hat{X}_s) ds. \tag{7.44}$$

This simple example extends to other component functions $f^r(y_i)$, provided that f^r is sufficiently smooth for Itô's rule to apply. Itô's rule provides a powerful way to separate the predictable and martingale components of $f^r(y_i)$. Since the martingale component has expectation zero, simulation is only required to estimate the expected value of the predictable component. In general, for functions $f \in C^2$, we can define

$$\hat{E}_b f^r(y_i) = \hat{E}_a f^r(y_i) - \int_0^{t_i} Df^r(\hat{X}_s) \cdot b(s, \hat{X}_s) d\hat{W}_s \qquad (7.45)$$

where Df^r denotes the derivative of f^r. Aside from notational complexity, the scheme extends immediately to the case $G > 1$. The basic idea also extends to convex and not necessarily differentiable choices for f^r. Combining $\hat{E}_b$ with the idea of averaging independent estimates, leads in an obvious way to an even more precise estimator of Ef_i, which we denote $\hat{E}_b^{(M)} f_i$.

In applications, a continuous-time specification has two parts: a specification for some underlying continuous-time process X, such as that given by (7.1); and a measurement scheme for the observed data, of the form $y_i = g_i(X)$. As noted previously, the measurement schemes that arise with financial data are many and varied. They include point-sampling ('stocks'), the integral of the process over an interval of time ('flows'), and the range of the process over an interval of time, as well as combinations of all three. Suppose the X process is point-sampled. Some of the components of X may be unobserved for some or all of the observations. The time between measurements may be irregular, or random and related to the values of the process. The data may be corrupted by measurement error. Even with very simple specifications for the latent X process, analytic results for the effect of these measurement schemes on the distribution of the observed data, or the expected value of functions of the observed sample, are often not available. By contrast, simulation can handle the computational difficulties introduced by various measurement schemes rather easily: simply replace $f_i(\hat{Y})$ by $f(g_i(\hat{X}))$ in the discussion above.

Simulation methods also allow the investigator to consider much richer specifications for the latent continuous-time process X. Conceptually, quite general specifications for the coefficients in (7.1) can be entertained as long as the integral still makes sense. Current methods require that at some 'deep' level the randomness introduced by simulating the semi-martingale integrators be held constant as we search over the parameter space. This means that the semi-martingale integrators must be expressible as a transformation of some other semi-martingales that don't depend upon unknown parameter values. Fortunately, this condition is easily met for continuous-path semi-martingales and for some discontinuous-path semi-martingales (such as Poisson processes). Conceptually, therefore, very general specifications for the semi-martingale integrators can also be entertained.

Although simulation methods for estimation of continuous-time processes are very promising, a good deal of work remains to be done.

APPENDIX

The purpose of this appendix is to collect some of the background concepts and definitions. There now exist a variety of textbook treatments of stochastic processes and their applications in finance (e.g., Duffie (1988)), but the material is still sufficiently novel that many readers may benefit from having an abbreviated summary. In what follows, I borrow freely from Jacod and Shiryaev (1987), Karatzas and Shreve (1988) and Protter (1990).

Let $(\Omega, \mathscr{F}, P)$ denote a probability space. For our purposes, a stochastic process is a family $X = (X_t; t \in \mathscr{R}_+)$ of $\mathscr{F}/B(\mathscr{R}^n)$-measurable mappings from Ω into $\mathscr{R}^n$, where $B(\mathscr{R}^n)$ denotes the Borel σ-field on $\mathscr{R}^n$. The collection of mappings $(X_t(\omega); t \in \mathscr{R}_+)$ for a fixed $\omega \in \Omega$ is called a path (sample path, trajectory, or realisation) of the process.

Let X and Y denote two processes. There are a variety of equivalence relations for processes, including:

(i) X and Y are indistinguishable if $P(X_t = Y_t, \forall t \in \mathscr{R}_+) = 1$
(ii) X is a modification of Y if, for every $t, P(X_t = Y_t) = 1$
(iii) X and Y have the same finite dimensional distributions if for every finite set of times $\{t_i \in \mathscr{R}_+; i = 1, \dots m\}$, and every set $A \in B(\mathscr{R}^{mn})$,

$$P[(X_{t_1}, X_{t_2}, \dots X_{t_m}) \in A] = P[(Y_{t_1}, Y_{t_2}, \dots Y_{t_m}) \in A]. \qquad (7.1A)$$

Clearly (i)$\Rightarrow$(ii)$\Rightarrow$(iii), but in general none of the reverse implications is true. Note that each of these three notions of equivalence depend upon the probability measure P.

It is useful to distinguish processes whose paths possess certain regularity properties. A process Y is right-continuous if, for each $\omega \in \Omega$ and $t \in \mathscr{R}_+$, $\lim_{s \downarrow t} Y(\omega, s) = Y(\omega, t)$. A process has left-limits if, for each $\omega \in \Omega$ and $t \in \mathscr{R}_+$, $\lim_{s \uparrow t} Y(\omega, s)$ exists. The definitions of left-continuous and right-limits are the obvious analogues. A process is continuous if it is both left- and right-continuous. A process $(Y = Y^1, \dots Y^m)'$ is increasing if each of its components is increasing, i.e., $Y^i(\omega, s) \le Y^i(\omega, t)$ for each $\omega \in \Omega$ and $s \le t$. Strictly increasing is defined analogously. A process that is both right-continuous and possesses left-limits is labelled RCLL. An alternative to RCLL is càdlàg ('continu à droite, limite à gauche'). The abbrevations RC (càd), LC (càg), etc. are also useful. If X is RCLL, we associate two more processes with it. X_{t-} denotes the left limit at time t, and $\Delta X_t \equiv X_t - X_{t-}$ denotes the jump of the process at time t. Both the convention $X_{0-} = X_0$ and $X_{0-} = 0$ are followed in the literature.

Probabilists traditionally ignore null-probability events. Therefore, if the process Y has any of the path properties above, then these properties are endowed to all processes X that are indistinguishable from Y. Under this more general definition, whether or not the process X is (say) continuous may depend upon the measure P.

The notion that information is revealed by the passage of time is captured by the concept of a filtration. A filtration, $\mathbf{F} = (\mathcal{F}_t; t \in \mathcal{R}_+)$ is an increasing family of σ-algebras (i.e. $\mathcal{F}_s \subset \mathcal{F}_t$ for $s \leq t$). $\mathcal{F}_\infty \equiv \mathcal{F}$ or $\mathcal{F}_\infty \equiv \sigma(\mathcal{F}_t; t \in \mathcal{R}_+)$ depending upon the author. A process X is said to be adapted (to the filtration $\mathbf{F}$) if X_t is $\mathcal{F}_t$—measurable, for every t. An older synonym for adapted is non-anticipative. Let $\mathcal{F}_t^X \equiv \sigma[X_s; 0 \leq s \leq t]$, i.e., the σ-algebra generated by the process up to time t. Heuristically, $\mathcal{F}_t^X$ contains all the events A for which we can determine whether $\omega \in A$ or $\omega \notin A$ based upon observing the history of the process X up to and including time t. $\mathbf{F}^X \equiv (\mathcal{F}_t^X; t \in \mathcal{R}_+)$ provides an example of a filtration (the so-called natural filtration), and X is adapted to $\mathbf{F}^X$ by construction. A probability space endowed with a filtration, denoted $(\Omega, \mathcal{F}, \mathbf{F}, P)$, is called a filtered probability space (or a stochastic basis).

For technical reasons (essentially concerned with measurability properties), further restrictions on $\mathbf{F}$ are often imposed. The filtration $\mathbf{F}$ is said to be right-continuous if $\mathcal{F}_t = \cap_{s > t} \mathcal{F}_s$. Associated with each filtration $\mathbf{F}$ is the P-augmented filtration $\mathbf{F}^P = (\mathcal{F}_t^P; t \in \mathcal{R}_+)$, where $\mathcal{F}^P$ is the P-completion of $\mathcal{F}$, and $\mathcal{F}_t^P$ is the σ-algebra generated by $\mathcal{F}_t$ and the null sets of $\mathcal{F}^P$. A filtration that is right-continuous and augmented is said to satisfy *the usual conditions*. The filtered probability space $(\Omega, \mathcal{F}^P, \mathbf{F}^P, P)$ is said to be complete.

It is natural to view a process as a mapping from $\Omega \times \mathcal{R}_+ \to \mathcal{R}^m$. This can be done by strengthening slightly the measurability requirements. Let $B([0, \infty))$ denote the Borel σ-field on $\mathcal{R}_+$, and $\mathcal{F} \otimes B([0, \infty))$ the product σ-field. Sets in $\mathcal{F} \otimes B([0, \infty))$ are called random sets. A process X is said to be measurable (jointly measurable) if it is $\mathcal{F} \otimes B([0, \infty))/B(\mathcal{R}^m)$-measurable. If X is measurable, then its sample paths are a Borel-measurable function of $t \in [0, \infty)$. Every right- or left-continuous process is measurable. When viewed as a function of $\Omega \times \mathcal{R}_+$, the analog of adapted is progressively measurable (progressive). Formally, X is progressively measurable with respect to the filtration F if, for every $0 \leq s \leq t \in \mathcal{R}_+, X_s$ is $\mathcal{F}_t \otimes B([0, t))/ B(\mathcal{R}^m)$-measurable. Every stochastic process X that is measurable and adapted to $\mathbf{F}$ has a progressively measurable modification. If, in addition, X is RC or LC then X itself is progressively measurable.

When viewed as a mapping on $\Omega \times \mathcal{R}_+$, two important sub-$\sigma$-fields stand out. Fix the filtration $\mathbf{F}$. The optional σ-field O on $\Omega \times \mathcal{R}_+$ is the σ-field that is generated by all RCLL adapted processes. A process or a random set that is O-measurable is called optional. Similarly, the predictable σ-field P on $\Omega \times \mathcal{R}_+$ is the σ-field generated by all LC adapted processes (this turns out to be the same as the σ-field generated by all continuous adapted processes).

A process or random set that is P-measurable is called predictable. Clearly, $P \subset O$.

Fix the filtered probability space $(\Omega, \mathscr{F}, \mathbf{F}, P)$. An integrable process X is an adapted process all of whose components X^i satisfy $E(|X_t^i|) < \infty$, for every $t \in \mathscr{R}_+$. A martingale (resp. submartingale, resp. supermartingale) is an integrable process X that is RCLL P-a.s. such that, for all $s \leq t \in \mathscr{R}_+$

$$X_s = E(X_t | \mathscr{F}_s) \quad (\text{resp. } X_s \leq E(X_t | \mathscr{F}_s), \text{resp. } X_s \geq E(X_t | \mathscr{F}_s)). \quad (7.2A)$$

A martingale is called square-integrable if each of its components satisfies $\sup_{t \geq 0} E(|X_t^i|^2) < \infty$. Note that if X^i is a square-integrable, then $|X_t^i|^2$ is submartingale, by Jensen's inequality.

A random time $T: \Omega \to [0, \infty]$ is a stopping time of the filtration $\mathbf{F}$ if the event $\{\omega : T(\omega) \leq t\} \in \mathscr{F}_t$, for every $t \in \mathscr{R}_+$. If X is a process and T is a stopping time then X^T is used to denote the process stopped at time T, i.e., $X_t^T \equiv X_{t \wedge T}$. Stopping times can be used to augment a class of processes by what is known as a localisation procedure. Let $\mathscr{E}$ be a class of processes. $\mathscr{E}_{\text{loc}}$ is used to denote the localised class defined as follows: a process X belongs to $\mathscr{E}_{\text{loc}}$ of and only if there exists a sequence $\{T_n\}$ of increasing stopping times with $T_n \uparrow \infty$ P-a.s. such that each stopped process X^{T_n} belongs to $\mathscr{E}$. Of course, $\mathscr{E} \subset \mathscr{E}_{\text{loc}}$.

A process A is said to be of finite variation (on finite intervals or on compacts) if it can be expressed as the difference between two adapted increasing processes.

A process X is called a semi-martingale if it can be expressed as $X = X_0 + M + A$, where X_0 is finite valued and $\mathscr{F}_0$-measurable, M is a local martingale with $M_0 = 0$, and A is a finite variation process with $A_0 = 0$. The decomposition is not unique in general. However, a further decomposition allows us to write $X = X_0 + X^c + M^d + A$, where X^c is a continuous local martingale. X^c is called the continuous martingale part of X and it is unique (up to indistinguishability). The space of semi-martingales is a vector space (as well as a vector lattice and an algebra) that is closed under a variety of transformations: stopping, localisation, 'change of time', 'absolutely continuous change of probability measure', and 'changes of filtration'. It is also the largest class of processes with respect to which it is possible to provide a 'reasonable' definition of the integral of all locally bounded predictable processes. Protter (1990) shows that an equivalent definition of a semi-martingale can be given in terms of its properties as a 'good' integrator.

To each pair (M, N) of locally square-integrable martingales is associated a process $< M, N >$ called the predictable quadratic covariation (variation if $M = N$) that is unique up to indistinguishability and has the following properties: $< M, N >$ is a predictable finite-variation process and $MN - < M, N >$ is a local martingale. More generally, to each pair (X, Y) of semi-martingales is associated a process $[X, Y]$ called the quadratic covariation. The quadratic variation is defined by $[X, Y] = XY - X_0 Y_0 - X_- \cdot Y - Y_- \cdot X$. The two processes are linked by the result $[X, Y]_t = <X^c, Y^c>_t + \sum_{s \leq t} \Delta X_s \Delta Y_s$.

Let f be a function of class C^2 on $\mathscr{R}^d$, and let X denote a d-dimensional vector of semi-martingales. Then $f(X)$ is a semi-martingale and we have

$$f(X_t) = f(X_0) + \sum_{i \leq d} D_i f(X_-) \cdot X^i + \frac{1}{2} \sum_{i,j \leq d} D_{ij} f(X_-) \cdot <X^{i,c}, X^{j,c}>$$
$$+ \sum_{s \leq d} [f(X_s) - f(X_{s-}) - \sum_{i \leq d} D_i f(X_s) \Delta X_s^i] \tag{7.3A}$$

where $D_i f$ and $D_{ij} f$ denote the first and second derivatives of the function f, and $H \cdot X$ denotes the stochastic integral of H with respect to the semi-martingale X. Equation (7.3A) is called Itô's formula (or sometimes the change-of-variables formula) for semi-martingales. Various extensions are available (see Protter (1990), section 4.5), including a version for f convex (and not necessarily differentiable).

Notes

Prepared for presentation at the Sixth World Congress of the Econometric Society, Barcelona, August 1990. The Social Sciences and Humanities Research Council of Canada provided financial support. Ken Vetzal provided research assistance. Without implicating them, I would like to thank Lars Hansen, Jim Stock, Stuart Turnbull and Ken Vetzal for their comments and valuable discussions.

1 Merton (1990, p.471) reaches a similar conclusion, albeit for somewhat different reasons than those given below. He writes 'the continuous-time model as an empirical hypothesis, strictly speaking, remains unproved'.

2 Métivier (1982) provides a brief but useful description of historical developments.

3 Métivier (1982) provides a discussion of some of the differences that can arise, even in the finite-dimensional case, when a 'vector' definition of the stochastic integral is used.

4 Most papers in the literature impose further restrictions on the coefficient a, but these restrictions vary across authors. In addition, γ is often restricted to the range [0,1] to allow for the explicit characterisation of the transition density using the results of Feller (1951). Note that for $\gamma \in (0,0.5)$ solutions may not be unique (see Karatzas and Shreve (1988), section 5.2).

5 Brandt (1990) provides an interesting example. He looks at the seasonal properties of grain prices in eighteenth-century China. The data are available 'monthly', but the Chinese followed a lunar calendar. Periodically, extra months were introduced in order not to deviate too far from a solar year.

6 Although the form of the restrictions has changed over time, this argument goes back at least to Bergstrom (1966).

7 Cox and Rubinstein (1985) provide a useful and broadly based bibliography on continuous-time topics in finance, covering the period up to the mid eighties.

8 The remark was made to conclude a discussion on the Phillips' curve that had gotten out of hand. Since A.W. Phillips was also one of the first economists to consider specification of continuous-time stochastic processes, I feel a little bit less guilty about taking the remark out of context.

9 In many applications, the ultimate objective is to price an asset and compare the predicted to observed option prices. Applied researchers need better tools not only to specify and estimate multivariate specifications, but also to solve for the associated asset pricing predictions. In some ways, however, these two problems are related. Both would benefit from faster, more accurate, and more powerful algorithms for computing the expectation (w.r.t. a given measure) of functionals of the path of a continuous-time process.

10 The use of implicit estimators of volatility probably accounts for a good deal of the popularity of the geometric Brownian motion specification. If you're not going to take the specification seriously, why get fancy?

11 See Bossaerts and Hillion (1990) for an interesting approach that breaks the deterministic link between the actual and the predicted option price.

12 For a recent study, see Lamoureux and Lastrapes (1990).

13 Bergstrom (1988) provides a very useful and interesting history of this literature.

14 Note that these conditions do not require $\xi([0, t])$ to be a martingale, but only that it have uncorrelated increments.

15 A famous theorem of Lévy characterises a vector of standard Brownian motions by continuity and $< M^i, M^j >_t = \delta_{ij} t$, where δ is Kronecker's delta.

16 Stock's (1988) specification also imposes a normalisation.

17 Ethier and Kurtz (1986) pursue this approach for time-homogeneous Markov processes.

18 Feller (1971, section 10.4) provides an introduction to general time-homogeneous Markov jump processes.

19 In private conversation, Andy Lo has suggested solving the partial differential equation numerically for those specifications where an analytical solution is unknown. I know of no papers that have pursued this scheme explicitly, but it may provide a useful interpretation of some of the approximation schemes described in section 6.

20 Neftci (1990), in a related context, provides an informal but useful discussion of recent developments in optimal discretisation of stochastic differential equations driven by Brownian motions.

21 Duffie and Singleton (1988) provide an example of just such a case and a rigorous treatment of the properties of $\hat{\theta}_a$. It should be noted, however, that many of the processes that arise naturally as specifications in finance do not fit into the stationary ergodic framework used in Duffie and Singleton (1988). For example, many specifications have the property that with positive probability they will reach an absorbing barrier (e.g., an asset price that hits zero must stay there) or 'explode' in finite time.

References

Ball, C.A. and Torous, W.N. (1983), 'A Simplified Jump Process for Common Stock Returns', *Journal of Financial and Quantitative Analysis*, 18: 53–65.

Bergstrom, A.R. (1966), 'Nonrecursive Models as Discrete Approximations to Systems of Stochastic Differential Equations', *Econometrica*, 34: 173–82.

—— (1976) (ed.), *Statistical Inference in Continuous Time Economic Models*, Amsterdam: North-Holland.

—— (1983), 'Gaussian Estimation of Structural Parameters in Higher-Order Continuous Time Dynamic Models', *Econometrica*, 51: 117–52.

—— (1984), 'Continuous time stochastic models and issues of aggregation over time', in Z. Griliches and M.D. Intrilligator (eds.), *Handbook of Econometrics*, Amsterdam: North-Holland, chapter 20, pp.1145–212

—— (1985), 'The Estimation of Parameters in Non-Stationary Higher-Order Continuous Time Dynamic Models', *Econometric Theory*, 1: 369–85.

—— (1986), 'The Estimation of Open Higher-Order Continuous Time Dynamic Models with Mixed Stock and Flow Data', *Econometric Theory*, 2: 350–73.

—— (1988), 'The History of Continuous-Time Econometric Models', *Econometric Theory*, 4: 365–83.

Black, F. and Scholes, M. (1973), 'The Pricing of Options and Corporate Liabilities', *Journal of Political Economy*, 3: 637–54.

Bollerslev, T., Chou, R.Y. Jayaraman, N. and Kroner, K.F. (1990), 'ARCH Modeling in Finance: A Review of the Theory and Empirical Evidence', Working Paper No. 97, Northwestern University.

Bossaerts, P. and Hillion, P. (1990), 'Arbitrage Restrictions Across Financial Markets: Theory, Methodology and Tests', unpublished manuscript, California Institute of Technology.

Brandt, L. (1990), 'Time-Series Properties of Eighteenth Century Grain Prices in China', unpublished manuscript, University of Toronto.

Brennan, M.J. and Schwartz, E.S. (1979), 'A Continuous Time Approach to the Pricing of Bonds', *Journal of Banking and Finance*, 3: 133–55.

—— (1980), 'Conditional Predictions of Bond Prices and Returns', *Journal of Finance*, 35: 405–16.

—— (1982), 'An Equilibrium Model of Bond Pricing and a Test of Market Efficiency', *Journal of Financial and Quantitative Analysis*, 17: 301–29.

Chambers, M.J. (1991), 'Discrete Models for Estimating General Linear Continuous Time Systems', *Econometric Theory*, 7: 531–42.

Clark, P.K. (1973), 'A Subordinated Stochastic Process Model with Finite Variance for Speculative Prices', *Econometrica*, 41: 135–55.

Courtadon, G. (1982), 'The Pricing of Options on Default Free Bonds', *Journal of Financial and Quantitative Analysis*, 17: 75–100.

Cox, J.C. and Rubinstein, M. (1985), *Options Markets*, Englewood Cliffs, N. J.: Prentice-Hall.

Dietrich-Campbell, B. and Schwartz, E.S. (1986), 'Valuing Debt Options: Empirical Evidence', *Journal of Financial Economics*, 16: 321–43.

Doléans-Dade, C. and Meyer, P.A. (1970), 'Intégrales stochastiques par rapport aux martingales locales', *Lecture Notes in Mathematics*, 124: 77–107.

Duffie, D. (1988), *Security Markets: Stochastic Models*, Boston: Academic Press.

Duffie, D. and Singleton, K.J. (1988), 'Simulated Moments Estimation of Diffusion Models of Asset Prices', unpublished manuscript, Graduate School of Business, Stanford University.

Ethier, S.N. and Kurtz, T.G. (1986), *Markov Processes: Characterization and Convergence*, New York: John Wiley.

Fama, E. (1965), 'The Behavior of Stock Market Prices', *Journal of Business*, 38: 34–105.

(1976), *Foundations of Finance*, New York: Basic Books.

Fama, E. and Miller, M. (1972), *The Theory of Finance*, New York: Holt, Rinehart and Winston.

Feller, W. (1951), 'Two Singular Diffusion Problems', *Annals of Mathematics*, 54: 173–82.

(1971), *An Introduction to Probability Theory and Its Applications*, Vol.II (second edition), New York: John Wiley.

Harvey, A.C. and Stock, J.H. (1985), 'The Estimation of Higher-Order Continuous Time Autoregressive Models', *Econometric Theory*, 1: 97–117.

He, H. (1989), 'Convergence from Discrete to Continuous Time Financial Models', Finance Working Paper 190, Haas School of Business, University of California, Berkeley.

Ikeda, N. and Watanabe, S. (1989), *Stochastic Differential Equations and Diffusion Processes* (second edition), Amsterdam: North-Holland.

Ingersoll, J.E. (1987), *Theory of Financial Decision Making*, New Jersey: Rowman & Littlefield.

Jacod, J. and Shiryaev, A.N. (1987), *Limit Theorems for Stochastic Processes*, New York: Springer-Verlag.

Jorion, P. (1988), 'On Jump Processes in the Foreign Exchange and Stock Markets', *Review of Financial Studies*, 1: 427–45.

Karatzas, I. and Shreve, S.E. (1988), *Brownian Motion and Stochastic Calculus*, New York: Springer-Verlag.

Kyle, A.S. (1985), 'Continuous Auctions and Insider Trading', *Econometrica*, 53: 1315–35.

Lamoureux, C.G. and Lastrapes, W.D. (1990), 'Forecasting Stock Return Variance: Toward an Understanding of Stochastic Implied Volatilities', unpublished mimeo, Washington University.

Lo, A.W. (1988), 'Maximum Likelihood Estimation of Generalized Ito Processes with Discretely Sampled Data', *Econometric Theory*, 4: 231–47.

Mandelbrot, B. (1973), 'Comment on: A Subordinated Stochastic Process Model with Finite Variance for Speculative Prices, by Peter K. Clark', *Econometrica*, 41: 157–9.

McFadden, D. (1989), 'A Method of Simulated Moments for Estimation of Discrete Response Models Without Numerical Integration', *Econometrica*, 57: 1027–57.

Melino, A. and Turnbull, S.M. (1990), 'Pricing Foreign Currency Options with Stochastic Volatility', *Journal of Econometrics*, 45 (Annals): 239–65.

(1991), 'The Pricing of Foreign Currency Options', *Canadian Journal of Economics*, 24: 251–81.

Merton, R. (1969), 'Lifetime Portfolio Selection under Uncertainty: The Continuous Time Case', *Review of Economics and Statistics*, 51: 247–57.

(1971), 'Optimum Consumption and Portfolio Rules in a Continuous-Time Model', *Journal of Economic Theory*, 3: 373–413.

(1973), 'The Theory of Rational Option Pricing', *Bell Journal of Economics and Management Science*, 4: 141–83.

(1975), 'The Theory of Finance from the Perspective of Continuous Time', *Journal of Financial and Quantitative Analysis*, 10: 659–764.

(1990), *Continuous-Time Finance*, Basil Blackwell.

Métivier, M. (1982), *Semimartingales: a Course on Stochastic Processes*, New York: W. de Gruyter.

Neftci, S.N. (1990), 'Discretization of Stochastic Differential Equations and Econometric Forecasting: An Application to Time Varying Autoregressions', unpublished mimeo.

Nelson, D.B. (1990a), 'ARCH Models as Diffusion Approximations', *Journal of Econometrics*, 45 (Annals): 7–38.

(1990b), 'Filtering and Forecasting with Misspecified ARCH Models I: Getting the Right Variance with the Wrong Model', unpublished manuscript, Graduate School of Business, University of Chicago.

Ogden, J.P. (1987), 'An Analysis of Yield Curve Notes', *Journal of Finance*, 42: 99–110.

Oldfield, G.S., Rogalski, R.J. and Jarrow, Robert A. (1977), 'An Autoregressive Jump Process for Common Stock Returns', *Journal of Financial Economics*, 5: 389–418.

Pakes, A. and Pollard, D. (1989), 'Simulation and the Asymptotics of Optimization Estimators', *Econometrica*, 57: 995–1026.

Pardoux, E. and Talay, D. (1985), 'Discretization and Simulation of Stochastic Differential Equations', *Acta Applicandae Mathematicae*, 3: 23–47.

Protter, P. (1990), *Stochastic Integration and Differential Equations: A New Approach*, Berlin: Springer-Verlag.

Robinson, P.M. (1977), 'The Construction and Estimation of Continuous Time Models and Discrete Approximations in Econometrics', *Journal of Econometrics*, 6: 173–98.

Sargan, J.D. (1976), 'Some Discrete Approximations to Continuous Time Stochastic Models', in A.R. Bergstrom (ed.), *Statistical Inference in Continuous Time Economic Models*, Amsterdam: North-Holland.

Schwert, G.W. (1989), 'Why Does Stock Market Volatility Change over Time?', *Journal of Finance*, 44: 1115–53.

Shimko, D.C. (1989), 'The Equilibrium Valuation of Risky Discrete Cash Flows in Continuous time', *Journal of Finance*, 44: 1373–83.

Stock, J.H. (1987), 'Measuring Business Cycle Time', *Journal of Political Economy*, 95: 1240–61.

(1988), 'Estimating Continuous-Time Processes Subject to Time Deformation: An Application to Postwar U.S. GNP', *Journal of the American Statistical Association*, 83: 77–85.

Stroock, D.W. and Varadhan, S.R.S. (1979), *Multidimensional Diffusion Processes*, New York: Springer-Verlag.

Tse, Y.K. (1990), 'On Estimating Continuous Time Financial Models', mimeo, National University of Singapore.

Van Loan, C. (1978), 'Computing Integrals Involving the Matrix Exponential', *IEEE Transactions on Automatic Control*, AC-23: 395–404.

Wu, R. (1985), *Stochastic Differential Equations*, Boston: Pitman Publishing.

Zadrozny, P. (1988), 'Gaussian Likelihood of Continuous Time ARMAX Models when Data are Stocks and Flows and Different Frequencies', *Econometric Theory*, 4: 108–24.

IV
Development economics

CHAPTER 8

Political instability, political weakness and inflation: an empirical analysis

Sebastian Edwards and Guido Tabellini

1   INTRODUCTION

In recent years there has been an increased interest in analysing the effects of political incentive constraints on macro-economic policy. More and more economists are now using elements of public choice and game theory in an effort to better understand why some countries, at some specific moments in time, choose specific macro-economic policies. This new research programme on endogenous economic policy addresses questions such as: why do some countries rely more heavily on the inflation tax than others; why are fiscal deficits so different across countries; why do different countries choose different exchange rate policies, and so on. The answers emphasise the role of government's strategic behaviour, and of institutions that determine policy-making.[1]

In spite of this mounting interest in the political economy of macro-economic policy, until now there has been relatively little empirical work on the subject.[2] The purpose of this chapter is to present the results of a comparative cross-country empirical analysis of the political determinants of the inflation tax. Our analysis differs from previous work in three respects: first, we use a *new* data set on cross country political events and political institutions. An advantage of using these new data is that they are free from some of the more serious limitations encountered in other data sets which have been previously used by political scientists and economists (including ourselves).[3] Second, in this chapter we use alternative definitions of the inflation tax and of seignorage in an effort to check for the robustness of the results. And third, we try to discriminate empirically between two alternative families of models that emphasise political explanations of inflation: models based on political instability and government 'myopia', and models of decentralised policy making that focus on the relative weakness (or strength) of the government in office.

The chapter is organised as follows: in section 2 we briefly discuss the emerging theoretical literature on the political economy of inflation. In doing this we make a distinction between models based on political instability and models based on political weakness. We argue that there are some rather simple ways of empirically discriminating between these two views regarding the inflation tax. Section 3 deals with empirical results. We first describe our new data set on the political characteristics of seventy-eight countries between 1971 and 1982. Next, we present a set of regression results that provide ample support to the view that political instability encourages governments to rely on the inflation tax as a source of revenue. The results, however, do not provide such a strong support to the political weakness hypothesis. In this section we also present a sensitivity analysis that shows that our results are highly robust. In section 4 we extend our analysis to the case of trade taxes, analysing whether political variables affect the degree to which countries rely on this source of government revenues. Section 5 presents some concluding remarks.

2   INFLATION TAX, POLITICAL INSTABILITY AND GOVERNMENT WEAKNESS

The inflation tax is a very distorting source of government income, particularly at the rates observed in many developing countries. Presumably the governments that rely in it extensively do not have alternative sources of revenue. This suggests that the analysis of the inflation tax should go hand in hand with the analysis of tax reforms. To explain why some countries collect so much revenue from the inflation tax, we should explain why they do not enact tax reforms that improve the efficiency of the tax system.

A recent body of research has emphasised the existence of political constraints in analysing why some countries fail to enact Pareto-improving tax reforms. Two different (but complementary) explanations have been proposed. One view, articulated in Cukierman, Edwards and Tabellini (1990), argues that the policy maker deliberately *chooses* not to improve the efficiency of the tax system, because in a politically unstable environment it does not expect to reap the benefits of a more efficient tax system in the future. The reason for this, of course, is that the government in office is uncertain about its future reappointment. The second view, proposed in several different papers (by Alesina and Drazen (1989), Aizenman (1990), Sanguinetti (1991), among others), argues instead that inefficient tax systems are maintained because the government *cannot* change the status quo, in the sense that it cannot find a consensus in favour of any tax reform. According to this second view, the inability to make a collective decision forces the government to rely on residual sources of revenue, such as seignorage or borrowing. We now briefly summarise these two approaches to the positive theory of the inflation tax.

2.1   Tax reform and political instability

Following Cukierman, Edwards and Tabellini (1990), consider an economy described by two simple equations: the budget constraint of the government equation (8.1) and of the private sector equation (8.2)

$$g_t + f_t \leq \tau_t(1 - \theta_{t-1}) + s_t \tag{8.1}$$

$$c_t \leq 1 - \tau_t - s_t - \delta(\tau_t) - \gamma(s_t). \tag{8.2}$$

Subscripts denote time periods. Each individual is endowed with one unit of output in each period. g_t and f_t are two different public goods in per-capita terms and c_t is private consumption, also per-capita. The government collects from each individual an amount s_t in the form of 'seignorage' and an amount τ_t of tax revenue. The main difference between taxes and seignorage is that a fraction θ_{t-1} of the tax revenue is wasted due to tax collection costs, whereas seignorage carries no administrative costs. Both taxes and seignorage impose deadweight losses on the private sector, equal to $\delta(\tau_t)$ and $\gamma(s_t)$ respectively. These distortions increase at an increasing rate. Thus

$$\delta'(\cdot) > 0, \qquad \delta''(\cdot) > 0$$
$$\gamma'(\cdot) > 0, \qquad \gamma''(\cdot) > 0.$$

Here, θ_{t-1} is a rough measure of the *efficiency* of the tax system. A lower value of θ implies a more efficient tax system in the sense of lower administrative costs. Thus, in this simple model, a tax reform amounts to a choice of θ, whereas a fiscal policy is a choice of g, f, τ and s. To capture the greater inertia in reforming the tax system than in changing fiscal policy, we assume that θ, but not the other policy variables, must be chosen one period in advance. Thus, θ_t is chosen at time t but exerts an influence on tax collection costs only at time $t+1$ (cf., equation (8.1)).

There are two possible policy-maker types, L and R, who randomly alternate in office. The policy-maker of type i, $i = L, R$ maximises

$$W_t^i = E_t \left\{ \sum_{k=0}^{\infty} \beta^k [U(c_{t+k}) + H^i(g_{t+k}, f_{t+k})] \right\}, \qquad 1 > B > 0 \tag{8.3}$$

where $E_t(\cdot)$ denotes the expectation operator, $U(\cdot)$ is a concave and twice continuously differentiable utility function, and $H^i(\cdot)$ is defined as follows. If $i = L$

$$H^L(g, f) = \frac{1}{a(1-a)} \text{Min}[ag, (1-a)f], \qquad 1 > a > 0 \tag{8.3'}$$

and if $i = R$, then $H^R(\cdot)$ is defined as in (8.3′), but with α replaced by $(1 - \alpha)$. Thus, these two policy makers differ only in the desired composition of the public good. For simplicity, their disagreement is parameterised by α. The more distant is α from $\frac{1}{2}$, the more they disagree. By construction, the overall weight given to private versus public consumption does not depend on α.

The political system is described as a Markov process with transition probabilities π and $(1 - \pi)$: the government in office at time t has a fixed probability $(1 - \pi)$ of being reappointed next period. With probability π, it is thrown out of office and the other policy maker type is appointed. Cukierman, Edwards and Tabellini (1990) show that this model yields two important results. First, a more inefficient tax system (a higher value of θ) forces the government to rely more heavily on seignorage. Second, a more unstable political system (a higher value of π) induces the government to accept a more inefficient tax apparatus. Combining both results, we obtain that, in equilibrium, political instability is associated with more seignorage. Intuitively, an inefficient tax system (i.e., one that facilitates tax evasion and imposes high tax collection costs) acts as a constraint on the revenue collecting policies of the government. This constraint may be welcomed by those who disagree with the goals pursued by the current government. In particular a government (or legislative majority) may deliberately choose to maintain (or create) an inefficient tax system, so as to constrain the behaviour of future governments with which it might disagree.

Hence, political instability gives rise to a '*collective myopia*'. The more unstable is the political system, the more important is this strategic determinant of tax reforms, the more inefficient is the equilibrium mix of government revenues, and the higher is the reliance on the inflation tax.

2.2   Decentralised government and inflation

An alternative view of why governments prolong inefficient and unsustainable economic policies posits that the policy maker is not a single decision maker (like a president or a pivotal voter in the legislature), but rather a collection of decision makers that behave non-cooperatively and that control some dimensions of policy making, such as different ministries, different public corporations or different states in a federation.

In this setting, policy is the outcome of a game between different policy makers. The game can be modelled in alternative ways: like a 'war of attrition', as in Alesina and Drazen (1989) or Drazen and Grilli (1990); or like a 'tax competition' between different taxing authorities, as in Aizenman (1990); or yet like a federation of taxing and spending authorities, as in Sanguinetti (1991). In any event, the equilibrium policy is inefficient and typically relies on 'too much' seignorage as a source of government revenue. Moreover, the inefficiency is generally stronger the more conflict and polarisation there is among the different policy makers, and the weaker is the central government authority. The empirical implication obtained by this line of research is that seignorage should be higher in countries in which the central government is weaker or in which the various functions of governments are dispersed across different political interests.

To summarise, the key difference between the two families of political economy models discussed here is the distinction between the *unwillingness* to reform the tax system and the *inability* to do so. In the first class of models the *inflation tax* is the result of a strategic decision of the government in office; in the second class of models, on the other hand, the *inflation* tax is the *outcome* of a power struggle within the government. This difference between *unwillingness* and *inability* to move away from the use of the inflation tax as a source of revenue can be exploited in the empirical analysis to distinguish between these two alternative political economy models. According to the myopic government model, in a cross-country regression analysis we would expect to see a positive relationship between *instability* of the political system and seignorage. On the other hand, the weak government model suggests that measures of government weakness and seignorage should be positively related.

3   EMPIRICAL RESULTS

In this section we present the results from a set of cross-country regressions on the determinants of the inflation tax and seignorage. A specific purpose of this empirical analysis is to discriminate between political *instability* (or government myopia) and the government *weakness* approaches to the political economy of the inflation tax, that were discussed in the preceding section.

Our basic regression equation is the following

$$INRE_n = \beta X_n + \gamma y_n + \delta z_n + u_n, \tag{8.4}$$

where $INRE_n$ is the inflation tax (or seignorage) revenue as percentage of GDP (or total government revenues) in country n; X_n is a vector of structural variables that capture the countries degree of development and geographical location and other important features of their economies; y_n is an indicator of political instability defined as the perceived probability of government change; z_n is an indicator (or indicators) of political weakness of the government in office; u_n is an error term; and β, γ and δ are parameters of interest. Under the government myopia approach to public behaviour we would expect that the coefficient of political instability (γ) will be positive; under the decentralised approach that emphasises the relative weakness of the government we would expect both γ and δ to be significantly positive

3.1   Data

Seignorage and Inflation Tax: Our data set covers a cross section of seventy-eight countries (the list is in the appendix). Two (related) dependent variables were used in the analysis. The first one corresponds closely to the concept of seignorage and was defined as follows

$$SEIG = \frac{\Delta B}{GOVREV};$$

where ΔB is the yearly change in monetary base and GOVREV is total government revenue (inclusive of ΔB) for that particular year. In the cross country regressions the average of *SEIG* for the period 1971–82 was used. The specific data sources are given in the appendix.

The second dependent variable corresponds to the steady state value of the inflation tax and was defined as

$$INFTAX_t = \frac{\pi_t m_{t-1}}{q_{t-1}};$$

where π is the rate of inflation in year t, m_{t-1} is the real stock of money (M1) in $t-1$ and q_{t-1} is real GDP in $t-1$. The data sources are in the appendix.

Structural Variables: As suggested by a number of authors, we assume that the costs of administering a tax system affect the degree to which countries rely on the inflation tax:[4] the higher these costs, the higher the reliance on the inflation tax. More specifically we follow Cukierman, Edwards and Tabellini (1990) in assuming that these administrative costs are captured by a set of structural variables. These variables fall into three categories: (1) The sectoral composition of gross domestic product, to account for differences in administering tax collection across sectors. We expect the agricultural sector to be the hardest to tax, and thus to have a positive coefficient in the regressions. The mining and manufacturing sector are assumed to be the easiest to tax, and thus to have a negative coefficient. We also include the ratio of foreign trade to GNP, since in many developing countries imports and exports are a cheap tax base; hence its coefficient too is expected to be negative. (2) Two measures of economic development: GDP per capita, and a dummy variable taking a value of 1 for the industrialised countries and 0 otherwise. We expect both variables to have a negative coefficient, since the technology for enforcing tax collection is likely to be more inefficient in less-developed countries. (3) A measure of urbanisation: since tax collection costs are likely to be smaller in urban areas than in rural areas, we expect a negative coefficient.

Political Instability: We use two measures of political instability. The first, which we call POLINST, is the *actual frequency* of transfers of power in the period 1971–82. This index measures the instability *of the political system* by capturing changes in the political leadership from the governing party (or group, in the case of non-democratic regimes) to an opposition party. In constructing this index we define transfer of power as a situation where there is a break in the governing political party's (or dictator's) control of the executive power. More specifically, under a presidential system a transfer of power would occur if a new government headed by a party previously in the opposition takes over the executive. Under a parliamentarian regime, a transfer of power is recorded when a new government headed by a party previously in the opposition takes over, or when there are major changes in the coalition that result in the leading party moving to the opposition. However, minor changes in the government party coalition are not recorded, nor are changes of head of government if the coalition remains basically unaltered, even if the new prime minister belongs to a party different from that of the outgoing prime minister. Finally, in the case of single-party systems, dictatorships or monarchies, a transfer of power only takes place if there are forced changes of the head of state. Appointments of a successor by an outgoing dictator (as in Brazil during the 1970s) are not recorded as transfers of power.

This measure of political instability differs from indexes used by other researchers in an important respect. Most previous empirical work was based on measures of instability of *the government* as defined in Taylor and Jodice (1983). Under their definition a government transfer corresponds to *any* change in the head of state, independently of whether it is a change within the same political party or whether the opposition took over the government. These two alternative measures of instability are very different from each other. For instance, Japan and Italy have very unstable *governments*, but yet they have very stable *political systems*. For the whole sample of countries, the simple correlation coefficient between our indicator of political instability and the frequency of government changes obtained from the Taylor and Jodice (1983) data is only 0.4.

The second measure of instability used is the *estimated probability* of power transfer (POLINSTEST) obtained from a probit regression on pooled cross-country time series data. In this probit analysis the dependent variable takes a value of 1 when there is a power transfer (as defined above) and a value of 0 otherwise. The independent variables in the probit model fall in three broad classes: economic variables, designed to measure the recent economic performance of the government; political variables, accounting for significant political events that may signal the imminence of a crisis; and structural variables, accounting for institutional differences and country-specific factors that do not change, or that change only slowly over time. These structural variables consist of three dummy variables that group countries in three categories, according to their political institutions: (a) democracies, (b) democracies in which the election date is determined by the constitution, and (c) democracies ruled by a single majoritarian party. Even though these three groups are too broad to account for the variety of existing political institutions, at least they discriminate between very different constitutional environments. The results obtained from these probit estimates are available upon request.[5] The appendix contains the data for all the political variables used in this chapter.

Our two indicators of political instability POLINST and POLINSTEST move closely together; they have a simple coefficient of correlation of 0.988.

Political Weakness: Three indicators were used as proxies of the extent of weakness of the government in office. The first one refers to whether the party or coalition of parties in office have the absolute majority of seats in the lower house of parliament. This indicator, called MAJ, takes in any given year a value of zero if the party (coalition) does *not* have majority; it takes a value of one if it has majority; and takes a value of two if the system is a dictatorship. A higher value of MAJ, then, reflects a stronger government. In the cross-country regressions the average of MAJ over the period 1970–81 was used.

The second indicator of political weakness that we used is the number of political parties in the governing coalition (NPC). This index takes a value of zero for monarchical or dictatorial systems, and the number of parties in the coalition in democratic regimes. (That is, if there is a single-party government NPC will take the value of one.) It is expected that the higher the number of parties in the coalition, the higher the probability of conflict of interest across ministries and, thus, the higher the reliance on the inflation tax.

The third indicator of government weakness is whether the government is a coalition government or a single-party government (COAL). This index takes a value of zero for dictatorships, a value of one for single-party governments and a value of two for coalition governments. To the extent that coalition governments are more likely to be subject to disagreements within the different ministries and government branches, it is expected that under the 'weakness hypothesis' a higher value of COAL will be associated with higher values of SEIG or INFTAX.

3.2   Basic results

Tables 8.1 and 8.2 contain the results obtained when OLS were used to estimate cross-country equations on INFTAX and SEIG. As can be seen the overall results provide broad support for the political instability hypothesis. In every equation the coefficient of the political instability indicators (POLINST or POLINSTEST) is positive, as expected, and significant at conventional levels. These regressions, however, do not support the 'political weakness' explanation of the inflation tax. After controlling for other variables, including political instability, the data do not support the hypothesis that countries with weaker governments (on average) tend to rely more heavily on the inflation tax. This result doesn't seem to be a consequence of the choice of the weakness indicators: in fact, independently of the index used the coefficients are in most cases insignificant. Moreover, in the one case where it is significant (column (10)), it has the wrong sign.[6] Additionally, when our indicators of political weakness are included jointly in a regression, the results reported in tables 8.1 and 8.2 still hold: the instability indices are significant, while the indicators of political weakness have the wrong sign and/or are not significant.

Regarding the structural variables, most coefficients have the expected signs and are significant. An interesting exception to this, however, refers to urbanisation. In every equation its estimated coefficient has a positive sign. A possible explanation is that this variable is capturing some political features of the countries in the sample, such as the degree of political polarisation and political conflict. In fact, a number of political scientists have for a long time argued that the degree of political clashes and conflicts increase with the degree of urbanisation.[7]

The fact that the coefficients of POLINST and POLINSTEST are significantly positive says little regarding the relative importance of the political variables in explaining inflation tax and seignorage. The computation of standardised beta coefficients indicates, however, that these political variables played a quantitatively important role in accounting for cross-country differentials SEIG and INFTAX. For example, in column (4) the beta corresponding to POLINSTEST is the second highest (in absolute terms) and is equal to 0.24; the highest beta corresponds to the urbanisation variable and is equal to 0.29.

It is interesting to compare our results with those obtained when the

Table 8.1. *Inflation tax and political variables: OLS estimates**

Dependent variable: INFTAX

Explanatory variables		All countries			
	(1)	(2)	(3)	(4)	(5)
Intercept	0.134 (3.709)	−0.160 (−1.839)	0.136 (3.715)	0.076 (1.332)	−0.032 (−0.513)
Agriculture	—	0.514 E-2 (3.580)	—	—	0.343 E-2 (3.001)
Mining and manufacturing	−0.120 E-3 (−0.873)	0.253 E-2 (1.047)	−0.112 E-2 (−0.877)	−0.900 E-3 (−0.711)	—
Foreign trade	−0.087 (−2.724)	−0.052 (−1.698)	−0.086 (−2.640)	−0.083 (−2.617)	−0.062 (−1.973)
GDP per capita	−0.452 E-5 (−0.960)	−0.879 E-5 (−1.810)	−0.497 E-5 (−0.937)	−0.583 E-5 (−1.112)	−0.490 E-5 (−1.313)
Urbanisation	0.986 E-3 (1.430)	0.275 E-2 (3.518)	0.103 E-2 (1.472)	0.116 E-2 (1.659)	0.220 (2.908)

	(1)	(2)	(3)	(4)	(5)
Industrialised	(−0.084) (−2.301)	−0.049 (−1.214)	−0.075 (−1.819)	−0.053 (−1.241)	−0.056 (−1.460)
POLINST	—	0.194 (2.647)	—	—	—
POLINSTEST	0.175 (2.246)	—	0.171 (2.183)	0.165 (2.117)	0.160 (2.134)
MAJ	—	—	—	0.036 (1.314)	—
COAL	—	—	—	—	−0.832 E-2 (−0.335)
NPC	—	—	−0.745 E-2 (−0.455)	—	—
R^2	0.260	0.387	0.262	0.279	0.351
N	76	76	76	76	76

Note:
* The numbers in parentheses are t-statistics. R^2 is the coefficient of correlation and N is the number of observations.

Table 8.2. *Seignorage and political variables: OLS estimates**

Dependent variable: SEIG

Explanatory variables		All countries			
	(6)	(7)	(8)	(9)	(10)
Intercept	0.105 (5.119)	−0.053 (−1.025)	0.109 (5.303)	0.070 (2.097)	0.031 (1.280)
Agriculture	—	0.003 (3.255)	—	0.001 (1.811)	—
Mining and manufacturing	0.221 E-4 (0.330)	0.002 (2.340)	0.132 E-3 (0.198)	—	0.252 E-3 (0.932)
Foreign trade	−0.057 (−3.153)	−0.041 (−2.290)	−0.055 (−3.027)	−0.047 (−2.587)	−0.054 (−3.140)
GDP per capita	−0.675 E-5 (−2.291)	−0.930 E-5 (−3.243)	−0.757 E-5 (−2.535)	−0.612 E-5 (−2.470)	−0.841 E-5 (−2.919)
Urbanisation	0.976 E-3 (2.134)	0.196 E-2 (4.442)	0.107 E-2 (2.881)	0.141 E-2 (3.520)	0.124 E-2 (3.400)

Industrialised	−0.064	−0.041	−0.049	−0.045	−0.031
	(−3.101)	(−1.929)	(−2.147)	(−2.011)	(−1.308)
POLINST	0.094	0.087	—	—	—
	(2.134)	(2.016)			
POLINSTEST	—	—	0.089	0.745	0.083
			(2.017)	(1.751)	(1.960)
MAJ	—	—	—	—	0.042
					(2.771)
COAL	—	—	—	(−0.019)	—
				(−1.367)	
NPC	—	—	−0.013	—	—
			(−1.395)		
R^2	0.366	0.445	0.383	0.421	0.429
N	78	78	78	78	78

Note:
* The numbers in parentheses are t-statistics. R^2 is the coefficient of correlation, and N is the number of observations.

popular (and in our opinion less desirable) indicator of instability based on the Taylor and Jodice (1983) data set is used. For instance, the following result was obtained when column (4) was re-estimated using the observed frequency of government transfer (FRETRAN):

INFTAX = 0.102 − 0.215 E-2 Manufacturing − 0.091 Foreign Trade
    (1.945) (− 1.559)   (− 0.864)

    − 0.363 E-5 GDP per capita + 0.112 E-2 urbanisation
    (− 0.680)   (1.658)

    − 0.081 industrialised + 0.084 FRETRAN + 0.390 MAJ $R^2 = 0.274$.
    (− 1.671)   (1.998)   (1.522)

As can be seen, although the coefficient of political instability is smaller and is estimated with less precision, the overall results are still broadly supportive of the political economy approach to explaining cross-country differentials in inflation tax.

As we pointed out above, while our new POLINST and POLINSTEST indicators capture the degree of instability of the *political system*, the Taylor–Jodice index is a measure of *government* instability. This suggests that including both indices jointly in an inflation tax regression could help us distinguish between the two political economy models of section 2. When this was done the following result was obtained

INFTAX = 0.137 − 0.200 E-2 Manufacturing − 0.092 Foreign Trade
    (3.793) (− 1.423)   (− 2.944)

    − 0.285 E-5 GDP per capita + 0.110 E-2 Urbanisation
    (− 0.546)   (1.619)

    − 0.112 industrialised + 0.167 POLINST + 0.057 FRETRAN $N = 76$
    (− 2.736)   (2.009)   (1.308) $R^2 = 0.291$.

The fact that our new index of instability of the political system is significant, while FRETRAN is not, provides additional support to the myopic government model of inflation tax.

3.3   Sensitivity analysis

A possible limitation of the results reported in tables 8.1 and 8.2 refers to the potential endogeneity of the political instability variables. We deal with this issue by estimating a set of instrumental variable regressions. We used as instruments the 1950–70 averages for the following political variables: regular executive transfers, frequency of successful coups, a majority government dummy, and the frequency of unsuccessful coups and executive adjustments.

Table 8.3 contains a summary of the results obtained from a set of IV regressions. As can be seen, the conclusions obtained in tables 8.1 and 8.2 are strengthened: the coefficients of the political instability indexes are still positive and are estimated with (slightly) greater precision. Also, the coefficients of the weakness proxies are still insignificant.

In order to analyse the possible role of outliers in the results reported above, an influence analysis based on Cook's distance measure was undertaken. This shows the presence of two outliers: Ghana and Uganda. When these outliers were excluded from the sample, the results were not affected significantly. Also, when the estimates were corrected for hetero-skedasticity the most important conclusions obtained above were maintained.

Summarising, the results reported in this section provide broad support to the political economy approach to inflation. They indicate that political variables are important for explaining cross-country differentials on the use of the inflation tax to finance government expenditures. More specifically, these results show that, while political instability plays an important role in affecting government's reliance on seignorage, the (average) degree of weakness of governments' in office does not affect the inflation tax. These results are robust to the definition of the political instability indicator, the political weakness index, the estimation procedure, outliers exclusion, heteroskedasticity correction and reversed causation.

4 DISTORTIVE TAXES AND POLITICAL INSTABILITY: FURTHER RESULTS

The model on the strategic use by a government of the characteristics of the tax system, which was presented in Section 2.1, has implications that go beyond seignorage and the inflation tax. In fact, the main implication of that model is that in an unstable political system the government in office will not fully discount the future (i.e., it will be myopic) and, thus, it will rely on inefficient forms of taxation.

An interesting empirical extension of this type of model is that the use of other inefficient taxes, other than the inflation tax, should also be positively related to political instability. Once such type of taxes are taxes on foreign trade. Thus, as in the case of seignorage, we would expect that, after controlling for other structural variables, political instability and the reliance on taxes on foreign trade should be positively related in cross-country data. In this section we test this. The dependent variable is the 1971–82 average ratio of trade taxes as a percentage of government revenues obtained from the IMF *Government Financial Statistics*. As in the previous section, structural and political variables are included as regressors. The results obtained from the OLS estimates were somewhat mixed: while the coefficients of POLINST and POLINSTEST were positive as

Table 8.3. *Inflation and political variables: instrumental variables estimates*

Dependent variable:	(11) INFTAX	(12) INFTAX	(13) INFTAX	(14) SEIG	(15) SEIG	(16) SEIG
Explanatory variables						
Intercept	−0.065 (−1.107)	−0.063 (−0.898)	0.112 (2.511)	0.085 (2.987)	0.024 (0.694)	0.004 (0.110)
Agriculture	0.339 E-2 (2.970)	0.347 (2.922)				0.928 E-3 (1.364)
Mining and manufacturing			−0.104 E-2 (−0.798)	0.309 E-3 (0.424)	0.384 E-3 (0.555)	
Foreign trade	−0.054 (−1.651)	−0.058 (−1.780)	−0.081 (−2.430)	−0.051 (−2.581)	−0.506 (−2.716)	−0.042 (−2.128)
GDP per capita	−0.325 E-5 (−0.731)	−0.398 E-5 (−0.875)	−0.441 E-5 (−0.809)	−0.709 E-5 (−2.149)	−0.790 E-5 (−2.716)	−0.533 E-5 (−1.937)
Urbanisation	0.216 E-2 (2.787)	0.228 E-2 (2.894)	0.111 E-2 (1.532)	0.115 E-2 (2.818)	0.129 E-2 (3.302)	0.147 (3.385)

Industrialised	−0.096 (−2.240)	−0.089 (−1.819)	−0.104 (−2.049)	−0.076 (−2.481)	−0.054 (−1.873)	−0.069 (−2.189)
POLINST	0.398 (2.147)	—	—	—	—	0.268 (2.292)
POLINSTEST	—	0.321 (2.009)	0.317 (1.993)	0.247 (2.570)	0.215 (2.325)	—
MAJ	—	—	—	—	0.037 (2.325)	0.024 (1.396)
COAL	—	0.244 E-2 (0.900)	—	−0.015 (−0.925)	—	—
NPC	—	—	−0.471 E-2 (−0.277)	—	—	—
R^2	0.308	0.307	0.225	0.273	0.350	0.323
N	76	76	76	78	78	78

expected, their t-statistics were rather low. The residuals from these OLS estimates, however, provided unmistakable evidence of heteroskedasticity. When these regressions on cross-country trade taxes were re-estimated using a more efficient weighted least-squares method, the following result was obtained[8]

$$TRATAX = 0.053 + 0.004 \text{ agriculture} + 0.368 \text{ GDP per capita}$$
$$\quad (0.521) \quad (2.600) \qquad\qquad (0.055)$$
$$\quad + 0.052 \text{ foreign trade} + 0.169 \text{ E-3 urbanisation}$$
$$\qquad (1.700) \qquad\qquad (0.171)$$
$$\quad - 0.112 \text{ industrialised} + 0.164 \text{ POLINSTEST} \quad R^2 = 0.743$$
$$\quad (-2.585) \qquad\qquad (2.229) \qquad\qquad\qquad N = 61$$

When the estimated instability index was replaced by the actual frequency of transfers of power POLINST, the results were not affected in any way: it was still the case that more unstable political systems were associated with a higher reliance on (inefficient) trade taxes. Interestingly enough, this was not the case when the variable on the frequency of executive transfers constructed from Taylor and Jodice was used.[9] For example, when in the previous regression POLINSTEST was replaced by FRETRAN the estimates coefficient turned out to be -0.008 with a t-statistic of -0.26. An interesting and plausible explanation for these radically different estimates is related to the different meanings of our instability measure and the Taylor and Jodice base indicators. By focussing on transfers of power from the ruling *party* to an opposition *party*, our new instability indexes measure the degree of instability of the political *system*. On the other hand, the frequency of executive adjustments indicator measures the degree of instability of the government in office. It records every time the head of state is replaced, independent of the new leader is from the opposition party or the same party as the outgoing leader. In this regard then, our indicators POLINST and POLINSTEST are more closely related to the instability concept of the models in section 2, while the Taylor–Jodice-based index FRETRAN can be considered to be a proxy of political weakness. Under this interpretation the results reported in this section provide further support to the view that the degree of instability of the political system is an important determinant of macro-economic policy; we haven't found evidence, on the other hand, in favour of the political weakness approach.

5   CONCLUDING REMARKS

There are very large differences in the monetary and fiscal policies implemented by different countries or in the same country at different points in time. In this chapter we have asked how can these differences be explained? In the previous pages we argued that this is one of the central questions to be addressed by the theory of economic policy, and we suggested that an answer can be found by focussing on the incentive constraints faced by the policy makers. In particular, we emphasised various political constraints and incentives. The theoretical models reviewed and formulated in this chapter offer at least two different hypotheses of how political instability and more generally political institutions influence the policy formation process. First, political instability determines the rate of time preference of society as a whole, and hence matters for any collective intertemporal decision. Second, political institutions and in particular the degree of political cohesion influences a society's capacity to make decisions and to change the status quo in the face of adverse economic circumstances. Weaker governments will be unable to implement politically costly adjustments and will, thus, resort to inefficient (but easy) sources of financing. Until now very little effort has been made to discriminate between these two hypotheses. This has been the purpose of this chapter. The results obtained in this chapter provide broad support to the myopic government hypothesis. We have found a significantly positive relationship between political instability, on the one hand, and seignorage, inflation tax and trade taxes, on the other hand.

APPENDICES

Data sources

Seignorage and inflation tax: International Monetary Fund; IFS and GFS.
Agricultural and manufacturing shares: World Bank.
Foreign trade: International Monetary Fund.
Taxes on trade: International Monetary Fund.
Urbanisation: World Bank.
MAJ: Banks; Delury (1983); Encyclopaedia Americana; Encyclopaedia Britannica; Mackie (1982); MacHale (1983), World Almanac of Books and Facts (1984); Cook (1989); Council of Foreign Relations; World Almanac of Books and Facts.
COAL: Encyclopedia Americana; Encyclopedia Britannica; Banks; Gunson (1989); Hoplins (1984); Keesing's Archives; McHale (1983); Council of Foreign Relations.
INST: Banks; da Graca (1985); Encyclopedia Americana; Encyclopedia Britannica; McHale (1983); Alexander (1982); Gunson (1989).
NPC: Banks; Encyclopedia Americana; Encyclopedia Britannica; McHale (1983); Council of Foreign Relations.

List of seventy-eight countries included in the study

Australia	Malaysia
Austria	Mauritania
Belgium	Mauritius
Bolivia	Mexico
Botswana	Morocco
Brazil	Netherlands
Burma	New Zealand
Burundi	Nicaragua
Cameroon	Nigeria
Canada	Norway
Central African Republic	Oman
Chad	Pakistan
Chile	Papua New Guinea
Colombia	Paraguay
Congo, Peoples Republic	Peru
Cote d'Ivoire	Philippines
Denmark	Portugal
Dominican Republic	Rwanda
Ecuador	Sierra Leone
El Salvador	Singapore
Ethiopia	Somalia
Finland	South Africa
France	Spain
Gabon	Sri Lanka
Germany, Federal Republic	Sudan
Ghana	Sweden
Greece	Tanzania
Honduras	Thailand
India	Togo
Indonesia	Trinidad and Tobago
Iran	Tunisia
Ireland	Turkey
Italy	Uganda
Jamaica	United Kingdom
Japan	United States
Jordan	Venezuela
Kenya	Zaire
Kuwait	Zambia
Lesotho	Zimbabwe

Notes

This is a significantly revised version of a paper presented at the World Meetings of the Econometric Society, Barcelona, August 1990. We are indebted to our discussants at the meetings, Michael Bruno and Felipe Morandé, for helpful comments. We are grateful to the University of California Pacific Rim Program and the National Science Foundation for financial support. Roberto Schatan, Tom Harris and Julio Santaella provided very able research assistance.

1 See, for example, Alesina (1988, 1989), Cukierman and Metzler (1986), Tabellini (1989), and Persson and Tabellini (1990).
2 Some exceptions are Alesina and Sachs (1978), Tabellini (1990), Cukierman, Edwards and Tabellini (1990), Edwards and Tabellini (1991), Roubini and Sachs (1988, 1989) and Grilli, Masciandaro and Tabellini (1990).
3 The most widely used data set has been assembled by Taylor and Jodice (1983).
4 See Cukierman, Edwards and Tabellini (1991) and the references therein.
5 See Cukierman, Edwards, Tabellini (1990) for very similar probits computed using the Taylor and Jodice government transfer variables.
6 These results coincide with those obtained by Grilli, Masciandano and Tabellini (1990) for a data set of 180 OECDE countries only. Their regressions, however, are limited to political variables, and use one index of 'weakness' only.
7 See, for example, Huntington (1968).
8 The average population for 1970–81 was used as a weight. A possible problem with this equation refers to the potential endogeneity of the foreign trade and instability variables. However, then this equation re-estimated using instrumental variables, the results were basically unaffected.
9 See Edwards and Tabellini (1991).

References

Aizenman, J. (1990), 'Debt and Contingencies', unpublished manuscript, Hebrew University.

Alesina, A. (1988), 'Credibility and Policy Convergence in a Two-Party System with Rational Voters', *American Economic Review*.

(1989), 'Macroeconomics and Politics', in *NBER Macroeconomics Annual*.

Alesina, A. and Drazen, A. (1989), 'Why are Stabilizations Delayed? A Political Economic Model', NBER Working Paper No. 3053, August.

Alesina, A. and Sachs, J. (1988), 'Political Parties and Business Cycles in the United States, 1948–1984', *Journal of Money, Credit and Banking*, 20(1): 63–82.

Alexander, R. (1982), *Political Parties of the Americas*, Westport, Conn.: Greenwood Press.

Banks, A. (various issues) *Political Handbook of the World*, Binghamton, N. Y.: CSA Publications.

Cook, C. (1989), *The Facts on File World Political Almanac*, New York: Facts on File.

Council of Foreign Relations (various issues) *The World this Year*, New York: Simon and Schuster.

Cukierman, A. and Metzler, A. 'A Theory of Ambiguity, Credibility and Inflation under Discretion and Asymmetric Information', *Econometrica*, 54(5): 1099–128.

Cukierman, A., Edwards, S. and Tabellini, G. (1990), 'Seignorage and Political Instability', Discusssion Paper No.381, Centre for Economic Policy Research, February.

da Graca, J.V. (1985), *Heads of State and Governments*, New York: New York University.

Delury, G. (1983), *World Encyclopedia of Political Systems & Parties*, New York: Facts on File.

Drazen, A. and Grilli, V. (1990), 'The Benefits of Crises for Economic Reforms', NBER Working Paper No. 3527, December.

Edwards, S. and Tabellini, G. (1990), 'Explaining Fiscal Policies and Inflation in Developing Countries', NBER Working Paper No. 2493.

    (1991), 'Explaining Fiscal Policies and Inflation in Developing Countries', *Journal of International Money and Finance*.

Encyclopedia Americana (various issues), Year Book, Danbury, Conn.: Grolier.

Encyclopedia Britannica (various issues), Year Book, Chicago: Encyclopedia Britannica.

Grilli, V., Masciandaro, D. and Tabellini, G. (1990), 'Political and Monetary Institutions and Public Financial Policies in the Industrial Countries', mimeo, Birbeck College.

Gunson, P. (1989), *Dictionary of Contemporary Politics of South America*, New York: Macmillan.

Hopkins, J. (1984), *Latin America & Caribbean Contemporary Record, 1982–83*, New York: Holmes & Meier.

Huntington, S. (1968), *Political Order in Changing Societies*, New Haven: Yale University Press.

Keesing's Contemporary Archives (various issues), London: Longman.

Mackie, T. and Rose, R. (1982), *The International Almanac of Electoral History*, New York: Facts on File.

McHale, V. (1983), *Political Parties of Europe*, Westport, Conn.: Greenwood Press.

Nueva Enciclopedia de Chile (1974), Argentina: Ediciones Libra.

Persson, T. and Tabellini, G. (1990), *Macroeconomic Policy, Credibility and Politics*, New York: Harvard Academic Publishers.

Roubini, N. and Sachs, J. (1988), 'Political and Economic Determinants of Budget Deficits in the Industrial Democracies', *European Economic Review*.

    (1989), 'Government Spending and Budget Deficits in the Industrialized Countries', *Economic Policy*.

Sanguinetti, P. (1991), 'Fiscal Deficits and Federal Government', mimeo, UCLA Economics Dept.

Tabellini, G. (1990), 'Domestic Politics and the International Coordination of Fiscal Policies', *Journal of International Economics*, 28(3–4) (May): 245–65.

Taylor, C. and Jodice, D. (1983), *World Handbook of Social and Political Indicators*, New Haven: Yale University Press.

World Almanac of Books and Facts, (1984), New York: Newspaper Enterprise Association.

CHAPTER 9

Credibility and the dynamics of stabilisation policy: a basic framework[1]

Guillermo A. Calvo and Carlos A. Végh

1   INTRODUCTION

The Southern-Cone stabilisation programmes of the late 1970s brought new challenges to economic theory.[2] The underlying idea behind these programmes was that by pegging the exchange rate to the dollar, the inflation rate would rapidly come down to international levels. However – and to the surprise of policymakers – the inflation rate failed to converge quickly to the preannounced rate of devaluation, which resulted in substantial real appreciation of the domestic currency. Real economic activity expanded in spite of the real appreciation. Later in the programmes – and even before the preannounced exchange rate system was abandoned – a recession set in. The eventual slump in economic activity that took place in the Southern-Cone programmes gave rise to the notion of 'recession now versus recession later', in comparing stabilisations based on controlling the money supply with stabilisations based on fixing the (rate of change of the) exchange rate (hereafter referred to as money-based and exchange-rate-based stabilisations, respectively). The idea was that, under money-based stabilisation, the costs (in terms of output losses) would be paid up-front, whereas, under exchange-rate-based stabilisation, the costs would be postponed until a later date. Thus, choosing between the two nominal anchors was viewed as choosing not *if* but *when* the costs of bringing down inflation should be borne.[3]

Almost half a decade later, the 'heterodox' programmes of Argentina, Israel, and Brazil brought to life once again some of the same – and still mostly unresolved – issues.[4] Real appreciation was very much part of the picture in spite of the use of wage and price controls. More puzzling, however, was the re-emergence of the pattern of an initial boom and a later recession. The Israeli recession was viewed as particularly hard to rationalise because of its occurrence in a fiscally sound and largely successful programme. It then became clear that economic theory had to come to grips with the issue of an eventual recession in an exchange-rate-based stabilisation programme.

Some observers, reminded of the old adage, 'the more things change, the more they remain the same', began to suspect that the similarities between the Southern-Cone and the heterodox programmes were not purely coincidental. In particular, Kiguel and Liviatan (1992) dug up older programmes, compared them to the programmes of the late 1970s and mid 1980s, and concluded that most of the puzzling features observed in the Southern-Cone programmes could be upgraded to the category of 'stylised facts'.[5] Specifically, the beginning of an exchange-rate-based stabilisation programme is characterised by sustained real appreciation and an overheated economy.[6] Furthermore, later in the programme, a recession takes hold. These stylised facts appear not to depend on whether the stabilisation is ultimately successful or not. The scanty evidence on money-based stabilisations in chronic inflation countries also lends support to the notion that the recession takes place at the beginning of the programme rather than later. The most notable case is the Peruvian stabilisation of August 1990 which led to a substantial fall in output during the first year of the programme. Thus, the recession-now-versus-recession-later hypothesis appears to hold in practice.

Early models that attempted to explain the phenomena observed in the Southern-Cone programmes (for instance, Rodriguez (1982) and Calvo (1983a)) were based on reduced-form behavioural equations. In both Rodriguez (1982) and Calvo (1983a), perfect capital mobility prevails and excess aggregate demand depends negatively on the real interest rate and positively on the real exchange rate (i.e., the relative price of tradable goods in terms of non-tradable goods). Rodriguez's (1982) key assumption is that expectations are adaptive rather than rational. Hence, a reduction in the rate of devaluation, which lowers the nominal interest rate, results in a fall in the real interest rate, because the expected rate of inflation of home goods is predetermined. The initial fall in the real interest rate causes an expansion (assuming that output of the home good is demand-determined). The domestic currency begins to appreciate in real terms as inflation of home goods remains above the devaluation rate. Eventually, the impact of the real appreciation comes to dominate the effect of the lower real interest rate, and output falls.

In contrast to Rodriguez (1982), Calvo (1983a) assumes rational expectations and staggered price setting in the home-goods sector. A non-credible (i.e., temporary) reduction in the devaluation rate causes a reduction in the inflation rate of home goods that falls short of the decline in the rate of devaluation, thus causing real appreciation. The fall in the domestic real interest rate that results from the expected real appreciation increases excess aggregate demand on impact.[7]

An explicit comparison between money-based and exchange-rate-based stabilisation in a reduced-form model is carried out by Fischer (1986). In Fischer's model, prices are flexible but wages are predetermined as a result of long-term nominal contracts. A money-based stabilisation is recessionary, while an exchange-rate-based stabilisation has an ambiguous effect on output. The reason is that the contractionary effect of the real appreciation could be more than offset by the expansionary effect of the fall in the real interest rate.[8]

A second group of models that attempts to explain the effects of exchange-rate-based stabilisations derives behavioural equations from utility-maximising consumers. These models include Obstfeld (1985), Calvo (1986b), Drazen and Helpman (1987, 1988), and Helpman and Razin (1987). Obstfeld (1985) and Drazen and Helpman (1987, 1988) include money as an argument in the utility function. Obstfeld (1985) studies a gradual reduction in the rate of devaluation, in the spirit of the Southern-Cone 'tablitas'. Obstfeld concludes that, if the cross-derivative between real money balances and consumption is negative, then, on impact, consumption of both tradable and home goods increases and the real exchange rate falls.[9] Drazen and Helpman (1987, 1988) assume that consumption and money enter separately in the utility function and study the effects of anticipated changes in fiscal policy. If the government freezes the exchange rate and announces that it will reduce spending on tradable goods in the future, then, on impact, consumption of tradable goods increases, the current account goes into deficit, and the real exchange rate falls. Helpman and Razin (1987) focus on a Blanchard-type model in which Ricardian equivalence does not hold. An initial expansion in consumption may result from an exchange rate freeze, accompanied by future taxes, that generates a positive wealth effect for the current generation.

Calvo (1986b) introduces money through a cash-in-advance constraint and examines a non-credible (i.e., temporary) reduction in the rate of devaluation. The assumption of perfect capital mobility implies that the temporary reduction in the rate of devaluation translates into a temporary reduction in the nominal interest rate, and thus in the cost of consumption (since the cost of consumption includes the opportunity cost of holding money). Hence, the consumer increases the demand for current tradable goods relative to future tradable goods, which results in a current-account deficit. When the policy is discontinued, consumption of tradable goods falls below its initial level. If it is assumed that the tradable good acts as the only input in the production of home goods, Calvo (1986b) shows that the real exchange rate falls on impact but remains constant thereafter until the policy is discontinued.

All the models just reviewed provide valuable insights into the effects of stabilisation policy. Some issues, however, remain unexplained. Specifically, a utility-maximising model of exchange-rate-based stabilisation has yet to account for the following features. First, at the beginning of the programme, the home-goods sector is operating above its full-employment level at the same time that the real exchange rate is falling. Second, the home-goods sector enters into recession (i.e., output falls below its full-employment level) either when or *before* the programme is discontinued. Third, the inflation rate of home goods remains above the rate of devaluation for a long period of time, resulting in a *sustained and cumulative* real appreciation of the domestic currency.

A review of the literature also suggests that there exists the need to bring together the various analytical pieces and provide a unified analytical framework within which exchange-rate-based and money-based stabilisation policy can be analysed. To this effect, this chapter develops an analytical framework which, first, accounts for the main stylised facts of exchange-rate-based stabilisation and, second, compares exchange-rate-based stabilisation with money-based stabilisation.

The four key ingredients of our model are: (i) intertemporal consumption substitution; (ii) liquidity-in-advance constraint; (iii) price-staggering in the home-goods sector; and (iv) currency substitution. None of these assumptions can be relaxed in our model without losing the capacity of explaining some of the key features of exchange-rate-based or money-based stabilisations. Thus, in this sense, this chapter provides a 'minimal' model for rationalising some of the puzzles associated with stabilisations.

The demand side of the model follows the Ramsey–Lucas tradition of a representative individual subject to a cash-in-advance constraint. Instead of just 'cash', we assume that the individual can hold domestic and foreign currency in variable proportions – an assumption that is known as 'currency substitution' – which explains the use of the term 'liquidity-in-advance' constraint. This assumption is highly relevant because it is well-known that in high-inflation countries foreign currencies are widely used for transactions purposes.[10]

There exist two types of goods: tradable and non-tradable (or home) goods. This distinction allows us to model and discuss the real exchange rate (i.e., the relative price of tradable goods in terms of home goods). Production of tradable goods is exogenous and subject to perfect price flexibility, while home goods exhibit staggered price setting à la Phelps–

Taylor (see Phelps (1978), Taylor (1979, 1980)) with a Calvo twist (Calvo (1983b)). Output of home goods is demand determined.

Under full credibility, a reduction in the rate of devaluation, and thus of the nominal interest rate, induces the consumer to substitute away from foreign currency and towards domestic currency. The resulting wealth effect – due to lower seigniorage payments on foreign currency – leads to higher consumption of tradable goods. Since, under fixed exchange rates and sticky prices, the relative price of tradable goods in terms of home goods (i.e., the real exchange rate) is given in the short run, the rise in the consumption of tradable goods must be accompanied by a corresponding increase in the demand for home goods. The inflation rate of home goods falls by less than the rate of devaluation and could even increase. As a result, the domestic real interest rate falls and the domestic currency begins to appreciate in real terms. Thus, the predictions of the model under full credibility are consistent with some of the stylised facts of exchange-rate-based stabilisations – in particular, the initial expansion and real appreciation of the domestic currency. However, the eventual recession is left unexplained.

A fully credible reduction in the rate of growth of the money supply also leads to higher consumption of tradable goods due to the wealth effect just discussed. However, there is a recession in the home-goods sector. The reason is that the excess demand for domestic money that results from a lower nominal interest rate necessitates a fall in consumption of home goods to equilibrate the domestic money market. The inflation rate of home goods falls by more than the nominal interest rate, so that the domestic real interest rate increases.

The model thus highlights key differences between the impact effects of exchange-rate-based and money-based stabilisation that are unrelated to credibility problems (to be discussed below). Specifically, under full credibility, an exchange-rate-based stabilisation (i) causes an expansion in the home-goods sector, (ii) may have little effect on the inflation rate of home goods, and (iii) reduces the domestic real interest rate. In contrast, a money-based stabilisation (i) results in a recession, (ii) sharply reduces the inflation rate of home goods, and (iii) increases the domestic real interest rate.

Discontinuation of stabilisation programmes is the focal point of the present chapter. Following Calvo (1986b), we analyse this issue in the simplest possible manner by focussing on the implications of *temporary* policy.[11] By definition, a temporary policy is one that will be discontinued in the future. A temporary policy is equivalent to the case in which the authorities intend to continue the present policy but the public does not fully believe it (i.e., there exists lack of policy credibility). Thus, our analysis is capable of killing two birds with one stone: (i) it addresses the issue of policy temporariness and (ii) it sheds some light on the implications of non-credible policies.

Consider, once again, the case of predetermined exchange rates, and imagine that the public expects inflation-as-usual to be resumed after a few months. The momentary lowering of the rate of devaluation brings down the domestic nominal interest rate which, in turn, lowers the effective cost of consumption (because the latter includes the opportunity cost of holding money). Given that this phenomenon is seen as transitory, it leads the public to increase the demand for present tradable goods (and, correspondingly, to decrease the demand for future tradable goods). Since the relative price of tradable goods in terms of home goods is given in the short run, the rise in the consumption of tradable goods must be accompanied by a corresponding increase in the demand for home goods. The rise in aggregate demand implies that the inflation rate of home goods falls by less than the rate of devaluation – and could even increase. Thus, a prolonged period of real appreciation sets in, as the inflation rate of home goods remains above the devaluation rate until the policy is discontinued. Thus, *an overheated economy coexists with sustained real appreciation for a prolonged period of time.*

After increasing when the devaluation rate is reduced, excess aggregate demand for home goods, and hence output, fall over time as the relative price of home goods increases. At some point in time – when the policy is expected to be discontinued or even before that – output falls below its full-employment level. Therefore, *a recession sets in later in the programme even if the policy has yet to be discontinued* (assuming that the policy is discontinued when it was expected to be).

Under money-based stabilisation, lack of credibility does not substantially alter the impact effect of a reduction in the rate of growth of the money supply. Both output and inflation (of home and tradable goods) fall on impact. Thus, *a money-based stabilisation is always contractionary irrespective of policy credibility.* The real exchange rate falls on impact and remains below its new steady-state value during the whole adjustment process. The model thus suggests that the simultaneous occurrence of an overheated economy and a real exchange rate lower than its steady-state equilibrium is not likely to be observed in stabilisation programmes that rely on flexible exchange rates. Furthermore, the model also suggests that real appreciation may be an unavoidable consequence of inflation stabilisation, regardless of whether the exchange rate or the money supply is used as the nominal anchor. A substantial real appreciation has indeed characterised the recent money-based Peruvian programme of August 1990.

Another important difference between exchange-rate-based and money-based stabilisation lies in the effects of lower credibility. Under flexible exchange rates, a stabilisation programme that enjoys very little credibility has basically no effect either on real variables or on inflation. In sharp contrast, under predetermined exchange rates, lower credibility only exacerbates intertemporal substitution effects and, therefore, all ensuing real effects. In this sense, therefore, *substantial lack of credibility is more costly under exchange-rate-based stabilisation than under money-based stabilisation.*

The chapter proceeds as follows. Section 2 discusses the basic model. Section 3 deals with exchange-rate-based stabilisation. Section 4 addresses money-based stabilisation. Section 5 discusses the role of nominal 'anchors' in stabilisation plans in the light of the theoretical analysis. Some final remarks close the chapter in Section 6.

2   THE MODEL

Consider a small open economy inhabited by a large number of identical individuals. The utility function of the representative individual is

$$\int_0^\infty u(c_t, c_t^*)\exp(-\beta t)dt, \tag{9.1}$$

where $u(.)$, the instantaneous utility function, is increasing, twice-continuously differentiable, and strictly concave; c and c^* denote consumption of non-tradable (or home) and tradable goods, respectively; and β is the positive and constant subjective discount rate.

There exists currency substitution in the economy, in the sense that both domestic (M) and foreign (F) currency are used to carry out transactions. Let E denote the nominal exchange rate (in units of domestic currency per unit of foreign currency), P^* denote the (constant) foreign currency price of the tradable good, and P denote the domestic currency price of the home good. Then, real domestic money balances, m, and real foreign money balances, f, are defined as $m \equiv M/EP^*$ and $f \equiv F/P^*$.[12] The relative price of tradable goods in terms of home goods, e, is defined as $e \equiv EP^*/P$. (To maintain the conventional terminology, e will be referred to as the 'real exchange rate'.) As usual, domestic and foreign money are assumed to be imperfect substitutes because of, say, legal restrictions or different transactions patterns.[13] Formally, the consumer is subject to a liquidity-in-advance constraint[14]

$$c_t/e_t + c_t^* \leq l(m_t, f_t), \qquad l_m > 0, l_f > 0, l_{mm} < 0, l_{ff} < 0, l_{mf} > 0, \tag{9.2}$$

where $l(.)$ is a linearly homogenous, twice-continuously differentiable function, which may be interpreted as a liquidity-services production function.[15] Equation (9.2) states that total real expenditure in terms of tradable goods cannot exceed liquidity services produced by domestic and foreign money.

The consumer also holds an internationally traded bond, b, whose (constant) rate of return, in terms of tradable goods, is r. Real financial wealth is thus

$$a_t = m_t + f_t + b_t. \tag{9.3}$$

The consumer's lifetime budget constraint is

$$a_0 + \int_0^\infty (y_t/e_t + y_t^* + \tau_t)\exp(-rt)dt = \int_0^\infty (c_t/e_t + c_t^* + i_t m_t + r f_t)\exp(-rt)dt, \tag{9.4}$$

where y and y^* denote income of home and tradable goods, respectively, τ stands for lump-sum transfers from the government, and i is the nominal interest rate.

The consumer's problem consists in choosing paths of c, c^*, m, and f, to maximise (9.1) subject to (9.2), (9.4), and initial real financial wealth, a_0. To simplify the analysis, it will be assumed that $u(c, c^*) = \log(c) + \log(c^*)$.[16] In addition to (9.2) – holding with equality – and (9.4), the other first-order conditions can be expressed as[17]

$$1/c_t^* = \lambda[1 + i_t/l_m(m_t, f_t)], \tag{9.5}$$

$$c_t/c_t^* = e_t \tag{9.6}$$

$$l_m(m_t, f_t)/l_f(m_t, f_t) = i_t/r, \tag{9.7}$$

where λ is the (time-invariant) Lagrange multiplier associated with constraint (9.4).[18] Equation (9.5) represents the familiar condition whereby the consumer equates the marginal utility of consumption of tradable goods to the shadow price of wealth times the 'price' of tradable goods. The relevant 'price' of the tradable good in this model – which will be referred to as the *effective* price – is given by the term in square brackets on the right-hand side (RHS) of equation (9.5). The effective price consists of the market price (unity) plus the cost of producing the liquidity services needed to purchase one unit of the good $(i/l_m(m, f))$. Intuitively, note that one additional unit of liquidity services is needed to purchase an additional unit of tradable goods. The production of a unit of liquidity services requires $1/l_m(m, f)$ units of m, whose cost is $i/l_m(m, f)$.[19] Equation (9.6) indicates that, at an optimum, the marginal rate of substitution between tradable and home goods equals the relative price of tradable goods in terms of home goods (i.e., the real exchange rate).

At an optimum, the marginal rate of substitution between domestic and foreign money equals the ratio of their opportunity costs, as indicated by equation (9.7). Equation (9.7) implicitly defines the demand for f relative to m as a function of i/r (recall that $l(m,f)$ is homogenous of degree one so that $l_m(m,f)$ and $l_f(m,f)$ are homogenous of degree zero):

$$f_t/m_t = \phi(i_t/r), \qquad \phi'(i_t/r) > 0. \tag{9.8}$$

An increase in the nominal interest rate induces a rise in foreign money balances relative to domestic money balances, which characterises the phenomenon of currency substitution.[20]

The sum of m and f will be referred to as 'real liquidity' and will be denoted by z (i.e., $z \equiv m + f$). Combining equations (9.2) – holding with equality – and (9.8) yields the demand for m, f and z:

$$m_t = (c_t/e_t + c_t^*)\Phi^m(i_t/r), \qquad \Phi^{m\prime}(i_t/r) < 0, \tag{9.9}$$

$$f_t = (c_t/e_t + c_t^*)\Phi^f(i_t/r), \qquad \Phi^{f\prime}(i_t/r) > 0, \tag{9.10}$$

$$z_t = (c_t/e_t + c_t^*)\Phi^z(i_t/r), \qquad \Phi^{z\prime}(i_t/r) > 0, \tag{9.11}$$

As one would expect, the demands for m and f depend positively on real expenditure $(c/e + c^*)$ and negatively on their respective opportunity costs, as equations (9.9) and (9.10) indicate. Under the assumption that $i > r$, the demand for z depends positively on i/r (equation (9.11)). In other words, an increase in i, for given $c/e + c^*$, reduces the demand for m by less than it raises the demand for f, which results in a higher demand for z. The reason is that the marginal productivity of m is higher, at an optimum, than that of f, because the opportunity cost of m is higher than that of f (recall equation (9.7)). Hence, for given real expenditure, a rise in i must reduce the demand for m by less than it increases the demand for f for liquidity services (and thus real expenditure) to remain constant.

Equations (9.7) and (9.8) can be used to express the effective price of tradable goods – given by the term in square brackets on the RHS of equation (9.5) – as a function of i/r, which will be denoted by $p(i/r)$:

$$p(i_t/r) = 1 + r/l_f[1, \phi(i_t/r)], \qquad p'(i_t/r) > 0. \tag{9.12}$$

A reduction in i lowers the effective price of tradable goods because it reduces the opportunity cost of one of the two monies that are used to produce liquidity services. First-order condition (9.6) implies that the effective price of home goods is $p(i/r)/e$, so that a reduction in i also lowers, for given e, the effective price of c. Changes in the effective price of consumption as a result of changes in the nominal interest rate will play a key role in the analysis.

Let us now turn to equilibrium conditions. The present discounted value of government transfers is given by

$$\int_0^\infty \tau_t \exp(-rt)dt = q_0 + \int_0^\infty (\dot{m}_t + \epsilon_t m_t)\exp(-rt)dt, \tag{9.13}$$

where q_0 denotes the government's initial stock of net foreign assets, and $\epsilon(\equiv \dot{E}/E)$ denotes the instantaneous rate of devaluation (or depreciation).
Equilibrium in the home-goods markets requires that

$$c_t = y_t. \tag{9.14}$$

Moreover, perfect capital mobility is assumed, which implies that

$$i_t = r + \epsilon_t. \tag{9.15}$$

Combining equations (9.4), (9.13), (9.14) and (9.15) (and imposing the usual transversality condition) yields the economy's resource constraint:

$$k_0 + \int_0^\infty y_t^* \exp(-rt)dt = \int_0^\infty (c_t^* + rf_t)\exp(-rt)dt, \tag{9.16}$$

where $k = f + b + q$ denotes the economy's stock of net foreign assets. Equation (9.16) states that the economy's wealth (i.e., the present discounted value of tradable resources) equals the present discounted value of consumption of tradable goods plus seignorage on foreign money paid to the rest of the world.[21]

To derive the current account, consider the consumer's flow constraint given by

$$\dot{a}_t = y_t/e_t + y_t^* - c_t/e_t - c_t^* + rb_t - \epsilon_t m_t + \tau_t. \tag{9.17}$$

Under predetermined exchange rates, the government's flow constraint indicates that the excess of revenues over spending results in asset (or reserve) accumulation; namely, $\dot{q}_t = \dot{m}_t + \epsilon_t m_t + rq_t - \tau_t$. Combining the latter with equation (9.17) yields the current-account balance:

$$\dot{k}_t = rk_t + y_t^* - c_t^* - rf_t. \tag{9.18}$$

As expected, the accumulation of net foreign assets (i.e., the current-account balance) equals the difference between income of tradable goods and expenditure on tradable goods. Expenditure on tradable goods comprises consumption of tradable goods plus the rental cost of foreign money holdings.[22]

Naturally, equation (9.18) also obtains under flexible exchange rates. To derive equation (9.18) under flexible exchange rates, note that the central bank accumulates no reserves. (The government's initial stock of bonds is taken to be zero.) The growth of real money balances is given by

$$\dot{m}_t/m_t = \mu_t - \epsilon_t, \tag{9.19}$$

where $\mu(\equiv \dot{M}/M)$ is the rate of growth of the nominal money supply. Transfers are given by $\tau_t = \mu_t m_t$. Combining the latter equation with (9.19) and (9.17) yields the current-account balance (9.18).

We now turn to the supply side of the model. To simplify the analysis, it will be assumed that the supply of tradable goods is exogenously given at the constant level y^* (i.e., $y_t^* = y^*$ for all t), while the home-goods sector operates under staggered price setting and supply is demand determined.[23] Following the staggered-prices model in Calvo (1983b), it is assumed that

$$\dot{\pi}_t = -\theta D_t, \qquad \theta > 0, \tag{9.20}$$

where π is the inflation rate of home goods, and $D = y - \bar{y}$, where $\bar{y}$ can be interpreted as 'full-employment' output. Thus, D is a measure of excess demand in the home-goods market. As shown in Calvo (1983b), equation (9.20) can be derived from a setup in which firms set prices in an asynchronous manner, taking into account the expected future path of the average price of home goods and the path of excess demand in that market. Equation (9.20) indicates that the *rate of change* in the inflation rate is a *negative* function of excess demand. Intuitively, the higher is excess demand at time t, the higher will be the prices set by those firms that revise their prices at time t. Therefore, the higher is excess demand at time t, the higher will be the rate of inflation of home goods at t, π_t. Furthermore, excess demand at time t is not taken into account by price setters at t', for all $t' > t$. Hence, the higher is excess demand at time t, the sharper will be the drop in the inflation rate after t, which is what equation (9.20) asserts.[24]

Substituting $D_t = y_t - \bar{y}$ into (9.20) and imposing home-goods market equilibrium (9.14) yields

$$\dot{\pi}_t = \theta(\bar{y} - c_t), \tag{9.21}$$

which constitutes one of the key dynamic equations.

We now derive the equilibrium path of consumption of tradable goods. First-order condition (9.5) and the economy's resource constraint (9.16) imply that (recalling that $y_t^* = y^*$ for all t)

$$c_t^* = \frac{y^* + rk_0 - r\int_0^\infty rf_t \exp(-rt)dt}{p(i_t/r)r\int_0^\infty [1/p(i_t/r)]\exp(-rt)dt}, \tag{9.22}$$

where the definition of the effective price of consumption of tradable goods, given by (9.12), has been used. The numerator in equation (9.22) represents permanent income. The inverse of the denominator can be interpreted as the equilibrium marginal propensity to consume (MPC) tradable goods out of permanent income (see Calvo and Végh (1990a) for details), and reflects intertemporal substitution effects. If the nominal interest rate is constant over time (and equal to $\bar{i}$), the denominator, and thus the MPC, becomes unity. The time path of the effective price is constant over time so that there are no incentives to engage in intertemporal consumption substitution. Specifically, if $i_t = \bar{\imath}$, for all t, consumption of tradable goods is given by (using (9.2), holding with equality, (9.6), (9.8) and (9.22))

$$c_t^* = \frac{y^* + rk_0}{1 + 2r/l[1/\phi(\bar{\imath}/r), 1]}, \tag{9.23}$$

which implies that consumption of tradable goods is constant over time. It follows that unanticipated and permanent changes in i will affect c^* only through the *wealth effect* that results from using a different stock of foreign currency.

In order to isolate the substitution effects that result from temporary policy, the analysis will abstract from the wealth effect when studying temporary policy. For future reference, then, note that, if we abstract from seignorage payments on foreign currency, equation (9.22) reduces to[25]

$$c_t^* = \frac{y^* + rk_0}{p(i_t/r)r\int_0^\infty [1/p(i_t/r)]\exp(-rt)dt}. \tag{9.24}$$

Since the wealth effect associated with substituting foreign for domestic currency is no longer present, unanticipated and permanent changes in i have no effect on c^* because $c_t^* = y^* + rk_0$ for *any* level of i, as long as i is constant over time.

Having introduced the analytical framework which is common to the cases of both predetermined and flexible exchange rates, we can now proceed to study stabilisation policy under each regime separately.

3   EXCHANGE-RATE-BASED STABILISATION

This section studies stabilisation plans based on lowering the (exogenously given) rate of devaluation. It will be assumed here – and throughout this section – that prior to any policy change at $t = 0$, the rate of devaluation, ϵ, is fixed at ϵ^h and is expected to remain constant forever. The economy is thus at a steady-state given by (steady-state values are denoted by a subscript 'ss')

$$i_{ss} = r + \epsilon^h, \tag{9.25}$$

$$\pi_{ss} = \epsilon^h, \tag{9.26}$$

$$c_{ss} = \bar{y}, \tag{9.27}$$

$$c_{ss}^* = \frac{y^* + rk_0}{1 + 2r/l\{1/\phi[(r + \epsilon^h)/r], 1\}}, \tag{9.28}$$

$$e_{ss} = \bar{y}/c_{ss}^*, \tag{9.29}$$

$$r_{ss}^d = r, \tag{9.30}$$

$$m_{ss} = 2c_{ss}^* \Phi^m [(r + \epsilon^h)/r], \tag{9.31}$$

$$f_{ss} = 2c_{ss}^* \Phi^f [(r + \epsilon^h)/r], \tag{9.32}$$

$$z_{ss} = 2c_{ss}^* \Phi^z [(r + \epsilon^h)/r]. \tag{9.33}$$

The nominal interest rate (equation (9.25)) follows from the assumption of perfect capital mobility (equation (9.15)). For the real exchange rate to remain constant, the inflation rate of tradable goods (i.e., the rate of devaluation) and the inflation rate of home goods must be the same, as indicated by equation (9.26). From equation (9.21), it follows that consumption of home goods must equal full-employment output for inflation of home goods to remain constant, as indicated by equation (9.27). Consumption of tradable goods, given by (9.28), follows from (9.23) and (9.25) because the devaluation rate, and thus the nominal interest rate, are constant over time. The steady-state level of the real exchange rate, given by (9.29), follows from (9.6) and (9.27). A higher steady-state consumption of tradable goods must be accompanied by a lower real exchange rate (i.e., a lower relative price of tradable goods). Equation (9.30) indicates that the steady-state domestic real interest rate, r^d (defined as $r^d \equiv i - \pi$), equals r, which follows from the definition and equations (9.25) and (9.26). Equations (9.31)–(9.33) follow from (9.9)–(9.11), using (9.6) and (9.25).

3.1 Permanent reduction in the rate of devaluation

Suppose that the economy is initially at the steady-state just described. At $t = 0$ (the 'present'), policy makers announce that the rate of devaluation will be immediately and permanently reduced from ϵ^h to ϵ^l.[26] Furthermore, the announcement is fully credible, in the sense that the public *expects* that the devaluation rate will stay at ϵ^l for the indefinite future.

Perfect capital mobility (see equation (9.15)) implies that the fall in the rate of devaluation causes the nominal interest rate to adjust immediately to its lower steady-state value, given by $r + \epsilon^l$. The reduction in the nominal interest rate lowers the opportunity cost of domestic money relative to foreign money, which induces the consumer to reduce the ratio of foreign to domestic currency. The adjustment to the new steady-state value is instantaneous, because, from (9.8), the ratio f/m depends only on the nominal interest rate. The consumer increases his or her holdings of real domestic money balances by exchanging foreign currency for domestic currency at the central bank.

Since the lower nominal interest rate is expected to prevail forever, consumption of tradable goods is given by equation (9.23). The constant path of the nominal interest rate implies that there are no incentives to engage in intertemporal substitution; in other words, the path of c^* will remain flat. The substitution of domestic for foreign money results in lower seignorage payments on foreign currency, which increases the present discounted value of tradable resources. This wealth effect causes c^* to adjust instantaneously to its higher level, as indicated by (9.23).[27]

We now turn to the behaviour of the real exchange rate, e, and inflation of home goods, π. Substituting (9.6) into (9.21) yields

$$\dot{\pi}_t = \theta(\bar{y} - e_t c_t^*).\tag{9.34}$$

Since $e \equiv EP^*/P$, it follows that (recall that P^* is constant)

$$\dot{e}_t = (\epsilon - \pi_t)e_t,\tag{9.35}$$

where ϵ denotes the constant rate of devaluation. The determinant associated with the linear approximation of the dynamic system (9.34) and (9.35) around the steady state equals $-\theta\bar{y}$, which, being negative, indicates that the system exhibits saddle-path stability.

Figure 9.1 depicts the phase diagram corresponding to the dynamic system (9.34) and (9.35). The initial steady-state is at point A where $\pi_{ss} = \epsilon^h$ and $e_{ss} = \bar{y}/c_{ss}^*$. The new steady-state is given by either B or D, depending on the magnitude of the fall in e_{ss}. The fall in e_{ss} depends, in turn, on how large is the increase in c_{ss}^*, and hence on the magnitude of the wealth effect discussed above.[28] If the increase in c_{ss}^* is relatively small (c_{ss}^* increases to, say, $c_{ss}^{*'}$), then the fall in e_{ss} is small as well (e_{ss} falls to e_{ss}', where $e_{ss}' = \bar{y}/c_{ss}^{*'}$); the new steady-state is thus at point B, and $B'B'$ denotes the corresponding saddle path. On impact, the inflation rate of home goods *falls* from A to C and then proceeds along the saddle path $B'B'$ towards point B. If the increase in c_{ss}^* is relatively large (c_{ss}^* increases to, say, $c_{ss}^{*''}$, where $c_{ss}^{*''} > c_{ss}^{*'}$), then the fall in e_{ss} is large as well (e_{ss} falls to e_{ss}'', where $e_{ss}'' = \bar{y}/c_{ss}^{*''}$); the new steady-state is thus at point D, and $D'D'$ denotes the corresponding saddle path. In this case, the inflation rate of home goods *increases* on impact from A to E and then the system proceeds along $D'D'$ towards point D.[29] In both cases, the real exchange rate falls over time towards its lower steady-state value.

The intuition behind the result that π can either increase or fall on impact lies in the presence of two opposing forces. The first force acting on π is the reduction in the devaluation rate. In the absence of any wealth effect – because of, say, fixed proportions between domestic and foreign money – π would instantaneously adjust to its lower steady-state level (i.e., π would jump from A to F in figure 9.1) because c^* would remain at its initial level. The second force acting on π is the wealth effect that results from substituting domestic for foreign currency. This effect tends to increase π because the higher c_{ss}^* necessitates a fall in the relative price of c^* (i.e., a fall

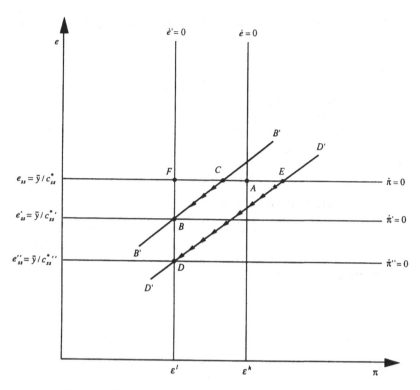

Figure 9.1 Permanent reduction in devaluation rate

in the real exchange rate). For a given rate of devaluation, this requires a rise in the inflation rate of home goods, π.

If π decreases on impact, then the average inflation rate – which is a weighted average of π (the inflation rate of home goods) and ϵ (the inflation rate of tradable goods) – also jumps downwards.[30] The wealth effect could, in principle, be strong enough for the rise in π to more than offset the reduction in ϵ and thus cause the average inflation rate to rise.[31]

Let us now examine the behaviour of consumption of home goods. It follows from equation (9.6) that, since e is given on impact, c must increase on impact as a result of the jump in c^*. Because c^* is time invariant (i.e., $\dot{c}^* = 0$), first-order condition (9.6) implies that, after increasing on impact, c declines over time towards its unchanged steady-state level, $\bar{y}$, as the real exchange rate falls. Hence, the domestic real interest rate must fall on impact and remain below the world real interest rate throughout the adjustment path to induce consumers to choose a declining consumption path.

We have thus shown that, *in the presence of currency substitution, an exchange-rate-based stabilisation programme results in an initial expansion, even if the programme enjoys full credibility.* The inflation rate of home goods falls by less than the devaluation rate – and could even increase – thus causing real appreciation. These predictions of the model are consistent with the stylised facts discussed in the introduction. However, the eventual recession is left unexplained. To account for such a feature, lack of credibility needs to be introduced into the picture.[32]

3.2   Temporary reduction in the rate of devaluation

Consider now a temporary reduction in the rate of devaluation.[33] Initially (i.e., before time 0), the devaluation rate is ϵ^h. At $t = 0$, the devaluation rate is set to a lower level, but at time T it is increased back to its original level. Formally, for some $T > 0$,

$$\epsilon_t = \epsilon^l, \qquad 0 \leq t < T, \tag{9.36a}$$

$$\epsilon_t = \epsilon^h, \qquad t \geq T, \tag{9.36b}$$

where $\epsilon^h > \epsilon^l$.

The path of the nominal interest rate under policy (9.36) follows from equation (9.15): i falls at $t = 0$ and remains at that level up to $t = T$, at which time it increases back to its initial level given by (9.25). This path of the nominal interest rate induces the consumption path of tradable goods illustrated in figure 9.2, panel A. Since the effective price of c^* is lower during $[0, T)$ than during $[T, \infty)$ (recall (9.12)), there is intertemporal substitution toward present consumption, which results in high consumption of tradable goods during $[0, T)$ and low consumption afterwards. The parameter T measures the 'degree of temporariness' of the policy. A lower T implies that the tradable good is cheaper for a shorter period of time, which exacerbates the intertemporal substitution effects. Hence, the smaller is T, the higher is the rise in c^* at $t = 0$. Conversely, the larger is T, the smaller is the initial rise in c^*.[34]

The current-account path, illustrated in figure 9.2, panel B, follows from equation (9.18) (abstracting from the last term on the RHS, which reflects seignorage payments, and recalling that $y_t^* = y^*$ for all t) and from the behaviour of consumption of tradable goods just described. On impact, the current account jumps into deficit due to the upward jump in c^*. The current account then deteriorates steadily during $[0, T)$, even though c^* remains constant, because interest income on net foreign assets declines

A. Consumption tradable goods

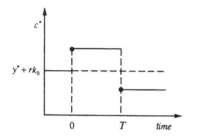

B. Current account

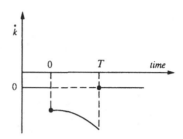

C. Inflation rate

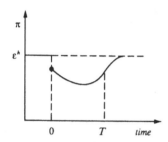

D. Real exchange rate

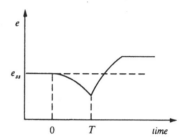

E. Consumption of home goods

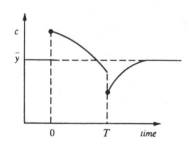

F. Domestic real interest rate

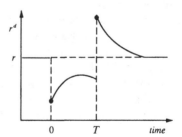

Figure 9.2 Temporary reduction in devaluation rate

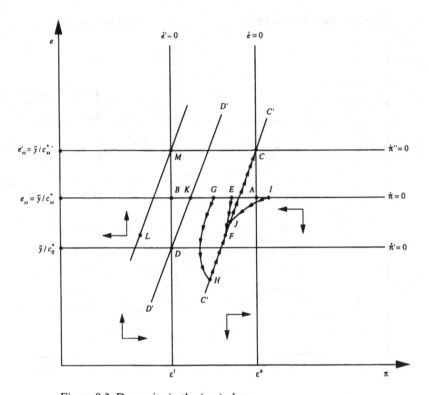

Figure 9.3 Dynamics in the (π, e) plane

throughout. At $t = T$, the fall in c^* brings the current account into balance. In the new steady-state, net foreign assets are lower than they were initially.

We now turn to system (9.34) and (9.35) to examine the behaviour of e and π. The fact that the system includes two exogenous variables (ϵ is a policy variable and c^* is exogenous to the system), both of which jump at $t = 0$ and $t = T$, does not prevent us from using standard graphical techniques, as will become clear below. Figure 9.3, which depicts the same phase diagram as figure 9.1, will be used to analyse temporary changes in the rate of devaluation.

As in the previous case, the initial steady state is at point A where $\pi_{ss} = \epsilon^h$ and $e_{ss} = \bar{y}/c_{ss}^*$. The final steady-state is given by point C where π_{ss} remains unchanged at ϵ^h but the steady-state real exchange rate, e_{ss}', is higher because steady-state consumption of tradables has declined to $c_{ss}^{*'}$. Since π is continuous at T, the system must hit $C'C'$ – the saddle path corresponding to point C – at $t = T$ in a continuous manner (i.e., neither π nor e is allowed to jump at T).[35] From our previous analysis, we know that c^* rises on impact; this implies that the $\dot{\pi} = 0$ schedule shifts downward at $t = 0$ to $\dot{\pi}' = 0$. At $t = T$, c^* falls and therefore the $\dot{\pi}' = 0$ schedule shifts upward to $\dot{\pi}'' = 0$. During the transition (i.e., during $0 \leq t < T$), the system is governed by equations (9.34) and (9.35) with $c_t^* = c_0^*$. (The directional arrows depicted in figure 9.3 correspond to the transition.) Therefore, the corresponding 'steady-state' is point D in figure 9.3, and the associated saddle path is $D'D'$. To find the equilibrium convergent path, we need to establish where π jumps on impact (recall that e is a non-jumping variable). It should be clear that π cannot jump to point K or to the left of K because, if it did, the system could not hit the saddle path $C'C'$ in a continuous fashion at $t = T$.

It can be shown that there exist three qualitatively different paths, which differ in the behaviour of the inflation rate of home goods. If T is large, the system jumps on impact to a point such as G, hits the saddle path $C'C'$ (point H) at $t = T$, and then proceeds towards point C. The path of π is illustrated in figure 9.2, panel C; π *falls* on impact, then decreases and, before the transition is over, begins to increase. If T is small, π may rise or fall on impact, depending on how large is the reduction in the rate of devaluation.[36] If the fall in ϵ is relatively small, the system jumps on impact from A to E, travels along an unstable branch to hit the saddle path $C'C'$ (point F) at time T, and then proceeds towards point C along the saddle path $C'C'$.[37] Thus, π falls on impact but, unlike the first case, always decreases during the transition. For large reductions in ϵ, the system jumps from A to I, travels along an unstable branch to hit the saddle path $C'C'$ (point J) at time T, and then proceeds towards point C. Thus, π *increases* on impact and decreases throughout the transition. The initial rise in π reflects the large increase in c^* (as a result of a large reduction in ϵ and a small T), which requires a large real appreciation of the domestic currency during the transition.

It follows from figure 9.3 that, qualitatively, the time path of the real exchange rate, illustrated in figure 9.2, panel D, does not depend on T. Since the inflation rate of home goods always falls by less than the rate of devaluation – and could even increase – the real exchange rate falls throughout the transition (i.e., during $[0, T)$). Furthermore, the less credible is the programme (i.e., the smaller is T), the more will the real exchange rate fall in the first stages of the programme. At $t = T$, when the devaluation rate returns to its original level, the real exchange rate begins to increase.

Figure 9.2, panel E, illustrates the time path of consumption of home goods (and thus output) for a large T. The fall in i induces an increase in the consumption of c^* on impact, as indicated earlier. Since the relative price of tradable goods in terms of home goods, e, does not change on impact, consumption of home goods increases as well (see (9.6)). During $[0, T)$, consumption of home goods falls over time as the relative price of home goods increases. Moreover, for a large T, consumption of home goods falls below its full employment level before T.[38] Thus, *the model can explain a recession in the home-goods sector (in the sense of output falling below its full-employment level), even before the programme is discontinued* (assuming that the programme is discontinued when it was expected to). For a small T, consumption of home goods remains above its full-employment level up to time T, at which point c falls below $\bar{y}$ accompanying the fall in c^*.

The behaviour of the domestic real interest rate (for a large T) is depicted in figure 9.2, panel F. Since $r^d \equiv i - \pi$, r^d falls on impact because, even if π decreases on impact, the fall in i exceeds that of π. The initial fall in the domestic real interest rate induces the consumer to increase consumption of home goods. During the transition, the domestic real interest rate remains below its initial value. At $t = T$, r^d jumps upward, and falls over time afterwards.[39]

It is important to highlight the effects of lower credibility in an exchange-rate based stabilisation. This aspect constitutes one of the key differences between exchange-rate-based and money-based stabilisation programmes. As suggested earlier, a smaller T (i.e., a lower degree of credibility in the programme) implies that the initial upward jump in consumption of tradable goods is larger. This, in turn, implies a larger increase in consumption of non-tradable goods because the real exchange rate is predetermined. Therefore, *the real effects of an exchange-rate-based stabilisation programme get more pronounced the less credible is the programme.* The reason is that the nominal interest rate gets 'anchored' at a low level by the reduction in the devaluation rate and the assumption of perfect capital mobility. The shorter the period of time during which the public believes the nominal interest rate will stay at that low level, the more pronounced the intertemporal substitution effects become.

We have abstracted from the wealth effect to isolate the effects of lack of credibility. In the absence of the wealth effect, the inflation rate of home goods adjusts instantaneously to its lower level if the public believes that policy makers will maintain the lower rate of devaluation forever.[40] But if the stabilisation programme lacks credibility and the public believes that the stabilisation attempt will be short lived (i.e., that it will end at T), the economy will behave during $[0, T)$ as though the authorities had announced a temporary reduction in the devaluation rate. If, when time T arrives, policy makers validate this belief by effectively raising the devaluation rate, the economy will behave from T on as described above.

It is interesting to examine some of the alternatives that policy makers face at T. Suppose, for instance, that at time T policy makers decided to stick to their announced policy and that, as a result, the public now *believed* that the rate of devaluation would be ϵ^l from T on. Interestingly, the paths of c^* and c would not be affected. To see why, note that, as far as the public is concerned (which is what matters), there is an unanticipated and permanent reduction in the devaluation rate at $t = T$ from ϵ^h to ϵ^l, because the public had acted on the expectation that the devaluation rate would be ϵ^h from T on. Therefore, the consumption of tradable goods does not change because, in the absence of the wealth affect, a permanent change in ϵ has no effects on c^*. Because the real exchange rate is given at T, the sharp drop in consumption of home goods still occurs and is in fact quantitatively the same as that which would occur if the authorities were to validate the public's expectations. To see why the path of c is unaffected, notice that if ϵ is expected to remain constant forever, system (9.34)–(9.35) can be expressed as follows

$$\dot{v}_t = \theta(e_t c_t^* - \bar{y}), \tag{9.34'}$$

$$\dot{e}_t = v_t e_t, \tag{9.35'}$$

where $v_t \equiv \epsilon - \pi_t$. Thus, the equilibrium solution for e is independent of ϵ. Hence, by (9.6) and the fact that $c_t^* = c_{ss}^{*\prime}$ for $t \geq T$, it follows that the path of c is entirely unaffected by the policy change.[41] However, the inflation path differs from what it would be if the authorities discontinued the stabilisation programme, i.e., if $\epsilon_t = \epsilon^h$ for $t \geq T$. Consider, for instance, the path AEF in figure 9.3. If policy makers decide at time T to stick to their policy, there is a sharp drop in inflation from point F to point L; π undershoots its steady-state value, now given by ϵ^l, and the system then travels towards point M. More precisely, by (9.34') and (9.35'), we know that, compared to the value that it would take if the authorities discontinued the stabilisation programme, inflation is lower by exactly $\epsilon^h - \epsilon^l$ for all $t \geq T$. We then conclude that, *if policy makers stick to their disinflationary policy, and if the public now becomes convinced that the policy is permanent, inflation is successfully brought down at no costs in addition to those that would have occurred had the public's expectations been validated.* This provides an interesting example in which adopting a 'tough' policy stance pays off if it results in substantive credibility gains.[42]

4   MONEY-BASED STABILISATION

This section analyses stabilisation policy under flexible exchange rates; that is, stabilisation policy based on the reduction of the rate of growth of the money supply. From an analytical standpoint, the case of flexible exchange rates is somewhat more involved than the predetermined exchange rates case. The reason is that the ratio of foreign to domestic money, f/m, is not necessarily time invariant, because the nominal interest rate may vary over time.[43]

It proves convenient to define a new variable, x, by

$$x_t \equiv z_t/(c_t/e_t + c_t^*), \tag{9.37}$$

which can be interpreted as real liquidity demand per unit of total consumption. Using (9.11) and (9.37), the demand for x can be expressed as an increasing function of the nominal interest rate:

$$x_t = \Phi^z(i_t/r), \qquad \Phi^{z\prime}(i_t/r) > 0. \tag{9.38}$$

As discussed in section 2, an increase in i raises the demand for f by more than it reduces the demand for m (thus increasing the demand for $z(\equiv m+f)$), because domestic money is more productive at the margin than foreign money. From (9.38), it follows that, in equilibrium,

$$i_t = rw(x_t), \qquad w(x_t) \equiv (\Phi^z)^{-1}(x_t), \qquad w'(x_t) > 0. \tag{9.39}$$

Equation (9.39) implies that if the demand for x is, say, increasing, the nominal interest rate is also increasing. Furthermore, using (9.39), the demand for f/m (equation (9.8)) can be re-written as

$$f_t/m_t = \eta(x_t), \qquad \eta(x_t) \equiv \phi[w(x_t)], \qquad \eta'(x_t) > 0. \tag{9.40}$$

If x is increasing, the nominal interest rate must be increasing as well – as follows from (9.39) – which induces the consumer to increase the ratio of foreign to domestic money, as (9.40) indicates.

It can be shown (see appendix) that x obeys the following differential equation

$$\dot{x}_t = [1/\Gamma(x_t)][rw(x_t) - \mu_t - r]x_t, \qquad \Gamma(x_t) > 0. \tag{9.41}$$

As shown in the appendix, differential equation (9.41) is unstable. Since x is a jumping variable, this ensures a unique converging equilibrium path for x.

The laws of motion of consumption of tradable and home goods can be expressed in terms of x and the domestic real interest rate. The law of motion of c^* is (see appendix)

$$\dot{c}_t^*/c_t^* = -\gamma(x_t)\dot{x}_t/x_t, \qquad \gamma(x_t) > 0. \tag{9.42}$$

Equation (9.42) states that if x is, say, increasing over time, consumption of tradable goods is decreasing. The reason is that, as already discussed, an increasing x is accompanied, in equilibrium, by an increasing i. In turn, a rising i implies that the effective price of consumption is increasing over time (recall equation (9.12)). Since consumption is getting more expensive over time, the consumer chooses a decreasing path of consumption, which is what equation (9.42) indicates. This effect on consumption will be referred to as 'the effective price channel'.[44]

The law of motion of consumption of home goods is given by[45]

$$\dot{c}_t/c_t = r_t^d - r - \gamma(x_t)\dot{x}_t/x_t. \tag{9.43}$$

In addition to the effective price channel, given by the last term on the RHS of (9.43), the path of consumption of home goods is affected by the familiar 'real interest rate channel', given by $r^d - r$ in (9.43), whereby consumption increases as long as the domestic real interest rate is above the world real interest rate.[46]

The *impact* effect of money-based stabilisation on consumption of home goods will be dictated by equilibrium in the domestic money market. It is convenient to define domestic real money balances in terms of home goods; namely, $n \equiv M/P$. (Note that n, unlike m, is a non-jumping variable, because both M and P are predetermined variables.)[47] Thus

$$n_t = e_t m_t. \tag{9.44}$$

Substituting (9.44) into (9.9), using (9.6), yields money-market equilibrium

$$n_t = 2c_t \Phi^m(i_t/r). \tag{9.45}$$

Since n cannot jump, an incipient excess demand for real money balances that results from a reduction in the nominal interest rate necessitates a fall in consumption of home goods to equilibrate the money market.

Consider now the high-inflation initial equilibrium. Suppose that prior to $t = 0$, $\mu_t = \mu^h$, and that μ is expected to remain at that level forever. The steady-state values are given by

$$\epsilon_{ss} = \mu^h \tag{9.46}$$

$$i_{ss} = r + \mu^h, \tag{9.47}$$

$$\pi_{ss} = \mu^h, \tag{9.48}$$

$$c_{ss} = \bar{y}, \tag{9.49}$$

$$c_{ss}^* = \frac{y^* + rk_0}{1 + 2r/l\{1/\phi[(r+\mu^h)/r], 1\}}, \tag{9.50}$$

$$e_{ss} = \bar{y}/c_{ss}^*, \tag{9.51}$$

$$r_{ss}^d = r, \tag{9.52}$$

$$n_{ss} = 2\bar{y}\Phi^m[(r+\mu^h)/r], \tag{9.53}$$

$$f_{ss} = 2c_{ss}^*\Phi^f[(r+\mu^h)/r], \tag{9.54}$$

$$x_{ss} = \Phi^z[(r+\mu^h)/r]. \tag{9.55}$$

Conceptually, the initial equilibrium does not differ from that under predetermined exchange rates.[48]

4.1   Permanent reduction in the rate of growth of the money supply

Suppose that, at $t = 0$, policy makers announce that the rate of growth of the money supply will be immediately and permanently reduced from μ^h to μ^l. The announcement is fully credible; therefore, the public expects the lower rate of growth of the money supply to prevail for the indefinite future.

The reduction in μ lowers the steady-state nominal interest rate (equation (9.47)), which in turn decreases the steady-state demand for real liquidity per unit of total consumption, x_{ss} (equation (9.55)). Since (9.41) is an unstable differential equation, x must adjust instantaneously to its lower steady state. This implies, by (9.39) and (9.40), that both the nominal interest rate and the ratio f/m adjust instantaneously to their lower steady-state values, as is the case under predetermined exchange rates.

Consider now the dynamics of n and π. The law of motion of real money balances, which follows from (9.19), (9.35) and (9.44) is

$$\dot{n}_t = (\mu - \pi_t)n_t. \tag{9.56}$$

From (9.2), (9.6), (9.40) and (9.44), it follows that $c_t = (1/2)n_t l[1, \eta(x_t)]$. Substituting this expression into (9.21) yields

$$\dot{\pi}_t = \theta\{\bar{y} - (1/2)n_t l[1, \eta(x_t)]\}. \tag{9.57}$$

Equations (9.56) and (9.57) constitute a dynamic system in n and π because the behaviour of x is exogenously given to the system by (9.41). The system, illustrated in figure 9.4, exhibits saddle-path stability since the determinant associated with the linear approximation equals $-\theta\bar{y} < 0$. Point A represents the initial steady state. When μ is reduced from μ^h to μ^l, the $\dot{n} = 0$ locus shifts to the left (to $\dot{n}' = 0$) and the locus $\dot{\pi} = 0$ shifts upward (to $\dot{\pi}' = 0$) so that the new steady state becomes point B, where real money balances are higher and inflation is lower. On impact, inflation falls from A to C and then the system travels along the saddle path $B'B'$ towards point B. The rate of inflation must fall below the new rate of monetary growth to accommodate an increase in steady-state real money balances.

The impact effect on consumption of home goods follows from the money market equilibrium condition, given by (9.45). Real money balances in terms of home goods, n, are given on impact. Hence, the fall in i, which causes an incipient excess demand for domestic money, necessitates a fall in c to restore equilibrium in the money market. To induce the consumer to reduce consumption of home goods on impact, the domestic real interest rate needs to increase.[49] Therefore, r^d rises on impact and decreases over time.[50] Consumption of home goods increases after the initial fall towards its full-employment level (as follows from setting $\dot{x}_t = 0$ in (9.43)).[51]

The absence of the effective price channel implies that $\dot{c}_t^* = 0$ for all t (as follows from setting $\dot{x}_t = 0$ in (9.42)). Although the effective price of

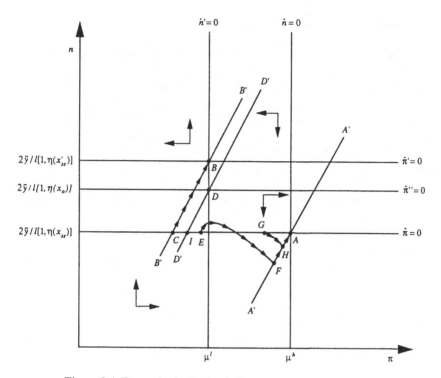

Figure 9.4 Dynamics in the (π, n) plane

consumption falls on impact due to the lower i, there are no incentives to engage in intertemporal consumption substitution, because the path of the effective price remains flat. It follows from (9.23) that c^* jumps upwards at $t = 0$ and remains at that level thereafter. The higher consumption of tradable goods reflects the wealth effect that results from the economy's lower holdings of foreign currency. Naturally, the current account remains balanced.

Since steady-state consumption of tradable goods increases, the steady-state relative price of tradable goods (i.e., the real exchange rate) must fall. On impact, the real exchange rate falls by more than in the steady-state, because it needs to accommodate not only the rise in c^* but also the fall in c. During the transition, the real exchange rate increases, as consumption of home goods rises.

Perfect capital mobility implies that $i = r + \epsilon$. Therefore, the rate of inflation of tradable goods (i.e., the rate of depreciation), ϵ, adjusts instantaneously to its lower steady-state value, μ^l. Since the inflation rate of home goods, π, remains below μ^l throughout the adjustment path, the average inflation rate will also be below μ^l throughout the adjustment path.

It is important to emphasise that, unlike the predetermined exchange rates case, the presence of the wealth effect resulting from a lower stock of foreign currency plays no role in affecting the outcome of a money-based stabilisation policy. Indeed, as should be clear from the analysis, the same effects on inflation and consumption of home goods would obtain if one were to abstract from this effect. The only difference would be that consumption of tradable goods would remain unchanged which would mean an unchanged steady-state value of the real exchange rate – although it would still fall on impact and increase thereafter. To understand why the wealth effect is irrelevant for the behaviour of c and π, consider an unanticipated and permanent increase in y^*. In that case, c^* and e would adjust instantaneously to their higher and lower steady-state values, respectively, but no other effects would result.

In summary, *a fully credible (i.e., permanent) reduction in the rate of monetary growth succeeds in bringing down inflation but only at the cost of an initial recession. The initial reduction in inflation is accompanied by a rise in the domestic real interest rate and real appreciation of the domestic currency.*

4.2   Temporary reduction in the rate of growth of the money supply

Consider a temporary reduction in μ. Initially (i.e., for $t<0$), $\mu_t=\mu^h$. At $t=0$, policy makers announce the following policy:

$$\mu_t=\mu^l, \qquad 0\leq t<T, \tag{9.58a}$$

$$\mu_t=\mu^h, \qquad t\geq T, \tag{9.58b}$$

for some $T>0$, and where $\mu^h>\mu^l$.[52] We first need to establish whether the path of x is continuous at $t=T$. Using equations (9.2), (9.5), (9.6) and (9.8) yields

$$2/\{m_t l[1,\eta(x_t)]\}=\lambda\{1+r/l_f[1,\eta(x_t)]\}, \tag{9.59}$$

which implies that x_t is continuous at time $t=T$ because the left-hand side of (9.59) is a decreasing function of x, while the right-hand side is an increasing function of x.[53] Therefore, c_t^* is continuous at $t=T$ (note that, from (9.2), (9.6) and (9.8), $c_t^*=(1/2)m_t l[1,\eta(x_t)]$). Furthermore, c_t is continuous at $t=T$ because $c_t=e_t c_t^*$ (and both e_t and c_t^* are continuous at $t=T$).

Having established that the paths of x, c^* and c, are all continuous at T, we can proceed with the analysis.[54] The instability of (9.41) implies that x jumps downward on impact (but falls short of the value it takes when the change in μ is permanent, x'_{ss}), and increases thereafter to reach its initial steady-state at $t=T$. Therefore, $\dot{x}_t>0$ for $0\leq t<T$. Equation (9.39) indicates that the nominal interest rate decreases on impact (but falls short of $r+\mu^l$), increases afterwards, and reaches its initial level at T.[55] By the same

token, from equation (9.40), it follows that f/m falls on impact, increases during the transition, and reaches its initial level at T. Intuitively, the reduction in μ lowers the nominal interest rate on impact, which induces the public to decrease its holdings of foreign money relative to domestic money. As the opportunity cost of domestic money increases, f/m increases.

The dynamics in the (π, n) plane are more involved than in the case in which the reduction in μ is permanent, because it is no longer the case that x adjusts instantaneously to its new steady-state. However, the same familiar graphical techniques may be used to characterise the equilibrium converging path.[56] Consider an 'auxiliary' system that consists of (9.56) and (9.57) but in which x_t has been 'frozen' at the value it takes at $t = 0$, x_0:

$$\dot{n}_t = (\mu - \pi_t)n_t. \tag{9.60}$$

$$\dot{\pi}_t = \theta\{\bar{y} - (1/2)n_t l[1, \eta(x_0)]\}. \tag{9.61}$$

Figure 9.4 illustrates the response of system (9.60) and (9.61) to policy (9.58). Since $x_0 < x'_{ss}$, the schedule $\dot{\pi} = 0$ shifts upward to $\dot{\pi}'' = 0$ – rather than to $\dot{\pi}' = 0$ as is the case when the rise in μ is permanent – so that the laws of motion drawn in figure 9.4 are those corresponding to point D. If T is large, the system jumps on impact to a point like E, hits the saddle path $A'A'$ (point F) at $t = T$, and then proceeds along the saddle path towards point A.[57] If T is small, the system would jump to a point like G and then follow the path GHA.

Let us now extend the results obtained in the 'auxiliary' system to the 'true' system. Inflation cannot initially jump to point I or to the left of I because, if it did, the system would follow a non-convergent path given that neither variable can jump at T. Because x increases between $[0, T)$, the schedule $\dot{\pi}'' = 0$ in figure 9.4 will be shifting downward during the same period. It can be readily checked that the 'true' system must follow the same laws of motion as the 'auxiliary' system does, because the 'true' system always lies below the shifting $\dot{\pi}'' = 0$ schedule. The continuity of x at T implies that the $\dot{\pi}'' = 0$ schedule gets arbitrarily close to the $\dot{\pi} = 0$ schedule as $t \to T$. It follows that, as suggested earlier, π cannot exceed μ^h during the transition because, if it did, the system would diverge. The path of the inflation rate, which is qualitatively independent of T, is illustrated in figure 9.5, panel A.

On impact, consumption of home goods must fall to equilibrate the money market, because the fall in i creates an excess demand for real domestic money balances (see equation (9.45)). Since π increases throughout the adjustment path, it follows from equation (9.21) that c is always below $\bar{y}$. Thus, *consumption of home goods falls on impact, and remains below the full-employment output level throughout the adjustment path*. Figure 9.5, panel B illustrates the path of consumption of home goods.[58]

A. Inflation rate

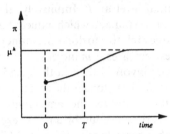

B. Consumption of home goods

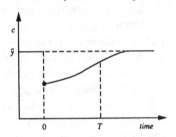

C. Consumption of tradable goods

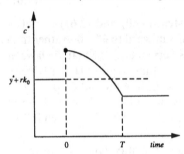

D. Current account

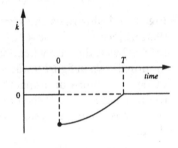

E. Real exchange rate

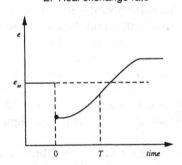

F. Depreciation rate

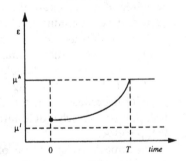

Figure 9.5 Temporary reduction in rate of monetary growth

Consider now how the initial fall in consumption of home goods is affected by T (the credibility horizon). Money-market equilibrium, given by (9.45), indicates that the magnitude of the initial fall in c depends on the size of the initial fall in the nominal interest rate. If T is small (the programme has low credibility), the fall in i is small as well. Therefore, *the smaller is T, the smaller is the inital fall in consumption*. In contrast, if T is large, the initial fall in c approaches that which occurs when μ is lowered permanently.

The behaviour of consumption of tradable goods, illustrated in figure 9.5, panel C, follows from equation (9.42). Equation (9.42), together with the path of x discussed above, imply that c^* decreases during $[0, T)$ and remains constant thereafter. Hence, it must be the case that c^* jumps upward on impact and reaches at T a value which is below its initial level, for, otherwise, the economy's resource constraint (given by (9.16) abstracting from seignorage payments) would be violated. Intuitively, because the effective price of consumption increases during the transition (since i increases), the consumer chooses a declining path of consumption.

The current-account path that results from the behaviour of c^* is illustrated in figure 9.5, panel D. The current account jumps into deficit at $t = 0$ but the deficit declines over time because the effect of a declining path of consumption of tradable goods more than offsets the reduced interest income on net foreign assets.[59]

The behaviour of the real exchange rate is illustrated in figure 9.5, panel E. The steady-state real exchange rate increases due to lower steady-state consumption of tradable goods. Since, on impact, c falls while c^* increases, the relative price of tradables, e, must fall to accommodate such changes (recall equation (9.6)). For large T, the real exchange rate begins to rise following the initial fall, as c is increasing and c^* is decreasing.[60]

Consider now the behaviour of the domestic real interest rate. Since $r_t^d = r + \dot{e}_t/e_t$, and $\dot{e}_t > 0$ at $t = 0$ (for large T), it follows that the domestic real interest rate increases on impact for large T. Alternatively, recall that for large T, the fall in inflation is larger than the fall in the nominal interest rate, which implies a rise in the domestic real interest rate. For small T, the jump in r^d tends to zero because the downward jumps of both i and π tend to zero.[61] The direction of r^d during $[0, T)$ is in principle ambiguous because both i and π increase. At $t = T$, r^d must lie above r because $\dot{r}_t^d = -\dot{\pi}_t < 0$ for $t \geq T$ and r_t^d is continuous at $t = T$.

Finally, consider the path of the depreciation rate, illustrated in figure 9.5, panel F, which follows from (9.15) and the behaviour of x discussed above. The depreciation rate falls on impact because of the fall in the nominal interest rate. The smaller is T, the smaller is the initial fall in ϵ, because the smaller is the initial fall in i. The rate of depreciation increases afterwards and reaches its unchanged steady-state level at $t = T$. Therefore, the inflation rate of tradable goods returns to its initial level at time T.

In summary, the presence of lack of credibility in a stabilisation programme under flexible exchange rates does not alter the qualitative behaviour of the home-goods sector. The fall in inflation is accompanied by a fall in consumption of home goods. In contrast, the behaviour of the tradable-goods sector (i.e., the current account) is dramatically altered by lack of credibility in the stabilisation programme. This is due to the existence of intertemporal substitution effects in consumption that are absent when the programme is fully credible. Therefore, *when a money-based stabilisation programme lacks credibility, the recession in the home-goods sector that accompanies the fall in the inflation rate co-exists with a current-account deficit.*

Finally, let us examine the consequences of lower degrees of credibility. Interestingly, the effects of lower credibility are dramatically different from those which obtain under predetermined exchange rates. *The basic result is that as the programme gets less credible* (i.e., $T \to 0$), *all real and monetary effects tend to vanish.* As discussed earlier, as $T \to 0$, the jump in i at $t = 0$ is very small (i.e., it tends to zero). This implies, in turn, that the fall in consumption of home goods which is necessary to equilibrate the money market tends to zero as well. The fall in the inflation rate of home goods, as well as the fall in the depreciation rate, are also very small. Because the fall in the nominal interest rate is small and consumption of tradables is continuous at $t = T$, the upward jump in c^* is also very small and, hence, so is the initial current-account deficit. *We conclude that very low credibility in the programme will mean no success whatsoever in bringing down inflation. But, at the same time, the programme's failure will not generate any real effects.* This conclusion stands in stark contrast to the effects of very low credibility under predetermined exchange rates, in which case the real effects of the programme are exacerbated.

5   ANCHORS

As suggested in the introduction, several attempts to stop high inflation in the 1970s and 1980s have shown once again that inflationary forces are not easily curtailed by just pulling at monetary policy strings. This phenomenon is clearly exhibited by our model. We have focussed on a feature of stabilisation programmes that is often mentioned as an explanation for their lacklustre performances; namely, imperfect policy credibility. In fact, we have shown that under imperfect credibility the dynamic response of the economy is quite different than under perfect credibility.

Imperfect credibility could arise due to a variety of factors. A stabilisation policy could not be credible, for example, because the fiscal programme is not in line with the inflation target. Indeed, lack of fiscal adjustment is a recurrent problem in stabilisation programmes, but the roots of the problem could be less obvious. For instance, a resumption of inflation could be feared because the public realises the fiscal-revenue potential of surprise departures from preannounced policy. A case in point is when there exists a relatively large stock of non-indexed domestic debt whose real value could be quickly reduced through surprise inflation or devaluation.

Our model does not tackle the issue of how credibility is affected by policy. Therefore, it is ill-suited to evaluate the chances of success of, for example, a so-called big-bang programme that eliminates all distortions and fiscal imbalances at once. However, the model sheds some light on any situation in which policy – either by fact or artifact – fails to restore full credibility.

Consider the choice between flexible and predetermined exchange rates. Independently of the credibility horizon, T, predetermined exchange rates are capable of stopping the inflation of tradable goods on its track. This is not the case for flexible exchange rates since, as shown above, inflation of tradable goods remains above μ^I, unless the programme is fully credible. In both regimes, however, the behaviour of the inflation rate of home goods has much life of its own, and its behaviour is strongly influenced by credibility factors. In particular, the analysis has shown that, when the credibility horizon is very small (i.e., when T tends to zero), inflation of non-tradable goods is approximately the same under the two exchange rate regimes. Consequently, if policy makers put a lot of weight on stopping, or at least dramatically decelerating, the rate of inflation – a typical situation when inflation seems out of control and about to devour the real economy, and credibility is at a low ebb – a regime of predetermined exchange rates could be highly appealing.

A drawback of predetermined exchange rates, however, is that large intertemporal substitution effects may result which, as shown in related models, could be quite costly (see Calvo (1987, 1988)). Furthermore, the intertemporal substitution effects get exacerbated the less credible is the programme. This contrasts sharply with the case of flexible exchange rates, in which stabilisation policy has almost no real effects when the credibility horizon is small. Therefore, a clear lesson is that the choice of nominal anchors could have implications for the real sector, aside from resulting in different inflation paths.

As a way to avoid unduly high current-account deficits at the beginning of the stabilisation programme, authorities might try to interfere with international capital flows. After all, one important avenue for the economy as a whole to carry out a significant amount of intertemporal consumption substitution is by means of accumulating or decumulating foreign assets.[62] Consequently, the model helps to rationalise an often-found additional anchor in exchange-rate-based programmes, namely, controls on international capital mobility.[63]

In practice, however, policy makers would have a hard time distinguishing between 'bad' capital flows (i.e., those arising from lack of credibility) and 'good' capital flows (i.e., those unrelated to credibility problems), which surely reduces the appeal of capital controls. In addition, the optimal time for removing capital controls would be hard to ascertain. Too early a removal may unleash the same credibility problems that capital controls were supposed to deal with in the first place. Too late a removal may lead to a resumption of inflation if the public believed that capital controls were a fundamental component of the stabilisation programme.

As previously noted, neither flexible nor predetermined exchange rates can do much to put a lid on prices of non-tradable goods. Thus, the policy maker might feel inclined to meddle directly with price/wage-setting mechanisms, as in the recent 'heterodox' programmes.[64] One 'neutral' way to institute price controls would be to force firms to set their prices *as if* the programme were fully credible. Thus, if the programme is actually followed as initially announced, no firm (or worker, for that matter) would have any serious ground for grievance because regulations would lead them to the same actions that they would have taken themselves had they known, in advance, that the policy maker was going to honour his or her announcements in full.[65]

A possibly serious problem with the above price-controls solution is that, in practice, there are many goods whose production and consumption are subject to a myriad of sector-specific random shocks. This information is both hard to obtain and hard to process in order to calibrate the price vector along its full-credibility equilibrium path. Therefore, the price-controls scheme is, at best, relevant only during the first few months of the programme. Perhaps an alternative that should be explored in the context of a stochastic model is the imposition of price/wage 'ceilings' which would hopefully be non-binding for all or most goods or labour services.

Price controls face two additional problems. First, they may be simply ineffective in economies in which black markets are relatively well organised. Second, like capital controls, the optimal time to remove price controls is hard to establish.

In summary, the model highlights the basic problems that arise from lack of credibility, and thus helps to rationalise the use of additional anchors, such as capital controls and price and wage controls, in exchange-rate-based stabilisations.[66] However, in order to establish whether these additional anchors are, in some sense, optimal would require a richer model in which both the costs and benefits of the additional anchors are explicitly incorporated.

6   FINAL WORDS

The model presented in this chapter is capable of explaining some of the puzzles that have arisen in connection with several recent stabilisation programmes based on the exchange rate as the nominal anchor (see Végh (1992) for an interpretation of the evidence in terms of this type of model). In particular, the model accounts for the following stylised facts: first, the co-existence of real appreciation and an overheated economy at the beginning of the programme; second, a recession late in the programme; and, third, the slow convergence of inflation to the devaluation rate. A key ingredient in explaining these features of exchange-rate-based stabilisation is the expectation that the stabilisation programme will be discontinued in the future, leading to a resumption of inflation. This is the critical 'credibility problem' emphasised in the chapter, which results in intertemporal consumption substitution.[67]

The analytical framework developed in this chapter also serves to highlight key differences between money-based and exchange-rate-based stabilisation. In particular, the costs, in terms of output, of bringing down inflation are borne at the beginning of the programme under money-based stabilisation, but only later in the programme under exchange-rate-based stabilisation. The consequences of low credibility are dramatically different under both regimes. Under exchange-rate-based stabilisation, real effects get more pronounced if the programme is less credible; in contrast, under money-based stabilisation, real effects tend to disappear as credibility decreases.

The discussion has dealt exclusively with qualitative results. Quantitative work is, of course, highly relevant but there is still little to report that is directly connected with the above kind of model. A first attempt to quantify the effects of lack of credibility in exchange-rate-based stabilisations can be found in Reinhart and Végh (1992). In the context of a simpler version of the model developed in this chapter, Reinhart and Végh derive a reduced-form equation for the change in consumption as a function of the intertemporal elasticity of substitution, the path of the nominal interest rate, and the credibility horizon, T. Using estimates for the intertemporal elasticity of substitution and the observed fall in nominal interest rates, Reinhart and Végh (1992) compare predicted and actual rises in consumption in seven major programmes of the late 1970s (the Southern-Cone tablitas) and the mid 1980s (the Austral, Cruzado, Israeli and Mexican plans). The model accounts for a large fraction of the observed increase in consumption (over 60 per cent) in the four heterodox programmes of the mid 1980s, but accounts for no more than 15 per cent in the case of the Southern-Cone tablitas. These contrasting results stem from the fact that the fall in nominal interest rates in the heterodox programmes of the mid 1980s was much larger than the one observed in the Southern-Cone tablitas. It is worth noticing, however, that the poor performance of the model for the Southern-Cone tablitas might be due to the omission of durable goods from the analysis.[68] We strongly believe that it is actually through the accumulation and decumulation of inventories that much of the intertemporal substitution effects take place.[69] Unfortunately, lack of data on consumption of durable goods in developing countries proves to be a formidable obstacle for an empirical rendition of the model.

Furthermore, at least the credibility horizon, T, should be treated as a random variable. This is essential because otherwise one would be unable to explain credibility-generated risk premia in domestic interest rates (an important feature of stabilisation programmes that is not exhibited by our model due to the assumption of perfect foresight).[70]

The chapter deals with the credibility issue as a completely exogenous phenomenon. We believe that this is a convenient and non-misleading analytical device, because we would expect that in any well-structured model of the public's beliefs, history should weigh heavily during the first stages of the stabilisation programme. This, of course, means that there will always be an element of exogeneity in the public's expectations. Thus, since stabilisation programmes normally start from unmanageably high inflation – and, not unusually, from a history of unsuccessful stabilisation programmes – our model's assumption that the public expects a future resumption of inflationary forces is likely to be a feature of any fully structured expectations model.

Nevertheless, the above observation does not relieve us of the duty of searching for more complete credibility models. In our view, however, this field of enquiry is still in its infancy. According to a dominant paradigm, for example, the public does not know the true characteristics of the policy makers (i.e., whether they are 'tough' or 'soft'), while policy makers know their type and, depending on their position in the spectrum of types, may prefer to try to reveal who they are, or to disguise themselves as members of some other type. All the interesting models along these lines assume that 'soft' is the dominant type (which, by assumption, is not good for making credible commitments), while the 'tough' ones (who are effective stabilisers) are rare in kind (see, for example, Backus and Driffill (1985) and Barro (1986)). The theory then revolves around the issue of the optimal deception strategy for the soft ones. The soft ones try to build a reputation that they are actually tough, which results in their implementing tough policies for a while. Thus, the reduced-form type of policy implied by this paradigm is not much different from that in our model. A major reservation about this line of research, however, is that policy makers are normally subject to rather close public scrutiny, so one might argue that their types are relatively well known. Moreover, even when policy maker types may be, to some extent, unknown by the public, it requires an unparalleled no-leaks system to be able not to reveal one's type in the course of everyday policy making, especially given that most major decisions are made by committees.

In this respect, Alesina and Drazen (1989) take a promising track by developing a model in which, in a sense, the policy maker himself is not fully aware of his type. They model this by assuming that the policy maker's decisions are dictated by a committee which operates according to majority rule. The committee members, in turn, play 'attrition' games against each other. Leaving aside the specific details of their model, we believe that this is a relevant line of research because casual empiricism shows that policy makers spend a lot of time looking for their constituencies' support. This behaviour will naturally give rise to stop-and-go cycles which could be incorporated in the basic structure presented above.

APPENDIX

This appendix derives differential equation (9.41). Substituting (9.39) and (9.40) into (9.5), taking into account that $l(m,f)$ is homogeneous of degree one, and differentiating with respect to time yields

$$\dot{c}_t^*/c_t^* = -\gamma(x_t)\dot{x}_t/x_t,$$

where

$$\gamma(x_t) \equiv rx_t \frac{w'(x_t)l_m - w(x_t)l_{mf}\eta'(x_t)}{l_m^2[1 + rw(x_t)/l_m]} > 0, \qquad (9.1A)$$

which is equation (9.42) in the text.[71] Using (9.2), holding equality, (9.6), and (9.40), and differentiating with respect to time yields

$$\dot{c}_t^*/c_t^* = \dot{m}_t/m_t + \zeta(x_t)\dot{x}_t/x_t,$$

where

$$\zeta(x_t) \equiv \frac{x_t l_f[1, \eta(x_t)]\eta'(x_t)}{l[1, \eta(x_t)]} > 0. \qquad (9.2A)$$

Combining (9.15), (9.19), (9.39), (9.1A) and (9.2A), implies that

$$\dot{x}_t = [1/\Gamma(x_t)][rw(x_t) - \mu_t - r]x_t, \qquad (9.3A)$$

where

$$\Gamma(x_t) \equiv \gamma(x_t) + \zeta(x_t) > 0,$$

which is equation (9.41) in the text. The linear approximation of (9.3A) around the steady-state is

$$\dot{x}_t = [rw'(x_{ss})x_{ss}/\Gamma(x_{ss})](x_t - x_{ss}), \tag{9.4A}$$

which shows that this is an unstable differential equation (recall, from (9.39), that $w'(x) > 0$). Since x is a jumping variable, this ensures a unique converging equilibrium path for x.

Notes

1 The authors are grateful to Michael Bruno, Willem Buiter, Pablo Guidotti, Mohsin Khan, Leonardo Leiderman, Felipe Morandé, Jonathan Ostry, Carmen Reinhart, Ratna Sahay, and seminar participants at CEMA (Buenos Aires, Argentina), Columbia University, and the VI World Congress of the Econometric Society (Barcelona, Spain, August 1990) for helpful comments and discussions. The views expressed in this chapter are those of the authors and do not necessarily reflect those of the International Monetary Fund.

2 The Southern-Cone programmes – which comprise the stabilisation plans in Argentina, Chile and Uruguay – have been discussed, among many others, by Harberger (1982), Corbo (1985), Fernández (1985), Hanson and de Melo (1985), Calvo (1986a), Ramos (1986), Edwards and Edwards (1987), Kiguel and Liviatan (1988) and Sjaastad (1989).

3 See, for instance, Fernández (1985).

4 These programmes are referred to as 'heterodox', because of the reliance on wage and price controls. For an account of these experiences, see, for instance, Blejer and Liviatan (1987), Bruno, di Tella, Dornbusch and Fischer (1988), Helpman and Leiderman (1988) and Kiguel and Liviatan (1989).

5 One notable exception appears to be the behaviour of real interest rates, which declined in the Southern-Cone stabilisations but rose in the heterodox programmes (see Végh (1992)).

6 'Overheating' is defined as an expansion of the non-tradable- (or home-) goods sector above its full-employment level.

7 Dornbusch (1982) also addresses the issues raised by the Southern-Cone programmes in a rational-expectations model. Dornbusch's key assumption is that there is inertia in the actual inflation rate, so that the inflation rate is predetermined at each point in time. The real appreciation is thus a direct consequence of the reduction in the inflation rate of tradable goods.

8 Interestingly enough, Fischer (1986, p.252) dismisses the possibility of an initial expansion, stating that '[i]ndeed, as a curiosity to be ignored henceforth, it is even possible that the real interest rate falls so much that (an initial) boom (results)'.

9 Throughout this chapter, the real exchange rate will be defined as the relative price of tradable goods in terms of home goods. Hence, a fall in the real exchange rate indicates real appreciation.

10 For evidence on currency substitution in small open economies, see, for instance, Ortiz (1983), Ramirez-Rojas (1985), El-Erian (1988), Canto and Nickelsburg (1989), Rojas-Suarez (1992) and Savastano (1992). For a review of the main policy and analytical issues associated with currency substitution in developing countries, see Calvo and Végh (1992).

11 In order to focus on the effects of lack of credibility, the analysis of temporary policy abstracts from the wealth effect discussed above.

12 Except for the real exchange rate – and unless otherwise indicated – the term 'real' refers to nominal variables deflated by the price of tradable goods.

13 Casual evidence in chronic-inflation countries suggests that foreign currency – usually US dollars – is used for large transactions while domestic currency is used for small transactions.

14 The liquidity-in-advance constraint has been used (with interest-bearing demand deposits in lieu of foreign currency) by Walsh (1984) and Calvo and Végh (1990a, b, c). Currency substitution has usually been modelled by making both monies arguments in the utility function (see, for example, Liviatan (1981), Calvo (1985), Végh (1988) and Rogers (1990)). For alternative approaches, see Poloz (1984) and Guidotti (1989) who model currency substitution in a Baumol-Tobin context, and Végh (1989a, b) who assumes that both monies reduce 'shopping' time.

15 A subscript on a function denotes partial differentiation. The assumption $l_{mf} > 0$ is equivalent to ruling out perfect substitutability between m and f. (Notice that if $l_{mf} = 0$, then, by Euler's theorem, $l_{mm} = l_{ff} = 0$, in which case $l(m,f)$ is a linear function.)

16 While the logarithmic form is critical in simplifying the analysis under flexible exchange rates, it would be straightforward to conduct the analysis of predetermined exchange rates under a general, but separable, utility function. Since it will be assumed that output of home goods is always demand determined, the consumer is not subject to any quantity constraints.

17 Equation (9.2) holds with equality at an optimum because the opportunity cost of both monies will be assumed to be positive.

18 It has been assumed that $\beta = r$ to ensure the existence of a steady state.

19 Formally, differentiate equation (9.2), as an equality, and set $d(c/e) = df = 0$, to obtain $dm/dc^* = 1/l_m(m,f)$.

20 An asset demand function such as (9.8) was the key building block in early models of currency substitution (see Kouri (1976) and Calvo and Rodriguez (1977)).

21 See Fischer (1982) for estimates of the cost, in terms of seignorage, of using a foreign currency.

22 The equilibrium path of reserves follows from the usual assumption that domestic credit expansion just compensates the consumer for the depreciation of real money balances, so that $\tau_t = rq_t + \epsilon_t m_t$. Substituting the latter into the government's flow constraint yields $\dot{q}_t = \dot{m}_t$. Thus, changes in reserves reflect changes in domestic real money balances.

23 A more symmetric, but analytically less convenient, formulation would assume that (i) output in each sector is produced by a neoclassical production function with labour as the only input, (ii) prices are flexible, and (iii) wages are set in a staggered manner. The basic results, however, would remain unchanged.

24 The micro-foundations of the staggered-prices model are discussed in Calvo (1982) and Romer (1989).

25 Equation (9.24) can be derived by proceeding in the same way as before. Formally, we are implicitly assuming that seignorage paid on foreign currency held by domestic residents is given back to the domestic economy.

26 Throughout the chapter, superscripts 'h' and 'l' stand for 'high' and 'low' levels, respectively, of a policy variable.

27 The rise in c^* increases the demand for foreign currency, thus *partially* offsetting the negative effect on the demand for foreign currency of the reduction in i. To see that f necessarily decreases as a result of the fall in i, note that if i, and hence c^*, are constant over time, so is f, as follows from (9.2), (9.6) and (9.8). Hence, equation (9.22) reduces to $c^* = y^* + rk_0 - rf$. The rise in c^*, which follows from (9.23), implies that f falls.

28 One would conjecture that, for a given reduction in ϵ, the higher the elasticity of substitution between domestic and foreign money, the larger the wealth effect, and thus the larger the rise in c^*.

29 As one would expect, simulations of the model suggest that a high elasticity of substitution between m and f is required for π to increase on impact.

30 The average inflation rate is defined as the proportional change in the marginal cost of increasing utility by one unit and equals $(1/2)(\pi + \epsilon)$, given that both goods have the same weight in the utility function.

31 The openness of the economy – as reflected in the weight attached to the inflation of tradable goods in the average inflation rate – should also play an important role in determining the direction of the initial jump in the average inflation rate. This could be easily incorporated into the present analysis by working with a more general utility function.

32 It is worth stressing that when foreign and domestic currency are held in fixed proportions, the adjustment is instananeous. This has two important implications. First, it is the substitutability between domestic and foreign currency rather than the presence of foreign currency in itself that causes a slow adjustment. Second, sticky prices need not imply slow adjustment to the new steady-state equilibrium. Hence, our model flatly contradicts the popular view that the presence of staggered prices results in slow adjustment towards the new full-employment equilibrium.

33 Later in the section, the temporariness of the policy will be interpreted as lack of credibility in the stabilisation plan. In order to isolate the effects of policy temporariness, the ensuing analysis will abstract from the wealth effect resulting from lower seignorage payments that was the focus of the previous case. (Note that, in the absence of the wealth effect, a permanent reduction in ϵ results in an instantaneous adjustment of π to its lower steady-state value.) Therefore, in what follows, equation (9.24) applies to consumption of tradable goods. Taking into account the wealth effect would only reinforce the expansionary effects of a temporary reduction in the devaluation rate analysed below.

34 Formally, the path of c^* and the effects of changes in T can be derived by substituting policy (9.36) into (9.24) (see Calvo and Végh (1990a)).

35 The continuity of π at T follows from Calvo (1983b).

36 It can be shown that as $T \rightarrow 0$, $\lim[\pi_0(T)] = \epsilon^h$; that is, in the limit π does not jump. If the reduction in ϵ is relatively small, then $\pi_0(T)$ is a decreasing function of T. For a relatively large reduction in ϵ, however, $\pi_0(T)$ may increase at first and then decrease (the existence of the latter case was established by simulating the model).

37 As indicated earlier, a smaller T implies that the initial jump in c^* is larger, which implies that the downward displacement of the $\dot{\pi} = 0$ schedule is larger. Similarly, because a smaller T implies that c_t^*, $t \geq T$, is higher, the $\dot{\pi}'' = 0$ schedule is closer to the $\dot{\pi} = 0$ schedule. To simplify the graphical representation, figure 9.3 abstracts from these considerations.

38 This follows from the fact that $\dot{\pi}$ becomes positive before T when T is large. Hence, from (9.21), c falls below $\bar{y}$.

If T is small, r^d always increases during the transition but still remains below its initial value.

39 As indicated in the introduction, real interest rates apparently fell at the beginning of the Southern-Cone programmes, which is in accordance with the predictions of the model. In other programmes, however, real interest rates rose (see Végh (1992)). In the context of the present model, high real interest rates at the beginning of the programme can be generated by assuming that the money supply is being used as an additional nominal anchor (see Calvo and Végh (1991)).

40 The wealth effect will not be present if (1) both monies are used in fixed proportion or (2) there is no currency substitution.

41 We have shown that, in the absence of the wealth effect, a permanent change in ϵ is *everywhere* superneutral; that is, a change in ϵ is superneutral even when the system starts outside the steady state.

42 It should be pointed out, however, that the important question of why the programme would become credible at T is left unanswered.

43 The logarithmic utility function plays a critical role in making the case of flexible exchange rates analytically tractable, unlike the predetermined exchange rates case in which only the separability between c and c^* is important.

44 Under predetermined exchange rates, the path of c^* is time invariant (i.e., $\dot{c}^* = 0$) because the nominal interest rate, and thus the effective price of consumption, are time invariant.

45 Equation (9.43) follows from equation (9.42), using first-order condition (9.6) and the definition of the domestic real interest rate.

46 Naturally, the real interest rate channel is absent from the law of motion of tradable goods (equation (9.42)), because the real interest rate in terms of tradable goods is constant and equal to r.

47 In what follows, the expression 'real money balances' will refer to n.

48 The reader is referred to the predetermined exchange rates case for the derivation of equations (9.46)–(9.52) and (9.54). Equations (9.53) and (9.55) follow from (9.38), (9.45) and (9.47).

49 Since the nominal interest rate adjusts instantaneously to its lower steady-state

value, the effective price channel is inoperative when the change in μ is permanent.

50 Formally, note that, by definition, $r^d \equiv i - \pi$. On impact, π falls by more than i does, so that r^d increases. Thereafter, r^d falls over time because i does not change while π increases over time.

51 It is worth noticing that the path of c is independent of the path of c^*, which would not be the case if the utility function were not separable.

52 As in the case of exchange-rate-based stabilisation, the analysis will abstract from seignorage payments when studying this case, in order to isolate the effects of temporariness. However, for the same reasons discussed above, the presence of the wealth effect would only affect the behaviour of consumption of tradables and the real exchange rate.

53 Note that $m(\equiv M/EP^*)$ is continuous at T because E cannot jump at T. If E jumped at T, there would be unbounded arbitrage profits, which is inconsistent with equilibrium.

54 Recall that, from Calvo (1983b), π is also continuous at T.

55 Note, for further reference, that, as $T \to 0$, the downward jump in x, and thus in i, tends to zero.

56 See Calvo and Végh (1990c) for a similar expository device.

57 Note that, in the auxiliary system, it could happen that π overshoots μ^h before T. We will show, however, that this path is not feasible in the 'true' system (i.e., when x is allowed to move over time). The position of the $\dot{\pi}'' = 0$ schedule depends on T: the larger is T, the closer the $\dot{\pi}'' = 0$ schedule is to the $\dot{\pi}' = 0$ schedule. For graphical simplicity, figure 9.4 assumes that the position of the $\dot{\pi}'' = 0$ schedule is independent of T.

58 For $t \geq T$, it follows from (9.43) that $\dot{c}_t > 0$, because $\dot{x}_t = 0$ for $t \geq T$ and, as discussed below, $r_t^d > n$ for $t \geq T$. The direction in which c moves during $[0, T)$ depends on the magnitude of T, which determines the relative strength of the real interest rate and effective price channels emphasised in equation (9.43). For large T, it can be shown that the real interest rate channel prevails at $t = 0$, so that $\dot{c}_0 > 0$. For small T, the change in r^d is small, so that the effective price channel dominates at $t = 0$, and $\dot{c}_0 < 0$. The monotonicity of the path of c during $[0, T)$ remains an open issue.

59 The path of the current account may not be necessarily monotonic during $[0, T)$.

60 It cannot be ruled out that the real exchange rate decreases over some range.

61 The issue of whether r^d could fall on impact for some value of T remains open.

62 Another important avenue, not treated in our model, is through the accumulation or decumulation of human or physical capital.

63 Controls on capital mobility have not been studied in the previous sections. However, they can be easily introduced by, for example, assuming that the private sector is not allowed to hold foreign bonds, b, and that the central bank ensures convertibility only on current-account type transactions (i.e., exports and imports). Those conditions ensure that the private sector would not be able to finance an initial consumption binge (see Calvo and Végh (1991)).

64 For a discussion of incomes policy in stabilisation plans, see Dornbusch and Simonsen (1987).

65 This idea was first exposed, in a different context, by Phelps (1978).
66 An important issue, which we have not addressed, is the viability of predetermined exchange rates in light of potential balance-of-payments crisis.
67 We would conjecture that the effects of the nominal interest rate on consumption discussed in this chapter could also result from the introduction of liquidity constraints – rather than from intertemporal substitution in consumption.
68 The expansionary effects of low real interest rates should also be taken into account for the Southern-Cone tablitas.
69 Durable goods can actually give rise to large intertemporal substitution effects even when there is perfect intertemporal complementarity of consumption, as shown in Calvo (1988).
70 Drazen and Helpman (1988) develop an interesting model in which T is random. In their model, the nominal interest rate includes a risk premium which reflects a discrete jump in the exchange rate when the predetermined exchange-rate regime is discontinued at T.
71 The arguments of l_m and l_{mf} have been omitted for notational simplicity.

References

Alesina, Alberto and Drazen, Allan (1989), 'Why Are Stabilizations Delayed?', unpublished manuscript, Harvard University and Princeton University.
Backus, David K. and Driffill, John (1985), 'Inflation and Reputation', *American Economic Review*, 75: 530–8.
Barro, Robert J. (1986), 'Reputation in a Model of Monetary Policy with Incomplete Information', *Journal of Monetary Economics*, 17: 1–20.
Blejer, Mario and Liviatan, Nissan (1987), 'Fighting Hyperinflation: Stabilization Strategies in Argentina and Israel 1985–86', *IMF Staff Papers*, 34: 403–38.
Bruno, Michael, di Tella, Guido, Dornbusch, Rudiger and Fischer, Stanley (eds.) (1988), *Inflation Stabilization: The Experience of Israel, Argentina, Brazil, Bolivia, and Mexico*, Cambridge, Mass.: MIT Press.
Calvo, Guillermo A. (1982), 'On the Microfoundations of Staggered Nominal Contracts: A First Approximation', unpublished manuscript, Columbia University.
(1983a), 'Staggered Contracts and Exchange Rate Policy', in Jacob A. Frenkel (ed.), *Exchange Rates and International Macroeconomics*, Chicago: University of Chicago Press for the NBER, pp.235–52.
(1983b), 'Staggered Prices in a Utility-Maximizing Framework', *Journal of Monetary Economics*, 12: 383–98.
(1985), 'Currency Substitution and the Real Exchange Rate: The Utility Maximization Approach', *Journal of International Money and Finance*, 4: 175–88.
(1986a), 'Fractured Liberalism: Argentina under Martinez de Hoz', *Economic Development and Cultural Change*, 34: 511–33.
(1986b), 'Temporary Stabilization: Predetermined Exchange Rates', *Journal of Political Economy*, 94: 1319–29.

(1987), 'On the Cost of Temporary Policy', *Journal of Development Economics*, 27: 245–62.

(1988), 'Costly Trade Liberalizations: Durable Goods and Capital Mobility', *IMF Staff Papers*, 35: 461–73.

Calvo, Guillermo A. and Rodriguez, Carlos A. (1977), 'A Model of Exchange Rate Determination under Currency Substitution and Rational Expectations', *Journal of Political Economy*, 85: 617–25.

Calvo, Guillermo A. and Végh, Carlos A. (1990a), 'Interest Rate Policy in a Small Open Economy: The Predetermined Exchange Rates Case', *IMF Staff Papers*, 37: 753–76.

(1990b), 'Fighting Inflation with High Interest Rates: The Small Open Economy Case under Flexible Prices', unpublished manuscript, International Monetary Fund. Forthcoming in *Journal of Money, Credit and Banking*.

(1990c), 'Interest Rate Policy in a Staggered-Prices Model', unpublished manuscript, International Monetary Fund.

(1991), 'Exchange Rate-Based Stabilization: The Dynamics of Non-Credible Policy', unpublished manuscript, International Monetary Fund.

(1992), 'Currency Substitution in Developing Countries: An Introduction', *Revista de Analisis Economico*, 7: 3–27.

Canto, Victor A. and Nickelsburg, Gerald (1989), *Currency Substitution: Theory and Evidence from Latin America*, Boston: Kluwer Academic Publishers.

Corbo, Vittorio (1985), 'Reforms and Macroeconomic Adjustments in Chile during 1974–84', *World Development*, 13: 893–916.

Dornbusch, Rudiger (1982), 'Stabilization Policies in Developing Countries: What Have We Learned?', *World Development*, 10: 701–8.

Dornbusch, Rudiger and Simonsen, Mario Henrique (1987), *Inflation Stabilization with Incomes Policy Support*, Group of Thirty.

Drazen, Allan and Helpman, Elhanan (1987), 'Stabilization with Exchange Rate Management', *Quarterly Journal of Economics*, 52: 835–55.

(1988), 'Stabilization with Exchange Rate Management under Uncertainty', in Elhanan Helpman, Assaf Razin and Efraim Sadka (eds.), *Economic Effects of the Government Budget*, Cambridge Mass.: MIT Press, pp.310–27.

Edwards, Sebastian and Edwards, Alejandra Cox (1987), *Monetarism and Liberalization: The Chilean Experiment*, Ballinger Publishing Co.

El-Erian, Mohamed (1988), 'Currency Substitution in Egypt and the Yemen Arab Republic', *IMF Staff Papers*, 35: 85–103.

Fernández, Roque B. (1985), 'The Expectations Management Approach to Stabilization in Argentina during 1976–82', *World Development*, 13: 871–92.

Fischer, Stanley (1982), 'Seigniorage and the Case for a National Money', *Journal of Political Economy*, 90: 295–313.

(1986), 'Exchange Rate versus Money Target in Disinflation', *Indexing, Inflation, and Economic Policy*, Cambridge, Mass.: MIT Press, chapter 8.

Guidotti, Pablo E. (1989), 'Currency Substitution and Financial Innovation', Working Paper 89/39, International Monetary Fund. Forthcoming in *Journal of Money, Credit and Banking*.

Hanson, James, and de Melo, Jaime (1985), 'External Shocks, Financial Reforms, and Stabilization Attempts in Uruguay during 1974–1983', *World Development*, 13: 917–39.

Harberger, Arnold C. (1982), 'The Chilean Economy in the 1970's: Crisis, Stabilization, Liberalization, Reform', *Carnegie-Rochester Conference Series on Public Policy*, 17: 115–52.

Helpman, Elhanan and Leiderman, Leonardo (1988), 'Stabilization in High Inflation Countries: Analytical Foundations and Recent Experiences', *Carnegie-Rochester Conference Series on Public Policy*, 28: 9–84.

Helpman, Elhanan and Razin, Assaf (1987), 'Exchange Rate Management: Intertemporal Tradeoffs', *American Economic Review*, 77: 107–23.

Kiguel, Miguel A. and Liviatan, Nissan (1988), 'Inflationary Rigidities and Orthodox Stabilization Policies: Lessons from Latin America', *The World Bank Economic Review*, 2: 273–98.

(1989), 'The Old and the New in Heterodox Stabilization Programs: Lessons from the 1960s and the 1980s', PPR Working Paper No. 323, The World Bank.

(1992), 'The Business Cycle Associated with Exchange Rate Stabilization', *The World Bank Economic Review*, 6: 279–305.

Kouri, Pentti, (1976), 'The Exchange Rate and the Balance of Payments in the Short Run and the Long Run: A Monetary Approach', *Scandinavian Journal of Economics*, 78: 280–304.

Liviatan, Nissan (1981), 'Monetary Expansion and Real Exchange Rate Dynamics', *Journal of Political Economy*, 89: (December): 1218–27.

Obstfeld, Maurice (1985), 'The Capital Inflows Problem Revisited: A Stylized Model of Southern Cone Disinflation', *Review of Economic Studies*, 52: 605–25.

Ortiz, Guillermo (1983), 'Currency Substitution in Mexico: The Dollarization Problem', *Journal of Money, Credit and Banking*, 15: 174–85.

Phelps, Edmund S. (1978), 'Disinflation without Recession: Adaptive Guideposts and Monetary Policy', *Weltwirtschaftliches Archiv*, 100: 783–809.

Poloz, Stephen S. (1984), 'The Transactions Demand for Money in a Two-Currency Economy', *Journal of Monetary Economics*, 14: 241–50.

Ramirez-Rojas, Luis, C. (1985), 'Currency Substitution in Argentina, Mexico, and Uruguay', *IMF Staff Papers*, 32: 629–67.

Ramos, Joseph (1986), *Neoconservative Economics in the Southern Cone of Latin America, 1973–1983*, The Johns Hopkins University Press.

Reinhart, Carmen M. and Végh, Carlos A. (1992), 'Nominal Interest Rates, Consumption Booms, and Lack of Credibility: A Quantitative Examination', unpublished manuscript, International Monetary Fund.

Rodriguez, Carlos A. (1982), 'The Argentine Stabilization Plan of December 20th', *World Development*, 10: 801–11.

Rogers, John H. (1990), 'Foreign Inflation Transmission under Flexible Exchange Rates and Currency Substitution', *Journal of Money, Credit and Banking*, 22: 195–208.

Rojas-Suarez, Liliana (1992), 'Currency Substitution in Peru', *Revista de Analisis Economico*, 7: 153–76.

Romer, David (1989), 'Staggered Price Setting with Endogenous Frequency of

Adjustment', NBER Working Paper No. 3134.

Savastano, Miguel A. (1992), 'The Pattern of Currency Substitution in Latin America: An Overview', *Revista de Analisis Economico*, 7: 29–72.

Sjaastad, Larry A. (1989), 'Argentine Economic Policy, 1976–81', in Guido di Tella and Rudiger Dornbusch (eds.), *The Political Economy of Argentina, 1946–83*, pp.254–75.

Taylor, John B. (1979), 'Staggered Wage Setting in a Macro Model', *American Economic Review, Papers and Proceedings*, 69: 108–13.

(1980), 'Aggregate Dynamics and Staggered Contracts', *Journal of Political Economy*, 88: 1–23.

Végh, Carlos A. (1988), 'Effects of Currency Substitution on the Response of the Current Account to Supply Shocks', *IMF Staff Papers*, 35: 574–91.

(1989a), 'Currency Substitution and the Optimal Inflation Tax under Labor Income Taxation', unpublished manuscript, International Monetary Fund.

(1989b), 'The Optimal Inflation Tax in the Presence of Currency Substitution', *Journal of Monetary Economics*, 24: 139–46.

(1992), 'Stopping High Inflation: An Analytical Overview', *IMF Staff Papers*, 39: 626–95.

Walsh, Carl E. (1984), 'Optimal Taxation by the Monetary Authority', NBER Working Paper No. 1375.